RICHARD

Smith and Keenan's
Company Law

Smith and Keenan's Company Law

Seventh Edition by Denis Keenan

Denis Keenan
LLB(Hons), FCIS, DMA, CertEd

of the Middle Temple, Barrister-at-Law
Formerly Head of Department
of Business Studies and Law,
Mid-Essex Technical College and School of Art
(now Chelmer Essex Institute of Higher Education)

Pitman

PITMAN PUBLISHING
128 Long Acre, London WC2E 9AN

© Kenneth Smith and Denis Keenan 1966
© Denis Keenan and Mrs K Smith 1970, 1975, 1976, 1981, 1983
© Denis Keenan 1986, 1987
Seventh edition first published in Great Britain 1987

British Library Cataloguing in Publication Data
Smith, Kenneth, *1910–1966*
    Smith and Keenan's company law.—7th ed.
    1. Corporation law—Great Britain
    I. Title   II. Keenan, Denis   III. Smith,
    Kenneth, *1910–1966*.   Company law
    344.106'66   KD2079

ISBN 0-273-02792-1

Printed in Great Britain at The Bath Press, Avon

Contents

liabilities – The Financial Services Act 1986 – Listed securities – Unlisted securities – Underwriting.

Preface

to Seventh Edition

This edition follows so soon upon the last because of the enactment of the Insolvency Act 1986, the Company Directors Disqualification Act 1983 and the Financial Services Act 1986. The Insolvency Act 1986 consolidates almost the whole of the Insolvency Act 1985 together with those Parts of the Companies Act 1985 that deal with company liquidations and receiverships. Those provisions of the Insolvency Act 1985 which were concerned with the disqualification of directors are consolidated in the Company Directors Disqualification Act 1986 on the grounds that some director disqualifications can take place in solvent companies.

There have also been some changes in case law to reflect the more important recent decisions, particularly in the area of minority rights.

A major change which was made in the sixth edition in the Appendix of Cases and Materials has been continued. Each case, or sometimes a group of cases, now has introductory material that enables the cases to be more easily studied independently of the text as well as with it. It is hoped that this change will make the book even more effective as a text and casebook combined.

In the preparation of this edition the publishers and I have had, as before, the invaluable assistance of my wife in terms of preparation and editing of the typescript, indexes and proofs, together with the general organization of sources of new material since the last edition.

I also express my thanks to Eric Dalton, Simon Lake, David Carpenter and all those members of staff at Pitman Publishing who have been involved with the book for their help throughout, and also the printers for their assistance in processing the typescript and the proofs.

As always, I must acknowledge the contribution of my students whose questions can sometimes expose a defect of exposition which leads to discussion and clarification of a particular point or points of law. The author must, of course, accept responsibility for any errors and omissions.

Maenan
April 1987

Denis Keenan

Table of statutes

Table of cases

Note. The reference in bold type indicates the number of the case in the Appendix. Page numbers in ordinary type refer to the pages on which the case is cited.

Bahia & San Francisco Railway Co, *re* (1868),   **93**, 144

Baillie *v* Oriental Telephone and Electric Co Ltd (1915),   **138**, 199, 207

Baily *v* British Equitable Assurance Co Ltd (1904),   75

Baker *v* Gibbons (1972),   **164**, 261

Balaghat Co, *re* (1901),   178

Balkis Consolidated Co Ltd (The) *v* Tomkinson (1893),   **94**, 144, 145

Bamford *v* Bamford (1969),   **68**, 77, 234

Banque de l'Indochine et de Suez SA *v* Euroseas Group Finance Co (1981),   443

Barclays Bank Ltd *v* Quistclose Investments Ltd (1968),   **177**, 282

Bargate *v* Shortridge (1855),   81

Barker (George) (Transport) Ltd *v* Eynon (1974),   325, 567

Barnett Hoares & Co *v* South London Tramways Co (1887),   562

Bateman *v* Service (1881),   33

Bayswater Trading Co Ltd, *in re* (1970),   406

Beattie *v* E and F Beattie Ltd (1938),   77, 474, 475

Beauforte (Jon) (London) Ltd, *re* (1953),   **42**, 60, 461

Bell *v* Lever Bros Ltd (1932),   261

Bell Houses Ltd *v* City Wall Properties Ltd (1966),   **27**, 51, 52, 53, 62, 63

Bellador Silk Ltd, *re* (1965),   193

Bellerby *v* Rowland & Marwoods's Steam Ship Co Ltd (1902),   **110**, 158

Belmont Finance *v* Williams (1980),   163, 164

Bentley-Stevens *v* Jones (1974),   **135**, 198

Berry and Stewart *v* Tottenham Hotspur FC (1935),   **200**, 337

Bersel Manufacturing Co Ltd *v* Berry (1968),   **174**, 270

Biba Group Ltd *v* Biba Boutique (1980),   442

Birch *v* Cropper (1889),   88

Bird Precision Bellows (1984),   193, 195, 523

Blaker *v* Herts & Essex Waterworks Co (1889),   316

Block (Stanley L) Inc *v* Klein (1965),   583

Bloomenthal *v* Ford (1897),   **97**, 145

Boardman *v* Phipps (1967),   550

Bond Worth Ltd, *re* (1979),   304

Borden (UK) Ltd *v* Scottish Timber Products Ltd (1979),   304

Borland's Trustee *v* Steel Brothers & Co Ltd (1901),   135

Bowling and Welby's Contract, *re* (1895),   13

Bowman *v* Secular Society (1917),   32

Bradford Banking Co *v* Briggs (1886),   **108**, 156, 180

Briess *v* Woolley (1954),   558

Briggs, *ex parte* (1866),   124

British Eagle International Air Lines Ltd *v* Compagnie

House Coal Colliery Co
(1895), 80
Cousins *v* International Brick
Co Ltd (1931), 213
Craven-Ellis *v* Canons Ltd
(1936), **161, 242**
Crichton's Oil Co, *re* (1902),
75, 86
Cuckmere Brick Co *v* Mutual
Finance Ltd (1971), 324
Cunliffe Brooks & Co *v*
Blackburn Building Society
(1884), 61
Cyclists Touring Club, *re*
(1907), **50, 65**

D H N Food Distributors Ltd *v*
Tower Hamlets London
Borough Council (1976), **7,**
19
Dafen Tinplate Co *v* Llanelly
Steel Co (1907) Ltd
(1920), **55,** 74, 199
Daimler Co Ltd *v* Continental
Tyre & Rubber Co (Great
Britain) (1916), **9,** 19, 46,
273
Daniels *v* Daniels (1978), **146,**
200
De Courcy *v* Clements (1971),
401
Derry *v* Peek (1889), **86,** 125
Destone Fabrics Ltd, *re* (1941),
309
Deuchar *v* Gas Light and Coke
Co (1925), **43,** 53, 60, 446
Development Co of Central and
West Africa, *re* (1902), 99
Devlin *v* Slough Estates Ltd
(1982), **147,** 201, 350
Dimbleby & Sons Ltd *v* NUJ
(1984), 433
Dimbula Valley (Ceylon) Tea
Co Ltd *v* Laurie (1961), 88,

284, 286
Dixon *v* Kennaway & Co Ltd
(1900), **96, 144**
Dorchester Finance Co Ltd *v*
Stebbing (1977), **169, 263**
Duck *v* Tower Galvanising Co
(1901), 80
Dunderland Iron Ore Co Ltd, *re*
(1909), 310
Duomatic Ltd, *in re* (1969),
160, 242, 243, 253, 267, 416
Durham Fancy Goods Ltd *v*
Michael Jackson (Fancy
Goods) Ltd (1968), **24,** 46,
444

East *v* Bennett Bros Ltd
(1911), 207
Ebrahimi *v* Westbourne
Galleries (1972), **129,** 20,
190, 192, 270, 523, 524, 528,
534
Eddystone Marine Insurance
Co, *re* (1893), **117,** 171,
172
Edgington *v* Fitzmaurice
(1885), **80,** 122
Egyptian Delta and Land
Development Co Ltd
(1907), **48,** 65, 66
El Sombrero Ltd, *re*
(1958), **155,** 207
Eley *v* Positive Government
Security Life Assurance Co
(1876), **64,** 77, 530
Ellis (Matthew) Ltd, *re*
(1933), **188,** 309
English and Colonial Produce
Co Ltd, *re* (1906), 27
Erlanger *v* New Sombrero
Phosphate Co (1878), 22
Estmanco Ltd *v* GLC (1982),
144, 199

1 The nature of a company

This text is concerned almost entirely with the law relating to *registered companies*. These are governed in the main by the Companies Act 1985 and relevant case law. Section references throughout the text are to the Companies Act 1985 unless otherwise indicated.

However, since a company is a corporation, it is necessary first to examine the nature of a corporation. A *corporation* is a succession or collection of persons having at law an existence, rights, and duties, separate and distinct from those of the persons who are from time to time its members.

The distinguishing features of a corporation are—

(*a*) It is a *persona at law*, i.e. an artificial not a natural person;

(*b*) It has perpetual succession, i.e. its existence is maintained by the constant succession of new persons who replace those who die or are in some other way removed.

Corporation sole. A corporation may be a corporation sole, i.e. it may consist of only one member at a time holding a perpetual office, e.g. the Bishop of London. Here the office is personified to distinguish it from the person who is from time to time the holder.

An example is provided by the Public Trustee which is a corporation sole created by the Public Trustee Act 1906. The Public Trustee is a civil servant who while he is in post is the sole member of the corporation. The corporation is trustee of much property and it would be inconvenient if all the trusts had to be transferred into the ownership of the new holder of the office every time there was a change. The office of Public Trustee was therefore personified as a corporation sole and the trust property is vested in the corporation and is not affected when the human holder of the office changes.

Corporation aggregate. A corporation aggregate consists of a number of persons so associated that in law they form a single person, e.g. a registered company. Here the undertaking is personified so that it may be distinguished from its members. (*Salomon v Salomon & Co Ltd*, 1897,[1] *Macaura v Northern Assurance*, 1925[2] and *Lee v Lee's Air Farming Ltd*, 1960.[3]) A company is a species of corporation and is an association of persons formed often for the purposes of some business or undertaking which is carried on in the name of the association.

Compulsory registration. It has always been the policy of company legislation to compel registration of all but the smaller associations of persons for the purposes of better control.

The maximum permitted membership for a partnership including, by reason of s. 46 of the Banking Act 1979, those carrying on the business of banking is 20. (S. 716(1).)

The limit is waived by s. 716(2) so that it is permissible for a partnership of more than 20 members to be formed to carry on practice as solicitors or accountants if all the members are professionally qualified, which so far as accountants are concerned means that they must be members of one of the chartered institutes in England and Wales, Scotland or Ireland, or of the Chartered Association of Certified Accountants, or to carry on business as members of a recognized stock exchange if all the members are members of a recognized stock exchange.

Section 716(3) gives the Department of Trade and Industry power to make regulations extending these provisions. Under regulations made to date it is possible, for example, for a partnership of patent agents or actuaries to have more than 20 members if they are all registered patent agents or fellows of the Institute or Faculty of Actuaries, in addition a partnership of more than 20 persons may carry on the practice of surveyors, auctioneers, valuers, estate agents, estate managers, or building designers if at least three-quarters of the partners are members of certain designated professional bodies; furthermore, a partnership of consulting engineers may have more than 20 members if a majority of them are recognized as chartered engineers. Exemption has also been extended to partnerships of loss adjusters.

An association which does not comply with the above provisions is illegal and void. Nevertheless, if the managers of the association make contracts in its name with a person who does not know that its membership is in excess of the permitted number, the managers are deemed to contract as agents for all its members and every member is personally liable to the other contracting party. However, so far as the association is concerned the contract is affected by the illegality and is not enforceable by the association or by its members. In addition, an association with a membership in excess of the permitted number is only made void if it is formed to carry on some *business* for the purpose of *gain*. (S. 716(1).) This definition covers most forms of commercial undertaking but an interesting exception is provided by the unit trust which is not an association affected by the above prohibitions. The members of such a trust deposit their funds with the managers for investment but are not in 'business' with them. (*Smith v Anderson* (1880) 15 Ch D 247.)

It should be noted that the inclusion of the word 'company' in the name is not essential and an association is not necessarily a company because it uses that word since many partnerships use the word 'company' in this way.

CLASSIFICATION OF COMPANIES

Section 716(1) refers to three main types of company.

1 Chartered companies

A chartered company is formed by grant of a charter by the Crown operating under either prerogative powers or special statutory powers. The procedure for the formation of such a company is for the promoters to petition the Privy Council for the grant of a charter. The petition is addressed to the Lord President and prays for the grant, a draft of the charter being annexed to the petition.

Charters are used to incorporate learned societies, professional bodies such as the Institute of Chartered Accountants in England and Wales, the Chartered Institute of Secretaries and Administrators, the BBC, public schools, and colleges of universities.

This form of incorporation is not now used by trading concerns, for whom registration is a better method, but some trading companies still operate under charters, mainly banks and insurance companies.

It is possible to have a *corporation by prescription*, and this occurs where it is presumed that a charter was granted but it has been lost. The City of London is a corporation by prescription.

A charter company can have any number of members but not less than two. There is generally no personal liability in the members unless the charter otherwise provides. The creditors must rely on the company's assets.

2 Statutory companies

Such companies are formed by special Act of Parliament. This method of company formation was formerly used for public utilities such as electricity, gas, water and railways, because these undertakings need special powers, e.g. for the compulsory acquisition of land, and these powers can only be conferred by legislation. Further, such undertakings need a monopoly in the area in which they operate. It would be intolerable to have (say) ten gas companies supplying gas in one area.

To ensure that there was some uniformity in the regulations controlling these companies, various public general Acts, called *Clauses Acts*,

3

e.g. the Companies Clauses Acts 1845–89, were passed containing general corporate powers and duties. These were deemed to be incorporated in the Private Act setting up a company, unless the Act provided to the contrary.

For all practical purposes the public utilities are now nationalized by public Acts under which their functions have been taken over by public corporations with some recent privatization. These organizations fall outside the scope of a book of this nature because large and important branches of company law do not apply to them.

As Denning L J said in *Tamlin v Hannaford* [1950] KB 18, 'The significant difference ... is that there are no shareholders to subscribe the capital or to have any voice in its affairs. The money which the corporation needs is not raised by the issue of shares but by borrowing; and its borrowing is not secured by debentures but is guaranteed by the Treasury. If it cannot repay, the loss falls on the Consolidated Fund ..., that is to say on the taxpayer. There are no shareholders to elect the directors or to fix their remuneration.... If it should make losses and be unable to pay its debts, its property is liable to execution, but it is not liable to be wound up at the suit of any creditor. The taxpayer would, no doubt, be expected to come to its rescue before the creditors stepped in.'

It should be mentioned that various other organizations owe their existence to statute; these include friendly societies, building societies, and industrial and provident societies (co-operative societies). These are not our concern and will not be dealt with.

3 Registered companies

Such companies are either formed under the Companies Act 1985 or were formed under previous Acts. In either case they are governed by the Companies Act 1985 and relevant case law, except that the articles of association of the company, if based on *Table A*, are those of *Table A* in the Act under which it was formed. Thus a company formed under the Companies Act 1948 is governed by *Table A* appearing in that Act as the First Schedule to it. The first Act allowing the registration of companies was the Joint Stock Companies Act of 1844, though they were not allowed limited liability until the Limited Liability Act of 1855. This book is concerned mainly with this type of company.

PUBLIC AND PRIVATE COMPANIES

Public companies

Section 1(3) defines a public company as a company limited by shares or by guarantee with a *share capital* whose memorandum states that

4

the company is a public company. By s. 1(1) only two persons are required to form a public company. By s. 25 the name of a public company must end with the words 'public limited company' or the Welsh equivalent if the registered office is situated in Wales. Section 27(1) and (4) provide that the abbreviation plc may be used and give the equivalent in Welsh.

If the company is a public company the authorized capital must under ss. 11 and 118 be at least £50,000, or such other sum as the Secretary of State for Trade and Industry may, by statutory instrument, specify instead. The certificate of incorporation of a public company states that it is and is conclusive evidence that the Acts have been complied with and that the company is a public company. (S. 13(7)(a) and (b).)

Under s. 117 a public company cannot commence business or borrow money unless the Registrar has issued a s. 117 certificate which private companies do not require. The certificate is issued if the company's allotted share capital is at least £50,000 and by reason of s. 101(1) not less than one-quarter of the nominal value of each issued share and the whole of any premium has been received by the company whether in cash or otherwise. The s. 117 certificate is conclusive evidence that the company is entitled to do business and exercise any borrowing powers.

Private companies

These are intended for the smaller business and may be formed by two or more persons. Under s. 1(3) a private company is a company which is not a public company. There are no restrictions on the right to transfer the shares of the company or on the number of its members unless the articles contain such restrictions. The only restriction on a private company is in s. 170 of the Financial Services Act 1986, which replaces s. 81 of the Companies Act 1985. Section 170 contains a provision which in general prohibits the issue of advertisements offering securities of a private company.

Private companies are further subdivided by ss. 247–256 which introduce the accounting exemptions. They give the benefit of confidentiality of information but involve the preparation of two sets of accounts—one for members and one for the Registrar of Companies. These exemptions then, draw a distinction between the reporting requirements in regard to the accounts which small or medium companies prepare for their members and those which they file with the Registrar of Companies. They are allowed to file what the Act refers to as 'modified accounts' with the Registrar.

(a) Small companies

Under ss. 248(1) and 249(4)(a) a small company is one which has been within the limits of *two* of the following thresholds for the current financial year and one before—
Turnover £2 million
Balance Sheet total (i.e. total assets) £975,000
Employees 50 (average)
The modifications in regard to filing are—

(*i*) there is no need to file a profit and loss account or a directors' report (Sched 8, Part I, para 3).

(*ii*) under Sched 8, Part I, para 2(1) and (2) a modified balance sheet may be filed showing only those items to which a letter or Roman numeral is assigned in the balance sheet formats of Sched 4, Part I, i.e. only main headings. However by reason of Sched 8, Part I, para 6(a) and (b) it is necessary to analyse the aggregate amounts shown for debtors and creditors into those amounts which fall due within one year and after more than one year from the date of the balance sheet. This may be done either on the face of the balance sheet or in the notes.

(*iii*) under Sched 8, Part I, para 5 the information required by Sched 4 to be given in notes to the accounts need not be given except—

(*a*) accounting policies,
(*b*) share capital,
(*c*) particulars of shares allotted,
(*d*) particulars of indebtedness (amounts repayable in excess of five years and details of secured liabilities),
(*e*) basis of translation of foreign currency amounts into sterling, and
(*f*) corresponding amounts for the previous financial year.

Disclosure requirements imposed by other sections still apply, e.g. s. 232 and Sched 6, Part I (transactions with directors and others, see p. 245).

(*iv*) under Sched 8, Part I, para 4 the information required by Sched 5, Parts V and VI, i.e particulars of directors' and higher paid employees' remuneration, i.e. currently those earning more than £30,000, need not be given.

(b) Medium companies

Under ss. 248(2) and 249(4)(b) a medium company is one which has been within the limits of *two* of the following thresholds for the current financial year and the one before—

Turnover £8 million
Balance Sheet total (i.e. total assets) £3·9 million
Employees 250 (average)

The modifications in regard to filing are only in the profit and loss account and the notes to the accounts as follows—

(*i*) under Sched 8, Part I, para 7 the *profit and loss account* may commence with 'gross profit or loss' which combines those items in the prescribed formats which would otherwise require disclosure of turnover, cost of sales information, and other operating income.

(*ii*) under Sched 8, para 8 there is no need to give *in the notes to the accounts* the analyses of turnover and profit which are otherwise required.

The reason for the modification in the filed financial statements of medium companies is that the details of turnover and profit were used sometimes to the unreasonable disadvantage of medium companies by competitors.

The Directors' report and Balance Sheet is required in full.

Groups

A holding company is entitled to file *modified group accounts* if the group as a whole qualifies to be treated as small or medium. (S. 250.)

As regards the *individual accounts* of a holding company, a holding company is treated as if it were the same size as the whole group. So if the whole group is medium sized so is the holding company even though on its own it would be a small company. (S. 250.)

Subsequent failure to qualify

If a company ceases to satisfy the exemption requirements for two years it must file full accounts for the second year. (S. 249(5).)

Exemptions inapplicable

Under s. 247(2) the exemptions do not apply if the company concerned is or at any time during its financial year was—

(*i*) a public company,

(*ii*) a banking, insurance or certain shipping companies,

(*iii*) a member of an 'ineligible group', i.e. a group containing any of the companies in (*i*) and (*ii*) above. There are to be separate accounting directives for banks and insurance companies and the 4th Directive on which the above provisions are based does not require member states of the EEC to apply the Directive to shipping companies for some years. The government is therefore requiring full disclosure from 'certain' shipping companies, i.e. those which are or have a subsidiary which is so designated by the Secretary of State for Trade and Industry and thought to be few in number.

Special directors' and auditors' reports

Modified accounts must under Sched 8, Part I, para 9 include *a statement by the directors* saying that they have relied on the exemptions because the company or group is small or medium as the case may be.

Paragraph 10(3) requires a special report by the auditor which they must provide to directors who propose to file modified accounts, stating whether, in their opinion, the requirements for exemption are satisfied.

Paragraph 10(1) also provides that when the accounts are actually filed they must be accompanied by a special auditors' report instead of the normal one. The special report states that the requirements for exemption are satisfied and that the modified accounts have been properly prepared in line with those exemptions and reproducing the full text of the normal audit report on the full accounts (which have gone to members).

Dormant companies

Certain private companies may be eligible to be regarded as dormant companies under s. 252. Such companies are the only ones which do not have to appoint an auditor though accounts must still be prepared and filed. However, they need only prepare one set of accounts, i.e. a modified balance sheet as for a small company.

A dormant company is a 'small' company (see above) which has had no 'significant accounting transaction' since the end of the previous financial year. A holding company required to prepare group accounts cannot be dormant. (S. 252(2).)

Section 252(5) provides that a 'significant accounting transaction' is *any* transaction which is required by reason of s. 221 to be entered in the company's accounting records other than one arising from the taking of shares in the company by a subscriber to the memorandum in pursuance of an undertaking to do so in the memorandum.

The members must pass a special resolution excluding s. 384 (obligation to appoint auditors). The directors, or them failing the members, must appoint auditors if the company ceases to be dormant which it does under s. 252(5)(*b*) on the occurrence of a significant accounting transaction.

A dormant company may in practice be a company which has transferred its business and assets but is being kept 'on the shelf' to preserve the name.

LIMITED AND UNLIMITED COMPANIES

The liability of a company to pay its debts is unlimited in the sense that it must pay all debts due from it so long as its assets are sufficient to meet them. However, the liability of the members may be limited.

Section 1(2) provides that a registered company may be—

(i) *Limited by Shares.* First it should be noted that limitation of liability refers to the members and not to the company itself. The liability of the company is always unlimited in the sense that it must discharge its liabilities so long as it has assets to do so.

Limitation of liability by shares may occur on formation, i.e. the company is registered as such. Where this is so the liability of each member to contribute to the capital of the company is limited to the nominal value of the shares that he has agreed to take up or, if he has agreed to take up such shares at a premium, i.e. at more than their nominal value, to the total amount agreed to be paid for such shares. Once the member has paid the company for his shares his liability is discharged completely and he cannot be made responsible for making up the deficiencies of the company or of other shareholders. Furthermore, he has no liability whatever in respect of unissued shares. However, in the case of a small private company, the advantages of limited liability tend to be illusory, since those who give the company credit facilities will in practice require personal guarantees from its directors and major shareholders.

(ii) *Limited by Guarantee.* Companies limited by guarantee could be registered with or without a share capital. Section 1(4) provides that companies limited by guarantee with a share capital may not be registered, though of course companies which had registered with a share capital before the Act remain in existence. Where there is no share capital the members have no liability unless and until the company goes into liquidation. When this happens those who are members at the time are required to contribute towards the payment of the company's debts and liabilities and the costs of winding up in accordance with the guarantee. The amount guaranteed will be whatever sum is stated in the memorandum and it is frequently £1·00, although in some cases the agreed liability may be substantial and much depends upon the type of company.

If those who are members at the date of winding up cannot meet their obligations under the guarantee then the liquidator may have access to those who were members during the year prior to the commencement of the winding up but only in respect of debts and liabilities incurred while they were members.

If a company limited by guarantee has a share capital its members have two liabilities. They must pay the issue price of their shares, and must honour their guarantee in the event of the company being liquidated. (S. 74(3), Insolvency Act 1986.) There is no benefit to the company in having such a dual liability and in practice companies limited by guarantee with a share capital were not formed. The device of the guarantee company is only used where no share capital is to be issued but the members of the company wish to limit their liability to contribute towards the company's debts and liabilities.

It is also possible to re-register an unlimited company as a limited one but this does not apply to a company which was previously a limited company but has re-registered as an unlimited one. (S. 51(2).) If the conversion is *to a private limited company* the conversion must be authorized by special resolution of the members. Following this copies of the memorandum and articles as altered are sent to the Registrar who will issue a new certificate of incorporation which is conclusive evidence that the conversion is in all respects valid. The Registrar will also advertise the issue of the new certificate in the *London Gazette*. (S. 711(1).)

If an unlimited company wishes to re-register *as a public company* which is by definition a company limited by shares, s. 48 applies and the procedure followed is that for the re-registration of a private company as a public company (see p. 339) except that the special resolution to convert must include two additional matters as follows—

(*a*) it must state that the liability of the members is to be limited by shares and what the share capital of the company is to be; and

(*b*) it must make such alterations in the company's memorandum as are necessary to bring it in substance and in form into conformity with the requirements of the Companies Act in regard to the memorandum of association of a public company limited by shares. This involves, e.g., changes in the company's name and capital clauses.

The re-registration as a public company is not available to unlimited companies which have re-registered as such having been previously limited companies. (S. 43.)

The effect on the liability of members of such a conversion is that those who become members after conversion are liable only to the extent of capital unpaid on their shares. Those who were members at the date of the conversion, and are still members at the date of winding up, are fully liable for debts and liabilities incurred before conversion. Those who were members at the date of conversion but have transferred their shares after conversion and before winding up are liable for debts and liabilities incurred before conversion up to three years after it took place. (S. 77(2), Insolvency Act 1986.)

(iii) *Unlimited*. The personal liability of members of this type of company is the reason why not many of them exist. However, some organizations, such as the Stock Exchange, will not admit a company to membership unless the members of the company are personally liable for its debts. In addition, there are advantages in having separate corporate status and perpetual succession even though these are not accompanied by limited liability.

Unlimited companies must be private companies since a public company is by definition a company limited by shares (or by guarantee with a share capital).

Unlimited companies may be formed as such, either with or without a share capital. A share capital may be used, for example, if the company is trading and making profits, since the shares are a basis for the distribution of that profit. As regards liability, where there is a share capital, the members must first of all pay for their shares and if this is not adequate to satisfy all the debts and liabilities of the company together with the costs of winding up, the members must contribute rateably according to their shareholding. Where there is no share capital, the members contribute equally until all the debts and liabilities of the company plus the costs of winding up are paid. In the event of any members defaulting the others are liable to make good the deficiency as much as is necessary to pay the whole of the company's liabilities and the costs of liquidation.

An unlimited company may also come into existence by being re-registered as such. Section 49(1) allows a company limited by shares or by guarantee to be re-registered as an unlimited company.

However, under s. 49(3) no public company may apply under this section to be re-registered as an unlimited company because a public company cannot be an unlimited company and therefore such a conversion involves a reduction in status from public to private. A public company which wishes to re-register as unlimited must use the procedure laid down in ss. 53–55 for conversion of a public company to a private company (see p. 341).

If, however, the company is private ss. 49 above and 50 apply and all the members must consent in writing and if this can be achieved there must be sent to the Registrar of Companies a statutory declaration by the directors that all the members of the company have consented together with copies of the memorandum and articles as altered. The Registrar will then issue a new certificate of incorporation which is conclusive evidence that the conversion is in all respects valid. In addition, the Registrar must publish the issue of the new certificate in the *London Gazette*. (S. 711(1).) We have already noted that there can be no conversion back to a limited company. (S. 51(2).) In addition, a company is excluded from re-registering as unlimited if it has previously re-registered as limited. (S. 49(2).)

There are certain special features relating to unlimited companies. For example, an unlimited company may reduce its capital by extinguishing liability on partly paid shares or even repaying capital to the members by passing a special resolution to that effect *and the permission of the court is not required*. In addition, an unlimited company may, if its articles permit, reduce its capital by buying back the shares of its members even to the extent of using its assets to do so.

These practices do not, in theory at least, reduce the funds available to creditors on a winding up because the members are liable to pay the debts and liabilities of the company in full on winding up. However, as regards reduction of capital by purchase of shares, if the company knew at the time of purchase that the members would not be able to meet their liabilities on winding up, the purchase would be set aside as a fraud on the creditors. (*Mitchell v City of Glasgow Bank* (1879) 4 App Cas 624.)

It will be noted in Chapter 4 that limited companies can also purchase their own shares under the provisions of Part V Chapter VII. However, limited company purchases are subject to the not inconsiderable restrictions of that Act. Unlimited companies are not subject to these restrictions and require only permission in the articles.

In addition, an unlimited company enjoys privacy in regard to its financial affairs because it need not deliver copies of its annual accounts and the relevant reports to the Registrar. (S. 241(4).) However, the price of privacy is the unlimited liability of its members. The provision in regard to the annual accounts does not apply if the company concerned is a subsidiary or holding company of a limited company or is *potentially* under the control of two or more limited companies because of share or voting rights which they hold even though these have not been exercised in concert for the purposes of control. (S. 241(4).)

Other situations of unlimited liability

(*a*) *Section 24* provides that if a company carries on business without having at least two members and does so for more than six months, a person who, for the whole or any part of the period that it carries on business after those six months, (*a*) is a member of the company, and (*b*) knows that it is carrying on business with only one member, is liable jointly and severally with the company for the payment of the company's debts contracted during the period or, as the case may be, that part of it. In addition, as soon as the membership falls below the statutory minimum there is a ground on which a petition may be presented for winding up by the court. (S. 122(e), Insolvency Act 1986.) This ground is provided to enable a member to escape personal liability for the company's debts which he will incur if the membership remains below the statutory minimum for more than six months.

Liability under s. 24 may arise on the death of a member since the personal representatives do not become members unless they are on the register. (*Re Bowling and Welby's Contract* [1895] 1 Ch 663.) Liability may also arise by transfer of shares from one member to the only other member. This liability may be avoided by the transfer of some shares to a trustee, or nominee, for the benefit of a member or members before the six months has elapsed.

As regards the nature of the liability, a creditor may sue the member personally and there is no need for him to ask for a winding up. Thus the situation is rather different from that pertaining in the case of an unlimited company where the creditor must ask for the winding up of the company before the liability of the members arises. If the member is required to pay a debt or debts he may ask for a contribution from the company. Additionally, because he has paid the company's debt, he may at common law have a complete indemnity against the company, though the Act gives a mere contribution.

It is possible for two persons to be liable for different periods and if there are no members, as where the sole member has died and the company is being run by a salaried director, the section does not apply at all.

Section 24 provides a difficulty for holding companies where the holding company owns all the shares in a subsidiary. In these circumstances there is a potential risk in the holding company of liability under s. 24. In practice holding companies take precautions to prevent this by having a few shares transferred to nominees, at least to make up the minimum number of members.

(*b*) *Section 214, Insolvency Act 1986. Wrongful trading.* Section 214(1), (2) and (7) provide that the court may on the application of a liquidator declare a director (including a shadow director) (see p. 223) of a company personally liable to make such a contribution to the debts of the company as the court thinks proper if it is engaged in wrongful trading.

The section applies where the company has gone into insolvent liquidation and the director, before the liquidation, knew, or ought to have known, that there was *no reasonable prospect* that the company would avoid going into insolvent liquidation and did not take the steps he ought to have taken to minimize the potential loss to creditors.

The following points should be noted—

(i) for the purposes of s. 214 a company goes into insolvent liquidation if it goes into liquidation at a time when its assets are insufficient for the payment of its debts and other liabilities and the expenses of winding up. (S. 214(6).)

(ii) The court will not make a declaration of liability in respect of a director who can show that he took every step with a view to minimizing the potential loss to the creditors of the company as he *ought* to have taken given his general knowledge, skill and experience which he either *has or could reasonably be expected to have*, in view of the functions he carries out within the company. (S. 214(3) and (4).)

This is an *objective* test and under it a declaration of liability may be made against a person even if he has done his best. A higher standard will be required of a qualified and/or experienced executive director or non-executive director than of a non-executive director who has less or no experience or relevant qualifications for the business concerned.

The test for liability under s. 213 is *subjective*. (See (c) below.)

(iii) To avoid liability those potentially liable under s. 214 should put the company into receivership, administration, or liquidation, as soon as possible.

(c) *Section 213, Insolvency Act 1986. Fraudulent trading.* Section 213(1) and (2) provide that if in the course of the winding up of a company it appears that any business of the company has been carried on with intent to defraud the creditors of the company or creditors of any other person or for any fraudulent purpose, the court, on the application of the liquidator of the company, may declare that any persons who were knowingly parties to the carrying on of the business in manner mentioned are to be personally responsible without any limitation of liability, for all or any of the debts or other liabilities of the company as the court may direct.

The following points should be noted—

(i) The section is wider than s. 214 because it covers *all liabilities*, e.g. damages for breach of contract, and not *merely debts*.

(ii) Section 213, Insolvency Act 1986 is available against directors and also against members or others who may participate. Section 214 (*ibid*) is a more likely jurisdiction as regards actions by *liquidators against directors*. Directors are potentially liable under s. 213 but the need to prove that the business was being conducted in a fraudulent manner makes it difficult to establish liability under it. Actions against those who are not directors will have to be brought under s. 213, since s. 214 is available only against directors.

In order to bring a person within the section it must be shown that he is taking some positive steps in carrying on the business in a fraudulent manner. (See, e.g. *Re Maidstone Buildings Provisions Ltd*, 1971.)[4]

(iii) The limitations of the section are that it can only be invoked on a winding up and the applicant must prove fraud. (For alleged conduct said to amount to fraud see in *Re Gerald Cooper Chemicals Ltd*, 1978.[5]) Section 214 of the Insolvency Act 1986 also applies only on a winding up, though it is not necessary to prove fraud.

(iv) For the purposes of civil liability fraud will not apparently be inferred merely because the company continues in business and to incur debts when, for example, the directors know that the company is insolvent. It is necessary to show an element of dishonesty involving real moral blame. The position was well put by Buckley J (as he then was) in *Re White and Osmond (Parkstone) Ltd*, 1960 (unreported) where he said:

'Lastly it is said that the directors continued to incur credit in carrying on the business of the company at a time when they knew the company was insolvent. In my judgment there is nothing wrong in the fact that directors incur credit at a time when, to their knowledge, the company is not able to meet all its liabilities as they fall due. What is manifestly wrong is if directors allow a company to incur credit at the time when the business is being carried on in such circumstances that it is clear that the company will *never* be able to satisfy its creditors. However, there is nothing to say that directors who genuinely believe that the clouds will roll away and the sunshine of prosperity will shine upon them again and disperse the fog of their depression are not entitled to incur credit to help them to get over the bad times.'

This test is *subjective* and means that a person cannot be made liable for the debts and other liabilities of the company so long as *he believed* that there was light at the end of the tunnel. The statement refers to directors. Liquidators will normally claim against directors under s. 214, Insolvency Act 1986 where the test is as we have seen *objective*. However, the statement is relevant to claims brought against persons other than directors under s. 213 by liquidators.

The statement was not approved by Lord Lane C J in *R v Grantham* [1984] 3 All ER 166 at p. 170. He and the other judges in the Court of Appeal in that case decided that for the *crime of fraudulent trading* (see below) it was not necessary for the prosecution to prove that there was no reasonable prospect that the company's creditors would *ever* receive payment. It was enough to show that the person concerned had *no good reason for thinking* that they would be paid. This test may increasingly be applied to cases brought against persons under s. 213 in regard to their *civil liability* for the debts of the company.

(v) A solution to the problems of fraudulent trading or wrongful trading was approved in *Re Kayford* [1975] 1 All ER 604. This is for the directors or others who may become involved to arrange for

15

money received from customers to be paid into a special bank account headed, e.g. 'Customer Trade Deposit Account'. On liquidation these monies would belong to the customers and would not form part of the general assets of the company because the opening of such an account creates a trust in favour of customers. A liquidator would therefore have to return the money to the customers who would not suffer because of the liquidation. However, it should be noted that in *Re Kayford* the customers were members of the public sending money in advance for mail order goods which the directors felt that the company would not be able to supply. It is therefore to some extent inherent in the judgment that the setting up of a special account was in the 'public interest'. To open such an account for advance payments from traders would probably be a preference under s. 239, Insolvency Act 1986 (see Chapter 17).

(vi) It is interesting to note that if the liquidator applies to the court under s. 213 any money received is distributed to creditors generally and forms part of the general assets of the company for distribution. (*Re William C. Leitch Ltd (No. 2)* [1933] Ch 261.) In other words, the money a director pays over to the liquidator is not used only to pay creditors whose debts were incurred during the period of fraudulent trading. It will increase the dividend payable to all creditors.

Presumably, any money received by a liquidator under s. 214, Insolvency Act 1986 will be distributed to creditors generally.

Under s. 10, Company Directors Disqualification Act 1986, the court, where it makes a declaration in regard to wrongful trading under s. 214 or in regard to fraudulent trading under s. 213 may make an order disqualifying the person concerned from acting as a director of a company. (See further p. 228.)

(vii) In addition to the civil aspects of s. 214, Insolvency Act 1986 and s. 213 which are considered above, s. 458 provides for a criminal liability in persons concerned in fraudulent trading by a company. The section provides that this criminal liability shall apply, whether or not the company has been or is in the course of being wound up. The civil law aspects under s. 214, Insolvency Act 1986 and s. 213 continue to depend upon a winding-up situation.

The test for criminal liability is proof of *fraud* which requires proof that the person involved *had no good reason for thinking* that funds would be available to pay the creditors concerned. (See *R v Grantham*, above.)

(c) *Section 117, Companies Act 1985.* It will be recalled that by reason of s. 117 a plc cannot commence trading or exercise borrowing powers unless and until it has received a s. 117 certificate from the Registrar. If it does so the transactions are enforceable against the company but if the company fails to meet its obligations within 21 days of being called upon to do so the directors are, under s. 117(8), jointly and severally liable to indemnify a person who has suffered loss or damage by reason of the company's failure to meet its obligations. This is a further example of liability in the directors to pay, e.g. the company's debts and no fraud is required.

(d) *Section 306, Companies Act 1985.* Under this section the memorandum of a company may provide that the liability of its members shall be limited but the liability of its directors shall be unlimited.

Under s. 307 a limited company, if authorized by its articles, may by special resolution alter its memorandum in order to make unlimited the liability of its directors or managers, or of any managing director. This alternative is hardly ever adopted in practice.

COMPANIES AND PARTNERSHIPS COMPARED

The major differences between companies and partnerships may be considered under the following headings—

Formation. A company is created by registration under company legislation. A partnership is created by agreement which may be express or implied from the conduct of the partners. No special form is required, though partnership articles are usually written, and, in the case of a limited partnership, must be written.

Status at law. A company is an artificial legal person with perpetual succession. Thus a company may own property, make contracts, and sue and be sued. It is an entity distinct from its members. (*Salomon v Salomon & Co Ltd*, 1897,[1] *Macaura v Northern Assurance Co*, 1925,[2] and *Lee v Lee's Air Farming Ltd*, 1960.[3]) A partnership is not a legal person though it may sue and be sued in the firm's name. Thus the partners own the property of the firm and are liable on the contracts of the firm.

Transfer of shares. Shares in a company are freely transferable unless the company's constitution otherwise provides; restrictions may, of course, appear in the articles of a private company. A partner can transfer his share in the firm, but the assignee does not thereby become a partner and is merely entitled to the assigning partner's share of the profits.

Number of members. A company whether public or private must have at least two members, though no upper limit is laid down. A partnership may not consist of more than 20 persons though this maximum does not apply to all partnerships (see p. 2).

Management. Members of a company are not entitled to take part in the management of the company unless they become directors. Partners are entitled to share in the management of the firm unless the articles provide otherwise.

Agency. A member of a company is not by virtue only of that membership an agent of the company, and he cannot bind a company by his acts. Each general partner is an agent of the firm and may bind the firm by his acts.

Liability of members. The liability of a member of a company may be limited by shares or by guarantee. The liability of a general partner is unlimited. In a limited partnership one or more of the partners may limit his liability for the firm's debts to the amount of capital he has contributed, though even a limited partnership must have at least one general partner.

Powers. The affairs of a company are closely controlled by company legislation and the company can only operate within the objects laid down in its memorandum of association, though these can be altered to some extent by special resolution. Partners may carry on any business they please so long as it is not illegal and make what arrangements they wish with regard to the running of the firm.

Termination. No one member of a company can wind up the company, and the death, bankruptcy or insanity of a member does not mean that the company must be wound up. A partnership may be dissolved by any partner at any time unless the partnership is entered into for a fixed period of time. A partnership is, subject to any agreement between the partners to the contrary, dissolved by the death or bankruptcy of a partner.

Advantages and disadvantages of incorporation

The main advantages put forward by professional advisers for the conversion of a business into a limited company can be summarized as follows:

(1) Perpetual succession of the company despite the retirement, bankruptcy, mental disorder, or death of members.

(2) Liability of the members for the company's debts limited to the amount of their respective shareholding.

(3) Contractual liability of the company for all contracts made in its name.

(4) Ownership of property vested in the company is not affected by a change in shareholders.

(5) The company may obtain finance by creating a floating charge (see Chapter 11) with its undertaking or property as security yet may realize assets within that property without the consent of the lenders during the normal course of business until crystallization occurs. *No other form of business organization can use such a charge.*

18

It is generally thought that the above advantages outweigh the suggested disadvantages of incorporation, which are—
(1) Public inspection of accounts.
(2) Administrative expenses, in terms, e.g. of filing fees for documents.
(3) Compulsory annual audit (unless a dormant company).

LIFTING THE CORPORATE VEIL

The principle enunciated in *Salomon v Salomon & Co Ltd*, 1897[1] is not always applied. There are two jurisdictions. The veil may be lifted by the judiciary or by statute.

(a) The judiciary

It is difficult to be precise about the circumstances in which a judge will lift the corporate veil. However, it may be said that the power to do so is a tactic used by the judiciary in a flexible way to counter fraud, sharp practice, oppression, and illegality.

Examples of areas of application are as follows—
(i) *Groups of companies.* The court has on occasion lifted the veil of incorporation to allow a group of companies to be regarded as one. (*Re Hellenic and General Trust Ltd*, 1975[6] and *DHN Food Distributors Ltd v Tower Hamlets LBC*, 1976.[7])

In addition, the concept of agency has sometimes been used by the courts under which a subsidiary is regarded as the agent of its holding company, even though there is no agency agreement as such between them in regard to the transaction concerned. The effect is that transactions entered into by a subsidiary are regarded as those of the holding company for which the holding company is liable. This doctrine has been implemented for purposes of liability to tax. (See *Firestone Tyre & Rubber Co Ltd v Lewellin*, 1957.[8])

It has not been used to control abuses in the area of holding and subsidiary companies in regard to trade creditors. If a subsidiary is insolvent only public and stock market opinion prevents the holding company from liquidating the subsidiary, leaving its creditors' claims unsatisfied, even though the group as a whole is solvent.

(ii) *Illegality.* The courts have been prepared to draw aside the corporate veil of incorporation in order to establish that a company was owned by nationals of an enemy country so that to deal with it would be illegal because there would be a trading with the enemy. (*Daimler Co Ltd v Continental Tyre & Rubber Co (Great Britain)*, 1916.[9])

(iii) *The personal relationship company.* A breakdown in the management of the company or the complete exclusion of a member director from participation in management have been redressed by winding up the company on the just and equitable ground by regarding the company as in fact, if not in form, a partnership. (See *Ebrahimi v Westbourne Galleries*, 1972, p. 519 and *Re A & B C Chewing Gum*, 1975, p. 523.)

(iv) *Sharp practice.* There is also the 'facade' or 'sham' concept which seems to apply where the company concerned has been formed primarily to evade existing liabilities or to defeat the law. Here the courts have been prepared to investigate sharp practice by individuals who are trying to hide behind a company front. Thus in *Gilford Motor Co v Horne* [1933] Ch 935 a former employee bound by a restraint of trade set up a company in order to evade its provisions, claiming that he as a person might be bound by the restraint but the company, being a separate entity, could not be. An injunction was granted against both him and his company which the court described as 'a device, a stratagem . . . a mere cloak or sham'.

(b) Statutory provisions

As we have seen, the Companies Act 1985 in ss. 24 and 117, and the Insolvency Act 1986 in ss. 213 and 214, effectively draw aside the corporate veil by making directors and others liable for the debts and in some cases other liabilities of the company, in appropriate circumstances. (See pp. 12–17.)

An additional situation occurs under s. 15, Company Directors Disqualification Act 1986. This provides that a person who is disqualified to act in the management of a company (see p. 228), or who is an undischarged bankrupt who acts without leave of the court in the management of a company is jointly and severally liable with the company for 'relevant debts' of the company.

In order to prevent disqualified and/or bankrupt directors from running a company through nominee managers s. 15(2) (*ibid*) provides that anyone who acts or is willing to act (without leave of the court) on instructions given by a person whom he knows (at the time of acting or being willing to act) to be the subject of a disqualification order or an undischarged bankrupt is also jointly and severally liable for 'relevant debts'.

Relevant debts are such debts and other liabilities as are incurred while the person concerned was involved in management or when he was acting or willing to act on instructions.

2 Promotion and incorporation

The promotion of a company consists in taking the necessary steps to incorporate it by registration under the Companies Act to see that it has share and loan capital, and to acquire the business or property which the company is formed to control.

THE PROMOTER

There is no general definition of a promoter in the Companies Act 1985, though reference is made to the expression for certain special purposes. The word appears in s. 67(1) in regard to persons liable for a Companies Act 1985 prospectus. The meaning of the word is dealt with by s. 67(3) which provides that the expression 'promoter' means 'a promoter who was party to the preparation of the prospectus or any portion of it containing the untrue statement, but does not include any person by reason of his acting in a professional capacity for persons engaged in procuring the formation of the company'. Thus a solicitor or accountant who merely advises the promoters on legal and financial matters respectively will not be considered as a promoter in respect of misrepresentations which appear in any prospectus issued to raise capital. Nevertheless accountants in particular may be liable as experts if any of their financial statements are included with their consent in a prospectus and turn out to be false. (See pp. 111 and 128.)

Furthermore, s. 56(1), referring to the matters which must be disclosed in a prospectus, deals with the promotional situation without mentioning the word 'promoter' as follows, '... any person who is or has been engaged or interested in the formation of the company'.

In addition the courts have not given the expression a precise definition although Cockburn C J, in *Twycross v Grant* (1877) 2 CPD 469 called a promoter 'One who undertakes to form a company with reference to a given project, and to set it going, and who takes the necessary steps to accomplish that purpose'. In addition Bowen J in *Whaley Bridge Calico Printing Co v Green* (1880) 5 QBD 109 said 'The term promoter is a term not of law, but of business, usefully summing up in a single word a number of business operations familiar to the commercial world by which a company is generally brought into existence'.

Thus it can be said that whether a person is a promoter or not is a matter of *fact* and not of *law*. However, a promoter will usually be in some sort of controlling position with regard to the company's affairs, both before it is formed and during the early stages of its existence and will be in a position analogous to that of a director during that period.

During the nineteenth century there was in existence a class of professional company promoters whose methods of raising capital from the investing public were often unscrupulous and thus it was necessary for the legislature and the courts to impose rigorous duties upon such persons to protect the public from fraud.

Those days have gone and in modern times companies are promoted as private companies by persons with an interest in the business who become directors and remain so. Obviously some protection is still required because such persons could defraud the company by, for example, selling property to it at exorbitant rates. However, they are not likely to do so because in the modern situation the promoter retains an interest in the company and would merely be defrauding himself, whereas the old professional promoter either did not take any shares in the company at all or if he did unloaded them to others shortly after its incorporation.

If, after incorporation as a private company, there is a need to raise capital from the public then there would be a conversion to a public company. In such a situation there is no need for a promoter but there would be a need for the services of an issuing house to raise the necessary capital from the public.

Duties of a promoter

In *equity* a promoter stands in a fiduciary relationship towards the company he is promoting but is not a trustee. Thus he is not absolutely forbidden to make a profit out of the promotion so long as he has disclosed his interest in the transaction out of which the profit arose and the company consents to the retention of the profit. As a general rule any profits which he makes on the promotion and fails to disclose must be surrendered to the company. (*Gluckstein v Barnes*, 1900.[10]) However, this is not the case where the profit arises from the sale by the promoter to the company of property which he acquired before he began to act as promoter (*Re Cape Breton* (1887) 12 App Cas 652 and see p. 23.)

In *Erlanger v New Sombrero Phosphate Co* (1878) 3 App Cas

1218, the House of Lords took the view that the disclosure mentioned above had to be made to an independent board of directors. This view was, however, too strict. The boards of private companies, for example, are unlikely to be entirely independent of the promoter of the company and since *Salomon*[1] where it was held that the liquidator of the company could not complain of the sale to it at an obvious over-valuation of Mr Salomon's business, all the members having acquiesced therein, it has been accepted that disclosure to the members is equally effective. Thus, if the company issues a prospectus disclosure to the shareholders may be made in it and the shareholders give their consent by conduct when they apply for the shares being issued under the prospectus. Disclosure by a person, in his capacity as promoter, to himself, in his capacity as director, is not enough. (*Gluckstein v Barnes*, 1900.[10])

A promoter will perhaps most often make a secret profit by selling his own property to the company at an enhanced price and this is further considered below. However, other forms of profit are possible, e.g. where the promoter takes a commission from the person who is selling property to the company (and see also *Gluckstein v Barnes*, 1900).[10] All such profits are subject to the rule of disclosure. The liability of promoters as vendors of property may be considered under two headings—

A. Where the property was purchased by the promoter before he began to act as a promoter. If the promoter does not disclose his interest in the sale, the company may rescind the contract, i.e. return the property to the promoter and recover the purchase price. If the company wishes to keep the property it may do so, but cannot recover the profit as such. The remedy is to sue the promoter for damages in tort at common law for negligence if damage has been suffered, as where the company has paid a price in excess of the market price. That this can be done follows from the decision of the Court in *Jacobus Marler Estates Ltd v Marler* (1913) 114 LT 640n, and also *Re Leeds and Hanley Theatres of Varieties Ltd* [1902] 2 Ch 809. There may, according to circumstances, be an action for fraud, or under s. 2 of the Misrepresentation Act 1967 where the promoter's misstatements, e.g. as to value, are made negligently. Therefore, if P acquired some land in 1986 for £10,000 and became the promoter of X Co in 1987, selling the land to the company for £20,000 through a nominee and without disclosing his interest, then the company may—

(i) rescind the contract; or

(ii) keep the property and recover damages for P's breach of duty of skill and care. If the property was worth only £18,000 in 1986, the company could recover £2,000, but in no circumstances could it recover the £10,000 profit.

B. Where the property was purchased by the promoter after he began to act as a promoter. Here again the remedy of rescission is available, but if the company does not wish to rescind, it is possible to regard the promoter as agent for the company when he purchased the property, and the company can recover the profit made by the promoter. Thus, in the example given above, if P had been the promoter of the X Co when he purchased the land, the company could have recovered the profit made, i.e. £10,000.

One of the first acts in promotion is normally to negotiate for the purchase of property. However, the courts have been reluctant to hold that the promoter's contract to buy property is the start of his promotion and this has deprived the rule about secret profits of much of its practical value. Obviously, if the public has been invited to subscribe for shares when the property is purchased the courts will regard the promotion as having commenced but things rarely happen in this way.

The remedy of rescission is not in general available against the promoter if it is not possible to restore the company and the promoter to the position they were in before the contract was made, as where the company has resold the property to a third party. In such a case the company must go on with the contract and sue the promoter for the profit made, depending on the promoter's position when he bought the property which he later sold to the company. However, where the property has been merely used and not sold, as where the company has worked a mine purchased from a promoter, the rule of full restoration to the former position does not appear to operate as any real restriction on rescission in view of the wide powers now exercised by the courts to make financial adjustments when granting rescission. This is particularly true where the promoter has been fraudulent.

The duties of a promoter to the company *at common law* have not been fully developed by the judiciary. They are not contractual duties because the company is not incorporated and cannot contract with the promoter. Nevertheless a promoter can be regarded as a quasi-agent working without a contract and as such would at common law owe a general duty in negligence to exercise reasonable skill and care in the promotion, i.e. to show reasonable business acumen in regard to transactions entered into.

Thus if he allows the company to buy property—including his own—for more than it is worth he may be liable to the company in damages for negligence. (*Re Leeds and Hanley Theatres of Varieties Ltd* [1902] 2 Ch 809.)

Again, if a promoter issues a prospectus which he knows to be false so that the company is liable to be sued by subscribers, the company may sue him at common law for damages. In the *Leeds* case the court proceeded on the basis of fraud but since the company does not itself act upon the fraud by subscribing for shares, the decision is felt to be based on negligence. (See p. 126.)

In other areas, e.g. the purchase by a promoter of a business which loses money, the standard required presumably depends upon the experience and/or qualifications of the promoter in business fields. A higher standard would be expected of a promoter who was, e.g. an experienced and/or qualified accountant, than would be of a person of no great experience or qualification in the field of business. The duty may well be analogous to that of directors (see p. 262).

The equitable and common law duties of a promoter are owed to the company which may enforce them by writ served by the company on the promoter. Also, by s. 212, Insolvency Act 1986, the court may in a liquidation, on the petition of the liquidator or a creditor, or a member, order a promoter to re-pay or restore property obtained by breach of duty. A shareholder may also bring a derivative action on behalf of the company against a promoter. However, because of the decision in *Foss v Harbottle*, 1843 (see p. 197), such an action can only be brought if the shareholder can bring his complaint within one of the exceptions to the rule in *Foss* as where the promoters are also the company's directors and majority shareholders and are preventing an action being brought in the company's name.

The duties are not owed to shareholders who are unable to bring a personal action unless this relates to false statements made by the promoter in a prospectus.

Trade creditors and debenture holders cannot sue for breach of duty. There was, for example, no action by trade creditors in *Salomon*[1] although he did not disclose to them his interest in the promotion. However, secret profits or damages recovered by the liquidator in a winding up are used to pay the company's debts.

The duties of disclosure and skill and care upon promoters do not end on the incorporation of the company, nor indeed on the appointment of a board of directors. However, once the company has acquired the property and/or business which it was formed to manage, the initial capital has been raised and the board of directors has effectively taken over management from the promoters, the latter's duties will terminate. Thus, in *Re British Seamless Paper Box Co* (1881) 17 Ch D 467, a promoter disclosed a profit which he had made out of the company's promotion to those who provided it with share capital when it commenced business. It was held that he was under no duty to disclose that profit to those who were invited to subscribe further capital some 12 months later and in these circumstances the company could not recover the profit from him by reason of his failure to do so.

Non-cash assets acquired from subscribers of public companies

Although a promoter is not bound to be a subscriber to the memorandum on incorporation of a public company, it is very likely that he will be. In these circumstances certain provisions of the Companies Act 1985 apply. These are as follows:

Section 104 provides that for two years following the date of issue of the certificate that a company *registered as a public company* is entitled to commence business, the company may not acquire non-cash assets from subscribers to the memorandum having an aggregate value equal to one-tenth or more of the nominal value of the issued share capital unless—

(*a*) the valuation rules set out in s. 109 are complied with. This means that the asset must have been valued by an independent accountant who must state that the value of the consideration to be received by the company is not less than the value of the consideration to be given by it; and

(*b*) the acquisition of the asset and the terms of the acquisition have been approved by an ordinary resolution of the company.

Under s. 104(4) the independent accountant's report must have been circulated to the members with the notice of the meeting. A copy of the resolution and the report must be filed at the Registry within 15 days of the passing of the resolution. Similar rules apply to a private company on re-registration as a public company if non-cash assets equal to at least one-tenth of the nominal value of the issued share capital at that time are acquired from persons who are members of the company at the time of re-registration. (See below.)

Under s. 104(6) the above rules do not apply if the asset is acquired in the ordinary course of the company's business, e.g. goods for resale.

If the above rules are not complied with then—

(*a*) if the non-cash asset has been paid for in cash, the cash may be recovered by the company or if the agreement has not been carried out it is void (S. 105(2)).

The Act is silent as regards recovery of the asset by the person who has repaid to the company the money he received for it. However, he could presumably recover it at common law on the basis of total failure of consideration;

(*b*) if the non-cash asset has been paid for by the company in whole or in part by an issue of shares then the subscriber is liable to make up the difference between the value of the non-cash asset and the value of the shares in cash plus interest on this amount since the shares were issued at what the Act refers to as 'the appropriate rate' (s. 105(3)(*b*)). Section 107 provides that the appropriate rate is 5 per cent per annum though this can be increased by statutory instrument.

By reason of s. 104(3) the above provisions apply when a private company converts to a public company and the non-cash asset is acquired from a person who is a member of the private company on the date of conversion, i.e. re-registration. The period is two years beginning with that date. Such members are also, in a way, promoters of the public company.

Payment to promoters

Promoters may be paid for their services to the company by cash or by the allotment of fully or partly paid shares. A payment in cash presents no problem, although disclosure of the amount paid is required in any 1985 Act *prospectus* issued within two years of the payment. (S. 56(1) and Sched 3, Part I, para 10(1)(*c*)). However, if the payment is in fully or partly paid shares, disclosure of the shares allotted to the promoters must be made in the prospectus and in addition, in the annual return, and also in the return as to allotments. The contract between the company and the promoters for their services, or particulars of that contract if it is not in writing, must be filed with the Registrar within one month of the allotment of the shares to the promoters. (S. 88(2)(*b*).)

Since a company cannot make a valid contract before incorporation, a promoter cannot legally claim any remuneration for his services, or an indemnity for the expenses incurred in floating the company. (*Re National Motor Mail Coach Co, Clinton's Claim*, 1908.[11]) The promoters could make a contract with the company *after* incorporation, though this would have to be under seal because the consideration given by the promoters will be past. However, it is more usual for the promoters to include a provision in the articles which allows the directors of the company to pay promotion expenses under their general management powers. (See *Table A, Reg 70.*) This does not bind the company in law (*Re English and Colonial Produce Co Ltd* [1906] 2 Ch 435) but, since the promoters or their nominees are likely to be the first directors, the payment will usually be made.

Pre-incorporation contracts

Promoters incur personal liability on contracts which they make on the company's behalf before its incorporation. (S. 36(4).)

The promoter is not merely liable to pay damages for breach of his implied warranty that he had authority to contract on the company's behalf. Thus, if the promoter has agreed before incorporation to buy land on behalf of the company, the vendor could obtain specific performance of the contract thus requiring the promoter to perform it and take and pay for the land. This personal liability applies whether the promoter contracts on behalf of the company as its agent or not. (*Phonogram Ltd v Lane*, 1981.[12])

The company cannot adopt the contract after its incorporation. Nevertheless, a contract may be *implied* from the way in which the company acts after its incorporation. However, it should be noted—

(*a*) that the acts of the company after incorporation must be unequivocally referable to the contract said to be implied. (*Natal Land and Colonization Co v Pauline Colliery and Development Syndicate*, 1904.[13]);

(*b*) even if the acts are unequivocally referable they amount only to an *offer* to be bound. (*Natal Land and Colonization Co v Pauline Colliery and Development Syndicate*, 1904.[13]) It should be noted that mere performance of the pre-incorporation contract by the company is not enough to amount to an offer, particularly if it is based on the belief that the contract is binding so that the company's performance is necessary in order to avoid legal liability. (*Re Northumberland Avenue Hotel Co*, 1886.[14]);

(*c*) the offer must be accepted by the other party. (*Natal Land and Colonization Co v Pauline Colliery and Development Syndicate*, 1904[13] and *Howard v Patent Ivory Manufacturing Co*, 1888.[15])

A company may therefore benefit from performance of services under a pre-incorporation contract without having to pay for the same. This rather unjust situation was reinforced by the decision in *Re National Motor Mail Coach Co*, 1908.[11]

The above difficulties do not worry, for example, a garage proprietor in a small way of business who is promoting a limited company to take over the garage business. Such a person will obviously be a director of the new company and will usually hold most of the shares in it. Being in control, he can ensure that the company enters into the necessary contracts after incorporation. However, where the promoter is not in control of the company after its incorporation, the difficulties outlined above are very real.

A promoter may overcome the difficulties facing him in the matter of pre-incorporation contracts in the following ways—

(i) He may incorporate the company before he makes contracts, in which case the problems relating to pre-incorporation contracts do not apply. There is no reason why a promoter should not take this course since the expenses of incorporation are not prohibitive, though they have increased considerably in the last few years.

(ii) He can settle a draft agreement with the other party so that when the company is formed it enters into a contract on the terms of the draft; but the parties are not bound other than morally by the draft, and unless the company and the other party make the contract after incorporation, there is no legal redress. *However, the promoter is not liable because there is no contract with him.*

(iii) The promoter may make the contract himself and assign the benefit of it to the company after it is incorporated. Since English law does not allow a person to assign the burden of his contract, the disadvantage of this method is that the promoter remains personally liable for the performance of his promises in the contract after the assignment to the company. Thus it is desirable for the other party to the contract to agree that the promoters shall be released from their obligations if the company enters into an identical contract with the other party after incorporation. Since the promoters will usually control the company at this stage, they should be able to ensure that the company does make such a contract with the other party and so procure their own release.

(iv) Where the promoter is buying property for the company, he may take an option on it for say three months. If the company, when it is formed, wishes to take over the property, the promoter can assign the benefit of the option to the company or enforce the option personally for the company's benefit. If the company does not wish to take the property, the promoter is not personally liable to take and pay for it, though he may lose the money he agreed to pay.

(v) It should also be noted that s. 36(4) states that the promoter is personally liable 'subject to any agreement to the contrary'. Thus the promoter could agree when making the contract that he should not be personally liable on it. (See the remarks of Lord Denning in *Phonogram Ltd v Lane*, 1981.[12])

Nevertheless the legal position is unsatisfactory and the Jenkins Committee on Company Law Reform which reported in June 1962 (Cmnd 1749) recommended legislation under which a company when formed could validly adopt a pre-incorporation contract by unilateral act, and Clause 6 of the Companies Bill, 1973 which never became law permitted a company after incorporation to ratify contracts which purported to have been made in its name or on its behalf before incorporation without the consent of the other party involved. At the present time such an act or ratification operates only as an offer to be bound which the other party must accept. (*Natal Land and Colonization Co v Pauline Colliery and Development Syndicate*, 1904.[13])

Public companies—commencement of business and borrowing

Under s. 117 a *public company*, registered as such on its initial incorporation, cannot commence business or exercise any borrowing powers unless the Registrar has issued what is known as a s. 117 certificate. A *private company* does not require such a certificate.

The certificate will be issued when the Registrar is satisfied that the nominal value of the company's allotted share capital is not less than the authorized minimum (£50,000) and not less than one-quarter of the nominal value of each issued share in the company plus the *whole* of any premium on such shares has been received by the company, whether in cash or otherwise. A share allotted in pursuance of an employees' share scheme may not be taken into account in determining the nominal value of the company's allotted share capital unless it is paid up at least as to one-quarter of the nominal value of the share and the whole of any premium on the share.

In order to obtain an s. 117 certificate the company must file with the Registrar a statutory declaration in prescribed form signed by a director or secretary of the company stating—

(*a*) that the nominal value of the company's allotted share capital is not less than the authorized minimum;

(*b*) the amount paid up at the time of the application on the allotted share capital of the company;

(*c*) the amount, or estimated amount, of the preliminary expenses of the company and the persons by whom any of those expenses have been paid or are payable; and

(*d*) any amount or benefit paid or given or intended to be paid or given to any promoter of the company and the consideration for the payment or benefit.

When a certificate is issued it is conclusive evidence that the company is entitled to commence business and exercise borrowing powers. (S. 117(6).) Failure to comply with s. 117 may result in a fine on the company and any officer in default. (S. 117(7).)

If a public company has not obtained an s. 117 certificate within a year of registration the Registrar may present a petition to wind it up. (Ss. 122(1)(*b*) and 124(4)(*a*), Insolvency Act 1986.)

If a company does commence business or borrow without an s. 117 certificate transactions with traders and lenders are nevertheless enforceable against the company. However, if the company cannot meet its obligations in terms of payment of a debt or repayment of a loan incurred during the period of unlawful trading, within 21 days of being called upon to do so, the directors of the company are jointly and severally liable to indemnify the trader or lender in respect of his loss resulting from the company's failure to meet its obligations.

INCORPORATION

Application for registration is made by filing certain documents with the Registrar of Companies.

They are as follows:

(i) *Memorandum of association.* If the company is a public company the memorandum must be in accordance with Table F of the Companies (Tables A–F) Regulations 1985 (SI 1985 No. 805) i.e. it must state that the company is a public limited company and its name must end with the words 'public limited company' and its authorized share capital must be at least £50,000.

(ii) *Articles of association.* Public and private companies limited by shares need not file special articles but may adopt *Table A* as set out in the 1985 Regulations.

The contents and purposes of the above documents will be dealt with later.

(iii) A *Statutory Declaration* made by a solicitor engaged in the formation of the company or by a person named as a director or secretary of the company in the statement of first directors and secretary delivered under s. 10 (see below) to the effect that s. 12(1) has been complied with must be delivered to the Registrar on registration and he may accept it as sufficient evidence of compliance with the Act. (S. 12(3).) The statutory declaration is made before a commissioner for oaths and if it contains false statements the person making those statements is liable to be prosecuted for perjury.

Section 12(1) provides that the Registrar shall not register the memorandum of a company unless he is satisfied that all the requirements of the Companies Acts in regard to registration have been complied with. If the company is a public company the share capital with which it proposes to be registered must be not less than the minimum authorized by the Act, i.e. £50,000.

Under s. 13(7) a certificate of incorporation of a public company states that it is a public company and is furthermore conclusive evidence that the requirements of the Act have been complied with and that the company is a public company. A certificate of incorporation issued to a private company is similarly conclusive evidence on the same lines as the above. (S. 13(7).)

(iv) *Form PUC I,* which contains a statement of nominal capital. This is required by the Finance Act 1973. However, under the Finance Act 1973 no capital duty is normally payable on registration but is paid at the rate of 1 per cent instead when the shares are issued.

(v) *The address of the registered office and a statement of directors and secretaries.* All companies are required to file on registration a notice of the address of the registered office and a statement of directors and secretaries. (S. 10(2) and (6).) The latter shows in respect of individual directors their names and any former names which they have used, their residential address, their nationalities, their business occupations, any other directorships which they hold, or have held during

31

the previous five years, and if the company is a public company or a subsidiary of a public company, the dates of their birth. Where a director is a corporation the notice must show its corporate name and the address of its registered or principal office. (See further p. 240.)

The statement must be signed by or on behalf of the subscribers of the memorandum and must contain a consent signed by each of the directors and secretaries named in it to act in the relevant capacity. (S. 10(3).)

Those persons named in the statement are deemed, on the incorporation of the company, to have been appointed as the first directors or secretary or joint secretaries of the company. Any appointment by the articles delivered with the memorandum of a person as director or secretary of the company is void unless he is named as a director or as a secretary in the statement. (S. 10(5).)

If the Registrar is satisfied with the contents of the documents, he will, on payment of certain fees, issue a certificate of incorporation. It should be noted that if the documents are in order and the company's objects appear legal, the Registrar has no discretion in the matter. He must grant a certificate and, since the Registrar is here acting in a quasi-judicial capacity, the subscribers may enforce registration by the prerogative *order of mandamus*. (*R. v Registrar of Companies, ex parte Bowen* [1914] 3 KB 1161.)

Effect of incorporation

The issue of a certificate of incorporation incorporates the members of the company into a *persona at law*, and limits their liability if the memorandum requires this. The certificate of incorporation is *conclusive* evidence that all the requirements of the Companies Act as to registration have been complied with, and if any irregularity had occurred in the registration procedure, it would not be possible to attack the validity of the company's incorporation. The evidence which was available to prove the irregularity would not be admissible. (*Cotman v Brougham*, 1918, see p. 455.) This provision, which is, as we have seen, contained in s. 13(7) means that all English companies registered under the Act are companies *de jure* (as a matter of law). In the United States of America, where this rule does not apply in every State, actions have been brought in the courts attacking the validity of a company's formation many years after incorporation. This cannot happen in England and Wales.

However, the certificate of incorporation is not conclusive evidence that all the objects of the company are legal; and if a company is registered with illegal or immoral objects, the House of Lords decided in *Bowman v Secular Society* [1917] AC 406 that the Crown could apply, through the Attorney-General, for the prerogative *order of certiorari* to cancel the registration made by the Registrar. In *Attorney-General v Lindi St. Claire (Personal Services) Ltd* (1981) 2 Co Law 69 the High Court quashed a decision by the Registrar of Companies to register the business of a prostitute as Lindi St. Claire (Personal Services) Ltd. The name was registered in 1979 after the Registrar had rejected Miss St. Claire's alternative titles, i.e. Prostitutes Ltd, Hookers Ltd and Lindi St. Claire French Lessons Ltd. Miss St. Claire's accountants advised her to register a company after receiving a letter from the Revenue's policy division stating that it considered prostitution to be a trade. The Attorney-General contended that the company should not have been registered because it was formed for sexually immoral purposes and was consequently against public policy and illegal. The High Court agreed and the registration was quashed.

In addition a company incorporated with unlawful objects may be ordered by the court to be wound up on the petition of a creditor or member, the ground for the petition being that it is just and equitable that the company should be wound up (s. 122(1)(g), Insolvency Act 1986), or on the petition of the Department of Trade and Industry (DoTI) where it has appointed an inspector to investigate the company's affairs and he has reported adversely on the legality of the objects for which it was formed. (S. 440.)

From the date impressed upon the certificate the company becomes a body corporate with perpetual succession, and with the right to exercise the powers given in its memorandum (s. 13). The company's life dates from the first moment of the day of incorporation. (*Jubilee Cotton Mills v Lewis*, 1924.[16])

There is no statutory requirement that the certificate should be displayed at the registered office or kept at any particular place.

Publicity in connection with incorporation

The Registrar is required by s. 711 to publish in the *London Gazette*:
   (a) the issue of any certificate of incorporation;
   (b) any report as to the value of a non-cash asset under s. 104 where a non-cash asset has been acquired from a subscriber.

Oversea companies

A company which is formed in a country outside Great Britain, whether incorporated by the law of that country or not, may carry on business in Great Britain without being incorporated under our legislation relating to companies, however large or small its membership may be. (*Bateman v Service* (1881) 6 App Cas 386.) However, if the company is an incorporated one and *establishes a place of business in Great Britain* then it must under s. 691 within a month of so doing file with the Registrar—

(*a*) a certified copy of the instruments defining the constitution of the company, and a certified translation if not in English;

(*b*) a list of directors and secretary;

(*c*) the name and address of at least one person resident in Great Britain authorized to accept service of notices on behalf of the company;

(*d*) the date on which the company's place of business in Great Britain was established.

Any alteration in the above particulars must be filed and the company must file annually the same accounts as a registered company. (Ss. 692 and 700.)

The company's name and country of incorporation (and, if the liability of its members is limited, a statement of that fact) must be stated on every place of business, every prospectus, and on all letterheads, notices, and official publications of the company in Great Britain. (S. 693.)

An overseas company is also subject to the same restrictions as a registered company in regard to the issue of a prospectus within Great Britain (ss. 72–79) (see further Chapter 5), and as to its name. (S. 694.) (See further Chapter 3.) If an overseas company ceases to have a place of business in Great Britain it must notify this fact to the Registrar who will remove the company from the Companies House index. (S. 696(4).)

Companies incorporated in the Channel Islands or the Isle of Man, which establish a place of business here, are thereafter subject to all the provisions of the Act as if they were registered companies, and must deliver to the Registrar all documents which would be required to register a company if it were incorporated in Great Britain. (S. 699.)

It should be noted that a foreign company with an office in Great Britain, e.g. for prestige reasons but which does not actually carry on business here, is not covered by the above rules. (*CPG Products Corporation v Shroder Executor and Trustee Co*, Chancery Division, 21 April 1980, unreported.)

3 The constitution of the company

The constitution of a registered company consists of two documents called the *memorandum of association* and the *articles of association*. The Memorandum contains the most important provisions setting out as it does the sort of activities which the company can carry on. The articles contain rules governing the internal management of the company such as the appointment of directors and the powers of the board, the rights of different classes of shareholders, and the holding of meetings of the company. The memorandum is of interest to outsiders who wish to deal with the company, while the articles are of interest mainly to shareholders and directors. However, since the powers of directors are, as we have seen, in the articles, they are on occasions also of interest to outsiders.

THE MEMORANDUM OF ASSOCIATION

Under s. 2 the memorandum must contain clauses setting out the following information—

(i) the name of the company with 'Limited' as the last word if the company is a private limited company. If the company is a public company the liability of its members must be limited and its name must end with the words 'public limited company';

(ii) in the case of a public company the statement 'The company is to be a public company';

(iii) whether the registered office is to be situated in England or in Wales;

(iv) the objects clause;

(v) a statement that the liability of the members is limited by shares (or by guarantee) where this is the case;

(vi) the amount of the share capital (if any) with which the company proposes to be registered and its division into shares of a fixed amount. This does not apply to unlimited companies. Where the company is a public company the share capital must be at least £50,000.

In the case of a company limited by guarantee the memorandum must state that each member undertakes to contribute to the assets of the company in the event of its being wound up, such amount as may be required, not exceeding a specified amount. The above, being statutory clauses, must appear in the memorandum and not for example in the articles, but the memorandum may contain other clauses, since the persons responsible for drafting the company's constitution have a choice between the memorandum and articles in the case of other provisions.

The memorandum is completed by the *Association Clause* in which the subscribers declare their intention to be associated as a company. The memorandum must be subscribed by at least two persons whether the company is public or private. (S. 1.) All subscribers must take at least one share (s. 2(5)(*b*)), and each subscriber must show opposite his name the number of shares he takes. (S. 2(5)(*c*).) Each subscriber must sign the memorandum in the presence of at least one witness who must also attest the signature. (S. 2(6).) The same witness may attest all the signatures.

Section 3 provides that the memorandum shall be in the form set out in the Tables contained in the Companies (Tables A–F) Regulations 1985 (SI 1985 No. 805) or as near thereto as possible, and Table B is appropriate for a private company limited by shares. The memorandum of a public company is in the form set out in Table F. In practice, however, considerable modifications are made. The memorandum once registered cannot be altered except in the cases expressly provided for in the Companies Act 1985. (S. 2(7).)

Since the memorandum is such an important document, it will now be examined in more detail.

1. THE NAME

Chapter II of Part I of the 1985 Act sets up a system for controlling company names.

COMPANY NAMES

On registration

Under s. 25(1) the name of a public company *as stated in its memorandum*, must end with the words 'public limited company' or, if its registered office is in Wales, the Welsh equivalent. Under s. 25(2) a private company limited by shares, or guarantee, must have 'limited' as its last word (or, as above, the Welsh equivalent) unless it is exempt under s. 30 (see p. 41).

Under s. 26 a new company may not be registered by a name which—

1. includes, otherwise than at the end of the name, any of the following words or their permitted abbreviations: 'limited', 'unlimited' or 'public limited company' (or their Welsh equivalent);
2. is the *same* as a name already on the index of names kept by the Registrar of Companies;
3. in the opinion of the Secretary of State would, if used, constitute a criminal offence or be offensive; e.g. a name which was obscene or blasphemous;
4. in the opinion of the Secretary of State would be likely to give the impression that the company is connected with local or central government;
5. includes any word or expression for the time being specified in regulations made under s. 29. These may be referred to as 'sensitive names', and are sensitive in the sense that they imply a prestigious connotation by implying an association with some well recognized institution or body, e.g. the Royal Family or a bank.

The above provisions apply to an existing company which wishes to change its name.

Index of names

Under s. 714 the Registrar is required to keep an index consisting mainly of the names of all UK registered companies and all overseas companies with a place of business in the UK.

Unless the name of a company is the SAME as a name on the index it will be registered but if the name is a sensitive name the company must have obtained the permission of the relevant department or body.

Sensitive company names

The Companies and Business Names Regulations 1981 (SI 1981/1685) and the Company and Business Names (Amendment) Regulations 1982 (SI 1982/1653) deal with sensitive company names in the following manner—

1. *A company would only be registered by a name containing the following words given by way of example if the applicant had obtained a letter of non-objection from the relevant department/body:*

Words	Department/Body
Royal, Royalty, King(s), Queen(s), Prince(s), Windsor, Duke(s), Royale, His/Her Majesty	Home Office (or Scottish or Welsh office respectively if the company's registered office were to be in Scotland or Wales)
Police	Home Office
Bank, Banking, Bankers, Deposit, Deposit Taker, Banker	Bank of England
Special School	Department of Education and Science
Chemist, Pharmacy, Pharmacist, Pharmaceutical, Drug, Druggist	The Pharmaceutical Society of Great Britain
Optician, Contact Lens	The General Optician Council
Dental, Dentist, Dentistry	The General Dental Council
Nurse, Nursing	General Nursing Council
Midwife(ives), Midwifery	General Midwives Board for England and Wales
Health Visitor	Council for Education and Training of Health Visitors
District Nurse	Panel of Assessors in District Health Nursing
Veterinary	Royal College of Veterinary Surgeons
Chemist/ry (Industrial/Scientific)	Royal Society of Chemistry
Health Centre, Health Service, Nursing Home, Pregnancy Termination/Abortion	Department of Health and Social Security
Horse/Pony Breed Society, Cattle Breed, Breed/Herd Society	Department of Agriculture, Fisheries and Food
Charity/Charitable	Charity Commission
University, Polytechnic	Department of Education and Science

2. *The consent of the Secretary of State for Trade would be required to the registration of a company by a name including the following words which:*
   (a) *Imply national or multi-national pre-eminence*
   International
   National

European
United Kingdom
Great Britain (or British)
England (or English)
Scotland (or Scottish)
Wales (or Welsh)
Ireland (or Irish)

(b) *Imply government connection, patronage or sponsorship*
Authority
Board
Council

(c) *Imply business pre-eminence or representative status*
Association
Federation
Institution (or Institute)
Society

(d) *Imply certain specific objects or functions*
Assurance/Insurance/Re-assurance/Re-insurance
Insurers/Assurers/Re-insurers/Re-assurers
Insurance broker(s)/Assurance broker(s)
Re-insurance broker(s)/Re-assurance broker(s)
Chamber of Commerce, Chamber of Trade, Chamber of Industry
Co-operative
Group
Holding
Post Office/Giro
Trust/Unit trust
Stock Exchange
Register/Registered
Friendly, Industrial, Provident Society
Building Society
Trade Union
Credit Union

Trade-marks

The name must not include a registered trade-mark unless the consent of the owner of the trade-mark is obtained. The Registrar does not consult the Trade-Marks Index when considering applications for a proposed new company name and the acceptance of a particular name is not an indication that no trade-marks right exists in it. Applicants are therefore advised in their own interest to avoid possible expense and inconvenience by investigating the possibility that others may have trade-mark rights in the names—or parts of such names—they require before applying to the Registrar. Searches may be made at the Trade-Marks Registry in London.

Change of name

(a) Voluntary change

Under s. 28(1), a company may, by special resolution, change its name and the Registrar will issue an altered certificate of incorporation. The new name must comply with the above-mentioned provisions relating to the prohibition on registration of certain names, and the change does not take effect until the altered certificate of incorporation is issued. (S. 28(6).)

(b) Compulsory change

(i) Section 28(2) provides that *within 12 months* of registration in a particular name the Secretary of State may direct a change in name within such period as he may specify if a registered name is the same or 'too like' that of a pre-existing company which appears (or should have appeared) on the index.

A complaints procedure exists and guidelines have been published but a major example of the 'too like' situation will be names with a distinctive element in common, e.g. Widget Holdings Ltd and Widget Ltd.

In a way these provisions are unsatisfactory because a newly registered company and one which has changed its name will be in doubt for 12 months as to the right to its name.

(ii) Section 28(3) deals with names obtained by deception and where it appears to the Secretary of State that a company has given misleading information in connection with its registration in a particular name the Secretary of State may *within five years of registration* direct a change of name within such period as he may specify.

(iii) Under s. 32 the Secretary of State has power to direct a company to change its name if it gives so misleading an indication of its activities as to be likely to cause harm to the public. The section is designed to deal with 'shell' companies as where a company named, e.g. 'Prosper Investments Trust' is acquired and used for the purpose of making cheap washing machines. The power under s. 32 is exercisable *at any time*. The company must comply with a request to change within six weeks but has a right to appeal to the court within three weeks after the DoTI's requirement is notified to it.

Where a company changes its name either voluntarily or compulsorily under the above provisions the change will not affect any of its rights or obligations or render defective any legal proceedings. (Ss. 28(7) and 32(6).)

On a change of name a new certificate of incorporation is issued by the Registrar who must publish the fact of issue in the *London Gazette*. (S. 711(1)(*a*).)

Companies exempt from requirement to use the word 'limited'

(*a*) *Companies eligible*

Section 30 makes provision for exempting certain companies from the requirement to use the word 'limited' in their names. Section 30 applies—

1. To private companies limited by guarantee, which for the future will be the only type of company to be allowed to apply for the exemption.
2. Where the objects of the company are to promote commerce, art, science, education, religion, charity, or any profession and anything incidental or conducive to any of those objects.
3. Where the company's memorandum or articles require that the company's profits or income be applied in the promotion of its objects. They must also prohibit payment of dividends and require all surplus assets on a winding up to be transferred to another body with similar or charitable objects.

Private companies limited *either by shares or by guarantee* which had a licence under s. 19 of the 1948 Act (a similar provision now repealed) may continue to omit the word 'limited', provided they meet the new criteria.

(*b*) *Formalities to obtain the exemption*

These are as follows—
1. The making of a statutory declaration *in the case of a company to be formed* by a solicitor engaged in the formation of the company or by a person named as a director or secretary of the company in the statement delivered under s. 10(2) (statement of first directors and secretary) or *in the case of a company changing its name to omit 'limited'*, by a director or secretary of the company (s. 30(5)(*c*)).
2. The statutory declaration is made to the Registrar and states that the company is one whose memorandum and articles are appropriately limited so that s. 30 applies (s. 30(4)).

(c) Provisions applicable after exemption

1. An exempt company may not alter its memorandum and articles so that they no longer comply with the exemption requirements (s. 31(1)).
2. If it appears to the Secretary of State that the company is breaking the limitations in its constitution, as where it is carrying on business for a profit he has power to direct the company to change its name by adding 'limited'. (S. 31(2).)

   There are fines on the company and its officers for contravention of s. 30. (S. 31(5).)
3. A company which is exempt from the requirements relating to the use of the word 'limited' and does not include the word as part of its name, is also exempt from the requirements of the 1985 Act relating to the publication of its name and the sending of lists of members to the Registrar of Companies with the annual return. (S. 30(7), see p. 184.)

   It should be noted that the exemption is not fully effective because s. 351(1)(d) requires a limited company exempt from the obligation to use limited as part of its name to mention in all business letters and order forms that it is a limited company, even though its name does not reveal that it is.

NAMES OF OVERSEA COMPANIES

Under s. 694, the Secretary of State may require an oversea company to carry on business in Great Britain *under a name other than its corporate name* if he is of opinion that it would be undesirable for that oversea company to carry on business in Great Britain in its corporate name. Thus if an oversea company has a name which is the same as one on the index or is 'sensitive' or 'too like' that of an existing company the Secretary of State may stop it from trading in that name, and if it wishes to go on trading here, it will have to change its name.

BUSINESS NAMES

Section 1 of the Business Names Act 1985 deals with the control of business names and s. 1(1)(c) applies the Act to companies which carry on business in Great Britain under a name which does not consist of the corporate name without addition. An addition indicating that the business is carried on in succession to a former owner does not make the name a business name. (S. 1(2)(c), *ibid.*) Section 2(1)(a) *ibid* provides that if a company uses a business name that name must not be one which would be likely to give the impression that the business is connected with local or central government nor must the name consist of or contain sensitive words (see above), unless permission has been granted by the appropriate authority, or the written approval of the Secretary of State has been obtained.

Section 1(1), *ibid*, applies the business names controls to oversea companies carrying on business here providing they have a place of business here.

Disclosure of names of those using business names

If Boxo Ltd trades through a number of retail outlets under the name 'Paris Fashions' then s. 1, *ibid*, applies the rules relating to business names to Boxo Ltd. These rules which are contained in s. 4, *ibid*, which requires the company to state in legible characters on all its business letters, written orders for goods or services to be supplied to the business, invoices, receipts, and written demands for payment of debts, the corporate name and an address within Great Britain at which service of any document relating in any way to the business will be effective. This will normally be the address of the registered office of the company. The corporate name and an address for service of documents must also be disclosed in a prominent position, so that it may easily be read by customers or suppliers, in any premises where the business is carried on *and to which* the customers or suppliers of any goods or services to the business have access.

Furthermore, s. 4(2), *ibid*, requires that the corporate name and an address for service be given immediately, in writing to anyone who is doing or negotiating business with the company and asks for them.

Breach of the provisions relating to business names

The criminal sanction consists of default fines on the corporation and also its directors and officers, e.g. secretary.

The civil sanction is that s. 5, *ibid*, applies to defeat a contractual claim by a person (in this context a company) carrying on business under a trade name where that person was in breach of the disclosure provisions of s. 4(1), *ibid* (disclosure on business letters, etc.), or s. 4(2), *ibid* (information to be given to person doing or discussing business) at the time the contract was made. Thus the company might not be able to claim successfully an unpaid contractual debt. However, the person being sued by the company must show—
1. that he has been unable to pursue a claim against the company himself because the company has failed to disclose the information required, *or* that he *has* suffered some financial loss as a result of failure to disclose; but

2. the court may allow the company's claim to proceed if it considers it just and equitable to do so; furthermore
3. Section 5, *ibid*, does not bar any counterclaim by the company if it is sued by, e.g. a customer.

An example to illustrate the operation of s. 5, *ibid*, would be to suppose that Joe Soap bought goods from Paris Fashions which were defective, and that Joe Soap was unable to pursue a claim against Boxo Ltd because he could not find out who was behind Paris Fashions. If Boxo Ltd sued Joe Soap for the price the court may decide that Boxo's claim should not proceed. The same might be true where Joe Soap had suffered financial loss as where he had sought a refund on goods returned but had been unable to get it and of course financial loss could presumably consist merely in the expense incurred in trying to trace the true owner of Paris Fashions. However, if Joe Soap were to sue Boxo Ltd for damages because, e.g. goods supplied by Paris Fashions were sub-standard then Boxo Ltd could counter-claim for the price if they had not been paid.

Other provisions not in company legislation

Statute has prohibited the use of certain names which have an association with recognized charitable organizations, in order to prevent private individuals from profiting by the goodwill which attaches to them. Thus, for example, a company's name may not comprise the words 'Red Cross' without the authority of the Army Council. (Geneva Conventions Act 1957, s. 6.)

At common law: passing off a name

As we have seen, apart from the special case of 'shell companies' under s. 32 where the DoTI can direct a change of name 'at any time', the registrar has under s. 28 only 12 months from incorporation or change of name to direct a change because a name has been registered which is the same or too like that of an existing company.

Once that time has passed and, say, the existence of a company with a 'too like' name has not been discovered by the first company to have the name then the first company can only seek redress at common law in the law of tort.

A company or other business organization which carries on or proposes to carry on business under a name calculated to deceive the public by confusion with the name of an existing concern commits the civil wrong (or tort) of *passing off*, and will be restrained by injunction from doing so. Where the offending business is a proposed company, an injunction can be obtained to prevent registration, if information is available in time. If an injunction is made against an existing company for passing off, it must either change its name or its business or wind up. (*Société Anonyme des Anciens Établissements Panhard et Levassor v Panhard Levassor Motor Co Ltd*, 1901.[17])

To constitute the tort of *passing off* the business carried on by the offending concern must be the same as that of the plaintiff, or it must be likely that custom will come to the offending concern because the public associate it with the plaintiff (see *Ewing v Buttercup Margarine Co Ltd*, 1917[18] and contrast *Aerators Ltd v Tollit*, 1902[19]); otherwise no injunction will be granted.

As a general rule an injunction will not be granted where the offending concern is trading in the name of its *proprietor* though, where a company is trading in a name which is merely that of one only of its members, then an injunction will be granted if confusion with an existing concern is likely to result. Neither will an injunction be granted where a company uses a name which consists of that of the person from whom the company bought its business, even though confusion results. (*Waring and Gillow Ltd v Gillow and Gillow Ltd*, 1916[20].)

Miscellaneous provisions of the 1985 Act regarding name

A company which is not a public company is guilty of an offence if it carries on any trade, profession or business under a name which includes, as the last part, the words 'public limited company' or their equivalent in Welsh. (S. 33(1).)

A public company is guilty of an offence if it carries on any trade, profession or business under a name which is likely to give the impression that that company is a private company. (S. 33(2).)

Publication of the name

Sections 348, 349 and 350 provide that the company's full name must appear legibly and conspicuously—

    (*a*) outside the registered office and all places of business;

    (*b*) on the common seal;

    (*c*) on all business letters, notices, and official publications; and

    (*d*) in all bills of exchange, cheques, promissory notes, orders for money or goods, receipts, and invoices signed or issued on its behalf.

Fines may be imposed on the company and its officers for failure to comply, and, in addition, the officers of the company may incur personal liability for any amount due unless it is paid by the company (s. 349(4)).

This liability may arise where an officer of the company signs or authorizes the signature, on behalf of the company, of any bill of exchange, promissory note, cheque or order for money or goods, and the name of the company is not mentioned thereon in legible characters. The rule of personal liability, which applies even though the officer signs as an agent, arises most often in connection with bills of exchange or cheques. It is probably not necessary to show that the third party concerned has been misled. (*Per* Lord Hunter in *Scottish & Newcastle Breweries Ltd v Blair*, 1967 SLT 72.)

Thus officers have been held personally liable where—

(*a*) *the word 'limited' was omitted* (*Penrose v Martyr*, 1858),[21] though it is enough if the full name appears anywhere on the bill and the abbreviation 'Ltd' can be used (*Stacey v Wallis*, 1912);[22]

(*b*) *the company was described by the wrong name* (*Hendon v Adelman*, 1973),[23] though the doctrine of equitable estoppel may prevent a person from enforcing his claim where he has himself written the words containing the misdescription (*Durham Fancy Goods, Ltd v Michael Jackson (Fancy Goods), Ltd*, 1968).[24]

(*c*) *where the bill was drawn and accepted in the company's business name and not its corporate name.* (*Maxform SPA v B. Mariani & Goodville Ltd*, 1979.)[25]

The basis of this personal liability derives from the fact that the legislature introduced limited liability on the understanding that persons dealing with the company would know that the liability of its members was limited. Since the officials of the company are the only persons who can ensure that the company's documents convey this impression it seems right to subject them to fines and personal liability where this is not so. However, in more recent times the section has been interpreted in a strict, rigid, and Draconian fashion, as cases such as *Hendon*[23] show.

2. THE REGISTERED OFFICE

Generally

The second clause of the memorandum must state whether the company's registered office is to be situated in England, Scotland or Wales (see below). (S. 2(1)(*b*).) If it is to be in England then registration is effected by the Registrar of Companies in London, and if in Scotland by the Scottish Registrar of Companies in Edinburgh. The situation of the registered office in England or Scotland fixes the company's nationality as British and its domicile as English or Scottish, as the case may be (but see *Daimler Co Ltd v Continental Tyre & Rubber*

Co Ltd, 1916),[9] though not its residence. Residence is fixed by ascertaining where the company's centre of control and management is. Thus a company may be resident in a number of countries where it has several centres of control in different countries. (*Swedish Central Railway Co Ltd v Thompson*, 1925.)[26] The residence of a company is important in connection with its liability to pay UK taxation.

A company must in all its business letters and order forms state whether it is registered in England or Scotland, the registration number assigned to it (as shown in the certificate of incorporation), and the address of its registered office. Furthermore, if reference is made on letters or order forms to the amount of the company's share capital, this must represent the paid up share capital. (S. 351.) There are penalties in case of default.

The actual address of the registered office is not set out in the memorandum but must be sent to the Registrar with the other documents required on incorporation. (S. 10(6).)

Companies with a registered offfice in Wales

Under s. 2(2) a company may state in its memorandum that its registered office is situated in Wales. Such a company may use 'cyfyngedig' as the last word of its name instead of 'limited' or 'Cyf' for 'Ltd'. (S. 25(2)(*b*).) However, a statement in English that the company is limited must appear in any prospectus and official publications of the company and at its place of business. (S. 351(3) and (4).) Companies with a registered office in Wales may register a memorandum and articles in Welsh with an English translation and documents required to be filed with the Registrar may be in Welsh with an English translation. A company with a registered office in Wales has a British nationality and an English domicile and registration is effected by the Registrar of Companies in Cardiff.

Purpose of registered office

The registered office is the company's official address. It provides a place where legal documents, notices, and other communications can be served. A document can be served on a company by leaving it at, or sending it by registered or ordinary post to, the registered office. (*T.O. Supplies Ltd v Jerry Creighton Ltd* [1951] 1 KB 42.) If the company has no registered office writs and summonses may be served on the directors or the secretary at an office which is not registered. Thus in *Re Fortune Copper Mining Co* (1870), LR 10 Eq 390 the registered office of the company had been pulled down and a writ was served on the secretary and the directors at an unregistered office. The court held that this was good service.

When the Registrar of Companies receives a communication returned as undeliverable at the registered office he will eventually set in motion the procedures for striking the company off the Register under s. 652, as a defunct company.

The following registers and documents which can be inspected either by shareholders, creditors, or the public are also kept at the registered office—

(i) *The register of members*, and if the company has one, the index of members, unless the register is made up elsewhere, in which case they can be kept where they are made up. Where the register and index (if any) is made up by an agent they may be kept at the agent's office (s. 353(1)) (see also p. 177).

(ii) *A copy of any instrument creating any charge* requiring registration under Part XII, Chapter I, of the 1985 Act (s. 406) (see also p. 311).

(iii) *The company's register of charges* affecting the property of the company (s. 407) (see also p. 314).

(iv) *The minute books* of general meetings (s. 383) (see also p. 222).

(v) *The register of directors and secretaries* (s. 288) (see also p. 240).

(vi) *The register of directors' interests* in shares in, or debentures of the company or associated companies, together with the index of names in the register unless it is in the form of an index. Where the register of members is not kept at the registered office the register of directors' interests may be kept where the register of members is kept (s. 325(5) and Sched 13, Part IV) (see also p. 181).

(vii) *The register of interests* in shares. This is a register of substantial shareholders' interests in five per cent or more of the nominal value of any class of issued share capital which is quoted and has unrestricted voting rights, together with an index of names in the register unless it is in the form of an index. If the register of directors' interests is not kept at the registered office then the register of shareholders' interests must be kept where the register of directors' interests is kept (s. 211(8)) (see also p. 182).

(viii) *The register of debenture holders*, if the company has one. If the register is made up at another office it may be kept where it is made up and where it is made up by an agent it may be kept at his office (s. 190(3)) (see also p. 295).

(ix) *A copy of each director's service contract* or a memorandum thereof. These may be kept at the registered office, or where the register of members is kept, or at the company's principal place of business if this is situated in the country in which the company is registered. The Registrar of Companies must be told where these documents are kept if they are not at the registered office. The directors referred to now include those directors who are employed by subsidiaries and those who work wholly or mainly outside the United Kingdom. (See further p. 241.) Contractual arrangements with shadow directors are also included. (S. 318(6).)

(x) *A copy of the report, if any, following an investigation by a company of interests in its shares on the requisition of its members.* This report must be available for inspection at the company's registered office for a period of six years from the date on which it first became available. (S. 215(7).)

The above registers and documents must be kept open to inspection by members free of charge during business hours, subject to reasonable restrictions leaving not less than two hours a day for inspection. The minute books of general meetings are only open to the inspection of members. Copies of instruments creating a charge and the register of charges are also open to the inspection of debenture holders and creditors without charge. The register of directors and secretaries, the register of directors' interests and the register of debenture holders are open to inspection by the public on payment of a prescribed fee subject to exceptions where the company is within Sched 5, paras 3 and 10 (exemption of a company from requirement to disclose in its accounts particulars of shareholdings in subsidiaries or other bodies corporate incorporated or carrying on business outside the UK in circumstances where disclosure would be harmful to the business of the company) (see also p. 351). The register of interests in shares and any report required by s. 215(7) to be kept at the registered office (see above) is available for inspection by any member of the company or any other person without charge and copies of the register or report must be given on request, though the company may charge a prescribed fee. Once again, there are exemptions in regard to inspection by the public where the company is within Sched 5, paras 3 and 10 (see above).

The actual location of the registered office is usually decided by the promoters and the address is filed with the memorandum and articles when these documents are presented for registration.

Change of address of registered office

A company incorporated in England cannot change the provision in its memorandum which states that the registered office will be situated in England or Wales. A move to Scotland would mean a change of domicile and require registration of a Scottish company in Edinburgh. Nevertheless the actual address of the registered office may be changed from one place in England or Wales to another place in England or

Wales. Movement of the registered office within England and Wales does not involve a change of domicile, the law of England and Wales being the same. The change of address can be done by an ordinary resolution of the members, i.e. a resolution passed by a simple majority. Quite often the power to change the address of the registered office is given to the directors by the articles, and where this is done, a resolution of the Board will suffice. *Table A, Reg 70*, which gives the directors of a *Table A* company wide management powers, would appear to give them, by implication, power to change the address of the registered office. The company must notify the Registrar of the change within 14 days. (S. 287(2).) The Registrar must publish in the *London Gazette* notice of the receipt by him of a change in the situation of the registered office. (S. 711(1)(*n*).) In addition, until this is done the change is not effective against any person who serves a document on the company at the old address and is unaware of the change. (S. 42(1)(*d*).)

3. THE OBJECTS CLAUSE

The third clause of the memorandum must set out the objects which the company is formed to pursue. A company is incorporated for certain specified objects or purposes and has no power to do anything which is not within those stated objects or fairly incidental thereto.

The original intention of Parliament when it introduced company legislation was that the *objects clause* should be a short statement of the company's objects, the ancillary powers required to carry out the objects being implied. Thus a company which has as its main object the making of steel castings may want to run its own transport in order to get its products to its purchasers. The transport aspect of the business would really be ancillary to the running of the business of making the castings, and ought to be implied so that it should not be necessary to provide for transport powers in the memorandum. Indeed, Tables B, C, D, E, and F in the Companies (Tables A–F) Regulations 1985 (SI 1985 No. 805) contain a short objects clause confined strictly to setting out the company's authorized business and the Act requires this specimen form to be adhered to as closely as circumstances permit (s. 3(1)) so that the longer form of objects clause is hardly a compliance with the Act. Certain early cases showed that the courts would take a liberal view and would allow activities not specifically mentioned in the objects clause. Indeed, the House of Lords in *A.G v Great Eastern Rail Co* (1880) 5 App Cas 473 held that a company was impliedly granted such necessary and incidental powers when it was incorporated. However, business men were not willing to leave the matter to implication, preferring to set out in the memorandum all the ancillary powers which might be needed. Hence, in more recent times it has been usual to set out at length the objects and powers which the company is likely to require for carrying on any conceivable kind of business or activity.

This type of drafting is encouraged by the *ultra vires* rule which states that when an act is performed or a transaction carried out which though legal in itself is not authorized by the objects clause, that act or transaction is *ultra vires* (beyond the powers of) the company and is void. However, although such drafting makes it less of a hazard to do business with a company, since transactions are less likely to be affected by the *ultra vires* rule, it inevitably results in less control over the activities of directors.

In more recent times two main developments have taken place to alleviate the effect of the *ultra vires* rule on those doing business with a company. These are as follows—

(*a*) a more liberal approach by the judiciary to the construction of objects clauses which has tended to widen the scope of permitted activities. (See *Bell Houses Ltd v City Wall Properties Ltd*, 1966[27] and *Re New Finance and Mortgage Co Ltd*, 1975[28]); and

(*b*) legislation which is now contained in s. 35 (see further p. 62).

Implied powers

(*a*) To carry on the main business

As we have seen the courts have on the lines of *AG v Great Eastern Rail. Co* (1880) 5 App Cas 473 been prepared to imply certain powers as distinct from objects in trading companies, and they can carry out certain activities even though there is no express power in the objects clause. For example, a trading company can according to the case law on the subject—

(i) borrow money and mortgage its property as security for the loan (*General Auction Estate & Monetary Co v Smith* [1891] 3 Ch 432) (see p. 564).

(ii) sell the company's assets, but not the entire undertaking (*Re Kingsbury Collieries Ltd* [1907] 2 Ch 259);

(iii) engage and dismiss employees and agents (*Ferguson v Wilson* (1866) 2 Ch App 77);

(iv) bring and defend legal proceedings (*Re Norwich Provident Insurance Society* (1878) 8 Ch D 334);

(v) pay gratuities and pensions to employees and ex-employees and their dependants whilst the company is a going concern. (*Henderson v Bank of Australasia* (1888) 40 Ch D 170.) This is what case law decides, but s. 719 gives a company statutory power to make provision for employees or ex-employees and those of its subsidiaries on the cessation of the whole or part of its business or on its transfer in a merger.

It should be noted, however, that *express powers* in respect of the foregoing matters would normally be included in the memorandum, and in addition there is often a concluding paragraph to the objects clause empowering the company 'to do all such other things as are incidental or conducive to the attainment of the above objects or any of them'. Some problems of interpretation of this type of clause remain in terms of whether it makes powers in the objects clause main objects which can be pursued in themselves or whether it merely operates to extend the range of powers not specifically mentioned in the objects clause if and only if they assist the company in carrying out main objects. In other words in the example given at p. 50 would such a clause enable the company to give up the making of steel castings and run a transport business, or would it merely assist in allowing the company to transport its goods if a transport power was not specifically included? In *Evans v Brunner, Mond & Co Ltd* [1921] 1 Ch 359 Eve J adopted a restrictive approach in respect of such a clause holding that the powers in earlier paragraphs were not made main objects and as powers they were still limited in scope to enable the real main objects to be carried out. However, in *Bell Houses Ltd v City Wall Properties Ltd*, 1966[27] the Court of Appeal held that such a concluding paragraph had the effect of widening the meaning of the earlier paragraphs so that they conferred ancillary powers and also created subsidiary and associated objects. However, in *Bell* the concluding paragraph was a little less wide than in *Evans* because in *Bell* the *directors* were to decide what was advantageous or incidental. As Salmon L J said: 'As a matter of pure construction, the meaning of these words seems to me to be obvious. An object of the plaintiff company is to carry on any business which the directors genuinely believe can be carried on advantageously in connection with or as ancillary to the general business of the company'.

The Jenkins Committee recommended that the Companies Act should be amended to provide that every company should have certain specified powers, except to the extent that they are excluded, expressly or by implication, by its memorandum; such powers being those which any company would normally need in order to pursue its objects. This recommendation has not, as yet, been implemented.

(b) To carry on additional business

In addition to powers which are required to carry on the main business, powers have been implied by the court to carry on an additional business which was fairly incidental. (*Deuchar v Gas Light & Coke Co*, 1925 (see p. 460) and the *Bell Houses* case[27].)

(c) Basis on which court implies powers

Before leaving the subject of powers it should be noted that before *implying* a power not set out in the company's constitution the courts have always insisted that its exercise must be, as is illustrated by the judgment of Eve J in *Re Lee, Behrens & Co Ltd*, 1932[29]—

    (i) reasonably incidental to the carrying on of the company's business;

    (ii) a *bona fide* transaction; and

    (iii) done for the benefit of and to promote the prosperity of the company.

The reason for the above requirements is to prevent the directors using the shareholders' money in an obviously improvident way. As Bowen LJ said in *Hutton v West Cork Railway* (1883),[30] 'The law does not say that there are to be no cakes and ale, but there are to be no cakes and ale except such as are required for the benefit of the company'.

This means, in essence, that a power to exercise generosity which has no commercial motivation will not be implied. This judicial view is based upon the notion that registered companies are formed primarily to make profit and not to give away their funds.

Gratuitous payments and in-house gifts

The question whether gratuitous payments, or in-house gifts, made by the directors of a company *without the approval of the members by ordinary resolution in general meeting*, are *ultra vires* and void unless made for the benefit of the company, has produced a considerable number of judicial decisions. Nevertheless, it is still difficult to draw firm conclusions as to the application of the law in all situations. It seems, however, that—

1. It is *a matter of construction* of the objects clause whether an express provision giving rise to the making of a gratuitous payment of the company's funds as by, e.g. the payment of a non-contractual pension to an employee or director may be exercised by the board without reference to the 'benefit' principle of Eve J in *Re Lee Behrens*, 1932.[29] Thus, a judge may take the view that no particular benefit need be shown as in *Charterbridge Corporation Ltd v Lloyds Bank Ltd*, 1969.[32]

2. If the company concerned does *not* have an express provision in its memorandum, e.g. to pay a non-contractual pension to a director, then Eve J's *first* and *third* tests must be complied with and if they are not the court will refuse to *imply* a power and the transaction will be *ultra vires* and void. (*Re Lee Behrens*, 1932[29] and *Re W & M Roith Ltd*, 1967.[31])

3. However, the comparatively clear and convenient formula set out in 1 and 2 above is disturbed because the issue of gratuitous payments often arises in a receivership or in a liquidation following insolvency, or on a sale or transfer of the company's business. In such situations the receiver and liquidator will be trying to cut down the number of claimants upon the company's funds by seeking to have their claims declared *ultra vires*, or they may be trying to recover for the secured or general body of creditors sums of money paid out gratuitously by the board while the company was in financial difficulties or insolvent. Where the company has sold its business one may find additionally that shareholders feel aggrieved because surplus assets have been reduced by gratuitous payments made by the board and they may try to recover these or prevent payment of them.

4. In circumstances such as those outlined in 3 above the court will be pre-disposed to protect creditors and shareholders by regarding the gratuitous transaction(s) as void. In *Hutton*,[30] *Lee Behrens*[29] and *Re W & M Roith Ltd*[31] this was achieved by invoking the 'benefit' rule and regarding the various transactions as *ultra vires* and void. Charity could sit at the board but only if the company was a going (and on-going) concern.

5. The above development was challenged by the court in *Charterbridge Corporation Ltd v Lloyds Bank Ltd*, 1969.[32] Pennycuick J said that if the transaction was entered into under an *express* power, the court could not challenge it on the 'benefit' principle, though this test had to be satisfied if the court was being asked to *imply* a power. Significantly, however, in the *Charterbridge* case Pennycuick J had found that the transaction concerned was for the benefit of the company and the company involved was a going and on-going concern anyway.

6. Nevertheless, the *Charterbridge*[32] judgment left the courts with a difficulty which related to how it could render invalid a gratuitous transaction emanating from an *express* power in a situation of insolvency or transfer of business. Cases such as *Lee Behrens*,[29] *Re Roith*[31] and *Hutton*[30] show that damage can be done to the claims of the creditors who have supplied goods or services to the company, and to members entitled to surplus assets by the directors making in-house gifts.

7. Where the company is in liquidation, the liquidator or any creditor or member may apply to the court under s. 212, Insolvency Act 1986. This section provides, amongst other things, that if, in the course of the winding up of a company, it appears that a person who has taken part in the management of the company has misapplied or retained, or become accountable for, any money or other property of the company, or been guilty of any misfeasance or breach of any fiduciary or other duty in relation to the company, that person may be compelled by the court to repay, restore, or account for the money or property or any part of it or to contribute such sum to the company's assets by way of compensation in respect of the misfeasance or breach of fiduciary or other duty as the court thinks just. The predecessor of this section was applied in *Re Halt Garage (1964) Ltd*, 1982[33] and was considered as a remedy in *Re Horsley & Weight Ltd*, 1982.[34] This approach leaves the transaction valid but requires the directors to compensate for any loss caused if they have disposed of the company's funds gratuitously in a situation of insolvency, this being regarded by the court as a breach of duty or use of their powers for an unauthorized or improper purpose.

8. Since s. 212 (*ibid*) applies only in a winding up, how would an aggrieved shareholder fare if he wished to challenge a gratuitous transaction entered into by the directors when the company was, and was likely to remain a going concern? The answer would appear to be—

(*a*) *If there was no express power* to do the act complained of but it required the court to imply a power, the transaction could be challenged successfully and declared *ultra vires* and void unless the directors could show benefit to the company. (*Re Lee Behrens*, 1932.[29]) According to the decision in *Hutton*[30] even a transaction approved by an ordinary resolution in general meeting is not valid unless it is for the benefit of the company.

(*b*) *If there is an express power* to enter into a transaction the court may—

(i) regard the directors as the best judge of what is for the company's benefit and refuse to intervene thus rendering the transaction good (*Charterbridge*[32]); or

(ii) regard the transaction as invalid on the basis that an express power has been used 'in furtherance of some purpose which is not an authorized purpose' *per* Vinelott J in *Rolled Steel Products (Holdings) Ltd v British Steel Corporation*, 1982.[35]

A major exception to the 'benefit' rule is to be found in s. 719 which gives power in certain circumstances to make provision for the benefit of employees or ex-employees of the company or its subsidiaries on the cessation or transfer of its business. The power may be exercised notwithstanding that to do so is not in the best interests of the company—company in this context meaning shareholders. (See further p. 254.)

Political donations by companies

Similar problems arise here. However, it seems likely that a company can make a donation to a political party by way of implied power if such a donation is reasonably incidental to the substantive objects of the company. The same rule would seem to apply even with an express object. A typical one is 'To support and subscribe to any charitable or public object, and any institution, society or club which may be for the benefit of the company or its employees'.

It was held by the Court of Appeal in *Re Horsley & Weight Ltd*, 1982[34] that acts carried out under express objects are beyond challenge by the judiciary only if they are substantive not ancillary. The abovementioned object would appear ancillary since a trading company will not normally have charitable donations as a main business. The exercise of an ancillary object must be to further the substantive objects of the company. If not, the act is *ultra vires* and void.

This is illustrated by an unreported decision of Mervyn-Davis J in the High Court on 24 May 1983 entitled *Simmonds v Heffer*. Janet Simmonds sued on behalf of herself and other members of the League Against Cruel Sports, a company limited by guarantee without a share capital. The first defendants were Eric Heffer and others representing the executive committee of the League. Janet Simmonds alleged that a donation of £80,000 made by the League to the Labour Party in respect of the general election of 1979 was *ultra vires* the objects of the League and void.

It appeared that £50,000 had been donated to the Labour Party general election fund and £30,000 for the 'cause of animal welfare generally and in particular that part of it within the objects and purposes of the League'. The Labour Party had express provisions in its manifesto for the abolition of blood sports. One of the express objects of the League was 'to affiliate, to combine, or to co-operate with, subscribe to, or support, any institution having objects similar to the League or any of them'.

The judge decided that the donation of £30,000 could be identified with the objects of the League. It was therefore *intra vires* and could be retained by the Labour Party whose representatives were the second defendants. However, the donation of £50,000 was *ultra vires* and void. It was therefore returnable to the League. The Labour Party's general objects went far beyond those of the League.

Donations to the Conservative or any other party would presumably have to pass the same test. Section 235 and Sched 7, Part I require the directors' report to state political donations in excess of £200. There are those who would think that this justifies the making of them. There is no judicial decision on the point. However, the above provisions are concerned with publicity and not necessarily validation. There are those who take the view that the publicity is designed to enable shareholders to stop an unlawful practice. After all, loans, etc. to directors have to be disclosed in the accounts, even if they are unlawful. (See further p. 245.) So publicity and validation are not necessarily the same thing. Parliament should make the matter clear by legislation.

Ownership of land

Regarding the ownership of land, corporations have been under a disability in the holding of land. In earlier times when land was held of a superior lord, the death of a tenant brought benefits to the lord arising out of the tenancy. However, if the land was conveyed to a corporation, these benefits did not accrue because a corporation never dies. Since the superior lord was often the Crown, it was decided that corporations should not be allowed to take land without licence in mortmain from the Crown. This prevented corporations holding land in their own right because a licence was not easy to obtain and these early difficulties have continued to influence the law relating to land holding by corporations.

Section 14 of the Companies Act 1948 gave to registered companies a statutory power to hold land without licence in mortmain, and so every company registered could hold land by virtue of the statute and regardless of any power given in the memorandum. The Charities Act 1960 abolished the law of mortmain and furthermore by Sched 7 repealed s. 14 of the Companies Act 1948. Thus *there is now no statutory power given to registered companies to hold land,* and if a registered company wishes to hold land other than for the purpose of carrying out its *objects*, it *must have such a power in its memorandum.* Without any express mention in its memorandum a registered company has power to hold land for the purpose of its trade or business. A company could buy land for building a steel foundry if steel making was its business; but if a company wishes to buy land merely as an investment, it would have to have as one of its objects the business of dealing in land, or have an express power to hold land in its memorandum.

The substratum rule

This rule states that although a company may include in the objects clause powers ancillary to the object or objects of the company, these powers cannot be pursued as ends in themselves. They are intended to assist the company in the carrying out of the main object only. Thus if the main object or *substratum* fails, the company cannot continue to operate a business merely under an ancillary power. Furthermore, the shareholders can petition for the winding up of the company where the whole *substratum* has gone and the court can order a liquidation under its power to do so whenever it is just and equitable. (S. 122(1)(g)) (*Re German Date Coffee Co*, 1882.[36])

Objects and powers—effect of special clauses in the memorandum

The person who drafts the memorandum can and commonly does insert in the objects clause a final clause stating that each clause of the memorandum of the company contains an independent main object, and in *Cotman v Brougham*, 1918,[37] the House of Lords decided that such a clause meant that each ancillary power must be treated as a main object which could be pursued as an end in itself. (And see also *Anglo-Overseas Agencies Ltd v Green*, 1960.[38]) However, some limit has been placed on this device, the court deciding in *Introductions Ltd v National Provincial Bank Ltd*, 1968,[39] that the borrowing or raising of *money* cannot be an independent object but must be read as a back-up or ancillary power to other activities since money is never borrowed for its own sake. (See now *Rolled Steel*, p. 457.)

The *ultra vires* rule

Origin

The fact that a company could not only be restrained from doing *ultra vires* acts at the suit of its members but that any contract entered into by the company beyond its powers was void and could not be enforced against it was finally settled in *Taylor v Chichester and Midhurst Rail. Co* (1867) LR 2 Exch 356 in spite of a powerful dissenting judgment by Blackburn J who sought to restrict the application of the doctrine to actions brought by members against their company for injunctions.

Theories

The theories behind the application of the *ultra vires* rule as regards registered companies were laid down by the House of Lords in *Ashbury*

Railway Carriage & Iron Co v Riche (1875) (see p. 458). They are as follows—

(*a*) That since what is now s. 1 of the 1985 Act refers to the incorporation of a registered company on the basis of a memorandum, the company is incorporated as subject to that memorandum including the contents of the objects clause.

(*b*) That because what is now s. 2(7), *ibid*, prohibits a company from altering its memorandum except in the manner authorized by s. 4, *ibid*, a company would in effect be altering its memorandum in defiance of the Act if it were allowed to pursue activities not authorized by the objects clause of its memorandum.

(*c*) That the memorandum and articles are a contract between the company and the members to comply with the memorandum and articles. Thus, part of the company's contract with its members is not to exceed the powers in the objects clause of the memorandum.

Actions by members to restrain ultra vires acts

A member of a company has the right to sue for an injunction to restrain the company or its directors from doing an *ultra vires* act. Creditors, including secured creditors, have no right to sue.

Contracts rendered invalid

A contract to do an act which is beyond the powers contained in the company's memorandum is deemed *ultra vires* and is void, unless the contract is made enforceable under s. 35, or the company has a modern long objects clause to which *Rolled Steel* (1985), p. 454 applies. The contract cannot be enforced against the company, and this is so even where the other contracting party did not know that the contract was *ultra vires*. (*Fountaine v Carmarthen Railway Co*, 1868.[40]) The reason for this is that the memorandum can be inspected at the Companies Registry before the contract is made, and every person who deals with the company is deemed to know the contents of the memorandum. The company cannot ratify an *ultra vires* contract after it has been made and so render it valid. (*Ashbury Railway Carriage and Iron Co v Riche*, 1875.[41])

If a person obtains a judgment against a company on a transaction which is *ultra vires* and the question of *vires* is not considered by the court giving judgment, then the company can have the judgment set aside; and if execution has been levied on the company's goods under the judgment, then the execution creditor must account to the company for the proceeds. Similarly where a company has created a mortgage over its property to secure an *ultra vires* loan, the lender will have to account to the company for the proceeds if he sells the mortgaged property. A judgment creditor who has obtained a judgment without the question of *vires* being considered cannot prove for the judgment debt in the company's liquidation. (*Re Jon Beauforte (London) Ltd*, 1953.[42])

An attempt has been made in s. 35 to help persons who enter into *ultra vires* transactions with companies. The position under the Act is dealt with at p. 62 but it can be said that it may not be very helpful. A much more important breakthrough is the development of the common law seen in *Rolled Steel* (1985), p. 454.

Rights of other party to an *ultra vires* transaction

A person who has entered into an *ultra vires* contract with a company will obtain some redress in the following circumstances—

(i) The contract may be enforceable if the acts, though not specifically authorized by the memorandum, are 'fairly incidental' to the company's objects as set out in it. (*Deuchar v Gas Light and Coke Co*, 1925.[43])

(ii) Since the law assumes that persons contracting with a company will have inspected its memorandum, it will enforce an *ultra vires* contract made with a company which is on the face of it *intra vires*, i.e. where, if the contract and the memorandum had been compared, the contract would have appeared to be *intra vires*. (*Re David Payne & Co Ltd*, 1904.[44]) The rule applies whether the memorandum has in fact been inspected or not.

(iii) The other contracting party who cannot enforce the contract against the company may sue the agent or agents who negotiated the contract on the company's behalf (usually a director) for damages for breach of warranty of authority.

Every agent warrants that his principal has power to make the contract which the agent is making on his behalf. (*Firbanks Exors. v Humphreys*, 1886.[45]) Where the company is a statutory one and its powers are therefore contained in a statute, it may not be possible to sue the directors, since everyone is deemed to know the contents of an English statute, and ignorance of the law is no excuse.

The doctrine of *constructive notice of the memorandum* could, of course, prevent an action against the directors of a registered company for breach of warranty, since the other contracting party could not rely on a warranty where he had knowledge of its falsity, even though that knowledge was merely constructive. However, though the point is not free from doubt, it is not thought that the doctrine of constructive notice will be allowed to prevent an action for breach of warranty, where the directors have made misleading statements as to the *operation* of the company's public documents as distinct from their *contents*, e.g. as where the directors state that the limits of borrowing have not been exceeded.

Furthermore it is likely that directors who wilfully misrepresent their own powers, or those of the company, will be liable in the tort of deceit to a person dealing with the company in spite of the doctrine of constructive notice which deems that an outsider knows the company's powers and cannot be misled. The company could also be sued being vicariously liable for the deceit of the directors. An action in deceit against the company and/or the directors would of course be difficult, if not impossible, to sustain where the other party *knows either from actual inspection of the memorandum or otherwise* that the company has no power to make the contract.

There is also the possibility of bringing an action for a negligent misstatement under *Hedley Byrne & Co v Heller & Partners*, 1963 (p. 494).

(iv) *At common law* property and/or money transferred to the company can be recovered because the company has not acquired ownership, the transaction being void.

However, the property must be identifiable. In the case of money, tracing at common law is available only if it is in a separate account.

There can be no recovery from *bona fide* third parties who have taken the property from the company for value without knowledge of the *ultra vires* transaction. Thus *intra vires* creditors who have been paid off with an *ultra vires* loan cannot be required to repay the money. However, in such a case the doctrine of *subrogation* applies and the lender may stand in the shoes of the creditor(s) paid off and sue the company as the creditors could have done if they had not been paid.

(v) Money which is in a mixed fund with the company's other money can be traced *in equity*. This aspect of the law is complex and it is unnecessary to consider the detailed rules in a text at this level.

(vi) It has been held that a lender can sue the guarantor of an *ultra vires* loan on the contract of guarantee if the guarantor has promised to pay, even though the contract is not enforceable. This seems to be at the root of the decision in *Garrard v James* [1925] Ch 616. If the guarantor's promise to pay is based upon the assumption that the company is legally bound to repay the *ultra vires* loan, the guarantee may be void. (See *Heald v O'Connor*, 1971.[46])

Rights of the company where a transaction is *ultra vires*

The company may, under the principles of tracing, be able to recover from the other party property which has passed under an *ultra vires* transaction provided it is still in his possession. (*Cunliffe Brooks & Co v Blackburn Building Society* (1884) 9 App Cas 857.)

The company's officers are also liable to make restitution to the company and they have rights of contribution as between themselves so that if one officer is called upon to make full restitution himself he may ask those of his fellow officers who were involved to pay their share. Contribution will be assessed by the court on the basis of what is found to be 'just and equitable', having regard to the extent of the individual's responsibility for the damage in question; although any person may be exempted from contribution or compelled to make a complete indemnity if the court considers it appropriate. (S. 2, Civil Liability (Contribution) Act 1978.) The right to seek a contribution is lost after two years from the date when the right to claim it accrued. (S. 10, Limitation Act 1980.) These provisions render the rules of 'equal contribution' between wrongdoers obsolete. It should be noted that officers of registered companies may be relieved of liability by the court under s. 727 (see further p. 267) if they have acted reasonably and ought to be excused.

It was once thought that if the company sued on the *ultra vires* contract for the recovery of its property the recipient could not resist the claim by setting up the company's incapacity as a defence. However, in *Bell Houses Ltd v City Wall Properties Ltd*, 1966 (see p. 445), Mocatta J, at first instance held he could. The Court of Appeal left the point open when they reversed the decision of Mocatta J and held that the transaction was *intra vires*. However, the view of Mocatta J is supported by *Anglo-Overseas Agencies Ltd v Green*, 1960,[38] where the defendants were allowed to raise the issue of *ultra vires* against the plaintiff company as a preliminary issue.

The *ultra vires* rule—the contribution of Parliament

In an attempt to give effect to the first directive issued by the Council of the European Communities for the harmonization of company law in the member states what is now s. 35 provides that in favour of a person dealing in good faith with a company any transaction decided on by its directors shall be deemed to be within the capacity of the company to enter into validly, and the other party to the transaction shall not be bound to inquire about the capacity of the company to engage in it and shall be presumed to have acted in good faith unless the contrary is proved.

The *ultra vires* rule is not abolished because the sub-section merely allows the other party to an *ultra vires* transaction with a company to enforce it against the company if the necessary conditions are fulfilled. Thus the sub-section does not—

(a) prevent a member of the company from obtaining an injunction to restrain the company and its directors from entering into an *ultra vires* transaction; or

(b) absolve the directors from liability for any loss they cause the company by carrying out such a transaction; or

(c) make the transaction enforceable by the company but only against it. Thus the other party can raise the defence of *ultra vires* if sued by the company (see *Bell Houses*).[27] However, if the other party sues the company it could plead defences. For example, if it were a contract of sale of goods and the company was being sued for the price it could raise defences, e.g. that the goods were not of merchantable quality.

However, *it does* abolish the rule of constructive notice in circumstances where the section applies.

Unfortunately the sub-section applies only if the transaction has been decided on by a majority of the directors acting collectively at a properly constituted board meeting. The use of the plural appears to mean all the directors of a company holding office at the relevant time. However, s. 35 applies and an *ultra vires* transaction is binding on the company where it is made on behalf of the company by a director to whom all actual authority to act for the board has effectively been delegated. (See *International Sales etc v Marcus*, 1982.[47])

Much more difficult, however, is the situation in which an *ultra vires* transaction is entered into by the executive of the company without ever going to the board which might often be the case in a large public company. Here it is at least questionable whether s. 35 would validate the transaction.

In addition to the problems outlined above it is necessary under the Act that the plaintiff should be 'dealing' with the company 'in good faith'. Good faith is not defined in the Act but the burden of proving lack of good faith is placed on the company. In addition to the circumstances in *International Sales etc v Marcus*, 1982[47] the following examples are put forward as an indication of the application of the 'good faith' principle—

(a) P (the person dealing with the company) has actual knowledge that the transaction is *ultra vires*, either because he has been so advised, or because he has read the memorandum and understood it correctly. Presumably, such a person would not be dealing 'in good faith'.

(b) P has read the memorandum and thus has actual (as opposed to constructive) knowledge of its terms. But he misunderstands their meaning and honestly believes the transaction to be *intra vires*. Subject to judicial interpretation it is felt that P would be protected by the Companies Act, 1985, s. 35 on the grounds that a person who has read the documents and misunderstood them cannot be regarded as having acted in bad faith. This was the view of the Jenkins Committee as regards failure to appreciate the effect of a company's constitutional document. (See para 42(c) of the Report.)

(c) P (like the bank in *Re Introductions Ltd*, 1968[39]) has always called for a company's memorandum and articles when doing business with it, such as lending money. Suppose that to avoid any doubt under (b) above P stops this practice. If he did so he might be regarded as acting in bad faith because he has adopted a policy of shutting his eyes to possible dangers.

As regards 'dealing' Lawson J held that there was no 'dealing with the company' in *International Sales*.[47] Such dealing as there was resulted only in a gratuitous handout of the company's funds. There was no contractual or property transaction.

In this connection s. 35 would not seem to protect those who have received gratuitous payments from a company. (See p. 53.) They are unlikely to be regarded as 'dealing' with the company since that presupposes a contract or property transaction with mutual consideration passing. This follows from the view of Lawson J in *International Sales*.[47] (And see also *Re Halt Garage*, 1982.[33])

Alteration of the objects clause

Section 4 provides that the objects clause may be altered by a *special resolution* for the purposes set out in s. 4. These are as follows—

(i) *To enable the company to carry on its business more economically or efficiently*. This paragraph does not allow alterations in the type of business which the company is conducting, but does allow alterations which will assist in the method of conducting it. The company may for example take power to acquire shares in other companies carrying on businesses similar to its own, to promote such other companies and to enter into partnership or profit-sharing arrangements with such other companies. (*Re Consett Iron Co Ltd* [1901] 1 Ch 236.)

(ii) *To enable the company to attain its main purpose by new or improved means*. Here again the company cannot alter its main objects but can merely alter its ancillary powers, or provide new powers to assist it in achieving its main objects. In spite of the ruling in *Cotman v Brougham*, 1918[37] (and see p. 58), under which by use of an appropriate concluding clause each clause in the objects clause can be regarded as a separate and independent main object and not a mere power, for the purpose of the *ultra vires* rule it is thought that the court would seek out the main object or objects in order to ascertain that the alteration was merely in a power and so was valid under this heading.

(iii) *To enlarge or change the local area of its operations.* No alteration in the company's business is allowed, though it may alter the objects clause to allow it to conduct that business in another part of the world, sometimes necessitating a change in the company's name. (*Re Egyptian Delta Land and Investment Co Ltd*, 1907.[48])

(iv) *To carry on some business which under existing circumstances may conveniently or advantageously be combined with the business of the company.* It seems that quite sweeping changes may be made under this paragraph even in the main objects of the company. The most sweeping change ever allowed was that in *Re Parent Tyre Co*, 1923.[49] The courts seem inclined to leave the question of convenience and advantage to the members, but the new objects must not be inconsistent with the existing business. (*Re Cyclists Touring Club*, 1907.[50]) It would seem that a company can insert a new object and later abandon its original object or objects so long as there is no manifest inconsistency at the time of the alteration.

(v) *To restrict or abandon any of the objects specified in the memorandum.*

(vi) *To sell or dispose of the whole or any part of the undertaking of the company.*

(vii) *To amalgamate with any other company or body of persons.*

Items (v) to (vii) above do not give power to alter the company's business, and since they are self-explanatory no more need be said about them.

Before the 1948 Act it was necessary to seek the confirmation of the court before a special resolution altering the memorandum could stand. (See *Re Parent Tyre Co*, 1923[49] and *Re Cyclists Touring Club*, 1907.[50]) Under the 1985 Act the special resolution stands unless certain persons object within 21 days of the passing of the resolution. If objections are raised, the special resolution must be confirmed by the court. Otherwise it takes effect without reference to the court.

Under s. 5 an application for cancellation of the special resolution may be made by petition to the Companies Court within 21 days after the date on which the resolution was passed by or on behalf of—

(*a*) holders of 15 per cent in nominal value of the company's *issued capital* or *any class of it, or if the company is not limited by shares, not less than 15 per cent of the members*; or

(*b*) holders of 15 per cent of the company's issued debentures. However, to have a right of objection the debentures must have been issued before 1 December 1947, or form part of a series the first of which was issued before that date. The debentures must in all cases be secured by a floating charge.

The holders of the shares or debentures must not have consented to or voted for the alteration.

On receipt of the petition the court may under s. 5—

(i) Confirm the resolution wholly or in part on such terms and conditions as it thinks fit. For example, in *Re Parent Tyre Co*, 1923[49] the court confirmed the resolution in part only. Furthermore, the court may require the company to change its name. (*Re Egyptian Delta Land and Investment Co Ltd*, 1907.[48])

(ii) Adjourn proceedings to enable the company to make arrangements for the purchase of the dissentient shares by individual shareholders. In addition, the court may, if it thinks fit, make an order providing for the purchase by the company of the shares of the dissentients and for a reduction accordingly of the company's capital. The court order may make such alterations in and additions to the memorandum and articles of the company as may be required. (S. 5(5).)

(iii) Refuse or confirm the resolution.

Where a court order under s. 5(6) requires the company not to alter the provisions of a court order altering the memorandum and/or articles, then no alteration can be made by the members of the company without the further permission of the court.

The provisions in (ii) above do not apply to debenture holders.

Section 6(4) provides that where 21 days have passed without the alteration being challenged, the validity of the alteration shall not be questioned in proceedings taken under s. 5 *or otherwise*. Thus, suppose one or more members wish to challenge the change not under s. 5 because they do not have the necessary shareholding, but on the grounds that the alteration was not made for one of the purposes specified in the Act and was therefore *ultra vires*. This action would have to be brought within 21 days otherwise s. 6(4) would prevent it from being brought. It should be noted however that any smaller proportion of members than 15 per cent would have to sue for a declaratory judgment or an injunction since they could not proceed under s. 5.

Under s. 6 when a company has passed a resolution altering its objects, a *printed* copy of the memorandum as altered must be delivered to the Registrar within 15 days from the end of the period allowed for making application to the court for cancellation. If an application has in fact been made, the company must *forthwith* notify the fact to the Registrar, and, within 15 days (or such extended time as the court may allow) after any order confirming or cancelling the alteration, deliver to the Registrar a copy of the court order and, if the alteration is confirmed, a printed copy of the memorandum as altered.

In view of the above provisions companies can, in practice, change their objects for any purpose whatsoever and regardless of what is said in s. 4 and the alteration cannot be challenged after the expiration of three weeks. The cases cited were decided under the Companies

Act 1929 or earlier legislation (but see p. 466) which provided that an alteration would not take effect unless it was approved by the court so that the court could ensure that no alteration came into effect unless it was made for one of the specified statutory purposes. These cases will now be relevant only if proceedings are taken to challenge the validity of the alteration within the period of 21 days allowed.

4. LIMITATION OF LIABILITY

The memorandum of a limited company states that the liability of the members is limited and where the company is limited by guarantee this clause may contain the terms of the guarantee, though this may appear in the articles of association. Even though the company has an exemption from the DoTI allowing it to dispense with the word 'Limited' as part of its name, the memorandum must still contain a statement that the liability of the company's members is limited.

The procedure for re-registration of limited companies as unlimited and *vice versa* has already been considered (see p. 10).

5. CAPITAL

Under s. 2(5)(*a*), the memorandum of a company which is limited by shares must state the amount of the company's share capital *and* its division into shares of a fixed amount, e.g. 'The share capital of the company is two hundred thousand pounds divided into two hundred thousand shares of £1 each'. Shares may also be divided into classes, e.g. ordinary shares and preference shares, though it is usual to do this in the articles. Guarantee companies formed since the coming into force of the Companies Act 1980 cannot have a share capital but since such companies are not usually formed to carry on business activities this is not a disability.

The nominal value of a company's shares is left to the discretion of those promoting it. Nominal values are rarely more than £1.00 because shares of high nominal value are difficult to sell, and it is not unusual to find shares with a nominal value of 50p, 25p, or even as low as 5p.

The amount of capital stated in this clause is known as the company's *nominal* or *authorized* capital and it can be of any amount in a private company but must be at least £50,000 if the company is a public company. The requirement of s. 2(5)(*a*) that the nominal capital be divided into shares of a fixed amount means that English companies cannot issue *no-par value shares*.

A *no-par value share* has no nominal value; its *no-par value* is the price at which the share can be sold and not merely what the original owner paid for it, and since many shares are issued at a premium today, even current *par values* do not represent what was paid for shares in the first place. Few other items of property are still referred to by their original cost since it is their current market price which is of interest. Thus a *no-par value* share would have certain advantages. Having no nominal value dividends are expressed as so much per share, e.g. £0.20 per share, and not as a percentage of a nominal value.

Suppose P buys a share in the X Co Ltd for £4, the nominal value of which was £1, and the company declares a dividend of 20 per cent which is £0.20 per share. This is only a return of 5 per cent on P's current investment, and the only person who actually gets 20 per cent on his money is an original purchaser of a share, if any such person exists. The rate of 20 per cent is therefore misleading in relation to the actual yield. A dividend of £0.20 per share declared in such terms is more realistic, and indeed although a company cannot issue *no-par value shares*, there is nothing to prevent its declaring dividends in such terms.

Other advantages which would accrue if *no-par value shares* could be issued would be the elimination of the need to open a share premium account when shares are sold for more than their nominal value and also the elimination of the need for provisions forbidding the issue of shares at a discount. (See Chapters 4 and 7.)

It is of interest to note that, since the 1985 Act does not require an unlimited company to divide its share capital into shares of a fixed amount, an unlimited company seems to be able to issue *no-par value shares*.

A limited company may increase, reduce, or re-organize its share capital but the requirements of company legislation in this regard can only be fully appreciated in the context of other rules relating to share capital and they are therefore dealt with in Chapter 4.

6. OTHER CLAUSES

The clauses which have been dealt with above *must*, by the provisions of s. 2, appear in every memorandum. However, other clauses may be included, the ones most commonly found providing for the special rights of different classes of shareholders. Where such rights are included in the memorandum, and no provision for the variation of rights is made either in the memorandum itself or in the articles, such rights can be varied either with the approval of the court under s. 425 (see p. 380) or with the consent of all the members. (S. 125(5).) However, they are not alterable by special resolution under the provisions of s. 17. (See below.) Where class rights are contained in the *articles*, they can always be altered by special resolution, and any provision in the company's constitution to the contrary is void. Alteration is, of course, subject to the requisite consent of the holders of the shares (see further p. 94).

The memorandum is the superior document and where shareholders' rights are contained in the memorandum, any contrary provisions in the articles do not apply. However, the articles may be looked at *but only to explain any ambiguities in the memorandum, or to supplement it (Re Duncan Gilmour & Co Ltd, 1952)*,[51] e.g. where the voting rights of certain shares are in the memorandum and dividend rights are included in the articles. This is to be expected because the contract which the shareholder makes with the company is contained in two documents, i.e. the memorandum and the articles, and they must be read together subject to the rule that in case of conflict the memorandum prevails.

7. ASSOCIATION CLAUSE

It is in this clause that the subscribers to the memorandum (at least two persons), declare that they desire to be formed into a company and agree to take the shares opposite their names. Their signatures must be witnessed by at least one person who is not a subscriber. It is usual for the subscribers to take one share each in the memorandum, and contract by another agreement for the balance of the shares they intend to take up.

8. ALTERATION OF THE MEMORANDUM GENERALLY

In addition to the methods of alteration of certain clauses already given, s. 17 provides that any condition contained in the memorandum which could have been contained in the articles, i.e. any clause other than the statutory ones, can be altered by special resolution unless the memorandum provides for some other method, or prohibits the alteration of the condition, or the condition relates to *class rights*, i.e. the special rights of any class of members. Since provisions dealing with class rights are the only important provisions which could be in either the memorandum or the articles, the result is that s. 17 is not very important in practice. Section 17 contains the same provisions as to cancellation of an alteration as s. 5 does for the objects clause, with the exception that debenture holders cannot apply for cancellation.

Neither the memorandum nor the articles can be altered so as to require a member, after he became a member, to take up more shares, or otherwise increase his liability, unless he consents in writing, either before or after the alteration is made. (S. 16.) Thus if a company is proving to be a bad investment and cannot get fresh capital from the public, it cannot coerce its present members into supplying more capital, by an alteration in the articles requiring this.

Where there is a court order under s. 461 to relieve a minority of shareholders, and in order to relieve the minority it was necessary for the order to alter the company's memorandum or articles, then the company cannot make a further alteration inconsistent with the order without leave of the court. The rights of minorities will be further considered in Chapter 7.

When a company has altered its memorandum in any respect all copies of it issued thereafter must contain the alteration in the sense that the text must be altered to include the amendments. (S. 20.)

9. THE ARTICLES OF ASSOCIATION

The articles of association regulate the rights of the members of the company *inter se* (among themselves), and determine the manner in which the business of the company shall be conducted. The articles deal with such matters as the appointment and powers of directors, general meetings of the company, the voting rights of members, the transfer of shares, and dividends. The rights of the different classes of shareholders may also be found in the articles.

A company may have its own articles or may adopt *Table A* as set out in the Companies (Tables A–F) Regulations 1985 (SI 1985 No. 805). However, even where a company has its own articles, *Table A* will still apply, except where it is excluded expressly or by implication in the company's special articles. Thus, if company promoters do not wish *Table A* to apply, they must see that the first provision in the company's articles is one which expressly excludes the whole of *Table A*.

Articles must be printed (not typewritten) and divided into paragraphs numbered consecutively (s. 7). The articles must also be signed by each person who subscribed the memorandum, and the signature must be attested (s. 7), though one witness for all the subscribers' signatures is enough.

A private company can have any number of members and need not restrict the right to transfer its shares but under s. 81 a private limited company and any officer in default is guilty of an offence if it—

(a) offers to the public directly any shares or debentures of the company (whether for cash or otherwise); or

(b) allots or agrees to allot shares or debentures to an issuing house with a view to an offer for sale to the public.

Section 81(3) provides that nothing in s. 81 shall affect the validity of any allotment or sale of shares or debentures or of any agreement to allot or sell shares or debentures, so that an issue in contravention of s. 81 would be valid, as a contract, the sanction being the default fines on the company and its officers which are set out in s. 81(2).

Section 81 is now repealed in favour of s. 170 of the Financial Services Act 1986 which, in general, prohibits the issue of advertisements offering securities of a private company.

10. ALTERATION OF THE ARTICLES

The articles may be altered by means of a special resolution. Such alteration is as valid as if contained in the original articles, and, subject to the provisions of the Act which gives, e.g. in s. 461, power to the court to change a company's constitution, can itself be altered only by special resolution. (S. 9.) This power cannot be taken away or limited by any provision in the company's memorandum or articles, nor can the memorandum or articles allow or require the alteration to be made by any other type of resolution e.g. ordinary resolution (see *Bushell v Faith*, 1969, p. 542).

Thus it is impossible to entrench a provision in the articles. In the memorandum it is possible to provide that a clause other than a statutory clause shall be unalterable, but the articles can be altered freely by means of a special resolution. However, in *Cane v Jones*, 1981[52] it was decided that *all* shareholders may by unanimous agreement change the articles without a meeting or a resolution in writing even in the absence of a provision allowing this in the articles.

An alteration of the articles may operate retrospectively. Thus, in *Allen v Gold Reefs of West Africa Ltd* [1900] 1 Ch 656 the articles originally gave the company a lien on partly-paid shares. The plaintiff was the only member with fully-paid shares but he also owned calls on certain other partly-paid shares which he owned. The company altered its articles to give itself a lien on fully-paid shares, thus putting itself in a position where it could refuse to transfer the plaintiff's fully-paid shares unless and until he had paid calls owing on his partly-paid shares. It was held that the alteration was valid and for the benefit of the company, even though it operated retrospectively so far as the plaintiff was concerned.

There are, however, the following restrictions on alteration—

(i) The articles cannot be altered so as to include an illegal clause, as where, for example, the articles are altered so as to require a four-fifths majority on resolutions altering certain articles. This was regarded as illegal in *Ayre v Skelsey's Adamant Cement Co Ltd*, (1904) 20 TLR 587 on the grounds that what is now s. 9 gives a legal right to alter *all* articles by a special resolution requiring only a three-quarters majority. It should be noted, however, that weighted voting rights are not illegal. (See *Bushell v Faith*, 1969, p. 542.)

(ii) An alteration to include a clause which contravenes a provision in the memorandum is of no effect. Thus, if the memorandum provides that holders of preference shares should have a preferential right to repayment of their capital in a winding up (which the courts can construe as meaning that they have no right to participate in surplus assets in a winding up), and the articles are altered to provide that in a winding up the surplus assets should be divided among all the members in proportion to the capital paid up on their shares, both preference and ordinary, the alteration would be of no effect.

(iii) No alteration of the memorandum or articles can impose a liability on members of the company at the date when the alteration is made to take more shares than they already hold, or to contribute more share capital or pay more money to the company than they have already agreed to contribute or pay, unless the member concerned agrees in writing. (S. 16.) The effect of the rule is to deny power to the company to raise further capital by coercing its members when it cannot raise the capital from them voluntarily.

(iv) Where the rights of different classes of shareholders are contained in the articles, then, obviously, these rights can only be changed so far as the articles are concerned, by special resolution of the members of the company. However, this is not enough since s. 125 states that such a resolution is ineffective unless holders of three-fourths of the issued shares of that class consent in writing, or by means of an extraordinary resolution passed at a separate general meeting of holders of the shares of the class. In addition, s. 127 applies and under that section 15 per cent of the class not voting for the variation may apply to the court within 21 days of the resolution which altered the articles. Once such an application has been made the variation will not take effect unless and until it is confirmed by the court.

The court is concerned, so s. 127(4) says, to see whether the alteration will 'unfairly prejudice' the shareholders of the class. This is a matter of fact to be decided on the circumstances of each case. However, let us suppose that A Ltd has 100,000 £1 ordinary shares and 10,000 14 per cent £1 cumulative preference shares. A Ltd has three members, Ernest, Edward, and James. Ernest, and Edward who hold all the ordinary shares and 8,500 of the preference shares have decided to alter the articles so that the dividend on the preference shares shall no longer be cumulative and the rate shall be reduced to 11 per cent. James who holds 1,500 of the preference shares could obviously dissent and the court would have to decide whether, e.g. the variation of the rights of the preference shares was, in view of the company's financial state, for the benefit of the preference shares or whether it was simply a scheme by Ernest and Edward to deprive James of an adequate share of profit in order to enhance their own position. If the latter the court would probably refuse to approve the variation.

Where a company which has special articles containing a provision relating to approval of shareholders on a variation, the special articles apply. Where a company has special articles which do not contain a provision relating to the approval of shareholders of the class on a variation of their rights, s. 125 applies and once again a special resolution to alter the articles in regard to class rights is ineffective except with the consent in writing of the holders of three-fourths of the issued shares of the class, or with the sanction of an extraordinary resolution passed at a separate general meeting of the holders of the shares of the class. Section 127 applies in respect of dissentients.

It should be noted that ss. 125 and 127 apply only if the company has more than one class of shares. The remedies available to shareholders where there is only one class of shares will be considered in detail later. Here we are concerned purely with the mechanics of alteration of the articles.

(v) The alteration must not deprive members of rights conferred on them by the court under s. 210 of the 1948 Act unless the court approves. (*Re Harmer Ltd*, 1958, see p. 524.)

It should be noted that s. 210 is now repealed and new minority protection is substituted in ss. 459–461. This in no way affects *Re Harmer* because the court has very similar powers under s. 461 and an order similar to that in *Harmer* could have been made under that section. It also allows the court as in *Harmer* to amend the company's constitution by court order and again, such an alteration cannot be altered by the members of the company unless the court approves.

(vi) Finally, the court has a jurisdiction to regard an alteration of the articles as invalid unless it is made for the benefit of the company as a whole. (*Per* Lindley MR in *Allen v Gold Reefs of West Africa Ltd* [1900] 1 Ch 656 at p. 671.)

The court has a jurisdiction to declare an alteration invalid if it is not for the benefit of the company, i.e. the whole body of members as where it is a fraud on the minority. It is impossible to understand the decisions on this branch of company law unless it is first realized what position the court takes up. It does not look solely at the company as it is at the time of the action (which would be a subjective test) but tries to see the company in equilibrium. That is to say the court envisages the company in a hypothetical situation in which shares and voting power are evenly distributed among the members, and assumes that members will vote independently of each other and not, as it were, combine to coerce other members.

Having viewed the company in this situation, the court then decides on the validity of the alteration. This is an objective test and is really the only one the court can adopt. If it were to test the validity of the alteration against the present state of the shareholding, then the day after the resolution was approved the shareholding may alter and there may be a shift in the centre of power in the company. Rather than cope with so many imponderables, the court decides the question by putting the company into a state of equilibrium (hypothetically at least) and then looking at the alteration.

However, the objective test is not altogether satisfactory and appears to operate unfavourably towards particular shareholders. (See, for example, *Greenhalgh v Arderne Cinemas Ltd*, 1951.[53]) The difficulty is that the court assumes, probably rightly, that those who are managing the company's affairs and, on occasion, a majority of the shareholders, know better than the court what is for its benefit. Thus shareholders may sometimes feel that they have not been dealt with fairly and yet the court will accept the alteration to the articles as valid and for the benefit of the company as a whole. (*Rights and Issues Investment Trust v Stylo Shoes*, 1964.[54])

Indeed the result of the objective test used by the court is that most alterations are allowed, and it is only those which give the company power to expel members which are regarded with suspicion. (*Dafen Tinplate Co v Llanelly Steel Co (1907) Ltd*, 1920.[55]) However, expulsion is allowed where it would benefit the members as a whole, as where the member expelled is competing with the company (*Sidebottom v Kershaw, Leese & Co Ltd*, 1920[56]), or is defrauding it. (*Shuttleworth v Cox Bros & Co (Maidenhead) Ltd*, 1927.[57])

Breaches of contract arising out of alteration of the articles

A company cannot by altering its memorandum or articles escape liability for breach of a contract into which it has entered. The difficulty has arisen with regard to the remedies of the other party to the contract.

In *Punt v Symons & Co Ltd* [1903] 2 Ch 506 it was said that the other party to the contract could sue the company for damages for breach, but could not obtain an injunction to prevent the alteration taking effect. Then followed a series of cases which revealed considerable judicial indecision on this point. For example, in *Baily v British Equitable Assurance Co Ltd* [1904] 1 Ch 374 the Court of Appeal seems to have been prepared to grant an injunction to restrain an alteration of the articles in breach of contract although in fact it was only asked to give a declaratory judgment as to the state of the law. However, in *Southern Foundries v Shirlaw*, 1940,[58] Lord Porter in an *obiter dictum* gave support to the view that the other party to the contract can sue the company for damages only, and cannot obtain an injunction to prevent the alteration from taking effect. It may be said, therefore, that although the matter is not free from doubt the present judicial opinion is that a company is quite free to alter its articles, though if in doing so it breaks a contract which it has made, it must face an action in damages by the party aggrieved. There may also be an action against those who voted for the alteration. (*Southern Foundries v Shirlaw*, 1940.[58])

The position is different where a person contracts with a company and the contract incorporates a provision of the memorandum or articles by implication. In such a case the other party is deemed to know that the company may alter its memorandum or articles, and therefore takes the risk of the contract failing because of such an alteration, even to the extent of failing in an action for damages. (*Shuttleworth v Cox Bros & Co (Maidenhead) Ltd*, 1927.[57]) However, there are certain limitations upon the above rule—

(i) Rights which have already accrued under the contract cannot be disturbed by the alteration. (*Swabey v Port Darwin Gold Mining Co*, 1889.[59])

(ii) As we have seen, no alteration of the memorandum or articles can affect the *express* terms of the contract. If a contract expressly provides for (say) the salary of a director, and the articles also carry a salary provision, then the contract would not be affected if the company altered the salary provision in the articles. In addition, the court may sometimes *imply* a term against alteration of the articles into a separate contract and then allow the party aggrieved to sue on the separate contract for a breach of this implied term. (*Southern Foundries v Shirlaw*, 1940.[58])

(iii) It is felt that the obligations of the other party cannot be made more onerous by an alteration of the articles. Thus, if the articles appoint a director to serve for a period of years on a part-time basis, he cannot be required to give his full time to the company by the company altering its articles so as to require him to do so.

(iv) As we have already seen, where the company has shares of more than one class, it cannot vary the rights of a class of shares merely by altering them in the memorandum or articles. Section 125 applies and requires the consent of three-quarters of the class and there are dissentient rights. (See further p. 94.)

The articles can, of course, be altered by a special resolution of the members, but the rights of the class are not affected by such changes made by the membership as a whole.

Finally, the court cannot rectify a mere drafting error in the articles although it has this power in respect of other contracts. Such an alteration is a matter for the members by special resolution. (*Scott v Frank Scott (London) Ltd*, 1940.[60]) Section 461(2)(*a*) gives the court a power to amend the memorandum and articles in any way it thinks fit, as part of its jurisdiction to regulate the conduct of the company's affairs in the future, where a petition is brought under that section by a member of the company who claims that the affairs of the company are being conducted in a manner which is unfairly prejudicial to some of the members, including himself. (See further p. 191.) When the court has amended the memorandum or articles under s. 461 they cannot, by reason of s. 461(3) and (4), if the court so orders, be further altered by resolution of the members so as to nullify the alteration which the court has imposed unless leave of the court is first obtained. Nevertheless, the court's power under s. 461 is limited to dealing with the unfairly prejudicial conduct complained of and no power is given by the section to rectify mere errors of drafting.

11. THE LEGAL EFFECT OF THE MEMORANDUM AND ARTICLES

The memorandum and articles when registered bind the company and its members in contract as if these documents had been signed and sealed by each member and contained covenants on the part of each member to observe the provisions of the memorandum and articles. (S. 14.)

The results of this statutory contract are as follows—

(i) The memorandum and articles constitute a contract between the company and each member. Thus each member *in his capacity as member* is bound to the company by the provisions in the articles. (*Hickman v Kent or Romney Marsh Sheepbreeder's Association*, 1915.[61]) Furthermore, although s. 14 does not state that the articles shall bind the company and the members as if they had been *signed and sealed by the company* and contained *covenants on the part of the company* to observe their provisions, the company is regarded as bound to each member in his capacity as member to observe the provisions in the articles. (*Pender v Lushington*, 1877.[62])

(ii) The memorandum and articles are also by reason of case law a contract between the members themselves. Thus one member can sue another if that other fails to observe a provision in the memorandum or articles. There is no need to call upon the company to sue. (*Rayfield v Hands*, 1958.[63])

(iii) No right given by the memorandum or articles to a member in a capacity other than that of member, e.g. as solicitor or director, can be enforced against the company.

The memorandum and articles are not a contract with outsiders but merely with the members in respect of their rights as members. (*Hickman v Kent or Romney Marsh Sheepbreeder's Association*, 1915[61] and see *Eley v Positive Government Security Life Assurance Co*, 1876[64] and *Beattie v E. and F. Beattie Ltd*, 1938, p. 474.)

However, a provision in the memorandum or articles can become part of a contract between the company and a member or outsider in the following ways—

(*a*) where there is an express contract and a provision in the memorandum or articles is *expressly incorporated* into that contract by a provision therein;

(*b*) where a provision in the memorandum or articles is *incorporated by implication* arising out of the conduct of the parties (*Re New British Iron Co, Ex parte Beckwith*, 1898[65] and see *Eley v Positive Government Security Life Assurance Co*, 1876[64]), or where an express contract between the parties is silent on a particular aspect, e.g. in the case of a director, the length of his appointment. In such a case reference may be made to the memorandum or articles to fill the gap, if those documents contain a relevant provision. (*Read v Astoria Garage (Streatham) Ltd*, 1952.[66])

Although the above decisions are concerned with a member enforcing or being bound by a provision in the articles which was *personal* to himself as member, e.g. a right to the vote attaching to his shares (*Pender v Lushington*, 1877),[62] the principles involved may go further than this. There is some authority for the view that *each member has a right under the articles to have the company's affairs conducted in accordance with the articles*. There are cases in which, despite the rule in *Foss v Harbottle*, 1843 (see p. 197) an individual member has been allowed to challenge the conduct of a company's affairs by a properly constituted board. (*Hogg v Cramphorn Ltd*, 1966,[67] and *Bamford v Bamford Ltd*, 1969.[68]) The same principle seems to allow for the indirect enforcement of the rights of outsiders by means of a member suing in his capacity of member to have provisions in the articles observed even where these involve the rights of outsiders. (*Salmon v Quinn and Axtens Ltd*, 1909, see p. 529.)

12. THE RULE IN *ROYAL BRITISH BANK v TURQUAND*

The rule which was laid down in *Royal British Bank v Turquand*, 1856[69] protects persons who deal with a company from *outside* against defects in the internal management of the company's affairs. The protection is given because, if the directors appear to be acting in accordance with the memorandum and articles, then those dealing with them *externally* are entitled to assume, because they cannot know, that the directors have the authority which they claim to have. The rule, which is also referred to as the 'indoor Management Rule' derives from the judgment of Lord Hatherley in *Mahony v East Holyford Mining Co* (1875) LR 7 HL 869, where he said, after referring to the fact that those dealing with companies were required to ensure that the transaction was in accordance with the memorandum and articles of which they had constructive notice, 'After that ... all that the directors do with reference to what I might call the indoor management of their own concern is a thing known to them and known to them alone ...'. The rule applies only to transactions which are within the company's powers but beyond the directors' powers. Thus the rule may cure defects in the authority of a company's representatives; it will not cure a transaction which is *ultra vires* the company itself.

The development of the rule may be traced through a number of major cases and s. 35, which have affected it so that in modern law it applies in three major situations as set out below.

Directors acting in excess of their authority

Under s. 35, a distinction must be made between two situations as follows—

(*a*) *Transactions authorized, effected or ratified by the board of directors*. Section 35 provides that if a company enters into a transaction 'decided on by the directors' which infringes a limitation on the powers of the directors under the memorandum or articles, the other party may treat the company as bound by it if he acted in good faith, and without *actual knowledge* of the limitation. (See p. 62.) Section 35 is wider than *Turquand*,[69] because a person dealing with the company in good faith is not deemed to have constructive notice of the memorandum or articles and is protected even if the company's constitution *expressly forbids* the transaction, e.g. a sale of the company's property which the articles expressly forbid (and see *Irvine v Union Bank of*

Australia, 1877).[70] Section 35 gives the same protection as *Turquand*[69] where correct internal procedures were not followed.

(*b*) *Transactions effected by managing and other directors of the company.* It would appear that the Act does not apply in this situation, but *Turquand*,[69] although normally requiring a collective act of the board, may be extended to cover acts of individual directors by the use of the ordinary principles of the law of agency. (See *Freeman & Lockyer v Buckhurst Park Properties Ltd*, 1964[71] and *Hely-Hutchinson v Brayhead Ltd*, 1968.[72]) In addition, although we refer to s. 35 and *Turquand's Case* as operating in the collective situation, we can assume that following *International Sales etc v Marcus*, 1982[47] s. 35 and *Turquand* would apply to a transaction entered into in excess of the board's authority by a director to whom all actual authority to act for the board had been effectively delegated. But whether the contract is made by the board collectively or by a managing or other director, the following cases are relevant—

(i) *Re Hampshire Land Co*, [1896] 2 Ch 743 which decides that if the articles contain a limit to directors' borrowing, which may be raised by ordinary resolution, a lender may assume the assent of members to the additional borrowing, even if he knows that the personal limit of the directors has already been reached.

(ii) *Irvine v Union Bank of Australia*, 1877,[70] which decides that where consent to borrowing or extra borrowing is by special resolution, the Rule does not apply. Registration of such a resolution is required and inspection at the Registry would reveal that it had not been passed. Failure to inspect is of no consequence because there is constructive notice of the company's file. *Irvine*[70] further states that *Turquand*[69] does not protect against absolute prohibitions in the company's constitution and that the person concerned has constructive notice of the constitution for this purpose.

However, s. 35 could well protect an outsider in the circumstances of *Irvine*[70] because those who rely on s. 35 have no constructive notice of the company's constitution and therefore are not constructively aware of absolute prohibitions, though of course if they have actual notice of the prohibition they cannot rely on s. 35. For example, s. 35 would presumably not work in the circumstances of *Howard v Patent Ivory Manufacturing Co*, 1888[15] where invalid debentures were issued to directors, who being 'indoors the management', were taken to *know* of the irregularity.

Directors acting despite defects in title to office

Section 285 may assist a person who has dealt with directors and finds that the validity of their acts is called into question. The section provides that the acts of a director or manager shall be valid notwithstanding any defect that may later be discovered in his appointment or qualification. (*Reg* 92 of *Table A* contains a similar provision.)

There are *certain differences in the protection* provided by the common law in *Turquand*'s case[69] and that provided by s. 285 as follows—

(*a*) The statutory provision applies only where there is some defect in the *procedure* involved in the appointment; it does not cover cases where there is no real appointment at all. (*Morris v Kanssen*, 1946.[73]) Thus the statute provides rather less protection than the common law.

(*b*) The common law rule in *Turquand*[69] operates to cure the defects only at the instance of the person dealing with the company; the company has no right to use *Turquand*[69] to validate a transaction. However, the company can take advantage of the provisions of s. 285, and can claim a transaction as valid and binding on the other party, even though the director was not properly appointed or qualified.

Directors acting on the basis of a decision taken at an improperly constituted board meeting

All the cases in which *Turquand*[69] has been quoted on this point have been concerned in the main with absence of a *quorum* at the relevant board meeting. It was decided in *County of Gloucester Bank v Rudry Merthyr Steam and House Coal Colliery Co* [1895] 1 Ch 629 that where the articles allow the directors to fix their own quorum an outsider is protected in respect of a transaction resolved upon at a meeting without a quorum, because he has no way of discovering how many directors should attend. In addition, it was decided in *Prince of Wales Assurance Society v Athenaeum Assurance Society* (1858) 3 CBNS 756 that where the articles fix a quorum an outsider is still protected because he is not concerned to see and cannot know that the proper number of directors attended the meeting. Finally, *Duck v Tower Galvanising Co* [1901] 2 KB 314 is authority for the view that an outsider is protected under the rule even where the act was done on behalf of the company *without a board meeting at all*, provided the person(s) who acted for the company did so with the knowledge of the directors, whether properly appointed or not. In that case a person formed his business into a company and continued to carry on the whole business of the company with the consent of the other members. Without any meeting he issued debentures to Duck for £500 under the seal of the company. The company's constitution gave power to issue debentures and it was held Duck was entitled to assume that the debentures were valid and he thus had priority over the other creditors on the basis of the security of the debenture.

It is uncertain whether s. 35 would apply to cure a transaction entered into by the board without a quorum. The section uses the phrase 'decided on by the directors' and this, perhaps, ought to be interpreted as meaning a properly-constituted board meeting so that s. 35 would not apply if there was no quorum.

Persons who may rely on the rule. The rule in *Turquand's*[69] case protects persons who deal with the company from *outside* against defects in the internal management of the company's affairs. Members of a company can take advantage of the rule and in *Bargate v Shortridge* (1855) 5 HL Cas 297 it was held that a member could rely upon a written consent purporting to be given by the board, as required by the articles, allowing him to transfer his shares, even though it was given by the managing director alone. The company could not set aside the transfer and restore the member's name to the register.

Directors and persons who act as such *in regard to the transaction in question* are regarded as *insiders* and cannot rely on the rule. Thus, an allotment of shares made to a director at a meeting at which he was present by a board, some or all of whom were not properly appointed, would be invalid. As Lord Simonds said in *Morris v Kanssen*, 1946[73] in regard to directors: 'To admit in their favour a presumption that that is rightly done which they themselves have wrongly done is to encourage ignorance and careless dereliction from duty'.

However, if a director *does not act as such in connection with a transaction* he may be able to rely on the rule. Thus in *Hely-Hutchinson v Brayhead*, 1968[72] it was held that a director who lent money to his company's subsidiary, and also guaranteed loans to it by other persons, could enforce an agreement to indemnify him given in the company's name by a fellow director who had assumed the functions of managing director on an irregular basis but with the acquiescence of the board. The company was represented in the transaction only by the fellow director, and the director who made the loan was not therefore prevented from relying on the rule.

Forged documents issued on behalf of the company

As regards the operation of the rule on forged documents it is necessary to distinguish between two types of forgery as follows—

(*a*) where A writes the name of B on a document issued on behalf of the company the document will not be validated by the rule. Thus, in *Ruben v Great Fingall Consolidated*, 1906 (see p. 500) where a company secretary forged the signatures of directors on a spurious share certificate in order to raise a personal loan, the certificate was said not to bind the company because it was a forgery;

(*b*) where A signs his own name on a document issued on behalf of the company without authority. This point was raised in *Kreditbank*

Cassel v Schenkers Ltd [1927] 1 KB 826 where a manager of a company signed a bill of exchange on behalf of the company in order to pay a personal debt. Again, it was said that the bill was not binding on the company because it was a forgery, i.e. it purported to be a different document from what it in fact was. It purported to be issued on behalf of the company in payment of its debt whereas it was issued in payment of the manager's own debt.

Nevertheless, the better view is that forgeries of the kind set out in (*b*) above can be validated by the rule. It seems that *Kreditbank* was based on the absence of any usual or apparent authority in the branch manager to sign bills of exchange on behalf of the company and it may be that this is why the bill was not binding on it. It is thus possible to say that if a director or some other agent of the company with usual or apparent authority forged a company document in the manner set out in (*b*) above the document would be validated by the rule and would bind the company if taken by a third party *bona fide* and for value.

In this connection the Law of Property Act 1925, s. 74(1) provides that persons dealing with the company in good faith in property matters may treat a *deed* as binding on the company if the deed bears the common seal of the company and appears to be properly attested by persons, e.g. directors and secretary, who would normally be authorized to attest the deed.

Remedies

If a transaction which is entered into on behalf of a company by a person who has no authority to make it does not bind the company, then the remedies of following and tracing are available to the third party on the same basis as when the contract is *ultra vires* the company. (See p. 61.) There is, however, an additional possibility which is that since the transaction is not *ultra vires* the company but only beyond the powers of the board or other individuals who entered into it on behalf of the company, the members may, if they wish, by ordinary resolution in general meeting ratify the transaction and cure the defect so that the company becomes bound by it. If the articles require a special or extraordinary resolution to validate the transaction then the members must pass such a resolution to ratify the transaction.

Reform of *ultra vires* rule

At the present time, unless s. 35 applies, an outsider is protected by the rule in *Turquand*'s case[69] only if the transaction appears proper if compared with the memorandum and articles *whether the outsider has looked at the documents or not.*

The Jenkins Committee recommended that legislation should provide in effect that outsiders could safely assume that all directors had authority to represent the company individually, in much the same way as partners may represent their firm, unless they actually knew that the memorandum or articles prohibited this.

In *Freeman & Lockyer v Buckhurst Park Properties Ltd,* 1964[71] Diplock L J said in effect that the Jenkins Committee proposal was already law and by doing so widened the rule in *Turquand's* case[69] by extending it through application of general principles of agency law to the acts of individual directors.

While this is an advantage to outsiders, it does have the effect of allowing individual directors to bind the company and makes inroads on the principle of *collective* management by the board. Those who regard it as beneficial for important decisions relating to the company's affairs to be taken in board meetings, if only on the ground that two or more heads are better than one, will be apprehensive about such an extension of the law. However, the courts seem willing to affirm that the apparent authority of a *managing director* is such that in all normal commercial transactions he can bind his company, even if not properly appointed, provided that the company has, by its conduct, held him out as having authority. (*Freeman & Lockyer v Buckhurst Park Properties Ltd,* 1964.[71]) Where no managing director has been appointed the courts seem also to be prepared to treat chairmen who are *de facto* chief executives as having the same apparent powers as managing directors. (*Hely-Hutchinson v Brayhead,* 1968.[72]) Interestingly enough s. 35 does not appear to extend to transactions which may be effected by managing or other directors or by other officers or agents of the company, since it applies only in respect of transactions decided on by the board (but see *Reg 72* of *Table A,* p. 233).

However, the judiciary have used the concept of the usual authority of an agent in order to allow a company secretary to bind the company in a contract which he made without actual authority. (See *Panorama Developments (Guildford) Ltd v Fidelis Furnishing Fabrics Ltd,* 1971, p. 562.) Furthermore, the rule in *Turquand's case*[69] does not apply where the circumstances put the third party upon enquiry. Thus in *A. L. Underwood Ltd v Bank of Liverpool* [1924] 1 KB 775 it was held that the bank at which a director of a company has his private account will be put on enquiry if that director pays cheques made out to the company into that private account, and the bank may be liable to pay damages to the company for conversion of its cheques.

4 Capital and its maintenance

When we talk of a company's capital we may have one of many things in mind, since the word capital has several meanings.

(*a*) **Nominal or authorized capital** is the total amount of capital which the company is allowed to issue. The initial amount on registration, which is set out in the memorandum, can be increased or reduced. (S. 121.)

(*b*) **Allotted capital** is that part of the company's nominal capital which has been actually allotted to the shareholders. A company is not bound to allot all its capital at once. Public companies must have a minimum allotted share capital of £50,000 with not less than one-quarter of the nominal value of each allotted share plus the whole of any premium on such share being paid up in cash or otherwise, though employees' shares may be excluded from this calculation. All other shares must be included.

(*c*) **Called-up capital** is the total amount called up by the company on the shares allotted.

(*d*) **Paid-up capital** is that part of the called-up capital which has been paid up by the shareholders. If a reference to a company's capital is made in its business letters or order forms, the reference must be to its paid-up capital. (S. 351(2).)

(*e*) **Uncalled capital** is the amount not called up on shares which the company has allotted. Uncalled capital is seldom encountered today because partly paid shares are not popular with investors in commercial companies. Such persons do not, in general, wish to be under a liability to pay money at any time when called upon by the company to do so. Thus nowadays most issues of shares are fully paid up within a very short time after allotment, and *reserve capital* (see (*g*) below) is comparatively rare.

(*f*) **Equity share capital** is that part of the company's allotted capital (usually the ordinary shares) which gives the holders a right to participate in dividends and distributions of capital *without limit*.

(*g*) **Reserve capital** is that part of the uncalled capital of a limited company which the company has by special resolution determined shall not be called up except in the event of winding up. (S. 120.)

It is not under the control of the directors and if charged by the company, e.g. as security for an issue of debentures, the charge is void.

(*h*) **Debentures.** Money raised by debentures is not *strictly speaking* capital, although it is often an alternative way of raising money needed for carrying on the company's business instead of issuing further shares. A debenture is distinguished from share capital in that it is a *loan* to the company; it is often *secured* by either a charge on a specific asset or assets, or a floating charge on all the assets or a combination of both; it carries *no voting rights or any share of control*; the interest charge must be met, whether profits are made or not, and may therefore, unlike the dividends on shares, be paid out of capital. These matters will be fully treated at a later stage.

CLASSES OF CAPITAL

A company may confer different rights on different classes of shares, the main types being *preference*, *ordinary* and *deferred* shares. It is necessary to refer to the articles, or to the terms of issue, in order to ascertain the rights attaching to the various classes of share. Although the share capital is stated in the memorandum, the types of shares and their respective rights need not be set out in it, and power may be taken in the articles to issue different classes of shares. (See *Table A, Reg. 2.*) But where the rights attaching to different classes of shares *are* set out in the memorandum, they cannot be altered *unless* the memorandum or articles provide a method of alteration, or the permission of the court is obtained for a scheme of arrangement under s. 425, or with the consent of *all* the members (s. 125). The question of arrangements will be dealt with more fully in Chapter 15, but by way of explanation here, s. 425 provides a procedure whereby the company can meet and discuss with the shareholders the question of variation of their rights so as to achieve an agreed alteration.

PREFERENCE SHARES

These shares are entitled to preferential treatment when dividends are declared. Thus a 10 per cent preference share must receive a dividend of 10 per cent out of profits before anything can be paid to the ordinary shares. Since there may be several classes of preference shares ranking one after the other, it is essential to refer to the company's articles, or the terms under which the shares were issued, to ascertain the precise rights of a holder of a particular preference share.

However, a right to preferential dividend without more is deemed a right to a *cumulative* dividend, i.e. if no dividend is declared on the preference shares in any year, the arrears are carried forward and must be paid before any dividend can be declared on ordinary shares (*Webb v Earle* (1875) LR 20 Eq 556). Thus, if the 10 per cent preference shares mentioned above received dividends of 5 per cent in 1983; 5 per cent in 1984; and nothing in 1985; they would be entitled at the end of 1986 to 5 + 5 + 10 + 10, or 30 per cent before the ordinary shareholders could have a penny.

However, it may be *expressly* provided by the terms of issue that they are to be non-cumulative but it is rare nowadays to find such a provision in the case of shares issued by public companies; and they may be held to be *non-cumulative by implication*, as where the terms of issue or the articles provide that dividends shall be paid 'out of yearly profits' (*Adair v Old Bushmills Distillery* [1908] WN 24) or 'out of the net profits of each year'. (*Staples v Eastman Photographic Materials Co* [1896] 2 Ch 303.)

Preference shares do not carry the right to participate in any surplus profits of the company unless the articles so provide. (*Will v United Lankat Plantations Co*, 1914.)[74] However, it is possible to create *cumulative and participating* preference shares, conferring on the holders of such shares a right to participate in surplus profits up to a given percentage, e.g. a right to a preferential dividend of 6 per cent plus a further right, after (say) 10 per cent has been paid to ordinary shareholders, to participate in surplus profits until a further 6 per cent has been paid but no more.

Arrears of preference dividend in a winding up

In the absence of an express provision in the articles, no arrears of preference dividend are payable in the winding up of a company unless the dividend has already been declared (*Re Crichton's Oil Co*, 1902),[75] and this is so even where the articles provide for the payment of dividends *due* at the date of winding up, for a dividend is not *due* until declared. (*Re Roberts and Cooper Ltd*, 1929.)[76] Where the articles do provide for payment of arrears they may be paid out of the surplus assets after payment of the company's debts, *even though those assets do not contain any undistributed profits*. (*Re Wharfedale Brewery Co* [1952] Ch 913.) Thus the general rule that dividends must not be paid out of capital does not apply in this sort of situation. However, unless there is a specific provision which says so, the right to arrears ceases at the date of liquidation. (*Re E W Savory Ltd* [1951] 2 All ER 1036.)

Even where the articles or terms of issue do contain a provision regarding the repayment of dividend and/or capital to preference shareholders in a winding up, problems of construction arise, i.e. problems arise with regard to the meaning of the words used. For example, in *Re Walter Symons Ltd* [1934] Ch 308, preference shares were issued with 'the right to a fixed cumulative preferential dividend at the rate of 12 per cent per annum on the capital for the time being paid up thereon . . . and to rank both as regards dividends and capital in priority to the ordinary shares *but with no right to any further participation in profits or assets*'. The court took the view that the italicized words envisaged a winding up, because it is only in winding up that the question of participation in *assets* arises. Therefore the rest of the clause must also apply in a winding up, and the preference shares had priority in a winding up for repayment of dividends unpaid at that date.

However, in *Re Wood, Skinner and Co Ltd* [1944] Ch 323, the preference shareholders had 'the right to a fixed cumulative dividend of 6 per cent per annum on the capital paid up on the shares', and were expressed to rank 'both as regards dividends and capital in priority to the ordinary shares'. In this case the court decided that since the latter part of the clause did not refer solely to the winding-up situation, the priority conferred was restricted to dividends declared whilst the company was in operation, and did not give the right to arrears of dividend once a winding up had commenced.

Of course a person drafting terms of issue today would normally make his intentions more clear than was done in the two cases cited above, and would certainly not use the phrases which were used then. Nevertheless problems do arise out of bad draftsmanship and the cases show how the court might deal with such situations.

A typical modern clause in the terms of issue of preference shares which more clearly expresses the rights intended to be conferred is as follows. 'The holders of preference shares shall be entitled to a fixed cumulative preferential dividend at the rate of X per cent per annum upon the amount paid up thereon, and in the event of the winding up of the company, to repayment of the amount paid up thereon together with any arrears of dividend calculated to the date of such repayment in priority to the claims of ordinary shares, but shall have no other right to participate in the assets or profits of the company.'

It should be noted that under such a clause unpaid preference dividends will be payable for periods up to the repayment of the preference capital, even though the dividends have not been declared and in spite of the fact that the company may not have earned sufficient profits to pay them while it was a going concern. (*Re Wharfedale Brewery Co* [1952] Ch 913.)

Repayment of capital on winding up

Preference shares have no inherent priority as to the repayment of capital in a winding up. If the assets are not enough to pay the preference and ordinary shares in full then, unless the articles or terms of issue provide to the contrary, preference and ordinary shares are paid off rateably according to the nominal value of their shares. (*Birch v Cropper* (1889) 14 App Cas 525.) Where, *as is usual*, the preference shares have priority either by the articles or terms of issue, they are entitled to repayment of their capital in full before the ordinary shareholders receive anything by way of repayment of capital. Where there are surplus assets left after the discharge of all the company's liabilities and the repayment of capital to all shareholders, the surplus is divided among ordinary and preference shareholders unless the articles provide to the contrary. Any rights given by the articles are exhaustive. Thus, where the articles give preference shareholders priority of repayment of capital in a winding up, but do not refer to any further rights in the capital of the company, the preference shareholders have no right to participate in surplus capital. (*Scottish Insurance Corporation v Wilsons and Clyde Coal Co* [1949] AC 462.)

The following is, therefore, a summary of the position—

(i) Where the preference shareholders have no priority in regard to repayment of capital, they share the assets rateably with the ordinary shareholders, including any surplus assets left after repayment of share capital and other liabilities.

(ii) If the articles or terms of issue give the preference shareholders priority for repayment of capital, they are repaid the nominal value of their shares before the ordinary shareholders *but no more.*

In addition it should be noted that if the articles give preference shareholders an *express* right to participate equally with the ordinary shareholders in surplus assets, they are entitled to share in such assets even though they include ploughed back profits of former years which could have been distributed as dividend to ordinary shareholders but which instead were placed in reserve. (*Dimbula Valley (Ceylon) Tea Co Ltd v Laurie* [1961] 1 All ER 769.) The fact that the ordinary shareholders are, while the company is a going concern, in charge of the profit, i.e. they can resolve upon a distribution within the provisions of Part VIII of the Companies Act 1985, does not prevent the preference shareholders having a right to participate in those profits which the ordinary shareholders have left undistributed.

Redeemable shares—generally

The Companies Act 1948 allowed companies to issue redeemable *preference* shares. The relevant section was repealed in favour of *new powers* which are now in the Companies Act 1985 allowing the issue of redeemable shares whether equity or preference.

The provisions are designed, amongst other things, to encourage investment in the equity of small businesses in circumstances where the proprietors, often members of a family, can, at an appropriate stage buy back the equity investments without parting permanently with family control.

Issue of redeemable shares

Under s. 159(1) a company limited by shares or guarantee with a share capital may, if authorized by its articles, issue redeemable shares. They may be issued as redeemable at the option of the company or the shareholder. Thus *Table A, Reg 3* authorizes the issue of redeemable shares.

Under s. 159(2) redeemable shares may be issued only if there are in issue other shares which cannot be redeemed. If a company's shares were *all* redeemable it could redeem the whole of its capital and end up with no members. This would circumvent s. 24 and s. 122(1)(e), Insolvency Act 1986 which have already been considered in Chapter 1 and which are designed to prevent a company continuing in existence with less than two members.

The redemption of redeemable shares

Under s. 159(3) redeemable shares may not be redeemed unless they are fully paid. The *issued capital* is the creditors' buffer and it is this figure and not the paid up capital which must be replaced.

Under s. 159(3) the terms of the redemption must provide that the company shall pay for them on redemption and not, e.g. at a later date as by creating a creditor. Creditors do not usually receive interest on an outstanding debt or a dividend so that failure to pay on redemption would give the company the resource of the share capital without cost.

Under s. 160(1) redeemable shares may only be redeemed out of distributable profits or out of the proceeds of a fresh issue of shares (which need not be redeemable) made for the purpose. Any premium payable on redemption must be paid out of distributable profits of the company, unless the shares being redeemed were issued at a premium. (See below.)

Private companies may redeem (or purchase their own shares not issued as redeemable) partly out of capital subject to certain restrictions. (See further p. 108.)

Under s 170(1) where shares are redeemed out of profits, a sum equal to the nominal value of the shares redeemed must be transferred from the company's profit and loss account to a capital reserve called the 'Capital Redemption Reserve'. The purpose of this provision is to preserve the capital of the company intact. The reserve cannot be utilized for the payment of dividends.

Under s. 160(4) shares when redeemed are to be treated as cancelled and this will reduce the issued share capital of the company by the nominal value of the shares redeemed. Authorized capital is not reduced.

Under s. 160(2) if the shares being redeemed were themselves issued at a premium, any premium on their redemption may be paid out of the proceeds of a fresh issue of shares made for the purposes of redemption up to an amount equal to—

(*a*) the aggregate of the premiums received by the company on the issue of the shares redeemed, or

(*b*) the current amount of the company's share premium account (including any sum transferred to that account in respect of premiums on the new shares) *whichever is the less*, and in that case the amount of the company's share premium account shall be reduced by a sum corresponding (or by sums in the aggregate corresponding) to the amount of any payment made by virtue of s. 160(2) out of the proceeds of the issue of the new shares.

The object of the above provisions is to tighten protection for creditors on a redemption (or purchase, see p. 108) of shares as the following example shows.

Some years ago Boxo plc issued 500 Class A redeemable preference shares at a premium of 10p per share and 500 Class B redeemable preference shares also at a premium of 10p per share. Boxo plc now intends as agreed to redeem the Class A shares at a premium of 20p per share. 350 new shares of £1 each have been issued at par for the purposes of the redemption.

(a) 1985 Act approach

Shareholders' funds	£ Before	£ After	
Preference share capital	1,000	500	(Class B)
Ordinary share capital	1,000	1,350	
Share premium	100	50	
Capital redemption reserve	—	200	

Capital and undistributable reserves			
(i.e. creditors' buffer)	2,100	2,100	(same)
Distributable profits	800	600	
Net assets	2,900	2,700	

(b) Under previous legislation

Prior to 1981 a company could utilize the whole of its share premium to pay premium on redemption. This could reduce the creditors' buffer (see below).

	£	£	
Shareholders' funds	**Before**	**After**	
Preference share capital	1,000	500	(Class B)
Ordinary share capital	1,000	1,350	
Share premium	100	—	
Capital redemption reserve	—	150	
Capital and undistributable reserves			
(i.e. creditors' buffer)	2,100	2,000	(reduced)
Distributable profits	800	650	
Net assets	2,900	2,650	

Under s. 160(5) a company which has issued all of its authorized capital need not increase it merely to issue the new shares necessary to redeem existing ones.

Miscellaneous matters relating to redeemable shares

Commonly, redeemable shares are made redeemable between certain dates. The holder thus knows that his shares cannot be redeemed before the earlier of the two dates, which is normally a number of years after the issue of the shares, in order to give him an investment which will last for a reasonable period. He also knows that the shares are bound to be redeemed by the later of the two dates mentioned.

As regards failure to redeem (or purchase) its shares, a company cannot be liable in damages for such a failure. (S. 178(2).) The shareholder may obtain an order for specific performance *unless* the company can show that it cannot meet the cost of redemption out of distributable profits. (S. 178(3).)

Following statements by Megarry J in *Re Holders Investment Trust* [1971] 2 All ER 289, a shareholder whose shares are not redeemed on the agreed date may be able to obtain an injunction to prevent the company from paying dividends either to ordinary shareholders or to any subordinate class of preference shareholder until the redemption has been carried out. *Re Holders* also confirms that such a shareholder may petition for a winding up under s. 122(1)(g), Insolvency Act 1986—the just and equitable ground.

If the company goes into liquidation and at the date of commencement of the winding up has failed to meet an obligation to redeem (or purchase) its own shares, and this obligation occurred before the commencement of the winding up, the terms of the redemption or purchase can be enforced by the shareholder against the company, *but not if* during the period between the due date for redemption (or purchase) and the date of commencement of the winding up the company could not have lawfully made a distribution (see further p. 283) equal in value to the price at which the shares were to have been redeemed or purchased. (S. 178(4) and (5).)

However, any money owed under s. 178(4) and (5) is *deferred* to claims of all creditors and preference shareholders having rights to capital which rank in preference to the shares redeemed or purchased but *ranks in front* of the claims of other shareholders. (S. 178(6).)

Sched 4, Part III, para 38(2) provides that the balance sheet must specify in the case of any part of the allotted capital that consists of redeemable shares, the earliest and latest dates on which the company has power to redeem those shares; whether those shares must be redeemed in any event or are liable to be redeemed at the option of the company or of the shareholder; and whether any (and, if so, what) premium is payable on redemption. Notice of redemption must be given to the Registrar within one month of the redemption. (S. 122.)

Preference shares which are already issued cannot be converted into redeemable preference shares since this is not considered to be an 'issue' within the terms of s. 159. (*Re St James' Court Estate Ltd* [1944] Ch 6.) This can, however, be done under s. 425 (see further p. 380) by cancelling the existing non-redeemable shares and replacing them with an issue of redeemable shares.

ORDINARY SHARES

The nature of an ordinary share is perhaps best understood by comparing it with a preference share. In this way we can ascertain the distinguishing features, and the advantages and disadvantages which arise from the holding of ordinary shares.

Disadvantages

Under this heading we must consider the fact that the ordinary shareholder is entitled to a dividend only after the preference dividends have been paid. Furthermore, where the preference shares have preference as to capital, the ordinary shares rank behind the preference shares for repayment of capital on winding up or where there is a reduction of capital by repayment. The preference shares must be fully repaid first. (See further p. 102.)

It is perhaps because of the above priorities given to preference shareholders that the ordinary shareholders are said to hold the *equity* share capital of the company, presumably by analogy with the *equity of redemption* held by a mortgagor in the law of mortgages. A mortgagor who pays off all the charges on his property has the right to redeem or recover it by virtue of this equity; indeed it is the last right he retains, for when that is gone, he has lost his property. Similarly the *equity shareholders* are entitled to the remaining assets of the company after the claims of creditors and of preference shareholders have been met.

Advantages

Here we may observe that the voting power of the ordinary shareholders in general meetings is such as to allow them to control the resolutions at such meetings. In fact this means that *the directorate really represents*, or can be made to represent, *the ordinary shareholders.*

It is not uncommon for companies to issue preference shares with no voting rights at general meetings, though if such shares are to be listed on the Stock Exchange, they must be given *adequate* voting rights by the company's articles. It would seem, however, that the voting rights of preference shareholders are *adequate* if they can vote—

(*a*) when their dividend is in arrear;

(*b*) on resolutions for reducing share capital and winding up the company; and

(*c*) on resolutions which are likely to affect their class rights.

A further advantage of ordinary shareholders is that their dividends are not fixed and may rise considerably with the profitability of the company. Furthermore if a prosperous company is wound up, the ordinary shareholders in most cases take the surplus assets, even if this means that they are paid many times more than the value of their shares.

A final advantage is that a company may issue bonus shares, or new issues (called rights issues) at prices lower than outsiders would have to pay, and these are generally offered to the company's existing ordinary shareholders.

VARIATION AND ABROGATION OF CLASS RIGHTS

If the shares of a company are divided into different classes the expression 'class rights' refers to the special rights of a particular class of shareholder concerning, e.g. dividends and voting. Section 125(8) makes it clear that *abrogation of class rights is included.* This means that class rights can be *extinguished entirely* as well as merely varied provided appropriate procedures as set out below are followed.

1. Meaning of variation

Case law decided that class rights are to be regarded as varied only if after the purported act of variation they are *different in substance* than before. Unless this is so consent of the particular class or classes of shareholders is not required. The courts have in general taken a narrow and, perhaps, over-literal approach to the meaning of variation of rights. (See e.g. *Greenhalgh v Arderne Cinemas*, 1936.[53])

2. Method of variation

The method by which the variation is effected will depend upon the source of the class rights.

(a) *Where the rights are conferred by the memorandum.* The company in general meeting must change the rights by a resolution of the type laid down in the memorandum. As we have seen, the general power to alter the memorandum by special resolution conferred by s. 17 does not apply to alteration of class rights. (S. 17(2)(b).) If neither the memorandum nor the articles provide for variation they may not be varied except with the consent of *all* the members under s. 125(5) (which operates to vary the rights and also gives permission to do so), or by a scheme of arrangement under s. 425 (see further p. 380).

(b) *Where the rights are contained in the articles.* In the case, e.g. of an article creating a class of preference share, or a redeemable ordinary share, the rights can be changed by a special resolution of the company in general meeting under the general provision in s. 9.

(c) *Where the rights are contained in a resolution setting out the terms of issue.* The articles or terms of issue must be followed. It may be that only an ordinary resolution is required.

3. Permission to vary

Subject to what has been said about the effect of s. 125(5) (see above), the resolution to vary the rights is of no legal effect unless the consent of the class or classes concerned is obtained.

Any procedures for obtaining the consent of the class specified in the memorandum or articles must be complied with. There are no such procedures in the current *Table A*. However, if the variation is concerned with the giving, variation, revocation, or renewal of an authority under s. 80 (authority for directors to allot shares) or with a reduction of capital under s. 135, it can, *regardless of what the memorandum and articles provide*, only be sanctioned by either the written consent of the holders of three-quarters in nominal value of the issued shares of the class or by an extraordinary resolution passed at a separate meeting of the class. *If the memorandum or articles impose more onerous requirements these must be followed.* (S. 125(3)(c).)

Where class rights are not in the memorandum, as where they are in the articles or a resolution containing the terms of issue, and there is no provision in the articles under which they can be varied, they can be varied with the three-quarters' consent or extraordinary resolution procedure described above. (S. 125(2).) The rules relating to the conduct of the class meeting are considered at p. 215.

4. Right to dissent

Dissentient members of a class may object to variation. Section 127 provides that the holders of not less than 15 per cent of the issued shares of the class, being persons who did not consent to or vote for the resolution to vary, may apply to the court to have the variation cancelled. If such application is made, the variation has no effect until confirmed by the court. Application to the court under s. 127 must be made within 21 days after the date on which the resolution was passed or the consent given. It may be made on behalf of all the dissentients by one or more of them appointed in writing. (S. 127(3).) The court's power on hearing a petition for cancellation of a variation of class rights is limited to approving or disallowing the variation. The court cannot amend the variation or approve it subject to conditions. (S. 127(4).)

Section 127(5) requires that the company send to the Registrar within 15 days of the making of the court order, a copy of that order embodying the court's decision on the matter of variation.

SPECIAL RIGHTS: REGISTRATION OF PARTICULARS

In order to ensure that the public has access to the details of a company's class rights s. 128 provides that *if a company allots shares* with rights which are not recorded in its memorandum or articles, nor contained in a resolution or agreement required by s. 380 (see further p. 218) to be sent to the Registrar of Companies, it must unless, by reason of s. 128(2), the shares have rights which are in all respects the same as those previously allotted, save that they do not carry the same rights to dividend during the 12 months immediately following allotment, deliver to the Registrar within one month of allotment a statement giving particulars of the class rights attached to those shares. (S. 128(1).)

The same procedure must be followed where there is a *variation of rights of existing shares* or *the renaming of them* by a method which does not require the filing of a resolution or agreement under s. 380. (S. 128(3) and (4).) Section 129 applies similar provisions to the rights of members of a company which does not have a share capital.

Further publicity as to the classes of shares (or members) which a company has is provided by s. 352(3) and (4) which state that the different classes of shares (or members if there is no share capital) must be identified in the register of members. (See further p. 177.)

Under s. 711(1)(j) the Registrar must publish in the *London Gazette* the receipt by him of any statement or notice delivered under s. 128. A company which fails to comply with s. 128 is liable to a fine as is every officer in default. (S. 128(5).)

ALTERATION OF SHARE CAPITAL

A company's share capital may be altered or increased provided the company follows the appropriate methods and procedures.

1. Increase of nominal or authorized capital

A company may, if authorized by its articles (see *Table A, Reg* 32(a)) increase its nominal or authorized capital by new shares of such amount as the resolution prescribes. Under *Reg* 32 this is done by an ordinary resolution in general meeting, and this power cannot by reason of *Reg* 70 (see further p. 231) be delegated to the directors. Notice of the increase must be given to the Registrar within 15 days of the passing of the resolution (s. 123). A copy of the resolution effecting the increase must also be filed with the Registrar (s. 123(3)). The resolution must be printed or in some other form approved by the Registrar, e.g. electrostatic photocopy.

Where the articles do not give power to increase or alter capital, a special resolution to alter the articles is required, but the alteration of the articles and the alteration of the capital can be achieved by the same *special resolution*. (*Campbell's Case* (1873) LR 9 Ch App 1.) The new shares may be ordinary or preference unless the memorandum otherwise provides. It is usual to increase the nominal capital only when all the existing nominal capital has been issued, but an increase can be made before this position is reached.

2. Consolidation of capital

A company may, if authorized by its articles, consolidate its capital by amalgamating shares of smaller amount into shares of larger amount, e.g. by consolidating groups of twenty shares of nominal value 5p into shares of nominal value £1. (S. 121(2)(*b*).) It is rarely that a company needs to consolidate, the tendency being to subdivide and go for lower nominal values which makes the shares easier to sell, since shares in public companies sell on the Stock Exchange for more than nominal value.

3. Conversion into stock

A company may, if authorized by its articles, convert its *paid-up* shares into stock, or reconvert stock into paid-up shares of any denomination. (S. 121(2)(*c*).) Stock is the holding of a member expressed in pounds instead of so many shares of a certain value each. Instead of saying A holds 10 shares of £1 each one would say A holds £10 of stock. Stock cannot be issued direct; if shares have been converted into stock and additional capital is subsequently issued, the new capital must be issued as shares and another resolution passed converting it into stock with effect from the date on which it becomes fully paid. Stock may be reconverted into paid-up shares of any denomination and the procedure is similar to that on conversion into stock.

4. Subdivision of shares

This is permitted by s. 121(2)(*d*) and would occur, for example, where a company subdivides every £1 share into 10 shares of 10p each. However, the proportions of amounts paid and unpaid must remain the same where the shares are partly paid (s. 121(3)); for example, if before subdivision every £1 share was 50p paid, then the new shares of 10p each must be treated as 5p paid. The company cannot regard some of the new shares as fully-paid and some as partly paid. A company may wish to subdivide shares to make them more easily marketable, e.g. a share having a nominal value of £1 may have a market value of £8 and this may restrict market dealings. If the company subdivides

97

its shares into shares of 10p each the market price would be 80p per share and dealings would be facilitated.

5. Cancellation of unissued nominal capital

Under s.121(2)(e) a company can reduce the amount of share capital available for issue and this does not operate as a reduction within the meaning of s. 135. A cancellation may be desirable following a scheme of arrangement or an amalgamation, or where a company wishes to get rid of onerous conditions attaching to a class of shares which have been created but not issued, e.g. preference shares giving the right to a preferential dividend of 30 per cent per annum.

The type of resolution required to make the alterations set out in 2, 3, 4, and 5 above is the one laid down in the articles. Where the articles are silent a resolution to alter the articles to give authority and to effect the change required is necessary. *Table A, Reg* 32 provides that an ordinary resolution is sufficient, but where a company has special articles these may require a special or extraordinary resolution to effect the change. When an alteration by way of consolidation, conversion, subdivision or cancellation has been effected, the company must notify the Registrar within one month of the alteration. (S. 122.)

MAINTENANCE OF CAPITAL OR PROTECTION OF THE CREDITORS' FUND

The acceptance by English company law of the concept of limited liability has led to a need to protect the capital contributed by the members of such a company since those members cannot be required to contribute funds to enable the company to pay its debts once they have paid for their shares in full.

A creditor of a company must expect that the company's capital may be lost because of business misfortune. However, he can also expect that the company's shares will be paid for in full and that the company will not return the capital to its members.

Company legislation therefore deals with the protection of the creditors' fund in two ways as follows—

(*i*) Provisions designed to prevent capital being 'watered down' as it comes in. These are to be found in ss. 97 and 98 in relation to underwriting commission (see p. 132).

(*ii*) Provisions designed to prevent capital going out of the company once received. These are to be found for example in Part VIII (distributions, see p. 283) and in the following chapters of the Companies

Act 1985, Part V—Chapter VI (financial assistance by a company for the purchase of its own shares, see p. 161), Chapter III (share premium, see p. 173), Chapter VII (procedure on redemption of redeemable shares, and purchase of own shares by a company, see pp. 89–90 and 108), Chapter IV (reduction of capital).

REDUCTION OF CAPITAL

A company limited by shares may, if authorized by its articles, reduce its share capital or share premium account or its capital redemption reserve. The method is by *special resolution* which must be confirmed by the court. (S. 135.) The meeting at which the resolution is passed may, in exceptional circumstances, consist of one shareholder (*X.L. Laundries*, 1969) (see p. 541). In addition, before a reduction of capital can proceed the consent of three-quarters of each class of shareholders affected is required. (S. 125.)

Under s. 135 share capital can be reduced 'in any way'. The section, however, envisages *three* forms of reduction in particular. These enable a company to reduce for the reasons set out below.

(*a*) *It may have more capital than it needs* and may wish to return some of it to shareholders. For example, a company may wish to return paid-up capital which is in excess of its requirements where it has sold a part of its undertaking and intends in the future to confine its activities to running the remaining part of its business. The company may achieve its purpose by reducing the nominal value of its shares. Suppose that before the reduction the company had a share capital of 50,000 shares of £1 each, fully-paid. On reduction it could substitute a share capital of 50,000 shares of 50p each fully-paid, and return 50p per share in cash to the members.

(*b*) *Share capital already issued may not be fully paid* and yet the company may have all the capital it needs. Reduction in these circumstances may be effected as follows. If the company's share capital before reduction was 50,000 shares of £1 each, 50p paid, the company may reduce it to 50,000 shares of 50p each fully-paid. However, liability for unpaid capital cannot be reduced by crediting a partly-paid share as paid up to a greater extent than it has in fact been paid up. (*Re Development Co of Central and West Africa* [1902] 1 Ch 547.) Thus, it is not possible to leave the nominal value of the shares at £1 and cancel one share from every two held by shareholders, regarding the remaining one of the two as fully paid.

(*c*) *Where capital has been lost by the wastage of assets* the company may wish to write off the loss and then pay dividends on the reduced capital value of the shares. Thus, if the company has a share capital of 50,000 shares of £1 each, fully-paid, and its assets are worth only £25,000, it may reduce its capital to 50,000 shares of £0.50 each, fully-paid.

In cases under (a) above a reduction may be confirmed by the court even though the money which is to be used to make the payment is borrowed. (*Re Nixon's Navigation Co* [1897] 1 Ch 872.) It may even be borrowed from the same shareholders whose shares are to be reduced. (*Re Thomas de la Rue & Co Ltd* [1911] 2 Ch 361.) Thus if a company wishes to simplify its capital structure by replacing all its preference shares by exchanging them for loan stock, it could do so under s. 135 on the authority of *Re Thomas de la Rue*. Alternatively, the company could use a reconstruction under s. 425 (see further p. 380).

As we have seen, the permissible modes of reduction are not limited to the situations outlined above. Thus in *Carruth v ICI Ltd* [1937] AC 707 the company had issued £1 ordinary shares and £0.50 deferred shares both fully paid, and the market value of the deferred shares was a quarter of that of the ordinary shares. The court approved a reduction of the deferred shares to £0.25 shares fully paid so that other resolutions passed by shareholders for converting the deferred shares into ordinary shares, on the basis of four deferred shares for one ordinary share, might be more conveniently carried out.

Protection of creditors

In methods (a) and (b) above the creditors are deprived of funds which might have been used to pay off the debts in a winding up. Accordingly before the company's petition for confirmation of the resolution is heard by the court, the company must file a list of agreed creditors and advertise inviting other creditors to submit claims. The court will not proceed to consider a company's petition for its sanction to reduction unless it is satisfied by affidavit of the company's solicitor and one of its officers that all creditors who are named in the filed list, or who have notified their claims, have been paid or have consented to the reduction. If not, the company must secure the amount claimed to the court's satisfaction or satisfy the court that the disputed claims are invalid. (S. 136(5).) The court may dispense with these requirements which protect creditors (s. 136(6)) where, for example, the company has deposited, e.g. with a bank, sufficient funds to cover all claims which may be made against it.

In method (c) above the creditors are not deprived of any funds because the assets have been lost. However, the court may still require the company to take the same steps as outlined above, if it thinks this necessary to protect the creditors. This might arise where the court does not think that the reduction is necessary or genuine, e.g. where the court suspects that the supposed loss of assets has not in fact occurred, so that after the reduction the actual value of the assets might exceed the reduced capital and the company might then distribute the excess amongst its shareholders as if it were profit and so diminish the assets available to pay its debts. It is also the function of the court to see that in method (c) the reduction is operated fairly as between shareholders.

Serious loss of capital

In addition, with regard to method (c) above it should be noted that where the net assets of a public company amount to half or less of the called-up share capital the directors of the company are required by s. 142 to call an extraordinary general meeting within 28 days of one or more of their number becoming aware of that fact. The meeting is to be held within 28 days of its being called so that it is held within 56 days of the directors becoming aware of the serious loss of capital. The meeting is to consider what, if any, measures should be taken to deal with the situation, i.e. winding up, or perhaps to resolve that in view of the measures being taken by the board no further action is required.

The ordinary rules as to notice apply so that the notice of the meeting must set out verbatim any special or extraordinary resolution that is to be proposed at the meeting together with the general nature of any other business. (S. 142(3).)

If there is a failure to convene an extraordinary general meeting as required by s. 142(1), each of the directors of the company who—

(a) knowingly and wilfully authorizes or permits that failure; or

(b) after the expiry of the period during which the meeting should have been convened, knowingly and wilfully authorizes or permits that failure to continue, is liable on conviction by the court to a fine. (S. 142(2).)

Section 142 is to some extent an unsatisfactory provision. It does reproduce the requirements of the EEC Second Directive but leaves doubts as to procedures to be adopted. The financial position of a company may vary greatly during a financial year and s. 142 requires asset valuation to make an appropriate assessment so that a balance sheet is required as well as management accounts.

It would seem to be a reasonable approach for directors to rely on the audited annual accounts as the trigger, if any, for compliance with s. 142, unless, of course, they become aware, presumably as a result of some catastrophe, that the asset value is materially below 50 per cent of the called up share capital.

The section does not state whether a reckless or uncaring director could be saddled with constructive notice. It is also silent as to what happens after the meeting if the deficiency continues. The holding of the meeting would seem to be all the section requires. Once this has been done its force is presumably spent.

Payment of shareholders on reduction

The matter of repayment of shareholders should be treated as if the company was being wound up. Thus if the capital is being repaid for the reasons given in methods (a) and (b) above, the preference shareholders should be paid first if they have priority in a winding up. If the reduction is due to loss of assets, the ordinary shareholders should be reduced before the preference shareholders. This order may, however, be varied if the preference shareholders consent. As a result of s. 125 the court has no discretion to confirm a reduction without separate class meetings of the shareholders affected.

It should also be noted that if a company has created reserves by the transfer of retained profits and subsequently suffers a loss of assets, it is the usual practice to write off the loss against the reserves and to reduce share capital only if the reserves are insufficient. Again, where the company has capital reserves such as a share premium account or a capital redemption reserve, the practice is to write off losses against them before reducing share capital. Losses may be written off against revenue reserves by making an appropriate adjustment in the accounts but losses may only be written off by reducing the share premium account or a capital redemption reserve fund if the same steps are taken as are required for reducing share capital. (S. 130(3) and s. 170(4).)

Procedure after confirmation by the court

If the court is satisfied that the creditors have consented or been paid off or secured, it may make an order confirming the reduction on such terms and conditions as it thinks fit. If the reduction is confirmed, the court will approve a minute giving the new capital structure of the company, and that minute must be filed at the Companies Registry. (S. 138.)

The Registrar of Companies, on production to him of an order of the court confirming the reduction, will issue a certificate of registration to the company. The minute when registered will be deemed to be substituted for the corresponding capital provision in the memorandum and is valid and alterable as if it had been originally contained therein. Copies of the memorandum issued after the date of registration must be altered accordingly. The reduction must be advertised as the court may direct, and the court may also require that the company shall publish reasons for the reduction, and may order the company to add the words 'and reduced' after its name for a period of time. (S. 137(3).) In practice these powers are not normally exercised by the court, but if such an order was made the words 'and reduced' would be inserted after the company's name on all documents, including business letters, on which the name of the company appears.

The provisions of ss. 137(3) and 138 do not apply where the reduction is of the share premium account or the capital redemption reserve, nor where shares are forfeited or surrendered (see p. 157).

Under s. 139, if the court reduces the issued share capital of a public company to below £50,000 it must re-register as a private company. The Registrar is required not to register the order confirming the reduction unless the company is first re-registered as a private one. To facilitate this the court may authorize re-registration without the company having passed the special resolution required by s. 53 in which case the court order will also specify and in effect make the necessary changes in the company's constitution, e.g. in the company's name.

A private company can in certain circumstances purchase its own shares *partly* from capital. (See further p. 108.) This provides, in effect, a much easier way of reducing capital. However, the shareholders concerned must be willing to sell their shares.

ACQUISITION OF OWN SHARES—GENERALLY

Section 143 prohibits a company (whether public or private) from acquiring its own shares (whether by purchase, subscription or otherwise). Exceptions under s. 143(3) are—

    (i) the redemption or purchase (see below) of any shares under Part V of the 1985 Act;

    (ii) the acquisition of shares in a reduction of capital duly made;

    (iii) purchasing shares under a court order as, for example, under s. 5—the buying out of dissentients on an alteration of objects, or under Part XVII—buying out an unfairly prejudiced minority (see pp. 191–5); or

    (iv) forfeiting shares or accepting a surrender in lieu in pursuance of the articles for failure to pay any sum payable in respect of those shares.

Under s. 143(3) a company may acquire its own fully paid shares as a gift and hold them directly in its own name.

Under s. 144, if a person has acquired shares in a company as nominee for that company, then if he fails to pay any sums due on the shares the other subscribers to the memorandum—if he acquired them as a subscriber—or the directors—if he acquired them in some other way—are, unless the court grants relief, jointly and severally liable with the nominee for payment of the sums due.

Such arrangements could in the past be engineered by the directors to keep themselves in secret control so that when faced with a take-over bid they could frustrate the bidder by arranging for shares to be acquired by nominees of the company, sometimes without too much attention as to when and how they were to be paid for, who would, of course, refuse to accept the bid. Under the 1985 Act a person who acquires shares as nominee for the company alone is liable to pay for them and the company is not regarded as having any beneficial interest. If the nominee fails to pay the amount of any call in respect of the nominal value or the premium within 21 days of his being called upon to do so, the subscribers to the memorandum (if the shares were issued to the nominee as a subscriber), or the directors at the time of the issue or the acquisition (in all other circumstances) are jointly and severally liable with the nominee for that amount. In addition in the case of a public company such shares must be disposed of or cancelled within three years and in the meantime any attempt to exercise voting rights in respect of them will be void. (S. 146.)

Relief may be granted by the court in cases where a subscriber or a director would otherwise be liable, if it appears to the court that he acted honestly and reasonably and he ought fairly to be excused, taking into account all the circumstances of the case. The relief may be granted either in any proceedings for the recovery of any amount due or upon the application of a subscriber or a director in anticipation of such proceedings.

In addition, under s. 146, *in the case of a public company*, where shares are forfeited or surrendered, no voting rights may be exercised by the company in respect of them and the shares must be disposed of or cancelled within three years. If the cancellation has the effect of reducing the company's allotted share capital below the authorized minimum, then the directors must apply for the company to be re-registered as a private company in the prescribed manner. In such a case there are relaxations in the conversion procedure provided for by s. 147. In particular only a directors' resolution is required to make the necessary reduction, application and any alterations to the memorandum that are necessary. The company does not need to apply to the court to obtain confirmation of the reduction in capital, but any resolution passed by the directors must be filed with the Registrar under s. 380.

Finally, s. 150 provides that a public company shall not take a lien (see further p. 156) or other charge over its own shares. However, a lien is permitted over partly-paid shares for amounts called or payable on the shares. In addition, charges over its own shares may be taken by a company which makes a loan in the ordinary course of a business so that a bank may take its own shares as a security for a loan by the bank.

PURCHASING OWN SHARES

Generally

Formerly the rule of capital maintenance designed to protect creditors prevented a limited company from using its resources to purchase its own shares from its shareholders. This principle was first enunciated in case law, the leading case being *Trevor v Whitworth* (1887) 12 App Cas 409, and later in company legislation. The strictness of that rule was later relaxed and purchase by a company of its own shares is allowed subject to safeguards.

Types of purchase—generally

There is a 'market purchase' and an 'off-market' purchase. Section 163 defines a market purchase to include only purchases of shares subject to a marketing agreement on a recognized investment exchange.

Section 163 defines an off-market purchase as a purchase of any other types of shares.

Any market or off-market purchases must, if they are to be legal, have authorization in the articles. (S. 162(1).)

Market purchase

Under s. 166 a company may make a market purchase of its own shares provided that the purchase has been authorized by an ordinary resolution of the members in general meeting. The resolution must:

(*a*) Specify the maximum number of shares which the company may acquire under the resolution;

(*b*) State the maximum and minimum prices which the company may pay for those shares. This could give rise to problems in volatile market conditions but is required by the Second Directive;

(*c*) Specify a date when the authority given by the resolution will expire. *This must not be later than 18 months after the passing of the resolution.*

The authority given may be varied, revoked or renewed by a further ordinary resolution of the members. (S. 166(4).)

Under s. 166(5) a company may complete a purchase after the date of the authority given by the ordinary resolution has expired given that the contract for the purchase was made before the expiry date and the terms of the ordinary resolution cover execution of the contract after the expiry date.

Section 380 applies to the ordinary resolution giving the authority and it must therefore be filed with the Registrar within 15 days of being passed and a copy must be embodied in or annexed to every copy of the articles issued thereafter.

Off-market purchases

Under s. 164 a company may make an off-market purchase under a *specific contract* which has received advance authorization by a special resolution of the company. That authorization may be varied, revoked or renewed by special resolution *and with regard to a public company* the resolution must give a date on which the authority will expire this being not later than 18 months after the date on which the resolution was passed.

The shareholder whose shares are being purchased should not vote on a special resolution to confer, vary, revoke or renew an authority. If he does the authority will not be effective unless the resolution would have been passed with the requisite majority without his votes. Any member of the company may demand a poll on the resolution.

A copy of the contract of purchase, or a memorandum of its terms if it is not in writing, must be available for inspection by any member at the registered office for at least 15 days prior to the date of the meeting at which it is to be passed and available at the meeting itself, otherwise the resolution is of no effect.

The contract, or the memorandum of it, must include or have annexed to it a written memorandum giving the names of the shareholders to which the contract relates, if they do not appear in the contract or memorandum.

The special resolution must be filed with the Registrar within 15 days of its passing and a copy of it must be embodied in or annexed to every copy of the articles issued after the resolution has been passed. (S. 380(1) and (2).)

Contingent purchase contracts

Under s. 165 a company may enter into a contract to buy its own shares on the future happening of a certain event, e.g. a contract to buy the shares of an employee on retirement. This is a 'contingent purchase contract' and can only be made if approved in advance by a special resolution and the following of the procedures of s. 164 (above).

Assignment and release

Section 167 provides that the rights of the company under any contract to buy its own shares pursuant to ss. 164, 165 or 166 are not capable of assignment so that the company *cannot sell or buy back* its rights to purchase a member's shares and so create a market in purchase contracts. The company *cannot release its right* to purchase under any contract approved under ss. 164 or 165 unless the release has been approved in advance by a special resolution. This is to prevent the company from providing funds to say selected shareholders by buying the right to purchase their shares and then later releasing that right, i.e. buying a sort of option which it is never intended to exercise.

Disclosure

Under s. 169 a company which has purchased shares under the Act must within 28 days afterwards deliver a return to the Registrar stating the number and nominal value of each class of shares purchased and the date on which they were delivered to the company and the amount paid for them. In addition the company must keep at its registered office any contract or contingent contract for the purchase of its shares and any variation thereof, or a memorandum of its terms if it is not in writing. These documents must be kept for 10 years after the final purchase of the shares, and must be open to inspection by any member of the company and in the case of a public company, to any other person.

Failure by company to purchase shares

Under s. 178 the company is not liable to pay *damages* in respect of a failure to purchase (or redeem) its shares. However, a shareholder may apply for specific performance of the contract of purchase (or the terms of redemption) but no order is to be made if the company can show that it could not pay the price from distributable profits.

Section 178 also deals with winding up and provides that in a liquidation a shareholder may enforce a contract of purchase (or the terms of redemption) against the company provided that the due date for purchase (or redemption) was before the date of commencement of the winding up, *unless* it is shown that the company could not at any time between the due date for purchase (or redemption) and the commencement of the winding up have paid for the shares from distributable profits.

Section 178 also provides that in a winding up all other debts and liabilities are to be paid in priority to the purchase price (or redemption price) as are shareholders with a prior right to return of capital, e.g. preference shareholders. Subject to that the purchase or redemption price is paid in priority to amounts due to other members in a winding up.

Provisions to ensure preservation of capital

Under s. 162, *all* companies may purchase (or redeem) shares from profits or from a fresh issue of shares. Under s. 170 where the purchase or redemption is from profits an amount equivalent to the nominal value of the shares purchased or redeemed must be transferred to a capital redemption reserve. This reserve can only be reduced under s. 135 (see p. 102), though it may be used for the purpose of paying-up unissued shares to be allotted to members as fully-paid bonus shares. Thus the creditors' fund is protected because the shares purchased (or redeemed) are replaced by a new issue of shares or a capital reserve.

Purchase or redemption out of capital—generally

The Companies Act 1985 gives a power to private companies to purchase or redeem shares *partly* from capital when the company concerned has neither sufficient distributable profits nor the ability, in the circumstances to raise all the money required by a new issue. These provisions allow, in effect, a private company to reduce its capital without going to the court under s. 135.

These provisions would be beneficial where, e.g. a controlling shareholder in a family company has died without leaving funds adequate to pay the tax required. A purchase by the company itself rather than by an outsider might suit the other members of the family better if they could not, or did not, wish to make the purchase themselves.

Conditions

Under ss. 171–177 the following conditions must be satisfied before a payment out of capital can be made—

(*a*) the articles of the company must authorize it;

(*b*) the payment must not exceed the 'permissible capital payment'. Under this rule the company is required to utilize its available profits and any proceeds arising from a new issue, if any, before making a payment out of capital. Only the deficiency, if any, can be met from capital;

(c) the directors must make a statutory declaration specifying the amount of the permissible capital payment and also that they are of the opinion that—
  (i) immediately following the purchase (redemption) the company will be able to pay its debts; and
  (ii) for one year immediately following also, so that the directors are saying in effect that the company can continue as a going concern throughout the year;

(d) annexed to the statutory declaration is a report by the auditors addressed to the directors stating that they have enquired into the company's affairs; that the permissible capital payment has been properly determined; and that they are not aware of anything to indicate that the opinion expressed by the directors is unreasonable;

(e) the payment must be approved by a *special resolution* of the members, to safeguard the interests of those members who are not selling. There is a mandatory right for any member to demand a poll. The resolution must be passed on, or within one week, after the date on which the directors make the statutory declaration. The resolution will be effective only if the statutory declaration and auditors' report is available for inspection at the meeting at which it is passed. The special resolution is invalid if it was passed only because the shares being purchased were voted. However, the member whose shares are being purchased may vote other shares if he has any on a poll but not on a show of hands;

(f) the payments out of capital must be made not earlier than five weeks nor later than seven weeks after the date of the resolution.

Publicity

Under s. 175 the company must publish in the *London Gazette* and a national newspaper within the week immediately following the date of the special resolution a notice of the proposed capital payment stating in particular that any creditor may at any time within the five weeks immediately following the date of the special resolution (which is given) apply to the court for an order prohibiting payment.

Similar publicity must be given to the fact that the directors' statutory declaration and the special auditors' report thereon are available for inspection at the registered office of the company. A copy of the statutory declaration and the auditors' report must be filed with the Registrar by the date of publicizing the proposed payment.

Dissentient shareholders/creditors

Under s. 176 a member or a creditor may within five weeks from the resolution apply to the court for an order cancelling the resolution. The right does not extend to a member who consented to the resolution.

Civil liability of past shareholders and directors

Under s. 76, Insolvency Act 1986—

(*a*) if winding up takes place within 12 months of a purchase (redemption) from capital and the company's assets are not sufficient to pay its debts and liabilities; *then*

(*b*) the person(s) from whom the shares were purchased *and* the directors who signed the statutory declaration; *are*

(*c*) jointly and severally liable to contribute to the assets of the company, to the amount of the payment received by the shareholder(s) when the company purchased (or redeemed) the shares. There is a right of contribution between those liable in such an amount as the court thinks just and equitable;

(*d*) those in (*b*) above are given a right to petition for a winding up on the grounds—

  (i) that the company cannot pay its debts; and

  (ii) that it is just and equitable for the company to be wound up.

Criminal penalties

There are a variety of criminal penalties on directors, e.g. for making a false statutory declaration, or refusing to allow its inspection.

5 Company flotations

It is necessary to distinguish offers of listed and unlisted securities. The former are governed by The Financial Services Act 1986 (see p. 130); the latter are governed by the Companies Act 1985 until replaced by the 1986 Act and Rules made under it.

THE PROSPECTUS—GENERALLY

Section 744 defines a prospectus as follows: 'Any prospectus, notice, circular, advertisement, or other invitation offering to the public for subscription or purchase any shares or debentures of a company'.

Section 56(2) states that it is unlawful *to issue any form of application for a company's shares or debentures* unless the form is issued with *a prospectus complying with the requirements of s. 56 as to contents.* This sub-section is at the heart of the whole matter. The issue of shares by a company is not a contract of utmost good faith at common law as an insurance contract is. Disclosure of matters material to an investor's decision to subscribe for the shares is not required by the common law. Thus statutory protection is required and is provided by the Companies Act 1985.

Section 56(3) states that s. 56(2) does not apply if it can be shown that the form of application was issued either—

(*a*) in connection with a *bona fide* invitation to a person to enter into an *underwriting agreement* with respect to the shares or debentures; or

(*b*) in relation to shares or debentures not offered to the public.

Section 56(3)(*a*) exempts underwriting agreements (see further p. 132) because those who underwrite shares in companies are experienced people and do not require statutory protection. Any documents, letters, and so on accompanying a form of application sent to an underwriter need not, therefore, comply with the contents requirements of s. 56.

Section 56(3)(*b*) narrows the requirement of statutory disclosure by making it clear that the statutory protection in terms of disclosure applies *only where the application form is available to the public.*

Thus in *Nash v Lynde* [1929] AC 158 several copies of documents marked 'strictly private and confidential' and containing particulars of a proposed issue of shares were sent, accompanied by a form of application, by the managing director of a company to a co-director who sent a copy to a solicitor, who, in turn, gave it to a client who passed it on to a relative. The documents were signed by all the directors and concluded with a statement that the writer was willing to discuss the proposition with anyone interested. It was held by the House of Lords that in this case there had been no offer to the public. However, the question of how wide an offer must be before it is to the public *is a matter of fact* to be decided upon the circumstances of each case and no general guidelines can be given.

However, s. 59 makes it clear that 'public' includes any section of the public, e.g. all women over 40 years of age, or however selected. Section 60 goes on to provide, however, that an invitation is not treated as being made to the public if it is not calculated to result in shares or debentures becoming available for subscription or purchase by persons who have not received it. This would cover a rights issue without rights of renunciation. It would also cover an offer by company A to acquire the undertaking of company B by offering shares in A to the shareholders of B, as in a take-over or merger. The offer of securities is not made to the public since it can only be accepted by the shareholders of B and, further, it does not involve a purchase or subscription. (*Governments Stock and Other Securities Investments Co Ltd v Christopher*, 1956.[77])

Section 60 also provides that an offer is deemed not to be made to the public if it is otherwise *the domestic concern* of the persons making and receiving it. It follows that if the promoters or directors of a company ask a number of friends to take shares, the rules relating to prospectuses will not apply. Under s. 60(3) and (7) there is a rebuttable presumption that an offer of shares or debentures of a private company is the domestic concern of the persons making and receiving it if it is made to an existing member or employee of the company, or a member of his family, i.e. husband, wife, widow, or widower, and children, including stepchildren and their descendants, and any trustee, acting as such, where the beneficiary of the trust is the member or employee or any of the relatives described above. An offer of securities to a market maker following an application for listing on the Stock Exchange is not deemed a prospectus. (S. 60(8).)

Section 56(5) states that s. 56(1) also does not apply—

(*a*) to the issue to existing members or debenture holders of a form of application relating to the company's shares or debentures—whether the applicant will or will not have a right to renounce in favour of other persons; or (*b*) to the issue of a form of application relating to shares which are or are to be in all respects uniform with shares or debentures previously issued and for the time being listed on a prescribed stock exchange.

These two exceptions apply to rights issues so that information issued in connection with such an issue does not have to be a s. 56 prospectus.

Contents of prospectus

By reason of s. 56(1) the prospectus must, *as regards matters to be stated*, comply with Part I of Sched 3 to the Companies Act 1985, and *as regards reports to be set out*, with Part II of that Schedule. (See further p. 116.) Section 57 provides that a condition requiring or binding an applicant for a company's shares or debentures to waive compliance with the provisions of s. 56, or purporting to affect him with notice of any contract, document, or other matter not specifically referred to in the prospectus is void.

Offers for sale

This is a commonly used method by which a company offers shares to the public. *It is not a sale by the company but more of a resale.* It involves the sale of a block of shares or debentures to an issuing house such as a merchant bank which resells the securities, normally at a higher price, to the public. There is no need to separately underwrite such an issue because the securities have already been sold to the issuing house which will retain those which it cannot resell to the public. The resale arrangement is covered by s. 58 which makes clear that the resale document is a prospectus which must comply with Sched 3 with the additional requirement that it must state the net amount of the consideration received or to be received by the company from the issuing house in respect of the shares or debentures to which the offer relates, and the place and time for inspection of the contract under which the shares or debentures have been or are to be allotted. (S. 58(4).)

Not all resales are caught by s. 58 but only those where the issuing house resells the securities within six months after itself taking, or agreeing to take allotment, or resales *at any time* if when the resale takes place the company has not received all that the issuing house owes to it in respect of the securities being resold. (S. 58(3).)

Oral sales of securities

It seems clear that the statutory provisions relating to prospectuses apply only where there is a written document of some kind used in the sale of shares. Oral sales of securities are to be regulated by the conduct of business provisions in Chapter V of Part I of the Financial Services Act 1986.

Registration of the prospectus

Before or at the time of issue of a prospectus a copy of it must be filed with the Registrar. (S. 64(1).) The copy must be dated (s. 63) and signed by every director and proposed director or his agent appointed in writing. (S. 64(1)(a).) It must also have endorsed on it or attached to it any consent to the inclusion in the prospectus of any statement made by an expert. (S. 64(1)(b).) Section 62 defines an expert as including an 'engineer, valuer, accountant, and any other person whose profession gives authority to a statement made by him'. Where a prospectus is issued generally, i.e. not only to existing members or debenture holders, there must, under s. 65, also be attached a copy of any material contract (see further p. 120) and a signed statement of any adjustments made to any report on the company by the persons responsible for them.

Authority to issue and pre-emption rights

Under s. 80 the directors of a public and private company cannot allot *shares* other than subscribers' shares or shares allotted under an employees' share scheme without the authority of the company given, either in general meeting, or by the articles. (See further p. 137.) So if the issue is of *shares* the directors must have s. 80 authority to issue them. Furthermore, section 89 requires public and private companies to offer new shares to existing members before they are allotted to others unless the pre-emption rights have been disapplied.

Since private companies cannot offer their shares or debentures to the public (see p. 71), the rules set out in the rest of this chapter will only apply, as regards shares, if the members of a *public company* have resolved to allow the directors to allot shares to outsiders under a prospectus.

Methods of offering shares and application of prospectus provisions

We shall now consider the five common methods by which shares are offered.

(i) *An invitation to the public at large or public issue.* Here the company makes a direct offer to the public by publishing a prospectus inviting the public to subscribe for the securities offered. Such an offer would normally be underwritten so that the company does not have to bear the loss if the issue is unsuccessful. The underwriters agree to take up any shares or debentures not applied for by the public and are paid a commission for this. It is unheard of in these days for a registered company to make this sort of direct offer to the public since companies do not have the specialist staff required to ensure that the public issue is successful in terms, for example, of its timing and dealing with applications. However, if this course is adopted, the document inviting subscriptions is a prospectus and must comply with the law.

(ii) *Offers for sale.* Where this method is used the securities are, as we have seen, offered to the public through a finance or issuing house which are organizations, such as merchant banks, specializing in the public issue of securities. The document inviting purchase of the shares by the public is a prospectus and must comply with the law.

(iii) *Public placing.* An issuing house or firm of brokers may place securities with dealers on the Stock Exchange so that they may be sold to the public. Where this is done advertisements in the press giving the public details in connection with the securities will be prospectuses if accompanied by an application form, because the issuing house or sponsoring brokers subscribed for the securities with a view to them being sold to the public by the dealers with whom the securities are placed. (S. 59(1).) Abridged advertisements may be published in other newspapers.

It will be unnecessary for the company to underwrite the issue because if the public do not buy the securities, the dealers will normally retain the securities. A public placing might be regarded as unfair in that it deprives the small investor of an opportunity to acquire securities at the price for which the company is prepared to sell them, though it must be borne in mind that the Stock Exchange requires a substantial proportion of a placing to be offered to the market.

In addition issuing houses, market makers and banks may, without subscribing for the shares, act as *agents* for the company and invite their clients to take the shares from the company. In such a case the agent receives a commission from the company called brokerage (see p. 134). The invitation by the agents to their clients is usually a prospectus must comply with the law.

(iv) *Rights issues.* Here the company offers the shares to existing members in proportion to their present holding, e.g. two for one, and the offer is made by means of a *letter of rights* and requires acceptance by the shareholder. Modern practice is for the company to anticipate acceptance by sending provisional letters of allotment, allotting the shares to which the existing member is entitled, although the member may, of course, refuse the allotment and renounce in favour of an outsider. The company may decide to underwrite a *rights issue* in case the members do not take up the shares offered.

The document which gives details of the rights issue is *not* a prospectus, and need not comply with the law even if it allows the members to renounce their rights to other persons who may be members of the public, who are not members of the company.

If the company has a Stock Exchange listing for its existing shares or debentures then the regulations of the Stock Exchange require that rights offers should normally be in renounceable form.

In this connection it should be noted that s. 89 gives pre-emption rights to all equity shareholders in both public and private companies, though these rights may be disapplied (see p. 138).

(v) *Private placing.* Here the company negotiates with individuals who, if they are interested, may subscribe for the shares offered. The document used to give information about the securities is not a prospectus and need not comply with the Act.

A *private company* cannot in general offer its shares or debentures to the public and can, therefore, only use a *rights offer* or a *private placing*. If it uses a rights offer, the letters of rights must be non-renounceable.

A *rights issue*, mentioned in method (iv) above, is a contractual offer made by the company to its existing members, and the members may or may not accept it. In a *private placing* the offer may be made by the company or the prospective member, and this will depend on the circumstances of each case.

THE PROSPECTUS—MANDATORY STATUTORY INFORMATION

By s. 56 the general rule is that every prospectus issued by or on behalf of a company must state the matters specified in Part I of Sched 3 to the 1985 Act and set out the reports specified in Part II of that Schedule, which will be replaced by Rules made under s. 162, Financial Services Act 1986. Section 57 provides that a condition, requiring or binding an applicant for shares in, or debentures of, the company to waive compliance with the requirements of s. 56(1), shall be void. The object of these provisions is to compel the company to give in the prospectus all necessary information required by potential investors so that they may decide whether or not to subscribe for the company's shares or debentures.

The matters required by Sched 3 to be set out in the prospectus come under the following headings—

1. *The number of founders' or management or deferred shares, if any, and the nature and extent of the interest of the holders in the*

property and profits of the company. It is not usual to issue such shares today, but in the days when they were issued they generally went to the vendors of property and to promoters. They usually carried larger voting rights than the ordinary shares and took a larger proportion of the profits in relation to their nominal value. In a successful company deferred shares might deprive the ordinary shareholders of a large part of the profits earned by the employment of capital contributed largely in the form of ordinary shares. It is, therefore, relevant for intending subscribers for ordinary shares to know the interests (if any) held by deferred shares.

2. *The directors' share qualification (if any) and any provision in the articles as to their remuneration.* This information is important today only in regard to the revealing of the method by which remuneration is determined (see *Table A, Reg* 82 which provides that it be determined by ordinary resolution of the company). The *amount* of remuneration need not be set out.

3. *The names, descriptions, and addresses of directors and proposed directors.* This will reveal whether the directors are persons of standing in the commercial world, as this may affect the prospects of the company and the particular issue.

Items 2 and 3 above do not apply in the case of a prospectus issued more than two years after the date at which the company is entitled to commence business.

4. *Particulars of the minimum subscription.* This is the amount of money which in the opinion of the directors must be raised by the issue of the shares to provide for—

(i) the purchase price of any property to be defrayed wholly or partly out of the proceeds of the issue;

(ii) the preliminary expenses and commission payable to persons who have agreed to subscribe or obtain subscriptions for shares;

(iii) the repayment of any monies borrowed by the company in respect of any of the foregoing; and

(iv) working capital.

The minimum subscription may be stated in the prospectus as a lump sum.

In addition the prospectus must state, where appropriate, the amounts to be provided for items (i) to (iv) above otherwise than out of the proceeds of the issue and the sources from which they are to be provided.

The above provisions are important only in connection with a first issue of shares *by a public company formed as such* because, unless the public subscribe for the shares in sufficient numbers to reach the minimum subscription, no shares may be allotted with the result that the issue will fail, although underwriting will normally ensure that this does not happen. The Act requires that prospectuses subsequent to the first still contain this figure, but failure to obtain it does not affect such subsequent issues. (But see s. 84, p. 137.)

5. *The time of the opening of the subscription lists.* No allotment of shares can be made until the beginning of the third day after that on which the prospectus is issued, or such later date as the prospectus may provide. (S. 82.) Since most prospectuses are advertised, the date of issue is the date of publication of the first newspaper advertisement. The purpose of this provision is to allow time for intending subscribers to consider the prospectus. However, applications may be made before the subscription list opens, and there is no guarantee that the first applications received will be dealt with first when the time arrives, although concerns such as banks who deal with such matters do deal fairly with applications.

No application for shares may be withdrawn until the fourth day i.e. after the expiration of the third day (as the Act says) after the opening of the subscription lists unless a person named in the prospectus as a director or expert has given public notice that he does not wish to be associated with it. (S. 82(7).)

This is a useful provision because in many public issues it is difficult to process applications for the shares to the point where acceptances can be posted and the contract made binding (see *Household Fire Insurance Co v Grant*, 1879, p. 495) before the public becomes aware of the result of the issue. If it is undersubscribed applicants cannot by reason of s. 82(7) withdraw their offers before the time when it can reasonably be expected that the company's acceptances will have been posted.

6. *The amount payable on application and allotment on each share including the amount, if any, payable by way of premium, and details of shares offered and allotted for cash within the previous two years and the amount paid on the shares allotted including the amount, if any, paid by way of premium.* This information will give a prospective subscriber some idea of his own commitment and details of the state of the company's recent issues.

7. *Where the company has given to a person or persons an option to subscribe for the company's shares or debentures, the prospectus must state who such persons are and the sum they will have to pay for the shares subject to the option, what consideration they gave for the option and for how long it is exercisable.* An option to subscribe for its shares or debentures can be given by any company and it is not necessary for the issue price payable on the exercise of the option to be equal to the *market value of the securities* either at the date when the option is given or when it is exercised. (*Hilder v Dexter*

[1902] AC 474.) Consequently if the market price is above the option price, option holders are in a privileged position, and a shareholder who is going to pay in full for his shares is entitled to know the extent of the options, because if they are extensive and given for an inadequate consideration, this will tend to water down the value of the shares being subscribed for. There cannot be an option to buy shares at less than their nominal value because this would operate as an issue at a discount which is forbidden for all companies by s. 100.

8. *Details of shares and debentures issued in the two preceding years for a consideration other than cash, with particulars of the consideration given.* Here again if the consideration is inadequate, the company will not be getting the true value of the shares, and the general effect will be to lower the value of the shares being subscribed for.

Of course, ss. 103 and 108 control the issue of shares for a non-cash consideration in public companies in order to ensure that the consideration is adequate (see p. 172).

9. *Where the company proposes to use the proceeds of the issue wholly or partly to pay for property which it has acquired or proposes to acquire, then the prospectus must state the names and addresses of the vendors and the total purchase price.* The amount of the purchase price to be paid to each vendor must be shown separately, along with the method of payment. The prospectus must also give particulars of transactions concerning the property now being purchased, during the last two years prior to the issue of the prospectus, in which the present vendors or a promoter or a director or proposed director had an interest. This will reveal whether the vendors bought at a price lower than that charged to the company, and whether this is due to a general rise in prices or to excessive profit.

A vendor is defined by Sched 3, Part I, para 9(2) as a person who has entered into any contract for the sale or purchase, or for any option of purchase, of any property to be acquired by the company, in any case where—

(*a*) the purchase price is not fully paid at the date of the issue of the prospectus;

(*b*) the purchase money is to be paid or satisfied wholly or in part out of the proceeds of the issue offered for subscription by the prospectus; and

(*c*) the contract depends for its validity or fulfilment on the result of that issue.

If A sells property to B for £200,000 and B contracts to sell it to the company for £250,000, then, provided the contract between A and B is completed before the prospectus is issued, B's name only need be given in the prospectus as vendor. Thus if the contract between A and B is completed on 30th June and the prospectus is issued on

1st July *A* need not be mentioned, but the price he received from *B* must be disclosed. If, however, the contract between *A* and *B* was not complete on 1st July then both *A* and *B* would have to be mentioned in the prospectus as vendors and the price at which *B* is buying from *A* must be disclosed.

10. **Where a business is being purchased with the proceeds of the issue, the amount being paid for goodwill must be shown separately.** If the valuation is excessive, the goodwill may have to be written off later with the result that profits available for distribution will have to be reduced.

11. **Underwriting commission.** The amount of such commission paid on issues during the preceding two years is required, including brokerage but not sub-underwriting commission (see p. 133). This will give an indication of the confidence of underwriters in the previous issues. If the rate of commission charged is high, this will indicate a low level of confidence, whereas a low rate of interest will indicate a high degree of confidence. However, in recent times, competition between institutions prepared to offer underwriting services has tended to equalize rates so that they are no longer any real indication of confidence.

12. **An estimate of preliminary expenses and the expenses of the issue is required.** These expenses include the legal fees incidental to the formation of the company, registration fees and stamp duty, the cost of the prospectus and the cost of promotion. Such expenses will have to be written off against profits, and, if excessive, will reduce seriously the amount of dividend available for distribution. They must, therefore, be disclosed to intending subscribers.

13. **Any amount or benefit paid or given within the two preceding years or intended to be paid or given to any promoter, and the consideration he gave for such payment or benefit.** Promoters' remuneration must, therefore, be disclosed if it has been paid during the last two years or is yet to be paid.

14. **The dates and parties to and the general nature of any material contract entered into within two years prior to the issue of the prospectus, not being a contract entered into in the ordinary course of business carried on or intended to be carried on by the company.** The term *material contract* is not defined by the Act, but it probably means every contract knowledge of which would affect, however slightly, the value of the shares to a purchaser. However, it should not be assumed that these are the only contracts to fall in the class. It has been said that a material contract is one which, whether deterrent or not, a potential investor ought to know about. (*Broome v Speak* [1903] 1 Ch 586.) Thus, the provision may necessitate the disclosure of all *important contracts* even in perhaps the rare case where they do not affect share values. Certainly the contracts set out in para 9

120

and para 10 above would be material, as would the contract with an issuing house under an offer for sale. It is difficult to be more definite since the question of materiality is not one of law but one of fact for the judge. Copies of material contracts must also be filed with the Registrar. (S. 65(2).)

15. *The names and addresses of the auditors of the company.* This information will enable the prospective investor to see whether the auditors are reliable and of good standing.

16. *The interest of each director (or any firm of which the director is a member) in the promotion of the company or the property to be acquired by it.* This will reveal the amounts (if any) paid to the directors to induce them to become directors and for their services during promotion, or their interests in any property being acquired by the company.

This paragraph, together with paragraphs 2, 3 and 12 (in so far as it is concerned with preliminary expenses) does not apply to a prospectus issued more than two years after the company is entitled to commence business.

17. *The rights attaching to the various classes of shares which form the company's capital.* This information will show the relative rights of the different kinds of shares in the matter of voting, dividend, and capital.

18. *The length of time for which the company's business or the business (if any) to be acquired by the company has been carried on, if less than three years.*

Reports required by Schedule 3, part II

The following are required—

(*a*) a report by the company's auditors on the financial position of the company and its subsidiaries if it has any; and

(*b*) a report by the company's accountants named in the prospectus regarding the financial position of any business to be acquired.

Schedule 3 requires that the accountant's report cover a period of five years.

If the auditors and accountants make any adjustment in the figures in the accounts, their report must indicate that such adjustments have been made, and a written statement of the reasons for the adjustments must be sent to the Registrar. (S. 65(4).)

SUBSCRIPTIONS INDUCED BY MISREPRESENTATION

Where a purchaser has bought shares on the faith of a prospectus which is misleading because of a misstatement in the prospectus, he may have legal remedy against the company or individuals, e.g. the directors or experts responsible, or both. Furthermore, there are criminal sanctions which may be invoked.

Suppose, e.g., the directors of a company do as they did in *Re Pacaya Rubber and Produce Co Ltd*, 1914[78] where the prospectus overstated the number of rubber trees on a rubber estate which were mature enough to yield latex. Persons invested on the strength of this and lost their money. What could they do? The range of remedies is set out below.

CIVIL LIABILITIES

The actions available at civil law may be analysed in the following manner.

Rescission

This is an action against the company and if it is successful the Register of Members will be rectified by the deletion of the subscriber's name and his money will be returned, with interest from the time of payment at a rate decided on by the court. (*In re Metropolitan Coal Consumers' Assn, Karberg's Case* [1892] 3 Ch 1.) The subscriber must show that the company is responsible for the prospectus. In this connection a company is responsible for a prospectus issued by its promoters before incorporation if it takes applications based upon such a prospectus. In addition, s. 58(2) makes the issuing house responsible in an offer for sale or a public placing by an issuing house, even though the issuing house merely publishes the prospectus.

Thus in the case of an offer for sale, rescission is of the contract to take shares from the issuing house. There is no remedy of rescission against the company. The issuing house has, in effect, to take the shares back and stay on the register of the company itself.

Statements made in experts' reports will form a basis for the action against the company because by incorporating such statements in the prospectus the company impliedly vouches for them unless the prospectus carries an express statement to the contrary. (*Re Pacaya Rubber & Produce Co Ltd*, 1914.)[78]

A plaintiff's case requires proof of a number of matters as follows—

(a) *False statement of fact.* The plaintiff must prove that what he complains of is a misrepresentation, whether fraudulent, negligent, or innocent (see below), of existing fact. (*Aaron's Reefs Ltd v Twiss*, 1896.[79]) However, in some cases a statement of intention or opinion may be a misrepresentation of existing fact if the intention or opinion is not put forward honestly. (*Edgington v Fitzmaurice*, 1885.[80])

It should be noted that misrepresentation does not arise solely from statements which are on the face of them untrue but also from statements which taken individually are true but which read together are misleading. (*R. v Kylsant*, 1932.[81])

It should be appreciated, however, that it is only when the prospectus puts something forward as an inducement to those who might subscribe that it must tell the whole truth about it. Apart from the provisions of statute law, a company is not required to disclose facts about itself which might be of interest to an intending investor. Thus in *Heyman v European Central Rail Co* (1868), LR 7 Eq 154 a prospectus did not disclose that the promoter of the company had given his own shares to certain of the directors in order to induce them to accept their directorships and also in consideration of their negotiating loans for the company. It was held that there was no misrepresentation and the subscriber for shares under the prospectus could not rescind.

(*b*) *The statement complained of must have been addressed to the plaintiff.* Before the plaintiff can rescind he must show that the false statement of fact was addressed to him by the prospectus whether issued by the company or under an offer for sale or placing.

A prospectus is not addressed to persons who buy securities from existing holders but only to those who subscribe for securities under the prospectus. Thus a purchaser from an existing holder cannot rescind even though he has seen and been influenced by the prospectus. (*Peek v Gurney*, 1873.[82]) However, the court may find as *a fact* that the prospectus induced purchases as well as subscriptions of shares. (*Andrews v Mockford*, 1896.[83])

If *A* receives from a company of which he is a member a renounceable letter of rights containing a false statement and *A* renounces to *B*, then *B* can ask for rescission because the company must envisage that *B* may take the shares and therefore its statements are addressed to him as well as to *A*. If, however, *B* takes under a provisional letter of allotment then he cannot rescind because he is then in a position of a purchaser from *A* and not from the company. (See p. 115.)

Finally, it should be noted that where a person applies for shares in a company without disclosing that he is acting on behalf of a principal, the only person entitled to rescind the contract on the ground of misrepresentation is the agent himself, and in order to succeed he must prove that he was induced by the misrepresentations to enter into the contract to take shares. It is not enough that the undisclosed principal was influenced. (*Collins v Associated Greyhound Racecourses Ltd* [1930] 1 Ch 1.)

(*c*) *The plaintiff must show that the false statement induced him to subscribe.* Thus the statement must have been material in the sense that it was capable of influencing him (*Smith v Chadwick*, 1884),[84] but a subscriber is not obliged to make any inquiries at all even if invited to do so and will not be prevented from rescinding by reason of failure to make inquiries. (*Central Railway Co of Venezuela v Kisch*, 1867.[85])

However, if a subscriber does inspect documents relating to the company which would reveal that the prospectus was false to a reasonable man, the subscriber is deemed to know that the prospectus is false and cannot rescind. (*New Brunswick and Canada Rail & Land Co v Conybeare* (1862) 9 HL Cas 711.)

Loss of right to rescind

The subscribers to the memorandum cannot rescind, largely because the company does not exist prior to incorporation and therefore can have no agents to deceive the original subscribers on its behalf. (*Re Metal Constituents Ltd. Lord Lurgan's Case* [1902] 1 Ch 707.)

Furthermore, rescission is not available to a shareholder who has affirmed the contract to take shares. A shareholder must not acknowledge, or appear to acknowledge, the fact that he wishes to continue the contract. So he must not sell, or try to sell, his holding, or part of it (*Ex parte Briggs* (1866), LR 1 Eq 483), or attend, or speak, or vote at a meeting of the company (*Sharpley v Louth and East Coast Rail Co* (1876) 2 Ch D 663), or sign a proxy, pay a call on the shares, or accept dividends (*Scholey v Central Rail Co of Venezuela* (1868) LR 9 Eq 266), unless before any of these acts is carried out he has elected to rescind as by commencing proceedings.

Lapse of time will also defeat the remedy. The subscriber must ask for rescission within a reasonable time after he discovers that he has been misled. In *Heyman v European Central Rail Co* (1868) LR 7 Eq 154 it was said that a shareholder who institutes a writ to be relieved of his shares because of misrepresentation more than three months after he has discovered the misrepresentation loses his rights to relief by delay. In addition where the company has actually told the shareholder that the statements are false he has nothing to check and must rescind straight away. A delay of 15 days in such a situation has been held to amount to waiver of the right to rescind. (*Re Scottish Petroleum Co* (1883) 23 Ch D 413.)

The right is normally lost on the commencement of any type of winding up, whether the company is solvent or not, unless the action for rescission was instituted before the commencement of the winding up. The reason for this is that on a winding up the rights of the company's creditors to compel shareholders to pay the unpaid capital on their shares in order to satisfy the company's debts is paramount and overrides the right to rescind.

Damages for fraud

A subscriber may have an action for damages on the tort of deceit. In connection with this action the following matters arise.

(*a*) *What must the plaintiff prove?* The plaintiff must prove the same matters as are required of him in rescission, i.e. that there was a false statement of fact which was addressed to him and induced him to subscribe. In addition, the plaintiff must prove that the defendant knew the statement to be false or did not honestly believe it to be true or made it recklessly not caring whether it was true or false. (*Derry v Peek*, 1889.[86])

(*b*) *Who may be sued?* An action on the tort of deceit may be brought—

(i) *Against the person or persons responsible for the issue of the prospectus.* Where the prospectus is issued by the company the directors will be responsible because they resolved that it should be issued. Directors not taking part at the relevant meeting or not agreeing to the issue of the prospectus will not be personally liable. Where an offer for sale or placing is used then the directors or partners of the issuing house and/or the market makers concerned are liable and in practice so are the directors of the company whose shares are being issued to the public. Their involvement arises because in the case of an offer for sale they sign the copy prospectus delivered to the Registrar and as regards a placing, the newspaper advertisement published in connection with the placing invariably contains a statement that the directors of the company concerned accept responsibility for the accuracy of statements made in connection with the placing.

(ii) *Against the company.* Since the company is vicariously responsible for the fraud of its officers the subscriber can recover damages from the company. The position is the same where the statements are made by an issuing house in the case of an offer for sale or by a market maker in the case of a placing. This arises because, as we have seen, the company will normally associate itself with the documents issued under an offer for sale or placing. However, before the subscriber can sue the company for damages for fraud he must rescind the contract (*Houldsworth v City of Glasgow Bank*, 1880)[87] and if he cannot rescind, he cannot sue the company but may still pursue his remedy against the persons responsible for the prospectus. Rescission is not a necessary preliminary to an action against them.

(c) *Measure of damages.* In general terms the loss suffered by the plaintiff as a result of the fraud will be the difference between the price he paid for the securities and their real value at the date when he took issue of them. (*McConnel v Wright*, 1903.[88])

Damages for negligence at common law

It has never been easy to prove fraud in civil actions and so the plaintiff may find it better, whether fraud potentially exists or not, to bring an action for negligence.

In this connection it has been suggested that the decision of the House of Lords in *Hedley Byrne & Co Ltd v Heller & Partners Ltd*, 1963[89] may provide assistance but the matter is not entirely clear because—

(a) in *Hedley Byrne*[89] Lords Morris and Devlin took the view that the duty of care set up in that case was not to be imposed on directors or others who invite the public generally to subscribe for securities by means of a prospectus;

(b) in a later case (*Mutual Life and Citizens' Assurance Co Ltd v Evatt* [1971] 1 All ER 150) the Privy Council took the view that generally a duty of care under *Hedley Byrne*[89] will arise only where the person giving the information or advice carries on a business or profession under which he normally gives information or advice of the kind in question. If this is so then company directors would be excluded from liability under *Hedley Byrne*[89].

However, in *Esso Petroleum Co Ltd v Mardon* [1975] 1 All ER 203 Lawson J felt that it was too restrictive to limit the duty in *Hedley Byrne*[89] to persons who carried on or who held themselves out as carrying on the business of giving information or advice, as did Ormrod LJ when the case was in the Court of Appeal ([1976] 2 All ER 5). The acceptance of these views that the duty can apply more widely could bring in company directors in terms that they could be liable on a personal basis for negligence.

In any case, the Stock Exchange, as part of admission of the shares to full or USM listing, requires that the prospectus shall state that the directors have taken reasonable care to ensure that the facts stated in it are true and accurate, that there are no misleading omissions, and that all the directors take responsibility for the prospectus.

In view of this statement, it is likely that a duty of care is owed only by the individuals involved in the making of the statements and not by the company as such. If this is so, no claim can be made against the company. This would accord with the general principle of capital maintenance inherent in the prospectus remedies, i.e. it is difficult to get one's money back from the company and easier to get compensation from directors or experts.

Hedley Byrne[89] applies very obviously to negligent misstatements by experts in their reports but, again, this has not been tested in a public issue context, but the words of Lord Salmon in *Anns v London Borough of Merton* [1977] 2 All ER 492 leave little room for doubt about the liability. He said: 'There are a wide variety of instances in which a statement is negligently made by a professional man which he knows will be relied on by many people besides his client, e.g. a well-known firm of accountants certifies in a prospectus the annual profits of the company issuing it and, unfortunately, due to negligence on the part of the accountants, the profits are seriously overstated. Those persons who invested in the company in reliance on the accuracy of the accountants' certificate would have a claim for damages against the accountants for any money they might have lost as a result of the accountants' negligence . . .'

Claim for compensation under s. 67, Companies Act 1985

The remedy under s. 67 is available where a misstatement is made innocently, but it can also be used in cases of fraud. Indeed, it is better to use it, because the burden of proof lying on the plaintiff, i.e. proof on a balance of probabilities not beyond a reasonable doubt, is lighter than that required for common law fraud. The action may be brought against those persons responsible for the issue of the prospectus (see p. 125), including promoters and experts, in respect of untrue statements made. However, the liability of such persons is not strict, because s. 68 provides them with certain defences, some of which are designed to make out that the defendant is not in fact a person responsible for the prospectus, and others, while admitting responsibility for its issue, raise some other defence.

Defences suggesting lack of responsibility. These are—

(i) that having consented to become a director he withdrew his consent before the issue of the prospectus and that it was issued without his authority or consent;

(ii) that the prospectus was issued without the defendant's consent or knowledge, and that when he knew it had been issued, he gave reasonable public notice of this fact;

(iii) that the prospectus was issued with his knowledge and consent, but after the issue of the prospectus and *before allotment* he became aware of the untrue statement, and withdrew his consent to the prospectus and gave reasonable public notice that he had done so and why.

Other defences

(iv) that the defendant had *reasonable grounds* for believing the statement to be true up to allotment.

(v) that the statement was made by an expert and the expert consented to the inclusion of his statement in the prospectus and that the defendant believed the expert to be competent.

(vi) that the statement was taken from a public official document or was made by an official, and was a correct and fair representation of the document or statement.

Experts' liability under s. 67. If an expert consents to the inclusion of his report in the prospectus and it is false, he is liable under the section. Again liability is not strict or absolute for the expert has the following defences—

(i) that he withdrew his consent in writing before the prospectus was registered;

(ii) that after the prospectus was registered but before the allotment, he discovered the statement to be untrue, and withdrew his consent, giving reasonable public notice of this fact and his reasons for so doing;

(iii) that he was competent to make the statement and up to the time of allotment believed on reasonable grounds that it was true.

The compensation awarded under s. 67 is assessed in the same way as damages for fraud. (See *McConnel v Wright*, 1903.)[88]

There can be no action under s. 67 unless the statement is made in a prospectus and so if it is made, e.g. orally, or in a letter of rights which has been renounced, there can be no statutory claim, but a claim in negligence or under the Misrepresentation Act of 1967 might be brought. Section 67 cannot be used in order to sue the company itself.

The Misrepresentation Act 1967

Section 2(1) of the 1967 Act allows a claim for damages (or rescission) against the company for negligent misrepresentation made, for example, by the directors on behalf of the company. The untrue statement must be made without reasonable grounds for believing it to be true, as where it is made without proper verification.

If, in spite of appropriate verification, a false statement is made innocently, there is no action, as such, for damages. Section 2(2) allows an action for rescission in such a case, but the judge has a discretion to award damages instead. The remedy of rescission must still be available and not lost under one or more of the rules described at p. 124.

The remedies under the 1967 Act are not available against those responsible for the issue of a prospectus personally. The Act gives rights only to those who have been induced to enter into a contract by a misrepresentation by, or on behalf of, the other party to it—i.e. the company (or the issuing house in an offer for sale).

Section 3 of the 1967 Act (as substituted by s. 8 of the Unfair Contract

Terms Act 1977) makes ineffective any clause in a contract which excludes or limits liability for misrepresentation, unless the court decides that it is reasonable. This has effect upon attempts to disclaim liability for misrepresentation in a prospectus.

It is not certain whether the *Houldsworth* case[87] applies to an action for damages under the 1967 Act. There is no express provision in the 1967 Act which covers it. However, as we have seen, s. 2(2) allows a judge to award damages in lieu of rescission. This seems to assume that *Houldsworth*[87] does not apply because it is the opposite of what *Houldsworth*[87] says.

Limitation of actions and contribution

The actions for damages referred to above and for compensation under s. 67 are barred after six years from allotment, though where a fraud has been concealed, the action is barred six years from the time when the fraud was discovered, or could with reasonable diligence have been discovered.

A person successfully sued under s. 67 may claim a contribution from the other persons responsible for the prospectus, and the same is true where one person is successfully sued in fraud, though here the contribution is confined to those who were also party to the fraud and no contribution can be claimed from a person not a party.

Remedies for misleading omissions

Omission of material facts may amount to misrepresentation. In *Coles v White City (Manchester) Greyhound Assn Ltd* (1929) 45 TLR 230 the prospectus stated that land to be acquired by the company was 'eminently suitable' for greyhound racing. No mention was made of the fact that approval of the local council was required in order to build public stands and kennels. This was held by the Court of Appeal to be a ground for rescission by the plaintiff.

However, the rule applies only where the statement is a half-truth, though it is extended to claims made under s. 67 by s. 71(*a*) which provides that a statement included in a prospectus shall be deemed to be untrue if it is misleading in the form and context in which it is included.

The half-truth principle is more difficult to apply in proving cases of fraud and negligence under *Hedley Byrne*,[89] though it has often supported an action for rescission.

The half-truth principle obviously does not apply to total non-disclosure. However, s. 56(2) is more powerful. It appears to give a remedy to those injured by a failure to specify the Sched 3, Companies Act

1985 matters in the prospectus, e.g. material contracts, such as the contract between the issuing company and the issuing house in an offer for sale. There is no right to rescind the contract (*Re South of England Natural Gas Co* [1911] 1 Ch 573), nor would the section appear to give any other remedy, e.g. damages against the company. The claim would seem to be one for damages against those responsible for the prospectus and by reason of s. 56(1) it is restricted to those taking under a prospectus, i.e. subscribers.

The omission would have to be material, and the plaintiff must show loss—for example, that if the required particulars had been given, he would not have purchased the shares. There are certain defences in s. 66(1), e.g. honest mistake of fact. It is thought that because there are defences there must be liability in damages against those responsible for the prospectus who cannot prove any of the defences. This was the view of the Court in *Re South of England Natural Gas Co* (see above).

THE FINANCIAL SERVICES ACT 1986

The Stock Exchange (Listing) Regulations 1984 (SI 1984/716) made a considerable impact on those requirements of English company law that relate to the breach of prospectus requirements. The Regulations, which came fully into force on 1 January 1985, implemented EEC Directives 79/279 (conditions for admission to listing); 80/390 (listing particulars) and 81/121 (regular information to be supplied by listed companies). The relevant provisions are now in the 1986 Act.

The Companies Act 1985 no longer applies to prospectuses issued by plc's with a full listing. It does apply to issues on the unlisted securities market (USM) until Rules are made under the 1986 Act.

LISTED SECURITIES

(a) Exclusion of Companies Act 1985

In practical terms where an application has been made to the Council of the Stock Exchange for the admission of any securities to listing and the Council has approved listing particulars then: (*a*) a form of application issued with a document which sets out the approved listing particulars, or indicates where they can be obtained, need *not* have with it a prospectus otherwise required by the Companies Act 1985; and (*b*) in relation to an offer of any of those securities made by means of a document as referred to in (*a*) the provisions of the Companies Act 1985 which would otherwise apply regarding liability do not apply.

Having excluded the Companies Act 1985, there is substituted the provisions of The Stock Exchange Listing Particulars. These reflect the provisions of EEC Directive 80/390.

(b) Liability (ss 146 and 150 of the 1986 Act)

This states that the listing particulars in the prospectus shall contain the information which, according to the particular nature of the issuer and of the securities, is necessary to enable *investors and their investment advisers* to make an informed assessment of the assets and liabilities, financial position, profits and losses and prospects of the issuer and of the rights attaching to such securities. The effect of this seems to be to give express liability to those responsible for the listing particulars for material misstatements, material omissions, and misleading opinions. It replaces s. 67 of the CA 1985 (compensation for subscribers misled by statement in prospectus) with a new type of action. However, any liability, civil or criminal, which a person may incur under the general law (as distinct from the Companies Act 1985) continues to exist. Thus a plaintiff could still sue for fraud, misrepresentation under the Misrepresentation Act 1967, or for a negligent misstatement under *Hedley Byrne v Heller* (1963)[89] and of course under s. 146.

(c) Who is responsible? (s. 152, Financial Services Act 1986)

This puts liability upon those responsible for the listing particulars as provided for in s. 152 of the Financial Services Act 1986. A prospectus must state the name and function of natural persons and the name and registered office of legal persons responsible for the listing particulars or for certain parts of them with, in the latter case, an indication of which parts.

So far as The Stock Exchange is concerned, it requires only that a prospectus (now strictly speaking the listing particulars) contains a responsibility statement from the directors and not, for example, from experts. However, responsibility will surely continue to be a matter of fact for the court. The former Stock Exchange rules also required a statement only by directors, but it was never felt that this was a bar to an action against, e.g., professional persons also involved and this is envisaged by s. 152.

(d) Defences (s. 151, Financial Services Act 1986)

This provides that a person responsible for non-compliance with or a contravention of s. 146 (see (b) above) shall not be liable if (*a*) he did not know of it; or (*b*) it was an honest mistake of fact on his part; or (c) it was in respect of a matter which in the opinion of the court was immaterial, or he ought, in any case, reasonably to be excused.

Comment. This seems wider than s. 68, Companies Act 1985 because there is no need to prove reasonable grounds for believing a statement was true. The defence seems to apply whether lack of knowledge was reasonable or not. It seems to encourage directors and others to remain in ignorance.

(e) Who can sue? (s. 146, Financial Services Act 1986)

This states that the duty is owed to 'investors and their investment advisers'. This would seem to include all subscribers, whether they have relied on the prospectus or not. Materiality appears to be the test and not reliance. So it seems a subscriber need not be aware of the error or even have seen the listing particulars.

Comment. S. 146 would seem also to cover subsequent purchasers in the market thus overruling *Peek v Gurney* (1873).[82] However, such a purchaser could surely only sue while the prospectus is the only source of information affecting the price of the securities. Once the company issues new information, or there have been published new factors, such as the loss by the company of a major contract, then it would be unreasonable to allow a claim.

(f) Contents of the prospectus

Sched 3 of the 1985 Act does not apply. A prospectus must contain the items laid down by The Stock Exchange in Listing Particulars made by the Council under s. 144, Financial Services Act 1986. These are not included here since questions on the contents of documents are seldom, if ever, asked in modern examinations, which are more conceptual.

UNLISTED SECURITIES

As we have seen, until Rules are made under the 1986 Act, the Companies Act 1985 applies and is relevant in this context only.

UNDERWRITING

Before a company's shares or debentures are issued to the public, agreement may be reached with persons who are prepared for a commission to take up (or underwrite) the whole or a part of the shares being offered if the public does not do so.

It is usual to underwrite even when a company is sound and the shares are popular, since changes, for example, in the international situation or the financial state of the country can affect an issue adversely.

Because the payment of underwriting commission could be used as a device to issue shares at a discount, the payment of underwriting commission is controlled by s. 97, 1985 Act which provides—

(i) that the payment of such commission must be authorized by the articles;

(ii) that the commission paid must not exceed 10 per cent of the price at which the shares are issued, or such less amount as may be authorized by the articles; and

Amendments to s. 97 made by the Financial Services Act 1986 will when implemented have the effect of saying that the figure of 10 per cent may be amended by Rules made under s. 169(2) of the Financial Services Act 1986. Section 169(2) empowers the Trade Secretary to make Rules regulating the terms of offers and the conduct of offerors of securities.

If there is in existence a *share premium account*, this may be applied to pay the commission on an issue of shares or debentures. (S. 130(2)(*b*).)

As consideration for underwriting, underwriters may accept an option to buy further shares in the company at par. This will be beneficial where the issue underwritten is at a premium.

Terms of the agreement

The underwriter agrees to underwrite a stated number of shares on the terms of a specified prospectus so that an alteration in the prospectus before issue may render the underwriting agreement void if it materially increases the risk taken by the underwriters. Thus in *Warner International & Overseas Engineering Co Ltd v Kilburn, Brown & Co* (1914) 84 LJ KB 365 a company altered the draft prospectus on which an underwriting agreement was based by reducing the minimum subscription to be received before allotment from £15,000 to £100 and by stating also that instead of buying a business it was to acquire by one payment from the proceeds of the issue it would buy the business by instalments out of future issues. It was held by the Court of Appeal that the underwriters were released from their contract.

The underwriter agrees to take up the balance of shares (if any) not taken up by the public, and also authorizes a director or other agent of the company to apply for the shares on the underwriter's behalf. This means that the company can ensure the allotment of the shares to the underwriter, and thus have an action for the full price, and not merely an action for damages if the underwriter merely refuses to apply for them. The authority to apply is expressed to be irrevocable.

133

Finally the company agrees to pay a certain percentage of the nominal value of the underwritten shares as commission.

The liability of the underwriter ends when members of the public subscribe for the shares, and he cannot be called on to pay if allottees do not meet their liabilities.

Disclosure

The total amount of underwriting commission paid during the year must be stated in the annual return. This is provided for by paragraph 3(f) of Sched 15 to the Companies Act 1985.

Sub-underwriting

Underwriters may enter into sub-underwriting contracts to relieve themselves of the whole or part of their liability. The underwriter pays a commission to the sub-underwriters and this need not be disclosed in the prospectus.

Brokerage

This is a commission paid over to a bank, stockbroker, or issuing house for placing shares. The difference between brokerage and underwriting is that the broker does not agree to take the shares himself, but merely agrees to try to find purchasers. The payment of brokerage could also lead to an issue of shares at a discount and yet it is not controlled by the Act, s. 98(3) providing that s. 97 shall not affect the power of any company to pay brokerage. However, it can only be paid to a bank, market maker, or issuing house and the rate must be reasonable, though the precise rate is a matter for negotiation according to the degree of risk. (*Metropolitan Coal Consumers' Association v Scrimgeour* [1895] 2 QB 604.)

6 Shares and their transfer

A share may be defined as a measure of the interest of the member in the company. It is clear from the judgment of Farwell J in *Borland's Trustee v Steel Brothers & Co Ltd* [1901] 1 Ch 279 at p. 288 that this interest consists in the rights and duties given and imposed by the constitution of the company and also by company legislation. As Mr Justice Farwell said: 'A share is the interest of a shareholder in the company measured by a sum of money, for the purpose of liability in the first place, and of interest in the second, but also consisting of a series of mutual covenants entered into by all the shareholders *inter se* in accordance with s. 16 of the Companies Act 1862 (now s. 14). The contract contained in the articles of association is one of the original incidents of the share.'

Thus under the Companies Act 1985 shareholders have a right to requisition meetings and to put resolutions on the agenda. They also have the right to inspect certain records and documents which a company is obliged to keep and the right to appoint a proxy to represent them at meetings of the company. Financially it represents what a member must pay or has paid for the share, and it provides a basis for the calculation of distributions of profits by means of dividends.

The assets of the company are owned *by the company*. The members do not have a legal or equitable interest in them (*Macaura v Northern Assurance*, 1925),[2] and although share capital is in a sense a liability, it is not in the nature of a debt owed by the company, and on a winding up the shareholders will receive what is left, if anything, after payment of the company's debts and liabilities.

Shares are personal estate and not real estate. (S. 182(1)(*a*).) They are, therefore, in the same category as money or goods. The section removes doubts raised by early cases as to whether shares in companies formed mainly to hold and manage land were not themselves of the legal nature of reality.

Subscribers' contract

Subject to certain special provisions of the Companies Act 1985, the general law of contract applies. Thus—

(i) The prospectus is merely an invitation to treat.

(ii) The application form sent in by intending subscribers is the offer to take the shares.

(iii) The company or the issuing house may or may not accept the offer.

(iv) If they do, allotment is made by resolution of the board and must then be notified to the offeror. In order to constitute a binding contract the allotment must be communicated by the company to the applicant. Where this is done, as is usual, by letter of allotment the contract is completed when the letter is posted, even if it is delayed or lost in the post. (*Household Fire Insurance Co v Grant*, 1879.[90])

However, communication of allotment may be made in other ways, e.g. by a letter from the company demanding payment of an instalment on the shares, *Forget v Cement Products Co of Canada* [1916] WN 259. Communication must take place within a reasonable time; otherwise the offer to take the shares will be deemed to have lapsed. (*Ramsgate Victoria Hotel Co v Montefiore*, 1866.[91])

Although at common law an application for shares can be revoked at any time before acceptance, the matter of revocation in this situation is currently subject to s. 82(7). (See p. 118.) Revocation of the offer made by the applicant must be communicated to the company. Revocation is *not effective* on posting but only when communicated. (*Byrne v Van Tienhoven* (1880) 5 CPD 344.)

It is a rule of the law of contract that acceptance must be unconditional, and if an issue is over-subscribed, the company could not under the general law allot fewer shares than the applicant had applied for, unless the applicant had agreed to this. It is for this reason that application forms when issued always contain a clause whereby the applicant agrees to accept an allotment of fewer shares than he applied for. Nevertheless an offer to take shares may be conditional. (*Re Universal Banking Co*, 1868.[92])

Statutory provisions affecting the contract to take shares

If the prospectus is issued *generally*, i.e. to persons other than the company's present share or debenture holders, e.g. as where the preemption rights of existing members have been qualified or withdrawn under s. 95 (p. 138), no allotment can currently be made until the third day after the prospectus is issued, or such later day as is named in the prospectus for the opening of the subscription lists. (S. 82(1).)

Further, there can be no revocation of the offer until the fourth day after the opening of the subscription lists unless a director or expert has given public notice that he does not wish to be associated with the prospectus. (S. 82(7).)

In addition, under s. 84 if a public company offers share capital for subscription (whether for cash or otherwise) no allotment of the shares shall be made unless—

(*a*) the capital is subscribed for in full; or

(*b*) if not, the terms of the offer state that the capital can be allotted even though not fully subscribed.

An applicant for shares cannot by agreement waive compliance with the section. (S. 84(6).)

It will be noted that the above requirements go beyond the current minimum subscriptions provisions in s. 83 by requiring the capital to be subscribed in full before allotment unless subscribers know it is a term of the offer that allotment may go ahead even though capital is not fully subscribed. It is, of course, possible to ensure full subscription by underwriting or through an offer for sale.

ALLOTMENT

Authority to issue

Before proceeding to the mechanics of allotment, it is necessary to note that under s. 80 directors of public and private companies must have the authority of the members by ordinary resolution in general meeting, or of the articles, before they exercise a power of allotment of shares or grant rights to subscribe for or convert securities into shares.

The authority of the members may be given each time there is an allotment or for up to five years in advance and the ordinary resolution(s) giving the authority are registrable at the Companies Registry under s. 380.

The authority, however given, must state the number of shares authorized and be expressed to expire not more than five years after it was granted unless revoked or varied before then. When such an authority expires it may be renewed for a further period not exceeding five years.

No authority is needed to allot shares to a person who is exercising an option previously approved or existing, or a conversion right, i.e. from loan stock to shares previously approved or existing, nor is it required for the allotment of shares made by the directors after the authority has expired where it was agreed during the currency of the authority that the allotment would be made and might involve the actual issue of the shares after the period of authority had expired.

Allotments made in contravention of the above provisions will not be invalid but the directors are liable to prosecution. Furthermore, the provisions do not apply to shares taken by subscribers to the memorandum or to shares allotted as part of an employees' share scheme or issued as part of a take-over. If members refuse to authorize directors to allot shares the power of allotment, except in relation to employees' shares, lies in the members themselves by ordinary resolution in general meeting

Pre-emption rights

As regards ordinary shareholders, s. 89 gives a right of pre-emption. This is designed to ensure that the rights of ordinary shareholders are not necessarily affected by the issue of further ordinary shares which has never been regarded as a variation of rights. Section 89 gives pre-emption rights to all equity shareholders in both public and private companies. Each ordinary shareholder must be offered a part of the issue *pro rata* to his existing holding. Equity shares may be offered to outsiders if they have not been taken up by existing shareholders within the offer period, which must be at least 21 days.

If s. 89 is not complied with the company and any officer in default is liable to compensate shareholders for their loss. Claims by shareholders must be brought within two years of the filing of the return of allotments under which s. 89 was contravened.

A private, but not a public, company may disapply pre-emption rights *without a time limit* by a provision in the memorandum or articles. (S. 91(1).) The pre-emption right is disapplied until such time, if any, as the memorandum or articles, as the case may be, are amended to remove the disapplication provision.

Both public and private companies may disapply pre-emption rights by a provision in the articles or by a special resolution of the members. *In either event the maximum period for disapplication is five years or such shorter period as the articles or special resolution may state.* (S. 95.)

The pre-emption provisions are triggered by an issue of equity shares *for cash*. (S. 89(4).) Thus pre-emption rights would not apply, e.g. to an issue of preference shares for cash or to the issue of equity shares for a non-cash consideration. In addition, pre-emption rights do not apply where shares are allotted under an employees' scheme. (S. 89(5).) Thus, if the company allots shares to employees under an employees' scheme, it is not obliged to make an offer of shares to the ordinary shareholders who are not employees. However, employees in a share scheme are entitled to participate in the pre-emption rights where an offer of equity shares is made to shareholders generally. (S. 89(1)(a).)

Thus if a company, A, has an authorized and issued share capital of £100,000 divided into 100,000 ordinary shares of £1 each and 50,000 of those shares are held under an employees' share scheme, then on an increase of capital and a proposal to issue 50,000 additional ordinary shares, each member will be entitled to an offer to subscribe for one share for every two ordinary shares which he currently holds.

Under s. 95(5) the directors must recommend the disapplication of pre-emption rights and no special resolution to allow it or a special resolution to renew a period of disapplication previously approved, may be proposed unless with the notice of the meeting the directors have circulated a written statement giving their reasons for recommending disapplication and stating the amount which will be paid when the equity shares which are the subject of the disapplication are allotted and giving the directors' justification of that price. Section 95(6) provides penalties for inclusion of misleading matter in this statement.

A shareholder may waive his pre-emption rights in which case he will not be entitled to receive shares under a pre-emptive offer. Under s. 89(3) shares which are offered on a pre-emptive basis may be allotted to a person in favour of whom the shareholder entitled to the offer has renounced his rights.

The Registrar must publish a notice in the *London Gazette* of the receipt by him of a special resolution passed in connection with disapplication of pre-emption rights. (S. 711(1)(e).)

Thus even when the directors have been given authority to issue shares they must still observe the pre-emption provisions of s. 89 as outlined above.

Public companies—the 25 per cent rule

It should also be noted that under s. 101 shares in a public company cannot be allotted until 25 per cent of the nominal value and 100 per cent of any premium have been received (in cash or otherwise) by the company, and also that the Companies Act 1985 contains restrictions upon the allotment of shares for a non-cash consideration (see p. 172).

An allottee who takes shares in a public company which are not paid up as required is liable to pay the company the balance up to the minimum the company should have received plus interest which is at present 5 per cent *per annum*. (S. 107.)

Allotment is usually made by the directors at a properly constituted board meeting, or by a committee of the board where the directors have power to delegate their powers to such a committee. The directors' powers of allotment are usually given by the articles and, even where the allotment is irregular because of some defect in the constitution of the board making it, the allotment may nevertheless be made binding on the company:

(*a*) under a clause in the articles similar to *Reg.* 92 of *Table A* (see p. 80); or (*b*) by reason of subsequent ratification by a properly constituted board (*Re Portuguese Consolidated Copper Mines Ltd* (1889) 42 Ch D 160); or

(*c*) under s. 285 or under the rule in *Royal British Bank v Turquand*, 1856[69] even without ratification.

As we have seen, allotment is effected by sending a letter of allotment to the allottee. The letter of allotment gives instructions for payment of instalments and registration and, in addition, often contains provisions under which the allottee may *renounce the whole* of the allotment in favour of another by signing the form of renunciation provided, or *renounce it partially* by 'splitting' the allotment with another. These renunciations become known to the company or issuing house when the relevant letters of allotment are returned. The following *restrictions on allotment by public companies* apply—

1. Minimum subscription

In the case of a first prospectus *issued generally* by a public company formed as such there can currently be no allotment of shares until the minimum subscription has been raised. The full amount of the minimum subscription need not have been received in application money so long as the company has received offers to subscribe for shares whose *total* issue price is at least equal to the minimum subscription. Cheques may be accepted so long as the directors have no grounds for thinking that they will not be met. (S. 83(2).)

If the minimum subscription is not subscribed within 40 days after the first issue of the prospectus *and the shares are not allotted*, the application money must be returned to the applicants. If it has not been returned within 48 days after the first issue of the prospectus, the directors become jointly and severally liable to repay it with interest at 5 per cent per annum from the expiration of the forty-eighth day, though it is a defence for them to show that the delay was not due to their misconduct or negligence, but was due to matters beyond their control. (S. 83(5).) The applicant's right to sue for the return of his money accrues against the company on the fortieth day after the prospectus was issued and against the directors on the forty-eighth day. He has six years from these respective dates within which to bring his action. (Limitation Act 1980, s. 9(1).)

If shares are allotted before the minimum subscription has been subscribed, or after 40 days from the first issue of the prospectus, the allottee may rescind the contract up to one month after allotment, and *even though the company is being wound up*. (S. 85(1).) However, the allotment is *not void*, and if the allottees wish to regard the contract as good, they may. It is not necessary to serve a writ commencing proceedings within one month. It was said in *Re National Motor Mail Coach Ltd* [1908] 2 Ch 515 that it was enough if notice of avoidance was given within one month followed by prompt legal proceedings.

Any director who knowingly contravenes these rules, or permits or authorizes an irregular allotment, is liable to compensate the company and the allottee for loss sustained as a consequence of the irregular allotment, but the action must be brought within two years from the date of the allotment. (S. 85(3).)

The object of the above provisions is to prevent the company from starting up in business with insufficient capital. They are re-inforced by s. 117 under which a public company cannot commence business or exercise any borrowing powers unless the Registrar has issued a s. 117 certificate (see p. 29).

2. Failure to apply for or obtain a Stock Exchange listing

It is most important in a contract to take shares in a public company that the shares be quoted on a recognized stock exchange, for if they are not so quoted, the shares have no market and there would be great difficulty in selling them. Therefore, where a prospectus states, as it currently may do, that application has been or will be made for permission for the securities to be dealt in on the Stock Exchange, any allotment made on an application under the prospectus is *void* if—

(i) the permission has not been applied for before the third day after the first issue of the prospectus (s. 86(2)) (Saturdays, Sundays and bank holidays not being counted: s. 83(3)); or

(ii) if the application has been refused within three weeks (or within such longer period, not exceeding six weeks as the Stock Exchange notifies to the company) after the date of the closing of the subscription lists. (S. 86(2).)

Until a Stock Exchange quotation is obtained, the money received from applicants remains their property and must be kept in a separate bank account in case it has to be returned. (S. 86(6).) In *Re Nanwa Gold Mines Ltd* [1955] 3 All ER 219, Harman J observed that what is now s. 86(6) created a kind of trust for applicants. The separate account, he said, was not part of the general assets of the company. It was not, therefore, subject to any floating charge or other claims against the company.

Where permission is not applied for or is refused, the company must forthwith repay without interest all money received from applicants, and if any such money is not repaid within eight days of the refusal of quotation or expiry of the time for applying, the directors are jointly and severally liable to repay the money with interest at 5 per cent per annum from the expiration of the eighth day. However, it is a defence for them to show that the failure to repay the money was not due to any misconduct or negligence on their part. (S. 86(5).)

Section 87 currently applies the above provisions to the offeror, i.e. issuing house, in an offer for sale.

3. Time of allotment

Where shares or debentures are offered for allotment or for sale by a prospectus issued generally, i.e. to persons who are not members or debenture holders of the company, no allotment of shares can currently be made until the third day after the prospectus is issued, or such later date as the prospectus may provide. (S. 82.) Contravention of these provisions renders the company and its officers who are in default liable to a substantial fine if the company has made the allotment. In an offer for sale the persons making the offer would be liable instead of the company and its officers. (S. 82(5) and (6).) It should be noted, however, that the allotment is *not* rendered void. (S. 82(5).)

RETURN AS TO ALLOTMENTS

Whenever a company makes an allotment of its shares, it must within one month of allotment deliver to the Registrar of Companies a *return of the allotments* stating the number and nominal value of the shares comprised in the allotment, the names and addresses of the allottees, and the amount paid up and unpaid on each share, whether on account of the nominal value of the share or by way of premium. (S. 88.)

Where shares have been allotted as fully or partly paid up otherwise than in cash as where, for example, the shares form the whole or part of the purchase price on a sale of land to the company, the consideration must be specified in the return, and if the contract is written, it must be sent with the return. (S. 88(2)(*b*1).) If the contract is not written, a written memorandum of its terms must be made out and filed with the Registrar. (S. 88(3).) These provisions are, of course, strengthened for public companies by s. 103 (requirement to file with return of allotment an expert's report on the value of non-cash consideration) (see p. 172).

Compliance with these requirements is enforced by a substantial fine on every director, manager, secretary or other officer of the company who is a party to the default. The court may grant relief where the omission to deliver any document within the time prescribed is accidental or due to inadvertence or it is just and equitable to grant relief, and may make an order extending the time for the delivery of the document for such period as the court thinks proper. (S. 88(6).)

SHARE CERTIFICATES

Every company must under the penalty of a fine for each day of the default within two months after allotment or transfer of shares or debentures have ready for delivery a certificate, unless in the case of an issue of shares the terms of the issue otherwise provide. (S. 185(1).) The terms of issue usually do exclude s. 185(1), because companies rarely issue a share certificate until the shares are fully paid which normally takes at least six months. Until the issue of a certificate, the subscriber has a letter of allotment which is renounceable or transferable. Where the transfer is through the Talisman system, s. 185(1) need not be complied with. (See s. 185(4) and p. 152.)

The form of the certificate is governed by the articles which may provide for the issue of share certificates under seal, though a seal is not required by law. The certificate will also specify the shares to which it relates and the amount paid up on the shares. (*Table A, Reg. 6.*) It will be signed by at least one director and the secretary. *Regulation 6* provides that every certificate shall be under the seal of the company (or under the official seal kept by the company by virtue of s. 40 specially for use on securities.)

If a listing on the Stock Exchange is required the certificate must, under the Rules of the Stock Exchange, be no larger than 22.5 cm × 20 cm (or 9 inches by 8 inches) dated and sealed and have a footnote stating that the transfer will not be registered without production of the share certificate. In the case of preference shares, it must state in addition the conditions conferred thereon as to capital and dividends.

Shares must be distinguished by an appropriate number, but if all the shares of the company are fully paid, or all the shares in a particular class are fully paid and rank *pari passu* in all respects, the distinguishing numbers can be dispensed with. (S. 182(2).)

A share certificate under the common seal of the company or the seal kept by the company by virtue of s. 40 specifying any shares held by any member is *prima facie*, but *not conclusive* evidence of the title of the member to the shares (s. 186.). However, it is not a contractual document and even though issued under the company's seal is not a deed. (*South London Greyhound Racecourses v Wake* [1931] 1 Ch 496.) Thus it is not deemed to have been properly executed under s. 74 of the Law of Property Act, 1925. (See p. 82.) The holders' legal rights depend upon entry on the register of members and not upon possession of the certificate.

The articles usually empower the directors to renew share certificates which have been lost or destroyed. A small fee is charged, but the shareholder must give the company an indemnity in case any liability should fall upon it by reason of the possibility of two share certificates in respect of the same holding being in existence. Where the certificate is defaced or worn out delivery of the old certificate to the company is required. (See *Reg. 7, Table A.*)

The doctrine of estoppel

By reason of the doctrine of *estoppel* a company may be unable in certain circumstances to deny the truth of the particulars in the certificate even though they are incorrect.

(a) **Estoppel as to title.** The mere fact that at some time the company has issued to X a share certificate stating that he is the holder of (say) 100 shares does not prevent the company from denying that X is the holder at some future date. The certificate is only *prima facie* evidence that X was entitled to the shares *at the date of issue of the certificate.* (See also s. 186, p. 143.)

However, if the company recognizes the validity of X's title by registering or certifying a transfer to Y on the basis of the certificate, the company is estopped from denying Y's title, because it has held out to Y that X has a title. (*Re Bahia & San Francisco Railway Co*, 1868[93] and *The Balkis Consolidated Co Ltd v Tomkinson*, 1893,[94] contrast *Longman v Bath Electric Tramways Ltd*, 1905.[95])

Where the transfer is a forgery, the original transferee under it will not normally obtain a good title and the company will not normally be estopped from denying his title even if it has issued a share certificate to him. But a purchaser from the original transferee, though not getting a good title, can hold the company estopped by the certificate issued to him because he did not take it under a forged transfer, the signature of the apparent owner being on the transfer form.

Thus if X owns some shares in a company and his clerk forges X's signature on a form of transfer and sells the shares to Y, then Y will not get a good title to the shares and the company will not be estopped by the certificate issued to him. If, however, Y transfers the shares to Z before the forgery is discovered, and Z is issued with a share certificate, then the company will be estopped as against Z, and will have to pay him the value of the shares as damages if he chooses to sue the company rather than Y. Nevertheless, Z will not become a member by virtue of estoppel and X's name must be restored to the register. (*Re Bahia & San Francisco Railway Co*, 1868.[93])

In appropriate circumstances the company may be estopped as against the original recipient under a forged transfer and against the person to whom the certificate was issued. (*The Balkis Consolidated Co Ltd v Tomkinson*, 1893.[94]) (*Dixon v Kennaway & Co Ltd*, 1900.[96])

(b) **Estoppel as to payment.** In similar circumstances to those outlined above the company may be estopped from denying that the shares are fully paid, or paid up to the extent stated on the certificate, and this is so even though the company is being wound up (*Bloomenthal v Ford*, 1897),[97] and even though the effect of this is that the shares are issued at a discount. However, the directors who issue the certificate are liable to the company for the unpaid share capital which cannot now be recovered. (*Hirsche v Sims* [1894] AC 654.) This estoppel does not apply to a person such as an original allottee under a prospectus who knows how much he has paid up on the shares but it can in appropriate circumstances be available to a person to whom shares were issued by the company. (*Bloomenthal v Ford*, 1897.[97])

The doctrine of *estoppel* does not operate if the certificate itself is a forgery and in addition is issued by a person without apparent authority (*Ruben v Great Fingal Consolidated*, 1906),[98] though if the forgery is part of a fraud perpetrated on a third party by a servant or agent of the company *in the scope of employment*, the company may be liable. (*Longman v Bath Electric Tramways*, 1905.[95])

The estoppel does not seem to be defeated by the fact that the entries in the register of members show who the true owner is (see *The Balkis Consolidated Co Ltd*),[94] even though the register is accessible to the public for inspection, but there can certainly be no estoppel in favour of a person who actually knows the true facts.

SHARE WARRANTS (OR BEARER SHARES)

Public and also private companies may, if authorized by their articles, issue in respect of fully-paid shares a share warrant under the common seal stating that the bearer of the warrant is entitled to the shares specified in it. (S. 188.) *Table A* does not authorize the issue of share warrants. Although share warrants could be issued under a prospectus, it has been the case in the past that they have been exchanged for registered shares and the procedures described below relate to that situation. When a share warrant is issued the company must strike out of the register of members the name of the holder of the shares and make the following entries in the register—

    (i) the fact of the issue of the warrant;

    (ii) a statement of the shares included in the warrant, distinguishing each share by its number, if the shares had numbers; and

    (iii) the date of issue of the warrant. (S. 355(1).)

The bearer of the warrant is, unless the articles provide to the contrary, entitled to be registered as a member on surrender of the warrant. (S. 355(2).)

When share warrants are issued the annual return (see p. 184) must show—

(i) the total amount of shares for which share warrants are outstanding at the date of the return;

(ii) the total amount of share warrants issued and surrendered respectively since the last return; and

(iii) the number of shares comprised in each warrant. (Sched 15, para. 3(j).)

Difficulties arise as to the rights of holders of warrants because, although they are always shareholders, they are not members, since they are not entered on the register of members, though the bearer of a share warrant may, if the articles so provide, be *deemed* to be a member of the company either to the full extent or for any purpose defined in the articles. (S. 355(5).) Their rights are in fact governed by the articles, but *dividends* are usually obtained by handing over to the company coupons which are detachable from the warrant, the payment of dividend being advertised. (S. 188(1).)

The articles may deprive the holders of share warrants of their *voting rights*, but usually they are given the right to vote if they deposit their warrants with the company, or, if the warrant is deposited at a bank, on production of a certificate from the bank. The holding of share warrants is not sufficient to satisfy a director's share qualification. (S. 291(2).)

A share warrant operates as an *estoppel* that the holder has a title now, and not that he once did when the warrant was issued. Hence *the company must recognize the holder* unless the warrant is a forgery issued by a person without apparent authority.

A share warrant is also *negotiable* so that a title to it passes free from equities on mere delivery. (*Webb, Hale & Co v Alexandria Water Co* (1905) 93 LT 339.) Since no stamped instrument of transfer is required, the state loses revenue on transfer, and stamp duty is commuted on the issue of the warrant which must be stamped with three times the stamp duty, i.e. 3 per cent (s. 1 and Sched 1, Stamp Act 1891; s. 59, Finance Act 1963). Share certificates do not bear stamp duty.

The main advantages of share warrants are anonymity, i.e. no one can find out from the company's public records who the owner of a warrant is, and the ease of transfer. Warrants are merely handed to the purchaser avoiding the formality and expense involved in transferring a registered share. The main disadvantage is that company law leaves it entirely to the company as to how it communicates with its warrant holders. Advertisements, e.g. of meetings, may not always been seen by warrant holders who may therefore not attend and vote.

146

CALLS

It is usual today for a company to specify in the terms of issue that money due on the shares is payable by stated instalments. These are not really calls but are contractual instalments which the member is bound to pay on the dates mentioned by virtue of taking an allotment of the shares. Where the method of instalments is used, the company cannot ask for the money sooner by relying on a general power to make calls under the articles.

A *call proper* is made in a situation where the company did not lay down a date for payment in the terms of issue of the shares. Since shares are generally fully paid up now within a short time after allotment under a fixed instalment arrangement, calls are not common today.

The articles usually give the directors power to make calls subject to certain restrictions, e.g. *Table A, Reg* 12, provides that subject to the terms of allotment, the directors may make calls upon the members in respect of any moneys unpaid on their shares (whether in respect of nominal value or premium) and each member shall (subject to receiving at least 14 days' notice specifying when and where payment is to be made) pay to the company as required by the notice the amount called on his shares. A call may be required to be paid by instalments. A call may, before receipt by the company of any sum due thereunder, be revoked in whole or part and payment of a call may be postponed in whole or part. A person upon whom a call is made shall remain liable for calls made upon him notwithstanding the subsequent transfer of the shares in respect whereof the call was made. *Regulation* 12 must be complied with otherwise there can be no action against the shareholders in respect of the call.

Regulation 13 of *Table A* provides that a call shall be deemed to have been made at the time when the resolution of the directors authorizing the call was passed. *Regulation* 14 provides that the joint holders of a share shall be jointly and severally liable to pay all calls in respect thereof.

If the articles do not give the directors power to make calls, then the company may make them by ordinary resolution in general meeting. The resolution of the board or the members must state the amount of the call and the *date* on which it is payable. (*Re Cawley & Co* (1889) 42 Ch D 209.) It is essential that calls be made equally on all the shareholders of the same class unless the terms of issue and the company's articles otherwise provide. (S. 119(a).) (*Galloway v Hallé Concerts Society*, 1915.[99]) *Table A, Reg* 17 authorizes such an arrangement, but that does not entitle directors to make calls on all shareholders except themselves (*Alexander v Automatic Telephone Co*,

1900)[100] unless the other shareholders *know* and *approve* of the arrangement.

An irregularity in the making of the call may render the call invalid. Any major irregularity in procedure, as where there is no quorum at the meeting, or where the directors are not properly appointed, will have that effect, though s. 285 may validate the call since it provides that the acts of a director or manager shall be valid notwithstanding any defect which may afterwards be discovered in his appointment or qualification. Minor irregularities will not invalidate a call. (*Shackleford, Ford & Co v Dangerfield*, 1868.[101])

Section 14(2) provides that all money payable by any member to the company under the memorandum or the articles shall be in the nature of a *specialty debt*, thus allowing the company to sue for unpaid calls up to 12 years after the date upon which payment became due. (Limitation Act 1980, s. 8.) The directors may charge interest on calls unpaid, and *Table A, Reg* 15 provides that if a call remains unpaid after it has become due and payable, the person from whom it is due and payable shall pay interest on the amount unpaid from the day it became due and payable until it is paid at the rate fixed by the terms of allotment of the share or in the notice of the call or, if no rate is fixed, at the appropriate rate (as defined by the Companies Act and currently 5 per cent (s. 107)) but the directors may waive payment of the interest wholly or in part.

The company may also accept payment in advance of calls if the articles so provide. (S. 119.) Such payments are loans, and interest is usually paid on them.

Calls must be made and calls in advance accepted in good faith and for the benefit of the company and the shareholders, and not for the personal benefit of the directors (*Alexander v Automatic Telephone Co*, 1900,[100] and *Re European Central Rail Co, Sykes' Case*, 1872)[102] though the directors are not trustees for the company's creditors. (*Poole's Case*, 1878.[103]) Default in payment gives the company a lien over the shares for the amount unpaid. (See further, p. 156.)

Table A, Regs 20 to 22 provide for forfeiture of shares (see p. 157) for nonpayment of a call or instalment.

MORTGAGES OF SHARES

Mortgages of shares may be either legal or equitable.

Legal mortgages

In order that there shall be a legal mortgage, the mortgagee or lender must be entered on the register of members. To achieve this, the shares which are being used as a security must be transferred to him. A separate agreement will set out the terms of the loan, and will also contain an undertaking by the lender to retransfer the shares to the mortgagor when the loan and interest are repaid.

With a legal mortgage the lender (mortgagee) is on the register and therefore appears to the outside world to be the absolute owner whereas he has a duty to transfer to the borrower on the repayment of the loan. Thus the borrower (mortgagor) should serve a 'stop notice' (see below) upon the company to prevent an unauthorized sale of the shares by the lender.

Equitable mortgages

Such a mortgage is more usual than a legal mortgage and may be achieved in the following ways—

(a) *Mere deposit of the share certificate with the lender.* This is sufficient to create an equitable mortgage, given that the intention to do so is present, but if the lender wishes to enforce his security, he must ask the court for an *order for sale*, and having sold the shares under the order, he must account to the borrower for the balance if the proceeds exceed the amount of the loan. Alternatively the lender can apply for an *order of foreclosure* which vests the ownership of the shares in him, and if such an order is made, the lender is not obliged to account to the borrower for any excess. For this reason foreclosure is difficult to obtain.

(b) *Deposit of share certificate plus a blank transfer.* Where the borrower deposits the share certificate along with a transfer form, signed by him but with the transferee's name left blank, the seller has an implied authority to sell the shares by completing the transfer in favour of a purchaser, or in favour of himself if he so wishes, and in such a case there is no need to go to the court. Once again a separate agreement will set out the terms of the loan, and provide for the delivery of the certificate and blank transfer on repayment of the loan plus interest.

The methods of equitable mortgage outlined above do not necessarily ensure the priority of the lender as against other persons with whom the borrower may deal in respect of the shares. Where the borrower obtains another certificate from the company and sells to a *bona fide purchaser for value* who then obtains registration, that purchaser will have priority over the original lender.

It is no use the borrower in a legal mortgage or the original lender in an equitable mortgage (L) writing to the company telling it of his interest, because by s. 360 and *Reg 5* of *Table A* a company cannot take notice of any trust or similar right over its shares. However, a borrower or lender, as appropriate, may protect himself by serving on the company a stop notice under the Rules of the Supreme Court. He will file at the Central Office of the Supreme Court an affidavit declaring the nature of his interest in the shares, accompanied by a copy of the notice addressed to the company and signed by the applicant. Copies of the affidavit and the notice are then served on the company.

Once the stop notice has been served, the company cannot register a transfer or pay a dividend, if the notice extends to dividends without first notifying L. However, after the expiration of eight days from the lodgment of the transfer, the company is bound to make the transfer or pay the dividend unless in the meantime L has obtained an injunction from the court prohibiting it.

A *judgment creditor* of a registered owner of shares may obtain an order *charging* the shares with payment of the judgment debt. Notice of the making of the order, or demand for the dividend, when served upon the company, has a similar effect to a stop notice (see above), in that until the charging order is discharged or made absolute the company cannot allow a transfer except with the authority of the court. A charging order has no priority over a mortgage created by deposit of the share certificate and a blank transfer *before* the date on which the charging order was made.

TRANSFER OF UNLISTED SHARES

Section 182 provides that shares are personal property and shall be transferable subject to any restriction contained in the articles. A company cannot register a transfer of shares or debentures unless a proper instrument of transfer (*Re Paradise Motor Co Ltd*, 1968),[104] duly stamped, has been delivered to the company and executed by or on behalf of the transferor. (S. 183(1).) Thus an article which provided for the automatic transfer of shares to a director's widow on his death has been held invalid. (*Re Greene* [1949] 1 All ER 167.) The directors usually have power under the articles to decline to register the transfer of a share, other than a fully-paid share, to a person of whom they do not approve, e.g. a minor or person of unsound mind who cannot be bound by the contract; and also to decline to register the transfer of a share on which the company has a lien. (*Table A, Reg* 24.) Any power of veto on transfer vested by the articles in the directors must be exercised within two months after the lodging of the transfer for registration and the transferee notified. (S. 183 and *Reg 25, Table A*.) If not the company may be compelled to register the transferee as a member. (*Re Swaledale Cleaners Ltd*, 1968.[105])

The purchase and sale of shares involves the following separate and distinct legal transactions—

(i) a contract for the sale of the shares which does not pass the property in the shares;

(ii) a transfer operating, like a conveyance of land, to vest in the purchaser a right to ask for registration;

(iii) the completion of the purchaser's title by entry on the register. Since specific performance may be ordered of the contract for the sale of shares *the equitable interest* passes to the purchaser on contract, though not if the agreement is subject to a condition precedent unless it is solely for the benefit of the purchaser and he is prepared to waive it. (*Wood Preservation Ltd v Prior*, 1969.[106])

The rights of persons to obtain registration or to claim under an equitable title are set out on p. 179. S. 127 of the Insolvency Act 1986 declares void any transfer of shares after the commencement of winding up by the court, unless the court otherwise orders.

Form of transfer

The Stock Transfer Act 1963 introduced two new transfer forms—a *stock transfer form*, which is for general use with unlisted shares, and a *brokers transfer form*, which is to be used together with the stock transfer form where a holding of stock or shares is sold on the Stock Exchange and is to be transferred to more than one buyer.

Registrars are required to accept for registration transfers in the form introduced by the Act because it overrides any contrary provision regarding transfer, whether statutory or not. The signature of the transferor need not be witnessed, and the transferee need not now sign the transfer, nor need it be in the form of a deed.

Procedure on transfer of unlisted shares

The method of transferring fully-paid shares or stock is as follows.

The shareholder executes a form, termed a *stock transfer form*, in favour of the purchaser, and hands it to the purchaser or the purchaser's broker or agent, together with the share or stock certificate. The purchaser, or his broker or agent, sends the stock transfer form along with the certificate to the company for registration. The purchaser need not sign the stock transfer form, nor need the form be under seal. The company secretary deletes the transferor's name from the register of share or debenture holders and replaces it with the transferee's name, and within two months, sends the share certificate to the transferee.

151

TRANSFER OF LISTED SHARES

The Stock Exchange operates a system under which the paperwork resulting from share transfers over a two or three week period has to be done in the few days around settlement on what is called 'account day'. To spread and computerize this paperwork the Stock Exchange has introduced a new computerized settlement system called 'Talisman' which spreads the time-consuming process of preparing sold stock for delivery to the buyer over a longer period. As soon as possible after the sale of shares the seller will transfer the legal title in the securities sold to a new Stock Exchange pool of nominees, a company known as 'SEPON Ltd'. SEPON will prepare the securities for delivery to the buyer and will vest the legal title in him on settlement. The Stock Exchange Centre will manage SEPON holdings and be responsible for the payment of Stamp Duty and the handling of dividends, bonus issues, rights issues and take-over bids relating to them. The operation of the system is a matter for the Stock Exchange but some changes in law were necessary to allow the system to function effectively. In the main, s. 185(4) exempts companies from the requirement to issue share certificates, debentures or debenture stock certificates under s. 185(1) when those securities have been allotted or transferred to a nominee of the Stock Exchange (SEPON). This will prevent the unnecessary burden on companies to issue certificates when the legal title in securities is transferred temporarily to SEPON in the course of settlement. Under the Talisman system a company will maintain a running list of securities held by SEPON until settlement day when the new shareholder will be placed upon the company's share register. There are no other changes in the law, though there are some changes in transfer forms which is more a matter of secretarial practice than company law.

Certification of transfers—unlisted and listed shares

The above procedure assumes that on completion of the sale of registered unlisted shares the seller delivers his share certificate to the purchaser together with the instrument of transfer. Where he is selling all the shares represented by the certificate the seller will do this, but if he is selling only part of his holding he will instead send the share certificate and the executed transfer of the shares which the purchaser is buying to the company so that the transfer may be certificated. (See below for Stock Exchange procedure for listed shares.)

The company secretary or registrar or transfer agent will compare the share certificate and the transfer with the register of members and if it appears that the seller is the owner of the shares mentioned in

152

the certificate and some of those shares are comprised in the transfer, the secretary, registrar, or agent, as the case may be, will write in the margin of the transfer a note that the share certificate has been lodged and will sign it on behalf of the company.

The certificated transfer is then returned to the seller, the share certificate being retained by the company or the transfer agents. The seller will complete the sale by delivering the certificated transfer to the purchaser who will accept it as equal to delivery of an uncertificated transfer accompanied by the share certificate. The purchaser will then lodge the transfer with the company or its transfer agents for registration and the company will issue a new share certificate to him for the shares he has bought and a new certificate showing the seller as the registered holder of the balance of the shares which he retains.

Under the new Talisman system the need for certification is avoided in a transfer of listed shares. The seller's certificate will be lodged with SEPON Ltd and forwarded by it to the company together with a request by the seller addressed to the company to issue him with a balance certificate in cases where all his shares are not being sold.

Liability arising out of certification

This is as follows—

(a) **Certification of unlisted shares by the company's officers or transfer agents.** Such a certification is not a warranty by the company that the person transferring the shares has any title to them, but it is a representation by the company that documents have been produced to it which show *prima facie* title in the transferor. (S. 184(1).)

Where, therefore, the company or its agent fraudulently or negligently makes a false certification a purchaser who acts upon the false certification may sue the company for any loss he may have incurred as a result. (S. 184(2).)

For example, if the company certifies a transfer without production of a certificate, it may be that the certificate has been used to make a transfer to another purchaser. If so, two purchasers now exist and both are eligible for entry on the register of members. If the later purchaser achieves registration first, he will establish his priority over the certificated transferee who will not then be registered and the company will be liable in damages to the certificated transferee for the loss he suffers thereby. However, if the company registers the certificated transferee and refuses the other purchaser it will not be liable to the latter because the share certificate does not operate as an estoppel except as on the date of issue.

(b) **Certification of listed shares under Talisman.** It will be noted that (a) above applies only to certification by the company's officers or transfer agents. Under Talisman the need for certification is avoided. The seller's certificate is lodged with SEPON Ltd and forwarded by it to the company together with a request by the seller addressed to the company to issue him with a balance certificate in cases where all his shares are not being sold. Although there have never been any problems arising from fraud or negligence of the officials of the Stock Exchange, it is presumably the case that the Council of the Stock Exchange would accept responsibility for loss caused by fraud or negligence of its officials.

Forged transfers

If a company transfers shares under a forged instrument of transfer, the transferor whose name has been forged must be restored to the register, and in so far as this puts the company to expense or loss, it can claim an indemnity from the person presenting the transfer for registration, even though he is quite innocent of the forgery. (*Sheffield Corporation v Barclay*, 1905.[107])

If the company issues a share certificate to the transferee under a forged transfer, the company is not estopped from denying his title to the shares, but if the original transferee sells or mortgages the shares to another person, who takes them *bona fide for value relying on the share certificate*, the company is so estopped, and will be liable in damages to such a purchaser or mortgagee in respect of any loss arising out of the fact that he does not obtain registration.

A company may inform the transferor that a transfer has been received for registration so as to give him a chance to prevent a fraudulent transfer, but a transferor is not prejudiced by the fact that he has received notice, and may still deny the validity of the transfer.

COMPANIES WHOSE ARTICLES RESTRICT TRANSFER

In the case of a company whose articles restrict transfer a transfer must be submitted to and approved by the board and any restriction must be the decision of the directors.

TRANSMISSION OF SHARES

This occurs where shares vest in another by operation of law and not by virtue of transfer. It occurs in the following cases—

(a) Death of a shareholder

The shares of the deceased shareholder vest in his personal representatives, either executors or administrators, who can sell or otherwise dispose of them without actually being registered. Section 187 provides that the company must accept probate of the will, or letters of administration, as sufficient evidence of the title of the personal representatives, notwithstanding anything in its articles.

Personal representatives can insist on registration as members in respect of the deceased's shares unless the articles otherwise provide. Under *Table A, Reg* 30 the directors have the same power to refuse to register personal representatives and trustees as they have to register transfers provided the shares are not fully paid. The company cannot insist that personal representatives and trustees be registered. If personal representatives or trustees are registered as members they become personally liable for capital unpaid on the shares but they receive the benefit of being entitled to vote at meetings of members. They are unable to do this before they are registered unless the articles expressly so provide. *Table A, Reg* 31 gives no voting rights to personal representatives or trustees unless they are registered as members.

The personal representatives receive all the benefits attaching to the shares without registering, but as we have seen unless the articles specifically allow it, they cannot vote unless they are registered.

(b) Mental Health Act patients

Transmission also occurs to the receiver of a person becoming a patient under the Mental Health Act 1983. The position of the receiver is similar to that of executors or administrators.

(c) Bankruptcy of a shareholder

On the bankruptcy of a member the right to deal with the shares passes to the trustee in bankruptcy, and he can sell them without actually being registered, or he can ask for registration. When the trustee sells the shares, the sale is effected by production to the company of the share certificate, together with the Department of Trade and Industry's certificate appointing the trustee and a transfer signed by him. A trustee cannot vote unless he is actually registered, but can direct the bankrupt on the way he must vote. (*Morgan v Gray* [1953] 1 All ER 213.)

A trustee in bankruptcy has a *right of disclaimer* under which he may disclaim shares as onerous property where there are calls due on them and they would have little value if sold. Disclaimer is effected by the trustee serving upon the company a notice in writing disclaiming the shares. The trustee is then not personally liable to pay the calls, and the estate of the bankrupt member is no longer liable as such. The company may, however, claim for damages, which in the case of shares of little value may not be as much as the calls due but unpaid. (*Re Hallet, ex parte National Insurance Co* [1894] WN 156.) Shares disclaimed may be re-issued as paid up to the extent to which cash has been received on them.

Trustees

If new trustees are appointed in a trust where the whole or part of the trust property consists of shares, the shares must be transferred to the new trustees in the usual way, i.e. by stock transfer form. There is no transfer by operation of law, nor under s. 40 of the Trustee Act 1925, where the new trustee is appointed by deed.

LIEN

The articles often give the company a first and paramount lien over its shares for unpaid calls, or even for general debts owed to the company by shareholders, but the Stock Exchange will not give a listing where there is a lien on fully-paid shares. Furthermore, s. 150(1) prevents, subject to some exceptions, e.g. for banks under s. 150(3), a public company from taking a lien or other charge over its own shares. However, under s. 150(2), a lien is permitted over partly-paid shares for amounts called or payable on the shares. It is usual also for the articles to give a power of sale. *Table A, Reg 9*, gives such a power of sale, but requires 14 days' notice in writing to the shareholder or his representatives before the sale takes place, during which time the money owed can be paid and the sale prevented. Since on a sale the shareholder or his representatives will probably not co-operate in the necessary transfer, the articles usually provide that a purchaser shall get a good title if the transfer is signed by a person nominated by the directors. (*Table A, Reg 10.*) If the articles create a lien but give no power of sale, the company would have to obtain an order for sale from the court.

A lien, other than for amounts due on the shares, cannot be enforced by forfeiture even if a power to forfeit is contained in the articles. (S. 143(3)(*d*).) Thus a company cannot enforce a lien for general debts by forfeiture even if its articles so provide.

The company's lien takes priority over all equitable interests in the shares, e.g. those of equitable mortgages, unless when the shareholder becomes indebted to the company, it has actual notice of the equitable interest. (*Bradford Banking Co v Briggs*, 1886.[108]) The lien attaches to dividends payable in respect of the shares subject to the lien (*Hague v Dandeson* (1848) 2 Exch 741).

FORFEITURE OF SHARES

Shares may be forfeited by a resolution of the board of directors if, *and only if*, an express power to forfeit is given in the articles. Where such an express power exists, it must be strictly followed, otherwise the forfeiture may be annulled. Further, the object of the forfeiture must be for the benefit of the company and not to give some personal advantage to a director or shareholder, e.g. in order to allow him to avoid liability for the payment of calls where the shares have fallen in value. (*Re Esparto Trading Co*, 1879.[109])

The articles usually provide that shares may be forfeited where the member concerned does not pay a call made upon him, whether the call is in respect of the nominal value of the shares or of premium.

The usual procedure is for a notice to be served on the member asking for payment, and stating that if payment is not made by a specific date, not earlier than 14 days from the date of the notice, the shares may be forfeited. If payment is not so made, the company may forfeit the shares and make an entry of forfeiture on the register of members. Once the shares have been forfeited, the member should be required to return the share certificate or other document of title so as to obviate fraud. A forfeiture operates to reduce the company's issued capital, since it cancels the liability of the member concerned to pay for his shares in full, but even so the sanction of the court is not required; a mere power in the articles is enough.

Shares cannot be forfeited except for non-payment of calls (s. 143(3)(*d*)), and any provision in the articles to the contrary is void.

Re-issue of forfeited shares

Forfeited shares may be re-issued to a purchaser so long as the price which he pays for the shares is not less than the amount of calls due but unpaid at forfeiture.

Suppose X is the holder of 100 shares of £1 each on which 75p per share has been called up, and X does not pay the final call of 25p per share, as a result of which the shares are forfeited. If they are re-issued to Y, then Y must pay not less than £25 for them, and any sum received in excess of that amount from Y will be considered as *share premium* and must be credited to a *share premium account*. Thus, although Y appears to have bought the shares at a discount, this is not so because the company has received the full amount of the called-up capital, i.e. £75 from X and £25 from Y.

The company's articles usually provide that if any irregularity occurs in the forfeiture procedure, the person to whom the forfeited shares are re-issued will nevertheless obtain a good title. (*Table A, Reg 22.*)

Liability of person whose shares are forfeited

Forfeiture of shares means that the holder ceases to be a member of the company, but his liability in respect of the shares forfeited depends upon the articles.

(a) *Where there is no provision in the articles* with regard to liability, the former holder is discharged from liability, and no action can be brought by the company against him for calls due at the date of the forfeiture unless the company is wound up within one year of it. In such a case the former holder may be put on the B *list of contributories* in the winding up, and may be called upon to pay the calls due at the date of the forfeiture unless they have been paid by another holder.

(b) *The articles may provide* (as does *Table A, Reg* 21) that the former holder shall be liable to pay the calls due but unpaid at the date of forfeiture, whether the company is in liquidation or not, unless they have been paid to the company by a subsequent holder.

Surrender of shares

The directors of a company cannot accept a surrender of shares unless the articles so provide. There is no provision in *Table A* but it would seem from decided cases that directors may accept surrender—

(a) where the circumstances are such that the shares could have been forfeited under the articles (*per* Lord Herschell in *Trevor v Whitworth* (1887) 12 App Cas 409) and

(b) where shares are surrendered as part of a scheme to exchange existing shares for new shares of the same nominal value, the new shares having perhaps slightly different rights and the old shares being either cancelled or available for re-issue.

In other circumstances surrender is not allowed. (*Bellerby v Rowland & Marwood's SS Co Ltd*, 1902.[110])

Treatment of forfeited and surrendered shares in public companies

The above material relating to forfeiture and surrender is still valid because it relates to the source of the power to forfeit or surrender and the surrounding circumstances. However, the treatment of forfeited and surrendered shares once this has happened is a matter for the Companies Act 1985. Section 146 of that Act provides that no voting rights may be exercised by the company so long as the shares are forfeited or surrendered and also that the company must dispose of the shares within three years. If they are not disposed of they must be cancelled. If the shares are cancelled and the cancellation has the effect of reducing the company's allotted share capital below the authorized minimum, then the directors must apply for the company to be re-registered as a private company. There are, however, under s. 147, certain relaxations in the procedures in this event. In particular, only a directors' resolution is required to make the necessary reduction, application, and any alterations to the memorandum that are necessary. The company does not need to apply to the court to obtain confirmation of the reduction in capital but any resolution passed by the directors must be filed with the Registrar. (S. 147(2).) If a company fails to comply with either the requirement to cancel or the requirement to re-register as a private company, the company and its officers in default become liable to a fine.

7 Membership and control

There are several ways in which membership of a company may be acquired: these are as follows—

(i) *By subscribing the memorandum.* When the company is registered, the persons who subscribed the memorandum automatically become members on subscription, and must be put on the register of members on registration of the company (s. 22(1)), though they are deemed to be members without such an entry and even without allotment.

(ii) *By making an application* under a prospectus or offer for sale for an allotment of shares.

(iii) *By taking a transfer* from an existing member.

(iv) *By succeeding to shares* on the *death* or *bankruptcy* of a member.

The persons mentioned in (ii), (iii) and (iv) above do not actually become members until their names are entered in the register of members. (S. 22(2).)

CAPACITY

The question of capacity is governed by the general law of contract, and anyone who has the capacity to make a contract may become a member of a company. Certain special cases must be considered—

1. Minors

A minor may be a member of a company unless the articles otherwise provide. Registration of a minor may give rise to difficulties in the case of partly-paid shares or unlimited companies, because a minor can repudiate the contract with the company at any time during minority and for a reasonable time thereafter. If he does repudiate, he cannot recover the money he has paid up to the time of repudiation if the shares have ever had any value. (*Steinberg v Scale (Leeds) Ltd*, 1923.[111])

The Family Law Reform Act 1969, s. 1 reduced the age of majority from 21 to 18 years. There is a general provision in the Act that a person attains a particular age, i.e. not only the age of majority, on the first moment of the relevant birthday.

A company always has power to refuse to accept a minor as a transferee or shareholder where it knows his age and can probably set aside a transfer to a minor once it learns the position. (*Re Contract Corporation, Gooch's Case* (1872) LR 8 Ch App 266.) However, if a company registers a minor knowing him to be such it cannot afterwards repudiate him.

2. Companies

A company may, if authorized by its memorandum, become a member of another company. It may attend meetings and vote by means of a representative (appointed by the board) (s. 375(1)(*a*)) or by proxy. However, a company cannot be a member of itself, i.e. it cannot purchase its own shares for a consideration because such a purchase would amount to a return of capital to the shareholders from whom the shares were bought, and would, therefore, operate as a reduction of capital without the consent of the court. A company limited by shares may acquire any of its own fully paid shares otherwise than for valuable consideration (s. 143).

Section 143 does not apply in relation to the redemption or purchase of any shares in accordance with Part V, Chapter VII of the Companies Act 1985; the acquisition of any shares in a reduction of capital duly made; the purchase of any shares in pursuance of an order of the court under s. 5 (alteration of objects); s. 54 (objection to resolution for company to be re-registered as private) or Part XVII (relief to members unfairly prejudiced); or the forfeiture of any shares or the acceptance of any shares surrendered in lieu in pursuance of the articles for failure to pay any sum payable in respect of those shares. (S. 143.)

The provisions of s. 143 could be avoided by the device of a loan or other assistance by the company to a person to enable that person to buy or subscribe for shares in the company; this is controlled by the provisions set out below.

Financial assistance for purchase of shares—previous position

The prohibition on the giving by companies of financial assistance for the purchase of their own shares or the shares of their holding companies was introduced by the Companies Act 1929 and retained in subsequent legislation until 1981.

The object was largely to defeat the asset stripper who might, e.g. acquire shares in a company by means of a loan from a third party so that he came to control it and once in control repay the loan from the company's funds and then sell off its assets leaving the company to go into liquidation with no assets to meet the claims of creditors. The company concerned was usually one whose shares were, perhaps because of the management policies of the board, undervalued. An example of another *modus operandi* can be seen in *Wallersteiner v Moir*, 1974.[112] ·

The sanction of the law designed to deter this sort of activity was a default fine which could be levied following *criminal proceedings*.

In addition there were civil law consequences since the transactions surrounding the acquisition of the company were illegal. Thus the loan by the third party was void and irrecoverable at law; if the company had given the lender a debenture to secure the loan; or a guarantee to repay it these securities were void and unforceable as was any guarantee or other security given by anyone else including the asset stripper himself.

The civil consequences are illustrated by *Heald v O'Connor*, 1971[46] and the same consequences would obtain in so far as a person infringed the present law set out below. Breach of the present law is stated to be 'unlawful' and is attended by criminal sanctions the maximum penalty being a term of imprisonment of two years and/or a fine of unlimited amount.

Problems created by previous legislation

The rule against the giving of financial assistance struck potentially at ordinary commercial transactions of companies as follows—

(*a*) *Management buy-outs*. This is the disposal of a company to its management. A holding company may use a buy-out to sell off a subsidiary whose business though successful does not fit the current development plan of the group.

However, the buy-out is more common in the case of private free-standing companies. Suppose that in a family business senior management has reached the age of retirement and is unable to find any purchaser of the business, who knows and can run it successfully other than those employees who are coming up as the next generation of management. In such a case those in management below the owner/directors may use a buy-out technique to acquire the business with the blessing of the owner/directors.

A *management buy-out is commonly achieved by* a bank lending the managers the money to buy the shares. Typically the managers can only provide between 10 and 20 per cent of the funds required. The loan is often secured on the assets of the company which management is acquiring and this is the giving of financial assistance and was an infringement of previous legislation.

Nevertheless it was a popular and useful technique which regrettably operated outside of the law.

(*b*) *Other transactions*. It was held by the Court of Appeal in *Belmont Finance v Williams (No 2)* [1980] 1 All ER 393 that there was an infringement of then existing legislation when Company A bought the share capital of Company B and the former owner of Company B used the money to buy shares in Company A.

Furthermore, there were even lawyers prepared to state that the purchase of shares in a company by an innocent recipient of dividends from it might be infringing the financial assistance rule!

Thus some not uncommon commercial transactions were rendered illegal by a rule which was not, it seems, intended to catch all of them.

The present law

This is designed to bring UK companies into line with US and Continental companies. It is contained in ss. 151–158. The provisions are set out below—

1. *The prohibition*. Section 151 makes it unlawful, as before, for a company to give financial assistance for the purchase of its own shares or those of its holding company, directly or indirectly, *whether before or at the same time as the shares are acquired*.

It will suffice for the moment to say that the S company is a subsidiary of the H company and the H company is the S company's holding company if—

(*a*) H is a member of S and controls the composition of S's board of directors;

(*b*) H holds more than half in nominal value of S's equity shares, in effect more than one-half of S's issued ordinary shares;

(*c*) S is a subsidiary of the Z company which is a subsidiary of H. (See s. 736(1).)

There is no prohibition on a subsidiary company providing financial assistance for the purchase of shares in its fellow subsidiaries or in a holding company providing assistance for the purchase of shares in one of its subsidiaries. Section 151(2) extends the prohibition to *assistance after acquisition* as where A borrows money to acquire shares in B Ltd and B Ltd later repays the loan or reimburses A after A has repaid the loan.

2. *Meaning of financial assistance*

(*a*) Under 152(1)(*a*)(i)–(iii), financial assistance is provided if the company concerned *makes a gift of the shares or a gift of funds to buy them*; or *guarantees a loan* used to buy its shares; or *gives an indemnity* to the lender; or *secures the loan by giving a charge* over its assets to the lender.

A company would also give assistance if it *waived or released*, e.g.

its right to recover a debt from a person A so that A could use the funds to buy shares in the company.

(*b*) Section 152(1)(*a*)(iv) is a 'sweep-up' sub-section which forbids any other financial assistance given by a company, the net assets of which are thereby reduced to a material extent or which has no net assets, i.e. a company which is insolvent, though the test is not liquidity but net worth based on the actual value of the assets. Thus a purchase by a company for cash at market value of a fixed asset from a person who later bought its shares would not be financial assistance because the company's net assets would not be reduced and cash would be replaced by the assets.

However, the section would catch artificial transactions affecting a company's assets, as where the company paid twice the market value for an asset in order to enable the seller to buy its shares.

Thus in *Belmont* the actual transaction was artificial and designed purely to assist the owner of Company B to acquire shares in A at the expense of the assets of A, because Company A paid far more for the shares of B than they were worth, i.e. £500,000 against a valuation of £60,000. The actual deal in *Belmont* would thus infringe s. 152(1)(*a*)(iv), although what happened is not otherwise a forbidden transaction under s. 152(1)(*a*)(i)–(iii).

For the purposes of s. 152(1)(*a*)(iv) 'net assets' is defined as the aggregate assets *less* the aggregate liabilities determined by reference to their *actual* rather than their *book* value. (S. 152(2).) Section 152(2) does not expressly state that actual as opposed to book values should be used but this was the view of the Government when the original provision which was in s. 87(4)(*c*) of the Companies Act 1980 was passed.

3. *When is financial assistance lawful?*

(*a*) *Under s. 153(1) and (2)*, the giving of financial assistance is lawful if the *principal purpose* of the company's action is not to give financial assistance OR such assistance is given as *an incidental part of some larger purpose of the company*. In addition the assistance MUST be given *in good faith* and *in the best interests of the company*.

The company's defence is therefore founded upon *the purpose* in giving assistance and since *this is a matter of fact* to be decided *on the evidence* it would be as well for the purpose to be set out clearly in the relevant Board minutes. A purpose must be established other than the mere giving of assistance. The provision could lead to much litigation. It should, nevertheless, prevent the kind of asset stripping referred to at the beginning of this section although there is little doubt that some, seeking to gain profit from purely artificial transactions at the expense of a company's assets, will try to dress up their dealings as some form, e.g. of 'reconstruction'.

Clearly, however, a legitimate management buy-out is allowed and other ordinary commercial transactions are no longer threatened by illegality. For example, A acquires B. B wishes to transfer its bank balances to A to effect a more efficient disposition of funds within the group. The Boards of A and B may both know that A intends to use those balances to reduce indebtedness, e.g. a loan incurred as a result of acquiring B but this is permitted because reduction of such indebtedness is merely incidental to a larger corporate purpose.

(b) *Under s. 153(3)* the following are also permitted:

(i) a distribution of assets in Company A by way of *dividend* or in *a winding up* where the distribution is used to buy shares in A or in its holding company or former holding company;

(ii) an allotment of bonus shares—which in a sense the company assists the shareholders concerned to acquire (the provisions relating to assistance cover acquisition of shares other than for cash but bonus shares are specifically exempt);

(iii) any arrangement or compromise under s. 425 or, s. 110 and Part I of the Insolvency Act 1986 which results, e.g. in a liquidator transferring the assets of Company A to Company B so that the shareholders of A receive shares in B into which A is merged which in a sense A's assets have assisted them to acquire (further details of reconstructions and amalgamations or compromises under s. 425 and s. 110 and Part I (*ibid*) are given in Chapter 15)

(iv) where the funds used to buy shares in the company or its holding company arise from:

(a) a reduction of its capital under s. 137; *or*

(b) a redemption or purchase of its shares under Chapter VII of Part V.

(c) *Under s. 153(4)* the following transactions are also permitted—

(i) A company may lend money to a person to enable him to acquire shares in it or its holding company if lending money is part of the ordinary business of the company. The fact that a company has power to lend money by its memorandum does not make lending money part of its ordinary business unless making loans is one of its main objects. Neither the loans it ordinarily makes nor the loan which facilitates the acquisition of the shares must be made for the specific purpose of acquiring the shares. The borrower must be free to use the loan as he wishes, and it must be merely coincidental that the borrower uses it to buy shares in the company. (*Steen v Law*, 1963.[113])

(ii) A company may provide money under a scheme to enable trustees to subscribe for or purchase fully paid shares in the company or its holding company to be held in trust for employees of the company, including salaried directors. This exception facilitates many of the profit-sharing and share subscription schemes operated by the larger companies. Under profit-sharing schemes a proportion of the company's profits is transferred annually to the trustees who acquire shares with it and distribute them among employees in the manner laid down in the scheme. Under share subscription schemes employees are given options to acquire shares at favourable prices from trustees who have subscribed for them with money advanced by the company.

Under s. 743 a company may finance an employees' share trust which benefits employees of the group and their dependents and not merely employees of the company.

(iii) A company may make loans to its employees, other than directors, to enable them to subscribe for or purchase fully paid shares in the company or its holding company to be held by them in their own right.

It should be noted that under s. 154(1) the lending set out in (i)–(iii) above is permissible in the case of a public company only if the company's net assets are not thereby reduced or, to the extent that those assets are thereby reduced, if the financial assistance is provided out of profits which are available for dividend. 'Net assets' in relation to a company for this purpose means the aggregate of that company's assets less the aggregate of its liabilities, including provisions, determined by their *book* value (see s. 154(2)(*a*)).

Finally, if shares are acquired by a *nominee for a public company* (not any other person) with financial assistance from the company, then (apart from any infringement of s. 151) under ss. 145–149 no voting rights may be exercised by that nominee and any purported exercise of such rights is void. Secondly, the company must dispose of the shares within one year and if this is not done it must cancel them. If the shares are cancelled and the cancellation has the effect of reducing the company's allotted share capital below the authorized minimum, the directors must apply for the company to be re-registered as a private company. Only a directors' resolution is required to make the necessary reduction, application and any alterations to the memorandum that are necessary. There is no need to apply to the court to obtain confirmation of the reduction but any resolution passed by the directors is subject to s. 380 and must be filed with the Registrar. (S. 147(2).)

Financial assistance—relaxation of restrictions: private companies: generally

A private company can give financial assistance in the same circumstances as a public company (see above 'When is financial assistance lawful?'), BUT in addition *a private company is not affected by the principal purpose rule* and could therefore provide assistance as the sole purpose and object of a particular exercise. (S. 155(1).)

However, a private company cannot give financial assistance for the acquisition of its own shares or those of its holding company if its net assets would thereby be reduced *except* that if the net assets will be reduced assistance can be provided if it comes from distributable profits. (S. 155(2).)

For this purpose net assets means the aggregate assets less the aggregate liabilities (including provisions) determined according to their *book* value. (S. 155(2).)

A private company cannot give assistance for the purpose of acquiring shares in its holding company unless it complies with the principal purpose rule, if the holding company or any intermediate holding company is a public company. (S. 155(3).) This is to ensure that public companies cannot avoid the principal purpose rule by a group scheme of some sort.

The practical effect of the above provisions is that a private company can give virtually any kind of financial assistance provided the company is solvent and the complicated procedure set out below is followed.

Procedure

Whether or not the financial assistance is the principal or only purpose or whether it is an incidental purpose, as in a management buy-out, a private company must follow a statutory procedure before the assistance is given. This is set out below:

(a) *Creditor protection: a statutory declaration and auditors report*

As we have seen a private company can give financial assistance if the company's net (book) assets will not be reduced, or if the financial assistance is provided from distributable profits. However, since *a private company is not required to take into account unrealized losses in determining distributable profits (see further p. 287) a statutory declaration of solvency is required* (s. 155(6)).

The directors of the company (and any holding company and intermediate holding company, if the assistance is for the purchase of shares in the holding company) giving financial assistance must make a statutory declaration in prescribed form. *Under s. 156(1) and (2) it must state*—

(i) particulars of the company's business and the assistance to be given and identifying the recipient of the assistance;

(ii) that the giving of the assistance will not prevent the company from paying its debts in the *immediate future*;

(iii) that *as regards the prospects of the assisting company for the following year* the company will be able to carry on its business as a going concern and will be able to pay its debts as they fall due throughout the year. If the assisting company is to be put into liquidation within a year but is now, e.g. assisting a purchase of shares in its holding company, the period must be the year following the start of the winding-up.

In forming an opinion on these matters contingent and prospective liabilities, e.g. commitments under hire purchase agreements, must be taken into account.

Under s. 156(4) the statutory declaration referred to above must have an *Auditors' Report* annexed to it.

The report which is addressed to the directors states that the auditors have enquired into the company's affairs and are not aware of anything indicating that the directors' opinion regarding the company's ability to pay its debts is unreasonable.

(*b*) *Shareholder protection: a special resolution.* Under s. 155(4) and s. 157(1), within a week of making the statutory declaration referred to in (*a*) above a *special resolution* must be passed by the company in general meeting (and if the financial assistance is for the purchase of shares in its holding company, by that holding company and any intermediate holding company) approving the financial assistance. If a company is a wholly owned subsidiary it is not necessary to pass a resolution for the reason that there are no shareholders to protect in the sense required by the 1985 Act.

Although a 75 per cent majority of those who vote is enough to pass the special resolution it is important in practice that every shareholder should vote in favour. If not, a four-week delay is imposed to enable possible dissenting shareholders to make application to the court (see below).

Under s. 156(5) the special resolution must be filed with the statutory declaration (or the statutory declaration alone for a wholly-owned subsidiary which need not pass a special resolution) plus the auditors' report within 15 days.

Giving the assistance: when can it be done?

Under s. 158 the financial assistance can, once the procedure outlined above has been followed, be given at any time within eight weeks from the date of the statutory declaration provided that *all* shareholders voted in favour of the special resolution in order to avoid the minority four-week delay which will otherwise have to come out of the beginning half of the eight week period. If there is an application to the court the timetable is then a matter for the court which may if there is delay in dealing with the dissentient's claim ask for another statutory declaration.

Dissentient rights

Under s. 157(2) the holders of not less than 10 per cent in aggregate of the nominal value of the company's issued share capital or of any class thereof; or not less than 10 per cent of the members, if the company is not limited by shares, who did not consent to the special resolution may apply to the court to cancel it. Under s. 157(3) the court *may require* the company to buy out the dissentients if necessary from the company's funds thus effecting a reduction of capital; *or make an order* cancelling the resolution which will then be ineffective.

Table A

The current *Table A* does not prevent the giving of financial assistance. *Table A* to previous Acts did so. Companies covered by previous *Tables A* or having a similar restrictive regulation must remove it before giving financial assistance.

Management buy-out and fair dealing by directors

Schemes of financial assistance given to *directors* to achieve a management buy-out would be caught and rendered illegal by Part X of the 1985 Act. (See p. 245.) Thus financial assistance for such a buy-out could only be given to management who were not at the time at board level.

Criminal penalties

There are a variety of penalties in terms of fines on the company and fines and/or imprisonment of its officers for various infringements of the financial assistance rules. (See s. 151(3) and s. 156(6) and (7).)

Acquisition other than for valuable consideration

There is nothing to prevent the transfer of shares in the company to a trustee who will then hold the shares on trust for the company, given that the transfer is voluntary and the shares are fully paid (*Kirby v Wilkins*, 1929[114]); and a gift to a company of fully-paid shares in the company is apparently not objectionable, so long as the shares are held by some other person on trust for the company. (*Re Castiglione's Will Trusts*, 1958.[115])

Section 143(3) provides that all companies limited by shares may acquire their own fully paid shares by way of gift and the effect of this provision is that the company may hold the shares directly in its own name. There is now no need to put such shares in the name of a nominee or trustee for the company. There is nothing to prevent the use of such a device but it is unnecessary in view of s. 143(3).

However, nominee holdings, as distinct from holdings as gifts, are governed by the Companies Act 1985. Section 144 provides that in the case of both a public and private company if a person has been issued with or has acquired shares in a company as nominee for that company, then if he fails to pay any sums due on the shares the other subscribers to the memorandum, if he acquired them as a subscriber, or the directors, if he acquired them in some other way, are, unless the court grants relief, jointly and severally liable with the nominee for the payment of the sums due. Furthermore, s. 146 provides that if the shares have been acquired by a person as nominee for a public company, the shares must be disposed of and if this has not been done within three years the company must cancel the shares and the formalities of ss. 135 and 136 of the 1985 Act do not apply to the reduction. In addition, the company's nominee must not exercise voting rights in respect of the shares and if he does the votes are void. (S. 146(4).)

Membership of a holding company

Another of Parliament's attempts to prevent devices which are tantamount to an acquisition by a company of its own shares is to be found in s. 23. Under that section a company cannot become a member of its holding company since the section regards this as in effect the acquisition of its own shares. If a subsidiary was already a member of its holding company on 1 July 1948 it may continue as such but it cannot exercise voting rights in regard to the shares it holds.

The above rules do not apply where the subsidiary holds the shares as a personal representative or a trustee unless the holding company or a subsidiary of it is beneficially interested under the trust, nor where the shares are held by the subsidiary as a security for a loan where the subsidiary's ordinary business is lending money. (S. 23(4).)

In addition, under Sched 2, para 2, the holding company is not deemed to be beneficially interested in a trust merely because it has a subsidiary trustee company through which it runs an employees' share scheme or pension scheme and that trustee company has shares in the holding company and the surplus assets of the trustee company go under the scheme to the holding company if the trustee company is wound up.

THE CONSIDERATION

Under s. 100(1) a member of a company must pay for his shares in full, and no arrangement between the company and the members can affect this rule. (*Ooregum Gold Mining Co of India v Roper* [1892] AC 125.) However, payment need not be in cash but may be for some other consideration. Where this is so issues at a discount may still in effect be made in private companies.

Payment in cash

This is generally effected by handing cash or a cheque to the company, but if the company pays an existing debt by an issue of shares to the creditor, this set off arrangement is deemed to be a payment in cash. (*Spargo's Case*, 1873.[116])

Considerations other than cash

(a) In private companies

Such considerations are legal, and the consideration very often consists in the sale of property to the company or the rendering of services. The consideration offered must be sufficient to support the contract in law and must not, for example, be past, though in private companies, at least, it need not be adequate. (*Re Eddystone Marine Insurance Co*, 1893[117], *Re Wragg Ltd*, 1897.[118]) The court will inquire into the agreement where there is fraud, or where the consideration is wholly illusory. (*Hong Kong and China Gas Co Ltd v Glen*, 1914.[119])

An agreement to allot shares for future services may mean that the allottee will become liable to pay for the shares in full, since if he does not render the services, the company would otherwise be reduced to a mere action for damages, and would not have an action for the actual price of the shares, and it is doubtful whether a company can replace the liability of a member to pay for his shares in full with a mere action for damages. (*Gardner v Iredale* [1912] 1 Ch 700.)

Where shares are issued for a consideration other than cash, the contract, or if the contract is not in writing written particulars of it, must be sent to the Registrar for registration within one month of the allotment of the said shares. (S. 88(3).) If there is no such registration within the time prescribed, the officers of the company are liable to a fine under the 1985 Act, but the allotment is not affected. It should be noted that *mere registration* of a contract under s. 88 will not make it binding on the company if there is no consideration for it. (*Re Eddystone Marine Insurance Co*, 1893.[117])

(b) In public companies

Under s. 102(1) a public company is only allowed to allot shares as fully or partly paid by an undertaking to transfer a non-cash asset to the company if the transfer is to take place within five years of the date of the allotment.

In addition, under ss. 103 and 108 allotment for a non-cash consideration is not to be made unless the non-cash asset has been valued by an independent accountant who would be qualified to be the auditor of the company (or by someone else approved by that independent accountant). In addition, the independent accountant must have reported to the company on his valuation during the six months prior to the allotment, and must state that the value of the consideration is at least equal to the value of the shares being allotted. A copy of the report must also have been sent to the allottee and filed at the Companies Registry with the return of allotments.

A valuation of the kind set out above is not required in a share exchange as in a take-over bid where Predator is acquiring Victim by exchanging Predator shares for Victim shares so that the consideration for Predator shares is the assets of Victim, but all the holders of shares in Victim must be able to take part in the arrangement.

Under s. 104 for two years following the date of issue of the certificate that a company registered as a public company is entitled to commence business, the company may not acquire assets from subscribers to the memorandum having an aggregate value equal to 10 per cent or more of the nominal value of the issued share capital unless—

(i) the valuation rules set out above are complied with; and

(ii) the acquisition of the asset(s) and the terms of the acquisition have been approved by an ordinary resolution of the company. A copy of that resolution must be filed at the Companies Registry within 15 days of its passing.

Similar rules apply on re-registration as a public company where non-cash assets equal to at least 10 per cent of the nominal value of the issued share capital at that time are acquired from persons who are members of the company at the time of re-registration. These provisions do not apply to assets acquired in the ordinary course of business.

In addition, under s. 106, the shares which a subscriber of the memorandum of a public company agrees in the memorandum to take must be paid up in cash, and under s. 99(2) a public company must not accept at any time in payment up of its shares or any premium on them, an undertaking given by any person that he or another should do work or perform services in the future for the company or any other person.

Where the above requirements are contravened s. 112 provides that the allottee and his successors, but not purchasers for value without notice, will be liable to pay to the company the amount outstanding in respect of the allotment with interest which under s. 107 is currently 5 per cent *per annum*. The company and any officer in default may also be liable to a fine. However, under s. 113 the court may grant relief where the applicant has acted in good faith and it is just and equitable to grant relief.

PROHIBITION ON ALLOTMENT OF SHARES AT A DISCOUNT

Section 100(1) prohibits the issue of shares at a discount. The power to pay underwriting commission under s. 97(1) is not affected. Where shares are allotted in contravention of s. 100(1), those shares shall be treated as paid up by the payment to the company of the amount of the nominal value of the shares less the amount of the discount, but the allottee shall be liable to pay the company the latter amount and shall be liable to pay interest thereon at the appropriate rate which, under s. 107 is currently 5 per cent *per annum*. (S. 100(2).) Persons who take the shares from the original allottee are jointly and severally liable with the original allottee to pay the amount mentioned above unless they are purchasers for value, and even a purchaser for value may be liable if he has actual knowledge of the contravention of s. 100 at the time of the purchase.

Debentures may be issued at a discount, though where there is a right to exchange the debentures for shares at par value the debentures are good but the right to exchange is void. (*Mosely v Koffyfontein Mines Ltd*, 1904.[120])

SHARES ISSUED AT A PREMIUM

Share premiums—generally

There is nothing to prevent a company issuing shares at a premium, e.g. £1 shares at a price of £1.25p; and, indeed, where it is desired to issue further shares, of a class already dealt in on the Stock Exchange at a substantial premium it is a practical necessity to do so.

However, s. 130(1) requires that such premium must be credited to a 'share premium account' to be treated as capital (s. 130(3)), except in so far as it may be written down to pay up fully-paid bonus shares, to write off preliminary expenses, commissions and discounts in respect of new issues, and to provide any premium on the redemption of any debentures. (S. 130(2).) It may also be used in a very restricted way to pay the premium on redemption of shares. (See p. 90.)

This is to prevent such premiums which are capital by nature from being paid away as dividends. Any balance on the share premium account must be shown in the balance sheet.

Section 130 in fact recognizes that the real capital of a company is the price which subscribers pay for its shares and not the somewhat artificial nominal value. This results, in effect, in an admission that shares are really of no par value. If no par value shares were issued the capital of the company would simply be the total paid for its shares by subscribers. This is known in the United States as the company's paid in capital. Where the whole of the issued price has not been paid, the total amount paid plus the total amount remaining to be paid is in the United States called the company's stated capital.

If it were possible to issue no par shares in England the accidental payment of dividends out of capital would automatically be precluded by the company's obligation to keep in hand assets worth at least the amount paid by subscribers plus the amount of the company's outstanding debts. However, until no par value shares are allowed the law can ensure that the issue price of the shares is not dissipated in paying dividends only by using the somewhat inelegant device of the share premium account.

The Companies Act 1985 requires share premiums to be credited to a share premium account whether the shares are issued for cash or otherwise. In consequence the Act always applies whether premiums are paid in cash or kind and so if a company issues shares for a consideration in kind which is worth more than the nominal value of the shares, a sum equal to the excess value of the consideration has to be transferred to share premium account. (*Henry Head & Co Ltd v Ropner Holdings Ltd*, 1952.[121]) (But see below.)

Share premiums—acquisition, mergers and group reconstructions

Sections 131–134 give relief, in certain circumstances, from the requirement to set up a share premium account under s. 130.

(a) Acquisitions and mergers

(i) *Acquisitions*. This involves a take-over where the predator company P makes an offer to the shareholders of the Victim company V either with or without the consent of the Board of V. The price offered is usually above the market price. If V is acquired, i.e. if there are sufficient acceptances from the shareholders of V, the investment of P in V must be shown in the books of P at its *true value*, i.e. the value of the consideration given. This has the effect of treating the reserves of V as pre-acquisition and therefore as undistributable and in particular pre-acquisition profits are locked up.

This position is unchanged by the 1985 Act and pre-acquisition profits must be locked up because if V pays a dividend to P out of pre-acquisition profits and P uses it to pay dividend to its shareholders P is returning the capital it used for the purchase of V's shares to its members because the pre-acquisition profits were represented in the price which P paid for V's shares.

(ii) *Mergers. Under s. 131* in the case of a merger between P and V involving a share for share exchange, e.g. P issues its equity shares to the members of V on a one for one basis, in exchange for the shares of the members of V, as a result of which P becomes the holder of 90 per cent or more of the equity shares of V then there is no need to value the investment in V at its true value. The value may simply be the nominal value of the shares exchanged and so no share premium account is created as was the case in *Henry Head* under the old law (see above). Thus the reserves of V need not be treated as pre-acquisition and pre-acquisition profits are not locked up.

The figure of 90 per cent must be achieved before s. 131 operates because it is at that figure that the law deems there has been a 'pooling of assets'. So far as accounting *practice* is concerned, reference should be made to the relevant Accounting Standard issued by the Accounting Standards Committee.

(b) Group reconstructions

Section 132 provides limited relief in the case of certain group reconstructions. The reconstructions to which the Act applies are those where the transactions are as follows—

(i) a wholly-owned subsidiary (the issuing company) has allotted some of its shares either to its holding company or to another wholly-owned subsidiary of its holding company;

(ii) the allotment is a consideration for the transfer to it of shares or any non-cash assets in another subsidiary of the holding company. This other subsidiary need not necessarily be wholly owned.

The purposes of reconstruction and the variety of changes that can be achieved by the use of the reconstruction sections of the Companies Act 1985 are further described in Chapter 15. (See pp. 377–99.)

However, let us assume that our holding company (H) holds 100 per cent of the shares in company A and 75 per cent of the shares in company B. A allots 1,000 £1 ordinary shares (valued at £6 per share) to H; in return H transfers its 75 per cent holding in B to A. If there was no relief in this situation A would have had to raise a share premium account in its books. However, under s. 132(2) A need only transfer to a share premium account an amount equal to the 'minimum premium value'.

This is the amount, if any, by which the base value of the shares in the subsidiary (B) exceeds the aggregate nominal value of the shares that the issuing company (A) allotted in consideration for the transfer (s. 132(3)1).

Base value is the lower of—

(a) the cost to the holding company (H) of the shares in B;

(b) the amount at which the shares of B were stated immediately prior to the transfer in the accounting records of H.

Thus if in our example the shares in B cost H £4,000 but are standing in the accounting records of H at £3,000 the base value is £3,000. The nominal value of the shares allotted by A is £1,000 so the minimum premium value is £2,000 and this must be transferred to A's share premium account, but not of course the true value of the consideration it received from B by allotting 1,000 shares to H.

Finally, it should be noted that the Act of 1985 imposes no obligation on a company to issue its shares at a premium when a premium could be obtained. Consequently, the issue of shares at par is valid even though a premium could have been obtained (*Hilder v Dexter* [1902] AC 474) but directors who fail to require subscribers to pay a premium which could have been obtained are guilty of breach of duty to the company and will be liable to pay the premium themselves as damages. (*Lowry v Consolidated African Selection Trust Ltd* [1940] 2 All ER 545.) Nevertheless, there are some exceptions to this ruling. For example, directors may issue shares at a price below their market value to existing shareholders in pursuance of a rights offer made to all the shareholders of the company, or to all the ordinary shareholders in proportion to the nominal values of their existing holdings. The reason for this is that all the shareholders concerned can avail themselves of the offer and if they do none of them will suffer a diminution of their percentage interest in the net assets or earnings of the company and consequently none of them will be harmed.

THE REGISTER OF MEMBERS

Section 352(1) to (3) requires every company to keep a register of its members. The register must contain the following information—

(i) the names and addresses of the members;

(ii) a statement of the shares held by each member, each share being distinguished by its number if it has one;

(iii) the amount paid or agreed to be considered as paid up on the shares of each member;

(iv) the date on which each person was entered in the register as a member;

(v) the date on which each person ceased to be a member.

Section 352 requires that where a company has more than one class of shareholders or stockholders the register must show to which class a member belongs and in the case of a company without a share capital having more than one class of members, the class to which the member belongs.

Failure to keep a register of members renders the company and every officer in default liable to a fine for each day of default for every day during which the default continues. (S. 352(5).) However, the duty of notifying changes of address is on the shareholders and the company is not required to trace shareholders where, for example, letters are returned or dividend warrants not encashed.

The register may be kept in any form, e.g. in the form of a loose leaf system, so long as proper precautions are taken to guard against falsification. (S. 722.) Section 723(1) allows the use of computers for company records, including the register of members, so long as the records can be reproduced in legible form. A company with more than 50 members must keep an index of its members, and if there is any alteration in the register, the index must also be altered within 14 days of such alteration. The above provisions do not apply if the register is kept in the form of an index. (S. 354.)

The register and index are to be kept at the registered office of the company, but if the register is made up elsewhere, then it may be kept at the place where it is made up. The index must be kept where the register is kept. (Ss. 353 and 354(3).) It is necessary to inform the Registrar of the whereabouts of the register if it is not kept at the registered office. (S. 353(2).)

Inspection of register

During business hours the register and the index must be kept open for inspection by any member free of charge, and by any other person on payment of a fee. The company must furnish either to a member or to any other person a copy of any part of the register, and may make a charge for this. If a request for a copy is made, the company must send the copy within ten days commencing on the day after that on which the company received the request. (S. 356(3).) If a company will not allow inspection of its register or give copies of it on request the company or any director or secretary who is responsible is guilty of an offence under s. 356(5). The person asking for inspection or a copy of the register can apply to the court for an order that the company will comply with his request. (S. 356(6).)

A person inspecting the register has no right himself to take extracts from or make copies of it (*Re Balaghat Co* [1901] 2 KB 665), and the right of inspection terminates on the commencement of winding up. (*Re Kent Coalfields Syndicate* [1898] 1 QB 754.) Any rights then existing are derived from the insolvency rules, and not from the Act, and may require an order of court.

A company may, if it gives notice by an advertisement in a newspaper circulating in the district in which its registered office is situated, close the register for any time not exceeding 30 days in each year. (S. 358.) This may be done to defer the entry of share transfers just prior to the annual general meeting at which a dividend is to be declared and shortly afterwards paid. It will also enable the company to prepare a list of its members as at a certain date in case a poll should be demanded at the annual general meeting.

Obsolete entries in the register

Section 352(6) provides that a company may now remove from the register any entry which relates to a former member where the person concerned has not been a member for at least 20 years.

Rectification of the register

The register of members is *prima facie* evidence of the matters which the Companies Act requires it to contain. (S. 361.)

Section 359 gives the court power to rectify the register if application is made to it where—

(*a*) the name of any person is without sufficient cause entered in or omitted from the register; or

(*b*) default is made, or unnecessary delay takes place, in entering on the register the fact that a person has ceased to be a member.

As well as rectification, the court may order the payment by the company of any damages sustained by any party aggrieved. (S. 359(2).) An order rectifying the register can be made even when the company is being wound up. (*Re Sussex Brick Co*, 1904.[122])

The circumstances set out in (*a*) and (*b*) above are not the only ones in which the court can order rectification. The power extends to all cases where a name stands on the register without cause. (*Burns v Siemens Bros Dynamo Works Ltd*, 1919.[123])

Notice of rectification must be given to the Registrar of Companies. (S. 359(4).)

Notice of trusts

Section 360, provides that no notice of any trust, express, implied, or constructive, shall be entered on the register of members of companies registered in England and Wales. The rule laid down by the section has two limbs—

(i) *The company is entitled to treat every person whose name appears on the register as the beneficial owner of the shares even though he may in fact hold them in trust for another.* Thus, if the company registers a transfer of shares held by a trustee, it is not liable to the beneficiaries under the trust, even though the sale of the shares by the trustee was fraudulent or in breach of the powers given to him in the trust instrument. (*Simpson v Molson's Bank*, 1895.[124])

(ii) *Where persons claim shares under equitable titles, the company is not made into a trustee if those persons merely serve notice on the company of the existence of their equitable claims.* (*Société Générale de Paris v Walker*, 1885.[125]) The correct method of protecting such an interest is by serving on the company a *stop notice* by the procedure already outlined. However, the section only protects the company; and where directors register a transfer, knowing it is being made in breach of trust or in fraud of some person having an equitable right, they may incur personal liability to the person injured.

If a trustee of shares is entered on the register, he is personally liable for the calls made by the company, though he can claim an indemnity to the extent of the trust property and, if this is not sufficient, from the beneficiaries personally. A company cannot put a beneficiary on the list of contributories in a winding up, though it can enforce the trustee's right of indemnity against the beneficiaries by the doctrine of *subrogation*. (*Per* James L J in *Re European Society Arbitration Acts* (1878) 8 Ch D 679.)

Where shares are purchased in the name of another person who has agreed to take the shares, the company cannot go behind the nominee to the beneficial owner in order to make him pay for the shares (*Re National Bank of Wales*, 1907[126]), though the company can apply for rectification to restore the name of the real owner to the register where the shares were applied for in a fictitious name, or the name of a person who had never agreed to take the shares. (*Re Hercules Insurance Co, Pugh and Sharman's Case*, 1872.[127])

A company claiming a *lien* on its shares will be affected by a notice of any charge which arose prior to the debt in respect of which the company's lien is being exercised. This is not regarded as a notice of trust, but is more by way of a notice of lien as between one trader and another. (*Bradford Banking Co v Briggs*, 1886.[108])

Table A, Reg 5 provides: 'Except as required by law, no person shall be recognized by the company as holding any share upon any trust and (except as otherwise provided by the articles or by law) the company shall not be bound by or recognize any interest in any share except an absolute right to the entirety thereof in the holder.'

Dominion register

A company which carries on business in some part of Northern Ireland or any part of Her Majesty's dominions outside the UK as listed in Sched 14, Part I, the Isle of Man and the Channel Islands may keep an overseas branch register of members resident in the country where it carries on business. (S. 362(1).) It seems that the purpose of such a register is to facilitate the transfer of the shares of these members. The Registrar of Companies must be informed of the situation of the office, where the overseas branch register is kept within 14 days of its opening, and must receive the same notice of its closure. (S. 362 and Sched 14, Part II, para 1(1) and (2).)

The overseas branch register is considered part of the company's main register and must be kept in the same manner. Copies of all entries on the register must be sent to the company's registered office as soon as possible after they are made, and the company must keep a duplicate of the register at the same place as its principal register. Rectification of the Dominion register is achieved by applications to the appropriate court in the place in which the register is kept. (S. 362, Sched 14, Part II.)

Termination of membership

Termination of membership is complete when the name of a former member is removed from the register. This may occur by—

(i) transfer of the shares to a purchaser or by way of gift (subject to liability to be put on the 'B' list of members for one year if the company goes into liquidation) (see further p. 418);

(ii) forfeiture, surrender, or a sale by the company under its lien;

(iii) the taking of a share warrant, though certain rights of membership may still be conferred by the articles;

(iv) redemption or purchase of shares by the company;

(v) the registration of a trustee in bankruptcy, or by his disclaimer of the shares;

(vi) death of the member;

(vii) rescission of the contract to take the shares arising out of fraud or misrepresentation in the prospectus, or by reason of irregular allotment;

(viii) dissolution of the company by winding up or amalgamation or reconstruction under s. 110, Insolvency Act 1986 (see also p. 379);

(ix) compulsory acquisition under s. 429 (see further p. 392).

SUBSTANTIAL AND NOMINEE SHAREHOLDINGS

As we have seen, the register of members merely gives the identity of the person in whose name the shares are registered. No indication is given of any interests in the shares which persons other than the registered holder might have. Indeed under s. 360 no notice of trust is to be entered on the register of members of a company registered in England. Where share warrants are in issue the position is, of course, worse since the names of the holders at any point of time are unknown, there being no form of registration.

This situation is capable of abuse. For example, it enables directors to traffic in the securities of their companies without this being known, or someone secretly to acquire control or a sizeable holding on which to base a bid for control. The Companies Act deals with this problem as follows—

(a) *Section 323* makes it a criminal offence for directors and their spouses and infant children (s. 327) to deal in options to buy or sell shares in, or debentures of, their companies or of any company in the group (i.e. the company, any subsidiary company, its holding company, or any other subsidiary of the latter), except where the shares or debentures are not quoted on the Stock Exchange. These provisions prevent a bad form of abuse in terms of insider dealing under which directors with inside information do not even buy shares in the company or the group, merely taking an option to buy or sell at a fixed price while waiting for the best time to buy or sell.

(b) *Sections 324, 325, 326, and 328* make provision for disclosure in relation to the purchase and sale of shares by directors.

Directors and shadow directors (see p. 223) have to notify the company in writing within 5 days of acquiring or disposing of any beneficial interest in shares or debentures of companies in the group. Interests of a spouse or infant child of a director are treated as interests of the director, as are interests held behind a nominee. Under s. 329 a quoted company must notify the Stock Exchange by close of business on the day following notification by the director.

The company must maintain a register of directors' interests and dealings and must enter thereon the information received within three days. This register is during business hours to be open to inspection by members without charge and by others on payment of a fee and copies may be obtained.

(c) *Part VI of the Companies Act 1985 also deals with disclosure of interests in shares. Under s. 198* a person is obliged to notify a *public company* of his *known* interests in the voting shares of that company *whether the company's shares are listed or not.* The notifiable percentage is under s. 201 5 per cent or more of the aggregate nominal value of the company's voting shares. Where the voting share capital is divided into different classes of shares the obligation to notify arises whenever a person is interested in 5 per cent or more of any class of shares (s. 198(2)). Under s. 200 notification must also be made where having reached the 5 per cent holding or more there is a *known* increase or decrease of more than 1 per cent in the interest.

Notification must therefore be made whenever a known change brings about a known increase above or below 5 per cent or a known increase or decrease of more than 1 per cent takes place in an interest exceeding 5 per cent.

No further notification is required once the interest is below 5 per cent unless and until it reaches 5 per cent or more again. Under ss. 203 and 208 a person has an interest if (i) he is the owner of the shares; (ii) his spouse or minor child owns them; (iii) a company in which he controls one-third of the voting power owns them; (iv) he is a beneficiary under a trust over the shares; (v) he owns them jointly with another (each owner is deemed to be interested in the entire holding); (vi) he has a stock exchange contract to buy the shares; (vii) he is a member of a 'concert party' (see below).

Under s. 202 the company must be notified within five days of the change and under s. 211(3) the company must record the details in a register of interests in shares within three days of receiving the notification. The register must be available for inspection without charge by any member or by any other person. (S. 219.)

Under s. 216 a person who fails to notify as required or gives false or misleading information is liable to a fine or imprisonment or both.

(d) *Concert parties.* A major difficulty which had arisen under previous disclosure legislation of the kind set out above was that several persons had held a non-disclosable interest, say, 4.9 per cent of a company's voting shares and had acted in concert, e.g. voted together, so that a position of strength had been built up in the company without the need for disclosure.

The Companies Act 1985 deals with this situation in ss. 204, 205 and 206, and the relevant provisions are set out below:

A concert party is defined as an agreement between two or more persons, whether legally binding or not, *to acquire shares in a public company*, and the agreement must include a provision for that. The agreement must also include provisions containing restrictions in respect of the use of the shares, e.g. as regards voting and disposal. Finally the shares must have been acquired because the person who bought them was doing so in order to carry out his agreement with the other or others.

Thus a group of shareholders who band together to oppose a particular plan of the board are not a concert party and therefore not subject to the provisions in the 1985 Act relating to concert parties.

If the three criteria for a concert party are established the obligation to notify the company of the *collective holding* at 5 per cent and of 1 per cent increases and decreases in an interest exceeding 5 per cent falls upon each member of the concert party and each member has an obligation to notify the other members of the concert party of his holding whether acquired under the agreement or not so that each is in a position to disclose the collective holding. The parties can appoint one of their number as an agent for the purposes of notification. The obligation to notify must be carried out within five days and there are criminal penalties for failing to do so. Once a concert party is established, the collective holding is *all* the voting shares held by each member and not merely those acquired in pursuance of the agreement.

(e) *Power of public company to investigate interests in shares.* Under ss. 212–216 a public company may make enquiries of *any person* (not merely a member) whom it knows or has reasonable cause to believe to be *interested* in any of its voting shares either at the present time or at any time during the preceding three years. This applies whether or not the company's shares are listed or dealt in on the unlisted securities market. It embraces present members, past members during the preceding three years, and persons, e.g. those holding behind a bank nominee who have never been registered as members. Failure to respond to an enquiry by a person who is or was interested or the giving of an incorrect response may result in a criminal prosecution leading to a fine and/or imprisonment. In addition the company may apply to the court for an order imposing the restrictions of Part XV (see further, p. 374) on the shares involved. These restrictions prevent transfer, voting, dividend payments, and the receipt of rights issues.

If the company (in practice the board) is not willing to commence an investigation members who hold at least 10 per cent of the paid-up voting shares may *require the board* to exercise the powers of investigation. There are fines and/or imprisonment on any officer of the company in default if the company is not caused to exercise the powers of investigation.

In addition, if the company fails to exercise its powers of investigation the 10 per cent (or more) requisitionists may apply to the court for the restrictions of Part XV to be put on the shares.

(f) *The role of Department of Trade and Industry investigations.* It should be noted that s. 446 confers a power on the Department of Trade and Industry to appoint an inspector to investigate possible breaches by the directors of their duties under s. 324, i.e. the duty to disclose share and debenture holdings in the company.

As regards the secret acquisition of control of companies, mention should also be made here of ss. 442–445 which give the DoTI power to investigate the ownership of a company's shares. These provisions will be dealt with at greater length in Chapter 14, but the sections have been used quite extensively in recent times in order to ascertain whether a person operating through nominees has acquired sufficient shares in a company to give rise to the making of a bid for the remainder as is required by the City Code, once 30 per cent of the voting shares have been acquired. (See further Chapter 15.)

THE ANNUAL RETURN

Every company which has a share capital must make *every year* a return to the Registrar of Companies. This return is called the annual return. (S. 363.) No annual return is required in the year of incorporation, nor if the company is not required to hold an annual general meeting during the following year, in that year either. A company is required to hold its first annual general meeting within 18 months of its incorporation, but if it was incorporated in (say) November, 1986, it would not have to hold an annual general meeting in 1986 or in 1987, but would be required to hold one not later than May 1988.

The annual return is required to contain the particulars set out in Sched 15, and to be in the form set out in the Schedule to the Companies (Annual Return) Regulations, 1983 (SI 1983/1023). *The particulars to be set out are—*

(i) The address of the registered office.

(ii) The place where the register of members and the register of debenture holders are kept if not at the registered office.

(iii) A summary distinguishing between shares issued for cash and shares issued as fully or partly paid up for a consideration other than cash, and specifying also calls made and received or unpaid, commissions paid or discounts allowed on shares or debentures, shares forfeited and surrendered, and share warrants issued or surrendered.

(iv) The amount of the indebtedness of the company in respect of all mortgages and charges which are required to be registered with the Registrar.

(v) *The annual return must also contain* a list of the names and addresses of all persons who on the fourteenth day after the annual general meeting are members, and of persons who have ceased to be members since the date of the last return. It must also state the number of shares held by each at the date of the return, specifying shares transferred since the date of the last return, and the dates on which the transfers were registered. If the names of the members are not in alphabetical order, there must be an index.

A complete return of the members and their holdings need only be made every third year and in the intervening two years only changes in membership need be detailed. (S. 363(5).) Where shares have been converted into stock, the same particulars of the stock must be given.

(vi) *The return must also give the same particulars of the directors and the secretary as are required to be entered in the register of directors and secretaries.*

The annual return must be made out as at the 14th day after the company's annual general meeting and a copy of it signed by a director and secretary must be sent to the Registrar of Companies within 42 days after that meeting. (S. 365(1) and (2).) Thus if the AGM is held after, say, 17 December 1985, and the return is not filed until 1986, a further return will have to be filed in 1986 as the 1986 return. If the annual return is not made, the company and every officer in default is liable to a fine.

Under s. 713 any member or creditor may make application to the court for a direction that the company shall make a return and the company is liable to pay the applicant's costs. In addition, the directors may become disqualified if they persist in failing to file the annual return or other documents. (See p. 228.)

It is often convenient and still in fact usual to lay the annual accounts before the annual general meeting and to deliver the accounts to the Registrar with the annual return, but the accounts requirements are, nevertheless, quite separate. (See further, p. 345.)

CONTROL OF THE COMPANY BY ITS MEMBERS

Although many functions are delegated to the directorate, the eventual power and control in a company rests with those shareholders who can command a majority of the voting power. Thus a person or group of persons controlling three-quarters of the votes would have complete control of the company, and a little more than half the votes would give almost complete control.

The principle of majority rule is well established and is emphasized in the matter of litigation by the rule in *Foss v Harbottle*, 1843. (See p. 527.) Generally it does little harm since most companies are managed fairly, even if at times there is not due concern for the rights of minorities which might lead to oppression. The problem is at its greatest in private companies because the shares of such companies are not listed on the Stock Exchange, the protection of the Stock Exchange rules is not available, and there is rarely any press comment on their activities.

There are a number of provisions in the Companies Act 1985 which may assist minorities and these will now be considered.

Rights of minorities to requisition meetings

The articles of a company usually provide that, apart from annual general meetings, meetings of the company can be convened by the directors whenever they think fit. The directors are, therefore, seldom under any obligation to call general meetings at which minority grievances can be put forward. However, s. 368 provides a method by which members holding not less than one-tenth of such of the company's paid-up capital as carries voting rights at the general meetings of the company can requisition a meeting. Thus, where a company has 200,000 £1 A ordinary shares, 50p paid, and (say) 50,000 B shares of £1 each, fully-paid, and all the shares carry voting rights, the requisitionists must have paid up on their shares, whether A or B ordinary one-tenth of £150,000, i.e. £15,000. Where the company does not have a share capital members of the company representing not less than one-tenth of the total voting rights of all the members having a right to vote at general meetings of the company may make a requisition.

The requisitionists must deposit at the company's registered office a signed requisition stating the objects for which they wish a meeting of the company to be held. The directors must then convene an *extraordinary general meeting*, and if they have not done so within 21 days after the deposit of the requisition, the requisitionists, or any of them representing more than one-half of their total voting rights, may themselves convene the meeting so long as they do so within three months of the requisition. The requisitionists can recover reasonable expenses so incurred from the company, and the company may in turn recover these from the fees of the defaulting directors.

The company's articles cannot deprive the members of the right to requisition a meeting under s. 368, although they can provide that a *smaller number* of persons may requisition, e.g. one-twentieth. An article would not be effective if it required a larger number than one-tenth. Section 368 is defective in the sense that although the directors are required to *call* the meeting they need not *hold* the meeting within any particular limit of time. Thus, they would appear to be within the section if they call the meeting for, say, six months hence, even though this might frustrate the purpose of the requisitionists, since once the directors have *convened* the meeting the requisitionists cannot do so. That this is so is confirmed by the unreported decision of Nourse J in *Re Windward Islands Enterprises (UK)* [1982] CLY 306.

The Jenkins Committee recommended that the requisitionists should be empowered to call the meeting themselves if the directors call the meeting to be held later than 28 days after the notice convening it was sent out. If this provision had become law it would limit the period of delay which the directors could impose to seven weeks from the date when the requisition was deposited with them.

However, *Reg 37* of *Table A* provides that the directors may call general meetings and on the requisition of members pursuant to the provisions of the Act, shall forthwith proceed to convene an extra-ordinary general meeting for a date not later than eight weeks after receipt of the requisition. This tightens up the provisions of s. 368 for those companies which have adopted *Table A* or have a similar article.

Section 370(3) provides that two or more members holding not less than one-tenth of the issued share capital of the company, or if there is no issued share capital, not less than 5 per cent in number of the members may call a meeting, *but the section has effect only in so far as the company's articles do not provide to the contrary*. Its main purpose is to allow members to call general meetings where there are no directors, or not enough to form a quorum, and *Table A, Reg 37*, confines its exercise to that sort of situation. The relevant part of the Regulation provides: 'If there are not within the United Kingdom sufficient directors to call a general meeting, any director or any member of the company may call a general meeting.'

Right of minorities to requisition members' resolutions at the annual general meeting

Section 376 provides that members representing not less than one-twentieth of the total voting rights of all members, or 100 or more members holding shares in the company on which there has been paid up an average sum of not less than £100 per member, can, by making a written requisition to the company, *compel the company—*
    (*a*) to give to members who are entitled to receive notice of the

next annual general meeting, *notice of any resolution* which may be properly moved and which they intend to move at that meeting; *and*

(*b*) to circulate to members who are entitled to have notice of any general meeting sent to them, any *statement* of not more than 1,000 words with respect to the matter referred to in any proposed resolution or the business to be dealt with at the meeting.

The amount which has been paid up on the shares is not material so, assuming that a company has 300,000 £1 ordinary shares 50p paid and 100,000 £1 preference shares fully paid all with voting rights, then the requisition could be made by the holders of 80,000 shares. If made by 100 requisitionists, then the amount paid up on their shares if added together would have to come to at least £10,000.

The requisition under s. 376 must be *signed* by the requisitionists, and must under s. 377 be *deposited* at the registered office of the company—

(i) if the requisition requires notice of a resolution, *not less than six weeks* before the meeting; and

(ii) if no resolution is required, as in (*b*) above, *not less than one week* before the meeting.

There must be tendered with the requisition a sum reasonably adequate to meet the company's expenses in giving effect to the requisition, otherwise the company is not bound to act upon it. All expenses must be borne by the requisitionists themselves, unless at the meeting the company otherwise resolves. The original recommendation in the report of the Cohen Committee said that the sum should be enough to cover the reasonable expenses of making copies of the resolution and/or statement to be sent to the members. Section 377(1)(*b*) states that there must be deposited or tendered with the requisition a sum reasonably sufficient to meet the company's expenses in giving effect thereto. Although there is no case law on s. 377(1)(*b*), this could be interpreted to mean the expenses of the whole meeting, e.g. the cost of printing the notice and proxy cards and in a large company this could well be in the region of £15,000/£20,000. Thus *bona fide* requisitionists could be put off by a board which chose to interpret s.377(1)(*b*) in that way because they just could not deposit enough money.

The company is not bound by s. 376 if the court is satisfied that its provisions are being abused in order to secure needless publicity for defamatory or abusive matter. (S. 377(3).) If the company calls an annual general meeting less than six weeks after the deposit of the requisition, the section is nevertheless deemed to have been complied with. (S. 377(2).) This is to prevent the directors defeating the rule as to notice by calling an annual general meeting before the notice has run its course.

Right to control the management of the company's business

The articles of a company (see, e.g. *Reg 70, Table A*) usually provide that the company's business shall be managed by the directors, and where this is the case, the company in general meeting cannot ordinarily deal with matters relating to such management. (*Scott v Scott*, 1943, see p. 545.) The following are ways in which the members can control the directors in the matter of management—

(*a*) *by altering the company's articles so as to cut down the directors' powers* (this would require a *special resolution* which a minority would not be able to obtain); *or*

(*b*) *by refusing to re-elect directors of whose actions they disapprove.* This course of action would require an ordinary resolution, i.e. voting power in excess of that possessed by a minority; *or*

(*c*) *by recourse to the provisions of s. 303*, which provides that a company may by *ordinary resolution* remove a director before the expiration of his period of office, notwithstanding anything in the articles or in any agreement between the company and him. Such a resolution requires *special notice* of 28 days to be given to the company of the intention to propose it. The section does not deprive a director so removed of any claim he may have for damages or compensation payable to him as a result of the termination of his appointment. (S. 303(5).) Section 303 would be satisifed by a majority of one, but a small minority would be unlikely to succeed in carrying such a resolution, and removal may be impossible if the directors have weighted voting rights on the resolution to remove them. (*Bushell v Faith*, 1969, see p. 542.)

In addition, *Pedley v Inland Waterways* [1977] 1 All ER 209 (see p. 271) decides that a minority wishing to remove a director must be of sufficient size to comply with s. 376 (if the directors are to be compelled to put a resolution on the agenda for removal at an AGM), or s. 368 (if the directors are to be required to call an extraordinary general meeting to consider the removal) (see further p. 271).

The topic of division of power between those who have a majority in general meeting and the board is considered at p. 231.

Other minority protections

There are a number of other sections in the Companies Act 1985 which enable a number of shareholders to defy the majority. For example, under s. 5 dissentient holders of 15 per cent of the issued shares can apply for cancellation of an alteration of objects. (See p. 65.) Furthermore, under s. 127 where class rights are varied in pursuance of a clause in the memorandum or articles, or under s. 125, dissentient holders of 15 per cent of the issued shares of the class can apply for cancellation of the variation. (See p. 95.) Furthermore, under s. 54, where a public company passes a special resolution to re-register as a private company, holders of not less than 5 per cent in nominal value of the company's issued share capital or any class thereof; or not less than 5 per cent in number of the members of the company, if the company is not limited by shares; or not less than 50 of the company's members may apply to the court to cancel the resolution. (See p. 341.)

Other examples are the right given by s. 157 to 10 per cent in nominal value of the company's issued share capital or any class of it or 10 per cent of the members if the company is not limited by shares, to object to the court where a private company gives financial assistance for the purchase of its own shares (see further p. 169); the right given by s. 176 to any member who did not consent or vote in favour of the special resolution approving the purchase by a private company of its own shares partly from capital to apply to the court for the cancellation of the resolution (see further p. 109); the misfeasance proceedings under s. 212 of the Insolvency Act 1986 which a member may bring against defaulting officers when the company is in liquidation (see further p. 419).

The rights of a minority to petition for a winding up; to petition the court under s. 459 and to seek a DoTI inspection are dealt with below.

Winding up on a petition by a minority

The court has a jurisdiction under s. 122(1)(g), Insolvency Act 1986 to wind up a company on the petition of a minority on the ground that it is 'just and equitable' to do so.

This ground is subjected to a flexible interpretation by the courts. In the context of minority rights, however, orders have been made where the managing director who represented the majority shareholder interests in his management of the company refused, e.g. to produce accounts or pay dividends (*Loch v John Blackwood Ltd*, 1924[128]) and where, in the case of a small company, formed or continued on the basis of a personal relationship, involving mutual confidence and which is in essence a partnership, the person petitioning is excluded from management participation and the circumstances are such as would justify the dissolution of a partnership. (*Ebrahimi v Westbourne Galleries*, 1972[129] and *Re A and B C Chewing Gum Ltd*, 1975[130] but see *Re a Company*, 1983, p. 521.)

The courts were at one time reluctant to wind up a company on the petition of a minority on the just and equitable ground, but by s. 125, Insolvency Act 1986 the court must make an order if the petitioners have made out their case. The section thus cuts down the area of judicial discretion in the matter, while making it clear that the court need not make the order if it is of opinion both that some other remedy is available to the petitioner and that he is acting unreasonably in seeking to have the company wound up instead of pursuing that other remedy. (See *Re a Company*, 1983, p. 521.)

Statutory protection of members against unfair prejudice

It will be appreciated that in many cases the winding up of the company will not benefit the minority shareholders because, amongst other things, the break-up value of the assets may be small and the only persons available to purchase the assets may be the majority share-holders whose activities have forced the minority to seek a remedy. In view of this the Companies Act 1985 provides in Part XVII, i.e. ss. 459–461 for a different kind of redress.

The provisions of Part XVII are as follows—

1. Under s. 459 any member of a company may apply to the court by petition for an order under Part XVII on the ground that the affairs of the company are being or have been conducted in a manner which is unfairly prejudicial to the interests of some part of the members (including at least himself), or that any actual or proposed act or omission of the company (including an act or omission on its behalf) is or would be so prejudicial.
2. Section 460 provides that if in the case of any company—
   (*a*) the Secretary of State has received a report under s. 437 (inspec-tors' reports, see p. 372) or exercised his powers under ss. 447 or 448 (inspection of company's books and papers, see p. 376), and
   (*b*) it seems to him that any ground exists by reason of which a member could apply to the court under s. 459 above he may himself, in addition to or instead of presenting a petition for the winding up of the company under s. 440, apply to the court by a petition for an order under this section.
3. Under s. 461(1) if the court is satisfied that a petition under Part XVII is well founded it may make such order as it thinks fit for giving relief in respect of the matters complained of.
4. Section 461(2) sets out some particular areas in which the court may make orders and states that the court may—
   (*a*) regulate the conduct of the company's affairs in the future;
   (*b*) restrain the company from doing or continuing any act com-plained of by the petitioner or require the company to do an act which the petitioner has complained it has omitted to do;
   (*c*) authorize civil proceedings to be brought in the name and on behalf of the company by such person or persons and on such terms as the court may direct;

(*d*) provide for the purchase of the shares of any member of the company by other members or by the company itself and, in the case of a purchase by the company itself, the reduction of the company's capital accordingly.

5. Under s. 461(3) where the court makes an order under this section which alters or adds to the memorandum or articles of the company, then the company concerned shall not have power without leave of the court to make any further alteration in or addition to the memorandum and articles inconsistent with the provisions of the court's order. Under s. 461(4) the court's order itself makes the alteration as if it had been duly made by the members in accordance with the provisions of the Act for altering these instruments.

6. An office copy of any order made under Part XVII altering or adding to or giving leave to alter or add to a company's memorandum or articles must within 14 days from the making of the order be delivered by the company to the Registrar of Companies for registration. If this is not done the company and every officer is liable to a default fine. (S. 461(5).)

7. Under s. 459(2) the provisions of Part XVII apply to a person who is not a member of a company but to whom shares in the company have been transferred or transmitted by operation of law and references to a member or members in the section are to be construed accordingly, thus a petition under the section may now be presented by the personal representatives of a deceased member or his trustee in bankruptcy.

In order to interpret Part XVII, examples may be taken from decisions under s. 210 of the Companies Act 1948 (now repealed) which would presumably be decided in the same way under Part XVII. *Re Harmer*, 1958[131] provides an example of an order under s. 461(2)(*a*) above and shows also the power of the court to make alterations in the company's constitution under 5 above. *Scottish C.W.S. v Meyer*, 1958[132] provides an example of an order which could be made under s. 461(2)(*d*) above.

Section 210, Companies Act 1948 and Part XVII, Companies Act 1985 compared

It may be useful, also, to examine some of the cases in which the petitioner failed to get a remedy from the court under s. 210 of the 1948 Act since Part XVII may not be a multipurpose weapon able to deal with all kinds of prejudicial conduct.

Thus the decision in the *Westbourne*[129] case would, according to Lord Grantchester QC in *Re a Company (No 004475, 1982), 1983* (see

p. 526), be unaltered because the conduct under Part XVII must be prejudicial *to the interests of members as such* and not to the interests of persons as directors. On the other hand, Vinelott J in *Re a Company*, 1983 (see p. 521), seems to have accepted that it might be prejudicial to the interests of a member that he had been expelled from management. This view was affirmed by Nourse J in *Re R A Noble (Clothing) Ltd*, 1983 (see p. 522), *Re Bird Precision Bellows*, 1984 (p. 523), and again in *Re London School of Electronics*, 1985 (p. 523).

However, since Part XVII is not set in the context of winding up, as was s. 210, it should not now be a ground for refusing to make an order, as was done in *Re Bellador Silk Ltd* [1965] 1 All ER 667, that the member cannot show that if the company were wound up there would be surplus assets. This is a requirement for a member petitioning under s. 122(1)(g), Insolvency Act 1986 but is not a requirement of Part XVII which merely states that the petition must be 'well founded'. Section 210 of the 1948 Act was couched in language which suggested that it was part of the court's winding up jurisdiction in the sense that it said that if a winding up would be prejudicial to a minority, but the circumstances were otherwise such that a winding up could take place, the court might instead make an order to relieve the oppressed minority under s. 210. Now, even if the company was in liquidation, the court could order the purchase of the Part XVII petitioner's shares by those in default at a price which would compensate him for injuries suffered.

Perhaps the greatest advance under Part XVII will be the possibility of bringing claims on behalf of the company against its directors for mismanagement. Negligence was not oppression for the purpose of s. 210 of the 1948 Act. However, negligence may give rise to unfair prejudice under Part XVII. Thus in *Re Five Minute Car Wash Service Ltd* [1966] 1 WLR 745, the petitioner, who was a minority shareholder, asked that the court should order the respondent shareholders to purchase his shares under s. 210 of the 1948 Act. He said that the respondents, and in particular a man named Mr Evison who was the major shareholder and its chairman and managing director, had lost some £200,000 in a period of five years by mismanagement such as the persistent non-payment of accounts which affected the company's goodwill, the buying of untested equipment and failure to remove incompetent staff. Mr Justice Buckley held that these allegations of mismanagement did not amount to oppression and refused relief. Negligence may be 'unfair prejudice' under Part XVII. However, negligent management normally affects *all* the members not just *part*, as s. 459 requires (see *re Carrington Viyella plc* (1983), *Financial Times*, 16 February) so there may be no claim under Part XVII.

The Jenkins Committee and Part XVII

Part XVII results from recommendations made by the Jenkins Committee which advocated the repeal of s. 210 of the 1948 Act and the substitution of new statutory arrangements. It is of value, therefore, to consider what sort of conduct the Jenkins Committee thought would be 'unfairly prejudicial'. They mentioned the following—

(a) directors appointing themselves to paid posts within the company at excessive rates of remuneration, thus depriving the members of a dividend or an adequate dividend;

(b) directors refusing to register the personal representatives of a deceased member so that, in the absence of a specific provision in the articles, they cannot vote, as part of a scheme to make the personal representatives sell the shares to the directors at an inadequate price;

(c) the issue of shares to directors and others on advantageous terms;

(d) failure of directors to declare dividends on non-cumulative preference shares held by a minority.

A general comment

Part XVII allows the court to restrain the doing of any act which covers *proposed conduct*. It is also clear that 'unfair prejudice' could result from *an isolated act*. A course of conduct is not necessary as it was under s. 210, where it was necessary to prove 'oppression'. The reference in Part XVII to 'omission', i.e. failure to act, is useful if the directors have consistently refused to declare dividends although distributable profits have been made. Furthermore, it would appear from s. 461(2)(b) that the court may *issue a prohibitory injunction* to prevent conduct unfairly prejudicial, or a *mandatory injunction* to compel performance of some positive act, e.g. to relieve the unfairly prejudicial situation.

Section 461(2)(c) is interesting because it allows the court to authorize civil proceedings to be brought in the company's name. *The action will not, therefore, be derivative* and clearly any proceeds of such an action will accrue to the company. The remedy will be useful where the unfairly prejudicial conduct is causing damage to the company and inflicting harm on the minority indirectly. It may enable actions to be brought in the company's name for directors' breach of fiduciary duty (see further p. 253), and negligence, though there is doubt since these matters affect all the members. (See re *Carrington Viyella plc*.)

To what extent s. 461(2)(c) has made the common law exceptions to the rule in *Foss v Harbottle*, 1843 (see p. 197) redundant in favour of an application under the sub-section, depends upon its interpretation in case law as this comes along. Certainly, it is not intended to overrule

Foss by allowing a minority to bring a claim for the company where the wrongful act has been approved by at least 51 per cent of the members in a *bona fide* manner, i.e. as where those committing the wrongful act are not in control of general meetings.

The major case law so far

In *Re a Company (No 004475 of 1982)*, 1983[133] Lord Grantchester QC held that no prejudice arose under what is now Part XVII of the 1985 Act simply because the directors of a company refuse to exercise their power to buy the company's shares; nor because they fail to put into effect a scheme which would have entitled the petitioners to sell their shares at a higher price than they might have been able to otherwise; nor because they proposed to dissipate the company's liquid resources by investing them in a partly-owned subsidiary. Lord Grantchester also said that it would usually be necessary for a member claiming unfair prejudice to show that his shares had been seriously diminished in value. However, in *Re R A Noble (Clothing) Ltd*, 1983 (see p. 522) Nourse J said that the jurisdiction under Part XVII was not limited to such a case and that diminution in the value of shares was not essential. In *Re Garage Door Associates* [1984] 1 All ER 434 Mervyn Davies J held that a member could present a petition for a winding up on the just and equitable ground *and* petition for the purchase of his shares under Part XVII. Such a procedure is not an abuse of the process of the court.

In *Re Bird Precision Bellows*, 1984 (see p. 523), and again in *Re London School of Electronics*, 1985 (see p. 523), Nourse J said that the removal of a member from the board was unfairly prejudicial conduct within what is now Part XVII. He made an order for the purchase of the shares of the petitioners in both cases by the majority shareholders and decided that in valuing the shares there should be no discount in the price because the holdings were minority holdings, unless the minority were in some way to blame for the situation giving rise to the alleged unfair prejudice. However, Nourse J did decide in *Re London School of Electronics*, 1985 (see p. 523), that there was no overriding requirement under what is now Part XVII that the petitioner should come to court with clean hands.

In *Re R A Noble (Clothing) Ltd*, 1983 (see p. 522), Nourse J decided that a director who had been excluded from management could claim unfair prejudice but not in the particular circumstances of the case because his exclusion was to a large extent due to his own disinterest in the company's affairs so that the other members of the board felt that they had to manage without him.

195

Department of Trade investigations

Minority shareholders may be able to avail themselves of those provisions of the Companies Act 1985, which provide for a Department of Trade and Industry investigation of the company's affairs.

The Act provides that the Department may appoint an inspector to investigate and report on the affairs of a company—

(a) in the case of *a company having a share capital*, on the application of at least 200 members *or* of members holding at least one-tenth of the shares issued (s. 431(2)(a)); and

(b) in the case of *a company not having a share capital*, on the application of at least one-fifth of the members on the register of members. (S. 431(2)(b).)

Any application must be supported by such evidence as the Department of Trade may require to show that there is good reason for the investigation (s. 431(3)), and the Department may require the applicant to give security for payment of the costs of the inspection in any amount not exceeding £5,000. (S. 431(4).)

A single complainant may also ask the Department to investigate the company's affairs under s. 432 if he can show that there are circumstances suggesting—

(i) that the company's affairs are being or have been conducted with intent to defraud its creditors or the creditors of any other person, or otherwise for a fraudulent or unlawful purpose, or in a manner which is unfairly prejudicial to some part of its members; *or*

(ii) that any actual or proposed act or omission of the company (including an act or omission on its behalf) is or would be so prejudicial, or that the company was formed for any fraudulent or unlawful purpose; *or*

(iii) that persons concerned with the company's formation or the management of its affairs have in connection therewith been guilty of fraud, misfeasance or other misconduct towards it or towards its members; *or*

(iv) that the company's members have not been given all the information with respect to its affairs which they might reasonably expect.

If from the inspector's report it appears that it is expedient in the public interest that the company should be wound up the Department of Trade and Industry may present a petition to the court under s. 440 for the winding up of the company on the ground that it is *just and equitable* to do so, or for an order under s. 460 to re-arrange the company's affairs satisfactorily under the unfair prejudice provisions of Part XVII.

Under s. 442, 200 members or the holders of one-tenth of the issued shares can apply to the Department of Trade and Industry for an investigation as to the ownership of the company. This provision relating to ownership of a company is, of course, directed at nominee holdings. It should also be mentioned that s. 446 confers a power on the Department of Trade and Industry to appoint an inspector to investigate possible breaches by the directors of their duty under s. 324, and under ss. 212–216 a public company may make enquiries of any person (not merely a member) whom it knows or has reasonable cause to believe to be interested in its voting shares. (See further p. 183.)

The above provisions regarding inspection have not worked too well in practice. The Department of Trade and Industry has been reluctant to appoint an inspector because such an appointment can have a serious effect on public confidence in the company even if the report is satisfactory. It is notable, for example, that Mr Moir (see *Wallersteiner v Moir*, 1974[112]) had in the course of a long legal battle sought in vain the assistance of the Department of Trade and Industry.

THE RULE IN *FOSS v HARBOTTLE*

The rule in *Foss v Harbottle*, 1843[134] states that in order to redress a wrong done to a company or to the property of the company, or to enforce rights of the company, the proper plaintiff is the company itself, and the court will not ordinarily entertain an action brought on behalf of the company by a shareholder.

Basis of the rule

Four major principles seem to be at the basis of the rule as the decided cases show—

1. *The right of the majority to rule.* The court has said in some of the cases that an action by a single shareholder cannot be entertained because the feeling of the majority of the members has not been tested, and they may be prepared, if asked, to waive their right to sue. Thus the company can only sue (*a*) if the directors pass a resolution to that effect where the power is delegated to them; or (*b*) if the company expresses its desire to sue by an ordinary resolution in general meeting, whether the power is delegated to the directors or not, since the power of the members to bring the company into court as a plaintiff is concurrent with that of the directors, and if the members wish to bring the company into court and the directors do not, the wish of the members by ordinary resolution will prevail.

2. *The company is a legal person.* The court has also said from time to time that since a company is a *persona at law*, the action is vested in it, and cannot be brought by a single member.

3. *The prevention of a multiplicity of actions.* This situation could occur if each individual member was allowed to commence an action in respect of a wrong done to the company. See James L J in *Gray v Lewis* (1873) 8 Ch App 1035 at p. 1051—a judgment which is particularly supportive of the multiplicity problem.

4. *The court's order may be made ineffective.* It should be noted that the court order could be overruled by an ordinary resolution of members in a subsequent general meeting. As Mellish L J said in *Mac-Dougall v Gardiner* (1875) 1 Ch D 13 at p. 25, '... if the thing complained of is a thing which in substance the majority of the company are entitled to do ... there can be no use in having a litigation about it, the ultimate end of which is only that a meeting has to be called, and then ultimately the majority gets its wishes'.

The decision of Plowman J in *Bentley-Stevens v Jones*, 1974[135] is an example of this approach.

Acts infringing the personal rights of shareholders

These actions are not so much genuine exceptions to the rule in *Foss*[134]; they are more in the nature of situations which are outside it. Thus in *Pender v Lushington*, 1877[62] the court dealt with the attempted removal of the plaintiff's right to vote without suggesting that the rule in *Foss*[134] in any way prevented the action from being brought. However, the matter must be one of substance and not a mere irregularity in the internal management of the company. Thus in *MacDougall v Gardiner* (1875) 1 Ch D 13 Mr Gardiner, the chairman of a meeting of a company, refused to take a poll on the question of whether or not to adjourn the meeting. The Court of Appeal would not give any remedy to the plaintiff shareholder who had requested the poll because it was a matter of internal management in which the court should not interfere.

Exceptions to the rule

Although the courts have not developed an entirely clear pattern of exceptions, those set out below appear to be the main areas in which the court will allow claims to be brought by shareholders as an exception to the rule in *Foss*.[134]

1. *Acts which are* ultra vires *or illegal.* Since no majority of the members can ratify or confirm such acts, there is no room for the operation of the rule in respect of activities which are *ultra vires* (*Simpson v Westminster Palace Hotel Co*, 1860[136]) or illegal. (*North-West Transportation Co v Beatty* (1887) 12 App Cas 589.)

This ground might be used by a minority to force the directors to comply with the law restricting, e.g. loans, quasi-loans, and credit given by the company to directors and their connected persons.

2. *Where the act complained of can only be confirmed by a special or extraordinary resolution.* *Foss*[134] is based on the principle that the majority, i.e. those who can obtain an ordinary resolution, should decide whether or not a complaint relating to the company should be brought before the court. Clearly, therefore, a simple majority of the members cannot be allowed to confirm a transaction requiring a greater majority. (*Salmon v Quin & Axtens Ltd*, 1909.[137]) In addition, the notice of the resolution must give fair and full particulars of the facts if it is to bind the minority. (See *Baillie v Oriental Telephone & Electric Co Ltd*, 1915[138] and *Kaye v Croydon Tramways Co*, 1898.[139])

3. *Where there is a fraud on the minority.* The rule in *Foss*[134] would create grave injustice if the majority were allowed to commit wrongs against the company and benefit from those wrongs at the expense of the minority simply because no claim could be brought in respect of the wrong. Thus, there is a major and somewhat ill-defined exception referred to as 'fraud on the minority'. The following headings describe the main areas of fraud.

(*a*) *Where the company is defrauded.*
   (i) *Misappropriation of corporate property.* Examples of this jurisdiction are to be found in *Menier v Hooper's Telegraph Works*, 1874[140] and *Cook v Deeks*, 1916.[141]
   (ii) *Breach of duty by directors.* These must in the view of the court be matters of substance and not merely ratifiable matters of internal management. (*Alexander v Automatic Telephone Co*, 1900.[100])

(*b*) *Where the minority as individuals are defrauded.*
   (i) *Expulsion of minority.* This will amount to fraud unless it is done *bona fide* and for the benefit of the company. A contrast is provided by *Brown v British Abrasive Wheel Co*, 1919[142]; *Dafen Tinplate Co Ltd v Llanelli Steel Co (1907) Ltd*, 1920[55] and *Sidebottom v Kershaw Leese & Co*, 1920.[56]
   (ii) *Inequitable use of majority power.* Examples of this jurisdiction are to be found in *Clemens v Clemens Bros Ltd*, 1976[143] and *Estmanco Ltd v GLC*, 1982.[144]

The exception of fraud on the minority depends *where the company is defrauded* on 'wrongdoer control', i.e. the individual shareholder must show that the wrongdoers control the company as where they control the board and general meetings and will not permit an action to be brought in the company's name. Furthermore, wrongdoer control is essential because cases of misappropriation of property and breach of duty can be ratified by a 51 per cent majority of the members which is not controlled by the wrongdoers.

The wrongdoers will obviously be in the above position if they have *voting control* as they had, for example, in *Menier*[140] and *Cook*.[141] However, in *Prudential Assurance Co Ltd v Newman Industries Ltd*, 1980 (see p. 554) Vinelott J held that *de facto* control was enough, i.e. the company does what the wrongdoers want even though the wrongdoers do not have voting control. They are able to persuade the majority to follow them. The Court of Appeal did not accept this reasoning but gave no guidance as to what might be meant by control. However, a judge could adjourn a hearing so that the company in question could hold a general meeting and with experience of the conduct of that meeting hope to ascertain areas of control not based purely on voting power.

4. **Fraud and negligence.** It is still not entirely certain whether damage caused by *negligence* can be brought under the heading of 'fraud' for the purposes of the exception of 'fraud on the minority'. In *Pavlides v Jensen*, 1956[145] the court held that negligence, however gross, was not included. However, in *Daniels v Daniels*, 1978[146] Templeman J, in distinguishing *Pavlides*,[145] said that a minority shareholder who had no other remedy should be able to sue whenever directors use their powers intentionally or unintentionally, fraudulently or negligently, in a manner which benefits them at the expense of the company. Vinelott J accepted this view in the *Newman* case. The Court of Appeal in that case did not give any guidance but the general approach of the Court was restrictive and suggests that negligence *which does not result in personal benefit* to the wrongdoers might still be ratifiable by a general meeting even with the votes of the wrongdoers and therefore not within the definition of fraud on the minority.

5. **Part XVII, Companies Act 1985.** This is a more recent exception which has already been considered. (See p. 191.) The Act gives the court power to waive the *Foss*[134] rule which may make the other exceptions redundant, developing perhaps, to the point where *Foss*[134] can be waived if to do justice requires this. It should be noted, however, that Vinelott J's attempt to establish such a broad exception in the *Newman* case (which was heard before what is now Part XVII became law) was turned down on appeal to the Court of Appeal on the grounds that it was too impractical.

Procedural aspects

When a shareholder is suing to restrain the majority from acting illegally or continuing to commit a personal wrong upon him he has a choice. He may sue in his own name or in the representative form on behalf of himself and other shareholders with whom he enjoys the right allegedly denied to him. The relief asked for will normally be a *declaratory judgment* saying what the law is and by which the parties intend to abide, or an *injunction* to restrain the conduct complained of if it is thought the majority will still continue to act unfairly.

Where the individual member is seeking a claim against third parties for the company's benefit so that he is trying to enforce a claim which belongs to the company, his claim is called *derivative.*

In a *personal* or *representative* claim the company is a real and genuine defendant. In a *derivative* action the company is joined as a nominal defendant because the directors and the majority of the members of the company will not bring the company into court as a plaintiff. The company is made a party to the action so that the judge may grant it a remedy by being brought in as a nominal defendant, the plaintiff naming the company as a defendant in his writ.

The remedy of damages is available in a derivative claim. The damages go to the company and not to the plaintiff. However, the plaintiff is entitled to an indemnity for his costs from the company. (*Wallersteiner v Moir (No 2)* [1975] 1 All ER 849.)

A derivative action is not available to challenge the form in which a company's accounts are prepared. The Companies Act requires the appointment of auditors who must report upon the accounts and this is the protection which statute law gives to the exclusion of other remedies. (*Devlin v Slough Estates Ltd*, 1982.[147])

A derivative claim is not available to a plaintiff whose own conduct is in some way tainted, as where he has been involved in the wrongdoing. (*Nurcombe v Nurcombe* [1985] 1 All ER 65.) This contrasts with petitions under Part XVII where, according to Nourse J in *Re London School of Electronics*, 1985 (see p. 195), there is no overriding requirement that the petitioner should come to court with clean hands.

The rule in *Foss*[134] is a *rule of procedure*. It is a matter to be decided *before* the trial of the allegations as to whether the plaintiff can be allowed to proceed to a trial under an exception to the rule. (See the comments of the Court of Appeal in the *Newman* case, p. 557.) The parties cannot waive this procedural rule. (*Heyting v Dupont*, 1964.[148])

8 Meetings and resolutions

A company is compelled by law to hold certain general meetings of shareholders, i.e., annual general meetings and in exceptional cases extraordinary general meetings. The articles of a company provide for the holding of general meetings, the relevant provisions of *Table A* being in *Regs* 36 and 37. All section references in this chapter are to the Companies Act 1985 unless otherwise indicated.

GENERAL MEETINGS

(a) Annual general meeting

Every company must in each year hold a general meeting as its annual general meeting, in addition to any other meetings in that year, and must specify the meeting as such in the notices calling it. (S. 366(1).) Not more than 15 months must elapse between the date of one annual general meeting and the next (s. 366(3)), but so long as a company holds its first annual general meeting within 18 months of its incorporation it need not hold it in the year of its incorporation or in the following year. (S. 366(2).) Thus a company incorporated between July and December, 1987, need not hold its first annual general meeting until 1989.

If default is made in calling an annual general meeting, the Department of Trade and Industry may, on the application of any member of the company, call or direct the calling of a general meeting of the company, and may give directions as to the conduct of it (s. 367(1)), and may direct that one person present in person or by proxy shall constitute a valid meeting. (S. 367(2).) Such a provision is useful where a company has only one member willing to attend and yet a meeting is required to decide certain issues.

There is no statutory provision which deals with the business which may be conducted at the annual general meeting and *Table A* contains no such provision.

The meeting is a safeguard for the shareholders in that it provides them with an opportunity of questioning the directors on the accounts and reports, which are usually, but not necessarily, presented to the AGM (see further p. 345), and on general matters. Moreover, it is a meeting which must be held whether the directors wish it or not.

(b) Extraordinary general meetings

Meetings of the members other than the annual general meeting are called extraordinary general meetings, and may be convened when the directors think fit. However, ss. 368 and 370(3) give a percentage of the members the right to convene a general meeting and the procedure has already been outlined in Chapter 7 (page 186). Section 371 gives the court power to call a general meeting if it is impractical to call one in the usual way, and the court may direct that one member of the company present in person or by proxy shall be deemed to constitute a valid meeting. This is a similar provision to that in s. 367(2) which gives the Department of Trade and Industry such power in respect of the annual general meeting.

In addition, under s. 391 an auditor has the right to requisition a meeting on his resignation (see p. 362), and s. 142 requires a meeting to be called if there is a serious loss of capital (see p. 101).

Convening of general meetings

General meetings are normally convened by the board of directors. *Regulation 37* states that the directors may call general meetings.

The company secretary or other executive has no power to call general meetings unless the board ratifies his act of doing so. (*Re State of Wyoming Syndicate* [1901] 2 Ch 431.)

As regards the time and place at which the meeting is to be held, this is in general terms a matter for the directors. However, it must be reasonably convenient for the members to attend and this probably prevents general meetings being held overseas. In addition the directors must act in good faith when they call a meeting. Thus, in *Cannon v Trask* (1875), LR 20 Eq 669 the directors called the annual general meeting at an earlier date than was usual for the company to hold it in order to ensure that transfers of shares to certain persons who opposed the board would not be registered in time so that they would be unable to vote. An action for an injunction to stop the meeting succeeded. It should also be noted that once the directors have called the meeting they cannot postpone it and the meeting may be held even though the directors try to postpone or cancel it. (*Smith v Paringa Mines Ltd* [1906] 2 Ch 193.) With the consent of the majority of those present and voting it could, however, once held, be adjourned.

The power of members to call meetings under s. 370(3) and s. 368 have already been considered as has the power of the Department of Trade and the court to call meetings under s. 367 and s. 371 respectively.

NOTICE OF MEETINGS

Regulations relating to notice of meetings are usually laid down in the company's articles and these must be referred to, although there are certain statutory provisions with regard to notice which must not be overlooked.

Length of notice

The company's articles must be followed, but s. 369(1) of the Act provides that any provision in the company's articles shall be void if it provides for the calling of a meeting of the company (other than an adjourned meeting) by a shorter notice than—

(a) in the case of the annual general meeting or a meeting to pass a special resolution (or under *Reg* 38 of *Table A* a meeting called for the passing of a resolution appointing a person as a director) not less than 21 days' notice in writing; and

(b) in the case of a meeting other than an annual general meeting, or a meeting for the passing of a special resolution, 14 days' notice in writing, or in the case of an unlimited company, seven days' notice in writing. (S. 369(1)(b).)

Where the company's articles do not make provision, the above periods apply. (S. 369(2).)

It should be noted that s. 369(3) provides that a meeting of a company, if called by a shorter period of notice than that prescribed in s. 369(1) or by the company's articles, shall be deemed *validly called* if—

(a) in the case of the annual general meeting, *all the members entitled to attend and vote* thereat *agree*; and

(b) in the case of any other meeting, *it is agreed by a majority in number* of the members having a right to attend and vote at the meeting, being a majority together *holding not less than 95 per cent in nominal value of the shares* giving a right to attend and vote at the meeting; *or* in the case of a company not having share capital, a majority representing *95 per cent of the total voting rights* at the meeting.

Since in both (a) and (b) above *all* the members of the company with voting rights would have to be in attendance the concession is in practice confined to meeting of private companies. Furthermore, it was held in *Re Pearce Duff & Co Ltd* [1960] 3 All ER 222 that the mere fact that all the members are present at the meeting and pass a particular resolution, either unanimously or by a majority holding 95 per cent of the voting rights does not imply consent to short notice and anyone who voted for a resolution in these circumstances can later challenge it. In practice a document setting out the agreement of the members to short notice should be signed by members at the meeting if all are present or if not, consent can be given by means of a number of documents sent out to members and returned by post. There would appear to be no reason why this should not be done *after* a meeting called by inadequate notice has taken place.

The days of notice must be 'clear days', i.e. exclusive of the day of service and the day of the meeting. (See further p. 206.)

Persons to whom notice must be given

The 1985 Act does not make any provision in this regard and it depends upon the class rights of the shareholders or on the articles. *Table A, Reg* 38 provides that notice shall be given to all the members, to all persons entitled to a share in consequence of the death or bankruptcy of a member, and to the directors and auditors. Section 387(1) provides that notice of every general meeting must be given to the auditors, and if notice of a meeting is not given to every person entitled to notice, any resolution passed at the meeting will be invalid (*Young v Ladies Imperial Club*, 1920[149]), though a provision in the articles may obviate this result. (See *Table A, Reg* 39 below.)

In the absence of a provision to the contrary in the articles, preference shareholders without the power to vote have no right to be summoned to general meetings. (*Re Mackenzie & Co Ltd* [1916] 2 Ch 450.)

Method of service

With regard to service of notice, the matter is again one for the articles, and a company is not compelled to post a notice to its members; it might, for example, use an advertisement or even a notice board. However, *Table A, Regs* 111–116 provide for service of notice and this sort of procedure is generally followed. These provisions are as follows—

(i) A *notice* may be given by the company to any member or his representative either personally or by sending it by post to his registered address. Where a notice is sent by post, it shall be deemed to be effected within 48 hours of properly addressing, prepaying and posting a letter containing the notice. This assists in complying with the 'clear days' notice requirement.

(ii) A notice may be given to *joint holders* by giving notice to the first joint holder named in the register of members.

(iii) *Notice* of every general meeting shall be given in the manner outlined above *to every member* who has supplied a registered address in the United Kingdom, and under *Table A, Reg* 38, to the personal representatives and trustee in bankruptcy of members, and *to the auditor* of the company. Section 387 also states that the auditor of the company is entitled to receive notices of general meetings. Where the company has share warrants, some arrangements will have to be made to advertise the meeting if the holders of the warrants have any right to attend under the articles.

The accidental *omission to give notice* of a meeting, or the non-receipt of notice of a meeting by any person entitled to receive notice, *does not invalidate the proceedings at that meeting.* (*Table A, Reg* 39.) Compare *Re West Canadian Collieries Ltd*, 1962[150] and *Musselwhite v C. H. Musselwhite & Son Ltd*, 1962.[151] Furthermore, in most cases the minimum number of days which must intervene between the day of posting the notice and the day of the meeting is not affected by the length of time which it takes for the Post Office to deliver the notice. The articles must, of course be looked at but under *Table A, Reg* 115 service of a notice of meeting is deemed to have been effected 48 hours after posting and other common form articles state that service is deemed to have been effected on the day of posting. Thus under *Table A* an annual general meeting due to be held on 25 March would be validly convened by notices sent on 1 March whether by first or second class mail.

The articles generally specify what the notice must contain, but *Table A, Reg* 38, provides that it must specify the time and place of the meeting, and the general nature of the business to be transacted.

If the meeting is the annual general meeting the notice must say so. (S. 366(1) and *Reg* 38.) If it is convened to pass a special or extraordinary resolution it must say so (s. 378(1) and (2)), and the resolution(s) must be set out verbatim (*McConnell v Prill* [1916] 2 Ch 57), as must ordinary resolutions of which special notice is required (s. 379), and resolutions put on the agenda of the annual general meeting by shareholders under s. 376. In addition, the notice must be adequate to enable members to judge whether they should attend the meeting to protect their interests. Thus in *McConnell v Prill* [1916] 2 Ch 57 a notice of a meeting called to increase the nominal capital of the company did not say by how much. It was held that the notice was bad because the eventual issue of the new shares (and there were no pre-emption rights then) could affect the rights of existing shareholders and they were therefore entitled to know by how much the nominal capital was to be increased. In addition, any interests which the directors may have in the passing of the resolution must be disclosed in the notice or the resolution is void. (*Kaye v Croydon Tramways,* 1898[139] and *Baillie v Oriental Telephone and Electric Co Ltd,* 1915.[138]) The notice must clearly state the right of the member to appoint a proxy. (S. 372(3).)

The provisions of s. 376 allow members' resolutions to be circulated along with the notice of the annual general meeting, and this procedure has already been described in Chapter 7 (p. 187).

QUORUM

The concept of quorum relates to the minimum of persons suitably qualified who must be present at a meeting in order that business may be validly transacted.

If the articles do not lay down the quorum required for general meetings, s. 370(4) provides that in the case of both public and private companies two members *personally* present, shall be a quorum.

Therefore, as a general rule and in the absence of a provision in the articles at least two members *present in person* are required to constitute a meeting. (*Sharp v Dawes,* 1876;[152] *In re London Flats Ltd,* 1969;[153] but see *X. L. Laundries,* 1969[154]), but the articles may provide that presence by proxy is enough. For example, *Table A, Reg* 40, provides that in both public and private companies two members present in person or by proxy shall be a quorum. Thus, under the regulation, one member holding a proxy for another could validly pass resolutions in general meeting. The persons who are to be counted in the quorum must be able to vote; mere presence is not enough. The reduction in the number of members to two was substituted in what is now *Reg* 40 by the Companies Act 1980, Sched 3. The amendment does not affect any company registered before 22 December 1980 and prior to the amendment the regulation read: 'three members present in person shall be a quorum'.

Where an annual general meeting is called by the Department of Trade or where an annual general meeting or other general meeting is called by the court, the Department or the court may decide upon the quorum which may even be one member present in person or by proxy. (Ss. 367(2) and 371(2).) (*Re El Sombrero Ltd,* 1958.[155]) Section 125(6) is concerned with the matter of quorum at class meetings fixing it at two persons holding or representing by proxy at least one-third in nominal value of the issued share capital of the class in question. At an adjourned class meeting the required quorum is, under s. 125(6) one person holding shares of the class in question or his proxy. (See p. 215.) However, in *East v Bennett Bros Ltd* [1911] 1 Ch 163 it was held by Warrington J that *one* member who held *all* the shares of a class constituted a valid class meeting.

Unless there is a quorum present, the meeting is null and void, but the articles must be looked at in order to ascertain whether a quorum is required throughout the meeting or only at the beginning. *Table A, Reg* 40 provides that a quorum is required throughout the meeting but if the articles are silent on this particular point, the better view is that a quorum need only be present at the beginning and need not be present throughout, though no valid resolutions can be passed if the number of persons present falls to one. (*In re London Flats Ltd*, 1969[153].) There is, of course, another argument which says that a company only *proceeds to business* when, e.g. it votes on a resolution, and if this view is taken a quorum must obviously be present throughout if business is to be validly transacted.

Table A, Reg 41 provides that if within half an hour from the time appointed for the meeting a quorum is not present, the meeting shall stand adjourned to the same day in the next week at the same time and place, or to such other day and at such time and place as the directors may determine. *The previous Table A provides that if at the adjourned meeting a quorum is not present within half an hour from the time appointed for the meeting, the members present shall be a quorum*, and it would seem that the attendance of one member is enough for the adjourned meeting (*Jarvis Motors (Harrow) Ltd v Carabott* [1964] 1 WLR 1101) where it was held that the Interpretation Act 1978, s. 6, applied to the articles of association of companies and that, therefore, words appearing in articles in the plural include the singular.

The italicized words set out above regarding quorum on an adjourned meeting were repealed by the Companies Act 1980 and do not apply to companies registered on or after 22 December 1980 so that for these companies there must be a quorum of two at the adjourned meeting or it is similarly adjourned until there is.

CHAIRMAN

It is his duty to preserve order, to call on members to speak, to decide points of order, such as the acceptability of amendments, and to take the vote after a proper discussion in order to ascertain the sense of the meeting. However, he is not bound to hear everyone. He must be fair to the minority but as Lindley MR said in *Wall v London & Northern Assets Corporation* [1898] 2 Ch 469, the majority can say: 'We have heard enough. We are not bound to listen until everybody is tired of talking and has sat down …'. The members present at the meeting may elect one of their number as chairman unless the articles otherwise provide. (S. 370(5).)

Table A, Reg 42, provides that the chairman (if any) of the board of directors shall preside as chairman at every general meeting of the company, of if there is no such chairman, or if he is not present within 15 minutes after the time appointed for the holding of the meeting, or if he will not act, the directors present shall elect one of their number to be chairman of the meeting, and if there is only one director present and willing to act he shall be chairman.

If no director is present, or no director present is willing to act within 15 minutes after the time appointed for holding the meeting, the members present shall choose one of their number to be chairman of the meeting. (*Table A, Reg* 43.)

VOTING

Unless the articles provide to the contrary, the voting is usually by show of hands. However, articles usually allow an initial vote by show of hands, particularly for routine matters, and each member has only one vote, regardless of his shareholding. There cannot be any voting in respect of proxies held, unless the articles provide. (S. 372(2)(*c*).) (*Table A, Reg* 54, does not allow proxy votes.) On controversial issues it is usual to demand a poll on which members can vote according to the number of shares they hold and proxy votes can be used. *Table A, Reg* 46 allows a poll to be demanded before a vote on a show of hands is taken. The provisions of *Table A, Regs* 55 and 57 respectively state that in the case of joint holders the person whose name appears first in the register of members shall be allowed to cast the vote in respect of the shares, and no member shall be entitled to vote at any general meeting unless all moneys presently payable by him in respect of the shares have been paid. *Regulation* 58 provides that objections to the qualification of a voter can only be raised at the meeting at which the vote is tendered. Objections are to be referred to the chairman of the meeting whose decision is final.

It should also be noted that a shareholder, even if he is a director, can vote on a matter in which he has a personal interest subject to the rules relating to prejudice of minorities. (See p. 199.) Furthermore, a bankrupt shareholder may vote and give proxies if his name is still on the register, though he must do in accordance with the wishes of the trustee. (*Morgan v Gray* [1953] Ch 83.)

If no poll is demanded the vote on the show of hands as declared by the chairman and recorded in the minutes is the decision of the meeting and under *Reg* 467 his declaration is *conclusive* unless there is an obvious error, as where the chairman states: 'There being a majority of 51 per cent on the show of hands, I hereby declare that the special resolution to alter the articles has been passed.'

The articles may set out the provisions governing the demand for a poll, but s. 373 of the Act lays down that such provisions in the company's articles shall be *void* in certain circumstances—

(*a*) *They must not exclude* the right to demand a poll at a general meeting on any question other than the election of the chairman or the adjournment of the meeting.

(*b*) *They must not try* to stifle a demand for a poll if it is made by—

    (i) *not less than five members* having the right to vote at the meeting; *or*

    (ii) *a member or members representing not less than one-tenth of the total voting rights of all the members* having the right to vote at the meeting; *or*

    (iii) *a member or members holding shares* in the company which confer a right to vote at the meeting and *on which an aggregate sum has been paid up equal to not less than one-tenth of the total sum paid up on all such shares.* For example, if the share capital of the company was 10,000 shares of £1 each with 50p per share paid the company would have received £5,000 from the shareholders and those wishing to demand a poll under this head would have had together to have paid up £500.

Thus the articles cannot prevent a fairly sizeable group of members from demanding a poll, and s. 373(2) also provides that the holder of a proxy can join in demanding a poll. Thus a proxy for five members could in effect demand a poll on his own.

Table A, Reg 46, contains provisions similar to those of s. 373, but also provides that the chairman can demand a poll, and indeed it would be his duty to do this if he felt it necessary to ascertain the sense of the meeting. It also ensures that the board can exercise its full voting rights. *Regulation* 46 also provides that *two* members present in person or by proxy can demand a poll, and no provision in the special articles can increase this number beyond five, as we have already seen.

The amendment to what is now *Reg* 46 allowing two members in person or proxy to demand a poll does not apply to companies registered before 22 December 1980. So far as they are concerned, at least three persons present in person or by proxy are required unless, of course, the company alters its *Table A* based articles to embrace the provision relating to two members in *Reg* 46.

Taking the poll

A poll, if demanded, is usually taken straight away, but the articles may allow the poll to be taken at a later date. *Table A, Reg 51*, provides that on any issue other than the election of a chairman or on the adjournment of the meeting, a poll may be taken at such time not being more than 30 days after the poll is demanded, as is directed by the chairman who then proceeds to the next business.

Persons not actually present at the first meeting may vote on the subsequent poll. Under *Reg 62(b)* in the case of a poll taken more than 48 hours after it is demanded, the proxies must be deposited after the poll has been demanded and not less than 24 hours before the time appointed for the taking of the poll. Under *Reg 62(c)* where the poll is not taken forthwith but is taken not more than 48 hours after it was demanded, proxies must be delivered at the meeting at which the poll was demanded to the chairman or to the secretary or to any director and an instrument of proxy which is not deposited or delivered in a manner so permitted is invalid.

Even where a poll is taken immediately, the result is not usually declared until a future date because of the problems involved in checking the votes and the right of the members to cast them. Postal votes are not acceptable. Where a proxy holder is acting for several principals, he need not use all the votes in the same way on a poll. (S. 374.) This enables him to vote in the way each principal directs.

It should not be assumed that the right to vote at general meetings of the company is of equal benefit to all shareholders. In many companies there are *numerical* majorities of shareholders whose *individual* voting power is too small to influence, for example, the appointment of directors. In this respect the introduction of legislation on the American pattern to require proportional representation on the board of directors might help. Under this system the election of several directors would be taken at the same time, the ones with the most votes being elected (say the first four). At present the election of each director is taken separately as if only one vacancy had to be filled (though a private company can put forward a composite resolution to elect all the retiring directors once). In consequence the holders of the major voting power can give *all* their votes to their nominees at the relevant election(s). Under the proportional representation system they would have to spread their votes over say four nominees at once thus reducing the vote effectiveness of their shareholding.

Chairman's casting vote

The chairman of the meeting has no casting vote unless the articles so provide. *Table A, Reg 50*, provides that in the case of an equality of votes, whether on a show of hands or on a poll, the chairman of the meeting shall be entitled to a second or casting vote.

Proxies

Before the Companies Act 1948 members had no right to appoint a proxy unless the articles so provided, and if they did the person appointed as a proxy very often had to be a member of the company. This latter provision in particular increased the control of the board because it was often difficult to find a member who would attend a meeting and oppose the board by voting against a resolution which the board supported.

Under s. 372 every member of a company having a share capital and entitled to vote at a meeting may appoint a proxy, and the person appointed need not be a member of the company. However, the proxy should have full legal capacity and the appointment of a minor is probably void; certainly The Insolvency Rules 1986/(SI 1986/1925) exclude minors as proxies in meetings concerned with winding up. (See rule 8.1.(3).) In addition, under s. 372(3), the notice of the meeting must make it clear that proxies can be appointed and failure to do this results in default fines on directors and the secretary but even so the meeting is valid. In public companies a member may appoint two or more proxies but in a private company only one unless the articles provide to the contrary. (S. 372(2)(b).)

The expression 'proxy' also refers to the document by which the voting agent is appointed. The articles frequently set out the form (see *Regs* 60 and 61) but a written appointment in reasonable form will suffice. (*Isaacs v Chapman* (1916) 32 TLR 237.) Furthermore, minor errors which do not seriously mislead will not render a proxy invalid. Thus in *Oliver v Dalgleish* [1963] 3 All ER 330 a proxy form gave the correct date of the meeting but said it was the annual general meeting and not an extraordinary general meeting as it in fact was. It was held by the High Court that the proxy was nevertheless valid.

Regulation 61 provides for two-way proxies, under which a member can indicate whether he wishes to vote for or against a particular resolution. This is the nearest which English law comes to a postal vote. There cannot in fact be a postal vote in English law because resolutions must in general terms be passed 'at a meeting' which means that the member or his proxy must attend and vote (but see p. 216). The articles of association must not forbid two-way proxies if the Stock Exchange is to give a listing. It is uncertain whether the company is bound by a two-way proxy as regards the choice of vote but the better view is that it is bound so that if a proxy tried to cast his votes differently from the way in which the member had indicated the

212

company ought not to accept the change. (*Oliver v Dalgleish* [1963] 3 All ER 330.)

The board may circulate proxy forms in favour of the board to members and meet the expense from the company's funds. (*Peel v L & NW Railway* [1907] 1 Ch 5.) However, these forms must be sent to *all* members entitled to attend and vote. (S. 372(6).) This provision prevents the directors merely soliciting the votes of those who are likely to vote in favour of the board's proposals. In addition, the directors may also send circulars with the notice of the meeting putting forward their views on various resolutions and pay for the circularization out of the company's funds. (*Peel v L & NW Railway* [1907] 1 Ch 5.) However, the circular must be issued in good faith to inform the members of the issues and must not be unduly biased in favour of the directors' views.

The right to appoint a proxy would be useless if it had to be made many weeks before the meeting. So, whatever the articles may provide, a proxy is valid if lodged not later than 48 hours before the meeting. (S. 372(5) and *Reg* 62(*a*).) If the articles do have an earlier requirement it is void and it appears that the company cannot then require any period of lodgement at all so that if the proxy turns up at the meeting with his form and votes his vote must be accepted.

As regards revocation of a proxy, this can be done expressly by telling the proxy not to vote or by the member exercising his right to vote in person, in which case his personal vote will over-ride that of the proxy if the latter votes. (*Cousins v International Brick Co Ltd* [1931] 2 Ch 90.) There is also automatic revocation of a proxy if the member who made the appointment dies or becomes bankrupt or of unsound mind. It should be noted that revocation is impossible if the proxy has an interest. Thus where L lends money to B and takes B's share certificates in X Ltd as security but is not registered it may be part of the agreement that L should always be appointed B's proxy at meetings of X Ltd. If so, the appointment of L as proxy is irrevocable until the loan is repaid.

All that is said in the above paragraph is subject to the articles of the company concerned. (*Spiller v Mayo (Rhodesia) Development Co (1908) Ltd* [1926] WN 78.) *Table A, Reg* 63 provides that a vote given or poll demanded by a proxy or by the duly authorized representative of a corporation shall be valid notwithstanding the previous determination of the authority of the person voting or demanding a poll unless notice of the determination was received by the company at the office or at such other place at which the instrument of proxy was duly deposited before the commencement of the meeting or adjourned meeting at which the vote is given or the poll demanded or (in the case of a poll taken otherwise than on the same day as the meeting or adjourned meeting) the time appointed for taking the poll.

Where a company is a member of another company the member company is entitled to appoint by resolution of its directors a representative to attend meetings. (S. 375.) If the member company is in liquidation the liquidator may also make the appointment. (*Hillman v Crystal Bowl Amusements* [1973] 1 All ER 379.) The representative is not a proxy and has the full rights of a member; thus he always counts towards the quorum, can move resolutions and amendments, can speak, even if the company is a public one, and can always vote on a show of hands. It is of some advantage to a company to appoint a representative, though if the meeting is not controversial a proxy will do just as well.

Under s. 375(1)(*a*) only one person can be appointed to represent the company. Thus where the company requiring representation is a nominee company holding shares for a number of persons with different interests, it should appoint proxies for the different holdings if each person requires someone to attend the meeting to represent his interest. More than one proxy can be appointed by a shareholder under *Table A, Reg 59*.

ADJOURNMENT OF THE MEETING

A meeting may be adjourned for various reasons, e.g. where the business cannot be completed on that day, or where there is no quorum. The adjourned meeting is deemed to be a resumption of the original meeting and the articles will provide as to the amount of notice required for it, but no business may be transacted at an adjourned meeting except that which was left unfinished at the original meeting.

Section 381 provides that where a resolution is passed at an adjourned meeting of the company, or at a class meeting or a meeting of the directors, the resolution shall be deemed for all purposes to have been passed on the date when it was in fact passed and not at the date of the earlier meeting. The section is thus important in deciding on what date to file a resolution which has to be filed within so many days of its being passed.

The articles usually determine who shall decide to adjourn, whether the members or the chairman. A chairman must not adjourn frivolously, and if he does so, the members may elect a new chairman and proceed with the meeting. *Table A, Reg 45*, provides that the chairman may (and *shall* if so directed by the meeting), with the consent of the meeting, adjourn the meeting from time to time and from place to place.

The chairman can of course adjourn under the common law without any resolution of the members where there is disorder at the meeting. However, he must exercise the power properly. Thus, if he adjourns the meeting immediately upon the outbreak of disorder without waiting to see whether it will subside, the adjournment will be invalid and the meeting may continue. (*John v Rees* [1969] 2 All ER 274.)

CLASS MEETINGS

Class meetings may be held in respect of shareholders and debenture holders. The articles must be looked at for the provisions relating to the class meetings of *shareholders*; in the case of *debenture holders* provisions are usually found in the trust deed under which they are issued. The only statutory provisions relating to class meetings of members are as follows—

(i) *Proxies.* Section 372, which provides for the appointment of proxies at general meetings, states in sub-s. (7) that the provision applies to class meetings.

(ii) *Representation of corporations.* Section 375, which provides that a corporation may be represented at meetings by a representative, applies also to class meetings.

(iii) *Resolutions passed at adjourned meetings.* Section 381, which provides that a resolution passed at an adjourned meeting shall be deemed for all purposes to have been passed on the date when it was in fact passed and not an earlier date, applies also to class meetings.

(iv) Section 125(6)(*a*) provides that the necessary quorum at a class meeting shall be at least two persons holding or representing by proxy one-third of the issued shares of the class, and that any holder of the shares of the class present in person or by proxy may demand a poll. At an adjourned class meeting, the required quorum is one person holding shares of the class in question or his proxy. At any class meeting, any holder of the shares of the class in question may demand a poll, whether he is present in person or by proxy. (S. 125(6)(*b*).) (And see also p. 94.)

RESOLUTIONS

Resolutions are of three kinds: (1) special, (2) extraordinary, and (3) ordinary. The type of resolution will depend upon the articles and is based on the nature of the business transacted; it has no necessary connection with the type of meeting. Thus all the above resolutions can be passed at any general meeting.

In addition, under *Table A, Reg 53*, a resolution in writing signed by or on behalf of all the members for the time being entitled to receive notice of, and to attend and vote at general meetings shall be as valid and effective as if the same had been passed at a general meeting of the company duly convened and held, and may consist of several instruments in the like form each executed by or on behalf of one or more members. *Regulation 53* applies to public and private companies and to ordinary, extraordinary and special resolutions, though in practice written resolutions are not likely to be a viable proposition in public companies. It should be noted that what is now *Reg 53* does not apply to companies registered before 22 December 1980 unless they have specifically incorporated it in their articles. However, such companies can achieve the same result in regard to written resolutions by reason of the decision in *Cane v Jones*, 1981.[52] Written resolutions must comply with the rules regarding the filing of resolutions with the Registrar.

1. Special resolutions

A special resolution is one passed by a majority of not less than three-quarters of such members as are entitled to and do vote in person, or, where proxies are allowed, by proxy, at a general meeting of which *not less than 21 days' notice* specifying the intention to propose the resolution as a special resolution has been duly given. (S. 378(2).)

A resolution may be proposed and passed as a special resolution at a meeting of which less than 21 days' notice has been given if it is agreed by a majority in number of the members having the right to attend and vote at any meeting, being a majority holding not less than 95 per cent in nominal value of the shares giving that right, or in the case of a company not having a share capital, a majority together representing 95 per cent of the total voting rights at the meeting of all members. (S. 378(3).)

The following matters must be carried out by special resolution and the memorandum and articles cannot provide to the contrary—

    (i) alteration of the objects (s. 4);

    (ii) alteration of the articles (s. 9(1));

    (iii) the changing of the company's name (s. 28(1));

    (iv) the reduction of the company's share capital (s. 135(1));

    (v) the creation of reserve capital (s. 120);

    (vi) rendering the liability of the directors unlimited (s. 307(1));

    (vii) a resolution that the company be wound up by the court (s. 122(1)(*a*), Insolvency Act 1986);

    (viii) a resolution to wind up the company voluntarily (s. 84(1)(*b*), *ibid*);

(ix) a reconstruction, i.e. the authorizing of the liquidator in the voluntary winding up of the company to sell the company's assets for shares in another company. (S. 110(3)(*a*), *ibid.*)

On the matter of special resolutions it should be noted that in *Bushell v Faith*, 1969,[156] Russell L J, was of the opinion that a provision as to voting rights which had the effect of making a special resolution incapable of being passed if a particular shareholder exercised his voting rights against a proposed alteration of the articles is not void under s. 9 of the Act of 1985.

2. Extraordinary resolutions

A resolution is an extraordinary resolution when it has been passed by a majority of not less than *three-quarters* of the members who are entitled to and do vote, in person or by proxy, at a general meeting of which notice specifying the intention to propose the resolution as an extraordinary resolution has been duly given.

The distinction between a special and an extraordinary resolution is not in the majority. The period of notice is different. Section 369(1)(*b*) applies and the minimum notice for an extraordinary resolution will be 14 days for limited companies and seven days in the case of unlimited companies.

An *extraordinary resolution* may be required by the articles for any business specified therein, but *must be used*—

(i) to wind up the company voluntarily when it cannot pay its debts (s. 84(1)(*c*), Insolvency Act 1986);

(ii) to authorize the liquidator to compromise or make an arrangement with creditors or contributories in a members' voluntary winding up (s. 165(2)(*a*), *ibid*).

3. Ordinary resolutions

An ordinary resolution is used where the articles so provide. Such a resolution is not defined by the Act, though notice must be given of the intention to pass such a resolution, and there must be more members voting for the resolution than against it. The majority is not a majority of the members of the company, but only a majority of those who attend and vote.

The chairman can put any resolution to the meeting without its being seconded though not if the articles forbid it. Whether a resolution requires a seconder and whether that seconder must be a member depends upon the articles. *Table A* does not require a seconder at all so that the motion or resolution could be put after proposal and no seconder is required at common law. (*Re Horbury Bridge Coal, Iron & Wagon Co* (1879) 11 Ch D 109.)

Registration of resolutions

Special and extraordinary resolutions must be registered with the Registrar of Companies. This is achieved by sending a printed copy of the resolution to the Registrar within 15 days after its passing. (S. 380.) Under s. 380(1) it is not necessary to send a *printed* copy of the resolution to the Registrar if instead the company forwards a copy in some other form approved by him. A copy of each such resolution must also be embodied in or attached to every copy of the articles of association issued after the passing of the resolution. (S. 380(2).)

A company need not forward to the Registrar of Companies a *printed* copy of a resolution authorizing an increase of its share capital, if instead it forwards a copy in some other form approved by him. (S. 123(3).)

Where, as will often be the case, a special resolution alters the company's memorandum or articles, the Registrar must advertise the filing of the resolution effecting the alteration in the *London Gazette*. (S. 711(1)(*b*).) The alteration is not effective against other persons who at the material time are unaware of it having been made until the advertisement is published. (S. 42(1).) 'Other persons' in this context would appear to mean persons other than the company and therefore includes shareholders and directors as well as outsiders. As regards the material time, this appears to mean the time when a transaction was entered into. In addition, when an alteration is made in the memorandum or articles (except in the case of a special resolution altering the objects under s. 4), a printed copy of the whole memorandum or articles as amended must be delivered to the Registrar with the resolution. (S. 18(2).) This helps when looking through a company's file at the Registry because there is no need to check back to the original memorandum and articles in order to see the overall effect of subsequent alterations.

An ordinary resolution need not be registered except where it has been used to increase the authorized capital when it must be filed with the Registrar within 15 days or to consolidate or subdivide shares, or to convert shares into stock or reconvert stock into shares. In this case notice of the resolution must be filed with the Registrar *within one month* after the change in capital has been made.

It has already been noted (see p. 158) that if shares in a public company are forfeited or surrendered to the company, the company must see to it that the shares are disposed of and if this has not been done within three years it must cancel the shares. If the result of this is that the company's issued share capital is brought below the authorized minimum, the company will have to apply for re-registration as a private company, and a resolution of the directors is sufficient to change the company's memorandum of association to prepare it for re-registration. That resolution of the directors is registrable with the Registrar within 15 days of it being passed.

ORDINARY RESOLUTIONS REQUIRING SPECIAL NOTICE

An ordinary resolution of which *special notice* has been given is required in the following cases—

(i) to remove a director before the expiration of his period of office, regardless of any provision in the articles or in any agreement with him; or to appoint another director in his place. (S. 303.) The section does not prevent companies from attaching special voting rights to certain shares on this occasion. (*Bushell v Faith*, 1969.[156])

(ii) to appoint or re-appoint a director who is over the age limit laid down by the Act or the company's articles. The age limit in the act is 70 years. (S. 293(2) and (5).)

(iii) appointing as auditor a person other than a retiring auditor; or

(iv) filling a casual vacancy in the office of an auditor; or

(v) re-appointing as auditor a retiring auditor who was appointed by the directors to fill a casual vacancy; or

(vi) removing an auditor before the expiration of his term of office. (S. 388.)

Where special notice is required, the resolution shall not be effective unless notice of the intention to move it has been given to the company not less than *28 days* before the meeting at which it is to be moved. The notice should be posted or delivered to the registered office of the company. The company shall give its members notice of any such resolution at the same time and in the same manner as it gives notice of the meeting, or if this is not possible, shall give them notice of it either by advertisement in a newspaper having an appropriate circulation or by any other method allowed by the articles, *not less than 21 days before the meeting*. If a meeting is called for a date 28 days or less after the notice has been given, the notice, though not given in time under the section shall be deemed to have been properly given. (S. 379(3).)

Section 379(3) is generally regarded as a provision to protect shareholders who give notice, e.g. to remove a director or auditor in case the board calls the meeting of members deliberately at less than 28 days so as to frustrate the removal of the director or auditor. However, in *Fenning v Environmental Products Ltd, Law Society Gazette*, 23 June 1982, the Court decided that s. 379(3) could operate also on the 21 days' notice for the meeting of members.

This is unfortunate because on the proposed removal of a director or auditor the person concerned is allowed to send written representations with the notice of the meeting at which his removal is to be discussed, or, if this is not possible, to make representations orally at the meeting. If the meeting can be held so quickly, i.e. at less than 21 days' notice as *Fenning* decides, then the time to prepare the case is cut down. If one looks at s. 369(3) the position is worse; that allows shareholders to agree to shorter notice—95 per cent of them are required in the case of an extraordinary general meeting, and 100 per cent in the case of an Annual General Meeting. As we have seen, since the figures are percentages of *all* the members of the company and not those attending the meeting, s. 369(3) is realistically confined to meetings of private companies. However, in such companies one could get a situation where A Ltd receives special notice to remove a director or auditor on 1 May, the company meets on 2 May, using s. 369(3) to waive notice, and removes the director or auditor quite validly. What chance in such a case does a director or auditor have to put his view? It is true that in the case of *Pedley v Inland Waterways* (see p. 271) Mr Justice Slade said that the requirement for the company to give 21 days' notice was strict and that the shareholders could not validly agree to shorter notice under s. 369, but since the Court in *Fenning* took a different view, at least on the need for 21 days' notice, and since both cases are at High Court level so that one cannot be preferred to the other, the matter is still unresolved.

Where a director gives the special notice it seems it must be acted upon by the board. However, where a shareholder who is not a director gives it, the directors are not, it would appear, bound to comply with it unless it is linked with a requisition under s. 376 (if removal of a director is to be at the AGM) or under s. 368 (if removal is to be at an EGM). (See further *Pedley v Inland Waterways Association Ltd*, 1977, p. 271.)

AMENDMENTS

As regards amendments to resolutions, which must be set out verbatim, such as special and extraordinary resolutions, it is often suggested that no amendment is possible since the Act requires *notice* of the resolution and some say, by implication, of any amendment, because if the resolution is changed by an amendment then proper notice has not been given of that part of it which was amended. It is generally believed that this ruling is too strict and indeed in *Re Moorgate Mercantile Holdings* [1980] 1 All ER 40 Mr Justice Slade decided that such a resolution could depart in some respects from the text of the resolution set out in the notice, e.g. on account of correction of grammatical or clerical errors, or the use of more formal language. However, apart from alterations of form of this kind, there must be no alterations of substance otherwise only where all the members (in the case of an AGM) or a majority in number and 95 per cent in value of members (in the case of any other meeting) have waived their rights to notice, could a special resolution be validly passed. The judge also decided that in the case of notice of intention to propose a special resolution nothing is achieved by the addition of such words as 'with such amendments and alterations as shall be determined on at the general meeting'. The facts of the case were that the company wished to reduce its share premium account on the grounds that it had been lost in the course of trade. The share premium account to be cancelled was stated in the notice to be £1,356,900.48p. That figure included the sum of £321.17 which had been credited to the share premium account under an issue of shares made on the acquisition of the outstanding minority interest in a subsidiary. This share premium could not be regarded as lost. At the meeting the chairman proposed to amend the special resolution and, although not all the members of the company were present, a special resolution was passed in the following form: 'That the share premium account of the company amounting to £1,356,900.48p be reduced to £321.17p'. The Court was then asked to agree to the reduction and the judge refused to do so on the grounds that the special resolution had not been validly passed.

Subject to what has been said above, once a resolution has been moved and, if the articles require, seconded, any member may speak and move amendments. No notice of the amendments is required unless the amendment effects a substantial change in the resolution, i.e. is the change such that a reasonable man who had decided to absent himself from the meeting would have decided to come if he had received notice of the amended resolution? This is a decision which the chairman must take and hope that if his decision is questioned in court the judge will agree with him. For example, in *Re Teede and Bishop Ltd* (1901) 70 LJ Ch 409 it was held that at a meeting to resolve that A Ltd should be sold to B Ltd and then that A Ltd should be wound up, it was not in order to accept an amendment that A Ltd be wound up without the sale to B Ltd unless notice had been given of it.

Amendments must be put to the vote before the resolution is voted upon. Improper refusal by the chairman to put an amendment renders the resolution void. (*Henderson v Bank of Australasia* (1890) 45 Ch

D 330.) Proxies cannot move resolutions or amendments or speak unless the company is a private one when a proxy may address the meeting. (S. 372.)

MINUTES

Section 382(1) requires every company to keep minutes of all proceedings of general and directors' meetings, whether they be meetings of the full board or a committee of the board, and to enter these into a minute book. If a minute is signed by the chairman of the meeting or of the next succeeding meeting, the minutes are *prima facie* evidence of the proceedings. (S. 382(2).) This means that although there is a presumption that all the proceedings were in order and that all appointments of directors, managers or liquidators are deemed to be valid (S. 382(4)), evidence can be brought to contradict the minutes. Thus in *Re Fireproof Doors* [1916] 2 Ch 142 a contract to indemnify directors was held binding though not recorded in the minutes. On the other hand, if the articles provide that minutes duly signed by the chairman are *conclusive* evidence they cannot be contradicted. Thus in *Kerr v Mottram* [1940] Ch 657 the plaintiff said that a contract to sell him preference and ordinary shares had been agreed at a meeting. There was no record in the minutes and since the articles of the company said that the minutes were conclusive evidence the court would not admit evidence as to the existence of the contract.

The minute books are to be kept at the registered office of the company, and the minutes of general meetings are open to the inspection of members free of charge. Copies or extracts from the minutes must be supplied and a charge may be made. The copy must be furnished within seven days of the request. Section 237(3) gives the auditor of the company a right of inspection at all times. Minute books may be kept on a loose leaf system so long as there are adequate precautions to prevent fraud. (S. 722.) However, it seems that some sort of visual record is required and s. 722 would not appear to envisage tapes being used.

9 Directors and secretaries

The management of a company is usually entrusted to a small group of persons called directors.

A company must have a board of directors numbering at least two in the case of a public company; one will suffice in the case of a private company. (S. 282.) Apart from this statutory provision the number of directors and the way in which they are to be appointed is left to be regulated by the articles. *Table A, Reg* 64 provides that unless otherwise determined by ordinary resolution, the number of directors (other than alternate directors) shall not be subject to any maximum but shall not be less than two. *Table A, Regs* 75 and 78 provide in effect that the company may from time to time by ordinary resolution increase or reduce the number of directors, and determine in what rotation the increased number is to retire.

Although the persons managing the company are usually called directors, other names are sometimes used, e.g. managers, governors, or committee of management. In this connection it is important to note the provisions of s. 741(1) which are that the term 'director' when used in the Act is taken to include any persons occupying the position of director by whatever name called. A director is also an officer of the company. (S. 744 provides that 'officer in relation to a body corporate includes a director, manager, or secretary'.)

It should also be noted that s. 741(2) extends the provisions of Part X of that Act (see p. 245) to a 'shadow director', being a person in accordance with whose directions or instructions the directors of a company are accustomed to act unless the directors are accustomed so to act only because the person concerned gives them advice in a professional capacity. Professional advisers such as accountants and lawyers are not, therefore, for that reason alone, shadow directors. Part X contains provisions that impose restrictions on certain dealings between the company and its directors because they could give rise to a conflict of interest. The restrictions relate in the main to contracts of employment and substantial property transactions which will be considered later in this chapter. Part X also contains provisions relating to the disclosure in the company's accounts of certain transactions relating to directors.

APPOINTMENT OF DIRECTORS

Directors may be appointed in the following ways—

(i) *By being named in the articles.* This method is sometimes used for the appointment of the company's first directors as an alternative to following the procedure laid down in the articles.

(ii) *By the subscribers to the memorandum.* As we have seen the subscribers to the memorandum, or a majority of them, may appoint directors; and again this method is sometimes used to appoint the first directors of the company.

However the first appointment is made, it is not effective unless the person concerned is named in the statement of directors and secretaries which is required by s. 10(2). The statement must be signed by or on behalf of the subscribers of the memorandum and must contain a consent signed by each of the directors named in it to act in that capacity. (S. 10(3).) Any appointment by any articles delivered with the memorandum of a person as director is void unless he is named as a director in the statement. (S. 10(5).)

(iii) *By an ordinary resolution of the members in general meeting.* (*Reg* 78.) In a public company the appointment of each director must be by a separate resolution, unless the meeting resolves with no dissentients that a composite resolution appointing several directors be put forward. (S. 292(1).) This is to prevent the board from coercing members into voting for the appointment of an unpopular director by putting him up for election along with others who are more popular. However, in the absence of some form of proportional representation, the appointments may not represent the wishes of the *numerical* majority of shareholders. (See p. 211.) The directors of a private company may by implication be appointed by a composite resolution. In addition, subject to any restrictions in the articles, which would be improbable, all members of companies, whether public or private can vote on a resolution for the election of directors whether they are themselves directors or not.

(iv) *By the board of directors.* The board may make appointments in two cases—

(*a*) to fill casual vacancies which may occur on resignation, disqualification, removal or death;

(*b*) to appoint *additional* directors up to a given maximum which may be set out in the company's articles. Any such appointment in excess of the permitted maximum is void.

Persons appointed in these two ways usually hold office until the next annual general meeting. However, if *Table A* applies the director concerned is not automatically eligible for re-election. The provisions of *Regs* 76 and 77 apply. *Regulation 76* states that no person other than a director retiring by rotation shall be appointed or reappointed a director at any general meeting unless—(*a*) he is recommended by the directors; or (*b*) not less than 14, nor more than 35 clear days before the date appointed for the meeting, notice executed by a member qualified to vote at the meeting has been given to the company of the intention to propose that person for appointment or reappointment stating the particulars which would, if he were so appointed or reappointed, be required to be included in the company's register of directors together with notice executed by that person of his willingness to be appointed or reappointed. *Regulation 77* provides that not less than 7 nor more than 28 clear days before the date appointed for holding a general meeting notice shall be given to all who are entitled to receive notice of the meeting of any person (other than a director retiring by rotation at the meeting) who is recommended by the directors for appointment or reappointment as a director at the meeting or in respect of whom notice has been duly given to the company of the intention to propose him at the meeting for appointment or reappointment as a director. The notice shall give the particulars of that person which would if he were so appointed or reappointed, be required to be included in the company's register of directors.

Table A, *Reg* 78, gives the members a concurrent power to appoint directors to fill casual vacancies and appoint additional directors, but this would involve the calling of an extraordinary general meeting.

Contractual rights to appoint directors

If by a company's articles directors are to be appointed by the members in general meeeting, the board cannot make a valid contract by which an outsider is empowered to appoint directors. (*James v Eve* (1873) LR 6 HL 335.)

However, if the company is governed by *Table A* it seems that the board may delegate its power to appoint additional directors (*Reg* 71) and this may prove useful when the board wishes, for example, to raise a loan or share capital from persons who are only willing to lend or invest if they can nominate a certain number of directors to the board to protect their interests.

If the articles expressly empower an outsider to appoint directors, his power to do so is undoubtedly valid, but whether the court would enforce the power by specific performance is doubtful. Generally, the court will not enforce contracts of personal service in this way.

However, in *British Murac Syndicate Ltd v Alperton Rubber Co Ltd* [1915] 2 Ch 186, Sargant J was of the opinion that the relation between a company and a director was not in the nature of a contract of service and tended to the view that a right to appoint a director could be specifically enforced. However, in *Plantations Trust Ltd v Bila (Sumatra) Rubber Lands Ltd* (1916) 85 LJ Ch 801, Eve J was of the opinion that an order of specific performance would not be granted. If the company refuses to accept an appointee in these circumstances there is, of course, always the solution in a quasi-partnership company of asking for a winding up. This method was adopted in *Re A & BC Chewing Gum* (1975).[130]

Assignment of office

Section 308 provides that if, under the articles or by reason of any agreement, a director or other manager of the company has power to *assign* his office to another person, such assignment will be of no effect unless it is sanctioned by a *special resolution* of the members in general meeting.

Alternate directors

These can be useful if the director has many outside commitments. There is no statutory authority for a director to appoint an *alternate* to act in his place in the event of his absence and alternate directors can only be appointed if the articles so provide. *Table A* provides in *Reg 65* that any director (other than an alternate director) may appoint any other director, or any other person approved by the directors and willing to act, to be an alternate director and may remove from office an alternate director so appointed by him. *Regulation 66* provides that an alternate director shall be entitled to receive notice of all meetings of directors and of all meetings of committees of directors of which his appointor is a member, to attend and vote at any such meeting at which the director appointing him is not personally present, and generally to perform all the functions of his appointor as a director in his absence but shall not be entitled to receive any remuneration from the company for his services as an alternate director. But it shall not be necessary to give notice of such a meeting to an alternate director who is absent from the United Kingdom.

Under *Regulation 67* an alternate director ceases to be an alternate director if his appointor ceases to be a director; but, if a director retires by rotation or otherwise but is reappointed or deemed to have been reappointed at the meeting at which he retires, any appointment of an alternate director made by him which was in force immediately prior to his retirement shall continue after his reappointment. Under *Regulation* 68 any appointment or removal of an alternate director shall be by notice to the company signed by the director making or revoking the appointment or in any other manner approved by the directors. Finally, under *Reg* 69 and save as otherwise provided in the articles, an alternate director shall be deemed for all purposes to be a director and shall alone be responsible for his own acts and defaults and he shall not be deemed to be the agent of the director appointing him.

An alternate director is a director of the company in his own right and his particulars should be lodged with the Registrar if he is not already a director of the company. All the other provisions relating to directors in company legislation apply to an alternate including, e.g. disclosure of interests in shares and debentures and material contracts.

Persons who cannot be appointed

This is to some extent a matter for the articles and they may, for example, provide that a minor or an alien shall not be appointed a director of the company. *Table A* does not contain any such restrictions, but the following statutory provisions apply—

(i) *Age Limit.* Section 293(1) and (2) provide that no person shall be appointed as the director of a public company, or of a private company which is the subsidiary of a public company, if at the time of his appointment he has reached the age of 70. However, the articles may set a higher or lower limit, or may simply exclude the section altogether. Furthermore, such a person may be appointed under s. 293(5) by the members in general meeting by an *ordinary resolution* of which *special notice* of 28 days has been given to the company. The special notice given to the company and by the company to its members must state the *actual* age of the person to whom it relates. (S. 293(5).) Where a director over the age limit has been appointed in some other way, the members may approve the appointment by a similar resolution.

Section 294(1) provides that any person who is appointed or to his knowledge is proposed for appointment as a director, and is over the age limit by virtue of the Act or the company's articles, shall give notice of the fact that he is over age to the company.

(ii) *Bankruptcy.* Section 11 of the Company Directors Disqualification Act 1986 makes it an offence for an undischarged bankrupt to act as a director of a company unless the court gives him the necessary permission to act. If he has such permission, he may take up an appointment unless the articles forbid his appointment with or without permission, in which case he cannot take the appointment. *Table A, Reg* 81(b) provides that a director who becomes bankrupt vacates office. The article does not prevent the appointment of a director who is already bankrupt, but such an appointment would not normally be made since the director could not act in that capacity.

(iii) *Persons disqualified by Court Order.* The Court may make a disqualification order. This is an order to the effect that a named person may not (unless the Court gives leave) perform any of the following activities during the period specified by the order—

(*a*) being a director (or liquidator or administrator receiver or receiver and manager) of a company;

(*b*) being concerned with or taking part in, directly or indirectly, the promotion, formation or management of a company. (S. 1, *ibid.*)

The circumstances in which a court may make an order are as follows—

  (i) where a person has been convicted of an indictable offence (whether tried on indictment or summarily) in connection either with the promotion, formation, management or liquidation or receivership of a company. (S. 2, *ibid.*)

 (ii) where a person has been convicted, whether or not on the same occasion, of three or more defaults in a period of five years in regard to delivery of documents to the Registrar, e.g. failure to file accounts or the annual return. (S. 3, *ibid.*)

(iii) where *in the winding up of a company* the person concerned has been guilty of fraudulent trading (see p. 14) (whether convicted of an offence under s. 458 or not) (s. 4, *ibid*); and also following wrongful trading (s. 10, *ibid*) (see p. 13).

(iv) where *in the winding up of a company* the person concerned has been guilty, while an officer, liquidator, receiver or manager of *any* fraud in regard to the company or any breach of duty. (S. 4, *ibid.*)

The following courts are empowered to make orders:

Magistrates courts, may make disqualification orders up to a maximum period of five years where the conviction is by a magistrates' court;

Higher courts, may disqualify for up to 15 years, but in the case of persistent default in filing documents under s. 3, *ibid* the maximum is five years whether in the magistrates' court or a higher court. (S. 3(5), *ibid.*)

The persons who may apply for a disqualification order are the Secretary of State; the official receiver; the liquidator; any past or present member or creditor of any company in respect of which the person who is to be disqualified has committed or is alleged to have committed an offence or default. (S. 16, *ibid.*)

228

(iv) *Disqualification of unfit directors of companies in liquidation.* Under s. 6 of the Company Directors Disqualification Act 1986 the court must make a disqualification order against a person in any case where on an application under the section (see below) the court is satisfied—

(*a*) that that person is or has been a director or shadow director of a company which has at any time gone into liquidation (whether while he was a director or shadow director or subsequently); and

(*b*) that that company was insolvent at the time; and

(*c*) that that person's conduct as a director or shadow director of that company makes him unfit to be concerned in the management of a company.

As regards (*c*) above, criteria for unfitness would be failure to ensure the production at appropriate intervals of management accounts and failure to take steps to minimize the loss to creditors.

Section 7(3), *ibid* places a *duty* on a liquidator in a voluntary winding up and on the official receiver in a compulsory winding up to report to the DoTI where he considers a director 'is unfit to be concerned in the management of a company'. It is then up to the Secretary of State to decide whether an application for disqualification should be made to the court. The period of disqualification shall not be less than two years. The maximum would be five years if the matter was taken in a magistrates' court and up to 15 years if taken in a higher court. (S. 6(4), *ibid*.)

(v) *Articles of association.* In addition to the above disqualifications imposed by law further disqualifications may be imposed by a company's articles. *Table A* imposes no such disqualifications, *Reg* 81 merely specifying the grounds on which directors will vacate office. Thus, unless there are such express provisions, a person is not disqualified merely because he is a minor or an alien and a company may be a director of another company.

Directors and employment law

Directors may be fee-paid supervisors acting in some ways as trustees for the shareholders, or senior executives or managers who work whole-time as directors of the company and who sometimes combine this with the giving of a professional service to the company, for example, as an accountant.

As we have seen, all directors may be removed by the members by ordinary resolution in general meeting under s. 303 and it is not necessary to allege any form of misconduct against them. Removal under s. 303 does not prevent the director removed from bringing an action for damages for wrongful dismissal if, but only if, he has a service contract which entitles him to a period of notice which the company has not given or if for a term of years which has not expired.

As regards claims for unfair dismissal and redundancy before industrial tribunals, directors who are employed under express service contracts will normally be engaged for a fixed term of one year or more and may have been required in the contract to waive the right to claim for unfair dismissal or redundancy if the contract is not renewed as s. 142 of the Employment Protection (Consolidation) Act 1978 (as amended by s. 8(2) of the Employment Act 1980) allows.

Otherwise, a director who is an employee and who is removed before his contractual term expires, has a claim before an industrial tribunal for unfair dismissal or redundancy, and this may be a quicker procedure than a court action for wrongful dismissal, though much depends upon salary as there is a ceiling placed on awards for unfair dismissal. Such claims are only available to employee directors, i.e. persons who under s. 153 of the Employment Protection (Consolidation) Act 1978 work under a contract of service, written or oral, express or implied.

DIRECTORS' SHARE QUALIFICATION

The articles may require the directors to take up a certain number of shares as a share qualification. The general purpose of this is said to be that, since they are to manage the company's affairs on behalf of the other shareholders, they should have a stake in it themselves to induce them to act diligently to ensure the company's progress. However, since it is not possible to ensure that directors have a beneficial interest in their qualification shares it seems that no useful purpose is served by a requirement of qualification shares.

Section 291(1) provides that it shall be the duty of every director who is by the articles of the company required to hold a share qualification, and who is not already qualified, to obtain the necessary shares within two months after his appointment, or such shorter time as may be fixed by the articles.

A director must be entered on the company's register as the holder of his qualification shares, but he need not hold them beneficially and could, for example, hold them on trust for others so long as his name appears on the register of members in respect of them. A director is not allowed to hold his qualification shares in the name of a nominee, since it would involve the company receiving notice of trust which is forbidden by s. 360. A director is not qualified by a share warrant. (S. 291(2).)

Special articles may require a director to hold his qualification shares 'in his own right', but even so it has been held that he need not be the absolute unfettered owner of the shares. (*Pulbrook v Richmond Consolidated Mining Co*, 1878.[157])

The modern trend is for articles of association not to require a share qualification for directors since it is now a generally held view that no useful purpose is served by the requirement. It does, of course, help to ensure a quorum at general meetings, though it carries a distinct risk that directors will become disqualified either by transfer, or during the currency of a take-over bid, where they have accepted an offer in respect of their own holdings. It is almost certain that far more cases of disqualification occur than might be supposed and that when the fact comes to light the directors concerned merely buy sufficient shares and carry on as before. In fact, of course, having been disqualified they ought to be re-appointed by the board or the members as the case may be, but probably very few are so re-appointed and it is unlikely that s. 285 (see p. 79) can be relied upon. The section does admittedly provide that the acts of a director shall be valid, notwithstanding any defect that may afterwards be discovered in his appointment or qualification. However, it is possible that s. 285 does not apply if there is no attempt at re-appointment, though the rule in *Turquand's case*[69] may be of assistance (see p. 78). Under s. 291(5) an unqualified person acting as director may be fined for each day that he continues to act.

DIRECTORS' POWERS

The board of directors and meetings of members of a company can between them exercise all of the company's powers. The distribution of those powers as between the members and the directors is, subject to the provisions of the Companies Act, left entirely to the discretion of those who frame the articles of association.

The board's powers can be as broad or as narrow as is desired, but if *Table A*, *Reg* 70 applies, then this confers on the board all the powers of the company, except those which the Companies Act 1985 and the articles require to be exercised by the members in general meeting.

The powers reserved to the members in general meetings by the Companies Acts are mainly the power to alter the memorandum and articles, the power to alter share capital, the power to appoint auditors and remove directors and the power to put the company into liquidation. Additionally, *Table A* reserves to the members the power to fix the rights to be attached to a new issue of shares and to effect variations of such rights, the power to appoint directors and the power to declare dividends though not in excess of the percentage recommended by the board and to capitalize profits and reserves.

In addition, under s. 80 directors of public and private companies must have the authority of the members by ordinary resolution in general meeting or of the company's articles before they exercise a power of allotment of shares or grant rights to subscribe for, or convert securities into shares. Furthermore, s. 89 requires public and private companies to offer new shares to existing members before they are allotted to others. However, a private company may exclude this requirement by its memorandum or articles or by special resolution and a plc may achieve the disapplication of pre-emption rights by a special resolution of its members. (See p. 138.)

Certain powers, even though given to the directors will be regarded as concurrent and exercisable by the members unless the articles make it clear that the power is exclusive to the directors. Thus a power for directors to appoint additional directors and to fill casual vacancies on the board or to fix the remuneration of the managing director will be treated as concurrent powers, unless the articles clearly show that it is to be exclusive to the directors (which *Table A* does not) and so resolutions passed by the members in respect of such matters will prevail over the directors' own decision. Although the directors have power to sue in the company's name, there is also a concurrent power in the members so that if the board decides not to sue in a particular case the members may by ordinary resolution resolve that the company shall sue.

Directors who carry out acts which are initially defective can have them validated by obtaining the sanction of the shareholders in general meeting (*Grant v United Kingdom Switchback Railways Co*, 1888[158]), assuming that the acts are not *ultra vires* (*Ashbury Railway Carriage Co v Riche* (1875)[41]) though the directors cannot cure acts which are in breach of their fiduciary duty to the company by obtaining an ordinary resolution of the members in general meeting if they control the voting at general meetings (*Cook v Deeks*, 1916[141]) or possibly control general meetings *in fact*, even though they do not have a majority of voting shares. (*Prudential Assurance v Newman*, 1980, see p. 554.)

If the company's constitution delegates certain powers to the board, the members can override that delegation: (*a*) by an ordinary resolution if the power is concurrent (*Scott v Scott* 1943[159]); or (*b*) by a special resolution where *Reg* 70 of *Table A* applies. This provides that subject to the provisions of the Act, the memorandum and the articles *and to any directions given by special resolution*, the business of the company shall be managed by the directors who may exercise all the powers of the company. No alteration of the memorandum or articles *and no such direction* shall invalidate any prior act of the directors which would have been valid if that alteration had not been made *or that direction* had not been given. The powers given by this Regulation shall not be limited by any special power given to the directors by the articles and a meeting of directors at which a quorum is present may exercise all powers exercisable by the directors.

If the members are dissatisfied by the way in which the directors are exercising their powers, then unless the power is in the limited area of concurrent powers, they must alter the articles so as to cut down the directors' powers, or refuse to re-elect the board when the opportunity arises, or, alternatively, remove them under s. 303. (See p. 270.)

Where there is a regulation such as *Reg* 70 of *Table A*, the members may give a direction by a special resolution under which the directors are required to act differently for the future.

Delegation of powers by the directors

The well-known maxim of the law of agency—'*delegatus non potest delegare*' (a delegate cannot delegate)—applies to directors, so that they cannot delegate their functions and powers to others without the permission of the members or the articles. Articles do usually allow delegation of powers to a committee of the board (*Table A, Reg* 72), though such delegation is revocable even if made for a fixed period of time. (*Manton v Brighton Corporation*, [1951] 2 All ER 101.) *Regulation* 72 also allows delegation to any managing director or any director holding any other executive office of such as the directors' powers as they consider desirable to be exercised by him.

Table A, Reg 71 also allows the board to employ agents and professional persons to carry out any functions which the board may itself carry out.

Board unable or unwilling to act

This situation may arise in the following circumstances:

(*a*) *Where the act is beyond the powers of the board*. Where the act is beyond the powers of the board authority for the transaction must be sought from the members in general meeting and the authorization may be given by ordinary resolution.

The members may authorize directors to do an act which is outside the directors' own powers, but within the company's power, by passing an ordinary resolution either before or after the directors' act. Per Bowen LJ in *Grant v United Kingdom Switchback Railways Co*, 1888.[158] In such a situation the members can, of course, revoke or vary the authority by ordinary resolution at any time. It is only necessary to amend the articles if the members wish to add the particular power to the powers of the board.

(*b*) *Lack of quorum at board meetings.* Directors may be unable to exercise the powers given to them by the articles because they have become so few in number that they cannot constitute a quorum, or because so many of them are, in a legal sense, interested in the transaction in question and are consequently disabled from voting by the articles, that a quorum of competent directors cannot be found.

As regards quorum, the articles usually empower the remaining directors to fill vacancies so as to make up a quorum (*Reg* 90), but if there are no directors at all, or if the remaining directors are unwilling to fill the vacancies, the members may exercise their powers until a board is properly constituted.

When a quorum of competent directors (i.e. directors who are not interested in the transaction) cannot be found, the board's powers temporarily revert to the members who may then authorize the remaining directors to act either in advance of their acting or by ratification afterwards.

(*c*) *The proper purpose rule.* If directors are unable to exercise their powers in a lawful manner because to do so would be a breach of their duty to exercise those powers for the purpose for which they were given (alternatively expressed as the Proper Purpose Rule), the members in general meeting may by ordinary resolution ratify what the directors have in fact done (*Bamford v Bamford*, 1969[68]), and it would seem that they may also authorize the directors *in advance* to do the act in question. (*Bamford v Bamford*, 1969,[68] per Russell LJ.)

If there is no such ratification or authorization by the members and the act of the board contravenes the Proper Purpose Rule, it is invalid. Thus, in *Galloway v Hallé Concerts Society*, 1915[99] where G was always late in paying calls made on him and once did not pay at all, so that the company had to take him to court to get the call, the directors made a call on G for the whole of the balance due from him, but they did not make calls on other members who were potentially liable. It was held that this was an improper exercise of the directors' powers to make calls and G was not liable to pay that call. Many of the cases which have been considered under the Proper Purpose Rule have been concerned with the use of the power of allotment to put off or assist a take-over bid (as for example *Bamford v Bamford*, 1969[68]) and it was consistently held that the power of allotment is given to the board to raise new capital for the company and if there are additional motives the allotment is invalid under the 'Proper Purpose Rule' unless the allotment has been approved by an ordinary resolution of the members. These cases are now of less importance because by s. 80 the directors of both public and private companies need express authority in the articles or by ordinary resolution of the members before making an allotment and that authority cannot last for more than five years and may be revoked (or renewed) by ordinary resolution even if conferred in the articles.

(*d*) *Dissension between members of the board.* If directors are unable to act because of a dissension between themselves, the members may exercise the powers of the board until a board is elected which can act. However, the dissension must result in deadlock before the members can intervene. It must, for example, be shown either that so many directors persistently absent themselves from board meetings that a quorum cannot be found, or that the dissenting parties have equal voting power at board meetings and resolutions cannot therefore be passed.

(*e*) *Powers of the court.* Where the board is unable to act because the directors are so few in number that a quorum cannot be found, or because of deadlock between the directors, the court may appoint a receiver of the company's business to manage it until a competent board can be constituted. Furthermore, if the power of the board which the members wish to have exercised is one which the court can conveniently exercise itself, the court may exercise the power and give any decision which the board could have given. (See *Re Copal Varnish Co Ltd* [1917] 2 Ch 349 where the court exercised a power to approve the transfer of shares.)

Managing director

It is usual to make one or more of the full-time directors managing director, and give him powers relating to the management of the business which are exercisable without reference to the full board.

Before such an appointment can be made the articles must so provide. *Table A, Reg* 84, provides for the appointment of a member of the board to the office of managing director, and further states that he shall not be subject to retirement by rotation, but that he shall cease to be a managing director if for any other reason he ceases to be a director, e.g. where he is removed or becomes disqualified. (*Southern Foundries v Shirlaw*, 1940.[58]) Thus under *Table A*, a managing director must also be a director but there is nothing in the Companies Acts which requires the chairman of the board to be a director. *Regulation* 84 allows the directors to fix the managing director's remuneration and *Reg* 72 allows the board to delegate any of their powers to him, subject to a right to review these powers from time to time. Where the articles are in the form of *Table A*, then *Reg* 72 will mean that the managing director is not wholly independent of the board, as he will be if his powers are outlined expressly in the articles.

Chairman

Companies are not required by the law to appoint a chairman. Since, however, they are bound to hold an AGM of shareholders (s. 366(1)) and articles such as *Table A*, *Reg* 88 envisage meetings of the board, there is obviously a need for a chairman to control proceedings.

A chairman of the company is therefore usually appointed. *Table A*, *Reg* 91 gives the board specific power to appoint a chairman of the board and *Reg* 42 states that the chairman of the board shall preside as chairman of general meetings, though provisions are made in each case for the chairman's absence and in practice a deputy chairman is often appointed.

Appointment of directors to executive posts

Under *Reg* 84 of *Table A* the directors may appoint one or more of their number to any executive office, e.g. finance director, under the company and may enter into an agreement or arrangement with any director for his employment by the company or for the provision by him of any services outside the scope of the ordinary duties of a director. Any such appointment, agreement, or arrangement, may be made on such terms as the directors determine and they may remunerate any such director for his services as they think fit. Any appointment of a director to an executive office will terminate if he ceases to be a director but without prejudice to any claim for damages for breach of the contract of service between the director and the company. A director holding executive office shall not be subject to retirement by rotation.

Furthermore, under *Reg* 72 the board may delegate to any director holding executive office such of their powers as they consider desirable to be exercised by him. Any such delegation may be subject to any conditions the directors may impose and either collaterally with, or to the exclusion of their own powers, may be revoked or altered.

Directors as agents

Reference should be made to pages 78–83 dealing amongst other things with the rule in *Turquand's Case*[69] and s. 35, since these have a bearing not only on the effect of the articles of association but also on the validity of acts of directors as agents.

BOARD MEETINGS

The powers of the directors must be exercised collectively at a board meeting and not individually, though an informal agreement made by them all will bind the company. This is envisaged by *Table A*, *Reg* 93 which provides that a resolution in writing signed by all the directors entitled to receive notice of a meeting of directors or of a committee of directors shall be as valid and effectual as if it had been passed at a meeting of directors or (as the case may be) a committee of directors duly convened and held and may consist of several documents in the like form each signed by one or more directors; but a resolution signed by an alternate director need not also be signed by his appointor and if it is signed by a director who has appointed an alternate director, it need not be signed by the alternate director in that capacity.

A meeting of the board can be called by any director unless the articles otherwise provide. *Table A*, *Reg* 88, provides that a director may, and the secretary shall at the request of a director, summon a meeting of the board.

Notice of board meetings

Notice of a board meeting should normally be given to all the directors and the time must be reasonable. This may be a matter of days, hours, or even minutes, depending on the circumstances. It has been held that three hours' notice to directors who had other business to attend to was insufficient, even though their places of business and the place where the board meeting was to be held were all in the City of London. (*Re Homer District Consolidated Gold Mines Ltd, ex parte Smith* (1888) 39 Ch D 546.) On the other hand, five minutes' notice to a director was held sufficient where neither distance nor other engagements prevented him from attending. (*Browne v La Trinidad* (1887) 37 Ch D 1.) Notice of a board meeting need not be given to a director whose whereabouts are unknown because, for example, he is travelling, and *Table A*, *Reg* 88, provides that notice need not be sent to a director who is for the time being absent from the United Kingdom, e.g. where he is absent on business, but unless the articles are in the form of *Table A*, notice must be given to all directors if their whereabouts are known.

The effect of failure to give proper notice is uncertain, but it is the better view that it does not render resolutions passed at the meeting void. The law is not entirely clear, but in *Re Homer, etc* (above) it was held that all resolutions passed at the meeting were void, but in *Browne v La Trinidad* (above) it was held that failure to give proper notice to a director merely entitles him to require that a second meeting be held if he does not attend the first. If he does not require a second meeting to be held within a reasonable time, then he waives his right to ask for it and the resolutions passed at the first meeting are then valid. The notice need only specify when and where the meeting is to be held. It is not necessary to set out the business to be transacted but in practice it is usual to do so.

Quorum

This is normally fixed by the articles, and *Table A, Reg* 89, provides that the quorum shall be fixed by the directors and unless so fixed shall be two. A person who holds office only as an alternate director shall, if his appointor is not present, be counted in the quorum. This does not, of course, apply to a private company with only one director. Certainly no business can be validly transacted without a quorum, and the quorum must if the articles so require (*Re Greymouth Point Elizabeth Rail & Coal Co Ltd* [1904] 1 Ch 32) consist of directors who are not personally interested in the business which is before the meeting, although in such a case interested directors are entitled to notice of the meeting and may attend and speak but not vote.

As regards personal interest, *Regs* 94 and 95 are relevant and provide as follows. Under *Reg* 94 a director shall not vote at a meeting of directors or of a committee of directors on any resolution concerning a matter in which he has, directly or indirectly, an interest or duty which is material and which conflicts, or may conflict with the interests of the company unless his interest or duty arises only because the case falls within one or more of the following paragraphs—

(*a*) the resolution relates to the giving to him of a guarantee, security, or indemnity in respect of money lent to, or an obligation by him for the benefit of, the company or any of its subsidiaries;

(*b*) the resolution relates to the giving to a third party of a guarantee, security, or indemnity in respect of an obligation of the company or any of its subsidiaries for which the director has assumed responsibility in whole or part and whether alone or jointly with others under a guarantee or indemnity or by the giving of security;

(*c*) his interest arises by reason of his subscribing or agreeing to subscribe for any shares, debentures, or other securities of the company or any of its subsidiaries, or by reason of his being, or intending to become, a participant in the underwriting or sub-underwriting of an offer of any such shares, debentures, or other securities by the company or any of its subsidiaries for subscription, purchase or exchange;

(*d*) the resolution relates in any way to a retirement benefit scheme which has been approved, or is conditional upon approval, by the Board of Inland Revenue for taxation purposes.

For the purposes of *Reg* 94 an interest of a person who is, for any purpose of the Companies Act connected with a director shall be treated as an interest of the director and in relation to an alternate director, an interest of his appointor shall be treated as an interest of the alternate director without prejudice to any interest which the alternate director has otherwise. *Regulation 95* provides that a director shall not be counted in the quorum present at a meeting in relation to a resolution on which he is not entitled to vote. *Regulation 97* enables a director to vote on the appointment of a fellow director to an office of profit under the company, but not on his own appointment. The company may by ordinary resolution suspend or relax to any extent, either generally or in respect of any particular matter, any provision of the articles prohibiting a director from voting at a meeting of directors or of a committee of directors. If the company is to have a listing on the Stock Exchange the rules of the Stock Exchange require that the company's articles follow *Regs* 94 and 95 in terms of directors' interests, otherwise a listing will not be granted.

Voting at board meetings

The voting at board meetings is usually governed by the articles and is normally one vote per director, but *Table A, Reg 94* provides, as we have seen, that directors with a personal interest in the business before the meeting are not allowed to vote. A majority of one will carry a resolution, though an equality of votes means that the resolution is lost, unless the position is resolved by the use of the chairman's *casting vote* if he is given one under the articles. *Table A, Reg 91* gives the directors power to appoint a chairman to preside at board meetings and *Reg 88* gives him a casting vote.

Minutes

Section 382 provides that every company shall cause minutes of all proceedings at directors' meetings and where there are managers all proceedings at meetings of managers, to be prepared and entered in books kept for that purpose. It further provides that when the minutes are signed by the chairman of the meeting, or by the chairman of the next succeeding meeting, they shall be *prima facie* evidence of the proceedings. The members have no general right to inspect the minutes of directors' meetings (*R v Merchant Tailors Co* (1831) 2 B & Ad 115), but the directors have.

PUBLICITY IN CONNECTION WITH DIRECTORS

Certain provisions of the Companies Act 1985 are designed to make available details regarding the executive of the company which may

239

be of assistance to members and persons dealing with it. The following should be noted:

(a) *The register of directors and secretaries.* The company must keep at its registered office a register of directors and secretaries and must notify the Registrar of any changes within 14 days of the happening thereof.

The contents of the register as to directors are as follows—

(i) Present Christian name or forename and surname.

(ii) Any former Christian name or forename and surname.

(iii) Usual residential address.

(iv) Business occupation.

(v) Any other directorships currently held or held within the preceding five years. (S. 289.) The object of including past directorships is to enable members and creditors or potential members and creditors to ascertain a director's past record, e.g. have certain of the companies of which he has been a director failed or at least not done well.

There are exemptions for both *present and past* directorships in companies which, for the whole five-year period, were dormant or within the same wholly-owned group of companies. (S. 289(3).) In addition, the company must include on the relevant forms sent to the Registrar on registration of a new company not only present directorships held by each director, but also those held in the preceding five years.

(b) *Trade catalogues and circulars.* Under s. 305 every company registered on or after 23 November 1916 must state on all letterheadings, on which the company's name appears, the names of all their directors *or none of them.* This does not apply to a name quoted in the text of a letter or to the signatory. Companies incorporated before 23 November 1916 do not come within these provisions and may, if they wish, show some and not all of the names of the directors.

(c) *Register of directors' interests in shares and debentures.* The provisions relating to this register were considered on page 181.

(d) *Inspection of directors' service contracts.* Every company must keep a copy of each of its directors' service contracts at its registered office or at its principal place of business in England, Scotland or Wales (depending on where it is registered), or the place where its register of members is kept. (S. 318(1)(a).)

If a director has no written contract, a written memorandum of the terms on which he serves must be kept instead. (S. 318(1)(b).)

The copy or memorandum must show all changes in the terms of the contract made since it was entered into. (S. 318(10).)

The company must notify the Registrar of Companies where the copies or memoranda of its directors' service contracts are kept unless they are kept at its registered office. (S. 318(4).)

There is no need for a copy or memorandum to be kept if the contract has less than 12 months to run, or if it can be brought to an end by the company within that time without payment of compensation. (S. 318(11).)

Members of the company may inspect such copies or memoranda without charge. (S. 318(7).) If inspection is refused the person wishing to inspect the contract may apply to the court which will make an order compelling inspection. (S. 318(9).)

The intention of the provisions of s. 318 is to assist members who wish to remove a director under s. 303. This publicity enables members to see what the cost of removal will be.

Section 318 also provides that—

(i) a director's service contract with a subsidiary (or a memorandum of it if it is not in writing) must also be open for inspection. (S. 318(1)(c).)

(ii) the *contract* of a director who works with the company or a subsidiary wholly or mainly outside the United Kingdom need not be available for inspection. In such a case there need only be available for inspection a memorandum containing—

(1) the directors' name;

(2) the name and place of incorporation of the subsidiary (if any) with which the contract is made; and

(3) the provisions in the contract as to its duration. (S. 318(5).)

(iii) Shadow directors, i.e. persons other than professional advisers, in accordance with whose instructions directors of a company are accustomed to act, are to be treated as directors for the purposes of this section. (S. 318(6).)

FINANCIAL ARRANGEMENTS WITH DIRECTORS

Remuneration

If a director is to receive remuneration by way of fees the articles must expressly provide for it, and in the absence of such provision, no remuneration is payable even if the members resolve in general meeting that it shall be (*Re George Newman & Co* [1895] 1 Ch 674.) Their proper procedure is to alter the articles or modify the contract to allow for it. *Table A, Reg* 82, provides that the remuneration of the directors shall from time to time be determined by the company in general meeting. It should be noted that a provision in the articles is not enough; there must also be an authorizing resolution by the company in general meeting. (*In re Duomatic Ltd*, 1969.[160]) The ability to fix the fees of directors is not within *Reg 70* (delegation of powers to board). (*Foster v Foster* [1916] 1 Ch 532.)

Directors are not entitled to any remuneration unless the articles so provide (*Hutton v West Cork Rail Co*, 1883[30]); and if they pay themselves remuneration out of the company's funds they may be compelled to restore it, even though they believed that the payment was permissible. (*Brown and Green Ltd v Hays* (1920) 36 TLR 330.) The directors cannot evade the rule by appointing themselves to salaried posts within the company. If they do the appointment is valid but it appears that the director would not be entitled to the salary applicable to the post. (*Kerr v Marine Products Ltd* (1928) 44 TLR 292.) *Reg* 83 provides for the payment of directors' expenses of office.

Where there is a provision for remuneration, it is *payable whether profits are earned or not* (*Re Lundy Granite Co* (1872) 26 LT 673), and in a winding up the directors rank for their remuneration with ordinary creditors and are not deferred, though they are not preferential creditors, except in respect of a salary which may be payable to them as where they occupy a managerial position, e.g. a company secretary, in addition to membership of the board.

Whether a director who vacates office before completing a year in office is entitled to a proportionate part of his yearly salary will depend upon the wording of the articles or his contract of service. The words 'at the rate of £S' per annum, or an express provision that the remuneration is to accrue 'from day to day', will mean that the director is so entitled; the words '£S per annum', or '£S in each year', will make the payment depend on a full year's service. (*Moriarty v Regent's Garage Co* [1921] 1 KB 423.) *Table A, Reg 82* provides that the directors' remuneration shall accrue from day to day.

If the director works for the company without a contract, he can recover a sum of money for his service under a *quantum meruit* (*Craven-Ellis v Canons Ltd*, 1936),[161] but this remedy is not available where the director has a contract which has used inappropriate words. (*Re Richmond Gate Property Co Ltd*, 1964.[162])

Section 311 provides that it shall not be lawful for the company to pay a director remuneration free of income tax, the company paying the tax.

Remuneration by way of contract of service is governed by different rules. *Reg 84* of *Table A* provides that service contracts may be made by the board with individual directors thus ousting the general fiduciary rule that a director may not contract with his company. *Regulation 85* allows the director concerned to be counted in the quorum at the meeting at which the company through its board decides to contract with him, though he cannot vote on his own appointment. Directors have, therefore, a largely unsupervised freedom to fix their own salaries and other terms of employment by using the contract of service approach.

As regards the power to pay, a company may remunerate its directors where this is 'reasonably incidental to the carrying on of the company's business', *per* Bowen LJ in *Hutton v West Cork Railway,* 1883.[30] This requirement will usually be complied with unless the company is not a going concern or has been sold as in *Hutton.*[30] Even then it would presumably be legal to pay the remuneration even if the company was not a going concern if the payment of directors' remuneration was made an express substantive object as were the pension arrangements in *Re Horsley and Weight Ltd,* 1982.[34]

Finally, remuneration may be paid even when the company is insolvent. There is no requirement that payment should be from distributable profits. (*Re Halt Garage (1964) Ltd,* 1982.[33])

Compensation for loss of office

Such compensation can be paid if authorized by the articles, but s. 312 provides that the payment must be disclosed to the members in general meeting and approved by an ordinary resolution. If it is not so disclosed the director holds the money on trust for the company, and must repay the sum involved to the company. (S. 313(2).) (*In Re Duomatic Ltd,* 1969.[160]) Furthermore, a director is also under a duty to disclose payment for loss of office made in connection with a transfer of shares on an offer, for example, to take over the company. In so far as the amount a director is to receive is not disclosed and approved by the shareholders, the director concerned holds the money on trust for persons who have sold their shares as a result of the offer. (S. 314.) The director concerned must bear the expense of distributing the compensation to them. (S. 315.)

A payment will be treated as compensation for loss of office only if the company is under no legal obligation to make it. Thus payment of damages to a director who is dismissed in breach of his service contract, whether the damages are settled out of court or assessed by the court, does not require the approval of members. (S. 316(3).) In addition, an amount which a director receives under the terms of his service contract on his resignation or removal from office in terms of severance pay is not treated as compensation for loss of office because the company is obliged by the contract to pay it. Thus it is payable unconditionally when the resignation or removal takes place and it does not require the approval of the members in general meeting. (*Taupo Totara Timber Co Ltd v Rowe* [1977] 3 All ER 123.)

Section 314 is a particularly weak provision in a take-over situation where the directors of the victim company remain in office within the group. The disclosure and approval provisions apply only on loss of office or retirement and if the director concerned does not lose his office or retire but continues as a director in the merged organization managing the same assets, there is no need to disclose or get members' approval of any compensation which is paid. (See further p. 393.)

Pensions

The company's implied power to pay pensions is in respect of employees only and not directors, but pensions may be paid to directors if the articles so provide, and *Table A*, *Reg* 87 allows this.

Disclosure of remuneration, etc

The various disclosures required which are set out below are derived from the Companies Act 1985, Sched 5, Part V unless otherwise indicated. Any provisions in the articles as to the power of directors in the absence of an independent quorum to vote remuneration, including pensions or other benefits to themselves, or any members of their body, must be disclosed in a prospectus issued by the company (Stock Exchange Listing Agreement, Section 3, Chapter 2, para. 6.9(b)). Sched 5 provides that the *notes to the accounts* of the company laid before the members in general meeting shall disclose—

(a) the aggregate amount of the directors' emoluments;

(b) the aggregate amount of directors' or past directors' pensions; and

(c) the aggregate amount of any compensation to directors or past directors in respect of loss of office.

When a company makes in its accounts the disclosures regarding directors' emoluments and particulars of directors' salaries, pensions and compensation for loss of office, it must also give the corresponding amount for the immediately preceding financial year.

The emoluments of the company's chairman, or if, in the financial year, more persons than one have been chairman, the emoluments of each of them, so far as attributable to the period during which each was chairman, must be disclosed in the accounts.

With regard to directors disclosure is required—

(a) of the number of directors who did not receive emoluments;

(b) of directors whose emoluments did not exceed £5,000; and

(c) by reference to each pair of adjacent points on a scale whereon the lowest point is £5,000 and the succeeding ones are successive integral multiples of £5,000, the number (if any) whose several emoluments exceeded the lower point but did not exceed the higher.

244

Disclosure is not required if the person's duties as chairman or director were wholly or mainly discharged outside the United Kingdom.

The emoluments of any one director receiving more than the chairman must also be disclosed. If two or more directors are receiving more than the chairman then the emoluments paid to them (in the case of equality) must be disclosed. Where their emoluments are not equal the emoluments of the director receiving the greater or, as the case may be, the greatest must be disclosed.

The expression 'chairman' means the person elected by the directors of the company to be chairman of their meetings and includes a person who, though not so elected, holds any office (however designated) which, in accordance with the constitution of the company, carries with it functions substantially similar to those discharged by a person so elected.

A company which is neither a holding company nor a subsidiary of another body corporate is not subject to the requirements of Sched 5, Part V if the emoluments of all the directors in the year do not exceed £60,000.

Under Sched 5, Part V and Section 3, Chapter 2, para. 6.3(b) of the Stock Exchange Listing agreement disclosure is also required of the number of directors who have waived rights to receive emoluments and the aggregate amount of those emoluments. Directors are under a duty to give the company the information it may require to make the above disclosures in the accounts. If the accounts do not comply with Sched 5, Part V the auditors must, so far as they reasonably can, include the required particulars in their report.

Loans and similar transactions: directors and shadow directors

The Companies Act 1980 brought about radical changes in this area of the law. The provisions are now in the Companies Act 1985 and are set out below.

Restrictions apply to all companies

Subject to the exceptions referred to later in the chapter, no company, whether public or private, may:

(a) make a loan to one of its directors or to a director of its holding company (s. 330(2)(a));

(b) give a guarantee or provide any security in connection with a loan made by any person to such a director (s. 330(2)(b)); this rule also applies to indemnities (s. 331(2));

(c) arrange for the assignment to it or the assumption by it of any rights, obligations or liabilities under a transaction which, if it had been entered into by the company, would have contravened (*a*) or (*b*) above. (S. 330(6).)

Thus if A makes a loan to B (a director of Boxo Ltd) and subsequently Boxo buys A's rights to recover the loan and interest by assignment, the assignment is illegal under the Act.

In addition, if A makes a loan to B as before and C guarantees the loan and subsequently Boxo assumes liability under the guarantee from which C is released, the transaction is illegal under the Act.

(*d*) Take part in any arrangement whereby—

    (i) another person enters into a transaction which, if it had been entered into by the company, would have contravened (*a*), (*b*), or (*c*) above; and

    (ii) that other person, in pursuance of the arrangement, has obtained or is to obtain any benefit from the company or its holding company or a subsidiary of the company or its holding company. (S. 330(7).)

This is a very broadly drafted provision but it is intended in the main to cover 'back to back' deals as where company A agrees to make loans to the directors of company B in return for loans made by company B to the directors of company A and also cases where a director persuades, for example, a bank to make loans on favourable terms to him in return for his company placing lucrative business with the bank.

In situations outlined in (*c*) and (*d*) above the mischief is that the company's resources are tied up indirectly in providing credit for its directors.

Restrictions applying to 'relevant companies' only

A 'relevant company' is defined by s. 331(6) as—

(*a*) a public company; or

(*b*) a company which is part of a group in which any one of the member companies is not a private company.

Again, subject to exceptions referred to later in the chapter, a relevant company may not:

(*a*) Make a *quasi-loan* to a person who is either one of its directors or a director of its holding company. (S. 330(3)(*a*).)

The expression 'quasi-loan' is new to English law, but some common examples are—(1) a company buys a railway season ticket for a director, the director to repay the company over an agreed period; (2) a director uses a company credit card to pay for personal goods or services, the director to repay the company at a later date (if the company credit card is used only for business expenses then no quasi-loan is given and the restrictions do not apply); (3) a company purchases airline tickets for a director's wife who is accompanying him on a business trip, the director to reimburse the company at a later date; (4) a company pays the account of a travel agent which includes amounts owing for private travel by the director and/or his wife, the director to reimburse the company; (5) a company lays out money for furniture and the redecoration of a director's flat, the director to reimburse the company at a later date.

(b) Make a loan or a quasi-loan to a person who is connected either with one of its directors or a director of its holding company. (S. 330(3)(b).)

The meaning of the expression 'connected person' is more precisely defined in s. 346, but in broad terms a person, who is not a director of the company, is regarded as connected with a director of a company only where he or she is the spouse, child or step-child of that director. Here it should be noted that 'child or step-child' includes any illegitimate child, but excludes any person aged 18 or over. Companies (called associated companies) in which the director and connected persons have together 20 per cent or more interest in the equity share capital, or control of 20 per cent of the voting rights, are connected, as are trustees of trusts whose beneficiaries include a director or a member of his family or associated company, though a person will not be connected where he is a trustee of an employees' share scheme or pension scheme, and, finally, a person who is acting as a partner of a director, or of any other person who is connected with him.

(c) Enter into any guarantee or give any security in connection with any loan or quasi-loan that was made by any person to a director or connected person. (S. 330(3)(c).)

(d) Enter into a credit transaction as creditor for such a director or connected person. (S. 330(4)(a).)

The expression 'credit transaction' includes supplying goods under a hire purchase or conditional sale agreement, leasing any land or hiring any goods in return for periodic payments, or dispositions of land or the supply of goods or services on the basis that the payment, regardless of the form it takes, is to be deferred.

Practical examples are—(1) a company sells furniture it either owns or has made to a director *by a contract* that payment be deferred for 12 months; (2) a company services a director's private car or that of his spouse (in a public company) *on the understanding* that payment shall be deferred (there is no need for a legal and binding contract); (3) a private company which runs a department store sells audio equipment to the wife of its public parent company's chairman under a hire purchase agreement. (This agreement is controlled because the private company is not free-standing. It is a subsidiary of a public company and therefore a 'relevant company'.)

(*e*) Enter into any guarantee, or provide any security, in connection with any credit transaction that was made by any other person for such a director or connected person. (S. 330(4)(*b*).)

It will be seen from what has been said above that the 1985 Act excludes private companies from the application of the extra rules regarding quasi-loans, credit and connected persons, unless the private company belongs to a group which includes a company which is not a private company. The main thrust is to protect members of the public who invest in companies and by and large the public is not to any great extent involved with private companies.

Permitted loans and similar transactions

The Companies Act 1985 exempts certain loans and similar transactions from the provisions set out above. These exemptions are set out below.

Category 1. Under s. 334 *all* companies may make loans to a director or a director of the holding company, but not connected persons, provided that the aggregate amount of the loan(s) does not exceed £2,500. Such loans require disclosure in financial statements under Sched 6 (see p. 353).

It is important to note that the aggregate amount of loans to the director concerned does not exceed £2,500. The relevant amounts are, by reason of s. 339, the value of the proposed loan and the amounts outstanding, if any, under any other loan to the director. The value of any existing quasi-loans or credit transactions does not have to be brought into account by reason of s. 339.

Category 2. This category relates to loans or quasi-loans to a subsidiary, or a fellow-subsidiary, of a *relevant company* and to the making of guarantees or the provision of securities in connection with loans or quasi-loans that any person makes to such a subsidiary. A relevant company is not prevented from entering into these transactions merely because a director of the company, or of its holding company, is associated with that subsidiary. 'Associated' means that the director, together with his connected persons, has an interest in at least 20 per cent of the share capital or controls 20 per cent of the voting power in that subsidiary. This exemption is to facilitate inter-group business. However, if the associated company is a trustee of a trust under which the director and/or his connected persons are beneficiaries, or the associated company is a partner of the director or his connected persons, the said associated company is to be regarded as connected. (S. 346.)

In addition, a quasi-loan made by a relevant company, either to one of its directors or to a director of its holding company, is permitted if—

(i) it contains a term under which the director must reimburse the company within two months of the quasi-loan being incurred, *and*

(ii) the aggregate amount of the quasi-loan and any outstanding quasi-loans does not exceed £1,000.

Category 3. This category covers credit transactions by *relevant companies.* The exemptions apply to—

(i) credit transactions or the making of guarantees or the provision of any security in connection with credit transactions for any director or connected person, where the aggregate of all of these transactions does not exceed £5,000.

This is what is known as a *de minimis* provision. The Act is not concerned to catch the smaller credit transactions, even though these may not be on a strictly commercial or arm's length basis. Thus a company may repair a director's car on credit in the company's workshops without infringing the provisions of the 1985 Act.

(ii) Credit transactions which are entered into on a commercial basis or at arm's length. There is no monetary limit on credit here provided that the ordinary business of the company involves, e.g. supplying goods on hire purchase or under leasing arrangements. However, the credit extended and the terms of the contract must be on ordinary commercial terms, i.e. in line with those that would be offered to a person who was unconnected with the company but who had the same financial standing as the director or connected person involved. The Act does not seek to prevent hire purchase companies, for example, from doing business with their directors provided it is on normal commercial terms.

Category 4. This category exempts all transactions by all companies in favour of their holding companies. Thus loans, quasi-loans, and credit transactions that a company makes for its holding company are not prohibited. The exemption extends to the entering into of guarantees and the provision of securities in connection with the above transactions.

This exemption is necessary because a holding company may be a director of the company offering the facility or a director of a subsidiary may be a substantial shareholder of the parent company so that the parent is a connected person. These exemptions are included because the Act is not concerned to interfere with legitimate group lending.

Category 5. This category relates to expenses incurred by a director to enable him to perform his duties. It includes the provision of funds by way of an advance and also the provision of goods, services, or credit.

Advances which a director receives in order to pay, e.g. hotel bills and travelling, are not included at all in this category. They are not loans because the director will not have to reimburse the company but only account for money spent and return the balance if any. The category is more concerned with e.g. a loan to purchase or furnish a flat or second home near to a branch of the company's business which the director may have to visit frequently. It could also be used to give a bridging loan for house purchase to a director if, because e.g. of promotion, he was moved to another part of the UK. However, the maximum allowed in a relevant company is rather small. (See below.)

There is no limit as to the aggregate amounts involved if the company is not a relevant company. However, the Act provides that only £10,000 of funds, etc. can be made available to each director of a relevant company under the exception and for all companies one of two conditions must be fulfilled—

(a) that the transaction is entered into with the prior authority of an ordinary resolution of the company in general meeting; or

(b) that the transaction contains a provision that if it is not approved by the company before the next annual general meeting, any liabilities under it must be discharged within six months of that annual general meeting.

Category 6. This category contains an exemption which relates only to moneylending companies (other than recognized banks). The exemption is limited to loans, quasi-loans and guarantees given in connection with such transactions made by a moneylending company in the ordinary course of its business. Such loans must be on normal commercial terms (see Category 3(ii) above) and, in the case of relevant companies, there is an upper limit of £50,000 which is an aggregate limit for each director taken together with his connected persons. Non-relevant moneylending companies have no limit, but the transaction must be on ordinary commercial terms.

It should be noted that loans made by a moneylending company to either its directors or directors of its holding company may be made, even though they are larger in amount or on more favourable terms than those which would normally be given in the ordinary course of business provided that the object of the loan is either to facilitate the purchase or improvement of a director's only or main residence, or to take over any similar loan that any other person has made to that director. In addition, the company must ordinarily make loans of that description to its employees on similar terms and the aggregate of the relevant amounts must not exceed £50,000.

As regards house purchase and house improvement loans, the financial limit applies to recognized banks also (see below).

Category 7—Recognized banks. Recognized banks are those granted

250

recognition by the Bank of England on the grounds that according to the Banking Act, 1979 they have established a high reputation and standing in the financial community. Such banks can, in general terms, lend to their directors without limit but the loans must be on commercial terms and disclosed to the shareholders (see below).

This exemption is necessary because banks would find it difficult to keep track of all transactions, particularly in the broad category of associated companies. However, as we have seen, the £50,000 limit for house purchase or home improvement does apply even in the case of recognized banks.

Relevant amounts

Section 339 provides that the financial limits are aggregate amounts, connected persons included. Existing transactions, i.e. loans, quasi-loans and credit, will therefore have to be aggregated before a new transaction is entered into. (See, however, the position with regard to the £2,500 loan at p. 248.)

A moneylending company may make a housing loan to a director not exceeding £50,000 and then make other loans to him in the ordinary course of business. Previously loans under both heads had to be aggregated and might prevent a loan for housing, though this did not affect recognized banks because they had, and still have, no limit on loans on ordinary commercial terms.

Loans, etc. to directors appear in diagrammatic form at the end of this chapter (see 'Other Materials', p. 275). For the provisions of the 1985 Act regarding disclosure of loans, etc. in the accounts see p. 353.

As we have seen, the above provisions restricting loans, quasi-loans, and credit, may interfere with the giving of financial assistance to directors in a management buy-out. (See p. 169)

Contravention of the provisions—civil remedies

In general terms a loan or similar transaction which contravenes the provisions set out above is *voidable* at the instance of the company. (S. 341(1).) In consequence the company will be able to recover property from those into whose hands it has passed except—

(i) where it is no longer possible to make restitution of any money or of any other asset that has been transferred under the transaction or arrangement. (S. 341(1)(*a*).) Thus any part of a loan that has been spent, e.g. on a cruise, would be irrecoverable as being quite unidentifiable.

(ii) Where the company has been indemnified for any loss or damage that it has suffered, e.g. by the borrowing director. (S. 341(1)(a).)

(iii) Where the avoidance of the arrangement or the transaction would affect rights that were acquired *bona fide* and for value and without actual notice of the contravention by anyone other than the person for whom the transaction or arrangement was made. (S. 341(1)(b).) This is the usual protection for third parties who take property for value from, e.g. a director, who has obtained it under a forbidden transaction but who have no knowledge that this is the case.

In addition, whether or not the transaction or arrangement has been rescinded, the director and, as appropriate, any connected person who was a party to the transaction or the arrangement, is liable—

(a) to account to the company for any gain that has been made either directly or indirectly from it (s. 341(2)(a)); and

(b) to indemnify the company for any loss or damage that has resulted from it. (S. 341(2)(b).)

It is important to note that this liability is extended also to any other director who has authorized the transaction or the arrangement.

Where the transaction is with a connected person, then the director with whom that person is connected will not be liable if he shows that he took all reasonable steps to ensure that the provisions of s. 330 were complied with. In addition, any director who authorizes the transaction or arrangement will not be liable if he can show that he did not know the relevant circumstances constituting the contravention at the time the transaction was made. (S. 341(5).)

As regards the possibility of enforcement by a minority as an exception to *Foss v Harbottle*, 1843,[134] (see pp. 198–9).

Contravention of the provisions—criminal liability

Section 342 sets out the criminal penalties for breach of s. 330. It is an offence for a director to authorize or permit contravention of the Act. The company is also liable; this should encourage shareholders to take what steps they can to prevent offences. Any other person who procures a prohibited transaction is also liable. However, a successful criminal prosecution requires full knowledge in the accused.

DUTIES OF DIRECTORS TO THE COMPANY

In general terms directors owe a duty to their company to manage it in accordance with the provisions of the law generally and the memorandum and articles of association. Thus they are liable to the company for loss caused by illegal or *ultra vires* acts, where, for example, they have paid dividends out of capital (*Flitcroft's Case* (1882), 21 Ch D 519) (see further p. 283).

It is not a defence that the director concerned is a nominee or alternate director who acts in accordance with the wishes of others as where, for example, he is appointed to the board by another company. (*Scottish CWS v Meyer*, 1958.[132])

In that case Scottish CWS appointed three of its own directors to the board of the subsidiary. These directors were held by Lord Denning to have subordinated the interests of the subsidiary to those of Scottish CWS and that they were equally liable with the other directors of the subsidiary for conducting the affairs of the subsidiary in a manner oppressive, or in modern times, unfairly prejudicial, to the minority.

Neither can the articles or a contract with a director exempt him from personal liability for fraud, negligence or breach of fiduciary duty. (S. 310(1).) However, the court may grant relief under s. 727 if the director concerned has acted honestly and reasonably. (*In Re Duomatic*, 1969.[160])

Fiduciary duties

The relationship between a company and its directors is that of principal and agent and as agents the directors stand in a fiduciary relationship to their principal, the company. These duties are not expressly limited to directors except where they depend on statutory provisions which are specifically so limited. Thus they can apply to any person, e.g. an executive, when acting as agent for the company.

The duties arise from case law or statute and are as follows—

(i) **Duty to exercise powers for the benefit of the company.** This duty requires directors to act in what they honestly believe to be the best interests of the company. It is not enough that the transaction is honest; if it is not in the interests of the company it is not binding on it. (*Re Lee Behrens & Co Ltd*, 1932[29] and *Re Roith Ltd*, 1967.[31]) In addition, it is not enough for directors to exercise a power honestly and for the benefit of the company; they must also exercise it for the purpose for which it was given to them. This is sometimes referred to as the 'proper purpose rule' and is illustrated by *Galloway v Hallé Concerts Society*, 1915.[99] It would appear, however, that if the power, e.g. to award a pension, is made *an express substantive object* of the company the directors do not necessarily have to exercise it for the benefit of the company. (See *Re Horsley and Weight Ltd*, 1982.[34]) The rule is still applicable to *express ancillary powers* and where the board seeks *an implied power*. (See further p. 53.)

(ii) **Duty to employees.** Although the phrase 'benefit of the company' has in the past been regarded as the benefit of the shareholders,

s. 309(1) states that the matters to which the directors of a company are to have regard in the performance of their functions shall include the interests of the company's employees in general as well as the interests of its members. However, s. 309(2) provides that this duty is owed by the directors 'to the company (and the company alone) and is enforceable in the same way as any other fiduciary duty owed to a company by its directors'.

It would, for example, be within s. 309 for the directors so to arrange the company's business as to save jobs, provided the company's interests were also served in a reasonable fashion. It would not be within s. 309 for the directors to carry on the company's business at a loss and put it at risk of liquidation in order to save jobs. There must be a balance of interests but the interests of the employees must be considered under s. 309.

The provisions of s. 309 cannot be enforced by employees unless they are also shareholders and even then a shareholder will have to bring himself within one of the exceptions to *Foss v Harbottle*[134] (see p. 198). In normal circumstances a shareholder should be able to do this on the grounds that if the directors are ignoring s. 309 they are doing an act contrary to law, i.e. an act contrary to the Companies Act 1985. However, unless there is damage to the company the most which a shareholder would be entitled to would be a declaration that the directors had failed to consider the interests of the employees in breach of s. 309.

While accepting that one cannot predict how the courts will interpret s. 309, it does appear to be a declaration of good intent and little more. It is unlikely that the company will take action to enforce the duty. However, if directors do acts favourable to the employees in balance with the rights of shareholders, they are not, at least, now breaking the law, which they would have been before the passing of s. 309 when the duties were to shareholders only.

Section 719(1) provides that the powers of a company are deemed to include, if they do not otherwise do so, the power to make provisions for its own, or a subsidiary's employees or former employees when the company itself or that subsidiary—

(i) ceases to carry on the whole or any part of its undertaking; or

(ii) transfers the whole or any part of its undertaking.

The Act specifically states that the exercise of that power need not be in the best interests of the company. (S. 719(2).)

This provision therefore reverses the decision in *Parke v Daily News Ltd* [1962] Ch 927. Briefly, the facts of that case were that the defendant company had sold the major part of its business and proposed to use the proceeds to make payments to employees by way of redundancy pay. However, the Court held that such payments were not for the benefit of the company, but rather for the benefit of the employees, and therefore the company had no power to make the payments.

Where a company has power to make provision for its employees only by reason of s. 719, then the exercise of the power must normally be approved by an ordinary resolution. However, this does not apply if the memorandum or the articles contain a provision whereby the power can be exercised by a directors' resolution or require its sanction by a resolution other than an ordinary resolution of the company in general meeting. (S. 719(3).) In addition, any other relevant requirement of the memorandum or articles must be complied with. (S. 719(3).)

The resolution can be implemented by a liquidator even though it was passed before the winding up. (S. 187(1), Insolvency Act 1986.) Furthermore, the power given by s. 719(1) may be exercised by the liquidator if the following conditions are satisfied—

(i) the company's liabilities have been fully satisfied;

(ii) provision has been set aside for the costs of the winding up;

(iii) the exercise of the power has been approved either by such a resolution of the company in general meeting as is required by the company's constitution or if there is no such requirement, by an ordinary resolution of the members; and

(iv) any other relevant requirements of the memorandum or the articles have been complied with. (S. 187(2), *ibid.*)

It should be noted that if any payment is made under s. 719 before the commencement of a winding up, then it must be made out of profits available for dividend as defined in the Companies Act 1985. In any other situation it must be made out of those assets of the company that are available to its members on its winding up. (S. 719(4) and s. 187(3), Insolvency Act 1986.) In other words a payment cannot be made in order to prejudice creditors.

In connection with the power of the liquidator to implement s. 719, it should be noted that s. 167(3), Insolvency Act 1986 applies so that in a compulsory winding up the liquidator exercises this power like all his others subject to the control of the court, and any creditor or contributory of the company may apply to the court with respect to the liquidator's exercise or proposed exercise of these powers if he does not agree with the way in which things are being done. In a voluntary winding up the liquidator may make an application to the court for directions under s. 112, *ibid* if he is in any doubt as to whether he should exercise the s. 719 powers.

(iii) **Duty to retain freedom of action.** This duty requires that directors shall not restrict their right to exercise their duties and powers freely and fully. Thus the directors cannot validly contract with one another or with third parties on the way in which they will vote at board meetings. Even a nominee or alternate director owes his duties to the company he serves, and not to interests responsible for his nomination. (*Scottish CWS v Meyer*, 1958.[132]) This duty would also prevent delegation of duties by directors but in practice a power to delegate is given in the articles.

(iv) **Duty to avoid a conflict of interest.** This duty requires that directors must not place themselves in a position in which there is a conflict of interest between themselves and the company unless the company consents. This duty manifests itself in regard to directors' contracts and substantial property transactions with the company and the making of secret profits.

(*a*) *Directors' contracts with the company.* Section 317 provides that every director who has an interest, whether direct or indirect, in a contract or proposed contract must disclose his interest either at the board meeting at which the contract is first discussed, or if his interest has not arisen at that time, then at the first board meeting after his interest arises.

If the director is a member of another concern which is doing business with the company, he may give a general notice of interest *either* orally to the board *or* in writing to the company, and this will cover a series of contracts made with the other concern. If a director fails to make proper disclosure of his interest, he is liable to a fine under s. 317(7).

A company can in any case rescind a contract made with a director because of the fiduciary duty that exists, but it must be possible to restore the *status quo, per* Lord Denning MR in *Hely-Hutchinson v Brayhead*, 1968 (p. 482). The articles may provide otherwise, or the members in general meeting may by ordinary resolution waive the company's right to rescind, but there can be no waiver by the board.

The provisions of s. 317 are now extended to cover any transaction or arrangement of a type set out in s. 330 (loans, etc.). The principle of disclosure applies whether or not the arrangement constitutes a valid and enforceable contract. (S. 317(5).) It should be noted that the interest of a connected person is treated for these purposes as an interest of the director. (S. 317(6).)

Section 317(8) extends the general principles of s. 317 to shadow directors. A shadow director is a person, who would not otherwise be treated as a director, on whose directions or instructions the proper directors of the company are accustomed to act. A person will not be a shadow director, however, if the directors act on his instructions or directions only because he is giving advice to them in a professional capacity. However, a holding company will not, by reason only of that definition, be a shadow director of any subsidiary.

It should be noted, however, that the interest of a shadow director must be declared by notice in writing to the directors and not at a meeting of the directors. (S. 317(8).) This notice may be specific in terms of a particular interest and given before the date of the meeting at which the shadow director would have been required to declare his interest if he had been a director (s. 317(8)(a)), or a general one (s. 317(8)(b)).

A director who has made a contract with the company can vote in favour of adopting it at a general meeting even where he controls the voting at general meetings. It will be remembered that he could not do this in order to ratify a secret profit, but he can in this case because the contract is voidable not because the director is in breach of any duty in actually making the contract but because of breach of the fiduciary relationship.

The provisions of Part X of the 1985 Act (loans etc.) are also relevant in regard to contracts and transactions between a company and its directors. In this connection it should be noted that for the purposes of Part X a person is to be treated as a director if the directors are accustomed to act on his directions or instructions, i.e. he is a shadow director.

As regards contracts of employment of directors, both public and private companies may not incorporate into any agreement a term under which a director's employment with the company or, if he is a director of a holding company, his employment with the group is to continue, or may be continued, except by the agreement of the company, for a period that exceeds five years, if during that period the company cannot terminate his contract by notice or his employment can be terminated by notice but only in specified circumstances. (S. 319(1).)

Under s. 319(7)(a) a contract for services is included. Thus the provisions relating to contracts of employment cannot be circumvented by directors who enter into long-term consultancy arrangements instead of contracts of employment. These arrangements could nullify to a large extent the provisions of s. 303 (see p. 270) in that directors could be removed from office under that section but long-term arrangements which they may have given themselves could involve massive compensation so that the company would, in practice, be unable to remove them.

The prohibition on long-term contracts applies to agreements between a director of a holding company and any of its subsidiaries. Thus a director is prevented from avoiding the provisions by entering into agreements with a company that is controlled by the company of which he is a director.

Section 319(2) contains provisions to prevent avoidance of the long-term contracts rules by the device of entering into a series of agreements. Thus if a director during the first year of a five-year contract which cannot be terminated by notice enters into a further five-year contract which cannot be terminated by notice, the period for which he is employed would be regarded as ten years and therefore a term would be implied into both contracts making the employment terminable by reasonable notice.

The provisions of s. 319 do not apply if the agreement continues after five years but once five years has passed it can be terminated at the instance of the company by notice. In addition, a term longer than five years may be valid if it has been first approved by a resolution of the company in general meeting and in the case of a director of a holding company, by a resolution of that company in general meeting also. However, in such a case a written memorandum setting out the proposed agreement and incorporating the term regarding length, must be available for inspection by the members of the company at the registered office for not less than 15 days ending with the date of the meeting and also the meeting itself. Finally, s. 319 does not apply to contracts given to the directors of a wholly-owned subsidiary. (S. 319(4).) The Act regards the subsidiary as a mere unit of management of the holding company so that the directors of these management units can have their conditions of service settled by the directors of the holding company. If a director of a wholly-owned subsidiary is also a director of the holding company then any contract in excess of five years will be caught by s. 319(1) (see above) and will be affected unless one of the exceptions applies.

A contract which contravenes the provisions of s. 319 is void and can be terminated by the company at any time after reasonable notice. Reasonable notice is not defined by the Act but in *James v Kent & Co Ltd* [1950] 2 All ER 1099 it was held to be an implied term of a company director's contract that he should be entitled to three months' notice.

Any term in the agreement, e.g. salary, which is distinct from the term relating to duration is valid and enforceable.

The Companies Act 1985 also places restrictions on substantial property transactions involving directors or connected persons. Thus there are restrictions on any arrangement under which—

(i) a director of the company or of its holding company (but not of any subsidiary company), or any person connected with such a director (see below) is to acquire one or more non-cash assets from the company (s. 320(1)(*a*)); or

(ii) a company acquires one or more non-cash assets from such a director or connected person. (S. 320(1)(*b*))

unless the arrangement is first approved by a resolution of the company in general meeting, and if the director or connected person is a director of its holding company or a person connected with such director, by a resolution in general meeting of the holding company.

A non-cash asset means any property or any interest in property other than cash (which includes foreign currency) and the acquisition of a non-cash asset includes the creation of an interest in property, e.g. a lease. (S. 739(2).) The prohibition relates to transactions both to and from a director or connected person as we have seen. However, the non-cash asset must exceed in value £50,000 or 10 per cent of the company's relevant assets, but the section does not apply where the value is less than £1,000. For this purpose 'relevant assets' means the value of the company's net assets as disclosed in its latest financial statements. (S. 320(2)(a).) However, where there are no such financial statements 'relevant assets' means the amount of the company's called-up share capital. (S. 320(2)(b).)

The prohibition does not apply in relation to any arrangement for the acquisition or disposal of a non-cash asset—

(a) Between a holding company and a wholly owned subsidiary in cases where the holding company is a director of the subsidiary. (S. 321(1).)

(b) If the non-cash asset in question is to be acquired by a holding company from any of its wholly owned subsidiaries or from a holding company or any of its wholly owned subsidiaries or by one wholly owned subsidiary of a holding company from another wholly owned subsidiary of that same holding company. (S. 321(2)(a).)

(c) If the arrangement is entered into by a company which is being wound up unless the winding up is a members' voluntary winding up. (S. 321(2)(b).)

(d) Section 321(3) makes clear that the prohibition on a director from acquiring one or more non-cash assets of the requisite value from the company does not apply to any arrangement under which a person is to acquire an asset from a company of which he is a *member* if the arrangement is made with that person *in his character as such member*.

The exception in (a) above did not permit arrangements between two companies in a group where a director of one of the companies was connected in terms of holding or controlling shares in the other. This created difficulties. For example a subsidiary might purchase supplies in bulk and then sell on to other members of the group and the sales would have to be approved in general meeting. But the provision in (b) above, which was first introduced by the Companies Act 1981, changes this and exempts arrangements between wholly-owned subsidiaries within groups and between holding companies and their *wholly owned* subsidiaries. However, where there is a minority interest as in the case of a partly owned subsidiary the Government feels that the minority must be safeguarded against the possibility of the directors of the holding company transferring assets from one partly-owned subsidiary in which they do not have a personal shareholding to one in which they do, and so the exemption relates only to wholly owned subsidiaries where there is no minority interest requiring protection.

As regards (c) above if a company in liquidation is insolvent, which is the case in a compulsory or creditors' voluntary winding up, the shareholders will have little interest in the disposal of its assets and so it is unnecessary to require general meeting approval in a situation where the liquidator plans to sell off some of the company's assets to its directors. The exception does not apply in a member's voluntary winding up because here the shareholders would still be interested in transactions between the company and its directors since the company is solvent and there will be or should be surplus assets for distribution to the members.

As regards (d) above this change is to avoid problems which a director might otherwise have experienced by receiving shares under a rights issue.

It should be noted that the Act refers to 'arrangements' for the transfer of property rather than to 'contracts'. The purpose of this is to catch a wide range of transactions even where these are not a firm legal arrangement.

As regards the effect of contravention of the provisions of s. 320 referred to above, the following rules apply—

(i) The arrangement is voidable at the instance of the company. However, the agreement or arrangement cannot be rescinded, where it is no longer possible to make restitution of money or property as where it is not identifiable, or where the company has been indemnified by the director or any connected person involved. In addition, there can be no avoidance against innocent third parties for value and also where, as we have seen, a general meeting has approved the transaction. If the arrangement is with a director of a company's holding company or a person connected with such a director, the arrangement must be confirmed by the holding company in general meeting.

(ii) The director and any connected person involved is liable to account to the company for any gain made directly or indirectly from the transaction and to indemnify the company for any loss or damage resulting. The liability is joint and several. Liability also extends to any other director who authorized the arrangement or any subsequent transactions, though there are defences where reasonable steps have been taken to ensure that the provisions of s. 320 have been complied with or the relevant circumstances were not known at the time the arrangement was made. 'Connected person' has already been defined and considered at p. 247.

There are of course other statutory restrictions on a director's freedom to contract with his company as follows—

(i) Under s. 311 a company may not pay a director remuneration (in any capacity) free of income tax.

(ii) Under Sched 5 disclosure is required to members through the annual accounts of the aggregate amounts of directors' emoluments, pensions and payments for compensation for loss of office.

(iii) Under Sched 5 disclosure is required of directors' emoluments *individually* in the case of the chairman and within prescribed bands in the case of others together with details of waived remuneration.

(iv) Under s. 318 directors' contracts of service or memoranda thereof and contracts or arrangements with shadow directors must be available for inspection by members of the company free of charge.

(v) Furthermore Sched 6 requires disclosure of certain transactions, e.g. loans and quasi-loans, in the accounts (see further p. 353).

(*b*) *Secret profits.* A director must account to the company for any personal profit he may make in the course of his dealing with the company's property. Thus, if a director buys shares in the company at par when the issue price is greater, he must account to the company for the difference; where he has sold at a profit, he must account for the profit. Again if a director receives gifts of money or shares from the promoters of the company or from persons selling property to it, he must account for these sums to the company. The reason for this is that there has been a *conflict of interest.* The director is supposed to negotiate for the company's benefit, and he can hardly have done so if he was taking gifts from the other party. He must also account for commissions received from persons who supply goods to the company. In addition a director who in the course of his employment obtains a contract for himself, is liable to account to the company for the profit he makes, even if it can be shown that the company would not necessarily have obtained the contract. (*Industrial Development Consultants v Cooley*, 1972.[163])

A director is not accountable for the profits of a competing business which he may be running (*Bell v Lever Bros Ltd* [1932] AC 161), unless the articles or his service contract expressly so provide, but he will be accountable if he uses the company's property in that business, or if he uses its trade secrets, or induces the company's customers to deal with him. Furthermore, a director of two or more companies takes the risk of an application under s. 459 if he subordinates the interests of one company to those of the other. (*Scottish CWS v Meyer*, 1958.[132]) A director is not allowed, either during or after service with a company, to use for his own purposes confidential information entrusted to him by the company. (*Baker v Gibbons*, 1972.[164])

A director may keep a personal profit if the company consents, but the consent must be given by the members in general meeting and not by the board, and a resolution in general meeting may be rendered invalid as prejudicial to the minority, if the director concerned controls the voting in general meetings. (*Cook v Deeks*, 1916.[141])

The general principles involved in this branch of the law are well illustrated by *Regal (Hastings) Ltd v Gulliver*, 1942[165] and of course *Industrial Development Consultants v Cooley*, 1972.[163]

However, a director may take advantage of a corporate opportunity on his own account if his company has considered the same proportion and *bona fide* rejected it. (*Peso Silver Mines Ltd (NPL) v Cropper*, 1966.[166])

Before leaving the subject it is important to note the position in relation to take-overs, where the general rules regarding secret profits have been supplemented by statutory provisions. The prevailing rules may be studied in connection with a particular method of take-over as follows—

(i) *Where the undertaking is sold.* It will be appreciated that since the directors are acting for the company they have a fiduciary duty to account to the company for any payments received by them. This duty appears in statutory form in s. 313 which provides that, in so far as a director has received sums by way of compensation for loss of office or retirement which have not been disclosed to and approved by the members, such sums are held on trust for the company.

(ii) *Sale of shares as a result of a general offer.* If in a take-over bid of this kind the directors bargain for extra payments to themselves these are held on trust for those shareholders who accepted the bid, unless disclosed to and approved by the members concerned. (S. 314.)

(iii) *Dealings with directors without a general offer to shareholders.* Sections 313 and 314 have application only where the undertaking (or part thereof) is being sold or a general offer is being made to shareholders. If a person seeks to obtain *de facto* control of a company by controlling the board, any payment made in order to induce, for example, the resignation of certain existing directors, is not covered by the statutory rules but may be caught by the general equitable fiduciary principles of disclosure laid down in *Regal (Hastings) Ltd v Gulliver*, 1942,[165] and in the case of quoted companies would be controlled by the extra-legal rules laid down in the City Code on Take-overs and Mergers. (See p. 393.)

Duty of skill and care

In addition to his fiduciary duties, a director also owes a duty of care to the company at common law not to act negligently in managing its affairs. The standard is that of a reasonable man in looking after his own affairs, and it might fairly be said that the earlier cases show that the duty is not a high one. (*Overend & Gurney v Gibb*, 1872,[167] and *Re City Equitable Fire Insurance Co*, 1925.[168]) However, in modern times when the directors of companies are often experts in certain fields, e.g. accounting, finance or engineering, a higher standard of competence may now be expected of them in their own sphere. Certainly directors *employed* by companies in a professional capacity, i.e. executive directors, have a higher objective standard of care to comply with (see *Lister v Romford Ice and Cold Storage Co* [1957] 1 All ER 125), and so have non-executive directors who are qualified or experienced in a relevant discipline. (*Dorchester Finance Co Ltd v Stebbing*, 1977.[169]) In addition, the directors' duty of care is owed only to the company and not to individual shareholders. (See *Prudential Assurance Co Ltd v Newman Industries (No 2)*, 1982 at p. 556.)

Section 13 of the Supply of Goods and Services Act 1982 imposes an implied contractual term that a supplier of a service acting in the course of business will carry out that service with reasonable care. SI 1982/1771 provides that s. 13 shall not apply to the services rendered by a company director to his company. It is evidently thought to be enough that they have to act in good faith, carry out fiduciary duties and meet the common law standard of reasonable skill and care.

DUTIES OF DIRECTORS TO SHAREHOLDERS

The directors do not owe any contractual or fiduciary duties to members of their company. (*Percival v Wright*, 1902.[171]) However, where there is a bid situation the City Panel on Takeovers and Mergers would be concerned and the Stock Exchange is beginning to look critically at the sort of insider dealing which took place in *Percival v Wright*, 1902,[171] at least where a listed company is concerned, and has introduced a code of dealing for directors. The rules which the City Panel has laid down do not, of course, have the force of law. However, the Panel can issue and publish a reprimand for insider dealing in the shares of a company prior to its take-over and this could have an adverse effect upon the career, particularly of a professional man. (See p. 389.)

The Stock Exchange, in consultation with the CBI, published a Model Code for Securities Transactions, to give guidance as to when it is proper for directors of listed companies to deal in the securities of the company. This Code received widespread acceptance and became part of the Listing Agreement. The main principles of the Code are—

(*a*) That directors *and executives* should not engage in short-term dealings, e.g. purchases and sales over short periods, because it is difficult to avoid the suggestion that such dealing is not based on inside knowledge.

(*b*) That directors and executives should not deal for a minimum period prior to the announcement of reports and results. Where results are announced half-yearly, the closed period for dealing should be the previous two months, but if announcements are more frequent, e.g. quarterly, the period should be discussed with the Quotations Department of the Stock Exchange.

Directors and executives should not deal either when an exceptional announcement is to be made which would probably affect the market price of the company's shares or when they are in possession of knowledge which, when accessible to the public, will affect the market price of the shares.

(*c*) That a minute book or record book of dealings should be kept by the chairman or another director and that the board as a whole should see that directors and executives comply with a practice to be established within the company on the above lines. In this respect a director should ensure that where he is a beneficiary under a trust the trustees notify him after dealing so that it can be recorded. In addition, a director must return dealings of a spouse or for infant children.

In addition the Company Securities (Insider Dealing) Act 1985 contains provisions relating to the *criminal offence* of insider dealing. Since the provisions are not confined to directors but apply to others who misuse price-sensitive information in terms of dealing in the company's shares, the topic is considered in detail in Chapter 15 at p. 395.

Directors may become agents of the members for a particular transaction in which case the situation of agency gives rise to fiduciary duties. (*Allen v Hyatt*, 1914.[172])

In addition, there appears to be a duty to shareholders in regard to the advice, if any, given by directors to those shareholders in regard to the acquisition or rejection of a take-over bid. Company legislation does not deal with this. However, in *Gething v Kilner* [1972] 1 All ER 1166, it was said that in a take-over the directors of the 'victim' company owe a duty to their shareholders to be honest and not to mislead as by suppressing, for instance, professional advice recommending rejection, and that the court might grant an injunction where this had happened, to prevent the bid going ahead.

DUTIES OF DIRECTORS TO OUTSIDERS

Again there is no contractual or fiduciary duty to outsiders, and the directors are not liable if the company breaks its contracts. However, where the directors make a contract with an outsider on behalf of the company, the directors may be liable, as other agents are, for breach or warranty of authority. The basis of this action is that an agent warrants to the third party that his principal has the capacity to make the contract and that he, the agent, is authorized to make it.

The action has been successful where a company having borrowing power has in fact exceeded it. (*Weeks v Propert*, 1873.[173]) The difference in the company cases is that the third party is deemed to have notice of the company's powers and cannot therefore be misled. It is not thought likely that the directors can be sued where the company is a statutory company and the contract is patently *ultra vires*, because this would involve the plaintiff's pleading ignorance of the statute, and ignorance of the law is not generally an excuse. The law has also regarded outsiders as having constructive notice of the objects clause of a registered company, but it is the better view that an action against the directors of a registered company would succeed because the directors are misrepresenting the contents of the memorandum and/or articles which would probably be regarded as a misrepresentation of *fact* and therefore actionable. It should, of course, be noted that where s. 35 (see p. 62) applies there will be no constructive notice in the outsider by virtue of that provision.

EFFECTS OF BREACH OF DUTY

As regards actions against directors for breach of duty, these may be brought as follows—

(*a*) *By the company.* The company can always sue the directors for breach of fiduciary duty or negligence and the action may be initiated by the board or by the members by ordinary resolution in general meeting. The power to bring the company into court as a plaintiff is concurrent as between the directors and the members where there is an alleged breach of duty, and the members' decision, if contrary to that of the directors, prevails.

(*b*) *By a member.* There is a potential action in a member to sue a director for breach of fiduciary duty but in most cases he will be met by the rule in *Foss v Harbottle*, 1842,[134] though his action may proceed where the member alleges fraud as distinct from mere breach of a fiduciary duty (*Menier v Hooper's Telegraph Works Ltd*[140]) or where the directors control general meetings, either by voting power (*Cook v Deeks*, 1916[141]), or possibly in other ways (*Prudential Assurance v Newman Industries*, 1980[170]). There is also an exception to *Foss v Harbottle*, 1984[134] in s. 459 of the Companies Act 1985 of which *Prudential Assurance v Newman Industries Ltd* may perhaps be regarded as an anticipatory example.

Under that section the court has power to order the bringing of civil proceedings in the name and on behalf of the company by such person or persons and on such terms as the court may direct. However, before the court can exercise that power, an individual shareholder must show that the affairs of the company are being or have been conducted *in a manner unfairly prejudicial* to the interests of some part of the members, including the petitioner, and the court must be satisfied that the petition is well founded. The breach by the directors would have, therefore, to be 'unfairly prejudicial' but, presumably, negligent mismanagement could be so regarded. To what extent breaches of fiduciary duty such as the taking of a secret profit will be regarded as unfairly prejudicial also remains to be seen. In small companies the taking of a profit could affect the value of the shares, but in large companies the value of the shares could be unaffected. However, Nourse J stated in *Re R A Noble (Clothing) Ltd*, 1983 (see p. 522) that it was not necessary to show a diminution in value of the shares and if this view is sustained s. 459 may give minorities improved rights over previous legislation. However, the decision in *Re Carrington Viyella* (see p. 193) suggests that s. 459 is available where *part only* of the members are affected; negligence and the taking of secret profits affect *all* the members. It is by no means certain, therefore, that the lot of minority shareholders in the bigger companies has been made any better by s. 459.

(*c*) *Under s. 212, Insolvency Act 1986.* In a winding up a liquidator or a creditor or a contributory may bring an action under s. 212 (*ibid*) against a director for breach of fiduciary duty, though not negligence. (*Re B Johnson Ltd* [1955] 2 All ER 775.) Application must be made to the court, the ground being misfeasance and the court may require the director to account. Compensation for loss of office, if not approved by the members, may be recovered for the company under s. 212 (*ibid*). (*Gibson's Exor v Gibson*, 1980 SLT 2 Ct Session, Outer House.) However, the assent of shareholders validates a benefit received by a director and prevents its recovery under s. 212 (*ibid*). Thus, in *Re Horsley and Weight Ltd*, 1982,[34] the company took out in 1975 in its own name a pension policy for the benefit of Mr Horsley who was a founder-member of the business involved. In 1977 the company was compulsorily wound up and the liquidator claimed the policy under what is now s. 212, Insolvency Act 1986 as an asset available to him in the winding up. The Court of Appeal said that it was not available; the pension arrangements were within the company's powers and the assent of all the shareholders to the scheme bound the company. There was no evidence of misfeasance by those shareholders in approving the scheme.

As regards exemptions, s. 310 provides that no provision in the articles may excuse a director for negligence or breach of fiduciary duty but under s. 727 the court may grant relief. (*Re Duomatic*, 1969.[160])

As regards limitation of actions, the writ must be served within six years of the breach of duty unless the director has a service contract under seal, when the period is 12 years. There is of course no limit where fraud is alleged. In addition where the director still has property obtained by breach of duty or its proceeds it is possible to follow or trace these without limit of time.

As regards the nature of the liability of directors, if all are involved in a breach of fiduciary duty or negligence then all are jointly and severally liable, though if one director has to pay compensation to the company, he has a right of contribution from the others. If only one director is involved then he is solely responsible and has no contribution from his fellow directors.

As regards the payment of dividends in contravention of the Companies Act 1985, the directors are liable to restore these to the company but may recover the sums involved from the shareholders who received payment, whether the shareholders knew or not that the payment was unlawful (*Moxham v Grant* [1900] 1 QB 88), unless they have changed their position, e.g. incurred an obligation to buy a property, in the belief that the dividends were lawfully paid. (*Skyring v Greenwood* (1825) 4 B & C 281.) In addition, under the Companies Act 1985, any member who receives an unlawful distribution is liable to repay it to the company if at the time he received it, he knew, or he had reasonable grounds to believe, that it was made in contravention of the Act. This provision is without prejudice to any other liability of a member to repay distributions that have been made to him unlawfully (s. 277(2)), thus the liability under *Moxham v Grant* (above) still applies where the directors have compensated the company first.

The *remedies* available against directors are as follows—

(*a*) an injunction is most useful where a breach of duty is threatened or where it is *continuing* and will forbid the breach on pain of a fine or imprisonment for contempt of court if the injunction is ignored;

(*b*) *damages* (or compensation, in respect of equitable claims for breach of fiduciary duty) result in *monetary* compensation for loss arising from the breach. Issues relating to the remoteness and *quantum* of damages are treated in accordance with the general principles of the law of contract, torts or trusts depending on the nature of the breach of duty. Third parties who knowingly participate in a director's breach of fiduciary duty are also liable (*Selangor United Rubber Estates Ltd v Cradock (No. 3)* [1968] 2 All ER 1073);

(*c*) *as we have seen property can be recovered* from the directors and from third parties who are not purchasers for value if it can be traced;

(d) *contracts made with the company in which a director was interested can be rescinded* provided the *status quo* can be restored and the rights of third parties have not accrued; and

(e) a director can be made to *account for secret profits* and his breach of duty may give rise to a right to summarily dismiss him.

VACATION OF OFFICE BY DIRECTORS

A director may vacate office for a variety of reasons.

1. Expiration of the period of office

The articles usually provide what the period of office shall be. *Table A, Reg* 73, provides that at the first annual general meeting all the directors shall retire from office, and at the annual general meeting in every subsequent year one-third shall retire, or if their number is not three or a multiple of three, then the number nearest to one-third shall retire from office. The directors retiring will be those longest in office since their last election. Difficulties may arise in the early years of the company's life if all the directors were appointed at the same time. If this is the case those retiring must, by reason of *Reg* 74, be ascertained by agreement between the board and on agreement failing, by drawing lots.

Regulation 80 provides that a retiring director shall be eligible for re-election, and *Reg* 75 provides that if the office vacated by a director on retirement by rotation is not filled, the retiring director shall, if he still offers himself for re-election, be deemed re-elected, unless the meeting expressly resolves not to fill the vacancy or unless the resolution for the re-election of such director has been put to the meeting and lost.

A director who is due to retire by rotation at, e.g. the 1988 AGM but reaches the age of 70 in 1987, will vacate office at the AGM in 1987 and, if re-elected, will fall to be be included in the directors retiring by rotation in 1988. If re-elected this time it will be until he next retires by rotation. All appointments would have to be by the special notice procedure.

Under *Reg* 79 the board may fill casual vacancies and appoint additional directors up to the maximum in the articles. Persons elected must stand for re-election at the next AGM and do not count in the one-third retiring, but are additional to that number. Furthermore, under *Reg* 84 the managing director and directors holding any other executive office, e.g. finance director, do not retire by rotation. They are subject to the terms of their contracts but cannot be either managing director or executive director unless also directors. Therefore they cannot continue in post if they are removed as directors by the members under s. 303 or under a provision in the articles. They would normally have a claim for breach of contract.

2. Disqualification

A director may become disqualified, and if so he automatically vacates office. The following are the reasons for disqualification—

(a) **Under a provision in the articles.** Table A, Reg 81, provides that the office of director shall be vacated if the director—

(i) ceases to be a director by virtue of any provision of the Act, e.g. removal under s. 303; or becomes prohibited by law from being a director, e.g. is disqualified by the court; or

(ii) becomes bankrupt or makes any arrangement or composition with his creditors generally; or

(iii) becomes of unsound mind; or

(iv) resigns his office by notice to the company; or

(v) has for more than six months been absent without permission of the directors from meetings of the directors held during that period and the directors resolve that his office shall be vacated. Under Table A one counts from the last meeting he attended and not the first meeting that he missed. It should be noted also that this provision covers involuntary absence, as where the director is ill.

The articles may be altered to provide additional reasons for disqualification (*Shuttleworth v Cox Bros*, 1927[57]), though an express contract is not affected by alterations in the articles and the director may bring an action for wrongful dismissal. (*Southern Foundries v Shirlaw*, 1940.[58])

(b) **Share qualifications.** Section 291 provides that the office of director shall be vacated if the director does not within two months from the date of his appointment, or within such shorter time as may be fixed by the articles, obtain his qualification shares, or if after the expiration of that time he ceases at any time to hold his qualification where a qualification is required.

(c) **Age limit.** A director may become disqualified if his age exceeds the limit laid down by s. 293 or by the articles. This matter has already been dealt with earlier in the chapter.

(d) **Bankruptcy and disqualification by the court.** A director may become disqualified for these reasons which have already been dealt with earlier, but we must note the following points. Where a director is disqualified by the court, he vacates office immediately. In the case of bankruptcy there is no automatic vacation unless the articles so provide, as does *Table A, Reg* 81.

3. Removal

A company may by *ordinary resolution* remove a director before the expiration of his period of office regardless of the way in which he was appointed and notwithstanding anything in its articles or in any agreement with him (s. 303), though weighted voting rights may render the section ineffective. (*Bushell v Faith*, 1969.[156]) *Special notice* of 28 days to the company is required of the intention to move the resolution. (S. 303(2).) This power is in addition to any other means of removal that may be provided in the articles, e.g. a power under which certain of the directors may remove others. (*Bersel Manufacturing Co Ltd v Berry*, 1968.[174]) Thus shareholders who wish to remove a director have a choice: either they can proceed under s. 303 or under a provision, if any, in the articles, and if the articles make removal more difficult, as where they require a special resolution, then s. 303 will be used. On the other hand, where the articles allow the directors themselves to carry out the removal, as in *Bersel Manufacturing Co Ltd v Berry*, 1968,[174] then of course it would be easier to do it through the power vested in the board.

The director concerned is allowed to put his case to the members by the circulation of his representations with the notice of the meeting, or if his representations are received too late for this, they are to be read out at the meeting. (S. 304(2) and (3).) (Note, however, the effect of *Fenning v Fenning Environmental Products Ltd*, *Law Society Gazette*, 23 June 1982.) The vacancy so created may be filled at the meeting, or if not so filled, may be filled as a casual vacancy (s. 303(3)), and any person appointed in the place of a director removed under s. 303 shall be deemed to hold office for as long as the director removed would have held it, and to retire when he would have retired. (S. 303(4).)

Nothing in s. 303 is to deprive a director so removed of any action he may have for dismissal (s. 303(5)), as where he has a contract outside of the articles appointing him for a specified period which has not expired. It should be noted that s. 318 allows members to inspect the service contract of a director in order to ascertain how much it will cost to remove him. Where the company is a personal relationship company a director removed under s. 303 may ask the court for a winding up order under s. 122, Insolvency Act 1986. (*Ebrahimi v Westbourne Galleries Ltd*, 1972[129] but see *Re a Company*, 1983, p. 521 and *Re London School of Electronics*, 1985, p. 523.)

At first sight s. 303 appears to give any member of a company who is not satisfied with the way in which a director is carrying out his duties the right to ask the members as a whole to consider passing an ordinary resolution in general meeting to remove him.

Let us suppose, as would be usual, that X, a member of the company, chooses the annual general meeting for this purpose. Let us further suppose that he serves special notice on the company secretary in the proper manner of his intention to propose a resolution to remove the director or directors concerned. Are the directors obliged to place that resolution on the agenda and take it at the annual general meeting? According to the decision of Slade J in *Pedley v Inland Waterways Association Ltd* [1977] 1 All ER 209, the answer is no, unless, that is, X or persons joining with him satisfy the requirements of s. 376. This section provides that members representing not less than one-twentieth of the total voting rights of all members or 100 or more members holding shares in the company on which there has been paid up an average of not less than £100 per member can, by making a written requisition to the company, compel the company in effect to put a particular item of business up at the annual general meeting. Therefore, if a particular member or members cannot satisfy, e.g. the one-twentieth voting rights provision, then the directors are not obliged to raise the question of the removal of one or more of their number at the annual general meeting. Thus it would seem that the rights given by s. 303, and indeed s. 386 (power to remove auditors), are much more restricted than might hitherto have been thought. It is impossible to use these sections unless the member or members concerned can satisfy the requirements of s. 376 at least so far as the annual general meeting is concerned. Although the *Pedley* case dealt only with matters regarding the removal of a director at the annual general meeting it would seem that an individual member is in an even worse position if he wishes to remove a director between annual general meetings. Unless the board are willing to call an extraordinary general meeting he, or members joining with him, will have to do so. This can be done under s. 368, but only by members holding not less than one-tenth of such of the company's paid-up capital as carries voting rights at the general meetings of the company. Even if a member can satisfy the requirements of s. 368 there is a further difficulty which is that under the section it would appear that the directors are not required to hold a meeting within any particular period of time. Thus if the board does call a meeting to be held many months ahead, thereby frustrating the wishes of the minority in terms of an early consideration of the removal of a director, the board has satisfied the requirements of s. 368 and the rights of the requisitionists to call the meeting them-selves, which are granted by the section, would appear not to arise.

4. Resignation

Regulation 81 does not require resignation in writing thus an oral resignation at a board meeting is effective. Once resignation has been made it cannot be withdrawn except with the consent of those persons who are entitled to appoint new directors.

5. Winding up

Where the winding up is by the court, the directors are dismissed when the court order is made. As regards a voluntary winding up, the position is not clear but the better view is that a resolution for voluntary winding up does not operate as an automatic dismissal of the directors unless the company is insolvent. (*Fowler v Commercial Timber Co Ltd* [1930] 2 KB 1.) However, whether the directors are dismissed by the winding up resolution or not, the liquidator can certainly dismiss them by excluding them from management under ss. 91 and 103, Insolvency Act 1986, or by selling the company's undertaking. (*Reigate v Union Manufacturing Co* [1918] 1 KB 592.)

6. Appointment of administrator/administrative receiver

The directors are not dismissed by the above appointments but their management powers to deal with the company's property are suspended during the administration/receivership. (But see *Newhart Developments Ltd v Co-operative Commercial Bank Ltd*, 1978.[175])

SECRETARY AND OTHER OFFICERS

The term 'officer' is partly defined in the Companies Act 1985 to include a director, manager, or secretary. (S. 744.) The term includes, for some purposes, the auditor, e.g. a misfeasance summons under s. 212 of the Insolvency Act 1986 (and see *R. v Shacter*, p. 584), but the auditor is not an agent of the company. (*Re Transplanters (Holding Company) Ltd* [1958] 2 All ER 711.)

Certain statutory provisions affect the liability of officers as well as directors. Thus, s. 310 applies and renders invalid any provision in the articles or in a contract purporting to relieve an officer from liability for negligence, default, breach of duty or breach of trust. Similarly, s. 727 applies to enable the court to relieve against liability. Under the Companies Act 1985, Sched 6, loans to officers, including directors, must be disclosed in the accounts. There are special provisions relating to proceedings against directors and officers for misfeasance or breach of trust discovered in the course of winding up (see s. 211 and 212, Insolvency Act 1986).

The secretary

A secretary owes fiduciary duties to the company which are similar to those of a director. (*Re Morvah Consols Tin Mining Co, McKay's*

Case, 1875)[176] and the criminal law takes a different view of his status as an organ of the company than does the civil law and regards him as a higher managerial agent whose fraudulent conduct can be imputed to the company in order to make it liable along with him for crimes arising out of fraud and the falsification of documents and returns.

Every company must have a secretary, and a sole director cannot also be the secretary. (S. 283(1) and (2).) A corporation may be secretary to a company but a company, X, cannot have as secretary a company, Y, if the sole director of company Y is also the sole director or secretary of company X (s. 283(4)). Section 284(3) provides that a provision requiring or authorizing a thing to be done by or to a director and the secretary shall not be satisfied by its being done by or to the same person acting both as director and secretary. By s. 288 the register of directors includes particulars of the secretary.

It is usual for the secretary to be appointed by the directors who may fix his term of office and the conditions upon which he is to hold office. *Table A, Reg 99* confers such a power upon the board together with the power to remove him. The secretary is a servant of the company. He is regarded as such for the purpose of preferential payments in a liquidation. (S. 175 and Sched 6, Insolvency Act 1986.)

The courts now recognize that the modern secretary is an important official who enjoys the power to contract on behalf of the company, even without authority. This is, however, confined to contracts in the administrative operations of the company, including the employment of office staff and the management of the office together with the hiring of transport. (*Panorama Developments (Guildford) Ltd v Fidelis Furnishing Fabrics Ltd*, 1971.[177]) However, his authority is not unlimited. He cannot without authority borrow money on behalf of the company. (*Re Cleadon Trust Ltd* [1939] Ch 286.) He cannot without authority commence litigation on the company's behalf. (*Daimler Co Ltd v Continental Tyre and Rubber Co Ltd* [1916] 2 AC 307.) He cannot summon a general meeting himself (*Re State of Wyoming Syndicate* [1901] 2 Ch 431) nor register a transfer without the board's approval (*Chida Mines Ltd v Anderson* (1905) 22 TLR 27) nor may he without approval strike a name off the register (*Re Indo China Steam Navigation Co* [1917] 2 Ch 100). These are powers which are vested in the directors.

Certain duties are directly imposed upon the secretary by statute. These include the submission of certain statutory declarations, e.g. before commencing business (s. 117), and the annual return (ss. 363–365) and as an officer the verification of certain statements, e.g. under s. 131 of the Insolvency Act 1986 in relation to the statement of affairs to be submitted to the Official Receiver in a compulsory winding up; under ss 22 and 47 (*ibid*) in relation to the statement of affairs to be submitted to an administrator and administrative receiver respectively.

Qualifications of the secretary of a public company

Section 286 provides that it shall be the duty of the directors *of a public company* to take reasonable steps to secure that the company secretary or each joint secretary, where appropriate, has the requisite knowledge and experience and comes within one of the following categories:

(*a*) He was in post as the secretary or the assistant or deputy secretary of the company on the day the section was brought into force.

(*b*) He has been the secretary of a public company for at least three out of the five years immediately preceding his appointment as secretary.

(*c*) He is a member of either the Institute of Chartered Accountants in England and Wales, or the Institute of Chartered Accountants of Scotland, or the Chartered Association of Certified Accountants, or the Institute of Chartered Accountants of Ireland, or the Institute of Chartered Secretaries and Administrators, or the Institute of Cost and Management Accountants, or the Chartered Institute of Public Finance and Accountancy. In addition, he will be suitable if he is a barrister, or an advocate or a solicitor who qualified in the UK. Furthermore, a person who 'by virtue of his holding or having held any other position or his being a member of any other body, appears to the directors to be capable of discharging' the duties and functions of a secretary is also acceptable (s. 286(1)(*e*)).

Thus, the directors of a public company may appoint a person who does not hold any of the specified formal qualifications.

It would seem that the duty of the board in regard to the secretary's qualification is a continuing one. Thus, if the secretary, being a member of one of the professional bodies listed, was struck off, then the directors would probably have to reconsider his position.

The word 'person' in s. 286(1)(*e*) includes a company.

The accountant

The accountant is an officer of the company. He owes a contractual duty to the company to prepare the accounts properly and like the auditor may, in some cases, owe a duty of care to third persons who act in reliance on his skill in their preparation. Seemingly, the accountant can acknowledge a debt on behalf of the company. (*Jones v Bellgrove Properties* [1949] 2 All ER 198.)

OTHER MATERIALS

Loans to directors

A. Companies which do not lend money

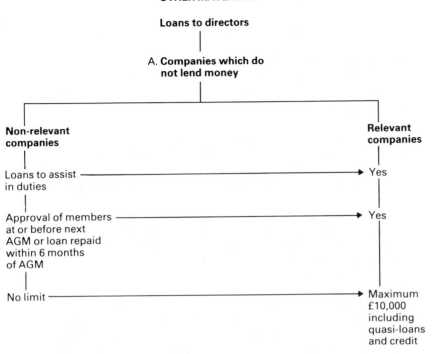

Non-relevant companies

Loans to assist in duties ⟶ Yes (Relevant companies)

Approval of members at or before next AGM or loan repaid within 6 months of AGM ⟶ Yes

No limit ⟶ Maximum £10,000 including quasi-loans and credit

Notes: Loans for purchase and improvement of director's main residence on employees scheme terms **not applicable**. Under s.334 **all** companies may make loans to a director or a director of its holding company but not connected persons, provided that the aggregate amount of the loan(s) does not exceed £2,500. Such loans require disclosure in financial statements under Sched 6 of the Companies Act 1985. They aggregate with any other loans but quasi-loans and credit are not aggregated with them.

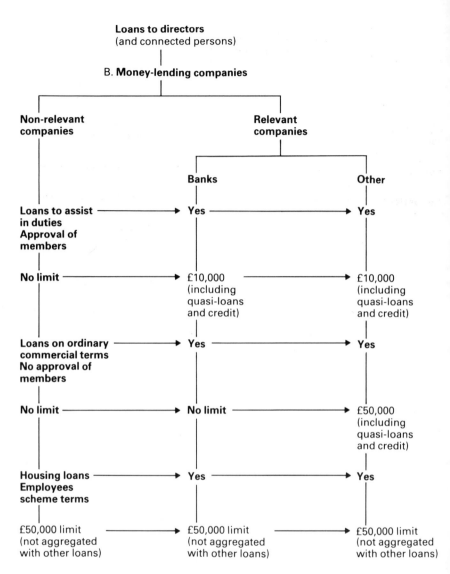

Loans to directors
(and connected persons)

B. **Money-lending companies**

	Non-relevant companies	Relevant companies	
		Banks	**Other**
Loans to assist in duties Approval of members	Yes →	Yes →	Yes
	No limit →	£10,000 (including quasi-loans and credit) →	£10,000 (including quasi-loans and credit)
Loans on ordinary commercial terms No approval of members	Yes →	Yes →	Yes
	No limit →	No limit →	£50,000 (including quasi-loans and credit)
Housing loans Employees scheme terms	Yes →	Yes →	Yes
	£50,000 limit (not aggregated with other loans) →	£50,000 limit (not aggregated with other loans) →	£50,000 limit (not aggregated with other loans)

Note: Under s.334 **all** companies may make loans to a director or a director of its holding company, but not connected persons, provided that the aggregate amount of the loan(s) does not exceed £2,500. Such loans require disclosure in financial statements under Sched 6 of the Companies Act 1985. They aggregate with other loans but quasi-loans and credit are not aggregated with them.

276

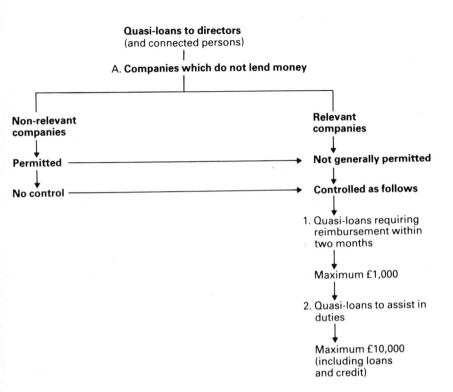

Quasi-loans to directors
(and connected persons)

A. **Companies which do not lend money**

Non-relevant companies

Permitted ──────────────────────→ **Relevant companies**

Not generally permitted

No control ──────────────────────→ **Controlled as follows**

1. Quasi-loans requiring reimbursement within two months

   Maximum £1,000

2. Quasi-loans to assist in duties

   Maximum £10,000 (including loans and credit)

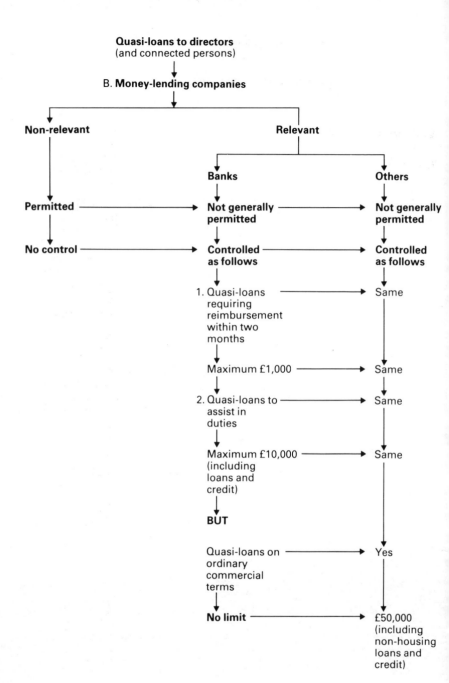

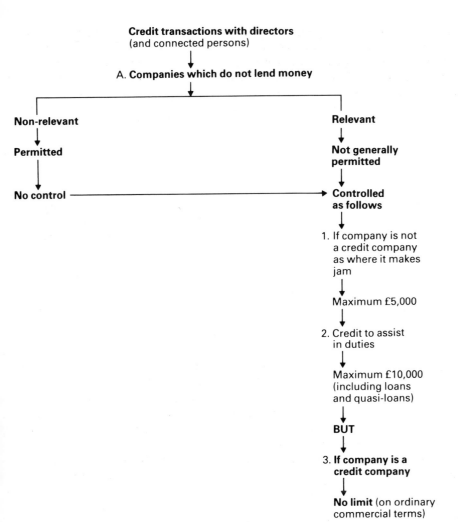

Credit transactions with directors
(and connected persons)

↓

A. **Companies which do not lend money**

Non-relevant

↓

Permitted

↓

No control ────────────→ **Controlled as follows**

Relevant

↓

Not generally permitted

↓

Controlled as follows

↓

1. If company is not a credit company as where it makes jam

↓

Maximum £5,000

↓

2. Credit to assist in duties

↓

Maximum £10,000 (including loans and quasi-loans)

↓

BUT

↓

3. **If company is a credit company**

↓

No limit (on ordinary commercial terms)

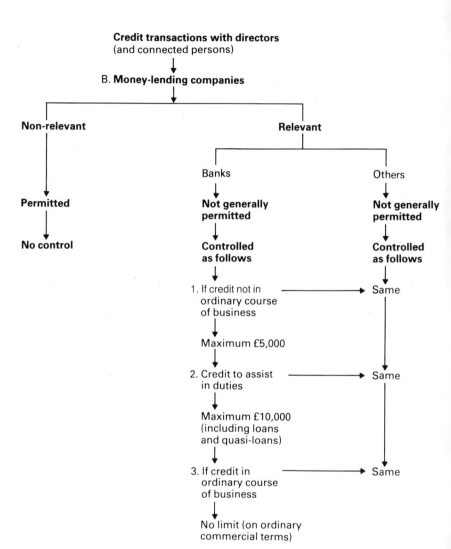

10 Dividends and profits

Dividends are sums of money authorized to be paid out of the profits made by the company amongst the members of the company in proportion to their share holding.

Declaration and payment

The question of declaration of dividends is usually dealt with by the articles. There is no absolute right to a dividend, and where the articles follow the pattern of *Table A*, *Reg* 102, the company, though it can declare dividends in general meeting, cannot declare a dividend higher than that recommended by the directors, and if the directors do not recommend payment of dividend, the members cannot declare one either on the preference or ordinary shares. Under a regulation such as *Reg* 102 the members in general meeting can reduce the dividend recommended by the directors. As regards the dividend payable in a particular year, the matter is usually a *fait accompli* because the dividend has been paid before the general meeting is held. However, the members could reduce the dividend recommended which would involve adjustments in the accounts for the following year.

Table A, *Reg* 104, provides that all dividends shall be declared and paid according to the amounts paid on the shares. Under such an article, no amount credited as paid in respect of calls in advance could be counted as paid for this purpose. Where the company's articles exclude *Table A* and yet do not provide for the method of payment of dividend, dividends are paid on the nominal value of the shares.

Unless the articles otherwise provide, dividends are payable in cash, but *Table A*, *Reg* 105, provides that the company may distribute specific assets in whole or in part satisfaction. *Table A*, *Reg* 106, provides that payment may be made by cheque sent through the post to the registered address of the holder. In the case of joint holders it shall be sent to the one whose name appears first on the register, or alternatively as the joint holders may direct *in writing*. Any one of two or more joint holders may give an effectual receipt.

Table A, *Reg* 107, provides that no dividend shall bear interest against the company, unless otherwise provided by the rights attached to the shares.

Dividends when declared are in the nature of a specialty debt and can be sued for up to 12 years from the date of declaration.

Where money is lent to a company to pay a dividend already declared the money is impressed with a *primary* trust in favour of the holders of shares whose dividend has been declared. Failing this primary trust a resulting trust arises in favour of the lender of the money. The loan does not become part of the general assets of the company and cannot be used for other purposes. (*Barclays Bank Ltd v Quistclose Investments Ltd*, 1968.[177])

Interim dividends

When the directors can see that the company is going to make a sufficient profit by the end of the financial year, they may declare a dividend part way through the year which is in the nature of a part payment of the dividend for the year as a whole. At the end of the year a final dividend is declared in respect of the balance. *Table A, Reg 103*, provides that the directors may from time to time pay to the members such interim dividends as appear to the directors to be justified by the distributable profits of the company. Under *Reg 103* an interim dividend does not require the approval of a general meeting of the members, and is not in the nature of a debt due from the company. Thus if it is not paid, it cannot be sued for, and there is nothing to prevent the directors subsequently rescinding or varying the dividend. (*Lagunas Nitrate Co v Schroeder* (1901) 85 LT 22.)

Under ss. 270 and 272 where the directors propose to pay an interim dividend, reference may have to be made to interim accounts, which in the case of a public company, must be such 'as are necessary to enable a reasonable judgment to be made': i.e. accounts complying with s. 228 (true and fair view) and signed by the directors under s. 238. Public companies must file these interim accounts with the Registrar before distribution. Interim accounts need not be audited.

Reference to interim accounts would be necessary if under the last annual accounts a distribution would be unlawful, as where the amount of distributable reserves calculated by reference to the last annual accounts is insufficient to make the distribution required.

Procedure for payment of dividend

The company may close its register for a short time before payment is made in order that the register shall remain static whilst the procedure for payment is carried out. *Dividend warrants* are prepared in favour of those persons whose names appear on the register, the dividend being declared according to the recommendation of the directors. The warrants are posted to the shareholders as soon as possible after the dividend is declared.

In the case of share warrants, the company will advertise that the dividend is payable in exchange for a coupon bearing a certain number, these coupons being attached to the share warrant. A dividend warrant is then made out in the name of the present holder of the share warrant.

It is current practice not to close registers but to declare a dividend payable to shareholders registered as at close of business on a given date (the striking date). It should be noted that companies are not concerned with equities when paying dividends. The registered share-holder (or the first named of joint holders) on the striking date or the first day on which the register is closed is the person to whom the dividend is paid. If such a person has recently sold his holding *cum* (with) dividend the buyer's broker will claim it through the seller's broker. If the sale was *ex* (without) dividend the seller keeps it and no claim arises. The purchase price of the share will take into acccount the *cum* or *ex* dividend element.

Many companies include a power in their articles to forfeit unclaimed dividends after a reasonable period. However, in the case of quoted companies Stock Exchange regulations insist that such a power shall not be exercised until 12 years or more have passed since the dividend was declared. *Table A, Reg* 108 provides that any dividend which has remained unclaimed for 12 years from the date when it became due for payment shall, if the directors so resolve, be forfeited and cease to remain owing by the company.

RESTRICTIONS ON DISTRIBUTIONS OF PROFITS AND ASSETS

Before the passing of the Companies Act 1980 the payment of divi-dends, in terms of the funds which could be used, was governed by case law which had got out of line with modern accounting principles, e.g. the prudence concept. The following are the major principles which had emerged from case law—

1. Company dividends could only be paid out of profit. (*Re Exchange Banking Co, Flitcrofts Case* (1882) 21 Ch D 519.)
2. Losses in previous years need not be made good. A dividend could be paid if there was a profit on the current year's trading. (*Re National Bank of Wales* [1899] 2 Ch 629.)
3. Profits of previous years could be brought forward and distributed

even if there was a revenue loss in the current trading period. (*Re Hoare & Co* [1904] 2 Ch 208.)
4. Losses on fixed assets in a current year need not be made good by depreciation before treating a revenue profit as available for dividend. (*Lee v Neuchatel Asphalte Co* (1889) 41 Ch D 1.) Thus case law distinguished between capital losses and revenue losses.
5. Unrealized capital profits on a revaluation of assets could be distributed by way of dividend. (*Dimbula Valley (Ceylon) Tea Co v Laurie* [1961] 1 All ER 769.)

The Companies Act 1980 made radical changes in regard to the distribution of profits and assets by companies. These principles are now contained in Part VIII of the Companies Act 1985. *Regulations 102* and *103* of *Table A* support the 1985 Act by providing that no dividend or interim dividend shall be paid otherwise than in accordance with the provisions of the Companies Act 1985 which apply to the company. The relevant provisions are considered below.

All companies

Under s. 263(1), companies, whether public or private, are not allowed to make distributions, e.g. pay a cash dividend, except out of 'profits available' for distribution. That is, accumulated realized profits both revenue and capital (s. 263(3)) (which have not previously been used as a basis for distribution or capitalized, as by being applied in financing a bonus issue or the purchase or redemption of the company's shares with a transfer to the capital redemption reserve (s. 280(2))) *less* accumulated losses both revenue and capital (s. 280(3)) (so far as not previously written off in a reorganization or reduction of capital). In addition, para 12(*a*) of Part II of Sched 4 states that 'only profits realized at the balance sheet date shall be included in the profit and loss account'. Provisions arising from a revaluation of *all* the fixed assets of the company can be ignored and excess depreciation arising from a revaluation of fixed assets can be added back to reserves in order to determine the accumulated, realized profits. Unrealized profits cannot be distributed or applied in paying up debentures or amounts payable on issued shares, but a company may, if its articles so provided before the 1980 Act came into force, issue fully or partly paid bonus shares out of unrealized profits. (S. 278.)

Section 263 applies to all companies and its main thrust is to prohibit the distribution of unrealized profits which the courts had permitted. Thus so far as the courts were concerned a revaluation of assets without the sale of those assets produced a surplus for distribution as dividend; this is no longer the case. In addition, under s. 263 companies with past revenue losses must make them good before current realized profits are distributable. Formerly a company could pay a dividend from its profits, even though it had made losses in the past; this is no longer possible.

We are now in a position to make some comparisons between the old law and the new law as means of understanding the new law.

Company dividends may only be paid out of profit (*Flitcrofts Case* (see above)).

Under the new law profit becomes 'realized' profit. (S. 263(1) and (3).) However, the 1985 Act does not fully define realized profit but leaves this to accountancy practice statements issued by the Accounting Standards Committee consisting of members of the major accounting bodies in the UK and Ireland.

For example, the Companies Act 1985 in Sched 4 states that the amount of any item in the accounts shall be determined on a prudent basis and in particular only profits realized at balance sheet date shall be included in the profit and loss account. Realized profits are defined in the Interpretation Schedule as such profits of the company as fall to be treated as realized profits for the purposes of those accounts in accordance with principles generally accepted with respect to the determination for accounting purposes of realized profits at the time when those accounts are prepared.

Statement of Standard Accounting Practice 2 amplifies the prudence concept by stating that revenues and profits are not anticipated but are recognized by inclusion in the profit and loss account only when realized in the form either of cash or of other assets, the ultimate cash realization of which can be assessed with reasonable certainty. The Act then reinforces the matching concept by requiring income and charges to be taken into account, without regard to the date of receipt or payment.

Furthermore, the word 'dividend', which meant a cash payment under the old law, has been changed to 'distribution' (see p. 290) which covers benefits other than the payment of a cash dividend. (See s. 263(2).)

The other rules may be considered in the context of questions.

Question 1. Boxo Ltd, a television and video hire company, makes a trading loss of £100,000 in 1986/87, but a profit of £80,000 in 1985/86. Can the company distribute this profit to members, either in cash or by reducing rentals to those of its members who hire equipment from it?

Answer. Under *Re National Bank of Wales* (see above) the answer would be yes, but under s. 263(3) losses of previous years must be made good before a distribution may be made, and under s. 263(2) distribution means every description of distribution of a company's assets to its members, whether in cash or otherwise, though there are exceptions, e.g. an issue of fully or partly-paid bonus shares.

However, a reduction in rentals would be regarded as a distribution.

Question 2. Boxo Ltd makes a trading profit in 1985/86 but a trading loss in 1986/87. Can it pay a dividend?

Answer. Under the rule in *Re Hoare & Co*, 1904 (see above) profits of previous years could be brought forward and distributed even if there was a revenue loss in the current trading period.

Under s. 263(3) if the trading loss in the current year is greater than the accumulated profit there cannot be a distribution.

Question 3. Boxo Ltd sells in the current year one of its branch office premises at 15 per cent below its book value, but makes a trading profit of £30,000. Can it pay a dividend?

Answer. Under the rule in *Lee v Neuchatel Asphalte*, 1889 (see above) losses on fixed assets in the current year need not be made good before treating a revenue profit as available for dividend. Under s. 275 *there is no distinction between capital and revenue losses.* This will be treated as a realized loss and must be set against profit made in the current year and/or previous years to see if there is a balance of profit, and if there is it may be used to pay a dividend.

If the premises had not been sold but revalued downwards by, say, 15 per cent, a private company could ignore this unrealized loss in deciding whether to pay a dividend, though it could if it wished make provision for it and treat it as a realized loss. Public companies are obliged to take into account unrealized losses. (See below—the capital maintenance rule.)

Question 4. Boxo Ltd revalues its fixed assets and shows a profit. The assets have not been sold and there are no trading surpluses in the current year. Can a dividend be lawfully paid?

Answer. Under the rule in *Dimbula Valley (Ceylon) Tea Company v Laurie*, 1961 (see above) unrealized capital profits on a revaluation could be distributed by way of dividend.

Under s. 263(3) unrealized gains are not distributable. However, s. 275 provides that if on the revaluation of a fixed asset an unrealized profit is shown to have been made and, on or after the revaluation, a sum is written off or retained for depreciation of that asset over a period, then an amount equal to the amount by which that sum exceeded the sum which would have been so written off or retained for depreciation of that asset over that period if that profit had not been made shall be treated as a realized profit made over that period.

For example, let us suppose we are depreciating a particular asset at 10 per cent per annum. The fixed asset at the beginning of the year was valued at cost, i.e. £2,000. It is revalued at £3,200 before depreciation. We would credit £1,200 to a revaluation reserve and depreciate the asset by £320. The charge to the profit and loss account is £320. Before revaluation we would have depreciated it by £200 so the excess depreciation is £120. This sum could be added back to the profits available for distribution in that year to arrive at the fund available for dividend. The entries in accounting terms are set out below.

	Dr £	Cr £
Fixed asset at cost (1986)	2,000	
Revaluation (end 1986)	1,200	
Revalued amount before depreciation	3,200	
Revaluation Reserve		
Fixed asset revaluation		1,200
realized		(120)
unrealized		1,080
Provision for depreciation		
Charge to P and L Account for 1986		
(10 per cent of revalued figure at end 1986)		320
(Excess depreciation over 1985 = 120)		

Public companies—a capital maintenance rule

By s. 264 which applies only in the case of a public company, a further restriction is introduced which is that distributions may only be made when the company's net assets will be (both before and after the distribution) not less than the aggregate of its called-up share capital and its undistributable reserves. In other words, unrealized capital losses must be taken into account by public companies but not necessarily by private companies. Under the provisions of s. 264 asset revaluation surpluses will not be available either for distribution or for making good realized losses. Furthermore, any past distributions out of unrealized profits must be made good by realized profits before any further distributions can be made.

The illustration in the following table shows how the computation of profit and capital maintenance rules work.

It should be noted that the capital maintenance requirement is a restriction imposed on public companies *as an addition* to the requirement to keep distributions to realized profits.

Public investment companies

Special rules apply to United Kingdom listed companies which fall into this class. The business of an investment company consists of

	Company A £		Company B £
Share capital	50,000		50,000
Surplus or deficit on re-valuation of fixed assets	4,000		(4,000)
Realized profits	7,000	7,000	
Realized losses	(2,000) 5,000	(2,000)	5,000
Total share capital and reserves/net assets	= 59,000		51,000
Distributable profit			
(a) if private company	5,000		5,000 (no capital maintenance rule)
(b) if public company	5,000		1,000 (capital maintenance rule applies)

investing its funds mainly in securities with the aim of spreading the investment risk and thus giving its members the benefit of the results of the management of its funds. (S. 266.) An investment company must indicate its status on its letters and order forms. (S. 351.) An investment company for the purposes of the 1985 Act is, in addition, a listed public company which has given notice in the prescribed form to the Registrar of its intention to carry on a business as an investment company.

If the capital maintenance rule in s. 264 were applied and an investment company had invested substantial sums in shares which had fallen, say temporarily in value, the net assets could at the normal time for dividend fall below cost and below the aggregate of the called-up capital and undistributable reserves and the company would be unable to make a distribution.

In other words, a deficit on the revaluation of the company's portfolio would have to be written off when deciding what income was available for distribution to shareholders. This could produce an unfair result since some of the shareholders may have income shares and others capital shares. Section 265 therefore gives such a company an option when making a distribution of using either the capital maintenance rule of s. 264 or an asset/liability ratio test under which it can make a distribution out of its accumulated, realized revenue profits less accumulated revenue losses so long as this does not reduce the amount of its assets to less than one and a half times the aggregate of its liabilities (including provisions for liabilities), immediately after the proposed distribution. The creditors are therefore safeguarded in such a case by requiring the assets to be at least equal to one-and-a-half times the aggregate of the liabilities.

Treatment of development costs

A company may incur expenditure upon a project before any revenue is received by its sale or use. Section 269 states that where development costs are carried forward in the accounts any amount so shown shall be treated for the purpose of s. 263 (see above) as a realized loss and for the purpose of s. 265 (investment companies) as a realized revenue loss.

However, if the directors feel that there are 'special circumstances' under which, e.g. future benefits can be reasonably anticipated, it might be their wish to defer the set off of expenditure on the development against future revenue, rather than treat it as a realized loss now. If so, they may decide not to treat it as a realized loss, but if they do so the company's financial statements must disclose this fact and also the circumstances relied upon by the directors in reaching that decision.

Insurance companies

Section 268 provides that an amount properly transferred to the profit and loss account of an insurance company from a surplus on its long-term business, e.g. life assurance, shall be considered as realized profit and available for distribution provided it is supported by actuarial investigation showing a surplus in the sense of an excess of assets over the liabilities attributable to the long-term business.

Relevant accounts

Section 270 specifies the accounts to which reference is to be made when determining the level of permitted distributions. In general they will be the last audited accounts filed at the Companies Registry. As we have seen for interim dividends, reference will have to be made in certain cases to interim accounts (see p. 282). It should also be noted that *initial accounts* will be required where a distribution is made during and before the end of the company's first accounting reference period. These will have to be filed with the Registrar where the company is public. Interim accounts need not be audited, as we have seen, but initial accounts prepared by a public company must have a report by the auditors stating whether in their opinion the accounts have been properly prepared.

If there is a qualified audit report and the company proposes to make a distribution, the auditor must make a written statement at the time of the report or later, saying whether in his opinion, the matter giving rise to the qualification is material in deciding whether a lawful distribution can be made. (S. 271.) If the matter is material a dividend can be paid but reduced to the level at which it is legal. Thus if the auditors qualify because of an inadequate provision for bad debts, or because of disagreement with the board over stock valuation as where the company has not kept proper records, then the dividend must be reduced to take account of this.

Section 277 provides that shareholders will have to repay the distribution if they knew or had reasonable grounds to believe that it was in contravention of the distribution provisions of the Act. In addition, as we have already seen, the directors are under a general duty to indemnify the company against a dividend paid unlawfully and if they have done this they are able to recoup the money from the shareholders. (See below.)

What is a distribution?

Section 263(2) defines a 'distribution' as meaning every type of distribution of a company's assets to its members in cash or in kind other than issues of fully paid or partly paid bonus shares, the redemption or purchase of any of the company's own shares out of capital (including the proceeds of any fresh issue of shares) or out of unrealized profits in accordance with Chapter VII of Part V of the Companies Act 1985, the reduction of share capital and the distribution of assets to members of the company on its winding up. Under s. 280(3) 'profits' and 'losses' refer unless the context otherwise requires to both capital and revenue profits or losses.

Distributions in kind

Section 276 is designed to facilitate demerger arrangements (see further p. 383). In a demerger property or shares in one or more companies in a group are distributed to other companies within the group. Some of these assets may have been revalued and contain an element of unrealized profit so that the distribution would offend s. 263. To prevent this s. 276 provides that a profit is to be treated as a realized profit where it arises in the following circumstances—

(a) a company makes a distribution of, or including, any non-cash asset; and (*b*) some part of the amount at which the asset is stated in the 'relevant accounts' (as defined by s. 270) represents an unrealized profit.

Payments out of capital

Exceptionally, shareholders can receive money out of capital in the form of interest. This can happen where interest is paid on calls in advance accepted by the company under s. 119 if the articles so provide; *Table A* does not.

Effect of paying dividends out of capital

Each director who is *knowingly* a party to the payment is jointly and severally liable to return to the company the amount of dividends so paid with interest, though he has a right of *indemnity* against each shareholder who received the dividend to the extent of the dividend received whether the shareholder concerned knew or not that it was paid out of capital. (*Moxham v Grant* [1900] 1 QB 88.)

CAPITALIZING PROFITS

The company may, as an alternative to paying a cash dividend, capitalize its profits. This may be achieved by the allotment of fully-paid-up bonus shares (or scrip issue, as it is sometimes called) by transferring to the capital account undistributed profit equal to the nominal value of the shares issued.

Profits, including unrealized profits, cannot be capitalized unless the articles so provide because, as we have already seen, in the absence of such a provision a shareholder is entitled to the payment of dividend in cash. *Table A, Reg* 110, provides for the capitalization of profits by an ordinary resolution of the members in general meeting upon the recommendation of the directors.

Where there is an allotment of bonus shares, the company must make a return of the allotment under s. 88, and since the shares are allotted for a consideration other than cash, the contract constituting the title of the allottees must be registered. *Table A, Reg* 110(*d*), allows the directors to authorize any person to enter into an agreement on behalf of the members who are to be allotted bonus shares, and this would obviate the need to make a contract with them all. However, since s. 88(3) allows particulars of the contract to be registered in lieu of the contract itself, the company need not actually file a contract but merely the particulars of it, and will in practice adopt this method.

It should be borne in mind that *an issue of bonus shares may necessitate an increase in the company's authorized capital.* The actual distribution of the bonus shares among the various classes of shareholders will be based on their right to receive dividend (*Reg* 110(*b*)) unless the articles or terms of issue otherwise provide.

RESERVES

A company is not in general bound to allocate certain of its profits to reserves. Although it must *on a redemption of shares* out of profits set up a *capital redemption reserve*, and it may be that the company is bound under a contract with its debenture holders to set aside a certain sum by way of a reserve to redeem the debentures.

Nevertheless the articles may provide for the directors to set up *reserve funds for dividend equalization* or *to meet future liabilities. Table A,* does not give such a power it being implied that provided the reserves are distributable the shareholders are entitled to them. However, where such a power exists, the directors may decide to set aside all the profits, even if this means that no dividend is paid on the preference or ordinary shares though in such circumstances there may be a petition under s. 459 by a member or members on the grounds of 'unfair prejudice'.

However, once again the decision in *Re Carrington Viyella* (see p. 193) would have to be overcome since failure to pay dividend affects *all* the members and not just *part* of them.

11 Borrowing powers

A trading company has implied power to borrow. (*General Auction Estate and Monetary Co v Smith*, 1891.[178]) Nevertheless it is usual for an express power to be given in the memorandum, and such express powers may impose some limit on the company's borrowing by stating a fixed sum beyond which the company cannot borrow, or by limiting the borrowing (say) to one-half of the issued share capital. A non-trading company has no implied borrowing powers and must take express power to borrow in its constitution.

A power to borrow, whether express or implied, carries with it by a further implication of law a power to give a security for the loan and to pay interest upon it. (*General Auction Estate & Monetary Co v Smith*, 1891.[178]) Once again it is usual for the company's constitution to give an express power to do these things, though an express power cannot override the Companies Act. Thus it would not be possible to charge the company's Reserve Capital since this is expressly forbidden by the provisions of s. 120 which renders such capital incapable of being called up except on a winding up. (See p. 84.)

ULTRA VIRES LOANS AND OTHER RESTRICTIONS ON BORROWING

Except where s. 35 applies borrowing which is in excess of the company's powers renders the loan *ultra vires* and void (*Fountaine v Carmarthen Rail Co*, 1868[40] but see *Re Introductions Ltd*, 1969[39]). Any security given is also void; nor can the company ratify the *ultra vires* loan by resolution in general meeting. (See *Ashbury Railway Carriage Co v Riche*, 1875[41], which states that *no contract* can be so ratified.) The *ultra vires* lender is not necessarily without a remedy, and may be able to sue on a guarantee, or by virtue of subrogation, or by tracing, and may also have a claim on any residuary assets in a winding up. These matters were dealt with in detail in Chapter 3.

Borrowing may also be within the company's powers but beyond those of the directors, and where this is so, there is no action against the company in respect of the loan unless—
  (i) the company ratifies it; or
  (ii) the rule in *Turquand's Case*[69] can be called in aid; or
  (iii) s. 35, Companies Act 1985 applies.
The new *Table A* in *Reg* 70 gives the board all powers to manage and there is no need for a *specific* power to borrow. There is no limit on the amount the directors can borrow so long as they remain within the company's power.

It should be noted that the power to issue debentures is subject to s. 80, i.e. the authority of the members is required if, e.g. the debentures are convertible, i.e. carry rights of conversion into share capital. (S. 80(2)(*b*).) (See also p. 137.)

Section 117 provides that a public company may not borrow money until it has received a certificate under that section allowing it to trade.

DEBENTURES

The most usual form of borrowing by companies is by means of debentures which are normally issued under the company's seal. The debenture also usually gives a charge on the company's property, or some other form of security. Section 744, which is the interpretation section of the 1985 Act, states that the term 'debenture' includes debenture stock, bonds and any other securities given by the company, whether constituting a charge on the assets of the company or not. The term is, therefore, an extremely wide one. (*Lemon v Austin Friars Investment Trust Ltd*, 1926.[179])

Debenture holders are creditors (but see p. 310) and not members of the company, and are entitled to interest on their debentures whether the company earns profits or not. Holders are provided with a safe if limited income, and debentures appeal to a cautious investor.

Debentures may also be *convertible* which means that they are issued with an option, tenable for a certain period of time, to exchange them for shares in the company. Debentures can be issued at a discount without restriction, but the issue of convertible debentures must not be allowed to operate as a device to issue shares at a discount as would be the case if a debenture for £100, issued at £90, were later to be exchanged for 100 shares of nominal value of £1 each. This would in effect be an issue of shares at a discount which is forbidden by s. 100.

TYPES OF DEBENTURES

Debentures may be issued in a series, e.g. where there is a public offer by prospectus, or alternatively they may be issued singly, e.g. to secure a bank loan or overdraft. They may also be issued in respect of either an existing debt or a fresh loan.

Where debentures are issued in a series, it is usual to provide expressly that they are to rank *pari passu*, i.e. equally. This is essential because loans rank for priority according to the time they are made, and if such an express provision were not made, the debentures in the series would rank for priority of payment and security according to the date of issue, and if all were issued on the same day, they would rank in numerical order. (*Gartside v Silkstone & Dodworth Coal & Iron Co Ltd*, 1882.[180])

Where debentures rank *pari passu*, there can be no action at law brought by an individual debenture holder merely in respect of his own rights, and any such action brought by him is deemed to be a representative action on behalf of all the debenture holders of the series.

Debenture stock may be issued so long as the stock is fully paid, and this affects transfer. A debenture must be transferred as a whole unit whereas debenture stock can be transferred in part, though the articles or the terms of issue usually fix a minimum amount which can be transferred, e.g. £1.

Debentures are usually *secured, registered*, and *redeemable*, though they may be unsecured, unregistered (i.e. bearer debentures) and irredeemable.

Secured debentures

These are normally secured by a charge on the company's assets, either by a provision to that effect in the debenture itself, or by the terms of the trust deed drawn up in connection with the issue. Sometimes a provision appears in both documents.

Registered debentures

These are recorded in the register of debenture holders, and the setting up of such a register is provided for by s. 190. Such debentures are transferable in accordance with the provisions of the terms of issue, but transfer is usually effected by an instrument in writing in a way similar to that of shares. The transferee of a debenture takes it subject to equities, and this includes claims which the company has against the transferor. However, the company's claims are normally excluded by the terms of issue of the debentures, these terms usually stating that the money secured by the debentures will be paid without regard to any equities between the company and previous holders. (*Re Goy & Co Ltd, Farmer v Goy & Co Ltd*, 1900.[181])

It should also be noted that when a company sets up a register of debenture holders, s. 360 does not apply to it, and the company would be bound by any notice of trust or other equity over the debentures. It is, therefore, usual to provide in the terms of issue that the company shall not be bound to recognize anyone other than the registered holder.

Redeemable debentures

Debentures are usually redeemable, and the company may provide a fund for their redemption. The annual amount so provided must be charged whether profits are made or not, though in some cases the terms of issue may stipulate that the fund shall be provided only out of profits, if made. Under the Sched 4, Part I, Section A, para 3(7)(*a*), amounts set aside for the redemption of debentures must be shown separately in the profit and loss account.

Debentures may be redeemed in the following ways—

(*a*) *By drawings by lot*, either at the company's option or at fixed intervals.

(*b*) *By the company buying them in the market*, and if the debentures are bought in the market at a discount, the consequent profit to the company is a realized profit available for dividend unless the articles otherwise provide.

(*c*) *By the company redeeming them either out of a Fund or possibly by a fresh issue of debentures*. A fresh issue is useful to the company where rates of interest have fallen, because the old debentures can be redeemed and the money reborrowed by the fresh issue at lower rates of interest. Where redemption is by a fresh issue, it is usual to allow the existing debenture holders to exchange the old debentures for the new ones if they so wish.

The company will redeem at a fixed future date, but usually has an option to redeem on or after a given earlier date, and this allows the company to choose the most convenient time for redemption.

Redemption may be at the issue price or at a higher price, and debentures may be issued at (say) 80 and redeemed at 100, or issued at 100 and redeemed at 110, thus giving the debenture holders a capital gain in addition to the interest payments made.

Re-issue

Section 194(1) allows the company to re-issue debentures which it has redeemed unless the company has resolved that the debentures shall not be re-issued, or unless there are provisions in the articles or terms of issue of the original debentures that they shall not be re-issued. A person to whom debentures are re-issued has the same priorities as had the original debenture holder. (S. 194(2).)

The articles and/or the trust deed under which the debentures are issued invariably forbid re-issue, and if there was a re-issue in that situation the purchasers of the re-issued debentures would be deferred to other persons holding debentures at that time.

Where a company has issued debentures to secure advances made from time to time on a current account such as a bank overdraft, the debenture shall not be considered redeemed by reason only of the account ceasing to be at a certain point in debit so long as the debentures are still deposited with the person making the advances. (S. 194(3).)

The Fourth Schedule requires that particulars of any redeemed debentures which the company has power to re-issue shall be disclosed in the notes to the company's balance sheet. (Fourth Schedule, Part III, para 41(2).)

Unsecured debentures

Such a debenture is no more than an unsecured promise by the company to repay the loan. The holder can, of course, sue the company on that promise, but is only an ordinary creditor in a winding up, although, since he is a creditor, he can petition the court for a winding up.

Bearer debentures

These are negotiable instruments and are transferable free from equities by mere delivery and it is not necessary to give the company notice of transfer.

Interest is paid by means of coupons attached to the debenture, these coupons being in effect an instruction to the company's banker to pay the bearer of the coupon a stated sum on presentment to the bank after a certain date. The company can communicate with the holders of bearer debentures only by advertisement, and it is often provided that the holders of such debentures may exchange them for registered debentures.

Irredeemable debentures

A debenture which is issued with no fixed date of redemption is an irredeemable debenture, though such debentures are redeemable on a winding up, and the liquidator is empowered to discharge them. In addition irredeemable debentures always empower the debenture holders to enforce their security should the company, for example, fail to pay interest on the loan and such enforcement will result in the payment of the debenture debt. Section 193 provides that such debentures may be issued, and this provision is necessary because otherwise the general rule of equity, that redemption of a mortgage cannot be postponed for too long a time, would apply. The result is that a company can create long mortgages over its land and other property by means of debentures, whether irredeemable or for a long contractual period prior to redemption. (*Knightsbridge Estates Trust Ltd v Byrne*, 1940.[182])

A debenture with no fixed date for redemption, but which gives the company the right to repay it at its option, is properly called a *perpetual* and not an irredeemable debenture.

ACQUISITION OF DEBENTURES

Debentures may be acquired either from the company itself or by transfer or transmission.

Issue by the company

A company may issue debentures either individually or in a series. The provisions of s. 100 forbidding the allotment of shares at a discount do not apply to debentures, and accordingly they may be allotted at par, at a discount, or at a premium, unless this is forbidden by the company's articles. However, if debentures are issued at a discount together with a right to exchange them for shares at par value, the debentures are good but the right to exchange is void. (*Mosely v Koffyfontein Mines Ltd*, 1904.[120]) Section 130 (share premium) does not apply to an issue of debentures and so if they are issued at a premium there is no need to open the equivalent of a share premium account.

If a person agrees to take a debenture from the company in return for a loan, the contract may be enforced by both the lender and the company by *specific performance*. Section 195 gives this right because, in the absence of such statutory provision, equity would not specifically enforce a loan.

The document offering debentures for sale on the USM is a prospectus and must comply with the Act, and an application form under which the debentures may be applied for must not be issued without a prospectus. (S. 56(2).) For listed companies see p. 130.

The provisions of s. 86 (see p. 141) regarding restrictions on allotment, where the company has applied for permission for the debentures to be dealt in on the USM, apply to debentures in the same way as they apply to shares.

The company must have certificates ready within two months after allotment or transfer, unless the terms of issue otherwise provide (s. 185(1)), though this sub-section is now restricted by s. 185(4) (see p. 152). If a company has issued any debentures during the financial year to which the accounts relate, the notes to the accounts must state the reason for making the issue, the classes of debentures issued, and as respects each class of debentures, the amount issued and the consideration received by the company for the issue.

Transfer

Registered debentures are transferable in accordance with the method laid down in the terms of issue, usually a stock transfer form as for shares. The company cannot refuse to register a properly stamped transfer, provided the terms of issue allow transfers and contain no restrictions, but a proper instrument of transfer must be produced to the company except in cases of transmission, or where the transfer is an exempt transfer under Stock Transfer Act 1982. (S. 183.) Where the company refuses to register a transfer, it must send a notice to this effect to the transferee within two months of the transfer being lodged. (S. 183(5).)

Certification by the company of an instrument of transfer has the same effect in the case of debentures as it has in the case of shares, i.e. it is a representation that documents have been produced to the company which show a *prima facie* title in the transferors. (S. 184.)

In the case of bearer debentures transfer is by mere delivery and the company is not involved.

Transmission

As in the case of shares, debentures pass by operation of law (*a*) to the holder's personal representatives on *death*, and (*b*) to the holder's trustee *on bankruptcy*, and the rights of such persons are similar to their rights when shares pass by operation of law. (See p. 154.)

FIXED AND FLOATING CHARGES

Debentures may be secured by a fixed or by a floating charge, or more commonly by a combination of both types of charge.

Fixed (or specific) charge

Such a charge usually takes the form of a legal mortgage over specified assets of the company, e.g. its land and buildings and fixed plant. A specific or fixed charge may be legal or equitable. Thus a company could create a specific charge over, say, a specific asset such as a warehouse, by giving the lender a legal mortgage over it which could be done, for example, by giving him a lease of 3,000 years over the property with a provision for the lease to cease when the company had repaid the loan. Alternatively, a legal mortgage could be created by a charge by deed expressed to be by way of legal mortgage under s. 85(1) of the Law of Property Act 1925. On the other hand, a company could create an equitable specific charge over the warehouse informally by handing the title deeds to the lender. In both cases the charge would be a specific charge because the warehouse is specific property over which the charge exists.

The advantage of a fixed charge from the debenture holders' point of view is that a particular asset (or group of assets) is available to satisfy their claims, and the company cannot dispose of the asset or create other charges ranking in priority to the present charge. On the other hand, the asset which has been chosen as a security may lose its value even when the other assets of the company are retaining their value or even appreciating, and since, under a fixed charge, the debenture holders' security is the asset chosen, they cannot proceed against other assets of the company, but are confined to the asset comprising the fixed charge.

The major disadvantage of a fixed charge from the company's point of view is that the company cannot dispose of the asset or assets subject to the charge without the consent of the debenture holders or their trustees.

Floating charge

This is a charge which is not attached to any particular asset identified when the charge is made. Instead it attaches to the company's assets as they may then be, if and when the charge *crystallizes*. The company is in the meantime free to dispose of its assets, and any new assets which the company may acquire are available to the debenture holders should the charge *crystallize*. Because such a charge does not fix at the time of its creation upon any particular asset, it is *equitable by nature*.

Floating charges restricted to companies

In theory a floating charge could be used by a sole trader or a partnership as a security but unless and until changes are made in Bills of

Sale legislation such a charge is not viable because a floating charge gives a proprietary interest in goods, e.g. stock in trade in circumstances where those goods are left in the company's possession. *This requires the registration of a bill of sale listing the property in the Bill of Sale Registry* if the charge is given by a sole trader or a partnership otherwise it is void. The floating charge does not lend itself to the listing of the property charged because its essential feature is that the assets charged are always fluctuating. The Bills of Sale Acts do not apply to charges given by companies. (See s. 17, Bills of Sale Act, 1882.)

Crystallization

A floating charge crystallizes—

(*a*) in the circumstances specified in the trust deed or in the debentures, e.g. failure of the company to pay interest or to redeem the debentures as agreed;

(*b*) if a receiver or administrative receiver is appointed for the debenture holders, either by the court, or by the debenture holders or their trustees under a power given by the terms of issue of the debentures, such appointment being out of court; or

(*c*) if the company commences to wind up.

Any disposition of the assets after the charge crystallizes means that the purchaser from the company takes the assets subject to the charge, i.e. the right of the debenture holders to proceed against them to satisfy their debt. However, rights such as set off and lien arising before the charge crystallizes are not affected, even though in the case of a lien the goods come into possession after the appointment of a receiver. (*Rother Iron Works Ltd v Canterbury Precision Engineers Ltd*, 1973.[183])

The advantage of such a charge to the company is that it has the free disposition of its assets until the charge crystallizes. From the debenture holder's point of view, a floating charge is advantageous because on crystallization they have a variety of assets available to satisfy the debenture debt, including recently acquired assets, if any.

Priorities between floating charges and other claims against the company

A person who lends money on the security of a specific mortgage of a company's property is always entitled to repayment of his loan from the proceeds of sale of the mortgaged property before any other creditor except, of course, a creditor with a prior specific charge. A person who takes a floating charge is not so secure. There are cases in which he has to give up assets to which his charge would otherwise attach so that they may be used to pay other creditors. The rules which govern competing claims by debenture holders secured by floating charges and other classes of creditors will now be considered.

Unsecured creditors

The owner of a floating charge cannot prevent the company from using its assets to pay unsecured creditors while the charge continues to float. However, as soon as it crystallizes he is entitled to repayment of his loan out of the assets to which the charge attaches before the company's unsecured creditors.

Preferential payments

There is one statutory exception to what has been said about unsecured creditors. When a floating charge crystallizes the claims against the company which would be preferential payments in a winding up must be paid out of the property to which the charge attaches before the debenture debt is paid. The debenture debt is deferred only to preferential payments accrued at the date of the appointment of an administrative receiver and not those which accrue subsequently. (S. 196.)

The preferential payments in a winding up will be dealt with in detail in Chapter 17, but, for example, the Crown has a preferential claim in respect of taxes for any one year ending on or before the preceding April 5th and employees of the company have preferential claims for wages and salaries in respect of services rendered during the immediately preceding four months up to a maximum of £800. When a floating charge crystallizes without the company being wound up these periods are calculated by reference to the date when an administrative receiver is appointed.

Sale of goods—reservation of title by seller

It has become fashionable in recent times for sellers of goods to try to protect themselves against the worst effects of a company receivership or liquidation by inserting retention clauses of one form or another into their contracts of sale.

These clauses have as their purpose the retention of the seller's ownership in the goods until the buyer has paid for them, even though the buyer is given possession of the goods and may use them in the manufacture of other goods which he will then re-sell. These clauses may also extend to the proceeds of resale.

If the clause works and the purchasing company goes into a receivership or liquidation because of insolvency, then the seller may seek to recover the goods which the purchasing company still has and the proceeds of resale by the purchasing company. The seller will normally find such a procedure more advantageous than—

(a) proving in a liquidation for whatever he can get by way of dividend leaving his goods to be sold for the benefit of creditors generally; or

(b) in a receivership leaving his goods with the administrative receiver who may in law continue the company's business without paying its existing debts, including that of the seller.

Retention clauses have been used extensively on the Continent for some time and are becoming popular in the UK. They are to some extent an understandable reaction by unsecured trade creditors to the increasing number of insolvencies in which a bank is found to hold a debenture giving a floating charge over the insolvent company's assets to secure an overdraft. The bank, being a secured creditor, takes the company's assets first through the medium of a receivership or liquidation, leaving trade creditors unprovided for.

The Romalpa case (Aluminium Industrie Vaassen BV v Romalpa Aluminium [1976] 2 All ER 552.) This was the first case in a series of three which alerted practitioners to the problems which retention clauses might cause in insolvency practice.

The facts of the case were that AIV sold aluminium foil to Romalpa, the contractual conditions of sale being—

(i) that the ownership of the material to be delivered by AIV would only be transferred to the purchaser when he had met all that was owing to AIV, no matter on what grounds;

(ii) that Romalpa should store the foil separately;

(iii) that if the foil was used to make new objects, those objects should be stored separately and be owned by AIV as *security* for payment;

(iv) that Romalpa could sell the new objects but in effect as agents of AIV.

In case the reader should feel that the expression 'new objects' is vague, it should be noted that the law report does not say what Romalpa's business was but it seems to have been some sort of processing.

Romalpa got into financial difficulties and was in debt to its bankers in the sum of £200,000. The bank had a debenture secured over Romalpa's assets and appointed a receiver under that debenture. At the time of the receiver's appointment Romalpa owed AIV £122,000 and in order to recover some of that money at the expense of the bank AIV sought, under their conditions of sale, to recover from Romalpa foil valued in round terms at £50,000 and the cash proceeds of resold foil of some £35,000. The proceeds had been received from third party purchasers from Romalpa after the receiver was appointed and he had kept the fund of £35,000 separate so that it was not mixed with Romalpa's other funds and was therefore identifiable.

The Court of Appeal held that the foil was recoverable and so were the proceeds of sale since there were two fiduciary relationships between AIV and Romalpa as follows—

(a) Romalpa was a bailee of AIV's goods because ownership had not passed to Romalpa; *and*

(b) Romalpa was AIV's agent for the purpose of the sale of objects made with the foil.

Therefore Romalpa was accountable to AIV for the foil and the proceeds of its sale and AIV could trace the proceeds into the hands of the receiver under the rule in *Re Hallett's Estate* (1880) 13 ChD 696 which provides for tracing between parties who are in a fiduciary relationship.

As regards a claim by counsel for Romalpa that the retention clause created a charge which should have been registered under what is now s. 395 and that the retention clause was inoperative because there had been no such registration, the Court decided that since ownership had not passed to Romalpa the charge was not over the property of Romalpa and so s. 395 did not apply, that section being confined, to charges over the property of the company. In addition, the Romalpa clause included a contractual charge over mixed objects. The Court did not give a decision as to the position in regard to this charge since there was no need in the case to use it. The claim was merely for foil remaining in the buyer's possession and for the proceeds of sale.

It should be noted that it is now the generally accepted view of the law that *one* fiduciary relationship, i.e. that of bailor and bailee is sufficient to allow recovery of goods *and* proceeds of sale. There is no need for an agency relationship.

Subsequent cases Since the decision in the *Romalpa* case the courts have had to deal with two main types of actions as follows—

1. Those cases where the supplier has been solely concerned to use that part of his retention clauses to retain the title over goods supplied under a contract of sale, and sometimes the proceeds of any resale of them, where the goods have not been used or changed or added to in manufacture as in the case of *Romalpa*. These actions will, it seems, succeed, without the need to register a clause as charge under s. 395. In other words, *Romalpa* would still, presumably, have been decided as it was originally.

2. Those cases where the supplier is trying to use a multi-purpose clause to cover goods supplied for use in manufacture, as in *Re Bond Worth Ltd* [1979] 3 All ER 919 (seller's Acrilan became carpet); *Borden (UK) Ltd v Scottish Timber Products Ltd* [1979] 3 All ER 961 (seller's resin became chipboard); *Re Peachdart Ltd* [1983] 3 All ER 204 (seller's leather became handbags); *Clough Mill Ltd v Martin*

[1984] 3 All ER 982 (seller's yarn became fabric); *Hendy Lennox (Industrial Engines) Ltd v Grahame Puttick Ltd* [1984] 2 All ER 152 (seller's diesel engines inserted in generators).

In the above cases the major difficulty facing the supplier in terms of recovering goods supplied for manufacture but not yet used in the process is that it is difficult to construe a bailment since it is intended that the goods be used in manufacture which must give the company some form of ownership over them. This was basically the reason why in all of the above cases except *Hendy Lennox* the High Court decided that there was no bailment of goods supplied for manufacture but still in stock. Where the goods have been mixed with the company's goods, or the company's workers have put their skill into the product (as in *Re Peachdart*) then the company owns the property and a retention clause will not normally succeed unless registered as a charge under s. 395.

Exceptionally, the court has allowed goods which were to be used in manufacture to be recovered, as in *Hendy Lennox* where the engines were already in generators but were readily identifiable, unchanged, and could be removed. Furthermore, in *Clough Mill* the Court of Appeal, while accepting the difficulty of construing a bailment of goods supplied for use in manufacture *while the contract continued*, felt that in the circumstances of the case where *the Receiver had repudiated the contract* and was refusing to pay for yarn in stock but not yet used in manufacture, a bailment could be construed and the yarn returned.

In a more recent case, *Four Point Garage Ltd v Carter, The Times*, 19 November 1984, a car was bought under retention arrangements until paid for. The supplier went into liquidation. Simon Brown J held that the car could not be recovered because the retention clause did not prevent the buyer from reselling it. A bailee cannot, he said, normally resell; so this was not a bailment and the ability to trace the property was not available.

Fixed or specific charges

A fixed or specific charge, whether legal or equitable, and whenever created, takes priority over a floating charge on the asset concerned. The only exception is where the floating charge expressly prohibits the creation of fixed charges in priority to the floating charge and the person taking the fixed charge knew this to be so. However, the registration of the charge at the Companies Registry does not give constructive notice of such a provision (*Wilson v Kelland*, 1910[184]) and there is in fact no means by which the debenture holders under a floating charge may ensure conclusively that all later mortgagees have notice of the restriction.

Other floating charges

If a company is to have power to create a second floating charge over its undertaking ranking before the first, the debenture securing the first charge must so provide expressly. (See *Re Automatic Bottle Makers Ltd*, 1926.[185]) Otherwise floating charges rank for priority in the order in which they were created.

Judgment creditors

If a creditor who has sued the company for his debt and obtained a judgment asks for and obtains a writ (*fieri facias*) which allows the sheriff's officers to take the company's goods and sell them to pay the debt, then the creditor cannot proceed with his execution if all that has happened before the floating charge crystallizes is that the sheriff has taken possession of the goods. The sheriff must surrender them to the administrative receiver *Re Opera Ltd* [1891] 3 Ch 260. However, if the sheriff has sold the goods or the company has paid the whole or part of the judgment debt to avoid a sale, the judgment creditor may be entitled to the amount received by the sheriff even though the money is still in the sheriff's hands when the floating charge crystallizes. However, the matter is not beyond doubt. There are no reported cases or statutory provisions and some practitioners take the view that an administrative receiver could have grounds for requiring the sheriff to pay such funds over to him.

A judgment creditor is entitled to the proceeds of sale or a payment by the company to avoid sale if the sheriff receives the money before crystallization.

Garnishee orders

If the company owes B £100 and will not pay then, provided B has sued the company for the debt and obtained a judgment in his favour, he may ask the court for a garnishee order over, for example, the company's bank account. Garnishee orders are either *nisi*, which gives a charge over the account, or absolute which require the bank to pay over the sum concerned to B.

If a judgment creditor obtains a garnishee order against a debtor of the company, such as the company's bank, he is entitled to the debt thus attached only if his garnishee order has been made absolute and the debtor, e.g. the bank, has paid the debt to him before the floating charge crystallizes. (*Cairney v Back* [1906] 2 KB 746.)

Hire purchase agreements

If a company obtains goods under a hire purchase agreement, it does not become the owner of them until the last instalment of the rental has been paid to the seller and the option to acquire the title to the goods has been exercised. Debenture holders have no better title to the goods than the company and the owner may recover the goods from an administrative receiver for the debenture holders where he could recover them from the company. It should be noted that the provisions of s. 90 of the Consumer Credit Act 1974 which prevent a creditor retaking possession of the goods without a court order when one-third of the price has been paid will not apply in the company situation. The provisions of the 1974 Act are designed to protect the ordinary consumer and for most purposes transactions by corporations are excluded. Whether the debenture holders have a specific mortgage or a floating charge makes no difference in this respect.

If the market value of the goods on hire purchase exceeds the outstanding instalments, it is probable that the owner will wish to take the goods from the administrative receiver. If the outstanding instalments exceed the market value the owner may leave the goods with him in case a purchaser can be found.

It should be noted that a debenture holder is sometimes able to claim that goods on hire purchase have become part of his security where they have been fixed or attached to buildings. This could apply, for example, where a sprinkler system had been installed in a factory on a hire purchase basis. (*Re Morrison, Jones and Taylor Ltd*, 1914.[186]) The matter is extremely complex and receivers and administrative receivers would normally obtain legal advice in each case. However, in general terms it may be said that goods on hire purchase may become part of the debenture holders' charge where they have been fixed or attached to land as described above.

Landlord

A landlord has a special right to enter the premises of his tenant in order to take goods for sale for non-payment of rent. As a general rule prior leave of the court is not required before distress can be levied. However, it is usually effected by a certificated bailiff, i.e. a person authorized by the court, to levy distress for rent.

The rights of a company's landlord are not affected by the crystallization of a floating charge. If he has distrained on the company's goods for arrears of rent before crystallization he may sell the goods thereafter and the debenture holders cannot require him to account for the proceeds of sale. He can also distrain for rent accruing after crystallization on goods in the debenture holders' possession, even though their charge has now attached specifically to those goods. However, if a receiver or administrative receiver appointed by the court is in possession of the company's goods, the landlord must apply to the court for leave to distrain which will always be given if there is rent owing.

Avoidance of floating charges on a winding up or administration order

By the Insolvency Act 1986, s. 245, a floating charge created by a company within one year before the commencement of its winding up or the making of an administration order is void as a security for any debt other than cash paid or goods supplied to the company in consideration of the charge at the time the charge was created or thereafter with interest thereon, if any, as may be payable under any agreement for interest. The period is two years if the person in whose favour the charge was created was connected with the company, e.g. one of its directors.

Section 245 does not apply if the company was solvent immediately after the creation of the charge. The purpose of the section is to prevent a company which is unable to pay its debts from preferring one of its unsecured creditors to the others by giving him a floating charge on its assets. There is no objection to the creation of a floating charge where the company actually receives funds or goods at the time or afterwards because these may assist it to carry on business and, indeed, avoid winding up.

The following hypothetical situations may make the application of the section clearer—

(a) A is an unsecured creditor of B Ltd. B Ltd gives him a floating charge over its assets to secure the debt. B Ltd is insolvent at the time and goes into liquidation within ten months. The security is void but the debt itself is not so that A can still prove as an unsecured creditor.

(b) The Barchester Bank agrees to advance money to B Ltd at the current rate of interest in return for a floating charge on its assets. B Ltd is insolvent at the time and goes into liquidation within ten months. The bank's charge is good and takes priority over unsecured creditors as regards the sums advanced with interest as agreed.

If the charge is created in favour of a person connected with the company, e.g. one of its directors, it can be avoided if made within two years from the commencement of winding up or the making of an administration order. As regards goods supplied, the charge extends only to the price which could reasonably have been obtained for them in the ordinary course of business at the time when they were supplied.

Thus the security would not extend to goods at an artificially high price.

Points arising from case law on this topic which should be specially noted are as follows—

(i) A floating charge is valid as a security for loans made after the date it was created if the lender promised to make such loans (covenanted loans) and even though the lender did not promise to make such loans (uncovenanted loans). (*Re Yeovil Glove Co Ltd*, 1965.[187]) Consequently advances made to an insolvent company by its bank on an overdraft account during the year before it is wound up are validly secured in the winding up by a floating charge given before the advances were made. The debenture creating the floating charge must, of course, expressly secure uncovenanted loans. (*Re Yeovil Glove Co Ltd*, 1965.[187])

(ii) The period of one year from the creation of the floating charge within which the company must be wound up or an administration order made if the floating charge is to be rendered valid is calculated from the date when the instrument imposing the charge is executed and not from the date when the debentures entitling their holders to the benefit of the charge are issued. Consequently, if more than a year before it commences to be wound up, a company executes a trust deed imposing a floating charge on its undertaking to secure a series of debentures, and the company issues some of the debentures as security for its debts within that year, the debenture holders are nevertheless entitled to the benefit of the charge and the statutory provision does not invalidate it. (*Transport & General Credit Corporation Ltd v Morgan* [1939] 2 All ER 17.)

(iii) If an unsecured creditor makes a new loan to the company on the security of a floating charge on the understanding that the loan will be applied immediately in paying off his existing unsecured debt, the floating charge is invalid unless the company is solvent. (*Re Destone Fabrics Ltd* [1941] 1 All ER 545 but see *Re Matthew Ellis Ltd*, 1933.[188])

(iv) Floating charges are invalidated by the Act only when the company is wound up or on the making of an administration order, and so if before it is wound up or such an order made, it redeems a floating charge which would have been invalid in those situations, the liquidator or administrator cannot require the owner of the charge to repay what he has received. (*Re Parkes Garage (Swadlincote) Ltd* [1929] 1 Ch 139.) However, if the redemption takes place within six months (two years if the debenture holder is a connected person) before the winding up, it may be a preference of the debenture holder in which case the liquidator can recover the amount paid from the debenture holder under s. 239, Insolvency Act 1986. (See further Chapter 17.)

THE TRUST DEED

When debentures are offered for public subscription, the company enters into a trust deed with trustees, usually a trust corporation such as an insurance company. The charge securing the debentures is made in favour of the trustees who hold it on trust for the debenture stock holders. The trustees are usually appointed and paid by the company to act on behalf of the debenture stock holders.

Debenture stock holders, unlike debenture holders, are not creditors of the company. Thus in *Re Dunderland Iron Ore Co Ltd* [1909] 1 Ch 446 it was held that the holder of debenture stock secured by a trust deed could not present a petition to wind up the company since he was not a creditor. The trustees are the creditors for the whole debenture debt, and the stock holder is an equitable beneficiary of the trust on which they hold that debt. Consequently, his remedies are against the trustees, but by suing them to compel them to exercise their remedies against the company, he can indirectly enforce the same remedies against the company as the holder of a single debenture can enforce directly.

The creation of a trust deed has the following advantages—

(i) *It enables a legal or equitable mortgage on specific assets of the company to be created.* The deeds of property can be held by the trustees, and where there is a legal mortgage, the legal estate can be vested in them. It could not be vested in hundreds or possibly thousands of debenture holders because, since the property legislation of 1925, the legal estate in land cannot be vested in more than four persons.

(ii) *The interests of the debenture holders are better safeguarded* by the employment of a professional trust corporation, or by a small number of expert trustees, than they would be if left to the debenture holders themselves. The latter are often widely dispersed and often lack the knowledge required to safeguard their interests properly.

Trustees usually have the power to call meetings of the debenture holders to inform them of matters of particular concern to them.

(iii) *The trust deed usually gives the trustees power to sell the property charged* without the aid of the court, and to appoint an administrative receiver should the company default, for example, in the payment of interest or repayment of the principal sums borrowed.

(iv) *The trust deed usually gives the trustees power to see that the security is properly maintained and repaired and insured.*

Where debentures are issued under a trust deed, the debentures themselves refer to the deed and thereby incorporate its terms.

Contents of the trust deed

The main clauses of a trust deed are as follows— (a) *The nature of the security.* Details of the assets charged are given, and it sets out the powers of the trustees to deal with them on default by the company and on a winding up.

(b) *The nature of the charge.* The deed will state whether the charge is a fixed or a floating charge. Usually there is a combination of both, i.e. a fixed charge on certain of the company's assets and a floating charge on the rest. There will also be a provision relating to the company's power to create other charges ranking equally with, or in priority to, the present charge.

(c) *The kind of debentures to be issued.* This clause will state whether the debentures are to be registered or bearer, or whether debenture stock is to be issued; and if stock, the minimum amount which can be transferred.

(d) *The method of redemption.* The clause will state whether there is to be an ordinary redemption by the company, or whether redemption is to be made by drawings or in the market, and when the redemption is to take place. This clause will also gve details of any fund which the company proposes to set up to provide for the redemption of the debentures.

A copy of any trust deed for securing any issue of debentures shall be forwarded to every holder of any such debentures on payment of a fee. (S. 191(3).)

REGISTRATION OF CHARGES

Section 395 provides for the registration of certain charges created by companies over their assets. Accordingly secured debentures must be registererd at the Companies Registry where the charges created are of the following kinds—

(i) A charge on uncalled capital of the company.

(ii) A charge created or evidenced by an instrument which, if executed by an individual, would require registration as a bill of sale, i.e. a mortgage of chattels. Where an individual wishes to create a mortgage of chattels *and yet retain possession of therm*, he may do so by a registered bill of sale filed at the Central Office of the Supreme Court. Where a company effects such a mortgage of chattels, registration at the Companies Registry is substituted for the normal bill of sale procedure.

(iii) A charge on land or any interest therein belonging to the company wherever situate. In this connection it should be noted that the deposit of the title deeds of property owned by a company gives rise to the presumption that an equitable charge over the property has been created and accordingly such a charge must be registered. (*Re Wallis & Simmonds (Builders) Ltd* [1974] 1 All ER 561.)

(iv) A charge on the book debts of the company.

(v) A floating charge on the undertaking or property of the company.

(vi) A charge on calls made but not paid.

(vii) A charge on a ship (or aircraft (Mortgaging of Aircraft Order SI 1972/1268)) or any share in a ship.

(viii) A charge on goodwill, on a patent or a licence under a patent, on a trademark, or on a copyright or a licence under a copyright.

(ix) A charge for the purpose of securing any issue of debentures. This would cover cases in which the charge was not one specifically set out in (i) to (viii) above. In fact, this is a 'sweep up' provision and would cover, for example, an investment company whose only assets were shares and debentures of other companies which would have to register charges made over those securities under heading (ix) even though they are not included specifically in the other headings.

As regards the acquisition of property by a company on which a charge already exists, s. 400 provides that where a company registered in England and Wales acquires any property which is subject to a charge of any such kind as would, if it had been created by the company after the acquisition of the property, have been required to be registered under the Act, the company shall cause the prescribed particulars of the charge, together with a copy (certified in the prescribed manner to be a correct copy) of the instrument, if any, by which the charge was created or is evidenced, to be delivered to the Registrar of Companies for registration in the manner required by the Act within 21 days after the date on which the acquisition is completed.

If the property is situate, and the charge was created, outside Great Britain, 21 days after the date on which the copy of the instrument could in due course of post, and if despatched with due diligence, have been received in the United Kingdom shall be substituted for 21 days after the completion of the acquisition as the time within which the particulars and the copy of the instrument are to be delivered to the Registrar. Failure to register a charge under s. 400 results only in a default fine. The validity of the charge is not affected.

The Registrar will issue a certificate of registration which is conclusive evidence that registration has been made (s. 401(2)(*b*)), (*In re C L Nye Ltd*, 1969[189]) and a copy of this certificate is endorsed on every debenture certificate issued. (S. 402(1).)

Effect of non-registration

If the charge is not registered as required by the Act, *the charge is void against the liquidator and creditors of the company*, and the debenture holder becomes an unsecured creditor in the company's winding up. However, the charge is *not void against the company whilst it is a going concern*, so that the debenture holder can enforce his security by sale or foreclosure and the liquidator in any subsequent winding up cannot set such sale or foreclosure aside. Charges created abroad by foreign companies with a place of business here or property in England and Wales are void for non-registration against foreign liquidators. (*N. V. Slavenburg's Bank v Intercontinental Natural Resources Ltd* [1980] 1 All ER 955.)

The effects of non-registration are such that it is obviously in the interests of the debenture holders that the charge be registered. Accordingly, although the duty to register is really that of the company, the registration of the charge may be effected on the application of any person interested therein. (S. 399(1).) Where such a person effects registration, he may recover the costs from the company. (S. 399(2).)

The court is given power by s. 404 to extend the time allowed for registration, and to rectify the register of charges in respect of errors in registration of the charge, if it is satisfied that the omission or error is accidental, or due to inadvertence, or some other sufficient cause, or is not likely to prejudice creditors or shareholders of the company, or that on other grounds it is just and equitable to grant relief, on such terms and conditions as the court thinks fit. A usual condition is that the late registration is to be allowed but 'without prejudice to the rights of any parties acquired prior to the time when the debenture was registered'. The interpretation of this phrase in *Watson v Duff Morgan and Vermont (Holdings) Ltd*, 1974[190] should be noted carefully.

In effect the unregistered charge ranks for priority as from the date of registration, though, of course, if it is registered while the company is a going concern, it has priority over unsecured creditors, but not if winding up has commenced before the charge was registered. Normally, late registration under s. 404 will be refused if the company is being wound up. In particular *Re Resinoid and Mica Products* [1982] 3 All ER 677 decides that the Registrar of the Companies Court is justified in refusing to extend the time in which a charge can be registered under the provisions of what is now s. 404 when the liquidation of the company is imminent and particularly should not do so after the company has gone into liquidation. However, registration out of time after commencement of winding up may be allowed in exceptional cases, as in *Re R. M. Arnold & Co* (1984) 11 *Current Law*, para

313

309 where the only other creditor who might have been affected had no objection to late registration.

Section 401(3) provides that the register of charges kept by the Registrar of Companies shall be open to the inspection of any person. No system of official search certificates exist, as is the case with land. When a charge is released or redeemed, the Registrar enters a memorandum of satisfaction on the register, but this cannot be taken as conclusive evidence of release or redemption, and the only certain way of ascertaining whether a charge has in fact been released or redeemed is to inquire of the owner of the charge.

COMPANY'S REGISTERS

Register of charges

Section 407 provides that every limited company shall keep at its registered office a register of charges and enter in the register all charges specifically affecting the property of the company, including floating charges on the undertaking or any other property of the company. The company must enter in the register a short description of the property charged, the amount of the charge, and the names of the persons entitled thereto, except in the case of securities to bearer.

Section 406 provides that the company shall keep at its registered office a copy of every instrument creating a charge which requires registration under the Act. The documents and register must be kept open to the inspection of members and creditors of the company free of charge, and to other persons on payment of a fee. (S. 408(1).)

As regards failure to register a charge in the company's register, there is a default fine on any officer of the company who knowingly and wilfully authorizes or permits the omission of any entry required to be made under the Act but the charge is still valid. In other words, it is only failure to register at the Companies Registry which affects the validity of a charge.

Register of debenture holders

Such a Register must be kept *if the terms of issue of the debenture require it*. The register must be kept at the Registered Office or at the place where it is made up, so long as that is within the country in which the company is registered. (S. 190(1) and (2).)

The Register may be inspected by those who are registered holders of debentures and shareholders in the company free, and by other persons on payment of a fee. (S. 191(1).) Members, registered holders of debentures, and other persons may require a copy of the register, and the company must provide copies of entries on payment of a fee. (S. 191(2).)

The register of directors' interests must show their debenture holdings also. This register is more fully dealt with on p. 181.

THE RIGHTS OF DEBENTURE HOLDERS

The two major rights of debenture holders are, of course, the right to receive interest and eventually the repayment of the principal sum lent.

Interest

The terms of issue usually provide for the rate of interest, and stipulate when interest shall be payable, e.g. every half year. Interest must be expressly provided for, since a debt does not carry interest at common law. Interest on debentures must be paid even if the payment is out of capital.

Principal

Debenture holders are entitled to repayment of principal in accordance with the provisions of the terms of issue. Where the debentures are irredeemable, there is no right to repayment of the principal except—

(a) if the company defaults in the payment of interest in accordance with the terms of issue; or

(b) if the company is wound up.

Debenture holders are also entitled to a copy of the company's balance sheet together with the documents attached thereto, that is the profit and loss account and the reports of the directors and auditors, except where the company has no share capital. (S. 240(1)(b).)

REMEDIES OF DEBENTURE HOLDERS

Unsecured debentures

The remedies available to the debenture holders are as follows—

(i) They may sue the company on its promise to pay interest or to repay the principal sum should the company fail to do these things.

(ii) As creditors, the debenture holders may, in the above circumstances, petition for the winding up of the company.

Where there is a trust deed, the trustees are the only persons who can exercise the above remedies, and if they refuse, the debenture holders may bring an action against the trustees requiring them to exercise the remedies available. The company may also be joined as co-defendant so that judgment may be given against it in the same action.

Secured debentures

Where the debentures are secured on the assets of the company, the following remedies are available—
  (i) *The property charged may be sold or leased;*
  (ii) *A receiver may be appointed to take possession of the property.*
Where the debentures are secured by a fixed charge, these remedies are available by virtue of the Law of Property Act 1925, because they are statutory remedies given to mortgagees. However, a floating charge may not be a mortgage for the purposes of that Act (*Blaker v Herts & Essex Waterworks Co* (1889) 41 Ch D 399). If this is so then the above remedies can only be exercised if given by the terms of issue.

After the assets are sold, any surplus after paying off the debenture holders and the costs of realization belongs to the company.

  (iii) *Application may be made to the court for a Foreclosure Order.*
If the application were successful, the debenture holders would become owners of the property charged, even if the property were more valuable than the sum secured. The remedy is rarely granted, the court preferring a sale.

The above remedies are exercised by the trustees if there is a trust deed, otherwise they may be exercised by a single debenture holder, suing on his own account. Where the action is brought by a single debenture holder and the debentures are in a series or rank *pari passu*, his action will normally be a representative action, i.e. on behalf of himself and the other debenture holders of the series. If the plaintiff debenture holder asks for foreclosure in his writ all debenture holders of a later class who have a floating charge which has not yet crystallized must be made defendants.

If no remedies are given to the debenture holders either by the terms of issue or by statute, they can always ask the court for an order for sale or to appoint a receiver. The main principles of the law of receivership are set out below.

They are set in the context of the appointment of an administrative receiver (formerly called a receiver and manager) by a bank, i.e. a single debenture holder, because the company cannot repay its overdraft which has been called in by the bank. This is a more usual context for the appointment of an administrative receiver. Appointments of such receivers are less often made by trustees of an issue of debenture stock.

RECEIVERSHIPS AND ADMINISTRATION

Appointment of an administrative receiver

A bank will not generally want to become the owner of the company's assets by foreclosure and the sale of assets will give only the break-up value of the property involved.

The best course is therefore to run the business for long enough to recover the overdraft from profits and then sell the company as a going concern. Thus the bank should appoint an administrative receiver or an administrator. (See p. 328.) We shall first consider the possibility of the bank appointing an administrative receiver and then follow with a description of the rather different office of administrator.

The quickest and cheapest way to do this is to appoint an administrative receiver out of court under the power given by the debenture. Having made clear at p. 328 the distinction between the two appointments, we shall now refer to an administrative receiver as a receiver.

Qualifications

An insolvency practitioner commits a criminal offence if he or she acts as a liquidator, administrator, or receiver, unless he or she has proper qualifications e.g. a Chartered Accountant. (S. 389(1), Insolvency Act 1986.) The Act provides for the issue of a certificate by the Trade Secretary or authorization by a recognized professional body. The certificate will not be issued unless there are adequate bonding arrangements. This was not formerly required except for persons appointed as liquidators in a compulsory winding up and receivers appointed by the court. All insolvency practitioners must now be covered by insurance against fraud, dishonesty and professional negligence. Finally, under s. 396, *ibid*, a tribunal is to be set up for appeals against refusal by the Trade Secretary to grant a certificate or the revocation of it.

Receiver appointed out of court

In theory anyone, apart from a body corporate (s. 30, *ibid*) or a bankrupt (s. 31) could be appointed, but in practice a receiver is an accountant of some experience.

Receiver's checks before accepting appointment

Before accepting an appointment a receiver should check that the charge under which he is to be appointed is valid, as follows:

(*a*) Was the borrowing *intra vires* the company?

(*b*) Was the charge registered properly and in time under s. 395?

(*c*) If the charge was created, e.g. in the previous six months, can it be invalid as a preference under s. 239, Insolvency Act 1986 if there is, e.g. a winding up?

(*d*) If the charge is a floating charge created within the last 12 months (or 24 months where the chargee is 'connected' with the company, e.g. as a director), is there a possibility that it might be declared invalid under s. 245, Insolvency Act 1986 in, e.g. a winding up?

(*e*) Has an administrator already been appointed? If so, no receiver can be appointed. (See p. 329.)

If the charge is or becomes invalid the receiver is a trespasser to the company's property and liable in conversion if he deals with it, though under s. 34 (*ibid*) the court may grant him an indemnity against his appointor.

In addition, of course, he may face problems if any seller of goods has reserved his title. (See *Romalpa* and subsequent decisions which were dealt with more fully earlier in the chapter.) Although reservation of title will not render the receiver's charge invalid, it may mean that there are fewer assets for him to receive.

Procedures on appointment and subsequently

These are as follows—

(*a*) The receiver's appointment, unless it is by court order, is in writing and may be under seal if the debenture requires this. It is signed by the debenture holder, e.g. a bank or the trustees for the debenture holders. The deed of appointment is the receiver's authority to act and he can produce it together with the debenture, or trust deed, as evidence of his authority should this be required.

(*b*) A debenture holder must, within seven days, give notice, that he has appointed a receiver, to the Registrar of Companies. (S. 405(1).) The receiver should obtain confirmation from the debenture holder that this has been done.

(*c*) Where, as in the case of our receiver, he is appointed for the whole or substantially the whole of the company's property, he must immediately give notice of his appointment to the company. (S. 46(1)(*a*), Insolvency Act 1986.) Within 28 days after his appointment, unless the court otherwise directs, he must send notice of his appointment to all creditors of the company so far as he is aware of their addresses.

(d) Within 21 days, or such longer period as the receiver or court may allow (there is no limit on the time which may be allowed) the company must let the receiver have a *statement of affairs* showing its assets and liabilities. (S. 47, Insolvency Act 1986.) This statement is verified by the affidavit of the secretary and one or more directors, and by other officers or the promoters or by persons who have been officers in the year before the appointment of the receiver. (S. 47, Insolvency Act 1986.)

The court may require verification by any officer or past officer or employee or past employee (being those who have left in the last 12 months) or of a corporate officer of the company, or by any person concerned in the promotion of the company in the last 12 months. There are also stringent powers in s. 235 of the Insolvency Act 1986 enabling office holders, i.e. a receiver or administrator or liquidator, to obtain information from the above persons by examination in court and by production of documents and papers. Under s. 236 absconders are liable to arrest or to examination outside the UK. Section 234, *ibid*, enables office holders to apply to the court for delivery of any of the company's property, or records, by members, bankers, trustees, and officers of the company.

The statement lists the assets at their estimated realizable market value at the date of appointment and lists the creditors in order of preference. It is the first major reporting requirement in a receivership and is often prepared by the company's auditors.

It assists the receiver to ascertain the financial position of the company and to establish the assets available to him. It is unlikely to be received within 21 days and a longer time may be allowed.

(e) Under s. 48 of the Insolvency Act 1986 where a receiver is appointed he must, within three months (or such longer period as the court may allow) after his appointment send to the Registrar, to the debenture holders by whom or on whose behalf he was appointed, and to any trustee for those debenture holders, a report as to the following matters, namely—

(a) the events which led up to his appointment;
(b) the disposal, or proposed disposal, by him of any property of the company, and the carrying on, or proposed carrying on by him of any business of the company;
(c) the amounts of principal and interest payable to the debenture holders by whom or on whose behalf he was appointed and the amounts payable to preferential creditors in accordance with s. 175 of the Insolvency Act 1986; and
(d) the amount (if any) likely to be available for the payment of other creditors

319

The receiver must also within three months (or such longer period as the court may allow) after his appointment either—

(i) send a copy of the report (so far as he is aware of their addresses) to all creditors of the company; *or*

(ii) publish a notice stating an address to which creditors of the company should write for copies of the report to be sent to them free of charge.

In either case, unless the court directs otherwise, the receiver must lay a copy of the report before a meeting of the company's creditors summoned for the purpose on not less than 14 days' notice.

A report under this section must include a summary of the statement of affairs made out and submitted to the administrative receiver under s. 47 (above) and of his comments, if any, on it.

Where a meeting of creditors is summoned under s. 48 of the Insolvency Act 1986, then under s. 49, *ibid*, the meeting may, if it thinks fit, establish a committee of creditors to receive information from the receiver. If a committee is established it may on giving at least seven days' notice require the receiver to attend before it and furnish it with such information relating to the carrying out by him of his functions as it may reasonably require. Its consent is not required for any act.

Effect of receiver's appointment

In general terms the appointment of a receiver paralyses the powers of the company and its administration in favour of the receiver. As was said in the House of Lords in *Moss Steamships v Whinney* [1912] AC 254: 'He entirely supersedes the company in the conduct of its business, deprives it of all powers to enter into contracts, or to sell, pledge or otherwise dispose of the property put into possession of or under the control of the receiver and manager. Its powers in these matters are entirely in abeyance.'

More particularly, s. 42 of the Insolvency Act 1986 and Sched 1 to that Act deal with the receiver's powers. This follows the recommendation of the Cork Committee that the powers of a receiver should be contained in statute so that it would not be necessary to refer to every specific debenture to find out what powers the receiver can exercise in a particular case. Under Sched 1 a receiver has the power to take possession of, collect, and get in the property of the company; to sell or otherwise dispose of the property of the company; to borrow money and grant security over the property of the company; to appoint a solicitor or accountant or other professionally qualified person to assist him in the performance of his duties; to bring or defend any action or other legal proceedings; to refer to arbitration matters affecting the company; to effect and maintain insurances; to use the seal; to draw, accept, make, and endorse bills of exchange; to appoint agents; to carry on the business of the company; to grant or accept a surrender of a lease; to make any arrangement or compromise; to call up any uncalled capital; to claim in the insolvency of companies or persons; to present or defend a petition for winding up of the company, and to do all things incidental to those powers.

Under s. 43 (*ibid*) the receiver may also seek a court order to sell property subject to certain charges and give the buyer a good title. The amount realized must be shown to be at least equal to open market value and the proceeds must be applied in discharging the security. Thus secured creditors cannot block advantageous sales.

Directors

The directors are not dismissed by the appointment of the receiver but their powers to deal with the company's property are suspended during the receivership. (But see *Newhart Developments*, 1978.[175])

Where the directors render management services in order to assist the receiver, he will have to make arrangements with regard to their remuneration. However, the receiver is not obliged to pay directors remuneration which is voted by the members either before or after the receiver's appointment, nor are the directors entitled to any fees granted to them by the articles.

If the continuation of the contract of service of a particular director is inconsistent with the position of a receiver and manager, his appointment will be terminated. This could well be the case with a managing director. (But see *Griffiths v Secretary of State for Social Services*, 1973.[191])

Employees

When a receiver is appointed out of court contracts of employment continue with the company because s. 44(1)(*a*) (*ibid*) states that such a receiver is deemed to be the agent of the company unless and until it goes into liquidation. If the receiver offers employees new contracts while he is running the company there is no breach in the continuity of their employment with the company. (*Re Mack Trucks* [1967] 1 All ER 977.) However, if he sells the whole business as a going concern the sale operates as a dismissal of all staff.

Receiver's relationship to the company and the debenture holder(s)

Under s. 44(1)(a) of the Insolvency Act 1986 the receiver is the agent of the company which is then responsible for his acts and defaults. However, in all cases, as will be seen below, the receiver is liable for his own contracts (s. 44(1)(b), Insolvency Act 1986), subject to an indemnity from the assets of the company. (S. 44(1)(c), *ibid.*)

Thus if he sells an asset at too low a price, the debenture holders will not be liable. However, the fact that he is an agent of the company does not mean that he must carry out its orders and he is not an officer of the company or liable *in general as such*. (*Re B. Johnson & Co (Builders)* [1955] 2 All ER 775.) However, liability is sometimes imposed on him by a specific reference in a section, e.g. s. 212(1)(b) of the Insolvency Act 1986 makes him liable for misfeasance proceedings under that section in a winding up.

However, the company may be able to control him by asking that an inspector be appointed under s. 432. (*R. v Board of Trade, ex parte Saint Martin's Preserving Co Ltd* [1965] 1 QB 603.)

Liability on contracts—generally

A receiver and manager will have to make contracts. Under s. 37(1)(a), and s. 44(1)(b), Insolvency Act 1986 he is personally liable on such contracts except in so far as the contract otherwise provides with a right to an indemnity out of the company's assets, but if these are insufficient he is liable personally for any shortfall. For this reason and because the assets may not be readily realizable he may take an indemnity from the debenture holders.

Contracts—detailed provisions

As regards contracts, the position is as follows:

(a) *Old contracts.* Contracts which were binding on the company when the receiver was appointed continue to bind the company; though any enforcement as by selling the company's assets is subject to the prior rights of the debenture holders over the assets. The receiver may in his discretion fulfil old contracts. However, although he has a discretion he should not disregard contracts if to do so would damage the company's goodwill or affect the realization of its assets, especially if it seems likely that the company will continue to trade. Thus in *Re Newdigate Colliery* [1912] 1 Ch 468 where the receiver and manager of a mining company could have made a greater profit by disregarding contracts for the forward sale of coal, he was not allowed to drop the contract because of the damage to the company's goodwill. Otherwise, he cannot only ignore old contracts, but may even take steps to frustrate their performance. (*Airlines Airspares v Handley Page*, 1970.[192]) As regards existing contracts, therefore, the receiver is able to select those he wishes to continue with knowing that his refusal to go on with contracts can only result in unsecured claims against the company for breach of contract which will not affect the receivership.

It seems, however, that the appointment of a receiver is no bar to an action for specific performance. Thus in *Freevale Ltd v Metrostore Ltd* [1984] 1 All ER 495, M had entered into a contract to sell land to F. It was held that F could apply for specific performance of the contract and that, on obtaining a decree, the contract must be carried out by the receiver who had been appointed after the contract was made.

Under s. 44(1)(b), Insolvency Act 1986 a receiver is liable—(*a*) *on general contracts* he makes; and (*b*) *on contracts of employment* which he may adopt. Under s. 44(2), *ibid* he is not regarded as having adopted an employment contract just because he has allowed an employee to work on for up to 14 days after the receivership. After that he is liable to pay employees unless he has repudiated the contracts.

Persons who have performed their contracts and have actions in debt may, of course, be able to petition for a winding up. This cannot happen, at least initially, on the appointment of an administrator who is to that extent in a stronger position than a receiver. (See further p. 328.)

(*b*) *New contracts*. A receiver is free to enter into new contracts in the course of carrying on the company's business. If the other party will accept it he may contract on terms that he should incur no personal liability. This is achieved, if acceptable, by overprinting or stamping all correspondence, orders and other documents which the receiver issues with the words 'The receiver contracts only as agent for the company and without personal liability'. But if this is not acceptable he will, in our situation, contract as an agent for the company but, as we have already seen, he will be personally liable also on the contract, with a right of indemnity against the company's assets but he may have taken an indemnity from the debenture holders.

Remuneration

This is paid by the company and will be fixed by those appointing the receiver. If it is excessive and the company is later wound up, the court has power to order a refund of what it regards as excessive remuneration.

Fiduciary duties

A receiver owes fiduciary duties to the company. In *Nugent v Nugent* [1908] 1 Ch 546 it was held that a receiver, in this case one appointed by the court, could not purchase land subject to the receivership. In addition, he must get the best price he can on a sale of the mortgaged assets. Thus in *Cuckmere Brick Co v Mutual Finance Ltd* [1971] 2 All ER 633 a receiver sold mortgaged land on the basis that it only had planning permission for houses when in fact it was more valuable since it had planning permission for flats. The receiver was held liable to make up the difference in value. It would seem, also, from *Standard Chartered Bank v Walker* [1982] 3 All ER 938, that there is a similar duty towards a person who has guaranteed the company's overdraft. In the case a bank appointed a receiver and he sold the company's property at an auction in mid-winter and during bad weather. Few people attended and the property did not raise enough to pay the bank. The defendant, who had guaranteed the overdraft, was sued for the balance but his claim against the receiver for loss was allowed to proceed to trial on the basis that there was a duty owed by the receiver to the defendant.

Functions of a receiver

The main aim of the receiver is to obtain enough money from the company to pay off his debenture holders. He may incidentally save the company or part of it. A contrast is provided by the office of administrator whose major purpose is to get the company on a profitable basis, or at least to dispose of its assets more profitably than in a liquidation. (See further p. 328.)

In our situation there is only one debenture holder and at the moment no other creditors are suing. In other situations our receiver may well have to hold a balance between a number of competing interests.

However, the following points should be noted—

(*a*) The receiver must collect and take possession of the company's assets. The bank's charge in our case authorizes him for that purpose to take any proceedings in the name of the company or otherwise.

(*b*) *Dealing with set-off and lien.* If A owes B £10 and B owes A £4, then in an action by B against A for £10 A can SET-OFF £4 and pay £6.

Also, if A owes B £10 and B has goods belonging to A, he may exercise a LIEN on them until he is paid.

In connection with receivership, the right of set-off and/or lien will not be available against the receiver if the claim to set-off or the claim to a lien only arises after the charge has crystallized. It is available if the claim was enforceable before crystallization (see *Rother Iron Works Ltd v Canterbury Precision Engineers Ltd*, 1973)[183] or arose in the same transaction as the debt which the receiver is trying to recover. (See *George Barker (Transport) Ltd v Eynom*, 1974, p. 567.)

(*c*) Our receiver is authorized by s. 42 and Sched 1, Insolvency Act 1986 to manage or to concur in the carrying on of the business of the company. For that purpose he can borrow money in priority to the bank's charge and with or without a charge on the property covered by that charge. For his power to deal with charged property see p. 330.

(*d*) Our receiver can sell property or lease it, surrender leases and can take by way of consideration shares in other companies.

Thus he is given by s. 42 and Sched 1, *ibid*, the broadest possible powers to do what he thinks is necessary to realize any part of the property charged.

Finally, he must, like an executor or liquidator, distribute the assets. The order of disposition of funds raised by realization is usually—

(i) The costs of collecting the assets.

(ii) The costs and remuneration of the receiver, including any indemnification of personal liability under ss. 37 and 44 of the Insolvency Act 1986.

(iii) If the charge is a floating charge the preferential debts, which would include such debts as a year's taxes due to the Crown, or wages and salaries for services rendered within four months prior to the receiver's appointment, not exceeding £800 per claimant. This is a statutory duty under s. 196, Companies Act 1985 and s. 175, Insolvency Act 1986. Further details of preferential payments appear at p. 423.

It should be noted that in so far as the charge is mixed, i.e. some specific charges and a floating charge over the rest of the assets, the realization of the property subject to fixed charges will not be available to the preferential creditors in preference to the debenture holders.

(iv) He will then satisfy the amount due to the debenture holders and the surplus (if any) will go to the company.

It should also be noted that a receiver is required by s. 405(2) to file with the Registrar a notice that he has ceased to act.

As our receiver is acting under a debenture holders' appointment he need not have all his actions approved by the court. Nevertheless, s. 35(1), Insolvency Act 1986 provides that a receiver appointed under an instrument such as a debenture may ask the court for directions in relation to any matter arising in the performance of his duties. This is a useful protection if the receiver finds that there are competing claims for an asset. The receiver can ask the court to decide who has the better title. This section is used e.g. to test retention clauses.

Vacation of office

Under s. 45(1), Insolvency Act 1986 a receiver may at any time be *removed* from office by order of the court (but not otherwise) and may *resign* by giving notice to his appointer or a liquidator if one is in post (r. 3.33). Under s. 45(2), *ibid*, a receiver vacates office if he ceases to be qualified as an insolvency practitioner.

Receiver appointed by the court

The bank in our case had extensive powers to appoint a receiver and did not need to resort to the somewhat expensive and clumsy procedure of applying to the court for an appointment.

However, if the company had issued a series of debenture stock under a trust deed giving the trustees power to appoint a receiver out of court which they were not for some reason prepared to do, an individual debenture holder might have been forced to bring a representative action on behalf of himself and the other debenture holders of the same series for the appointment of a receiver and manager to take charge of the company's property. In the action he would join the trustees as defendants.

Regardless of any power in a trust deed or debenture, the court has power to appoint a receiver and manager in three cases—

(*a*) when the principal sum has become repayable or interest is in arrear;

(*b*) if the company is wound up—even if this is only for the purposes of amalgamation or reconstruction;

(*c*) if the security is in jeopardy, even though interest is being paid.

The following is a list of circumstances in which the court has regarded the assets as in jeopardy:

(i) where a petition for winding up has been presented (*Re Victoria Steamboats Ltd, Smith v Wilkinson*, 1897[193]);

(ii) where creditors have obtained judgment against the company and are about to levy execution (*Re London Pressed Hinge Co Ltd*, 1905[194]);

(iii) where the company's business has been closed, or is about to be closed (*McMahon v North Kent Ironworks Co*, 1891[195]);

(iv) where the company is distributing its reserves to shareholders, or is disposing of its assets for an inadequate consideration (*Re Tilt Cove Copper Co Ltd*, 1913[196]).

The general effect of the appointment of a receiver by the court is the same as an appointment out of court but the following differences should be noted—

(1) A receiver appointed by the court needs the approval of the

court for almost everything he does, e.g. to sue, to sell property, to make compromises with creditors and to distribute the assets.

(2) He must give security though this does not apply if the Official Receiver is appointed receiver. He must also be a qualified and approved insolvency practitioner. (See further p. 317.)

(3) Since he is an officer of the court, interference with his duties is a contempt of court. Thus no actions can be brought against him or in respect of property in his control without leave of the court.

(4) Employees of the company are automatically dismissed. (*Reid v Explosive Co* (1887) 19 QBD 264.)

(5) His remuneration is fixed by the court.

(6) He is not an agent of the debenture holders or of the company and so neither is liable on contracts which he makes. He has the same right of indemnity out of the assets charged as a receiver appointed out of court.

The effect of a winding up on a receivership

Up to now we have assumed that our unsecured creditors are standing happily by while our receiver concentrates on the bank's interests alone.

Suppose, however, the unsecured creditors become restless and initiate a winding-up. How will this effect the receiver? The following points should be noted—

(*a*) There is nothing to prevent a winding-up order being made by the court for a compulsory winding up or a resolution being passed for a voluntary winding up while a receiver is in possession.

(*b*) The receiver continues in possession of the property subject to the charge and is not prevented from selling it, for example, by s. 127, Insolvency Act 1986 which forbids a disposition of the property of a company after the commencement of winding-up. Thus the liquidator may have to be patient and wait until the receiver has raised enough to pay his debenture holders.

(*c*) There is, however, a technical difference in the position of the receiver in that although s. 44, Insolvency Act 1986 makes him agent of the company he can no longer be so. The company cannot now trade and any contracts he makes are as a principal. However, the basic receivership powers remain. Thus in *Sowman v David Samuel Trust Ltd* [1978] 1 All ER 616 a receiver signed a contract to sell freehold land belonging to the company *after* the company had gone into liquidation and the contract of sale was held valid. Thus being an agent is not really the essence of a receiver's position.

By s. 37, Insolvency Act 1986 and s. 44(1)(*b*), Insolvency Act 1986 he is personally liable on those contracts but has the same indemnity from the assets of the company as he would have if there were no liquidation so that he is not really worse off.

(*d*) The commencement of winding-up may affect the receiver's charge as follows—

(i) it may be void against the liquidator if not registered under s. 395, Companies Act 1985;

(ii) it may be a preference under s. 239 of the Insolvency Act 1986 if created, e.g. in the previous six months;

(iii) it may be void under s. 245, Insolvency Act 1986 if created in the previous 12 months (or 24 months if the chargee is connected with the company, e.g. is a director of it) if the company was insolvent at the time of creation of the charge and the charge was not given for cash received or to be received by the company or goods.

The effect of a receivership on a winding-up

Even though a winding-up has commenced the debenture holders are not prevented from appointing a receiver or asking the court to appoint one. However, the receiver would have to apply to the liquidator or to the court for permission to take over any property of which the liquidator was already in possession.

ADMINISTRATION ORDERS

Generally

The object of administration orders, which were recommended by the Cork Committee, is to allow a company to be put on a profitable basis if possible, or at least disposed of more profitably than would be the case if other forms of insolvency proceedings, such as liquidation, were used. It is intended that creditors should play an active role. Section references are to the Insolvency Act 1986 unless otherwise indicated.

Method of appointment

A majority of the directors or the members by ordinary resolution or *any* creditor, regardless of the amount owed to him, can petition the court for the appointment of an administrator, though s. 231(1) seems to envisage joint appointments. From the date of the petition until any order made under it is discharged all methods of enforcement of the company's debts, including executions against its property, or insolvency proceedings, are stayed except with leave of the court. Those with charges over property in the company's possession are prevented from enforcing their security.

The administration order

Before making an order the court must be satisfied that the company either is, or is becoming, unable to pay its debts and also that an order is likely to promote the survival of all or part of the business as a going concern or the more advantageous realization of assets than on a winding up. (S. 8.)

Directors may well have a special incentive to petition since the seeking of an administration order would be a way of avoiding personal liability for the company's debts under s. 214, since it shows the taking of steps to minimize loss to creditors under s. 214(3). (See further p. 13.) Individual directors or members do not appear to be able to apply but individual creditors (even if unsecured) can, regardless of the amount of the debt owed.

Administrative receivers under a floating charge

The court must dismiss the petition if an administrative receiver (formerly called a receiver and manager) under a floating charge over substantially the whole undertaking has been, or is to be, appointed. (S. 9(3).)

To protect the rights of those who commonly take floating charges, such as banks, so that the availability of business credit is not reduced, a person petitioning for an administration order must give holders of floating charges notice that he is lodging a petition. A holder of a floating charge may then appoint, or take steps to appoint, an administrative receiver or agree to the appointment of an administrator and can in fact be a petitioner for an administrator himself. If an administrator is appointed no administrative receiver can then be appointed, and if an administrative receiver has been appointed he vacates office. (S. 11(1).)

Power to deal with charged property

Section 15 gives an administrator power *without the permission of the court,* to dispose of assets subject to a charge and give the purchaser a good title. The charge continues to apply as a floating charge over the proceeds of sale and any assets purchased therewith.

The intention of the Act is that property should be at the administrator's disposal but that the charge should not be destroyed. For example, if the administrator sells plant and machinery subject to a floating charge, the chargeholder's security would attach as a floating charge to the money obtained from the sale and then to any assets procured with the money.

Successful trading by an administrator with the proceeds of sale of charged assets will normally bring new assets within the floating charge and this will increase its value.

Section 15 also provides that the court may, to assist the objectives of the administration order, give the administrator permission to dispose of property subject to a charge, or security and goods subject to hire purchase leasing or retention arrangements *without the charge or other rights of the owner attaching to the proceeds*. However, the net proceeds after deducting any costs of disposal *must* be applied towards discharging the sums secured by the charge or payable under the HP, leasing or retention arrangements.

Sales which the court determines to be at less than market value must have the balance made up and applied towards discharging the sums secured by the charge or payable under the HP, leasing or retention arrangements. It will be noted, therefore, that the administrator must go to the court for permission to dispose of property free of any charge or encumbrance.

In most cases it will be for the parties to negotiate suitable terms between themselves for the continued use or disposal or property charged etc. In the event of failure to agree terms then the administrator is entitled to seek an order of the court for the sale of the goods so long as a net amount equivalent to the open market value is paid to the other party towards discharge of the debts owed to him.

As regards the power of an administrative receiver to deal with charged property etc, s. 43 applies. The distinction between the powers of the administrator and an administrative receiver is that an administrative receiver can only apply to the court for an order authorizing the sale of property subject to a charge which ranks in front of the one held by his appointer. There are no provisions allowing disposal of property subject to a charge without court permission the charge attaching to the proceeds, nor can the administrative receiver dispose of goods under hire purchase, leasing, or retention arrangements.

If the court gives an administrative receiver permission to sell, the net proceeds of sale go towards satisfying the charge, and if the court considers the sale to have been at less than open market price, the deficiency must be made good.

The powers given to an administrative receiver are designed to enable him to sell a property free from a security and give a good title to it, provided that the court is satisfied that the sale is likely to promote a more advantageous realization of assets. The section also prevents the inhibition of a company rescue scheme where the administrative receiver cannot negotiate successfully a deal with a particular charge-holder to enable him to sell the charged property.

A copy of any court order giving an administrator or administrative receiver permission to sell assets must be sent to the Registrar of Companies within 14 days of its being made. (S. 15(7) and s. 43(5).) This will then appear on the company's file and be notice to those who wish to know that the administrator or administrative receiver, as the case may be, was authorized to sell and give a good title.

Purpose of administration

If the business succeeds during the period of administration it is handed back to the directors. If it fails, or is not sold, or its assets disposed of, then a winding up will normally follow. If the administrator realizes all the assets a liquidator must nevertheless be appointed to formally wind up the company. The administrator can make payments to creditors under a scheme agreed with them. (See below.)

Discharge of administrator

Section 18 provides that the administrator (and only he) may apply to the court for discharge of the administration order if he is of opinion that its purposes have been achieved or are impossible or if the creditors require him to do so.

On discharge of the order the court may grant the administrator a release from any liability and if he dies or resigns he is released from the date on which notice of either event is communicated to the court.

Removal of administrator

By reason of s. 27 any creditor or member of the company may apply to the court for such order as the court may think fit on the grounds that the acts or omissions of the administrator are operating to the prejudice of some, one, or more of the creditors or members. The court's order could require the administrator to do, or not to do, any act, or carry out any course of conduct, or could discharge the administration order altogether.

331

Liability of administrator

By reason of ss. 212 and 20(3) he remains liable for misfeasance and breach of duty towards the company but a claim in respect of this can only be made in the winding up of the company.

Legal position of administrator

He is made an agent of the company. (S. 14(5).) He is personally liable on the contracts he makes unless the contract otherwise provides, but he is entitled to an indemnity from the assets of the company.

The administrator's remuneration and expenses and debts or liabilities incurred under contracts he has made or which he has adopted, e.g. an employment contract, are a charge on any property of the company which he has and this charge has priority over other charges. (S. 19(4).) Thus, if our bank appoints or allows the appointment of an administrator, he will have an indemnity out of the assets subject to the charge before the bank.

General powers of an administrator

Section 14 gives a general power to manage the company plus a number of specific powers set out in Sched 1. These specific powers also apply to an administrative receiver and they cover everything an administrator or administrative receiver is likely to want to do. In particular, both office-holders are given specific powers to use the company's seal and to move the address of the registered office.

In exercising his powers the administrator does so as the agent of the company and not of the person who applied for his appointment. He also has power to dismiss and appoint directors and is protected by the Insolvency Act from any powers conferred on the company or the directors, either in legislation or in the company's constitution which might hinder him in the discharge of his functions. He can thus assemble a new management team or a combination of new and old, which is particularly important where the objective of the administration order is the survival of the company. Directors are not automatically dismissed by the appointment of an administrator but their powers of management are exercisable only if he consents.

The administrator can also call meetings to consult with members and creditors on matters of importance and may apply to the court for directions in relation to any particular matter arising in connection with the carrying out of his functions. A person dealing with an administrator shall not be concerned to enquire whether he is acting within his powers. Outsiders are thus protected if he should exceed the powers of the company or the powers of the directors provided the outsider acts without actual knowledge of the lack of power.

Duties of administrator

These are in the main as follows—
(*a*) to notify the Registrar of Companies and the company of his appointment and publicize it, e.g. on orders for goods and business letters (s. 12);
(*b*) to notify all creditors within 28 days. (S. 46(1)(*b*).)

Statement of affairs

The company has 21 days from his appointment to submit to the administrator a statement of affairs. However, he may extend the time. (S. 22(5)(*b*).) The statement will normally be verified by one or more of the directors and by the secretary. The administrator may require verification by any officer or past officer or employee or past employee who has left the company in the preceding 12 months, or by any person concerned in its promotion in the previous 12 months.

Proposals of administration

Within three months of appointment, or such longer period as the court may allow, the administrator must lay his proposals for the company before a meeting of all the creditors. He must send copies of it to all members and the Registrar. (S. 23(1).)

The meeting of the creditors may ask for modification of the proposals but the administrator is not required to implement them unless he approves. If no agreement can be reached with the creditors the court may, under s. 24(5), discharge the administration order. There is no need for the court to approve the proposals; its function is limited to discharging the administration order if the proposals are not approved.

The meeting which approves the administrator's original proposals may establish a creditors' committee. This may call for information about the administrator's activities. Its consent is not required for any act. (S. 26.)

If the administrator is going to make substantial revision to his proposals, then he must send copies to all the creditors and the members and call a meeting of all the creditors at which agreement must be reached on any revisions proposed either by the administrator or the creditors. (S. 25.)

In the event that there is no agreement it would seem that the administrator may resign or be removed by the court under s. 19. Alternatively, a creditor or a member could apply under s. 27 on the ground of prejudice and ask for a court order to continue the administration on particular terms, or to discharge it.

Section 18(2) makes it a duty for an administrator to apply for his discharge if the purpose for the achievement of which the order was made has been achieved, or that neither of the possible purposes can be achieved. Obviously, this would arise if the creditors would not agree to his proposals for the company or a modification of them.

As regards meetings of creditors, the administrator has power to summon them at any time and 10 per cent of the creditors in value can, under s. 17(3), require him to do so. The court has a general power to summon meetings in any proceedings before it.

Transactions at an undervalue and preferences

Under s. 238 an administrator (but not, however, an administrative receiver) has the same powers as a liquidator to apply to the court for restitution under s. 238 of any property which a person has received by preference or where he has benefited by a transaction with the company at an undervalue. (See p. 422.) Section 244 gives him power to ask the court to set aside an extortionate credit transaction or to vary it. Under s. 245 the rules which invalidate floating charges on a liquidation apply also in an administration where the charge is created within 12 months before the administration, or 24 months where the person obtaining the charge is connected with the company, e.g. one of its directors. Finally, the Companies Act 1985 is amended so that charges are, in any case, void against an administrator as they are against anyone else if not properly registered under s. 395 of the Companies Act 1985.

12 Private companies and holding and subsidiary companies

PRIVATE COMPANIES

Generally

Section 1(3) states that a private company is a company which is not a public company. Thus private companies are a residual class. A private company must not offer its shares or debentures to the public. (S. 170, Financial Services Act 1986.) This provision, which replaces s. 81 of the Companies Act 1985, contains a general prohibition on the issue of advertisements offering securities of a private company. All unlimited companies are of necessity private companies because a public company must be a limited company. (S. 1(3).) In view of the prohibition on offers of shares and debentures to the public in private limited companies, it may be desirable to incorporate into the memorandum or articles of such a company a provision similar to that contained in *Table A*, *Part* II of the Companies Act 1948, i.e. 'Any invitation to the public to subscribe for any shares or debentures of the company is prohibited'. *Table A*, *Part* II was repealed by the Companies Act 1980 though it continues to apply to private companies registered before 22 December 1980 and it is no longer essential for such a provision to be in a private company's memorandum or articles, but it would be wise to include it so that it also forms part of the contract with the members.

Section 160 of the 1986 Act exempts issues of a 'private character' to be prescribed by rules expected to be that an offer of shares or debentures in a private company will be regarded as the domestic concern of those making it and those receiving it and therefore not an offer to the public if it is any of the following categories—

  (i) any offer to any:
    (*a*) member
    (*b*) employee
    (*c*) member of a member's or employee's family
    (*d*) debenture holder
  (ii) an offer of shares to be held in an employees' share scheme

(iii) an offer within (i) or (ii) above which allows renunciation in favour of any person who is mentioned in (i) above or the person who is entitled to hold shares under an employees' share scheme which is in force.

It should be noted that where a private company's articles contain a prohibition regarding an invitation to the public to subscribe for its shares or debentures, invitations in circumstances corresponding to those set out above will be regarded as not within that prohibition.

In addition, the prohibition of offers to the public does apply to the issue of debentures to the public by private companies which are limited by guarantee and do not have a share capital and to private companies which are unlimited companies. If these unlimited companies have a share capital they may not offer shares and debentures to the public.

It is, of course, still possible for private companies to have provisions in their articles placing a restriction on the number of members which the company may have and also restrictions on the right to transfer the company's shares. If the restriction on the number of members does not extend to members who are employees or ex-employees, in order to facilitate employees' share schemes, then provided a person becomes a member in respect of some shares whilst employed by the company, the articles would not be violated if he bought more shares after leaving the company's employment.

As regards restrictions on the right to transfer shares, these take two forms—

(i) a power in the articles giving a right of first purchase (or *pre-emption*) to other members of the company; and

(ii) a provision in the articles giving the directors power simply to refuse to register transfers.

The right of pre-emption

This means that when a member of a private company wishes to sell his shares, he must first offer them to other members of the company before he offers them to an outsider. The price is usually to be calculated by some method laid down in the articles, e.g. at a price fixed by the auditors of the company. In this context it should be noted that the auditor can be sued by the seller of the shares if the valuation is lower than it should be because of the auditor's negligence. This is an important claim because the seller will not normally be able to avoid the contract of sale because that contract usually makes the auditor's valuation final and binding on the parties.

If the other members do not wish to take up the shares, the shares may then be sold to an outsider. The other members must apparently be prepared to take *all* the shares that the vendor member is offering. (*Ocean Coal Co Ltd v Powell Duffryn Steam Coal Co Ltd*, 1932.[197])

The right of pre-emption can be enforced as between the members (*Rayfield v Hands*, 1958[63]), and also by the company, which may obtain an injunction against a member who is not complying with the articles in this matter. (*Lyle & Scott Ltd v Scott's Trustees*, 1959.[198]) The decision in *Lyle & Scott Ltd* could make it very difficult for a take-over bidder to take over a private company because if there is a pre-emption clause the board can ask the court for an injunction requiring a member to sell his shares to another member rather than to the bidder.

Rejection of transfers

Where the articles give the directors power simply to refuse or approve the registration of transfers, that power must be exercised in good faith (*Re Accidental Death Insurance Co, Allin's Case*, 1873[199]); but where the power to reject is exercisable for reasons specified in the articles, the transferee need not be told which is the reason for this rejection if the articles so provide. (*Berry and Stewart v Tottenham Hotspur FC*, 1935.[200]) The position is the same where the articles merely provide that the directors may reject a transfer 'without assigning reasons therefor'.

Where there is an equality of votes, a transfer cannot be deemed rejected, but must be accepted (*Re Hackney Pavilion Ltd*, 1924[201]), though it is usual for the chairman to have a casting vote which he can use to decide the issue. Similarly, a transferee can ask the court to rectify the register so that his name is included on it where one director, by refusing to attend board meetings, is preventing a directors' meeting from being held to consider the registration. (*Re Copal Varnish Co*, 1917, see p. 235.) In addition, the powers vested in directors to refuse to register a transfer must be exercised within a reasonable time. (See *Re Swaledale Cleaners*, 1968.[105])

Unless the articles otherwise provide, rights of pre-emption and rejection apply only on a transfer by a member, and do not arise on transmission through death or bankruptcy. Neither do they arise where the shares are still represented by a renounceable letter of allotment. (*Re Pool Shipping Co Ltd*, 1920.[202])

A restriction in a company's articles upon the transfer of shares covers only the transfer of the legal title, i.e. a transfer in the title of the person on the register of members, and does not include transfer of the beneficial interest. Thus if A and B are the only shareholders in a company and B has a majority holding, then if on the death of B his executor, C, holds the shares on trust for beneficiaries, X and Y, and C proposes to vote in accordance with the wishes of X and Y so that X and Y will control the company, then A cannot claim that there has been a transfer of the shares of B entitling A to the implementation of a pre-emption clause under which A might require the shares held by C to be transferred to him (A). (*Safeguard Industrial Investments Ltd v National Westminster Bank* [1982] 1 All ER 449.)

Distinctions between a public and a private company

(i) In a private company proxies may speak at meetings, as well as vote on a poll, though not on a show of hands unless the articles provide. (S. 372(1).)

(ii) A private company need have only one director and a secretary; a public company must have at least two directors and a secretary. (Ss. 282 and 283.) The secretary of a private company need not be qualified in the terms required of a secretary of a public company by s. 286.

(iii) In a private company two or more directors may be appointed by a single resolution. (S. 292(1).)

(iv) The age limit placed upon directors does not apply to a private company, unless it is a subsidiary of a public company. (S. 293.)

(v) *As regards registration.* The name of a public company must include 'public limited company' or 'p.l.c.'. A private company's name must only include 'limited' or 'ltd.'. (S. 25.) The memorandum of a public company must state that it is. (S. 1(3).) Furthermore, a public company can only commence business on the issue of a s. 117 certificate by the Registrar of Companies, whereas a private company can commence business on incorporation. (S. 117.) The minimum number of members is now two in each case. (S. 1.)

(vi) *As regards share capital.* The minimum allotted share capital of a public company is £50,000, whereas there is no minimum capital requirement for a private company. (S. 11.) A public company has an unrestricted right to offer shares or debentures to the public, whereas this is prohibited in the case of a private company (above). The pre-emption rights of the 1985 Act apply to public companies which must offer equity share capital first to existing shareholders. These provisions apply also to a private company though they may be excluded by the memorandum or articles. (S. 91.) Where a public company has lost half or more of its share capital it must call an extraordinary general meeting, whereas this provision is not applicable to private companies. (S. 142.) Finally, as regards a lien or charge on its own shares, this is restricted in the case of public companies. (See p. 156.) The provisions are not applicable to private companies which may take a lien or charge on their shares. (S. 150.)

(vii) *As regards payment for shares*. In the case of public companies, any agreement under which shares are to be allotted by an undertaking to carry out work or perform services is prohibited but is allowed in the case of private companies. (S. 99.) The subscribers to the memorandum of a public company must pay for their shares in cash, whereas in a private company payment may be in cash or some other consideration. (S. 106.) In public companies there is a minimum payment for shares, i.e. at least one-quarter of the nominal value plus the whole of any share premium must be paid up, but in private companies there is no minimum payment requirement. (S. 101.) Where shares are to be paid for by a non-cash asset, public companies are required to ensure that the asset is to be transferred by contract within five years of the allotment whereas there is no special requirement for private companies. (S. 102.) Furthermore, public companies must have an independent accountant's report on the value of the non-cash asset. This requirement does not apply to private companies. (S. 103.)

(viii) *Acquisition of non-cash assets*. A public company cannot validly acquire non-cash assets from subscribers to the memorandum in the first two years of its existence unless an independent accountant's report is received. These restrictions do not apply to private companies. (S. 104.)

(ix) *As regards distribution of profits and assets*. Where interim accounts are used to support a proposed distribution these accounts must, in the case of a public company, be filed with the Registrar of Companies, whereas there is no filing requirement for private companies. (S. 272.) Private companies need only fulfil the basic requirement of profits available for distribution. Public companies must also comply with the capital maintenance rule of s. 264 whereas private companies need not. (See further p. 287.)

(x) *As regards loans to directors*. Quasi-loans and credit transactions for directors and the directors of the company's holding company are prohibited with certain exceptions in the case of public companies (s. 330), as are loans, etc. to persons connected with the directors and the directors of any holding company. (Ss. 330 and 346.) (See further p. 245.)

Conversion of companies from private to public and vice versa

Private to public. This is covered by ss. 43–45. Under s. 43 a private company may be re-registered as a public company if

(*a*) the members pass a special resolution which alters the company's memorandum and articles so that they fit the statutory requirements of a public company;

(*b*) the requirements of s. 45 as regards share capital are met. This means that the nominal value of the allotted share capital is not less than £50,000 and in respect of all the shares, or as many as are needed to make up the authorized minimum, the following conditions are satisfied—

(i) no less than one-quarter of the nominal value of each share and the whole of any premium on it is paid up;

(ii) none of the shares has been fully or partly paid up by means of an undertaking to do work or perform services where this has not already been performed or otherwise discharged; and

(iii) where any share has been allotted as fully or partly paid up for a non-cash consideration which consists solely or partly of an undertaking to do something other than to perform services, i.e. usually an undertaking to transfer a non-cash asset, either the undertaking has been performed or otherwise discharged or there is a contract between the company and the person involved under which the undertaking must be performed within five years;

(c) an application for the change is made to the Registrar on a form signed by a director or secretary of the company;

(d) the application is accompanied by the following documents—

(i) a printed copy of the memorandum and articles as altered and added to by the special resolution;

(ii) a copy of the balance sheet prepared as at a date not more than seven months before the date of the application, but not necessarily in respect of an accounting reference period. The balance sheet must be accompanied by a copy of an unqualified report of the company's auditor in relation to the balance sheet. If there is a qualification the auditor must state in writing that it is not material in determining whether at the date of the balance sheet the company's net assets were at least equal to the sum of its called up capital and non-distributable reserves, e.g. share premium account;

(iii) a copy of a written statement by the company's auditors that in their opinion the balance sheet referred to in (ii) above shows that the amount of the company's net assets at the date of the balance sheet was not less than the aggregate of its called up share capital and non-distributable reserves, e.g. share premium account and capital redemption reserve;

(iv) a statutory declaration by a director or secretary of the company that: (a) the requirements in regard to the making of necessary changes in the company's constitution have been complied with; and (b) that between the balance sheet date and the application for re-registration there has been no change in the financial position of the company which has caused the net assets to become less than the aggregate of called up share capital plus non-distributable reserves.

If between the date of the balance sheet and the passing of a special resolution to convert to a public company the company has allotted shares which are wholly or partly paid for by a non-cash consideration, then by reason of s. 44 it shall not make an application for re-registration unless before application is made—

(*a*) the consideration has been valued in accordance with s. 103, i.e. by a person or persons who are qualified by law to audit a public company's accounts who may themselves appoint other suitable persons to assist them;

(*b*) a report regarding the value has been made to the company by the persons referred to in (*a*) above during the six months immediately preceding the allotment of the shares.

If the Registrar is satisfied with the application for re-registration and provided that there is not in existence any court order reducing the company's share capital below the authorized minimum, he will retain the documents which have been sent to him and issue a certificate of incorporation stating that the company is a public company.

The company then becomes a public company and the alterations in its constitution take effect. The certificate of incorporation is conclusive evidence that the re-registration requirements have been complied with and that the company is a public company.

Public to private. This is permitted by s. 53 and the procedure is as follows—

(*a*) the members must pass a special resolution altering the memorandum so that it no longer states that the company is a public company and also in terms of the name; and

(*b*) application is then made on the prescribed forms signed by a director or secretary. The application is delivered to the Registrar together with printed copies of the memorandum and articles as altered or added to by the special resolution.

It should be noted that as regards the special resolution there are dissentient rights. Within a period of 28 days after the passing of the resolution dissentient holders of at least 5 per cent in nominal value of the company's issued share capital or any class thereof, or not less than 50 members, may apply to the court under s. 54 to have the resolution cancelled and the court may cancel or affirm it. If there is no application to the court or if it is unsuccessful and the court affirms the special resolution the Registrar will issue a new certificate of incorporation as a private company.

It should also be noted that under s. 54 the court may, in addition, adjourn the proceedings brought by dissentients in order that satisfactory arrangements may be made for the purchase of the shares of those dissentients. The purchase may obviously be by other shareholders but the company's money may also be used for this purpose and if this is the intention the court will make the necessary order to provide for the purchase by the company of its own shares and to reduce its share capital. The order may also make any necessary alterations in or additions to the memorandum and articles of the company.

Reduction below authorized minimum of issued share capital of a public company. Under s. 139 if the court reduces the share capital of a public company to below £50,000 it must re-register as a private company. The court may authorize re-registration without the company having followed the s. 53 procedures and the court order may specify and make the necessary changes in the company's constitution. Thus a reduction under s. 135 may now have the further consequence of changing the company's status from public to private.

HOLDING AND SUBSIDIARY COMPANIES

Although it is a fundamental principle of company law that a company is a separate entity, the Companies Act 1985 limits this concept where companies are in association, largely to ensure that the group publishes its total financial position by means of consolidated accounts.

Thus if company H holds a controlling interest in 20 other companies, many of which are private as is often the case, the accounts of company H would, without the provisions of the Companies Act, merely show the income which company H had received from other concerns. In order to ascertain the real position, it would be necessary to look at the accounts of the other 20 concerns to try to get a composite picture of the group, and this would be made difficult by the fact that it would not be easy to find out the names of the 20 concerns in order to refer to their accounts. The Companies Act 1985 requires the publication of group or consolidated accounts showing the financial position of the group.

Under s. 736, company X is considered to be a subsidiary of company Y if, and only if—

(i) company Y is a member of company X and controls the composition of the board of directors of company X; *or*

(ii) company Y holds more than half in nominal value of the X company's *equity share capital*; or

(iii) company X is a subsidiary of (say) company Z which is a subsidiary of company Y. Company X may in such circumstances be referred to as a sub-subsidiary of company Y.

The *equity share capital* mentioned above means the issued share capital of the company concerned, *excluding* shares which have a limited right to share in profits during the company's lifetime and in the capital on winding up. (S. 736.) The equity share capital is in fact its ordinary share capital and does not include preference share capital.

Control of the composition of the board

The composition of a company's board of directors is considered to be controlled by another company if, and only if, the other company can by the exercise of some power, and without the consent of any other person, appoint or remove all or the majority of the directors; and in particular there is the necessary control when—

(*a*) a person cannot be appointed to the board unless some other company exercises a power in his favour; *or*

(*b*) a person becomes a director of the subsidiary automatically on appointment as director of the holding company; *or*

(*c*) the directorship is held by the holding company itself or a subsidiary of it. (S. 736(2).)

Shares held or powers exercisable by companies holding the shares as trustees, or in any fiduciary capacity, are ignored for the purpose of establishing the relationship. Furthermore, the relationship of holding and subsidiary company cannot be established by company Y exercising control of company X by virtue of powers given in the *debentures* of company X which are held by company Y. (S. 736(4).)

Thus the test of control adopted by the Act has three branches, and the necessary control exists—

(1) if company Y holds more than half of the equity share capital of company X;

(2) if company X is a sub-subsidiary and company Y is the head holding company;

(3) if company Y is a member of company X and controls the composition of company X's Board of Directors. In this case the number of shares held by company Y is irrelevant, as long as it holds some.

13 Accounts and reports

The main statutory requirements relating to the accounts of registered companies are set out below. It should be noted that the details which have to be shown in the profit and loss account and the balance sheet and the notes to the accounts are set out in the Fourth Schedule to the Companies Act 1985. The detailed contents of this Schedule are better dealt with in accounting texts in terms of preparation of the accounts and have therefore been omitted, as have references to the various accounting standards and exposure drafts which lay down standards of practice observed by the accountancy profession but do not have the status of law.

ACCOUNTING RECORDS

Section 221 requires the directors of a company to keep accounting records sufficient to show and explain the company's transactions. They must disclose with reasonable accuracy *at any time* throughout the financial year, the financial position of the company *at that time*. They must also enable a balance sheet and profit and loss account to be prepared to give a true and fair view of the company's state of affairs and profit and loss. They must contain: (a) entries from day to day of all sums of money received and expended with details of transactions, and (b) a record of assets and liabilities.

Additionally, a company dealing in goods must keep statements of stock held at the end of the financial year, and of stocktaking from which the year end statement is made up and of all goods sold and purchased, other than retail trade transactions, showing goods, buyers and sellers, so as to allow identification.

Accounting records must be open for inspection by the officers of the company at all times and kept for six years (public company) and three years (private company).

As regards statements of work in progress, the Act does not specifically require these to be kept on the grounds that many small companies have little or no work in progress and those for whom it is significant will have to keep statements as part of the general requirement to keep records sufficient to disclose the financial position of the company and to enable accounts to be prepared.

Failure to keep accounting records as required is an offence for which officers of the company are liable. The offence is punishable with a maximum of two years imprisonment and/or a fine.

Company legislation does not deal specifically with the legality of keeping accounting records on computer but such records are generally regarded as complying with the law. In particular, s. 723 provides ... 'that the power conferred on a company by s. 722(1) to keep a register *or other record* by recording the matters in question otherwise than by making entries in bound books includes power to keep the register *or other record* by recording the matters in question otherwise than in legible form so long as the recording is capable of being reproduced in legible form'. The words in italics would seem to apply to any record and not merely the register of shares and debentures.

Accounting reference periods and accounting reference dates

Section 224 gives a new definition of 'financial year'. Under s. 227 directors must prepare accounts based on an *accounting reference period*. This begins on the day after the date to which the last accounts were prepared, e.g. if 31 December, 1 January, and ends on the last day of the company's normal financial year, called the *accounting reference date*, though the directors may, in their discretion, move the reference date to seven days before or after the last day of the company's normal financial year.

The accounts, which need not be printed, and the auditors' and directors' reports must be laid before a general meeting (s. 241(1)) and, except for certain unlimited companies which are exempt, filed with the Registrar (s. 241(3)) within seven months of the reference date (public companies) or ten months (private companies). (S. 242(2).) The Department of Trade and Industry may extend these periods (s. 242(6)) if there are special reasons, e.g. in the smaller company, illness of a sole director.

Non-compliance with the requirement to lay before a general meeting and file with the Registrar can result in conviction of the directors. It is a defence to have taken reasonable steps to comply. (S. 243(2).)

In addition, failure to comply with the requirement to file accounts with the Registrar makes the *company* liable for penalties which are recoverable by the Department of Trade in *civil* proceedings. There is no defence for the company. (S. 243(3) and (4).)

Additionally, if there is failure to comply with the filing requirements, a member or creditor or the Registrar may serve a notice on the directors asking for compliance and if the directors do not comply within 14 days after service of the notice the above-named persons may ask the court for an order directing compliance, the costs being borne by the the directors. (S. 244.)

Under s. 225, at any time during the course of an accounting reference period a company may give notice to the Registrar specifying a new accounting reference date lengthening the current and subsequent accounting reference periods of the company. This may be done after the end of an accounting reference period so as to change the date by which accounts would normally be laid and filed only if the company is a holding or subsidiary company, and the change is in order to coincide the accounting reference dates of both. The change cannot be made in any case if the periods of seven or ten months have expired. There is no need for a resolution of members but merely a board resolution and minute.

Notice under s. 225 must state whether the new period is shorter or longer than the current period. Extension is not possible if a current period plus the extension is more than 18 months. Unless the Department of Trade and Industry otherwise directs, extensions are not allowed more than once in five years except to coincide the accounting periods of holding and subsidiary companies. These restrictions do not apply where an accounting reference period is shortened. The above provisions apply also to group accounts. Finally, it should be noted that new companies must notify an accounting reference date on or within six months of incorporation.

COMPANY ACCOUNTING AND DISCLOSURE

General provisions in respect of the form and content of accounts

The main features of the 1985 Act affecting the *form* and *content* of accounts are—

(i) a Schedule, i.e. the Fourth Schedule, listing disclosure requirements and introducing detailed rules for the content and format of accounts and the accounting principles and rules that must be followed;

(ii) a statement of the statutory requirements in respect of the preparation of a company's accounts, the overriding requirement still being that the balance sheet and profit and loss account must give a true and fair view.

Modified accounts

Under ss. 247–251 small and medium companies are permitted to file modified accounts. Small companies are permitted to file only a modified balance sheet. Such companies will, additionally, not be required to file a profit and loss account or a directors' report. A company will qualify to be treated as a small company if it does not exceed more than one of the following thresholds:

Turnover £2 million;
Balance sheet total £975,000;
Employees 50.

A major feature of the modified accounts of small companies is that there is no need to disclose directors' remuneration either in the aggregate or bands (see p. 348) or the remuneration of higher-paid employees. (See p. 349.) However, loans, etc., and material transactions with directors must be disclosed in notes to the accounts under Sched 6.

Medium-sized companies are to be permitted not to include in modified accounts details of their turnover and gross profit margins. In addition the note disclosing turnover and profit by class of business and turnover by geographical market may be excluded. This was intended to prevent competition and the poaching of markets by larger organizations. A company will qualify to be treated as a medium-size company if it does not exceed more than one of the following thresholds:

Turnover £8 million;
Balance sheet total £3.9 million;
Employees 250.

The thresholds set out above are also applicable to a group of companies taken together to determine whether the group may be treated as small or medium-sized for the purpose of its group accounts.

Companies in the following categories, regardless of size, are not eligible to be treated as small or medium-sized;

Public companies
Banking companies
Insurance companies
Certain shipping companies
Members of groups containing public, banking, insurance or shipping companies.

The banking, insurance, and shipping companies concerned are defined in s. 257. However, the Act enables banking companies, insurance companies, and shipping companies (in each case as defined) to continue to prepare accounts broadly on the basis of existing statutory requirements including the former Sched 8 of the Companies Act 1948, rather than comply with the new provisions of the 1985 Act.

As regards *publication of accounts*, s. 255 deals with publication otherwise than by delivery to the Registrar. Published full or modified accounts must be accompanied by any group accounts, and they and any group accounts must be accompanied by the auditors' report. Published abridged accounts, e.g. in a newspaper, must state that they are not full accounts and whether full accounts have been delivered to the Registrar. A company may not publish the full auditors' report with abridged accounts but must say whether such a report has been prepared and whether it is qualified.

Section 252 creates a new regime for *dormant companies*—those companies eligible to be treated as small companies and in respect of which no significant accounting transaction has taken place during the period in question. Such companies are relieved from the requirement to have their accounts audited; accounts delivered to the Registrar of Companies must state that the company is dormant.

Profit and loss account

The profit and loss account will now follow one of the formats in the Fourth Schedule. Most companies will use the vertical format No 1. The statutory provisions as to contents appear below.

Emoluments of Directors and Chairmen. In the notes to the accounts must be shown the aggregate of directors' emoluments, pensions and compensation payments for loss of office. (Sched 5.)

Under Sched 5 the emoluments of the company's chairman, or if in the financial year more persons than one have been chairman, the emoluments of each of them, so far as attributable to the period during which each was chairman, must be disclosed in the accounts.

With regard to directors disclosure is required—

(a) of the number of directors who did not receive emoluments;

(b) of directors whose emoluments did not exceed £5,000; and

(c) by reference to each pair of adjacent points on a scale whereon the lowest point is £5,000 and the succeeding ones are successive integral multiples of £5,000 the number (if any) whose several emoluments exceeded the lower point but did not exceed the higher. Thus the note will show the number of directors in range £5,001–£10,000; £10,001–£15,000, and so on.

Disclosure is not required if the person's duties as chairman or director were wholly or mainly discharged outside the United Kingdom.

Schedule 5 also provides that the emoluments of any one director receiving more than the chairman must also be disclosed. If two or more directors are receiving more than the chairman then the emoluments paid to them (in the case of equality) must be disclosed. Where their emoluments are not equal the emoluments of the director receiving the greater or, as the case may be, the greatest must be disclosed.

Schedule 5 states that 'chairman' means the person elected by the directors of the company to be chairman of their meetings and includes a person who, though not so elected, holds any office (however designated) which, in accordance with the constitution of the company, carries with it functions substantially similar to those discharged by a person so elected.

Schedule 5 also states that a company which is neither a holding company nor a subsidiary of another body corporate is not subject to the above requirements if the emoluments of all the directors in the year in question do not exceed £60,000.

Under Sched 5 disclosure is also required of the number of directors who have waived rights to receive emoluments and the aggregate amount of those emoluments. Directors are under a duty to give the company the information it may require to make the above disclosures in the accounts.

Employees' Emoluments. Disclosure is required of the emoluments of highly paid employees who are not directors, and who are not working wholly or mainly outside the United Kingdom. The relevant provision which is in Sched 5 states 'that there shall be shown by reference to each pair of adjacent points on a scale where on the lowest point is £30,000 and the succeeding ones are successive integral multiples of £5,000 beginning with that in which the multiplier is seven, the number (if any) of persons in the company's employment (other than directors of the company and employees working wholly or mainly outside the United Kingdom) whose several emoluments exceeded the lower point but did not exceed the higher'. Once again, the notes to the accounts would commence with a band of £30,001–£35,000; and then £35,001–£40,000, and so on.

Under Sched 5, if a company's accounts do not comply with the above requirements the auditors are required to include in their report so far as they reasonably can do so a statement giving the required information.

Balance sheet

Every balance sheet and profit and loss account of a company must give a true and fair view of the state of affairs of the company and its profit or loss at the end of its accounting reference period. (S. 228(2).)

The general provisions relating to the contents of the balance sheet are set out in the Fourth Schedule. Formats also appear in the Fourth Schedule and most companies use the vertical format No 1.

Statement of source and application of funds

This statement is invariably included in audited accounts. It is not a statutory requirement but stems from SSAP 10. It identifies the movement in assets, liabilities and capital which have taken place during the year and the result and effect on net liquid funds.

Supplementary current cost accounts

Once again, this is not a statutory requirement but stems from SSAP 16. The standard provides for current cost information to be included in annual financial statements in addition to historical cost information. SSAP 16 was withdrawn in 1985, partly because of falling levels of compliance by companies; less than 20 per cent were observing it at that time. A new exposure draft ED 38, entitled 'Reporting the Effects of Changing Prices on Earnings', is currently under discussion.

Form of accounts and minority rights

It has already been noted that a shareholder cannot bring a derivative action on behalf of a company to seek declaratory relief as to the form in which the accounts have been drawn up. (*Devlin v Slough Estates Ltd*, 1982, see p. 201.)

GROUP ACCOUNTS

If a company has subsidiaries, group accounts showing the state of affairs and profit or loss of the company and the subsidiaries must be laid before the company at the general meeting at which the company's own balance sheet and profit and loss account is laid. (S. 229(1).)

However, *group accounts are not required* if the company is, at the end of its financial year, the wholly owned subsidiary of another body corporate incorporated in Great Britain. (S. 229(2).) Group accounts need not deal with a subsidiary of the company if the company's directors are of opinion that—

(*a*) it is *impracticable*, or would be of *no real value* to members of the company, in view of the insignificant amounts involved, or would involve *expense or delay* out of proportion to the value to members of the company; or

(b) the result would be *misleading*, or *harmful* to the business of the company or any of its subsidiaries; or

(c) it is *unreasonable* because the business of the holding company and subsidiary are so different that they cannot reasonably be treated as a single undertaking.

The permission of the Department of Trade is required before a subsidiary can be omitted from the group accounts on the grounds of *unreasonableness* and where the directors allege that *harm* would accrue by the inclusion of the subsidiary. (S. 229(4).)

Any director who fails to take all reasonable steps to secure compliance with the statutory requirements regarding the accounts, is liable to imprisonment and/or a fine. However, it is a defence for a director to prove that he took all reasonable steps for securing compliance with the requirements of the Companies Act.

Identity of subsidiaries and other companies in which shares are held. Sched 5, Part I, para 1 requires a statement to be made in the notes to the accounts of a holding company showing the name of each subsidiary, the country (if other than Great Britain) in which it was incorporated, the identity of the class of shares held and the proportion of the nominal value of the allotted shares of the class which the company holds. If the holding company is registered in England and the subsidiary is registered in Scotland or vice versa, the statement must also show the country of registry of the subsidiary.

Under Sched 5, Part I, para 3 the above information regarding subsidiaries need not be given if the subsidiary is incorporated outside the United Kingdom, or, if incorporated in the United Kingdom, it carries on business abroad, and the information required would, in the opinion of the directors of the holding company, be harmful to the business of the holding company or its subsidiaries, and Department of Trade consents to non-disclosure.

Sched 5, Part I, para 4 provides that if, in the opinion of the directors of a company having, at the end of its financial year, subsidiaries and the number of such subsidiaries is so great that compliance with para 3 would result in particulars of excessive length being given, full compliance will be excused. However, para 1 must still be complied with in respect of subsidiaries the business of which, in the opinion of the directors, principally contributed to the amount of profit or loss of the group or to the amount of its assets.

Sched 5, Part I, para 5 states that if advantage is taken of para 4, the statement made at the end of the financial year shall say that it deals only with subsidiaries principally contributing to the profit or loss, or assets of the group and full compliance with para 1 is

351

later required in a statement to be sent with the annual return first made by the company *after* copies of its accounts have been laid before it in general meeting.

The accounts are also required to show details of companies in which there is more than a 10 per cent holding and also companies where there is more than a 20 per cent holding. (Sched 5, Part II, paras 7 and 9.) Details to be given are the country of incorporation (or registration and operation), the holding itself, and the proportion of that holding in the company as a whole.

Under Sched 5, Part II, para 10 the information required under paras 7 and 8 need not be given if company B is incorporated outside the United Kingdom, or if incorporated in the United Kingdom, it carries on business abroad and the information required would in the opinion of the directors of company A be harmful to the business of company A or B, and the Department of Trade and Industry consents to non-disclosure.

Where the disclosing company holds shares in a large number of companies and particulars of excessive length would have, to be given, paras 11 and 12 of Part II of Sched 5 provide for non-compliance in the same terms as paras 4 and 5 of Part I of Sched 5 above.

Ultimate holding company. Schedule 5, Part IV, para 20 states that where at the end of its financial year a company is a subsidiary of another company, the notes to the accounts of the subsidiary must state the name of the company regarded by the directors of the subsidiary as its ultimate holding company and, if known to them, the country in which it is incorporated.

Under para 21, *ibid*, the above disclosure is not required by a company which carries on business outside the United Kingdom if, in the opinion of the directors of the subsidiary, it would be harmful to the interests of the subsidiary, the ultimate holding company, or any other companies in the group. Section 260(2) states that when a company makes in the notes to its accounts the disclosures regarding directors' and employees' emoluments and particulars of directors' salaries, pensions, etc, required by Sched 5, it must also give the corresponding amount for the immediately preceding financial year.

Under 260(3) a director who fails to take reasonable steps to see that 260(2) is complied with shall be liable to imprisonment or a fine. However, it shall be a defence for a director to show that he had reasonable ground to believe and did believe that a competent person was charged with the duty of seeing that the provisions were complied with and was in a position to discharge that duty. Furthermore, no person shall be sentenced to imprisonment unless, in the opinion of the court, there is wilful default.

Disclosure of loans and other substantial contracts with directors

Schedule 6 of the Companies Act 1985 applies. Under this Schedule the notes to the accounts of the company must show—(a) loans and guarantees etc whether permitted or prohibited; and (b) any other transaction with the company or its subsidiary in which a director of the company or its holding company had a material interest; (c) under Sched 6, Part I, para 1 disclosure is not only of transactions, etc made with a director of the company in question, or his connected persons, but also of transactions, etc made with a director of its holding company.

The new disclosure provisions distinguish between directors and officers other than directors (see below) and holding and other companies and under Sched 6 are as follows—

(i) *Holding companies preparing group accounts.* Group accounts must give details of transactions or arrangements under s. 330. Disclosure of credit transactions is subject to the *de minimis* provisions of the Act and no disclosure of these is required if they have not exceeded in aggregate £5,000 in terms of directors and connected persons at any time during the year. Details of any agreement to enter into any transaction must also be shown. Thus disclosure is required of a transaction and even of an agreement to enter into it. Disclosure of any other transaction not specifically covered by the above is required if a director of the company has a material interest in it. (See below.)

(ii) *Companies which are either subsidiaries or free-standing companies,* i.e. companies which do not prepare group accounts. These are required to give the same details in their accounts as those in (i) above.

(iii) *Parent companies which do not prepare group accounts.* These are companies which do not produce group accounts by reason of an exception under s. 229(4). (See p. 351.) They must give the same details in their accounts as those in (i) above.

Material interests

Schedule 6 also provides that a director of the company or its holding company is deemed to be interested in a transaction or arrangement if he is involved in it himself or because a connected person is. It also says that a transaction is material if the majority of the board thinks so (excluding the director interested, of course). Thus the onus is placed on a director who is interested in a transaction with a company other than one which the Act specifically requires to be disclosed to seek the opinion of his fellow directors. If he does not materiality will be determined by the court if proceedings are brought for non-disclosure. For example, transactions made with persons other than the specified range of connected persons might have to be disclosed here as where a director has a material interest in a contract between his company and a company run by his brother (who is not a connected person).

Under Sched 6 it is not necessary to disclose a material interest if it did not at any time during the relevant period exceed in the aggregate £1,000 or, if more, did not exceed £5,000 or one per cent of the value of the net assets of the company preparing the accounts in question, whichever is the less.

Furthermore, SI 1984/1860 exempts from disclosure any transaction in which a director has a material interest if that transaction is entered into at arm's length and in the ordinary course of business, as where a director sells the goods of his separate business to the company: and any transaction between members of a group of companies which would have been disclosable only because of a director's being associated with the contracting companies, provided no minority interests in the reporting company are affected. This facilitates inter-group deals.

Other exemptions from disclosure are—(*a*) loans between companies merely because they have a common director; (*b*) contracts of service (covered by s. 318), and (*c*) arrangements which did not subsist during the financial year in question. However, this does not detract from the true and fair principle and disclosure of an arrangement may be required under s. 228 if it is a significant post-accounting event. Sanctions for failing to disclose apply to a director who fails to take all reasonable steps to secure compliance with company legislation in regard to the accounts.

Thus under the Companies Act 1985 details of loans, etc., to the company's directors and officers and directors' interest in material contracts now require disclosure in the accounts and if not so disclosed then in the auditors' report. Disclosure of loans, etc., and material contracts *are now subject to audit.*

Schedule 6 sets out particulars to be disclosed in the accounts as follows—

1. *Loans and related transactions*—(*a*) a statement of the transaction and the name of the director or connected person for whom it was made. (*b*) The amount of the loan liability (i.e. principal and interest) at the beginning and at the end of the period. The maximum amount of that liability at any time during the period, i.e. the opening position, the highest point reached in the year and the closing position. The amount of interest due but not paid and any provision in the accounts for non-recovery.

2. *Guarantees and securities.* If a company has guaranteed, or provided security for, a loan the amount for which it was liable at the

beginning and the end of the financial year must be shown; the maximum potential liability and the amount of any liability actually incurred by the company in, e.g. meeting a guarantee.

3. *Material interest in transactions.* The name of the director and the nature of the interest together with the value of the transaction.

Schedule 6 also provides for the disclosure in company accounts of the aggregate amount of loans, quasi-loans and credit transactions made in favour of officers other than directors of all companies. These should be disclosed in the aggregate. As regards recognized banks, only the aggregate of all such transactions with their directors and their connected persons need be disclosed.

Under Sched 6, a threshold of £2,500 is applied to the disclosure requirements in relation to officers who are not directors. Disclosure is not required of amounts owed by an officer where the aggregate amount of transactions, etc outstanding at the end of the relevant period in respect of *that* officer does not exceed £2,500.

Section 343 requires recognized banks to keep an internal register containing details of all relevant transactions and to produce a statement available to shareholders at, and for at least 15 days before, the annual general meeting containing the details that other companies would be required to produce in their accounts. The auditors must examine the statement and make a report to the members on it. The auditors' report must be attached to the statement before it is made available. If the statement does not give the necessary particulars, the auditors' report must. No details are required where the aggregate value for a director or his connected person did not at any time during the financial year exceed £1,000. (S. 344(1).)

The Companies Act 1985 places a duty on auditors to include in their report a statement giving the particulars (as far as possible) of any loans and other transactions of the kind described in ss. 330–344 which have not been disclosed in the accounts.

Powers of Department of Trade and Industry

The Companies Act 1985 gives the Department of Trade and Industry certain general powers to modify the accounting provisions of the Act. In particular s. 256 entitles the Department to alter or add to the requirements by statutory instrument. Section 258(4) entitles the Department on the application of, or with the consent of the directors, to modify in relation to any company any of the statutory requirements as to matters to be stated in the balance sheet or profit and loss account, except that there can be no waiver of the 'true and fair view' rule.

Section 256 also enables the Secretary of State to alter the requirements of the Companies Acts as to the directors' report.

DIRECTORS' REPORT

This is annexed to the balance sheet and circularized and publicized with it. The statutory contents of the directors' report are set out in Sched 7 and may be listed under the following headings.

Principal activities and business review

This is to include a description of the principal activities of the company and of its subsidiaries during the course of the year and any significant changes in the year. There must also be a fair review of the development of the business of the company and its subsidiaries during the financial year ending at the balance sheet date and of their position at the end of the year, together with an indication of likely future developments in the business of the company and its subsidiaries.

Events occurring since the date of the balance sheet

The report should give particulars of any important events affecting the company or any of its subsidiaries which have occurred since the end of the year.

Research and development

An indication should be given of the activities, if any, of the company and its subsidiaries in the field of research and development.

Significant changes in the fixed assets and market value of land and buildings

The report should give significant changes in the fixed assets of the company or any of its subsidiaries if any have occurred during the year, and give particulars of the changes and if, in the case of such of those assets as consist in interests in land, their market value, as at the end of the year, differs substantially from the amount at which they are included in the balance sheet and the difference is, in the opinion of the directors, of such significance as to require that the attention of members of the company or of holders of debentures thereof should be drawn thereto, indicate the difference with such degree of precision as is practicable.

Directors

The directors' report must state the names of the persons who, at any time during the financial year, were directors of the company.

The report will also show the interests of the directors in shares and debentures of the company and its subsidiaries. Alternatively, the directors' interests in shares and debentures may be included in the notes to the accounts.

Acquisition of company's own shares

The report should also include purchases of shares by the company during the year. Included under this heading also should be other acquisitions, e.g. by way of forfeiture or surrender or lien.

Charitable and political contributions

The report should also give details of charitable and political contributions made during the year. However, these particulars are not required if the charitable and political contributions in the United Kingdom do not exceed £200 in aggregate.

Employment of disabled persons

The report should include a statement of the company's policy in regard to applications for employment from disabled persons and in respect of employees that become disabled and in terms also of training, career development, and promotion of disabled persons. This information is not required if the company employs an average of 250 or fewer persons in the United Kingdom.

Health and safety at work

Information required to be included in directors' reports include such information concerning arrangements for the health, safety, and welfare at work of employees of the company and its subsidiaries, and protecting others against risks to health and safety consequent on the activities at work of those employees as may be described in regulations. Such regulations may make different provisions for different classes of company. At the time of writing no regulations have been issued.

Employee involvement

Directors' reports must also include a statement describing the action which the company has taken during the year to introduce, maintain, or develop arrangements for employee involvement. Where the directors' report is attached to group accounts, the requirement applies to the holding company. However, this provision does not apply to directors' reports of companies which employ an average of 250 or fewer persons in the UK.

Penalties of imprisonment or fine are provided for in respect of a director who fails to take all reasonable steps to comply with the provisions regarding the directors' report. However, it is a defence for him to prove that he had reasonable grounds to believe that a competent and reliable person was charged with the duty of securing compliance. There shall be no sentence of imprisonment unless in the opinion of the Court dealing with the case the offence was committed wilfully.

Members of the company, debenture holders and persons entitled to receive notices of general meetings of the company, have a right to receive copies of the directors' report.

It is the duty of the auditors of the company in preparing their report on the company's accounts, to consider whether the information given in the directors' report relating to the financial year in question is consistent with those accounts. If the auditors are of opinion that the information given in the directors' report is not consistent with the company's accounts for the financial year, they shall state that fact in their report under s. 236.

AUDITORS' REPORT

The auditors' report is attached to any circulated or published copies of the accounts. (S. 238). The contents of the report are dealt with in the chapter on Audits and Investigations. (See p. 364.)

14 Audits and investigations

An audit is a process which is concerned to establish and confirm confidence in the accounting information yielded by the company's records and systems so that an opinion may be given upon the accounts which have been prepared by the company from those records and systems. The audit is carried out primarily for the shareholders as a check upon the directors' stewardship, but it is obviously also of benefit to creditors and potential investors.

Section 384(1) requires companies to appoint auditors unless they can be classified as dormant. (See p. 348.)

ELIGIBILITY AS AUDITOR

Under s. 389 only those persons recognized as qualified by the Chartered Institutes of England and Wales, Scotland, and Ireland, and the Chartered Association of Certified Accountants, and persons with overseas qualifications recognized by the Department of Trade and Industry may act as auditors.

In the past the Department has had power to authorize persons not so qualified on the basis that they had adequate knowledge and experience. Persons who are authorized may continue to act but no further authorizations will be made by the Department. It should be noted that there is no automatic authorization for an overseas accountant coming from a country which provides reciprocal privileges. The qualification of the individual must be adequate and satisfy criteria as to training laid down in the United Kingdom. Thus an accountant qualified in, say, Transylvania, is not automatically allowed to practise here merely because some English accountants are allowed to practise there.

The following persons cannot be appointed as auditors to a company even though they are qualified or authorized—

(*a*) An officer or servant of the company. Although an auditor is an officer of the company for some purposes, the provision means officers other than the auditor for the time being.

(b) A person who is employed by or is the partner of an officer or servant of the company. 'Officer' includes a director, manager or secretary. (S. 744.)

(c) A body corporate. Thus a limited company cannot be appointed as auditor.

(d) Officers and servants of the company's holding or subsidiary companies and their employees or partners. (S. 389(7).)

Section 389(9) and (10) make it an offence for an unqualified person to act as an auditor. If anyone does so act he is guilty of an offence and liable on conviction to a fine.

In this connection the case of *Secretary of State for Trade and Industry v Hart* [1982] 1 All ER 817 should be noted. H acted as an auditor of a company when he was also a director of that company and therefore disqualified from acting under what is now s. 389(6). He was charged with that offence and acquitted by the magistrates but the prosecutor appealed to the Divisional Court who dismissed the appeal, finding H not guilty, by reason of the wording of what is now s. 389(9). The sub-section says that no person shall act as auditor of a company at a time when he knows that he is disqualified for appointment to that office. H contended, successfully, that he was not aware of the statutory provision which disqualified him and therefore could not be guilty of an offence. The Divisional Court upheld H's contention; a person was not guilty unless he *knew* that he was disqualified. The case is rather unusual in that it is a general rule of English law that ignorance of the law is no defence but it would appear that s. 389(9) is worded in such a way as to require knowledge of the Act itself. As Lord Justice Ormrod said in his judgment: 'If it means that he (the auditor) is entitled to rely on ignorance of the law as a defence, and in contrast to the usual practice of the usual rule, the answer is that the section gives him that right.' Parliament may have to look at the section again, and, incidentally, in order to catch H it would have been necessary to redraft sub-section (9) of s. 389 so that it read something like: 'No person shall act as an auditor of a company at a time when he is disqualified for appointment'. This would have made it a strict offence not requiring guilty knowledge or *mens rea*.

APPOINTMENT AND REMOVAL OF AUDITORS

At each general meeting at which accounts in respect of an accounting reference period are laid the members must appoint auditors who will hold office until the conclusion of the next general meeting at which accounts in respect of an accounting reference period are laid. (S.

384(1).) If no appointment is made the Department of Trade must be told within one week whereupon the Department may make an appointment. (S. 384(5).)

As regards the first auditors, they may be appointed by the directors to hold office until the conclusion of a general meeting at which accounts are laid. If the directors fail to make an appointment the company in general meeting may appoint. (S. 384(2) and (3).) As regards casual vacancies, these may be filled by the directors or by the members in general meeting. (S. 384(4).)

The members of a company may remove the auditors before the expiration of their office and if this is done the Registrar must be informed within 14 days of removal. (S. 386(1) and (2).) As regards procedure, special notice of 28 days is required for an ordinary resolution at a general meeting—

(a) appointing as auditor a person other than retiring auditor; or

(b) filling a casual vacancy in the office of an auditor; or

(c) re-appointing as auditor a retiring auditor who was appointed by the directors to fill a casual vacancy; or

(d) removing an auditor before the expiration of his term of office. (S. 388(1).)

In cases (a) and (d) above the auditor may make representations in writing to the company and require the notification of these representations to the members of the company. Failing such notification he may require that the representations be read out at the meeting and in any case he has the right to be heard orally at the meeting. If the court is satisfied, on the application of the company or any other person who claims to be aggrieved, that these rights are being used to secure needless publicity for defamatory matter, the representations need not be sent out or read out at the meeting. (S. 388(2)–(5).) In this connection reference should be made to the problems presented to the auditor if short notice of the meeting is allowed. (See *Fenning v Fenning Environmental Products Ltd*, *Law Society's Gazette*, 23 June 1982, p. 220.)

RESIGNATION OF AUDITORS

An auditor of a company may resign his office at any time by depositing at the registered office of the company a notice in writing to that effect. The date of his resignation is the date of the notice or such later date as may be specified in the notice. (S. 390(1).) Under s. 390(2) the notice of resignation must contain a statement either—

(a) to the effect that there are no circumstances connected with his resignation which he considers should be brought to the notice of the members or debenture holders of the company; or (*b*) of any such circumstances (the s. 390(2)(*b*) statement).

Under s. 390(3) the company must, within 14 days of receipt of such a notice send a copy to:

(*a*) the Registrar of Companies in any case; and

(*b*) if the notice contains a s. 390(2)(*b*) statement to members and debenture holders.

Under s. 390(4) and (5) the court may order that the copies of the s. 390(2)(*b*) statement need not be sent out if it is satisfied that the auditor is using the notice to secure needless publicity for defamatory matter provided that the company or any person who claims to be aggrieved, applies to the court for such an order within 14 days of receipt of a notice containing such a statement.

Under s. 390(6) the company must within 14 days of the court's decision send to members and debenture holders a statement setting out the effects of the order, or if no order is made, a copy of the notice containing the s. 390(2)(*b*) statement.

Under s. 391(1) where an auditor's notice of resignation contains such a statement he may deposit with the notice a requisition signed by himself calling on the directors of the company to convene an extraordinary general meeting of the company for the purpose of receiving and considering such explanation of the circumstances connected with his resignation as he may wish to place before the meeting.

Under s. 391(4) within 21 days of the receipt of such a requisition the directors must convene a meeting to be held within 28 days of the date of the notice convening the meeting.

Section 391(2) provides that where an auditor's notice of resignation contains a s. 390(2)(*b*) statement he may request the company to circulate to the members a statement in writing (a s. 391(2) statement) not exceeding a reasonable length setting out the circumstances connected with his resignation—

(*a*) before the general meeting at which his term of office would otherwise have expired; or

(*b*) before any general meeting at which it is proposed to fill the vacancy caused by his resignation or convened on his requisition.

Under s. 391(3) the company is then required (unless the statement is received too late for it to do so) to inform its members in the notice of the meeting that the s. 391(2) statement has been made and to send a copy to every member.

If the statement is not sent out either because it is received too late or by default of the company, the auditor may require that it be read out at the meeting. (S. 391(5).) This statement also need not be sent out or read out on the application of the company or any person who claims to be aggrieved (e.g. a director) if the court is satisfied that the right is being abused to secure needless publicity for defamatory matter. (S. 391(6).)

The resigning auditor is entitled to attend any such meeting and to be heard on any part of the business of the meeting which concerns him as a former auditor. (S. 391(7).) Section 390 deals with a situation where an auditor resigns his office in mid-term because things are wrong and he wishes to avoid having to qualify the accounts or have further responsibility for the company's affairs.

However, he cannot resign quietly but must make a statement. This protects shareholders and debenture holders and may make a weak auditor face up to his responsibilities.

The difficulty is, of course, that an auditor must make a living. A person who acquires a reputation of being a vocal auditor may find it difficult to get work, human nature being what it is.

An auditor who does not seek re-appointment at a general meeting at which accounts are laid, or who is not re-elected, is not in the same position. He has finished his audit and will have qualified his report if necessary and must make a report, so that there is no need for a further statement.

The power of an auditor to requisition a general meeting is useful and is designed for the auditor who resigns in mid-term. Under the relevant provisions he can requisition an extraordinary general meeting and put his views before it.

POWERS OF AUDITORS IN RELATION TO SUBSIDIARIES

Section 392 requires the auditor of a subsidiary incorporated in Great Britain to give the auditors of the holding company such information and explanation as they may reasonably require for the purposes of their duties as auditors of the holding company.

Before the Companies Act 1976 the auditors of a holding company had no right of access to the accounting records of subsidiaries, nor had the officers of the holding company a legal duty to obtain from subsidiaries information which the holding company's auditors needed and should have.

The Consultative Committee of Accounting Bodies asked for this provision because although in practice there is often consultation between the auditors of a holding company and subsidiaries, the section is useful if good practice breaks down.

FALSE STATEMENTS TO AUDITORS

Under s. 393 an officer of a company who knowingly or recklessly makes misleading, false or deceptive statements, orally or in writing to the company's auditors in connection with the audit commits an offence punishable with a maximum of two years' imprisonment and/or a fine.

This was a recommendation of the inspectors in their report on London County Securities and indeed goes further. It is an offence to give false or misleading information to an auditor, either knowingly or recklessly, i.e. not caring whether true or false, but only in his role as auditor and not on some other matter. (*Prudential Assurance Co Ltd v Newman Industries Ltd*, 1980.[170])

REMUNERATION

The remuneration of the auditors is fixed by the company in general meeting or in such way as the company in general meeting may determine, e.g. the company may delegate the fixing of remuneration to the directors.

Where the auditor is appointed by the directors or the Department of Trade and Industry, his remuneration is fixed by the directors or the Department as the case may be.

Money paid to the auditors by way of expenses shall be deemed included in the expression *remuneration*. (S. 385(3).)

The auditors' remuneration, including any sums paid by the company in respect of his expenses, must be shown separately in the notes to the profit and loss account. (Sched 4.)

DUTIES, RIGHTS AND LIABILITIES OF AN AUDITOR

An auditor has *two main duties:* (1) *To audit* the accounts of the company; and (2) *To report* to the members of the company on the accounts, i.e. on every balance sheet and profit and loss account and all group accounts, if any, laid before the company in general meeting during his tenure of office. (S. 236.) The auditors' report must be read before the company in general meeting and must be open to inspection by any member. (S. 236.)

Under s. 236(2) the report must state—

(*a*) whether, in the opinion of the auditors, the balance sheet and profit and loss account and (in the case of a holding company submitting group accounts) group accounts have been properly prepared in accordance with the Companies Act 1985, and

(*b*) whether in their opinion a true and fair view is given—

(i) in the case of the balance sheet, of the state of the company's affairs at the end of its financial year;

(ii) in the case of the profit and loss account (if not framed as a consolidated profit and loss account), of the company's profit and loss for its financial year;

(iii) in the case of group accounts, of the state of affairs and profit or loss of the company and its subsidiaries so far as concerns members of the auditors' client company.

If the auditors are of the opinion that proper accounting records have not been kept or received by them, or that the balance sheet and profit and loss account are not in agreement with the accounting records, they must say so in the report. (S. 237(2).)

Where auditors have not obtained all the information and explanations which they think necessary for their audit they must say so in the report. (S. 237(4).)

Furthermore, if the accounts do not contain particulars of the directors' emoluments the auditors' report should include the information required. (S. 237(5).) In addition, where any accounts do not comply with the disclosure requirements of the Sixth Schedule, the auditors must include in their audit report a statement giving the required particulars so far as they are reasonably able to do so. (S. 237(5).)

The articles of association cannot preclude the auditors from availing themselves of all information required for their report. (*Newton v Birmingham Small Arms Co Ltd* [1906] 2 Ch 378.)

The auditors are also required to show that in preparing the report they have carried out investigations so as to be able to form an opinion as to—

(i) whether proper books of account have been kept by the company, and proper returns adequate for the audit were received from branches not actually visited by the auditors;

(ii) whether the company's balance sheet and profit and loss account agree with the company's accounting records. (S. 237(1).)

If (i) and (ii) above have not been complied with the auditor must make this clear in his report.

If the directors do not give the auditors sufficient time in which to make these investigations they must either refuse to make a report or make a qualified one. (*Re Thomas Gerrard & Son Ltd*, 1968.[203])

It was decided in *Re Allen, Craig & Co (London) Ltd* [1934] Ch 483, that auditors perform their duty if they send their report to the secretary of the company and are not responsible if the secretary does not put the report before members.

The auditors have a *right of access* at all times to the books and accounts and vouchers of the company, and are entitled to require from the officers of the company, such information and explanations as they think necessary for the proper performance of their duties as auditors. (S. 237(3).)

Auditors are also entitled to attend any general meeting of the company, and to receive all notices and other communications relating to any general meeting which the members are entitled to receive. They also have a right to speak at any general meeting which they attend on any part of the business which concerns them as auditors. (S. 387(1).)

The case law on the duties of auditors may be summarized as follows—

(a) It is not their duty to see that the business is being run efficiently or profitably or to advise on the conduct of the busines. The auditors' concern is to ascertain the true financial position of the company at the time of the audit. However, the auditor is not an insurer and does not guarantee that the accounting records show the true state of the company's affairs. (*Re London and General Bank*, 1895.[204])

(b) An auditor may have to value shares and in this connection it should be noted that if on the facts of the case the court takes the view that the auditor was employed in the capacity of arbitrator rather than expert there is no liability in negligence. However, in most cases the auditor will be regarded as valuing as an expert because the parties are seldom in dispute with regard to the value of the shares and are simply seeking a professional valuation. Where the auditor values as an expert he will be liable in negligence under the rule in *Hedley Byrne & Co v Heller & Partners*, 1963[89] if he reaches a valuation without the exercise of proper skill and care. In addition, the auditors' valuation of shares is generally binding on the parties even if it is wrong. The courts are reluctant to set aside a professional valuation in the absence of fraud, or collusion (*Baber v Kenwood Manufacturing Co* [1978] 1 Lloyds Rep. 175) and this makes the remedy against the aud:tors more attractive provided, of course, negligence can be established.

(c) The auditor should be familiar with the company's constitution, i.e. its memorandum and articles (*Re Republic of Bolivia Exploration Syndicate Ltd*, 1914[205]) and must, of course, check and verify the company's accounts. (*Leeds Estate, Building and Investment Co v Shepherd*, 1887.[206])

(d) The auditor is not under a duty to take stock and can accept as honest any statements made by the company's officers and servants so long as he acts reasonably in so doing and the circumstances are not suspicious. (*Re Kingston Cotton Mill Co*, 1896.[207]) In other words he must act as a reasonably careful and competent auditor would.

It should be borne in mind, however, that the cases relating to the general duty of care of the auditor are rather old and that professional standards have risen in recent times. Thus, it is now generally accepted that an auditor should not rely on the accuracy and honesty of other persons even in the matter of stocktaking, and that he should carry out a check on at least one or more sample items. The standard of care required of an auditor at the present time was probably more accurately expressed by Lord Denning in *Fomento (Sterling Area) Ltd v Selsdon Fountain Pen Co Ltd* [1958] 1 WLR 45 at p. 61 where he said—

'An auditor is not confined to the mechanics of checking vouchers and making arithmetical computations. He is not to be written off as a professional "adder-upper and subtractor". His vital task is to take care to see that errors are not made, be they errors of computation, or errors of omission or commission, or downright untruths. To perform this task properly he must come to it with an enquiring mind—not suspicious of dishonesty...—but suspecting that someone may have made a mistake somewhere and that a check must be made to ensure that there has been none.'

This higher duty of care was to some extent applied in *Re Thomas Gerrard & Sons Ltd*, 1968.[203]

An auditor is an officer of the company and is liable for misfeasance under s. 212, Insolvency Act 1986, which gives the court power to assess damages payable to the company by delinquent officers during a winding up (*Re Thomas Gerrard & Sons Ltd*, 1968.[203]) Furthermore, an auditor may also be liable under s. 206(1)(*d*), *ibid* (making any false entry in any book or paper) and s. 207, *ibid* (frauds by officers of companies which have gone into liquidation), and s. 223 (liability where proper accounts not kept). (*R. v Shacter*, 1960.[208]) However, he is not ordinarily an *agent* whose acts bind the company. Thus the auditors' certificate on a balance sheet is not an acknowledgement of the company's indebtedness for the purpose of limitation of actions. (*Re Transplanters (Holding Co) Ltd* [1958] 2 All ER 711.)

An auditor is liable to pay damages to the company where he is in breach of duty or acts fraudulently, as for example where dividend has been paid out of capital because of his breach of duty. (*Re Thomas Gerrard & Sons Ltd*, 1968.[203])

The auditor's duty is to the company and the members, and there was formerly no duty to third parties in respect of the accounts (*Candler v Crane, Christmas & Co*, 1951[209]) but in view of the decision in *Hedley, Byrne & Co v Heller and Partners*, 1963[89] there is now a duty to third parties whom he *knows* will rely on the audited accounts unless there is a disclaimer of liability. It would seem from the decision in *JEB Fasteners v Marks Bloom* [1983] 1 All ER 583 that the liability of the auditor has been considerably extended in terms that he may now be liable to persons who rely on the audited accounts even though he did not *know* that they would do so. In the case A, who was intending to take over J Ltd, relied upon accounts prepared by the defendants.

A later alleged that the accounts did not show a true and fair view of the company and were negligently prepared in that it was alleged that some sales and purchases had been omitted and there had been a failure to make provision for interest due on the company's over-drawn account and that the valuation of stock was at a figure in excess of cost of approximately £13,500. As a consequence it was alleged that whereas the certified trading and profit and loss account had shown a profit of £11, there was in reality a loss in excess of £13,000. Mr Justice Woolf at first instance found that the defendants did owe a duty of care to A, *even though it was admitted that A was a stranger to the defendants at the time of the audit.* However, Mr Justice Woolf found that the defendants were not liable because A would not have acted differently and would still have gone ahead with his takeover even if he had known the true position. In the circumstances, although the defendants owed a duty of care to A, their alleged negligence was not a cause of A's loss. It appeared that A's main purpose in making the take-over bid was to acquire the services of two directors of J Ltd. The Court of Appeal dismissed an appeal by A and upheld Mr Justice Woolf's findings as regards the lack of causal connection between A's loss and the defendants' alleged negligence. It was, there-fore, not necessary to the decision of the Court of Appeal to determine the scope of an auditor's liability for professional negligence. In these circumstances Mr Justice Woolf's ruling on the matter retains some authority but the law is to some extent uncertain and obviously in a stage of development.

Nevertheless, the move from *knowledge* of the person who will rely on the accounts to the broader objective test of *foresight* seems likely to be established in future cases. This does not mean that an account-ant/auditor will be deemed to foresee everyone who relies on his ac-counts. In *JEB* it was held that the auditor foresaw the possibility of reliance because from the accounts he knew, or must be deemed to have known that the company would require money before the next accounts were completed. Therefore Woolf J said he could foresee that the accounts might be relied on, e.g. by a lender, such as a bank; by an investor of share capital, or by a person contemplating a take-over of a company which was in some difficulty. In *Twomax Ltd v Dickson McFarlane & Robinson*, 5 March 1982, Lord Stewart in the Scottish Court of Session found auditors liable in circumstances similar to *JEB* but where the controlling shareholders had relied on the accounts and did not have any other motive for acquiring the company.

Section 310 states that any provision in the articles of the company, or in any contract, exempting the auditor from liability for default, negligence or breach of duty, or agreeing to indemnify him in respect of it, shall be void. The court may, however, relieve the auditors if they have acted honestly and reasonably, and ought in all the circumstances fairly to be excused. (S. 727.)

INVESTIGATIONS

The powers given in the Companies Act to the Department of Trade and Industry to appoint inspectors to investigate the affairs of a company have three main purposes. *In the first place*, the provisions of the Act assist members to obtain information about the company's affairs where there is not sufficient disclosure by the management. *Secondly*, the provisions provide relief in cases of oppression of a minority, and this aspect of the matter has already been discussed in dealing with minority rights. (See p. 196.) *Thirdly*, under s. 177, Financial Services Act 1986, the Trade Secretary may appoint inspectors to investigate insider dealing.

Appointment of inspectors

The Department of Trade and Industry *may* appoint an inspector on the application of 200 members, or of members holding not less than one-tenth of the shares issued, or where the company does not have a share capital, e.g. a guarantee company without a share capital, on the application of not less than one-fifth in number of the persons on the company's register of members whether that fraction is more or less than 200. (S. 431(1) and (2).)

The application must be supported by such evidence as the Department may require in order to show that there is good reason for the investigation asked for. Furthermore the Department may, before appointing an inspector, require the applicants to give security up to an amount not exceeding £5,000 for the costs of the investigation. (S. 431(4).)

The company may also apply to the Department and the application would normally be initiated by the directors or by the members by ordinary resolution. (S. 431(2)(c).)

The power to appoint inspectors is exercised by a Department official called the Inspector of Companies who acts on behalf of and in the name of the Secretary of State for Trade and Industry. The usual practice is to appoint two inspectors: an eminent accountant and a barrister (usually a QC). It should be noted that the power in s. 431 is permissive in that the Department *is not bound* to appoint inspectors. As regards the requirement of 'good reason', the Department is not obliged under s. 431 (or s. 432, see below) to reveal what the reasons are or who has supplied the information leading to the appointment of inspectors. (*Norwest Holst Ltd v Secretary of State for Trade* [1978] 3 All ER 280.) It is apparently not possible to appoint inspectors if all that is alleged is negligent mismanagement of the company's affairs by its directors. (*Re SBA Properties Ltd* [1967] 2 All ER 615.)

The Department *must* appoint an inspector where the company asks that its affairs be investigated, or the court by order so decides. (S. 432(1).)

Under s. 432(2) the Department may independently appoint an inspector to a company where it is brought to the notice of the Department that there are circumstances suggesting—

(i) that its affairs are being or have been conducted with intent to defraud its creditors or the creditors of any other person or otherwise for a fraudulent or unlawful purpose, or in a manner which is unfairly prejudicial to some part of its members or that any actual or proposed act or omission of the company (including an act or omission on its behalf) is or would be so prejudicial, or that it was formed for any fraudulent or unlawful purpose; *or*

(ii) that persons concerned with its formation or the management of its affairs are defrauding the company or its members or are involved in 'other misconduct' towards them; *or*

(iii) that the members of the company are not being given all the information with respect to its affairs which they might reasonably expect.

The powers in (i)–(iii) above apply even though the company is in voluntary winding up and all references to 'members' include those who have taken a transfer or who are personal representatives but who are not on the register of members.

It will be noted that s. 432(2) is a permissive power. An application could be made to the court under s. 432(1) by an individual shareholder, in particular to reverse a decision of the Department not to appoint inspectors under s. 432(2) (i), (ii), (iii) (see above).

The use of what is now s. 432(1) is rare but it has been of advantage to the company as a method of controlling a receiver. Thus in *R. v Board of Trade, ex parte St. Martin's Preserving Co Ltd* [1964] 2 All ER 561 the debenture holders had appointed a receiver and a successful application was made under what is now s. 432(1) to allow the directors and members of the company to check, through the medium of an inspector, the way in which the receiver was conducting the company's affairs and in particular to investigate his disposal of the company's shareholding in a sub-subsidiary.

Section 432(2) is the sub-section which is of most use to a minority. Under it *anyone* can complain to the Department, e.g. one shareholder, regardless of holding, and even non-members, e.g. the Panel on Take-overs and Mergers which initiated the Pergamon Press investigation. The Department, when appointing an inspector need not reveal to the company involved which of the grounds of s. 432(2) (i), (ii), (iii) (see above) it is relying on. (*Norwest Holst Ltd v Secretary of State for Trade* [1978] 3 All ER 280.)

Section 432(2) (iii) (see above) is not confined to information to which a shareholder is entitled by law. The Department may initiate an investigation even though the members have received all the information which the Companies Act requires to be disclosed in the accounts and directors' report. This is of particular importance to minorities, since a major weakness of a minority in terms of seeking redress is that the directors have access to all the company's records, some of which a minority shareholder is not allowed by company legislation to inspect, e.g. minutes of board meetings.

The expression 'other misconduct' in s. 432(2) (ii) does not extend to negligence so that the Department cannot initiate an investigation merely because of allegations of negligence on the part of the directors. (*Re SBA Properties Ltd* [1967] 2 All ER 615.)

It should be noted that the Companies Act 1980 substituted for the words 'in a manner oppressive' in what is now s. 432(2) the words 'unfairly prejudicial to some part of the members'. This may widen the scope of the section. The word 'oppressive' has received a restricted interpretation by the courts. In particular, negligent mismanagement of the company's affairs by the directors causing losses has not hitherto been regarded as oppressive. (*Re Five Minute Car Wash Service Ltd* [1966] 1 All ER 242.) The new provision could extend to negligent mis-management, but note the decision in *Carrington Viyella* at p. 193. The 1985 Act also makes it clear that 'member' includes a personal representative of a deceased member or a trustee in bankruptcy of a member or any other person to whom shares have been transmitted by law. The 1985 Act also provides that an inspector can be appointed, even though the company is in voluntary winding up so that the majority cannot put the company into liquidation in order to avoid an investigation of its affairs.

Inspector's powers

An inspector appointed under ss. 431, 432 or 442 (see below) has the following powers—

(i) He can investigate the affairs of other companies where they are or were at the relevant time part of a group of companies to which the company being investigated belongs or belonged. The inspectors may report on these other companies so far as is relevant to the main investigation. (S. 433.) If inspectors wish to look at companies, the affairs of which may be relevant to their inquiries but which do not fall within the provision of s. 433, they may ask the Department to extend the investigation to these companies.

(ii) He has power to examine and require production of documents during an inspection. Thus s. 434 obliges *all officers and agents* of the company to produce documents and attend before the inspector to answer questions and give any other assistance. If the inspector wishes to examine those persons on oath s. 434 allows this and removes the previous requirement under which the inspectors had to apply to the court.

Section 434 obliges *persons other than officers or agents* of the company to produce books and documents and generally to give assistance and to attend before the inspectors who may examine them on oath.

If any person refuses to comply with the lawful requirement of an inspector the inspector may certify the refusal to the court and the court may in the absence of a satisfactory defence punish the person concerned as if he had been in contempt of court. (S. 436.) It seems that mere refusal to answer a question on the ground that it might incriminate will not be punished as contempt. (*McClelland, Pope & Langley v Howard*, 1966.[210])

Under s. 435 inspectors are empowered to investigate the private bank accounts of any of the company's directors. However, certain events must have occurred before the power to inspect arises. The main events are as follows—

(i) his emoluments have been paid into the account but omitted from financial statements contrary to Sched 5;

(ii) money has been paid into the account in respect of a contract with the company not disclosed in financial statements, e.g. a loan;

(iii) money has been paid in or out of the account, being money related in any way to misconduct, whether fraudulent or not.

Although proceedings before inspectors are only administrative and not judicial or quasi-judicial, inspectors are required to act fairly and so if they are disposed to criticize or condemn anyone in their report, they must give him an opportunity to correct or contradict that allegation. (*Maxwell v Department of Trade and Industry*, 1974.[211])

Inspector's report

An inspector may, and if the Department require it must, make interim reports to the Department. There must be a final written or printed report made to the Department at the end of the investigation. (S. 437.)

The Department will forward a copy of the inspector's report to the registered office of the company, and if the Department think fit to members or creditors of the company investigated, or of any other company dealt with in the report, *on request and on payment of a fee*. Where the inspector was appointed under s. 431, the persons who applied for the investigation are entitled to a copy on request. Where the inspector was appointed under s. 432 in pursuance of a court order, a copy of the report must be sent to the court. The Department may also decide to have the report printed and published. (S. 437.)

Expenses of Investigation. The expenses of the investigation, where the inspector is appointed by the Department, are payable in the first place by the Department, subject to the Department's right to recover from certain persons e.g. any company in whose name proceedings are brought is liable to repay to the extent of money or property recovered by it as a result of the proceedings. (S. 439.)

Evidential Value of the Inspector's Report. A copy of any report of any inspector appointed under ss. 431 or 432 of the Act, authenticated by the seal of the company whose affairs have been investigated, shall be admissible in any legal proceedings as evidence of the opinion of the inspector in relation to any matter contained in the report including the possible disqualification of a director. (S. 441.)

Investigations as to ownership

Appointment of Inspectors to investigate the Ownership of a Company. Where the Department of Trade thinks that there is good reason for going behind a company's register of members in order to ascertain who actually controls the company, as where the shares are held by nominees, the Department may appoint one or more inspectors to investigate and report on the membership of the company. (S. 442(1).) The inspector's appointment will normally define the scope of his inquiries and in particular may limit it to certain shares or debentures. (S. 442(2).)

An investigation of this kind can be requested by 200 members, or holders of not less than one-tenth of the shares issued, or where the company does not have a share capital, by not less than one-fifth of the members. When such a request is made, the Department must appoint an inspector to investigate the matters required by the applicants, unless it thinks that the request is vexatious or its scope is unreasonable. (S. 442(3).)

The inspector has power, subject to the terms of his appointment, to investigate arrangements or understandings relevant to the purposes of his investigation which, while not legally binding, are being or have been or may be observed in practice. (S. 442(4).) The expenses of any investigation under s. 442 are to be paid by the Department out of money provided by Parliament. (S. 443(4).)

Power to Investigate Ownership of Shares or Debentures without Appointing an Inspector. If the Department thinks that there is a good reason to investigate the ownership of any shares or debentures of a company and that it is unnecessary to appoint an inspector for the purpose, the Department may require any person whom they have reasonable cause to believe to be interested in the said shares or debentures, or to have acted as the solicitor or agent of some other person interested, to give the Department such information as they can as to the present and past interests in the shares or debentures, and the names and addresses of persons interested, and of any persons who have acted or do act on behalf of them. (S. 444(1).)

Power to impose Restrictions on Shares or Debentures. Where there has been an investigation under s. 442 or 444, and it appears to the Department that there is difficulty in finding out the relevant facts about the shares or debentures either issued or about to be issued, because the person concerned will not assist, the Department may by order direct that the shares or debentures shall until further notice be subject to the following restrictions—

(i) Any transfer or issue of the shares or debentures shall be void.

(ii) No voting rights shall be exercisable.

(iii) No rights issues shall be made in respect of the shares.

(iv) No payment shall be made of any sum due from the company on the shares or debentures, whether in respect of capital or otherwise, e.g. a dividend, except in a liquidation. (Ss. 445 and 454.)

Penalties of fines and imprisonment are provided for persons who ignore the restrictions.

It should be noted that nothing in ss. 431 to 446 requires disclosure to the Department or any inspector appointed by the Department of any information which a person would in the High Court be entitled to refuse to disclose on the grounds of legal professional privilege. This applies whether or not the person in question is a lawyer, but in the latter case the name and address of his client must be disclosed. Privilege may be waived by the client. (S. 452.)

The main reason for the inclusion of the above powers was to expose foreign control of United Kingdom companies, particularly newspapers. However, the provisions have been used by shareholders who felt that a certain person or syndicate was getting into a position of control of the company behind nominees and was therefore able to change the management style. In addition, they have been used by the existing directors controlling the company to ascertain the identity of a potential take-over bidder. Of particular importance in this context is Rule 9 of the City Code (see p. 391) which requires a person, or persons acting in concert, who have acquired 30 per cent of the equity shares of a listed company to make a mandatory bid for the rest of those equity shares. An investigation into ownership of shares may lead to the City Panel's insistence on the making of a mandatory bid.

The criminal penalties available against persons failing to give information about their holdings or giving false information are moderately severe, i.e. at a maximum, imprisonment for two years and a fine of unlimited amount. However, these penalties are not available against persons living outside the jurisdiction, which is a major weakness, though the sanctions under s. 445 in regard to restrictions over the securities involved can be applied regardless of the whereabouts of the owner.

Restrictions imposed by the Department under s. 445 can be lifted by the court in appropriate circumstances. Thus in *Re Ashbourne Investments Ltd* [1978] 2 All ER 418 the court released restrictions placed by the Department on transfer of shares in Ashbourne, as part of an investigation into ownership, so that the shares could be acquired after the making of a mandatory bid in accordance with the City Code by the syndicate which the investigation had revealed to be in a mandatory bid situation.

In the past the court had a complete discretion to lift the restrictions. Now the court (or the Secretary of State) may lift the restrictions only—

(i) if the relevant facts regarding the shares have been disclosed;

(ii) no unfair advantage has accrued to any person as a result of the earlier failure to make disclosure.

Before leaving the subject of ownership of shares, it should be noted that the Companies Act 1985 contains provisions under which a public company may make enquiries of persons believed to have an interest in its voting shares. (See p. 183.)

Power of Trade Secretary to present a winding up petition

Under s. 440 the Department may present a petition to the court that a company be wound up if the court thinks it is just and equitable for this to be done where an investigation of the company's affairs reveals that this is expedient *in the public interest*, and without having to show as before that the company was being run *fraudulently*. Further, under s. 460 the Department may ask the court for an order giving relief to minority shareholders unfairly prejudiced.

Civil and criminal proceedings

The Department may also institute criminal proceedings for offences revealed by inspectors' reports without having to refer to the Director of Public Prosecutions.

Section 438 provides that the Department may also bring civil proceedings if it feels that it is in the public interest to do so. These proceedings may be brought by the Department in the name, and on behalf, of the company. The Department must indemnify the company against costs or expenses incurred by it in connection with such proceedings. If civil proceedings are properly brought under s. 438 and there is no evidence to show that the company will be able to pay the defendant's costs if the defence succeeds, the defendant is fully protected by the indemnity provision in the section under which the Department must indemnify the company against costs or expenses which it cannot pay, and security cannot be ordered under s. 726. (*Selangor United Rubber Estates Ltd v Cradock (No. 3)* [1968] 2 All ER 1073.)

An inspector may, at any time in the course of his investigation, give the Department a more informal briefing. Section 437(1A) provides that any persons who have been appointed under ss. 431 or 432 *may* inform the Trade Secretary (and *must* if he so directs) of any matters coming to their knowledge as a result of the investigation.

Power to require production of documents

In the past, the Department was reluctant to appoint inspectors because such an appointment often cast doubt and suspicion on a company even if the report was good. However, many of the powers given in earlier legislation in connection with production of the company's books and papers arose only on the appointment of an inspector. Now ss. 447–453 give the Department the right to require production of documents without first appointing an inspector and without revealing to the public any interest which the Department may have in the company.

The powers are potentially effective in that the Department can apply for a warrant to get a company's books and papers (where the company's officers will not supply them), by entry and search of premises. Quite severe penalties are imposed for concealment or destruction of information.

Investigation—insider dealing

Section 177 of the Financial Services Act 1986 gives the Trade Secretary power to appoint inspectors to investigate and report on suspected infringements of insider dealing legislation. (See p. 395.)

15 Amalgamations, reconstructions, take-overs and insider dealing

The ways in which companies can alter their structures are set out below.

Objects clause

We have already considered the provisions of ss. 4–6 which contain procedures under which a company may alter its objects clause to incorporate a new business. (See further p. 65.)

Reduction of capital

If the company merely wishes to reduce its share capital it may do so under the procedures set out in ss. 135–141. The reduction requires the passing of a special resolution and the subsequent confirmation of the court. (See p. 99.)

Variation of shareholders' rights under the Memorandum and Articles or under s. 125

If the company wishes to alter the rights of shareholders this can be effected by the approval of the variation at class meetings followed by a special resolution of the company. There is, of course, always the possibility that dissentients within the class will apply to the court under s. 127. (See p. 95.)

The relevant sections apply only to registered companies and in addition do not enable any variation to be made in the rights of creditors, including debenture holders. Often, however, the trust deed of an issue of debentures will contain a similar variation clause under which the rights of debenture holders can be varied. In such a case, however, s. 127 does not apply, nor does s. 459: the only remedy of dissenting debenture holders being to plead a general fraud on the minority.

Purchase of own shares and financial assistance

As we have seen, s. 162 allows the purchase by a company of its own shares (see further p. 105), while ss. 151–158 lay down procedures under which a company may give, in appropriate circumstances, financial assistance for the acquisition of its shares. (See further p. 161.)

Re-registration

It should also be borne in mind that a private limited company may now re-register as unlimited (s. 49), but only with the consent of all the members (s. 49(8)) and that an unlimited company may re-register as a private limited company (s. 51), though with the preservation of the liability of former members. (S. 77, Insolvency Act 1986.)

Other methods of changing corporate structures

In addition to the areas of reconstruction described above for most of the transactions which a company wishes to enter into, the powers of the board combined with the approval of 51 per cent of the members in general meeting will suffice. Why, then, is it necessary to include in the Companies Act 1985, s. 425 and in the Insolvency Act 1986, s. 110 to deal with arrangements and reconstructions?

The reason is that the provisions referred to above do not permit a company to *compel* a shareholder to sell or otherwise dispose of his shares, except as part of a s. 135 reduction when he is, for example, paid off, or under s. 429 in a take-over (see below). Nor do they allow the rights of creditors to be affected or enable the liability of members to be increased without their individual consent. Nor, again, do they provide a means of amalgamating two or more companies or the transfer of the undertaking of one company to another, or the demerger or partition of a company into separate management in another company or companies.

Section 425 and s. 110 of the Insolvency Act 1986 provide procedures for these kinds of changes to be made in a corporate structure.

In addition, there are some companies which cannot remedy internal problems by the use of the specific procedures referred to above. For example, the provisions of s. 125 allowing variation of shareholders' rights do not apply to companies which do not have a share capital. Therefore, if the rights of members are to be varied, s. 425 will be used. (See *NFU Development Trust Ltd*, 1973.[212])

AMALGAMATIONS AND RECONSTRUCTIONS

The term 'reconstruction' is not defined by company legislation. However, it may be said that in a reconstruction the undertaking of the company concerned is preserved and is carried on *after* reconstruction by substantially the *same people* as it was before.

The contrast with an 'amalgamation' is that while a reconstruction consists of the reorganization of one company or group, an amalgamation involves two or more companies (e.g. A and B) being brought together under one. That one may be either a new company, C, to absorb both A and B, or one of the companies, say B, may absorb the other, A.

The take-over

Section 110 of the Insolvency Act 1986 is useful in obtaining mergers where the boards of the companies concerned are willing for the merger to take place. If they face opposition from members and/or creditors, then s. 425 would be the better approach.

In a take-over proper, the board of the company to be acquired, say B is not willing to co-operate so that the company seeking to acquire is forced to address an offer direct to the shareholders of B. This area of corporate activity is, as we shall see, not covered by the law, control depending upon the extra-legal rules of the Panel on Take-overs and Mergers, though there are now criminal penalties for insider dealing generally and during a take-over, under the Companies Act 1985.

In an amalgamation or take-over involving A and B where A and B are in a similar line of business or are complementary, as where A makes the goods and B markets them, there is potentially a monopoly and the Director of Fair Trading has, under the Fair Trading Act 1973, power by statutory instrument to impede the merger or dismember the integrated undertaking if the amalgamation has taken place.

AMALGAMATION (OR RECONSTRUCTION) UNDER S. 110, INSOLVENCY ACT 1986

Section 110 gives a liquidator power to accept shares as consideration for the sale of the property of a company, so that if A is in voluntary liquidation it may empower its liquidator by special resolution to sell its business and assets to B in exchange for B's shares.

The section would be used where there was no real opposition to an *amalgamation* by the members of A and no compromise with creditors was necessary. There are no provisions for variation of creditors' rights. Creditors are still entitled to prove in the liquidation of A.

If, in order to effect a *reconstruction*, the transfer of the undertaking of one company, A, to another, B, is to be associated with the liquidation of A, the scheme may be carried out under s. 110 provided no compromises are required. For example, the section may be used to *demerge*, as where the various business activities of one large company, A, are placed under separate management in a number of other companies, B, C, and D, and A is wound up. It may also be used to *partition* companies, as where a family company, E, is carrying on various activities and certain members of the family wish to carry on the activities separately through independent companies, F, G, and H, and E is to be wound up.

Procedure

This is as follows—

(*a*) The company proposing to be wound up voluntarily will pass a special resolution for winding up and appoint a liquidator.

(*b*) It will authorize the liquidator by special resolution to transfer the company's assets to a new company in return for shares in the new company. The new company may be one formed for the purpose or it may be an existing company.

(*c*) Such shares will be distributed among the members of the old company.

(*d*) Any member who did not vote in favour of the resolution can express his dissent by serving a written notice on the liquidator within seven days requiring him either—

    (i) to abstain from carrying the scheme into effect, or

    (ii) to purchase his shares at a price to be fixed by agreement or by arbitration, and the company must not be wound up until any such dissentient has been paid off, so that opposition from too many members could be costly.

(*e*) In *Payne v The Cork Co Ltd*, 1900[213] it was held that any provision in the articles preventing a member from dissenting was void.

(*f*) If an order for the compulsory winding-up of the company is made within a year, the special resolution authorizing the transfer is void unless the leave of the court is given (s. 110(6)).

(*g*) It should be noted that in the case of a creditor's voluntary winding up, the consent of the liquidation committee or the court is necessary. (S. 110(3)(*b*).) Apart from this there is no provision for a compromise with creditors.

AMALGAMATION (OR RECONSTRUCTION) UNDER S. 425

If, on a company *reconstruction*, any compromise or arrangement is proposed between the company and its members or creditors s. 425

must be used. The use of this section is essential for *amalgamation* where rights of members, debenture holders and creditors are to be compromised.

Procedure

This is as follows—

(i) The court has to be consulted at the outset and must be asked to direct the holding of meetings of members, creditors and debenture holders to discuss the proposed scheme. At this first stage the court will not exercise its discretion to call the meetings if, having regard to the opposition to the scheme by the holders of the majority of the votes, the meetings will serve no useful purpose. In addition, the court is concerned to see that the meetings are properly constituted. For example, a class meeting of shareholders may not be enough if there are groups within each class with different interests. (*Re Hellenic and General Trust Ltd*, 1975.[6]) The same problems can exist with creditors who may have different interests, e.g. some may have securities and others not.

If the court agrees, the meetings will be summoned and full details of the scheme presented. The scheme may involve a winding up of the company and a transfer of assets under s. 427 (see below) or it may be an internal reconstruction of the kind seen in *NFU Development Trust Ltd*, 1973.[212] In particular, the scheme must disclose the effect of the amalgamation upon directors, especially where it involves the retirement of some of them and payment to them of compensation for loss of office. This must be disclosed in the notices and sanctioned by the members. (Ss. 313 and 314.)

Where the rights of debenture holders are affected, a reference to the material interests, if any, of the trustees for the debenture holders must be disclosed as for directors.

(ii) The scheme must be approved by a majority in number and three-quarters in value of the members, creditors, and debenture holders. For example, if a company has 100 members and A has got 901 shares of £1 each, and the other 99 members have one share each, then the rest cannot force a scheme on A. Equally, A plus 49 of the rest cannot force a scheme on the remainder but A plus 50 of the rest can force the scheme on the others. The same rules apply to creditors and debenture holders. The court must then be asked to consent to the scheme as approved. The court will have to be satisfied in particular that creditors are not being prejudiced by the scheme of arrangement proposed by the company; and creditors have not only the right to hold their own meeting before the court hearing, as we have seen, but also to be represented in court on the issue of the court's approval. In practice, the company will make sure at a very early stage that creditors are fully satisfied with the proposed scheme and will not raise objections. Furthermore, the court must be satisfied that there is a genuine 'compromise or arrangement' within the meaning of s. 425; this implies some element of accommodation on each side, so that a scheme involving the total surrender of the rights of one side will not be approved. (See *NFU Development Trust Ltd*, 1973.[212])

(iii) If the court approves the scheme it will do so by order and a copy of the court order certified by the Office of the Supreme Court is delivered to the Registrar at which point the scheme becomes binding on all concerned.

Although any member or creditor can ask the court to convene meetings under s. 425, provided some compromise or arrangement is proposed, it appears that the court cannot do this unless the company has generated, or at least approves of, the scheme. Thus in *Re Savoy Hotel Ltd* [1981] 3 All ER 646, Trusthouse Forte had made a bid for the shares of Savoy but could not get acceptance from the major class of voting shareholders. Trusthouse Forte asked the Court to convene a meeting of those shareholders under s. 425 so that the bid might be discussed with them, and hopefully they might be convinced to accept it. Nourse J held that he had no power to convene the meeting because the Savoy Company had not generated the scheme, nor did the board or the voting members appear to approve of it.

The provisions of s. 427

Where a scheme under s. 425 involves a winding up, either to an internally reconstructed new company having the same members, debenture holders and creditors, or to a new or existing company as part of a merger, the court may by order—

(i) Transfer assets to the other company.

(ii) Allot shares or debentures to members and debenture holders of the old company.

(iii) Allow the old company's actions to be brought in the name of the other company.

(iv) Dissolve the old company without a winding up.

(v) Provide for dissentients otherwise than outlined in the scheme, e.g. by requiring them to be paid off.

Orders made under s. 427 must be filed with the Registrar.

Examples of schemes of internal reconstruction approved by the court under s. 425

Where s. 425 is used internally it represents a means by which a company can enter into a compromise or arrangement with its creditors and/or members without going into liquidation. Schedule 4, Part I of the Insolvency Act 1986 allows a compromise with creditors in the context of a winding up, though Part I of the 1986 Act provides a procedure for compromise with creditors, even though the company concerned is not in course of winding up. These provisions are considered in more detail at p. 399.

The court has approved the following types of internal reconstructions under s. 425—

(i) Debenture holders have given extension of time for the payment of their loan capital.

(ii) Debenture holders have accepted a cash payment less than the par value of the debentures.

(iii) Debenture holders have given up their security, thus releasing it to secure further loans.

(iv) Debenture holders have exchanged their debentures for shares.

(v) Creditors have taken cash in part payment of their debt and the balance in shares.

(vi) Preference shareholders have given up their right to arrears of dividend.

(vii) To simplify the capital structure of companies within a group as where H is the holding company of several partly-owned subsidiaries, all of which have old-fashioned complex capital structures comprising many types of shares carrying widely varying rights. The capital structure of the group has been simplified by exchanging all the subsidiary companies' shares held by minority shareholders for ordinary shares or even loan stock in the holding company by means of a scheme of arrangement under s. 425.

As (vii) above shows, reconstruction does not necessarily involve compromising with creditors, nor is it always set in a context of financial difficulty. It is, for example, a technique used for demerging and incentives to dismantle a large group of companies are given, as we have seen, by the Companies Act 1985 in terms of share premium (see p. 175), and also by revenue law, which is not considered here.

An example of a demerger attracting share premium relief appears below. The activities of the companies are indicated, as is the holding of H in each.

Old group structure

Procedure

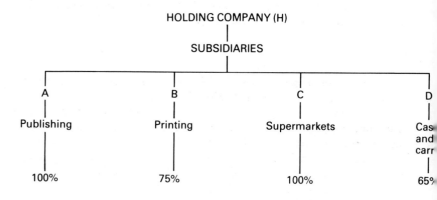

(a) A allots 1,000 £1 ordinary shares (valued at £6.00 per share) to H.

(b) H transfers its 75 per cent holding in B to A.

(c) C allots 1,000 £1 ordinary shares (valued at £6.00 per share) to H.

(d) H transfers its 65 per cent holding in D to C.

(e) H is then wound up, its holdings in A and C being sold, e.g. by a public placing.

New demerged structure

Share premium relief: s. 132

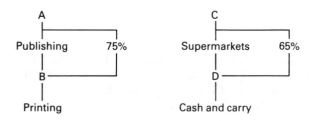

A and C need only transfer to share premium the 'minimum premium value'. This is the amount, if any, by which the base values of the

384

shares in B and D exceed the aggregate nominal value of the shares A and C allotted to H.

Base value is the lower of the cost to H of the shares in B and D and the amount which the shares of B and D were stated immediately prior to the transfer in the accounting records of H.

Example

(1) Shares in B and C cost H £4,000 in each case but stood in the accounting records of H at £3,000: base value £3,000.

(2) Nominal value of shares allotted by A and C was £1,000, so minimum premium value is £2,000. This goes to a share premium account in the books of A and C, but not the true value of the consideration received from B and D by allotting shares to H. The true value, of course, is the total value of the assets of B and D which could run into many thousands or millions of pounds.

It should be noted that share premium relief under s. 132 is available where the consideration for the issue of the shares consists of any *non-cash assets* of the company providing the consideration and not merely of shares in another subsidiary of the holding company. (SI 1984/2007.)

TAKE-OVERS

Definition

On the assumption that A Ltd is acquiring B Ltd, a take-over may be defined as an offer to all the shareholders of B or one or more classes of shareholders of B, to buy their shares for cash and/or securities in A, the purpose being that A will obtain control of B. A's offer is normally conditional upon sufficient acceptances to ensure control.

A take-over proper occurs when the directors of B do not support the bid. In such a situation A must deal direct with the shareholders of B. As we have seen, if the directors of B do support a merger with A, then they can call the necessary meetings and in general terms organize an amalgamation by methods set out in s. 110, Insolvency Act 1986 or s. 425 which have already been dealt with.

Why the City Code?

The City Code and the Panel on Take-Overs and Mergers which administers it are required because at the present time there is no legal control in regard to the following—

(i) *The offer document*, which is used to convey the offer to the shareholders of the company to be acquired, in this case B. The reason for this is that it is not a prospectus within the meaning of s. 56. The offer is not to the public, nor is it an offer to subscribe for shares, 'subscription' having been defined in *Government Stock, etc v Christopher*, 1956[77] as taking for cash; nor is there a purchase of the shares within the meaning of s. 56 which in *Christopher's case* was defined as meaning the purchase of shares already in issue, whereas in the take-over situation the shares are unissued until the bid is accepted and goes ahead.

However, the documents issued by the offeror (or the offeree board, giving, e.g. advice to its members whether or not to accept) are governed by Section J of the City Code Rules 23–27. The full details are beyond the scope of a book of this nature (but see p. 390). However, Rule 23.1 expresses the general standard of care as follows: 'Each document or advertisement issued to shareholders in connection with an offer must, as is the case with a prospectus, satisfy the highest standards of accuracy and the information contained therein must be adequately and fairly presented. This applies whether it is issued by the company director or by an advisor on his behalf'.

(ii) *Partial bids*. In the absence of the City Code there would be nothing to prevent a company making a partial bid in order to achieve control of a company 'on the cheap' as it were. It is not in practice necessary to acquire 50 per cent or more of the voting power of a company in order to control it. The making of partial bids is controlled by the Code and there are provisions under which a mandatory bid must be made for the remainder of the shares of the company to be acquired once a certain number of shares in that company has been obtained. These matters will be considered in more detail later.

(iii) *Insider dealing*. The Code deals with insider trading in quoted companies and the City Panel can publish reprimands in respect of those who deal inside. These are extra-legal sanctions, the 1985 Act providing for criminal sanctions. (See p. 395.)

(iv) *Misleading profit forecasts*. Directors and other officers of companies do, from time to time, make public statements as to the future profits of companies which are misleading. The Panel has been active in this area in requiring the publication of corrections of misleading statements.

In addition, when a forecast of profit before taxation appears in a document addressed to shareholders, there must be included forecasts of taxation, extraordinary items and minority interests.

(v) *Tactics of directors*. The directors of the company to be acquired have in the past used tactics such as the issue of additional shares to a company or persons who would not accept the bid and so frustrate it. See, for example, *Hogg v Cramphorn*, 1966.[67] But for the Code redress in such cases could only be obtained by the expensive and slow procedure of an action at law to nullify the allotment, as was done in *Hoggs's Case*. The Panel could now take action on the basis of the Code's General Principle 7 which states—

'At no time after a bona fide offer has been communicated to the board of an offeree company or after the board of an offeree company has reason to believe that a bona fide offer might be imminent may any action be taken by the board of the offeree company in relation to the affairs of the company, without the approval of the shareholders in general meeting, which could effectively result in any bona fide offer being frustrated or in the shareholders being denied an opportunity to decide on its merits.'

In the past directors' tactics used to frustrate a bid have often consisted of the issue of additional shares to a company or person(s) who would not accept the bid, without consulting the shareholders of the victim company as to whether this tactic of the directors was acceptable. Obviously General Principle 7 would apply to such a situation but now s. 80 provides that the authority of the company is required before the allotment of certain securities by the directors. (See p. 137.) This is reinforced by Rule 21 which carries a similar provision regarding the issue of shares but extends to the making of other contracts otherwise than in the ordinary course of business.

However, there are some situations where General Principle 7 and Rule 21 would be the only sanction. For example, where the directors lease off the company's property to put it beyond the control of the bidder so that he does not continue with his bid. If we assume that company B, our victim company, owns the freehold of a large block of flats which a bidder for company B wishes to demolish in order to develop the site, then if the directors of B were to lease out the block of flats for say, 99 years, thus preventing the bidder, even if he were successful, from demolishing the premises for that period so that he did not proceed with his bid, then such a tactic would, unless approved by ordinary resolution of the members, infringe General Principle 7 and Rule 21 and could be the basis of a complaint to the Panel and action by it to prevent infringement of the Code.

Has the Code any teeth?

Since the whole of this chapter is based on the acquisition of companies where at least one is a *listed* company, the answer is 'yes'. This is based on the fact that every company which seeks the Stock Exchange as a market for purchase and sale of its securities is required to enter into a 'listing agreement' with that body which binds the company to observe certain rules and procedures. The ultimate sanction for breach of the agreement is in essence very simple and consists in the deprivation of the facilities of the market. The regulations of the Stock Exchange do not have the force of law but it will be readily understood that with a sanction of the nature mentioned above the simple directive in Section 6 of the rule book for listing of shares: 'The Council attach great importance to observance of the City Code on Take-Overs and Mergers . . .' is no doubt sufficient to gain compliance with these regulations, even though compliance with the regulations is, strictly speaking voluntary.

In addition, the membership of the Panel covers a wide range of services within the City and therefore a flagrant flouting of the Code could lead to problems in addition to the loss of the Stock Exchange market for purchase and sale of securities. The Code is issued on the authority of the Panel on Take-Overs and Mergers and certain member bodies of that Council are represented on the Panel. They are as follows:

The Bank of England
The Accepting Houses Committee
The Association of Investment Trust Companies
Association of British Insurers
The Committee of London and Scottish Bankers
The Confederation of British Industry
The Issuing Houses Association
The National Association of Pension Funds
The Financial Intermediaries, Managers and Brokers Regulating Association
The Council of the Stock Exchange
The Unit Trust Association
The Consultative Committee of Accountancy Bodies
The Foreign Bankers in London
The Foreign Brokers in London
The Institute of Chartered Accountants in England and Wales

In addition, the Panel publishes reprimands which may even appear in the professional press. The publication of this sort of information should have some effect upon practitioners for publication leads to knowledge in their colleagues that they have transgressed the ethics of the Code.

The system works efficiently. At any time before or during the offer period any party or his adviser can contact any member of the Panel executive and get a speedy ruling—usually within a day. At very short notice an appeal can be made to the Panel itself, the members of which will review the decision of the executive. Further appeals go to the Appeal Committee which comprises an independent chairman and three members of the Panel who have not previously dealt with the matter under review. It is quite rare in practice for the appeal procedures to be invoked, even though the executive takes many decisions every day.

All that now remains is to consider some of the major steps in a take-over bid and see how the various rules of the Code affect the position. In addition we must give special consideration to the duties of directors in take-overs since this is not only the greatest area of practical problems but is also most likely to be required for examination purposes.

In all situations company A is attempting to acquire company B.

Secrecy during negotiations—insider dealing

The relevant provisions, which are set out in Rules 2 and 4, are designed to prevent insider dealing and they are *extra-legal* in their operation. The *legal* provisions, under which insider dealing may, in certain circumstances, be a criminal offence punishable by a fine and/or imprisonment, are set out in the Company Securities (Insider Dealing) Act 1985.

Rule 2, which is concerned with keeping bids secret before public announcement, states: 'The vital importance of absolute secrecy before an announcement must be emphasized'.

Rule 4 requires all persons who have confidential price-sensitive information concerning an offer or contemplated offer to treat it as secret and not pass it on to anyone else unless it is necessary to do so, as where it is part of a person's work to pass it on as, e.g. by one member of an audit team to another as part of the audit function.

Additionally, there must not be dealings in securities of the offeree or the offeror company by persons (other than the offeror) who have price-sensitive information prior to the announcement of an approach by a bidder, or an actual bid or of the termination of negotiations. Dealing is allowed in the shares of the offeror company where the bid will not significantly affect the value of the offeror's shares, which may often be the case. It is the shares of the offeree company which are most likely to be affected by a bid.

If those involved in the negotiations feel that secrecy cannot be maintained they should ask the Stock Exchange for a temporary halt in dealings.

Failure to comply with Rules 2 and 4 may result in a reprimand from the Panel which may be published.

The Rules of the Code are now preventive and information suggesting that insider dealing has taken place which might be revealed by dealings on the Stock Exchange would be passed by the Stock Exchange to the Department of Trade and Industry for investigation.

Offer document—contents

These derive from Section J (consisting of Rules 23–27) of the City Code. Of major importance is the requirement that if profit forecasts or asset revaluations are made, there must be a report on this by auditors, consultant accountants or other experts. In addition, terms of the bid must be received by the board of B three days before its despatch to the shareholders of B. Furthermore, recommendations by the directors of B to their own shareholders must disclose all their holdings in A and B and, additionally, whether they intend to accept the offer themselves.

More important than the contents of the offer document is what an individual shareholder can do if he is misled by the contents of the offer document. While accepting that this branch of the law is not well developed, the judgment of Brightman J in *Gething v Kilner* [1972] 1 WLR 337 would seem to justify the following statement—

'If an offer document or a recommendation circulated by the directors of the offeree company contains a false or misleading statement made knowingly, or presumably, if such a document omits information known to the persons issuing it which the law or good practice requires it to contain, any shareholder of the class to whom the bid is addressed may apply to the court for an injunction to restrain the offeror from proceeding with the bid or declaring it unconditional'.

Partial offers and mandatory offers

In this connection a knowledge of Rule 36 (partial offers) and Rule 9 (mandatory offers) is of importance. However, before considering the Rules relating to partial offers which can result in a bidder obtaining control of a company 'on the cheap', as it were, the nature of a partial bid should be understood. If we take three shareholders of the target company and their holdings to be Mr A (100 shares), Mr B (50 shares), and Mr C (40 shares), then a 50 per cent partial bid will involve an offer to take 50 of A's shares, 25 of B's shares, and 20 of C's. When this sort of bid is being contemplated, Rule 36 must be followed. Under the Rule the Panel's consent is required for any partial offer.

In addition, the following subrules of Rule 36 should be noted.

In the case of an offer which would result in the offeror holding shares carrying less than 30 per cent of the voting rights of a company, consent will normally be granted. (36.1)

Any offer which would result in the offeror holding shares carrying 30 per cent or more of the voting rights of a company must normally be conditional, not only on the relevant number of acceptances being received, but also on approval of the offer, normally signified by means of a separate box on the Form of Acceptance and Transfer, being given by shareholders holding 50 per cent of the voting rights not held by the offeror and persons acting in concert with it. This requirement may on occasion be waived if over 50 per cent of all voting rights of the offeree company are held by one shareholder. (36.5)

Where an offer is made for a company with more than one class of equity share capital which would result in the offeror holding shares carrying 30 per cent or more of the voting rights, a comparable offer must be made for each class. (36.8)

Rule 9. In connection with mandatory offers, the following subrules should be noted.

Except with the consent of the Panel, where (a) any person acquires, whether by a series of transactions over a period of time or not, shares which (taken together with shares held or acquired by persons acting in concert with him) carry 30 per cent or more of the voting rights of the company; or (b) any person who together with persons acting in concert with him holds not less than 30 per cent but more than 50 per cent of the voting rights and such person, or any person acting in concert with him, acquires in any period of 12 months additional shares carrying more than 2 per cent of the voting rights, such person shall extend an offer on the basis set out below to the holders of any class of share capital which carries votes and in which such person or persons acting in concert with him hold shares. A comparable offer shall be extended to the holders of any other class of equity share capital, whether such capital carries voting rights or not. (9.1)

The rule in 1(b) above is to cover those who have made a bid which has failed because of insufficient acceptances but who are left with, e.g. a 35 per cent holding. Such a holder would, on acquisition of more than 2 per cent in the circumstances of (b) above be required to make a mandatory bid.

Immediately upon an acquisition of shares which gives rise to an obligation to make an offer under this Rule, the offeror shall make an announcement of its offer giving the information required by the Code. The announcement of an offer under this Rule should include confirmation by a financial adviser or other appropriate independent party that resources are available to the offeror sufficient to satisfy full acceptance of the offer. (2.5)

Except with the consent of the Panel, no nominee of the offeror or persons acting in concert with it shall be appointed to the board of the offeree company, nor shall the offeror and persons acting in concert with it transfer, or exercise the votes attaching to, any shares in the offeree company, until the offer document has been posted. (9.7)

The Code defines 'acting in concert' as follows: 'Persons acting in concert comprise persons who, pursuant to an agreement or understanding (whether formal or informal), actively co-operate, through the acquisition by any of them of shares in a company, to obtain or consolidate control of that company.'

Then follows a list of persons who will be presumed to be persons acting in concert with others in the same category unless the contrary is established. These include a company, its parent, subsidiaries, and fellow-subsidiaries, and their associated companies.

For this purpose ownership or control of 20 per cent or more of the equity share capital of the company will be regarded as a test of associated company status. Other persons presumed to be acting in concert are a company with any of its directors (together with their close relatives and related trusts); a company with any of its pension funds; a person with any investment company, unit trust or other funds whose investments such person manages on a discretionary basis, a financial adviser with his client in respect of the shareholdings of the financial adviser and all the funds which the financial adviser manages on a discretionary basis, where the shareholdings of the financial adviser and any of those funds in the client total 10 per cent or more of the client's equity share capital, and finally, directors of a company which is subject to an offer or where the directors have reason to believe a *bona fide* offer for their company may be imminent.

It should be noted that although an interest of under 30 per cent does not constitute control in the Takeover Panel's eyes, the Office of Fair Trading may take the view that it could constitute a merger giving the Office of Fair Trading power to refer the matter to the Monopolies Commission with a view to preventing the take-over going ahead if it is thought by the Monopolies Commission to be undesirable in the public interest.

Compulsory acquisition

Section 429 is a section which can be used but only by a corporate bidder who has made a bid to acquire compulsorily the shares of a small minority who have not accepted the offer. The provisions of the section are as follows—

(a) Where A already has not more than 10 per cent of B or no holdings in B at all, then if 90 per cent of B's shareholders, or other shareholders have accepted the offer within four months A may within two months after the reaching of the 90 per cent threshold serve a notice on dissentients that it intends to acquire their shares. The dissentients have one month from the date on which the notice was given to appeal to the court. If there is no appeal or the court does not order otherwise, A acquires the shares.

(*b*) Where A has more than 10 per cent of B, then under s. 428 of the 1985 Act three-quarters in number and 90 per cent in value of B's other shareholders must accept within four months of the offer.

The court will seldom interfere if the offer is fair but will not allow the section to be used for improper purposes such as the expulsion of a minority. (See *Re Bugle Press Ltd* [1960].[214])

Reverse acquisition

Under s. 430A where A has acquired 90 per cent of B but does not intend to buy out the dissentients, then A must notify the dissentients of its acquisition of 90 per cent of B's shares. The dissentients then have three months to request A to buy them out and on receipt of such a request A must do so.

Directors' duties in a take-over by general offer

Suppose that in a bid situation the directors bargain for additional payments to themselves, what can the other shareholders do?

Apart from the provisions of the City Code, if the directors of B retire from office 'golden handshakes' are covered by ss. 314 and 315 and such sums are held in trust for those shareholders who sold their shares as a result of the offer, if the payments were not disclosed and approved by ordinary resolution of the members.

If they do not retire s. 314 does not apply and additional payments made to directors are not recoverable under the 1985 Act. Thus if no change is made in the directorship but, for example, the board are paid £10,000 to persuade them to recommend the offer to the other shareholders, or are paid an increased price for their shares because they hold a large block, it seems there can be no recovery under the section.

It will be apparent, therefore, that there are situations in which the directors, in connection with a take-over bid, may receive additional payments without being liable to account for them under the statute.

The Code also applies and provides that unless the Panel consents the offeror, or persons acting in concert, may not make arrangements to deal or buy or sell shares of the offeree company during an offer or when one is in contemplation, if those arrangements have attached to them favourable conditions not being extended to all shareholders.

The City Code and the supervision of the Panel should in most cases prevent this occurring in the case of public companies but it could still occur in the case of private ones where in fact some of the worst abuses have occurred in the past.

Where a private company is concerned or, in the case of a public company if the Panel is not effective, the most hopeful line, in terms of getting the money back from the directors, is to allege a breach of their fiduciary duties towards the company. The general equitable principle exemplified in *Regal (Hastings) Ltd v Gulliver*, 1942[165] could apply. However, the action is not straightforward because the wrong covered in that case is basically one to the company and payments made to directors to secure favourable recommendation to the shareholders in a bid situation seems merely to be a payment to them in their capacity as directors, no corporate action being involved, though the extra money received is, of course, an undisclosed benefit or profit from office and is recoverable by the company on the basis of a breach of fiduciary duty.

However, it is somewhat futile to allow the company to recover in cases where those who are really wronged are the other shareholders who have sold. Section 315 provides that moneys paid as a result of retirement are held on trust for the shareholders but the judge-made equitable rules as seen in the *Regal Case* do not necessarily extend to shareholders. However, American courts are ahead of ours and have allowed recovery by the individual shareholders who have suffered, notwithstanding that the basic principle in the case was that a duty to the company had been broken.

Dealings in shares during offer period

Another problem which can arise if the directors have been offered incentives to recommend a bid is that the bid price for the shares may be lower than it should be. Where this is so, the offeror company (A) may, in order to enhance its chances of successful control, purchase shares in B on the market at a price higher than the bid price.

Since it is not desirable to fetter the market in shares, Rule 8.1 of the Code provides that dealings in relevant securities by the parties to a take-over and by any associates, for their own account, or the account of discretionary investment clients, must be disclosed daily to the Stock Exchange, the Panel and the press not later than 12 noon on the business day following the date of the transaction. Such disclosures must state the total of all relevant securities of any offeror or the offeree company purchased or sold on any day during the offer period, in the market or otherwise, and the prices paid or received.

In this connection, Rule 6.2 provides that if the offeror or persons acting in concert purchases securities during the offer period at above the offer price, then it shall increase its offer to not less than the highest price paid for the securities so acquired. Rule 7.1 provides that an announcement of any such purchase and the consequent increased offer must be made immediately.

The Code provides that a person with a significant commercial interest in the outcome of an offer should not, without the consent of the Panel, deal in the shares of an offeror or an offeree company during an offer period.

INSIDER DEALING

The matter of insider dealing is covered by the Company Securities (Insider Dealing) Act 1985 and section references are to that Act unless otherwise indicated.

The deals covered

By reason of ss. 1 and 4 the shares concerned must have a published price and so shares quoted on the Stock Exchange are covered, as are shares dealt in on the Unlisted Securities Market, and by companies such as Harvard Securities which make a market in the shares of certain public companies.

However, the Act does not apply the insider dealing provisions to *private, or face-to-face transactions* so that *Percival v Wright*, 1902[171] is unaltered on its own facts.

The sanctions for insider dealing

The sanctions are criminal, not civil. Section 8(1) provides for a maximum of two years' imprisonment and/or an unlimited fine if the offender is convicted on indictment, or a maximum of six months' imprisonment and/or a fine not exceeding £2,000 if there is a summary conviction before magistrates.

To prevent frivolous or vexatious prosecutions s. 8(2) provides that proceedings shall not be instituted except by the Trade Secretary or by, or with the consent of, the Director of Public Prosecutions.

Section 8(3) provides that no transaction is void or voidable by reason only that it contravenes the insider dealing rules. Thus the remedy of rescission of the contract to take shares is not possible. However, ss. 35–38 of the Powers of Criminal Courts Act 1973 give power to the criminal courts to grant monetary compensation to victims of crime and these provisions could be used to compensate a victim of insider dealing for the loss suffered on the transaction. In addition, it may be possible to institute civil proceedings for damages for participating in a criminal conspiracy.

Insiders—generally

Section 1 provides that an insider is a person who is, or at any time in the six months preceding the deal has been 'knowingly connected' with the company whose shares are dealt in. He must also be in possession of unpublished price-sensitive information (psi) in relation to the securities dealt in, which he holds because of his *connection* with the company. Once the information is more than six months old there may be dealing on the basis of it, but this is obviously unlikely because its usefulness will normally have passed with time.

Who is connected with a company?

The reason for the requirement of connection with the company is to avoid the possible prosecution of persons against whom the insider dealing rules are not aimed. For example, the tea lady may, while in the course of serving tea in the board room, overhear psi in relation to the company's shares e.g. an imminent take-over of the company. She may pass this on, or even deal in the shares herself. However, she would normally be saved from prosecution by the fact that she is not connected with the company in the sense required by the Act.

Section 9 deals with those who are connected with a company. There are, broadly speaking, three categories as follows—

(a) *Access relationships.* These are persons with access relationship to the psi in the course of their duties and include directors and senior employees of the company. Clearly, the tea lady does not have an access relationship. In the situation described above the information comes to her by accident and does not arise *from her duties as such*.

(b) *Professional relationships.* These will include accountants, auditors, bankers, and solicitors and the senior employees of their firms or companies.

(c) *Business relationships.* These are more difficult, but in the absence of case law it could include customers of the company, i.e. those who buy or sell goods from or to the company, or a trade union official who is entitled to financial information for the purposes of collective bargaining.

It should be noted that the prohibitions also apply in the case of information about take-over bids and to public servants in relation to information obtained by them in their official capacity. The provisions do not at present extend to employees of nationalized industries or local authorities but the Trade Secretary may make relevant orders.

When is an insider liable?

Under s. 1 an insider is liable if—
   (a) he deals himself; or

(*b*) he counsels or procures another to deal. The person who deals here may also commit an offence if he is a tippee (see below).

An insider is not liable if he gives the psi to another as part of his job. In most cases when he does this he will give it to another insider. For example, suppose X, the finance director of A plc, tells a representative of the company's bankers that the company requires funds to acquire B plc, then X commits no offence, but Y would if he dealt in the shares of either A or B. The representative of the bank would be an insider, i.e. a person connected with the company by reason of a professional relationship.

Tippees

Under s. 1 a tippee is a person *who receives the psi* from an insider knowing that he does not need to give it as part of his job. If the tippee deals he is liable and so is the insider. Those who receive advice to deal but not the psi are not tippees and will not commit an offence by dealing.

Thus if X, the finance director of A plc who has psi regarding a takeover of the company tells his son, Y, that he ought to buy shares in A plc and no more, then X is guilty of an offence, but Y is not. If, on the other hand, X tells Y the details of the bid and then Y deals, both X and Y are liable.

Price-sensitive information

According to s. 10 this means information on *specific matters* relating to, or of concern to the company involved, and which is not generally known to those persons who deal or are likely to deal in its securities, but which would, if generally known to them, be likely materially to affect the price of those securities. For the purposes of the Act a person deals in securities if he buys or sells, or agrees to buy or sell any securities, whether as principal or agent.

The provisions of the Act are therefore restricted to information about *specific* matters and exclude *general overall impressions*, e.g. that a bid might be made. In the absence of case law it is not easy to define specific unpublished information but it must relate to specific matters and not be simply of a general nature. Specific matters could be taken by the court to include those items of company information which the listing agreement of the Stock Exchange requires to be notified to the Quotations Department. The following matters fall into this category—decisions to pay or to pass dividends or interest payments, preliminary announcements of profits, whether annual, half-yearly, or for any period, changes in directorate and proposed changes in capital structure. As regards information which would be of a general nature, the practice in the United States of America indicates that the following would be regarded as general—pricing trends, sale trends, cost trends, accounting policies, company organization concerning structure and changes below directorate, and merger and acquisitions policy which does not relate to specific mergers or specific acquisitions. It cannot be assumed that these views would be followed by judges in this country but they do provide some indication.

Exemptions

A person may deal with impunity even with psi when he deals 'otherwise than with a view of making a profit'. Thus, those who sell to pay a pressing debt are excused and there are also protections for receivers, liquidators, and trustees in bankruptcy. These are extended also to executors and trustees in respect of sales of shares with psi to complete the winding up of an estate or trust. In addition, if trustees receive advice, e.g. from an accountant who is, in fact, an insider, they will be protected unless they *know* that the accountant is prohibited from giving the advice. In other words, the trustees receiving the advice will not be regarded as tippees. There are also protections for those recognized by the Council of the Stock Exchange as carrying on the business of market maker.

MODEL CODE FOR SECURITIES TRANSACTIONS BY DIRECTORS OF LISTED COMPANIES

The Stock Exchange has a Model Code for Securities Transactions, to give guidance as to when it is proper for directors of listed companies to deal in the securities of the company. The Code received widespread acceptance and became part of the Listing Agreement. The main principles of the Code are—

(a) That the directors should not engage in short-term dealings, e.g. purchases and sales over short periods, because it is difficult to avoid the suggestion that such dealing is not based on inside knowledge.

(b) That directors should not deal for a minimum period prior to the announcement of reports and results. Where results are announced half-yearly, the closed period for dealings should be the previous two months but, if announcements are more frequent, e.g. quarterly, the period should be discussed with the Quotations Department.

Directors should not deal either when an exceptional announcement is to be made which would probably affect the market price of the company's shares, or when they are in possession of knowledge, which when accessible to the public, will affect the market price of the shares.

(c) That a minute book or record book of dealings should be kept by the chairman or another director and that the board as a whole should see that directors comply with a practice to be established within the company on the above lines. In this respect a director should ensure that where he is a beneficiary under a trust, the trustees notify him after dealing so that it can be recorded. In addition, a director must return dealings of a spouse or for minor children.

VOLUNTARY ARRANGEMENTS—INSOLVENCY ACT 1986

Part I, i.e. ss. 1–7 of the Insolvency Act 1986 introduces a new voluntary procedure for companies in financial difficulties. It can be put into operation by a liquidator or by an administrator or, in other circumstances, by the directors of the company. The existing provisions under s. 425 of the Companies Act 1985, which are expensive and appropriate only to major reconstructions, continue to be available.

The court is not required to approve any Part I arrangements, though it is available to settle disputes under a procedure allowing a decision to accept the voluntary arrangements to be challenged. If voluntary arrangements are instituted by a liquidator or administrator, they should summon meetings of the company's creditors to consider them and supervise the arrangements if approved. However, directors of a company not in liquidation or administration can initiate voluntary arrangements by approaching an insolvency practitioner with proposals (accompanied by a statement of the company's affairs) to put to creditors and shareholders. If the practitioner is of the opinion that the proposals are workable he will make a report to the court in those terms and call the necessary meetings. If both the creditors' meeting and the members' meeting accept the proposals, or accept them as modified, then they will be binding on all notified creditors and on the company.

There is no need for class meetings of creditors or members, and the court's formal approval is not required. It is the duty of the relevant chairmen to report the result of the meeting to the court. Any person who considers that he has been unfairly prejudiced by it may apply to the court for relief within 28 days of the report.

However, no proposal which affects the right of a secured creditor to enforce his security or of a preferential creditor shall be approved without his consent. If a voluntary arrangement is approved the court can stay all proceedings in a winding up or discharge an administration order. It can also give directions to facilitate the implementation of the approved composition or scheme.

16 Winding up: generally

A company's life can be brought to an end by a process known as *winding up*. This process is carried through by a *liquidator* whose functions are—

   (i) to settle the list of contributories;

  (ii) to collect the company's assets;

 (iii) to discharge the company's liabilities to its creditors;

 (iv) to redistribute the surplus (if any) to the contributories according to the rights attaching to their shares of the company's capital.

There are two methods of winding up—

 (1) a compulsory winding up by the court;

 (2) a voluntary winding up, which may be either a *members'* winding up or a *creditors'* winding up;

We shall now proceed to examine the general characteristics of these various types. Section references are to the Insolvency Act 1986 unless otherwise indicated.

COMPULSORY WINDING UP

A company may be wound up by the court when a number of situations occur—the most common being when the company is unable to pay its debts.

A petition for winding up may be presented by the company or by the Department of Trade and Industry, but is normally presented by a creditor.

When there is a petition for winding up, the court is not forced to make an order, but if it does, it will appoint the liquidator, who realizes the assets and pays the creditors, handing over the surplus (if any) to the shareholders. When the company's affairs are fully wound up, the court will make an order dissolving the company. The order is registered with the Registrar of Companies by the liquidator, and the Registrar makes an entry on the Register dissolving the company from the date of the court order.

VOLUNTARY WINDING UP

A company may be wound up voluntarily, under s. 84—

(a) When the period, if any, fixed for the duration of the company by the articles expires, or the event, if any, occurs, on the occurrence of which the articles provide that the company is to be dissolved, and the company in general meeting has passed an *ordinary resolution* requiring the company to be wound up voluntarily. A limitation on a company's duration is in practice very rare;

(b) If the company resolves by *special resolution* that the company be wound up voluntarily for any cause whatever.

(c) If the company resolves by *extraordinary resolution* to the effect that it cannot by reason of its liabilities continue its business, and that it is advisable to wind up.

When a company has passed a resolution for voluntary winding up, it must give notice of the resolution by an advertisement in the *Gazette* within fourteen days. (S. 85.) The voluntary winding up is deemed to commence at the time of the passing of the resolution. (S. 86.)

Declaration of solvency

Where it is proposed to wind up a company voluntarily, the directors, or a majority of them if there are more than two, may at a meeting of the board make a statutory declaration that they have made a full inquiry into the affairs of the company and have formed the opinion that it will be able to pay its debts in full within a period of 12 months from the beginning of the winding up. To be effective such declaration must be made within the five weeks before the passing of the winding up resolution or on that date but before the resolution was passed, and must be delivered to the Registrar of Companies for registration, and must embody a statement of the company's assets and liabilities as at the latest practicable date before the making of the declaration (s. 89), though errors and omissions will not necessarily render the statement invalid. Thus, in *De Courcy v Clements* [1971] 1 All ER 681, the statement of the company's assets and liabilities was held to be valid even though it omitted to state that a debt of £45,000 was owed by the company to a third party. Megarry J observed that what is now s. 89 did not require absolute perfection since, amongst other things, a liquidator who forms the opinion that the company will not be able to pay its debts in full within the period specified in the declaration of solvency must forthwith summon a creditors' meeting and put the matter to them. (See now p. 413.) The creditors can petition for a compulsory winding up, notwithstanding the voluntary liquidation, and might therefore be regarded as adequately protected. Directors making such a declaration without reasonable grounds are liable to heavy penalties.

The advantage to the company of such a declaration is that the winding up is then a 'members' voluntary winding up.' In the absence of such a declaration, it must be a 'creditors' voluntary winding up.' (S. 90.)

MEMBERS' VOLUNTARY WINDING UP

The company in general meeting must appoint one or more liquidators for the purpose of winding up the company and distributing its assets, and may fix the remuneration to be paid to him or them. The appointment may be made at the same meeting at which the resolution for winding up was passed.

On the appointment of the liquidator all the powers of the directors cease, except in so far as their continuance is sanctioned either by the company in general meeting or by the liquidator. (S. 91(2).) However, a resolution for voluntary winding up does not automatically dismiss all servants, but if it takes place because the company is insolvent it does operate as a discharge. (*Reigate v Union Manufacturing Co (Ramsbottom)* [1918] 1 KB 592.)

If a liquidator dies, resigns, or otherwise vacates his office, the company may in general meeting and subject to any arrangement with its creditors, fill the vacancy. Such a meeting may be convened by any contributory or, if there were more liquidators than one, by those continuing. (S. 92.) However, as a general rule a single shareholder cannot constitute a meeting for the purpose of making a valid appointment of a liquidator under s. 92. (*In Re London Flats Ltd*, 1969.[153])

Meetings

If the liquidator at any time forms the opinion that the company will be unable to pay its debts in full within the period stated in the statutory declaration, he must forthwith summon a meeting of creditors. When the liquidator calls the meeting of creditors the company is deemed to be in a creditors' voluntary, and that meeting may exercise the same powers as a creditors' meeting at the beginning of a liquidation which is initiated as a creditors' winding up, including appointing their nominee as liquidator and a liquidation committee. (Ss. 95 and 96, Insolvency Act 1986.)

In any event if the winding up continues for more than a year, the liquidator must summon a general meeting of the company at the end of the first year and of each succeeding year, or at the first convenient date within three months from the end of the year, or such longer period as the Department of Trade and Industry may allow. He must lay before the meeting an account of his acts and dealings, and the conduct of the winding up during the preceding year. (S. 93.)

As soon as the affairs of the company are fully wound up, the liquidator must make up an account of the winding up showing how it has been conducted, and how the property of the company has been disposed of, and then call a general meeting of the company in order to lay the account before it and explain it. (S. 94.) The meeting is called by advertisement in the *Gazette*, specifying the time, place and object of the meeting. This advertisement must be published at least one month before the meeting.

Within one week after the meeting the liquidator must send to the Registrar of Companies a copy of the account, and make a return to him of the holding of the meeting and its date. If no quorum was present at the meeting, the liquidator makes a return to the effect that the meeting was duly summoned and no quorum was present, and this is deemed to constitute compliance. The Registrar must publish in the *London Gazette* notice of the receipt by him of the return of the holding of the meeting. (S. 711(1)(*r*), Companies Act 1985.)

The Registrar then registers the account and return as to the meeting, and three months after such registration the company is deemed to be dissolved. The liquidator or any interested person may apply to the court for the deferment of dissolution and, if the grounds seem adequate, the court may defer the date as it thinks fit. The court may at any time within 12 years after the dissolution make an order declaring the dissolution void, again on the application of the liquidator or any interested person being someone who has a claim against its assets, e.g. a creditor who has not in fact received notice of the winding up. (S. 651.)

Where the liquidator has been obliged to call a meeting of creditors because of insolvency, these procedures are modified and those appropriate to a creditors' voluntary winding up apply.

CREDITORS' VOLUNTARY WINDING UP

Where a company proposes to wind up voluntarily and the directors are not in a position to make the statutory declaration of solvency, the company must call a meeting of its creditors not later than the fourteenth day after the members' meeting at which the resolution for voluntary winding up is to be proposed. Notices of this meeting are to be sent by post to creditors not less than seven days before the day of the creditors' meeting. (Insolvency Act, 1986, s. 98(1).)

The company must advertise a notice of the creditors' meeting once in the *Gazette* and once at least in two local newspapers circulating in the district where it has its registered office or principal place of business. (*Ibid*, s. 98(1)(*c*).)

The directors must place before the creditors' meeting a full statement of the company's affairs, together with a list of creditors and the estimated amount of their claims, and appoint a director to preside at the meeting. The notice of the meeting must give the name and address of an insolvency practitioner who will give creditors information about the company or state a place where a list of creditors can be inspected. (*Ibid*, S. 98(2).)

Appointment of liquidator

The creditors and the company at their respective meetings may nominate a liquidator. If the creditors do not nominate one, the company's nominee becomes the liquidator. If the creditors and the company nominate different persons, the person nominated by the creditors has preference. However, where different persons are nominated, any director, member, or creditor of the company may, within seven days after the date on which the nomination was made by the creditors, apply to the court for an order to appoint the company's nominee to act either instead of or in conjunction with the creditors' nominee, or alternatively to appoint some other person. (S. 100.)

At the same meeting the creditors may, if they think fit, appoint a liquidation committee to act with the liquidator. (S. 101.) On the appointment of a liquidator all the powers of the directors shall cease, except in so far as the liquidation committee, or, if there is no such committee, the creditors sanction their continuance. (S. 103.)

If a vacancy occurs, by death, resignation or otherwise, in the office of liquidator, other than a liquidator appointed by, or by the direction of the court, the creditors may fill the vacancy. (S. 104.)

Where the winding up continues for more than a year, the liquidator must summon a general meeting of the company and a meeting of the creditors at the end of the first and each succeeding year, or within three months of that time, and lay before the meetings an account of the conduct of the winding up during the preceding year. The Department of Trade and Industry may allow modifications to the time limit. (S. 105.)

Final meetings and dissolution

As soon as the affairs of the company are fully wound up, the liquidator makes an account of the winding up, and calls a general meeting of the company and a meeting of the creditors to lay before them the account and give an explanation of it. This meeting must be advertised in the *Gazette*, specifying the time and place and object, the advertisement being published one month at least before the meeting. (S. 106.)

Within one week after the date of the meeting or, if they are not held on the same date, after the date of the later meeting, the liquidator must send to the Registrar a copy of the account and a return of the holding of the meetings and their dates. If a quorum is not present at either meeting, the return should specify that the meeting was duly summoned and that no quorum was present and this will suffice. As with a members' voluntary liquidation, the Registrar registers the returns and the company is dissolved at the end of three months, subject to the rights of the liquidator or of interested persons to apply for the date to be deferred. The Registrar must cause to be published in the *London Gazette* notice of the receipt by him of the return of the holding of the meeting. (S. 711(1)(r), Companies Act 1985.)

Applications to court

The liquidator or any contributory or creditor may apply to the court to determine any question arising in the winding up of a company, or to exercise, as respects the enforcing of calls or any other matter, all or any of the powers which the court might exercise if the company were being wound up by the court, and the court may accede to these requests and make such orders as it thinks just. A copy of any such order must be sent forthwith by the company, or otherwise as may be prescribed, to the Registrar of Companies for minuting in his books relating to the company. (S. 112.)

Rights of creditors and contributories

Notwithstanding the fact that the company is being wound up voluntarily, a creditor or contributory may still apply to have it wound up by the court, but the court must be satisifed that, in the case of a contributory, the rights of the contributories will be prejudiced by a voluntary winding up. (S. 116.)

DEFUNCT COMPANIES

The Registrar may strike a *defunct company* off the register. Where the Registrar of Companies has reasonable cause to believe that a company is not carrying on business or is not in operation, he may adopt the following procedure—

1. He may send to the company by post a letter inquiring whether the company is carrying on business or in operation.

2. If he does not receive an answer within a month, he must within a further fourteen days send a registered letter referring to the first letter, stating that no answer has been received, and that if no answer is received within a further month, a notice will be published in the *Gazette* with a view to striking the name of the company off the register.

3. If he receives no answer within the month, or if he receives an answer to the effect that the company is not carrying on a business or in operation, he may publish in the *Gazette*, and send to the company by post, a notice that at the end of three months from the date of that notice, the name of the company will, unless cause is shown to the contrary, be struck off the register and the company will be dissolved. (S. 652.)

Where a company is being wound up, and the registrar has reasonable cause to believe either that no liquidator is acting or that the affairs of the company are fully wound up, and the returns required to be made by the liquidator have not been made for a period of six consecutive months, the registrar must publish in the *Gazette*, and send to the company or the liquidator, the notice mentioned in the last paragraph, and once again, after the lapse of the three months, he may publish a notice in the *Gazette* to the effect that he has struck the company off the register as from the date of the notice.

Nevertheless the liability, if any, of every director, managing officer, and members of the company continues as if the company had not been dissolved, and the court still has power to wind up a company so struck off if such course turns out to be appropriate. (S. 652.)

If in actual fact the company was carrying on business or in operation, it is open to any member, or personal representative of a deceased member (*In Re Bayswater Trading Co Ltd* [1970] 1 All ER 608), or creditor to make application to the court, before the expiration of twenty years from the publication of the notice in the *Gazette*, for the restoration of the company's name to the register. (S. 653.) If the court is satisfied with the application, the Registrar may be ordered to restore the name of the company to the register and it will be deemed to have continued in existence as if its name had never been struck off. Thus in *Re Regent Insulation Co, The Times*, 4 November 1981 an employee of the company contracted asbestosis. By the time this was diagnosed the company had been struck off by the Registrar. It was then discovered that the company had been insured in respect of the industrial diseases of employees. The company was restored to the register so that the employee could pursue a claim against it. The court may also make such provisions, and give such directions as seem just, for placing the company and other persons in the same position as they would have been if the company had not been struck off. In addition to the power to restore a company's name to the register under s. 653 the court can also declare the dissolution *void* under s. 651 (*Re Test Holdings (Clifton) Ltd* [1969] 3 All ER 517) and proceedings may then be taken against the company as if it had not been dissolved.

The notices mentioned above may be sent to the liquidator at his last known place of business, and in the case of a company to its registered office, or (if no office was registered) to some officer of the company whose name and address is known, or to each of the persons who subscribed the memorandum at the address mentioned in it. (Ss. 652 and 653.)

The provisions of s. 652 provide a proper alternative to winding up where a company has no realizable assets or funds available to pay the expenses of liquidation.

17 Winding up: in context

Having outlined the methods of winding up in terms of a broad overview, we now consider in this chapter the likely course of a winding up. Section references are to the Insolvency Act 1986 unless otherwise indicated.

Let us assume that we are dealing with a small manufacturing company which has suffered from a recession in trade and is now in difficulties in terms that its creditors are pressing for payment which it cannot make. In addition, let us consider the problem from the point of view of the unsecured or trade creditors who do not wish to appoint an administrator.

Two courses are open to them as follows—

(i) To initiate a winding up by the court. This is slow and expensive.

(ii) To convince the directors that the company cannot continue in business and that it would be advantageous to initiate a creditors' voluntary winding up.

Both procedures will be considered in turn.

WINDING UP BY THE COURT

Grounds

The grounds for compulsory winding up under s. 122(1) are as follows—

(i) a special resolution by the members to wind up;

(ii) failure to start business within one year of incorporation or suspension of business for a whole year;

(iii) if the number of members falls below two;

(iv) if the company is unable to pay its debts;

(v) if it is just and equitable that the company be wound up.

In addition, a newly-incorporated public company may be wound up if it does not obtain a certificate under s. 117 of the Companies Act 1985 within one year of incorporation. The petition may be presented by the Secretary of State. We have already considered the more important cases under (v) above (see p. 190).

It is only the fourth ground (which is the commonest and most important) that will be dealt with in any detail here.

A company's inability to pay its debts is defined in s. 123(1) as follows—

(i) If a creditor to whom the company is indebted in a sum exceeding £750 has served a demand in writing for payment and within three weeks the company has failed to pay the sum due (or given a security or entered into a compromise acceptable to the creditor).

Note that it is not merely the failure to pay the debt which gives the ground for winding up. Thus, if a company can satisfy the court that it has a defence to the claim a winding up order will not be made. In consequence it is advisable for a creditor to sue the company to judgment before serving a demand for payment of the judgment debt.

(ii) If a judgment creditor has tried to enforce his judgment by execution on the company's property and the execution has failed to satisfy the debt.

(iii) If the court is satisfied that the company is unable to pay its debts, i.e. is insolvent.

Petitioners

For our purposes six classes of persons can present a petition as follows—

(i) the company itself;

(ii) the Official Receiver who can present a petition even after the commencement of a voluntary winding up;

(iii) the Department of Trade and Industry, following an investigation;

(iv) a contributory;

(v) a creditor;

(vi) the Trade Secretary where a public company does not obtain an s. 117, Companies Act 1985 certificate in time.

Only a petition by a contributory or creditor will be considered in any detail here.

(*a*) *Contributory*. The following points should be noted—

(i) A contributory is defined by s. 79(1) as meaning everyone who is liable to contribute to the assets of the company should it be wound up.

(ii) Although at first sight the term would appear to cover only shareholders whose shares are partly paid, it applies also to holders of fully paid shares since all members are liable to contribute subject to any limits on their liability provided for by s. 74. (*Re Anglesey Colliery Co* (1886) 1 Ch App 555.) Section 74 of course provides that a person who has fully paid shares is not liable to contribute but nevertheless he is within the definition of a contributory. So contributory is merely another name for member.

(iii) By s. 124(2) a contributory cannot petition unless—(a) the number of members is reduced below two; or (b) he took his shares as an original allottee; or (c) by transmission from a deceased shareholder; or (d) he has held the shares for six out of the last 18 months. This is presumably a precaution to prevent the purchase of shares with a view to an immediate wrecking operation on the company.

(iv) Finally, a contributory cannot petition unless he has an interest in the process, e.g. it must be likely that there will be surplus assets. Thus, if a company is insolvent, a contributory cannot petition, though he can and has an interest if the membership is below the statutory minimum of two.

(b) *Creditors.* The following points should be noted—

(i) The creditor is the most usual petitioner. A creditor is a person who is owed money by the company and who could enforce his claim by an action in debt.

Thus an unliquidated (or unascertained) claim in contract or tort is not enough. Thus it is better for the creditor petitioner to have the debt made precise as to amount by suing the company to judgment before winding up, then on petition the company cannot, by reason of the judgment, deny that it owes the money, or that it is an unliquidated sum.

(ii) The debt owed to the creditor to be at least £750. If it is not, he will no doubt find other creditors to make a joint petition with him so that the total debt is at least £750.

The figure of £750 has been adopted by the judiciary from the amount specified in s. 123(1)(a), though that section does say: 'exceeding £750'.

(iii) Even if the debt on which the petition is based is not disputed, but there are some creditors who think that their best chance of recovering their money lies in the company continuing business, then the court may, in its discretion, refuse a winding up order. S. 195(1)(a) gives the court power to have regard to the wishes of the creditors which in practice usually means the wishes of the majority in value.

Thus, in *Re ABC Coupler & Engineering Ltd* [1961] 1 All ER 354 a judgment creditor for £17,540 petitioned as his debt was not paid. He was opposed by various creditors whose debts were slightly more, namely, £18,328. The company had extensive goodwill, orders worth £110,000 and its assets were worth almost £700,000 more than its liabilities. The court found that the wishes of the majority for the company to continue were reasonable.

Presentation of the petition

As soon as a petition is presented the court may take charge of the company's affairs by appointing a provisional liquidator. (S. 135.) This is usually the Official Receiver.

Liquidator

Under s. 136 of the Insolvency Act 1986 the Official Receiver becomes the liquidator of any company ordered to be wound up by the court. Section 136, *ibid*, prescribes the steps to be taken to secure the Official Receiver's replacement as liquidator by an insolvency practitioner. For this purpose he may summon meetings of the company's creditors and members to choose a person to replace him and, under s. 141, to decide whether to establish a liquidation committee to supervise the performance by the liquidator of his functions in the winding up. Alternatively, the Official Receiver may ask the Trade Secretary to make an appointment of a liquidator. If one quarter in value of the company's creditors request him at any time to call the meetings of creditors and members referred to above the Official Receiver must do so.

Under s. 139 if the members and creditors nominate different persons to be liquidators, the creditors' nominee becomes liquidator. Under s. 140 where a winding-up order follows immediately upon the discharge of an administration order, the court may appoint the former administrator to be liquidator.

Statement of affairs

Under s. 131(1), *ibid*, where the court has made a winding-up order or appointed a provisional liquidator, the Official Receiver may require the submission of a statement of affairs of the company giving, e.g. particulars of its assets and liabilities and details of its creditors.

The persons who will most usually be called upon to make the statement are the directors or other officers of the company. However, s. 131(3), *ibid*, empowers the Official Receiver to require other persons connected with the company to produce or assist in the production of the statement, e.g. employees or those employed within the last 12 months.

Investigation by Official Receiver

Section 132 places a duty on the Official Receiver to investigate the affairs of the company and the reasons for its failure and to make such report, if any, to the court as he thinks fit.

Public examination of officers

Section 133 gives the court power on the application of the Official Receiver to require the public examination of persons connected with the company, e.g. its officers or an administrator. Those who without reasonable excuse fail to attend the examination may be arrested and books or papers in their possession seized. (S. 134.)

Effect of winding up

This is as follows—

(i) Immediately an order is made all actions against the company are stopped. (S. 130(3).)

(ii) The company ceases to carry on business except with a view to a beneficial winding up. For example, it may be necessary to carry on the company's business for a while in order to realize its assets at a better price but realization must not be long delayed.

(iii) The powers of the directors cease. (*Fowler v Broads Patent Night Light Co* [1893] 1 Ch 724.)

(iv) Employees are automatically dismissed (*Chapman's Case* (1866) LR 1 Eq 346) though the liquidator may have to re-employ some of them until the winding up is completed.

VOLUNTARY WINDING UP

This is a more common method of winding up. If in our situation the directors can be persuaded to take the view that the company has no future and agree it would be best if its existence came to an end, then a voluntary winding up would be a cheaper method of achieving this purpose.

What sort of voluntary winding up is applicable?

If we want a members' voluntary winding up the directors would, as we have seen, have to make a *statutory declaration of solvency*, as it is called, in the five weeks before the special resolution for winding up was passed, or on that date but before the resolution was passed. (S. 89.) In the declaration they would have to say that in their opinion the company will be able to pay its debts in full within a stated period of time which must not be longer than 12 months, and a statement of assets and liabilities must be attached. Since the directors and the members control the process in a members' voluntary winding up, there is a strong temptation for the directors to make a declaration, even if it is not fully justified.

False declarations—what are the penalties?

Section 89 provides that if the declaration is made without reasonable grounds the directors are liable to imprisonment and/or an unlimited fine; *and* if the debts are not in fact paid within the stated period it is *presumed* that the directors did not have reasonable grounds so that they will have to prove that they did which is not an easy matter.

Furthermore, if during a members' voluntary winding up the liquidator is of the opinion that the company will not be able to pay its debts although a declaration of solvency has been given, s. 95, Insolvency Act 1986 provides that he must summon a meeting of creditors within 28 days of that opinion and put before it a statement of assets and liabilities.

As from the date when the liquidator calls the meeting of creditors, the company is deemed to be in a creditors' voluntary, and that meeting may exercise the same powers as a creditors' meeting at the beginning of a liquidation which is initiated as a creditors' winding up, including appointing their nominee as liquidator and a liquidation committee.

If he does not follow s. 95 the liquidator is liable to a fine; and if he does then the directors are liable to the s. 89 penalties for making a declaration of solvency without reasonable grounds.

The liquidator who has been nominated by the company on the basis that there would be a members' voluntary winding up can, between the date of summoning the meeting and the meeting taking place, act only with the sanction of the court, except for taking all property under his control to which the company appears entitled. He may also dispose of perishable goods and do all such other things as may be necessary for the protection of the company's assets but no more.

Filing the declaration of solvency

The declaration must be filed with the Registrar before the expiry of the period of 15 days immediately following the date on which the resolution for winding up the company is passed. The company must give the usual 21 days' notice to its members of the extraordinary general meeting to consider the special resolution to wind up voluntarily.

If the statutory declaration is not delivered within the 15-day period, the liquidation remains a members' voluntary liquidation but the company and its officers are liable to a default fine. (S. 89(6).)

Can we use a members' voluntary winding up?

Unfortunately, our directors are only too well aware that the company will not be able to pay its debts within 12 months, so we shall have to have a creditors' voluntary winding up and proceed as follows under s. 84—

(*a*) Summon an extraordinary general meeting.

(*b*) To pass an extraordinary resolution that the company cannot by reason of its liabilities continue in business.

(*c*) It is the resolution which marks the start of a voluntary winding up. (S. 86.)

(*d*) The liquidator is appointed by the company if it is a members' voluntary winding up (s. 91); in a creditors' voluntary winding up, though the members may by ordinary resolution have nominated their choice, the creditors have powers to override and appoint their own nominee, subject to the right of any member or creditor to appeal to the court within seven days. (S. 100.) If the company nominates five persons for what is called the liquidation committee, both in a voluntary winding up and also in a compulsory winding up, the creditors can now nominate five more and veto the company's nominees, subject again to a right of appeal to the court. (S. 101.)

Purpose of liquidation committee

The purpose of such a committee is to provide a small representative body to help the liquidator and also to keep an eye on him. Moreover, if there is a major creditor, who regards the assets of the company as virtually his own, the committee may provide him with a useful safety valve. The liquidator becomes involved in many kinds of businesses but a major creditor, with his knowledge of the trade, can control the committee, and supervise the winding up, and see that the run-down of the company is carried out to the best advantage. Since a liquidation committee or creditors can exercise certain powers, such as, for example, approving payment to any class of creditors, it will save the liquidator the necessity of calling a full meeting of creditors, whose approval would otherwise be necessary.

From now on we will combine consideration of the compulsory and voluntary winding up processes.

414

THE DUTIES OF A LIQUIDATOR

Appointment

The following points should be noted—

(i) If it is a compulsory winding up the Official Receiver, who automatically became provisional liquidator on the winding up order (if not earlier on the presentation of the petition) will commonly continue as the liquidator.

(ii) In the case of a voluntary winding up a person, other than a corporate body or a bankrupt, can be appointed, provided he is a qualified insolvency practitioner. (S. 390, Insolvency Act 1986.) (See further p. 317.) The liquidator is usually an experienced accountant. The present requirements of the Institute of Chartered Accountants in England and Wales for the grant of a licence as insolvency practitioner are 600 hours insolvency work spread over three years; or 750 hours spread over five years; or 1,000 hours spread over eight years. One of the above-mentioned years can be prequalification.

(iii) In a voluntary winding up the liquidator will have to notify his appointment to the Registrar of Companies and publish it in the *Gazette* both within 14 days. (S. 109(1).)

General position of the liquidator

Section 143(1) of the Insolvency Act 1986 states that the functions of the liquidator of a company *which is being wound up by the court* shall be to secure that the assets of the company are got in, realized and distributed to the company's creditors, and, if there is a surplus, to the persons entitled to it.

Beyond this there is no clear definition of his role; it is a mixture of common law and statutory duties and obligations. He partakes partly of the nature of a trustee, partly of an agent of the company and partly of an officer of the company.

(*a*) *As Trustee.* A liquidator is clearly not a trustee in the sense of the Trustee Act 1925, because the property of the company does not automatically vest in him as does trust property in trustees, although the court, under s. 145, can make an order so vesting it. However, he takes over the powers of directors who equally, without being trustees, owe fiduciary duties to the company. His duty, like that of the directors, is owed to the company as a whole and not to individual contributories. Also, like a trustee, he cannot, by reason of the Insolvency Rules 1986, SI 1986/1925 buy the company's property without leave of the court, or make a profit out of sales to the company.

Moreover he is in a more vulnerable position than a lay trustee because he is always paid to assume his responsibility and in *Re Home & Colonial Insurance Co* [1929] All ER Rep 231 the court referred to the 'high standard of care and diligence' required from him. 'His only refuge was to apply to the court for guidance in every case of serious doubt or difficulty'.

Furthermore, although it has not been definitely decided, it does not appear that the liquidator can claim the protection of s. 61 of the Trustee Act 1925 if he has acted honestly and reasonably and ought to be excused. In *Re Windsor Steam Coal Ltd* [1929] 1 Ch 151 the Court of Appeal held on the facts that the liquidator had not acted reasonably in paying a claim without the directions of the court, but left open the question of whether s. 61 was available as a defence.

(*b*) *As Agent*. The liquidator can be described as an agent for the company in that he can make contracts on behalf of the company for winding up purposes.

He has, of course, the paid agent's obligation to bring reasonable skill to his duties. However, he is not a true agent in that he controls the actions of his so-called principal, the company.

(*c*) *As Officer*. The liquidator is not named as an officer of the company in the definition section of the 1985 Act, i.e. s. 744, but he is named in s. 212 of the Insolvency Act 1986 as a person against whom proceedings may be taken for misfeasance, which will be referred to again later. Neither is it certain that he is entitled to the protection of s. 727 of the 1985 Act whereby the court can relieve any officer who, though negligent or in breach of trust, has acted honestly and reasonably and ought to be relieved. We have already seen an example of this section in operation in *Re Duomatic* (1969).[160]

Control by the court

Finally, the liquidator is subject to constant control by the court because under s. 168(5) any person aggrieved by an action or decision of a liquidator in a winding up may apply to the court. However, it would seem that the court is not anxious to upset his acts. Thus in *Leon v York-O-Matic* [1966] 3 All ER 277 where the liquidator was charged by a member of the company with selling assets at an undervalue, Plowman J construed s. 168(5) by saying that in the absence of fraud there could not be interference in the day-to-day administration of the liquidator, nor a questioning of the exercise by the liquidator in good faith of his discretion, nor a holding him accountable for an error of judgment.

Powers of liquidator

The following points should be noted—

(i) In a compulsory winding up s. 167 provides that something like half of his powers can only be exercised with the approval of the court or of the liquidation committee, e.g. to bring or defend actions, to carry on the business of the company so far as may be necessary for its beneficial winding up, and to pay any class of creditors in full. Otherwise he can do most acts on his own authority, e.g. sell the company's property or raise money on the security of the company's assets.

(ii) In a creditors' voluntary winding up, he can exercise all the powers on his own except three which need the sanction of the court, liquidation committee or the creditors. These powers are: to pay creditors; to make a compromise with creditors; and to compromise calls and debts. (S. 165.)

(iii) While the liquidator in a voluntary winding up has a freedom from supervision by the court which is not available in a compulsory winding up, he can always get support and guidance by applying to the court on any matter arising out of the winding up. (S. 112.)

Collection of the assets

(i) The liquidator will take charge of all assets which can be physically brought under his control, including money in the bank.

(ii) He will not be able to touch money subject to a trust. Thus in *Re Kayford* [1975] 1 All ER 604 a mail order company in anticipation of liquidation had put customers' deposits for goods which the company might not be able to supply in a special 'Customer Trade Deposit Account' and it was held that these deposits were returnable to the customers and did not come under the control of the liquidator. However, if there are any other assets in the hands, for example, of a sheriff who is intending to sell the goods as part of a judgment creditor's execution, the liquidator will be able to recover these assets if the process of sale has not been completed before the winding up commenced.

(iii) The liquidator will normally in a compulsory winding up pay all money into the Companies Liquidation Account at the Bank of England, but in a voluntary winding up he need not do so unless he has in his hands assets unclaimed or undistributed for six months.

(iv) He can bring actions to enforce debts due to the company (ss. 165 and 167) and he is not bound by an agreement for settlement of debts which would have prevented the company itself from suing, e.g. the rules of the International Air Transport Association for settling debts by payment of the balance to a clearing house. (*British Eagle*

417

International Air Lines Ltd v Compagnie Nationale Air France,
1975.[215])

(v) He will settle the list of contributories and he can ask the court
to exercise its powers under s. 237 of the Insolvency Act 1986 to
order an officer or any person who has previously held office as administrator or liquidator of the company or as a receiver or manager and
any trustee for or any banker or agent or officer of the company to
hand over any property or money or books, papers or records of the
company under his control. Set-off is not allowed to a contributory
until all the creditors have been paid in full. (S. 149(3).) In the unlikely
event of there being uncalled capital, he can call it up, and will settle
the A list of present members and the B list of persons who have
been members in the 12 months preceding winding up. The B list
members will only be liable for debts contracted while they were
members to the extent that their successors failed to pay the balance
due on their shares. (S. 74.)

Swelling the assets

It is the duty of the liquidator to swell the assets by recovering any
sums due from the directors or officers of the company. His ability
to recover may arise under a number of headings as follows—

(a) *Secret profits.* It may be that the directors have made an unauthorized profit out of their position. As we saw in *Regal (Hastings) Ltd
v Gulliver*, 1942,[165] the directors had helped the parent company out
by putting up money for shares in a subsidiary company, but were
made to repay to the parent company a profit on those shares when
they were sold. Alternatively, the directors may have paid themselves
unauthorized salaries which may be recovered. As we have seen, officers
of the company can be summoned before the court for examination
if they are suspected of having property of the company in their possession. (S. 237, Insolvency Act 1986.)

(b) Reference should also be made to s. 213 of the Insolvency Act
1986 (fraudulent trading) and ss. 214 and 216, Insolvency Act 1986
(wrongful trading etc) under which the company's officers and others
may be personally liable for certain debts of the company. (See further
pp. 13 and 20.)

If the liquidator recovers money under ss. 214, 216 and 213 (above),
it goes into a fund for all the creditors. (*Re William C Leitch Ltd
(No 2)* [1933] Ch 261.) In the past if an individual creditor, such
as the Revenue was paid his debt by the directors as a result of his
bringing an application under s. 213, then he could keep the money.
(*Re Cyona Distributors* [1967] 1 All ER 281.) This will not arise now
because only the liquidator may apply under s. 213.

(c) *Section 212, Insolvency Act 1986.* This section allows the court on the application of the Official Receiver, the liquidator, a creditor or a contributory to examine the conduct of any promoter, past or present director, manager, liquidator, administrator, administrative receiver or officer of the company. If it appears that such a person has misapplied or retained or become liable or accountable for any money or property of the company, or been guilty of any misfeasance or breach of trust in relation to the company, the court can order him to repay or restore or to contribute to the assets of the company by way of compensation such a sum as the court thinks just.

Creditors—proof of debts

The following points should be noted—

(i) The liquidator will normally have written to every known creditor on first appointment, sending him a copy of the statement of affairs, and he will advertise in the *Gazette* and a local newspaper (Insolvency Rules 1986, SI 1986/1925) for details of debts to be submitted within a definite period, and he will normally require debts to be verified by affidavit. Then he will examine and decide on every debt, and a rejected creditor can appeal to the court. (Rule 4.77.)

(ii) The admission of debts will depend on whether the company is solvent or not. If the company is solvent all debts can be proved which could have been enforced against the company if it had not gone into liquidation. However, statute-barred debts are only payable if all the members agree, and future debts are payable subject to a rebate of 5 per cent per annum because they are paid early.

(iii) If the company is insolvent the following rules apply and certain debts are non-provable as follows—

(a) Claims for unliquidated damages in tort. Damages for breach of contract or trust are provable on an estimate. Thus if a claim can be framed in either contract or tort, as might be the case where an injury was caused to a passenger by the negligence of a bus driver, it may be possible to include the claim as one of contract rather than of tort. This is a useful rule for a liquidator because he does not have to await the outcome of tort proceedings before winding up the company. However, in *Re Islington Metal and Plating Works* [1983] 3 All ER 218, Harman J decided that if a company which started liquidation as insolvent later became solvent, where, as in this case, an action by the liquidator on behalf of the company against its directors for misfeasance might succeed, debts of all descriptions could be proved. In such a situation, once the claims of the undoubted creditors were satisfied and the costs provided for, the tort claimants would be entitled to make claims before distribution of any surplus.

(b) Debts incurred after notice of a transaction at undervalue or preference (see below) or that the company could not pay its debts as they fell due and had suspended payment of debts.

(c) Contingent debts when the value cannot be fairly estimated. In *Re Patent Floor Cloth Co* (1872) 26 LT 467, two persons Dean and Gilbert were employed by the company as travellers for a period of three years on commission. In the first year they made £400 each and then the company was wound up. The court held that an estimate could be made of their entitlement to commission for the purposes of the winding up but this would have been impossible if there had not been a first year commission on which to base it.

(d) Debts barred by the Limitation Act 1980 at the commencement of winding up are not enforceable, though time stops running on the commencement of the liquidation and if the debt is not statute-barred then it will not become so because of delay in payment arising out of the liquidation.

(e) Illegal debts and unenforceable debts are not provable. For example, a debt on a contract for the sale of land which is not evidenced in writing as is required by s. 40 of the Law of Property Act 1925 is not provable. Nor would an illegal debt be provable as where a builder has built premises for a company knowing that there was no planning permission.

If a debt cannot be proved the creditor gets no dividend and has no rights as a creditor, e.g. to attend and vote at meetings.

There are also certain *deferred debts*. These are provable but no dividend is payable nor is there a right to vote until all provable debts have been paid with interest in so far as they are overdue. The deferred debts are as follows—

(a) loans under a written agreement that the lender is to receive a rate of interest varying with the profits of the company, and

(b) where the vendor of a business sold to the company is receiving a share of the profits as payment.

As regards secured creditors, a secured creditor must state in his proof that he is a secured creditor and either—

(a) surrender the security and prove for the whole debt, or

(b) value the security and prove for the balance which then remains. If the creditor underestimates the value he is bound by it and can only re-estimate if the court approves.

If the creditor values the security and proves for the balance, then the liquidator may—(i) redeem the security by paying the creditor the amount of the valuation, or (ii) require the security to be sold by auction to establish its value.

The creditor may at any time after lodging his proof by notice in writing require the liquidator to choose between (i) and (ii) above. The liquidator then has six months from receipt of the notice to make a choice. If he does not make a choice the creditor owns the security and may prove for the balance.

Section 189 of the Insolvency Act 1986 provides for the surplus remaining in any winding up after payment in full of proved debts to be applied in the payment of interest to the extent specified on the amount of those debts before it is available for members. The rate of interest payable under the section in respect of any debt is which ever is the greater of—

(a) the rate specified in s. 17 of the Judgments Act 1838 on the day on which the company went into liquidation (currently 15 per cent *per annum* (SI 1985/437)); and

(b) the rate applicable to that debt apart from the winding up, e.g. the contract rate of interest, if any.

Section 244 entitles the court on the application of the liquidator to vary or set aside any extortionate credit transaction between the company and a creditor.

Provisions which may invalidate a charge or debt

There are various provisions, some of which have been considered briefly already, which may invalidate a charge granted by the company or any other disposition it has made or any debt which it has incurred. These are as follows—

(i) A charge will be invalid against the liquidator or creditors if it is not registered under s. 395, Companies Act 1985 within three weeks with the Registrar. If it is invalid the holder falls to the level of an unsecured creditor. It will be remembered that under s. 401, *ibid*, the Registrar issues a certificate of registration stating the amount secured, and the certificate is conclusive evidence that the Act has been complied with. If there was a mistake and the charge was overlooked at the time of execution and then some months later the solicitor responsible for registration put in the date when the charge came to light and registered it within three weeks of that date, then according to *Re C L Nye*, 1969,[189] the certificate is conclusive and the charge is still valid. On the question of priority, even though there is several months delay in the registration of a charge, it may still have priority over a subsequent charge registered in time. In *Watson v Duff Morgan & Vermont Holdings Ltd*, 1974[190] both first and second debentures were created on 22 January 1971. The second debenture was registered within 21 days but the first not until 5 November after the court had extended the time for registration but subject to any rights acquired prior to the actual date of registration. It was held that the rights of the second debenture were acquired on the day it was executed and that failure to register the first debenture within the 21-day period did not give the second debenture any new rights. In these circumstances the first debenture retained its priority.

(ii) Section 241 of the Insolvency Act 1986 enables the court on the application of the liquidator to make orders for restoring the position of the company and its creditors to what it would have been if the company had not entered into a transaction at an undervalue or given a preference to a creditor before the commencement of the winding up. A sale at an undervalue and preferences within six months from the commencement of winding up can be set aside. The period is two years if with a connected person, e.g. a director.

The section applies to the creation of a charge and to any delivery of goods or the payment of money. A simple example from previous legislation is *Re Kushler* [1943] 2 All ER 22, where ordinary creditors were ignored but the company paid some £700 into the bank merely to clear the overdraft guaranteed by the directors. Repayment was ordered.

(iii) As we have seen by s. 245, Insolvency Act 1986, a floating charge created by a company within the year before the commencement of its winding up or within two years if given to a connected person, e.g. a director, may be void. (See further p. 308.)

The purpose of this section appears to be similar to s. 241, to prevent a company, while it is unable to pay its debts from preferring an unsecured creditor by giving him a charge on its assets.

(iv) It may be necessary to look at the *ultra vires* rule, namely that a company can only carry out transactions permitted by the objects clause in the memorandum of association or any reasonably incidental thereto. An *ultra vires* debt is invalid and the liquidator need not pay it, though the creditor may follow and trace his property into the company's assets. (See p. 61.)

Section 35, Companies Act 1985 may operate to render a particular transaction valid. There are difficulties involved in the application of the section since the transaction has to be 'decided on by the directors'. The position under s. 35, *ibid*, was considered in Chapter 3.

(v) If the liquidator can prove fraudulent trading or wrongful trading, against e.g. a director or officer under s. 213 or s. 214, Insolvency Act 1986 which have already been considered, the court may order that person to become personally liable for the debt. (Note also s. 216 (management by disqualified persons), p. 20.)

(vi) Finally, the liquidator has a very powerful weapon in the right to disclaim given to him by ss. 178 and 179, Insolvency Act 1986. The sections allow him to disclaim property, e.g. stock or shares, unprofitable contracts, property unsaleable or not readily saleable or land burdened with onerous covenants. As regards the latter, an illustration is provided by *Re Nottingham General Cemetery Co* [1955] 2 All ER 504 where contracts between the company and the owners of the grave plots prevented its use for a purpose other than a cemetery. The liquidator can, of course, disclaim such land and if he does it vests in the Crown subject to the right of any interested party, e.g. a local authority, to ask that the land be vested in him.

The liquidator must disclaim in writing within 12 months (this does not apply if he is the Official Receiver) and if he hesitates, anyone concerned can ask him to decide within 28 days what he will do. If he fails to tell the court within 28 days that he intends to disclaim he will lose his right. The court can assist persons affected by the disclaimer because, although they can no longer prove as creditors in the liquidation, they are entitled to damages. These damages may or may not equal the full amount of the debt. An illustration taken from the law of bankruptcy, which is the same on this point, is *Re Hooley, ex parte United Ordnance & Engineering Co*, 1899.[216]

Distribution of assets

The liquidator is now able to distribute the assets. The order laid down for a compulsory winding up under the Insolvency Rules is usually followed. The order is as follows—

(i) First come the costs of the winding up. In broad terms these cover the costs of getting in the assets, of the petition, of making the statement of affairs, the liquidator's remuneration and the expenses of the committee of inspection.

(ii) Then come the preferential debts (see Sched 6, Insolvency Act 1986). These debts rank equally between themselves so that if the property of the company is not sufficient to pay them all in full they will have to abate proportionately. The main preferential debts are as follows—

(a) Income Tax (but not Corporation Tax) and Capital Gains Tax assessed on or before 5 April next before the relevant date but not exceeding the whole of one year's assessment (the Crown may choose the year in question and may choose different years for different taxes);

(b) PAYE deductions (including deductions on account of tax from payments made to certain independent subcontractors particularly in the construction industry) which were made or ought to have been made in the 12 months next before the relevant date;

(c) Value Added Tax for the 6 months next before the relevant date;

(d) The amount of any Car Tax for the 12 months next before the relevant date;

(e) sums due in respect of general betting duty, gaming licence duty or bingo duty within 12 months next before the relevant date;

(f) wages or salaries of employees due within four months next before the relevant date up to a maximum of £800 for each employee;

(g) all accrued holiday remuneration of employees;

(h) earnings related social security contributions and redundancy fund contributions in the 12 months next before the relevant date.

(iii) Next come charges secured by a floating charge which take second place to preferential creditors.

(iv) These are followed by the unsecured ordinary creditors.

(v) Lastly come the deferred debts. These have already been referred to but one could add at this stage sums due to members in their capacity as members, such as dividends declared but not paid.

If there is money left at this stage the company is solvent and debts such as unliquidated damages in tort will be admitted.

Finally, any surplus will be distributed among members according to their rights under the articles or the terms of issue of their shares.

Insolvency—protection of employees

Under the Employment Protection (Consolidation) Act 1978, s. 122 (as amended) an employee who loses his job when his employer (in this case a company) becomes insolvent can claim through the Redundancy Payments Fund arrears of wages, holiday pay and certain other payments which are owed to him, rather than rely on the preferential payments procedure.

Any payments made must be authorized by the Secretary of State for Employment and the legal rights and remedies in respect of the debts covered are transferred to the Secretary of State, so that he can try to recover from the assets of the insolvent employer the costs of any payments made, up to the preferential rights the employees would have had. Major debts covered are as follows—

(i) Arrears of pay for a period not exceeding eight weeks up to a rate of £158 per week.

(ii) Pay in respect of holidays actually taken, and accrued holiday pay up to a rate of £158 per week, up to a limit of six weeks.

(iii) Payments in lieu of notice at a rate not exceeding £158 a week, up to the statutory minimum entitlement of a particular employee under the Employment Protection (Consolidation) Act 1978.

(iv) Any payment outstanding in regard to an award by an industrial tribunal of compensation for unfair dismissal.

(v) Reimbursement of any fee or premium paid by an apprentice or articled clerk.

There is no qualifying period before an employee becomes eligible and virtually all people in employment are entitled. Claims on the redundancy fund will not normally be admitted if the liquidator can satisfy the Secretary of State that the preferential payments will be paid from funds available in the liquidation and without undue delay.

Completion of winding up

The final stages of the winding up are as follows—

(a) *Compulsory winding up.* Once the liquidator has paid off the creditors and distributed the surplus (if any) and summoned a final meeting of the company's creditors under s. 146, Insolvency Act 1986 he may vacate office and obtain his release under s. 174, *ibid.* Under s. 205, *ibid,* the company is dissolved at the end of three months from the receipt by the Registrar of the liquidator's notice that the final meeting of creditors has been held and that the liquidator has vacated office.

(b) *Voluntary winding up.* In a voluntary winding up the liquidator will call final meetings of the company and creditors for approval of his accounts. Within a week he will file with the Registrar his accounts and a return of the meetings, and two months later the company is dissolved. (S. 201.) Release is under s. 173.

Whether it is a compulsory or voluntary liquidation, the court can restore the company to the Register within two years if, for example, further assets are discovered which should be distributed to creditors.

We have now completed a consideration of the two main methods of winding up. However, it is possible for a company which is in voluntary liquidation to be compulsorily wound up and this is referred to in the next section.

Compulsory winding up by a company in voluntary liquidation

The following points should be noted—

(i) Section 116 provides that a voluntary winding up does not bar the right of a creditor or contributory to have the company wound up by the court, though it is necessary to show one of the grounds for a compulsory winding up. If a creditor applies to the court, the court will take into account the wishes of all the creditors and the majority view would almost certainly prevail.

In the case of contributories, the Act provides that the court must be satisfied that the rights of contributories will be prejudiced by a voluntary winding up and that a compulsory order would be justified if, e.g. the voluntary winding up was being conducted in a fraudulent manner or there were suspicious circumstances and a searching investigation was required.

(ii) Section 124(5) allows the Official Receiver to present a petition but the court will not order winding up unless it is satisfied that the voluntary winding up cannot be continued with due regard to the interests of the creditors and contributories. Thus, in *Re Ryder Installations* [1966] 1 All ER 453 the liquidator in a voluntary winding up had not after eight years called a meeting of creditors and he had five convictions for failing to make the appropriate returns. Here the court ordered a compulsory winding up by the court.

(iii) The Secretary of State can also present a petition for a compulsory winding up after a voluntary winding up has been started. Thus, in *Lubin, Rosen & Associates* [1975] 1 All ER 577 the Secretary of State for Trade petitioned because an investigation suggested there had been fraud and the company, formed to build flats in Spain, never had sufficient share capital for its activities. 198 creditors with claims totalling £540,000 opposed compulsory winding up. Megarry J held that while such opposition by creditors was a formidable obstacle, the petition of the Secretary of State carried great weight and that when there were circumstances of suspicion it was highly desirable that the winding up should be by the court with all the safeguards that that provided. Consequently he ordered a compulsory winding up.

Appendix of Cases and Materials

Where the case is dated before the enactment of the legislation which it illustrates it was decided on identical (or similar) legislation which is now consolidated. Section references are to the Companies Act 1985 unless otherwise indicated.

THE NATURE OF A COMPANY

Legal personality—a registered company is, like any juristic person, an entity separate from its members.

1. Salomon *v* Salomon & Co Ltd [1897] AC 22

Salomon carried on business as a leather merchant and boot manufacturer. In 1892 he formed a limited company to take over the business. The memorandum of association was signed by Salomon, his wife, his daughter, and four of his sons. Each subscribed for one share. The company paid £39,000 to Salomon for the business, and the mode of payment was to give Salomon £10,000 in debentures, secured by a floating charge on the company's assets, and 20,000 shares of £1 each and the balance in cash. Less than one year later the company fell on hard times and a liquidator was appointed. The debts of the unsecured creditors amounted to nearly £8,000 and the company's assets were approximately £6,000. The unsecured creditors claimed all the remaining assets on the ground that the company was a mere alias or agent for Salomon. *Held*—The company was a separate and distinct person. The debentures were perfectly valid, and Salomon was entitled to the remaining assets in part payment of the secured debentures held by him.

Comment. (i) Salomon's charge securing his debentures might today have been rendered ineffective by s. 245, Insolvency Act 1986. This provides, e.g., that a charge securing debentures is ineffective if liquidation follows within a year and the company cannot be proved to have been solvent when the charge was created. In these circumstances Salomon would have been reduced to an unsecured creditor and would not have had a prior claim to the remaining assets.

(ii) There was no fraud upon creditors or shareholders. The creditors of the old business had been paid off. The unsecured creditors concerned in this case were creditors of the new company. The House of Lords took the view that they must be deemed to know the risk they were taking if the company went into liquidation with insufficient funds. The members who had fully paid shares could not be required to pay more. Any profit which Mr Salomon might have made as a promoter selling his business to the company was fully disclosed and approved by the shareholders, i.e. his family.

Legal personality—the assets of a company belong to it and not to the members. Shareholders do not have an insurable interest in the assets; nor do creditors unless they have a security.

2. Macaura v Northern Assurance Co Ltd [1925] AC 619

Macaura was the owner of a timber estate in County Tyrone and he formed an estate company and sold the timber to it for £42,000. The purchase money was paid by the issue to Macaura and his nominees of 42,000 fully-paid shares of £1 each. No other shares were issued. He also financed the company and was an unsecured creditor for £19,000, its other debts being trifling. Macaura effected an insurance policy on the timber in his own name, and not in that of the company or as agent for the company, and on 23 February 1922 most of the timber was destroyed by fire. Macaura claimed under his policies, but he was *held* not to have an insurable interest. He could only be insuring either as a creditor or as a shareholder of the company, and neither a simple creditor nor a shareholder has an insurable interest in a particular asset which the company holds, since the company is an independent entity.

Comment. Unlike a shareholder a debenture holder can insure the property of the company on which his debenture is secured. (*Westminster Fire Office v Glasgow Provident Investment Society* (1888) 13 App Cas 699.) The difference in the debenture holder's position is justifiable since as a secured creditor he has an interest in the company's property which of course the shareholder does not have.

Legal personality—a company may enter into a valid and enforceable contract to employ one of its members.

3. Lee (Catherine) v Lee's Air Farming Ltd [1960] 3 All ER 420

In 1954 the appellant's husband formed the respondent company which carried on the business of crop spraying from the air. In March 1956, Mr Lee was killed while piloting an aircraft during the course of top soil dressing, and Mrs Lee claimed compensation from the company, as the employer of her husband, under the New Zealand Workers' Compensation Act 1922. Since Mr Lee owned 2,999 of the company's 3,000 £1 shares and since he was its governing director, the question arose as to whether the relationship of master and servant could exist between the company and him. One of his first acts as governing director had been to appoint himself the only pilot of the company at a salary arranged by himself. *Held*—Mrs Lee was entitled to compensation because her husband was employed by the company in the sense required by the Act of 1922, and the decision in *Salomon v Salomon & Co*[1] was applied.

Comment. In *AG's Reference (No 2 of 1982)* [1984] 2 All ER 216 the Court of Appeal held that two directors who were also shareholders of several companies were capable of stealing from those companies. Money from the companies, which had raised large loans from various institutions, had been used, it was alleged, to support the extravagant lifestyle of the directors and their wives. There had, it was alleged, been a spending of the company's money in hotels and restaurants and on cars, yachts, and house improvements, silver and antiques. The effect on creditors was obviously uppermost in the mind of the Court which felt that a criminal sanction was needed. By applying the rule of corporate personality the directors could, as a matter of law, be liable for stealing from a company which they owned.

To be 'knowingly parties' to fraudulent trading under s. 213, Insolvency Act 1986 some positive step must be taken by those concerned.

4. Re Maidstone Buildings Provisions Ltd [1971] 3 All ER 363

A partner in a firm of accountants which acted as auditors to Maidstone was appointed secretary of the company. He attended board meetings and pointed out that the company was making large losses. Nevertheless, trading continued and debts were incurred which the company had no reasonable prospect of being able to pay. Eventually, Maidstone went into liquidation owing £99,000. The liquidator sought to make the secretary personally liable alleging that he had been 'a party to' fraudulent trading because he had not advised the directors to stop trading. It was *held* by Pennycuick V-C that the secretary had no duty to advise the directors to stop trading and the proceedings must be dismissed.

'The steps he omitted to take were to give certain advice to the directors. It seems to me impossible to say that mere inertia on the part of (the secretary) and that is all that is alleged against him, could represent being a party to the carrying on of the business of the company, and if that is right, that is the end of the matter' (*per* Pennycuick V-C).

Comment. This was presumably an exempt private company where an auditor could also be an officer or servant of the company. Section 389(6) forbids this for plc's and private companies. The exempt private company was abolished by the Companies Act 1967.

Liability under s. 213, Insolvency Act 1986 can arise if one creditor is defrauded in a single transaction.

5. Re Gerald Cooper Chemicals Ltd [1978] 2 All ER 49

In 1976 a consortium who had interests in a company called Jimlou Ltd agreed to provide £150,000 to Gerald Cooper Chemicals Ltd (Cooper) so that it could buy and install at a factory at Poplar plant for making indigo. Cooper agreed to repay the sum by 30 June 1976 and a further £1,350,000 to Jimlou Ltd by March 1977. It was expected that both sums would be available from profits made by the sale of indigo.

In the event the £150,000 was not enough and repayment was deferred by agreement until 10 August 1976. It was claimed that the consortium knew that Cooper was insolvent and would continue to be so unless additional and substantial sums of money were forthcoming.

On 19 August Mr Cooper as agent for Cooper, agreed to deliver 5,000 kilos of indigo to Harrisons Ltd during September 1976. On 20 August Harrisons paid the purchase price of £125,698 in advance and on that day Cooper paid £110,000 to Jimlou Ltd in part repayment of the loan of £150,000. Following these transactions Harrisons claimed that the business of Cooper, which was now in liquidation, had been carried on by the consortium and Mr Cooper with intent to defraud creditors for the purposes of s. 332(1) of the Companies Act 1948 (now s. 213, Insolvency Act 1986) since the payment to Jimlou Ltd rendered Cooper powerless to deliver the indigo or to repay Harrisons the purchase price.

Harrisons submitted that they were entitled to pursue their allegations by means of the machinery of s. 332 instead of commencing proceedings against the consortium as trustees of the £110,000 or in tort on the basis of fraud.

As a defence it was submitted that Harrisons' points of claim did not establish that the business of Cooper was carried on with intent to defraud creditors or, alternatively that the defendants were knowingly parties to the carrying on of the business of the company. Furthermore, one transaction could not amount to the carrying on of a business with intent to defraud creditors.

Templeman J rejected the submission that Harrisons' points of claim that the business was carried on with intent to defraud creditors disclosed no cause of action. The allegations, if true, appeared to meet the requirements of s. 332. Cooper was carrying on the business of selling indigo and if the allegations were true carried on business with intent to defraud as soon as it accepted a deposit of the purchase price knowing that it could not supply the indigo and would not repay the deposit.

In addition, a creditor could be a party to the carrying on of a business with intent to defraud creditors if as was alleged he accepted money which he knew had been obtained by carrying on the business with intent to defraud creditors for the purpose of making the payments.

Since there was the possibility of further proceedings under s. 332 by the liquidator of Cooper, his Lordship asked that the liquidator be advised of these proceedings so that the defendants should not be put in double jeopardy. All his Lordship was deciding at this time was that Harrisons' points of claim appeared to establish a case which invited investigation under s. 332. There was no actual finding of fraud. Under s. 213, Insolvency Act 1986 only the liquidator can bring a claim. Creditors and members could also claim under s. 332 which is now repealed.

Drawing aside the veil of incorporation—the courts have on occasion recognized the reality of the group.

6. Re Hellenic and General Trust Ltd [1975] 3 All ER 382

A company called MIT was a wholly-owned subsidiary of Hambros Ltd and held 53 per cent of the ordinary shares of Hellenic. A scheme of arrangement was put forward under which Hambros was to acquire all the ordinary shares of Hellenic for a cash consideration of 48p per share. The ordinary shareholders met and over 80 per cent approved the scheme, MIT voting in support. However, the National Bank of Greece, which was a minority shareholder, opposed the scheme because it would be liable to meet a heavy tax burden under Greek law as a result of receipt of cash for its shares. Templeman J refused to approve the scheme on a number of grounds. However, the one which interests us here is that he ruled that there should have been a separate class meeting of ordinary shareholders who were not a wholly-owned subsidiary of Hambros, thus in effect regarding the holding company, Hambros, and the subsidiary, MIT, as one economic unit in the class meeting.

7. DHN Food Distributors v London Borough of Tower Hamlets [1976] 3 All ER 462

DHN Food Distributors (DHN) was a holding company which ran its business through two wholly-owned subsidiaries, Bronze Investments Ltd (Bronze) and DHN Food Transport Ltd (Transport). The group collected food from the docks and distributed it to retail outlets. Bronze owned the premises in Bow from which the business was conducted and Transport ran the distribution side of the business. Tower Hamlets compulsorily acquired the premises in Bow for the purpose of building houses. This power of compulsory acquisition arose under the Housing Act 1957 and compensation was payable under the Land Compensation Act of 1961 under two headings (a) the value of the land, and (b) disturbance of business. Tower Hamlets was prepared to pay £360,000 for the value of the land but refused to pay on the second heading because DHN and Transport had no interest in the land. This was unfortunate for the group as a whole since the loss of the premises had caused all three companies to go into liquidation, it being impossible to find other suitable premises. The practical answer would have been, of course, to have conveyed the premises from Bronze to DHN when compulsory acquisition was threatened. This had not been done although the conveyance would have been exempt from stamp duty since it would have been a transfer between associated companies. However, Lord Denning in the Court of Appeal drew aside the corporate veil and treated DHN as owners of the property whereupon Tower Hamlets became liable to pay for disturbance of business. The basis of Lord Denning's judgment was that company legislation required group accounts and to that extent recognized a group entity which he felt the judiciary should do also.

Comment. It cannot be said from this case that there is *a general principle of group entity*. Much depends upon the circumstances of the case. Thus in *Woolfson v Strathclyde Regional Council* (1978) 38 P & CR 521 the House of Lords did not follow *DHN Foods* in what was a similar situation because in *Woolfson* the subsidiaries were active trading companies and not, as in *DHN Foods*, mere shells. Again, in *Multinational Gas and Petrochemical Co v Multinational Gas and Petrochemical Services Ltd* [1983] 2 All ER 563 the Court of Appeal held, following *Salomon*,[1] that wholly-owned subsidiaries in a group were separate entities and not the agents of the holding company or each other in the absence of a specific agency agreement. Furthermore, in *Dimbleby & Sons Ltd v NUJ* [1984] 1 All ER 751, a group of companies was regarded as a series of separate entities so that the picketing of one company within the group by workers employed by another company within the group was regarded as unlawful secondary picketing for the purposes of s. 17 of the Employment Act 1980.

Drawing aside the veil—presumed agency of subsidiary.

8. Firestone Tyre & Rubber Co Ltd *v* Lewellin [1957] 1 All ER 561

An American company formed a wholly-owned subsidiary in England to manufacture and sell its brand of tyres in Europe. The American company negotiated agreements with European distributors under which the latter would place orders with the American company which the English subsidiary would carry out. In fact the distributors sent their orders to the subsidiary direct and the orders were met without any consultation with the American company. The subsidiary received the money for the tyres sold to the distributors and, after deducting its manufacturing expenses plus 5 per cent, it forwarded the balance of the money to the American company. All the directors of the subsidiary resided in England (except one who was the president of the American company) and they managed the subsidiary's affairs free from day-to-day control by the American company. *Held*—by the House of Lords—that the American company was carrying on business in England through its English subsidiary acting as its agent and it was consequently liable to pay United Kingdom tax.

Drawing aside the veil—to determine whether a company is an enemy alien.

9. Daimler Co Ltd *v* Continental Tyre & Rubber Co (Great Britain) Ltd [1916] 2 AC 307

After the outbreak of war with Germany, the tyre company, which was registered in England and had its registered office here, sued the Daimler Company for money due in respect of goods supplied to Daimler before the outbreak of war. Daimler's defence was that, since the tyre company's members and officers were German, to pay the debt would be to trade with the enemy, and that therefore the claim by the tyre company should be struck out. Evidence showed that all the members of the tyre company save one were German. *Held*—by the House of Lords—that the action must be struck out. Although the place of registration and the situation of the registered office normally governs the company's nationality and domicile for the purposes of actions at law, the court has a jurisdiction to draw aside the corporate veil in some cases to see who the persons in control of the company's affairs are. If, as here, the persons in *de facto* control of the company were enemy aliens, the company could be so regarded for the purposes of the law relating to trading with the enemy.

PROMOTION AND INCORPORATION

A promoter may not make an undisclosed profit while acting as such.

10. Gluckstein *v* Barnes [1900] AC 240

In 1893 the National Agricultural Hall Co Ltd owned a place of entertainment called the Olympia Company which was being wound up. A syndicate was formed to raise funds to buy Olympia and resell it, either to a company registered under the Companies Acts for the purpose, or to another purchaser. If a company was formed, the appellant Gluckstein and three other persons Lyons, Hart and Hartley, who were members of the syndicate, had agreed to become its first directors and to promote it. In the event a company was formed, called the Olympia Company Ltd, and the promoters issued a prospectus stating that the syndicate which was promoting the company had purchased Olympia for £140,000 and was selling it to the company for £180,000 thus quite properly disclosing a profit of £40,000. What they did not disclose but referred to vaguely as 'interim investments', was the fact that they had purchased certain mortgage debentures in the old Olympia Company for less than their face value, and that these mortgage debentures were to be redeemed at their face value out of the proceeds of the issue of shares. This meant that the syndicate made a further £20,000 on the promotion. The company afterwards went into liquidation, Barnes being the liquidator, and he sought to recover the undisclosed secret profit. *Held*—The profit of £20,000 should have been disclosed and the appellant was bound to account to the liquidator for it.

Comment. The following points of interest arise from this case—

1. There had been disclosure by the promoters in regard to the £40,000 and £20,000 profit to themselves as directors but of

course this was useless because disclosure must be to an independent board.

2. The prospectus said that the £40,000 profit did not include profits on 'interim investments' but the court held that this was not a disclosure of the profit of £20,000.

3. The case also illustrates that liability of promoters is joint and several for recovery of profit because Mr Gluckstein tried to defend himself by saying he was only liable for a proportion of the profit.

The House of Lords held him liable to account for it all with a right of contribution against his fellow promoters.

A promoter has no legal claim for the expenses of promotion.

11. Re National Motor Mail Coach Co Ltd, Clinton's Claim [1908] 2 Ch 515

A company, called the Motor Mail Coach Syndicate Ltd, promoted another company, called the National Motor Mail Coach Co Ltd, to acquire the business of a motor mail contractor named Harris. The promoters paid out £416 2s. 0d. in promotion fees. The two companies were subsequently wound up and Clinton, who was the liquidator of the syndicate, proved in the liquidation of the National Motor Mail Coach Co Ltd for the promotion fees. *Held*—Clinton's claim on behalf of the syndicate could not be allowed because the company was not in existence when the payments were made, and could not have requested that they be made. The syndicate was not acting as the company's agent or at its request, and the fact that the company had obtained a benefit because the syndicate had performed its promotion duties was not enough.

Pre-incorporation contracts—liability of promoters and others acting for the company. (S. 36(4).)

12. Phonogram Ltd v Lane [1981] 3 All ER 182

In 1973, a group of pop artists decided that they would perform under the name of 'Cheap Mean and Nasty'. A company, Fragile Management Ltd (Fragile) was to be formed to run the group.

Before the company was formed, there were negotiations regarding the financing of the group. Phonogram Ltd, a subsidiary of the Hemdale Group, agreed to provide £12,000, and the first instalment of £6,000 being the initial payment for the group's first album, was paid. Fragile was never formed; the group never performed under it; but the £6,000 was not repaid.

The Court of Appeal was asked who was liable to repay it. It appeared that a Brian Lane had negotiated on behalf of Fragile and a Roland Rennie on behalf of Phonogram Ltd.

A letter of 4 July 1973 from Mr Rennie to Mr Lane was crucial. It read: 'In regard to the contract now being completed between Phonogram Ltd and Fragile Management Ltd concerning recordings of a group ... with a provisional title of "Cheap Mean and Nasty", and further to our conversation of this morning, I send you herewith our cheque for £6,000 in anticipation of a contract signing, this being the initial payment for initial LP called for in the contract. In the unlikely event that we fail to complete within, say, one month you will undertake to repay us £6,000. ... For good order's sake, Brian, I should be appreciative if you could sign the attached copy of this letter and return it to me so that I can keep our accounts people informed of what is happening.'

Mr Lane signed the copy 'for and on behalf of Fragile Management Ltd.' The money was paid over, and went into the account of Jelly Music Ltd, a subsidiary of the Hemdale Group, of which Mr Lane was a director.

The court had first to consider whether or not Mr Lane was personally liable on the contract? Clearly, Fragile could not be sued, since it never came into existence. Lord Denning took the view that Mr Lane was, as a matter of construction, liable on the contract without recourse to what is now s. 36(4), because the letter, which was in effect the contract, said: 'I send *you* herewith our cheque for £6,000', and 'in the unlikely event that we fail to complete within, say, one month, *you* will undertake to repay us the £6,000'.

However, Mr Justice Phillips at first instance had decided on the basis of a lot of evidence which he had heard that Mr Lane was not as a matter of construction liable personally, and Lord Denning and the rest of the Court of Appeal proceeded on the assumption that Mr Lane was not liable on the basis of intention and construction.

Lord Denning then turned what is now s. 36(4). This states: 'Where a contract purports to be made by a company, or by a person as agent for a company, at a time when the company has not been formed, then subject to any agreement to the contrary the contract has effect as one entered into by the person purporting to act for the company or as agent for it and he is personally liable on the contract accordingly.'

This seemed to Lord Denning to cover the case before him and render Mr Lane liable. Mr Lane made the contract on behalf of Fragile at a time when the company had not been formed, and he purported to make it on behalf of the company so that he was personally liable for it.

Mr Lane's counsel drew the attention of the court to the Directive (68/151) on which s. 36(4) is based. This states that its provisions are limited to companies *en formation* (in course of formation), whereas Fragile never commenced the incorporation process.

Lord Denning rejected this submission saying an English court must under Article 189 of the Treaty of Rome abide by the statute implementing the Directive, and that contained no restriction relating to the need for the company to be *en formation*.

Article 189 states: 'A Directive shall be binding, as to the result to be achieved, upon each member State to which it is addressed, but shall leave to the national authorities the choice of form and method.'

Counsel for Mr Lane also suggested that the word 'purports' must mean that there has been a representation that the company already exists. Lord Denning did not agree with this, saying that a contract can purport to be made on behalf of a company, or by a company, even though both parties knew that the company was not formed and was only about to be formed.

The court also decided that the form in which a person made the contract—e.g. 'for and on behalf of the company' as an agent or merely by signing the company's name and subscribing his own, e.g. 'Boxo Ltd, J. Snooks, managing director', where the form is not that of agency—did not matter and that in both cases the person concerned would be liable on the contract.

As regards the words 'subject to any agreement to the contrary', the court dealt with academic opinion which had suggested that where a person signs 'for and on behalf of the company'—i.e. as agent—he is saying, in effect that he does not intend to be liable and would not be on the basis of the words 'subject to any agreement to the contrary'.

On this, Lord Denning said: 'If there was an express agreement that the man who was signing was not to be liable, the section would not apply. But, unless there is a clear exclusion of personal liability, (the section) should be given its full effect. It means that in all cases such as the present, where a person purports to contract on behalf of a company not yet formed, then however he expresses his signature he himself is personally liable on the contract.'

Comment. The court did not consider, because it did not arise, whether an individual such as Mr Lane could have *sued* upon the contract. Section 36(4) talks about the person or agent being 'personally *liable*' on the contract. Perhaps it should say, 'Can sue or be sued'. However, lawyers have generally assumed that the court would give an individual like Mr Lane a right to sue if it arose, since it is, to say the least, unusual for a person to be liable on a contract and yet not be able to sue upon it.

A company cannot ratify (or adopt) a contract made before its incorporation either expressly or by conduct.

13. Natal Land and Colonization Co *v* Pauline Colliery and Development Syndicate [1904] AC 120

Prior to incorporation the P Company contracted to take an option to lease land belonging to Mrs de Carrey if it was coal bearing. After incorporation, the company entered on the land and made trial borings. The land was found to be coal bearing and the P company asked for a lease. Mrs de Carrey had transferred her interest in the property to the N company and they would not grant a lease. The P company sued at first instance for specific performance of the contract. *Held*— The P company could not enforce the option because—

(i) its own conduct in merely boring did not unequivocally evidence an intention to take a lease; *and*

(ii) even if it had, it was merely an offer, and there was no evidence of acceptance either by Mrs de Carrey or the N company.

Comment. United States Courts are more generous. They take the view that a contract made before incorporation is an offer open for acceptance by the company. So any act done by the company after incorporation which is unequivocally referable to the offer, operates as an acceptance and not an offer as in English company law.

The fact that a company following incorporation acts on a pre-incorporation contract because its directors think it is binding is not evidence of an offer to make a new contract. However, if after incorporation the terms of the pre-incorporation contract are considered and varied, this may amount to a fresh offer to be bound.

14. Re Northumberland Avenue Hotel Co (1886) 33 Ch D 16

A written agreement was entered into between W and D, the latter making the agreement on behalf of the Hotel Company. Under the agreement W, who had an agreement for a building lease from the Metropolitan Board of Works, agreed to grant a sub-lease of the land to the company so that an hotel could be built on it. The company was registered on the following day, there being no mention of the agreement in the memorandum, though the articles adopted it and provided that the company should carry it into effect. No fresh agreement was signed or sealed on behalf of the company, but the company did take possession of the land and spent money on building, and in general acted on the agreement because the directors thought it was binding. The company failed to complete the buildings, and the Metropolitan Board of Works re-entered into possession of the land. The company was then in the course of winding up, and the trustee in bankruptcy of W brought an action for damages against the company for breach of the agreement. *Held*—by the Court of Appeal, affirming Chitty J at first instance—that the agreement having been made before incorporation was incapable of ratification, and since the acts of the company were done under the erroneous belief that the contact between W and D was binding on the company, there was no evidence of a fresh offer in the company's acts. There was, therefore, nothing for W to accept, and so there was no contract and the trustee's claim failed.

15. Howard *v* Patent Ivory Manufacturing Co (1888) 38 Ch D 156

On 25 April 1885, a contract was entered into between the promoters of the company and certain vendors of property under which the company agreed to purchase some leasehold mills, together with plant and machinery, at a price of £36,500, payable £6,500 in cash and £30,000 in fully-paid shares in the company. On 29 April 1885, the company was registered, its memorandum and articles containing provisions for the adoption of the contract by the company. On 27 May 1885, the directors of the new company resolved that the agreement of 25 April 1885, be adopted by the company, and on 6 June 1885, the vendors agreed to vary the original agreement by accepting £3,000 in cash and £3,500 worth of debenture stock, plus the £30,000 in fully-paid shares as before. This had the effect of converting £3,500 of the purchase price into a loan to the company. The company's seal was not affixed to any agreement, but 35 debentures of £100 each were issued to the vendors and the company went into possession of the premises. On 6 November 1886, a winding-up order was made against the company, and a liquidator was appointed. This action was brought by Howard, one of the debenture holders, on behalf of himself and the others, to test the validity of the debentures. *Held*—

(i) The pre-incorporation contract did not bind the company, but by taking possession of the premises and offering to give debentures to the vendors, the company had made a fresh offer after incorporation which the vendors had accepted, and the contract was to that extent good. (*Re Northumberland Avenue Hotel Co*, 1886,[14] considered and distinguished.)

(ii) *Regulation* 95 of the company's articles provided that the directors could borrow up to £1,000 only, and after that required a resolution in general meeting. Since this had not been obtained (as the vendors were taken to know because they were directors and 'indoors the management', see p. 78), the debentures were valid only up to £1,000 so the first ten were valid taking them in order of number.

A company comes into existence on the date stated in the certificate of incorporation and from the first moment of that day.

16. Jubilee Cotton Mills *v* Lewis [1924] AC 958

Lewis was a promoter of a company formed to purchase a cotton mill and to carry on the business of cotton spinning. The memorandum and articles of the company were accepted by the Registrar of Companies on 6 January 1920, and the certificate of incorporation was dated on that day. However, the certificate, it appeared, was not signed by the Registrar till 8 January 1920. On 6 January a large number of fully-paid shares were allotted to the vendors of the mill, and they were later transferred to Lewis. The question of the validity of the allotment arose in this case, and it was *held* that the certificate was conclusive as to the date on which the company was incorporated. A company is deemed to be incorporated from the day of the date on its certificate of incorporation, and from the first moment of that day. Therefore, the allotment was not void on the ground that it was made before the company came into existence.

THE CONSTITUTION OF A COMPANY

Company names—the tort of passing off.

17. Société Anonyme des Anciens Établissements Panhard et Lavassor *v* Panhard Levassor Motor Co Ltd [1901] 2 Ch 513

The plaintiffs, a French company, had no agency in England but their cars were used in England. An English company was formed and registered with a capital of £100 and only seven members, the object being to prevent the French company from being registered in England in their own name so as to stop them competing more successfully with English companies. It was *held* that the name of the English company must be struck off the register and the members of the English company were ordered either to change the name or to wind up the company.

18. Ewing v Buttercup Margarine Company Ltd [1917] 2 Ch 1

The plaintiff had since 1904 been carrying on a business dealing in margarine and tea, and had upwards of 150 shops of his own selling 50 tons of margarine a week in all. The plaintiff's concern was called 'The Buttercup Dairy Co'. The plaintiff's shops were situated in Scotland and in the North of England, but he was planning to expand his business into the South of England. The defendant company was registered in November 1916, and as soon as the plaintiff heard about it, he complained to the management of the concern, and later brought this action for an injunction to prevent the defendant company from trading in that name. It appeared that although the defendants were in the business of selling margarine, they were wholesalers, whereas the plaintiff was a retailer, and the defendants put this forward as a defence suggesting that there would be no confusion. Another defence was that the company would operate only around London and there would be no confusion with a Northern concern. *Held*—by the Court of Appeal—that an injunction would be granted to the plaintiff restraining the defendant company from trading in that name. Although the defendants were at the moment wholesalers, the objects clause of the memorandum did give power to retail which they might exercise in future. Further the plaintiff intended to open up branches in the South of England where there would be confusion.

19. Aerators Ltd v Tollitt [1902] 2 Ch 319

The plaintiff company was formed to work a patent for the instantaneous aeration of liquids. The defendants were the subscribers of the memorandum and articles of a proposed new company to be called Automatic Aerator Patents Ltd. The plaintiffs sought an injunction to restrain the defendants from registering that name because it would deceive the public, the word 'Aerator' being associated with the plaintiff company. The plaintiff's patent was a portable aerator for use in syphons, whereas the defendant's company was concerned with large installations in public houses where a large amount of aeration of beer was required. *Held*—There was no evidence of the probability of deception, and an injunction would not be granted. The action was an attempt to monopolize a word in ordinary use and must be dismissed.

20. Waring and Gillow Ltd *v* Gillow and Gillow Ltd (1916) 32 TLR 389

W. and G. Ltd, well-known furniture, carpet and rug dealers and auctioneers, sought an injunction restraining G. and G. Ltd from carrying on a business as auctioneers of carpets (formerly the business belonged to L. C. Gillow, an auctioneer, who continued to be actively concerned with the business).

The court held that on the facts the two businesses were not likely to be taken one for the other and the injunction sought was not granted. In addition, since L. C. Gillow was actively concerned with the business, the company was allowed to incorporate his name. Furthermore, since the defendant company had purchased the business from L. C. Gillow, it was allowed to use his name in order to take advantage of the goodwill purchased.

Comment. There is no similar protection for a first name or nickname. In *Biba Group Ltd v Biba Boutique* [1980] RPC 413 the defendant whose surname was Gill had been known since infancy by the nickname 'Biba' and she ran a boutique in that name. The plaintiffs, who were in a similar line of business, obtained an injunction against her. Whitford J said that whatever the right of a person to use his own surname it did not extend to the use of a first name or nickname.

Incorrect identification of a company: liability of officers.

21. Penrose *v* Martyr (1858) EB & E 499

A limited company was described on a bill of exchange as 'The Saltash Watermens' Steam Packet Company, Saltash'. The bill was drawn on the company and was accepted by the secretary in the following form—'Accepted. John Martyr, Secy. to the sd. Coy'. The bill when presented for payment was dishonoured by the company and in this action it was *held* that the secretary was personally liable because the company's correct name did not appear on the bill. 'The intention of the enactment plainly was to prevent persons from being deceived into the belief that they had a security with the unlimited liability of common law when they had but the security of a Company Limited.' *per* Crompton J.

22. Stacey & Co Ltd *v* Wallis (1912) 28 TLR 209

A bill was drawn on a company as 'J & TH Wallis Ltd' and accepted by three persons in the following form—'James Wallis, Thomas Wallis, Henry Bowles, Secty'.

It was *held* that the correct name of the company was mentioned in the bill as required by the Companies Act. The name appeared on the face of the bill as drawee and in these circumstances it did not matter that it did not appear on the acceptance. Furthermore, the abbreviation 'Ltd' could be used for the word 'Limited'. The persons who had signed the acceptance were not liable on the bill.

Comment. It was *held* by Goff J in *Banque de l'Indochine et de Suez SA v Euroseas Group Finance Co* [1981] 3 All ER 198 that the abbreviation of 'company' to 'co' on a cheque is an appropriate mention of the company's name within what is now s. 349 and an officer of the company is not liable on the instrument if it is not met by the company. The judge applied the approach of *Stacey*. 'Co' is a commonly accepted abbreviation as 'Ltd' is.

23. Hendon *v* Adelman, *The Times*, 16 June 1973

A cheque signed on behalf of L & R Agencies Ltd omitted the amper-sand in the company's name so that the company's name was printed on its cheques as 'L R Agencies Ltd', the bank having left out the ampersand. *Held*—that the directors who had signed the cheque had not complied with the Companies Act and were accordingly personally liable on it.

24. Durham Fancy Goods Ltd *v* Michael Jackson (Fancy Goods) Ltd [1968] 2 All ER 987

On 18 September 1967, the plaintiffs drew a bill of exchange on the first defendants, Jacksons, which was accepted by M Jackson who was a director and company secretary. The bill and form of accept-ance, both of which were drawn up by the plaintiffs, referred to 'M Jackson (Fancy Goods) Ltd' whereas the proper name of the company was 'Michael Jackson (Fancy Goods) Ltd'. The bill was dishonoured and the plaintiffs brought an action against Mr Jackson contending that by signing the form of acceptance he had committed a criminal offence under the Companies Act and had made himself personally liable on the bill because he should either have returned the bill with a request that it be readdressed to Michael Jackson (Fancy Goods) Ltd and the form of acceptance changed, or he should have accepted it 'M Jackson (Fancy Goods) Ltd p.p. Michael Jackson (Fancy Goods) Ltd, Michael Jackson'. It was *held*—by Donaldson J that the mis-description was in breach of what is now s. 349 and that Mr Jackson was liable under the section. However, as the plaintiffs were responsible for the misdescription they were estopped from going back on their implied representation that it was acceptable to them.

Comment. A holder other than the plaintiffs might have been able to bring an action against Mr Jackson under what is now s. 349 since such a holder would not have been affected by the equity in that he would not have drawn the bill in an incorrect name.

25. Maxform SPA *v* B Mariani & Goodville Ltd [1979] 2 Lloyd's Rep. 385

Maxform was an Italian company which agreed to sell furniture to Italdesign which was the name under which the defendants, an English company, carried on business. Mariani was the sole director of the defendants. Maxform drew a bill of exchange on 'Italdesign' for the price of the furniture. The bill was accepted by Mariani without any addition to his signature and there was no mention of the defendant company. The price was not paid and so Maxform brought an action to recover the sum due under what is now s. 349(4). The defendants contended that the appearance on the bill in legible characters of 'Italdesign' was sufficient compliance with the Act, and also that Maxform was estopped from arguing that there had been a breach of it by reason of the wording used by Maxform in drawing the bill. *Held*—by Mocatta J—that there would be judgment for Maxform since it was not possible to take the view that the word 'name' in what is now s. 349(4) meant other than the registered corporate name of the company, and furthermore the facts were not sufficient to found an estoppel and in this regard *Durham Fancy Goods Ltd v Michael Jackson (Fancy Goods) Ltd*[24] was distinguished.

Comment. The decision of Mocatta J was affirmed by the Court of Appeal [1981] 2 Lloyd's Rep. 54.

The situation of the registered office fixes the company's nationality and domicile but not its residence.

26. Swedish Central Railway Co Ltd *v* Thompson [1925] AC 495

The company was incorporated in 1870 to construct a railway in Sweden, the registered office of the company being in London. Later the management of the company was moved to Sweden but the registered office remained in London, dealing only with formal administrative matters such as share transfers. All dividends were declared in Sweden, and no part of the profits was ever sent to England, except payment of dividend to English shareholders. The Commissioners of Income Tax assessed the company for tax on income received in Sweden. *Held*—A company could have more than one residence, though only one nationality and domicile. This company was resident in Sweden and London, and since residence was relevant for income tax purposes, the assessment of the Commissioners was affirmed.

Doctrine of *ultra vires*: a company's objects may be set out in such a way as to leave it to the directors whether to expand into other activities.

27. Bell Houses Ltd *v* City Wall Properties Ltd [1966] 2 All ER 674

The plaintiff company claimed £20,000 as commission under an alleged contract with the defendant company for the introduction of the latter to a financier who would lend the defendant company £1,000,000 for property development. As a preliminary issue the defendant company alleged that the contract was *ultra vires* and could not be enforced against them.

The principal business of the plaintiff company was the development of housing estates, and therefore the occasional raising of finance formed a necessary part of its activities. In consequence the company had obtained valuable knowledge of various sources of finance and because of this was able to arrange finance for the defendants. The defendants contended that the plaintiff company, in arranging finance for an outside organization, was, in effect, embarking on a new type of business, i.e. 'mortgage broking', and since this was not expressly included in the objects, nor reasonably incidental thereto, it was *ultra vires*. One of the sub-clauses in the objects clause of the plaintiff company was as follows: 'To carry on any other trade or business *whatsoever* which can *in the opinion of the board of directors* be *advantageously* carried on by the company in connection with, or as ancillary to, any of the above business or the general business of the company.' *Held*—by the Court of Appeal—that the alleged contract was *intra vires* in particular because of the clause set out above. In the court's view the *bona fide* opinion of the board, in this case represented by the managing director who arranged the finance, that the contract could be advantageously carried on with the company's principal business, was enough no matter how unreasonable in the *objective* sense that opinion might seem to be.

Comment. (i) This decision suggests that an objects clause can be drafted in such a way as to allow a company to carry on any business the directors choose.

(ii) It also illustrates that infringement of the *ultra vires* rule can be pleaded by both parties since the plaintiffs were claiming commission on a loan procured for the defendants under a contract, and it was the defendants who pleaded (unsuccessfully) that the contract was *ultra vires*.

(iii) The decision also rested on the alternative ground that the transaction was fairly incidental to certain of the company's objects. (See also *Deuchar*'s case, p. 460.) The Court did, however, accept that the sub-clause gave the directors power to extend the business into areas not fairly incidental.

(iv) The fact that the new business was to be carried on *with the company's main business* is an important restriction. The Court would not, it seems, have been prepared to accept an objects clause with no specified business which merely said, e.g. 'The company can do anything the directors think fit'.

Doctrine of *ultra vires:* liberal interpretation of objects clause.

28. Re New Finance and Mortgage Co Ltd [1975] 1 All ER 684

Under a sub-clause of the objects clause of its memorandum the company was empowered to carry on business as 'Financiers, capitalists, concessionaries, bankers, commercial agents, mortgage brokers, financial agents and advisers, exporters and importers of goods and merchandise of all kinds and merchants generally'.

The company was the proprietor of a petrol filling and service station on premises held under an underlease from Total Ltd. The underlease contained a tie clause which required the company to purchase all its fuel from Total. The company went into voluntary liquidation and Total lodged a proof for motor fuels sold and delivered to the company. The liquidator rejected the proof on the ground that the debt had arisen from *ultra vires* trading. *Held*—by Goulding J—that the words 'and merchants generally' extended to all purely commercial occupations and were thus wide enough to cover the company's business as a petrol filling and service station proprietor.

Comment. The legislation now contained in s. 35 was not considered in this case because all the material events happened before it came into force. The wide construction placed by the judge upon the words, 'and merchants generally' is certainly beneficial to those who transact business with companies. However, the statement of the company's objects is also intended to protect shareholders in terms that they may learn from it the purposes for which their money can be used. If phrases such as 'and merchants generally' can be construed to extend to all purely commercial occupations, the modern objects clause appears to serve no useful purpose as a shareholder's protection.

Gratuitous payments out of the assets of the company under *implied* powers can only be made if reasonably incidental to the business, *bona fide* and for the benefit of the company.

29. Re Lee Behrens & Co Ltd [1932] 2 Ch 46

Some three years before a company was wound up the board of directors decided that the company should enter into an agreement to pay a pension to the widow of a former managing director. The company's memorandum of association contained an express power to provide for the welfare of persons in the employment of the company or formerly in its employment, and the widows and children of such persons and others dependent upon them by granting money or pensions, providing schools, reading rooms or places of recreation, subscribing to sick or benefit clubs or societies or otherwise as the company might think fit. *Held*—that the agreement was not for the benefit of the company or reasonably incidental to its business and was for those reasons *ultra vires* and void. No thought had been given to the question whether the agreement was for the benefit of the company, indeed the sole object was to make provision for the widow.

'It is not contended, nor in the face of a number of authorities to the contrary effect could it be, that an arrangement of this nature for rewarding long and faithful service on the part of persons employed by the company is not within the power of an ordinary trading company such as this company was, and indeed in the company's memorandum of association is contained (Clause 3) an express power to provide for the welfare of persons in the employment in the company ... by granting money or pensions. ...

'But whether they be made under an express or implied power, all such grants involve an expenditure of the company's money, and that money can only be spent for purposes reasonably incidental to the carrying on of the company's business, and the validity of such grants is to be tested, as is shown in all the authorities, by the answers to three pertinent questions: (i) is the transaction reasonably incidental to the carrying on of the company's business? (ii) Is it a *bona fide* transaction? And (iii) Is it done for the benefit and to promote the prosperity of the company? ...' (*per* Eve, J)

Comment. (i) The two paragraphs from the judgment quoted above were, of course, critically examined by Pennycuick J in *Charterbridge* (see case 32 below).

(ii) Eve J based his judgment on the fact that he was implying a power. The express power to make payments to employees did not, to his mind, include directors. Executive directors such as the managing director are regarded in more modern law as employees.

(iii) It will be noted that Eve J began his paragraph on the 'benefit' test in terms that it applied to express and implied powers. However, his views on express powers are *obiter*.

30. Hutton *v* West Cork Railway Co (1883) 23 Ch D 654

The West Cork Railway Co had entered into an agreement to sell its undertaking to the Cork and Bandon Railway Co and remained in existence purely for the purpose of winding up. After the sale had been completed, the shareholders resolved at a meeting to spend £1,050 of the purchase money in compensating the salaried employees of the company for their loss of employment and £1,500 to the directors, who were not servants, as remuneration for their past services. It appeared that the directors had always understood that they were going to serve the company for nothing and there was in fact no power in the company's constitution to pay them. Hutton, a dissentient shareholder, challenged the validity of the resolution. *Held*—by the Court of Appeal—that although these payments might be made whilst the company was a going concern, a gratuitous payment could not be justified once the company had ceased to be a going concern. Therefore the payments could not be made. 'A railway company, or the directors of the company, might send down all the porters at a railway station to have tea in the country at the expense of the company. Why should they not? It is for the directors to judge, provided it is a matter which is reasonably incidental to the carrying on of the business of the company; and a company which always treated its employees with Draconian severity, and never allowed them a single inch more than the strict letter of the bond, would soon find itself deserted—at all events, unless labour was very much more easy to obtain in the market than it often is. The law does not say that there are to be no cakes and ale, but there are to be no cakes and ale except such as are required for the benefit of the company.... I think the resolution as to compensation is clearly wrong. The directors have no right to give it. It might in some instances be worth the while of the company to compensate a meritorious, but dismissed officer, but that kind of justification cannot exist in the case of a dying company. I think that makes the resolution bad...' *per* Bowen L J.

Comment. (i) Section 719 gives companies a statutory power to make provision for employees or ex-employees on the cessation of the whole or part of its business. This, of course, overrules that aspect of the Court of Appeal's decision which was concerned with employees. However, the case is still relevant in terms of its illustration of payments to non-executive directors, who are not servants, when the company has ceased to be a going concern.

(ii) The view of the majority of the Court in this case was that the payment was not validated by the fact that the members had approved it by ordinary resolution. Bowen L J said: 'The money which is going to be spent is not the money of the majority. ... It is the money of the company, and the majority want to spend it. ... They can only spend money which is not theirs but the company's if they are spending it for the purposes which are reasonably incidental to the carrying on of the business of the company.' This view has not been accepted in more recent cases—see Re Horsley and Weight, 1982.[34]

31. Re W & M Roith Ltd [1967] 1 WLR 432

In this case the controlling shareholder and director of two companies wished to provide for his widow but did not want to leave her his shares. Accordingly he entered into a service agreement with one of the companies under which his widow was entitled to a pension for life on his death. It was *held* in the liquidation of the company that the transaction was not binding on the company.

Comment. In the above case the company's constitution authorized this sort of payment, though the authorization was in the nature of a power. Clearly, it was not the main object of the company to make these payments.

The test of 'benefit' is quite inappropriate to the scope of express powers.

32. Charterbridge Corporation Ltd v Lloyds Bank Ltd [1969] 2 All ER 1185

A property developer by the name of Pomeroy owned several companies through which various developments were carried out. These companies formed a group in that each one was owned by Pomeroy. The main company in the group, P Ltd, was not the holding company of the other companies in the group but did co-ordinate their activities providing, amongst other things, finance and administration services. One of the companies in the group, Pomeroy Developments (Castleford) Ltd, held a long building lease of a piece of land at Castleford and this company gave a guarantee to Lloyds Bank in respect of a large overdraft owed to the bank by P Ltd, the guarantee being secured by giving to the bank a first legal charge on the land at Castleford. The first paragraph of the objects clause of the memorandum of Pomeroy Developments (Castleford) Ltd, gave *express* power to enter into guarantees of obligations incurred by anyone who had an undertaking in which Pomeroy Developments (Castleford) Ltd, was concerned or interested.

The Charterbridge Corporation, which was not within the group, had entered into an agreement to buy the land at Castleford from Pomeroy Developments (Castleford) Ltd but did not wish to take the land subject to the charge in favour of Lloyds Bank and now sought to show that it was *ultra vires* and void. Charterbridge relied in the main on the decision in *Re Lee Behrens & Co Ltd*, 1932,[29] contending that the guarantee, and therefore the charge securing it, was *ultra vires* unless created for the benefit of Pomeroy Developments (Castleford) Ltd and for the purposes of its business. Since the guarantee was given for the benefit of P Ltd and the group of companies as a whole, the interests of Pomeroy Developments (Castleford) Ltd were not the primary consideration. In addition these facts were known to the bank and therefore the guarantee and charge were void. *Held*—by Pennycuick J—that in considering whether the exercise of an *express* power in the memorandum of a company is *ultra vires* it is irrelevant to ask whether it is for the benefit of and to promote the prosperity of the company. Where a company is carrying out the purposes expressed in its memorandum and acts within the scope of an express power the act is *intra vires*. (*Re Lee Behrens & Co Ltd*, 1932,[29] distinguished.) However, if that view of the law was wrong the guarantee and charge were in any case valid because they were clearly made for the benefit of Pomeroy Developments (Castleford) Ltd. It would have been disastrous for that company if P Ltd had collapsed. Regarding benefit to the company the judge said—'The proper test, I think ... must be whether an intelligent and honest man in the position of a director of the company concerned, could, in the whole of the existing circumstances, have reasonably believed that the transactions were for the benefit of the company'.

Comment. (i) Pennycuick J agreed that Eve J's tests were '... probably appropriate to the scope of an implied power of a company where there is no express power. ...'

(ii) It will be noted that Pennycuick J was not dealing with an insolvent company and in any case he had found as a fact that there was benefit to the company.

Gratuitous payments: use of s. 212, Insolvency Act 1986.

33. Re Halt Garage (1964) Ltd [1982] 3 All ER 1016

The entire issued share capital of the company was owned by a husband and wife, Mr and Mrs Charlesworth, who were also the only directors. During its early years the company prospered. Both husband and wife worked very hard. Later, the company got into financial problems and went into what eventually became compulsory insolvent liquidation.

The liquidator issued a summons against husband and wife under what is now s. 212, Insolvency Act 1986. He wanted the court to decide that they were jointly and severally liable to repay to him certain sums paid to them both as directors under an express power now in *Reg* 82 of *Table A* which provides that: 'The directors shall be entitled to such remuneration as the company may by ordinary resolution determine . . .' during the period when the company had been making a loss. In regard to the husband's remuneration, the liquidator wanted repayment of that part of it which it was alleged had exceeded the market value of the work he had done. In regard to the wife, repayment was sought of the whole of her remuneration during the periods when she could not work by reason of illness. Counsel for the liquidator said quite simply that the payments to Mr and Mrs C were presents which the company had no power to make and which could not be ratified by the shareholders. Counsel for Mr and Mrs C said that the company had an express power to determine and pay directors' remuneration and that in the absence of fraud on the creditors or on minority shareholders, the amount of such remuneration was a matter for the company.

Mr Justice Oliver (as he then was) decided that—

(i) the amount of remuneration awarded to a company director was a matter of company management. Provided there has been a genuine exercise of the company's power to award remuneration and in the absence of fraud on the creditors or minority shareholders, it was not for the court to determine it or to decide to what extent it was reasonable.

(ii) Since there was no evidence, having regard to the company's turnover, that Mr C's drawings were obviously excessive or unreasonable or that they were disguised gifts of capital, the court would not inquire whether it would have been more for the benefit of the company if he had taken less. That was a matter for the company. The claim for misfeasance in regard to Mr C's drawings failed.

(iii) As regards Mrs C's drawings, the company's articles (now *Reg* 82 of *Table A*) gave power to award remuneration to a director on the mere assumption of office. It was not necessary that he should be active in any sense. To this extent the liquidator's claim that he should recover everything paid to Mrs C during periods of absence failed. However, where a director was not active, the court could examine the amount of the drawings. In the circumstances Mrs C was entitled to £10 per week (she had drawn £30) merely for being a director even during the period in which she was not active. Amounts drawn in excess of this were *ultra vires* and repayable to the liquidator.

Comment. (i) It would appear from this decision (affirming *Re Lundy Granite Co Ltd, Lewis's Case* (1872) 26 LT 673) that there is no requirement that directors' remuneration must come only from profits. Indeed, any requirement that it must would in some cases bring companies to a standstill and prevent those which had fallen on hard times from being brought round. The creditors' right to have the capital kept intact is subject to the consideration that directors may be paid remuneration.

(ii) The judge also said that the voting of directors' remuneration was valid even though in the circumstances the *Lee Behrens*[29] tests were not fully complied with.

(iii) Oliver J seemed to be of opinion that what is now s. 35 would not validate gratuitous payments because there would be no 'dealing' with the company. Obviously, this statement was *obiter* because he did not have to decide the point.

34. Re Horsley and Weight Ltd [1982] 3 All ER 1045

The issue in this case was the validity of a pension provided by the company to a working director of long service who was shortly to retire. The pension was arranged for a lump sum premium of £10,000 followed by an annual premium of £1,000. The two other directors who arranged it did not do so at a board meeting, nor was a general meeting held to discuss it. However, they were the only directors active in the management of the company at the time and between them they owned all the company's share capital.

Subsequently, the company went into compulsory insolvent winding up. The liquidator alleged that the pension arrangements were *ultra vires* and even if *intra vires* the pension arrangements had been made without the sanction of a board or general meeting, i.e. by way of misfeasance under what is now s. 212, Insolvency Act 1986. Therefore the pension-holder held the pension on trust for the company.

Evidence showed that there was an *express power* to grant pensions to directors and others and that there was a concluding clause rendering each clause in the objects clause a separate and distinct object.

On the point of *ultra vires* Buckley L J said that on a true construction of the objects clause the pension clause was a substantive and not an ancillary object of the company. The law does not require that the objects of a company should always be commercial in nature. The pension arrangements were therefore *intra vires* and constitutionally correct since they had been approved by

452

the unanimous consent of all the shareholders which in appropriate circumstances such as these could be given informally.

Comment. (i) In addition, the Court found that when the pension arrangements were made the accounts showed that business was expanding; that there were no discernible cash flow problems and that past profits were sufficient to absorb half of the payment for the pension, leaving the other half to be absorbed in the future.

There seemed, therefore, to be every indication that with the profits anticipated and the possibility of reducing directors' salaries if necessary, the remainder of the payment for the pension could be absorbed by the company. The Court made it clear that in those circumstances it was not possible to convict the directors of fraud, misfeasance, or negligence, and that their good faith in granting the pension could not in any way be impugned.

(ii) It is likely, however, that if the evidence had shown that the directors should at the time have appreciated that a pension was likely to cause loss to creditors they could well have been open to legal proceedings under s. 212, Insolvency Act 1986 and the director/pensioner would have held the pension on trust for the company whether or not the pension was granted under an express substantive object.

Gratuitous payments: use of an express object to further an unauthorized purpose: *ultra vires* in the narrow and wide sense.

35. Rolled Steel Products (Holdings) Ltd *v* British Steel Corporation [1982] 3 All ER 1057

The facts of this case are complex. It is of assistance to simplify them in order to make the essential points.

A Ltd owed (say) £100 to B Ltd. B Ltd owed (say) £1,000 to C Ltd. C Ltd provided funds to A Ltd so that A Ltd could pay its debt to B Ltd. In return A Ltd guaranteed that B Ltd would pay its debt to C Ltd and in addition gave C Ltd a debenture over its assets to secure the guarantee. B Ltd's debt to C Ltd had previously been guaranteed by S, a director of A Ltd. He was not released when A Ltd gave its guarantee and security.

At a later stage A Ltd was unable to pay its unsecured creditors and this action was brought to decide whether the guarantee and debenture were *ultra vires* in so far as the excess of £900 over what C Ltd had paid to A Ltd was concerned.

Vinelott J *held* that the guarantee and debenture were void as to the £900 excess. He distinguished between *ultra vires* in the narrow sense and in the wide sense. The former means the exercise of a power which the company does not have. (See, e.g. the pig-breeding business in *Re Introductions Ltd* (p. 456).) The latter refers to the exercise of a power which the company has but 'in furtherance of some purpose which is not an authorized purpose'.

A Ltd had an express power to lend and give guarantees but as a matter of construction this was intended only for the purpose of the company's authorized business which was wholesalers of steel, mainly to the motor trade.

The guarantee and debenture were issued to accommodate C Ltd. C Ltd knew this and so the transactions were *ultra vires* in the wider sense.

Comment. (i) Once again note that A Ltd was insolvent and there was no discernible benefit to it in the transaction as regards the surplus of £900. In *Charterbridge*[32] Pennycuick J had found the guarantee to be of benefit to the company and there was no insolvency. Clearly the two situations are distinguishable.

(ii) The Court of Appeal [1985] 2 WLR 908, affirmed the decision of Vinelott J but not his reasoning. Now if a company has the usual long objects clause and a *Cotman* (see case 37) concluding clause, then the doing of things covered by those clauses will not be *ultra vires*. But if the directors, as in *Introductions* (see case 39), use the clause for an improper purpose, the transaction is not void but can be avoided, but only if the outsider *knows* they did, as was the case in *Introductions* and *Rolled Steel*.

A company whose principal object (or *substratum*) has failed may be wound up under s. 122(1)(g), Insolvency Act 1986.

36. Re German Date Coffee Co (1882) 20 Ch D 169

According to the memorandum of association, the company was formed to work a German patent for manufacturing coffee from dates, and also to obtain patents for improvements and modifications of the said inventions, and to acquire or purchase other inventions for similar purposes together with other powers. The intended German patent was never granted, but the company did purchase a Swedish patent and established a works in Hamburg, where they made coffee from dates without a patent. When it was found that the German patent could not be obtained, many shareholders withdrew from the company, but a large majority of those who remained wished to carry on the company which was solvent. On a petition presented by two shareholders, one of whom held 100 shares and the other 10, it was *held* that the substratum of the company had failed, and it was impossible to carry out the objects for which the company was formed. Although the petition was presented within a year of incorporation, it was just and equitable that the company be wound up. The case was a marginal one, but the name German Date Coffee Co Ltd was material in determining the real object of the company, and on a consideration of the memorandum, the company was basically formed to work a German patent in Germany.

As regards the *ultra vires* rule, a clause in the memorandum stating that each clause contains a separate and independent object prevents a restrictive interpretation of the objects clause into objects and powers.

37. Cotman *v* Brougham [1918] AC 514

The parties to this action were liquidators. Cotman was liquidator of the Essequibo Rubber Estates Ltd, and Brougham was liquidator of Anglo-Cuban Oil Co. It appeared that E underwrote the shares in A-C although the main clause of E's objects clause was to develop rubber estates abroad. However, a sub-clause allowed E to promote companies and deal in the shares of other companies and gave numerous other powers. The final clause of E's objects clause said in effect that each sub-clause should be considered as an independent main object. The E Company, not having paid for the shares which it had agreed to underwrite, was put on the list of contributories of A-C, and E's liquidator asked that his company be removed from that list because the contract to underwrite was *ultra vires* and void. *Held*— by the House of Lords—that it was not, and that the E Company was liable to pay for the shares underwritten. The final clause of E's objects clause meant that each object could be pursued alone, because the Registrar had accepted the memorandum in this form and had registered the company. All the judges of the House of Lords deplored the idea of companies being registered with an objects clause in this wide form, and thought that the matter ought to have been raised by mandamus by the Registrar refusing to register the company. However, since the certificate of incorporation had been issued, it was conclusive; and matters concerning the company's registration could not be gone into.

Comment. It is clear from the judgment of Lord Parker of Waddington in this case that if the court is asked to construe the objects clause for the purposes of winding up under s. 122(1)(g), Insolvency Act 1986 because the *substratum* has gone, a concluding clause such as that found in *Cotman* is of no effect. The court can in spite of it, ascertain the main object and if this is not being pursued, wind up the company. A *Cotman* clause is, of course, effective in limiting the effect of the *ultra vires* rule.

38. Anglo-Overseas Agencies Ltd v Green [1960] 3 All ER 244

The company's main object was exporting and importing a wide variety of goods, but paragraph E of the objects clause empowered the company to 'acquire any concessions, contracts, rights ... and to perform and fulfil the terms and conditions thereof, and to carry the same into effect, operate thereunder, develop and turn to account, maintain and sell, dispose of and deal with the same'. The company employed Green, an architect, and the second defendants, who were estate agents, to assist in obtaining for the company a valuable building lease offered for sale by Merton and Morden Urban District Council. Later the company sued the defendants for conspiracy and breach of contract whereby the company had lost the lease to a rival firm. This was a preliminary issue raised by the defendants against the company to decide whether the purchase of the building lease was *ultra vires*. The concluding words of the company's objects clause made each object a separate and independent object. *Held*, by Salmon J, following *Cotman v Brougham*, 1918,[37] that the contract would, if obtained, have been *intra vires* the company, because each paragraph of the objects clause was separate and independent, and paragraph E was wide enough to cover the building lease.

Are all powers, e.g. borrowing powers, capable of being objects, just because the memorandum states that they are?

39. Introductions Ltd v National Provincial Bank Ltd [1968] 2 All ER 1221

Introductions Ltd was incorporated in 1951 and the objects of the company were to promote and provide entertainment and accommodation for overseas visitors. This business was not successful and in November 1960, the company embarked on a new business, pig farming. The company ran short of cash and arranged to borrow money from the defendants. The company executed certain debentures in favour of the bank for its indebtedness, which at the time of the winding up order in November 1965, was £25,571.

The bank now wished to enforce its security under the debentures and recover the loan. The liquidator of the company claimed that the loan was *ultra vires* and void, and the bank did not dispute that it was aware that the company's business was that of pig breeding and had notice of the company's objects. However, one of the sub-clauses of the memorandum related to borrowing and the bank said it was entitled to lend money on the strength of the sub-clause alone as it formed one of the objects of the company. There was a proviso to the memorandum which clearly stated that all sub-clauses of the memorandum were to be treated as separate and independent objects. *Held*—by Buckley J—that the loan was *ultra vires* and void, saying that the bare power to borrow contained in the sub-clause could not legitimately stand alone. The company must have had in view purposes to which the money was to be applied, i.e. for the purposes of the objects of the company. This being so the sub-clause did not authorize the raising or borrowing of money for something which was not an object of the company.

Comment. (i) This decision was affirmed by the Court of Appeal [1969] 1 All ER 887. If the bank had not known the purpose for which the money was required the loan would have been valid because the bank was not bound to inquire as to its purpose. (See *Re David Payne & Co Ltd*, 1904, p. 461.)

(ii) This case provides an example of Vinelott J's theory of *ultra vires* in the narrow and wide sense. (See *Rolled Steel Products (Holdings) Ltd v British Steel Corporation*, 1982.[35]) The pig-breeding business was *ultra vires* in the narrow sense, i.e. the company had no object relating to it. The borrowing was expressed to be an independent object but was exercised to further an unauthorized purpose. The borrowing was *ultra vires* in the wide sense. The Court of Appeal would say it was *intra vires* but invalid because made for an improper purpose known to the bank.

Ultra vires: **outsiders may be put on inquiry as to the extent of a company's powers.**

40. Fountaine *v* Carmarthen Railway Co (1868) LR 5 Eq 316

The company had issued debentures to the amount of £60,000, being the full amount it had power to borrow under its special Act of Parliament. Nevertheless the company issued a further debenture for a loan of £500 to a person named Walter Weeks. Later two debenture holders obtained judgment against the company for £500 each, and levied execution on the company's property to pay off the judgment. Subsequently the company borrowed on debentures £1,000 from the plaintiff and other persons. This action was brought by the plaintiff for an account of what was due to him, and for the appointment of a receiver. On the question of the validity of the debentures, the court *held* that Fountaine's debenture was good, but that the debenture issued to Weeks was *ultra vires* and void.

Comment. (i) In this case the lender could not recover from the company even though he was unaware of the extent of the previous borrowing. The memorandum gave him notice that there was a limit to the amount which the company could borrow and an enquiry would have shown that the limit was being exceeded. Of course, if he had enquired of the directors and was falsely told that his loan would be *intra vires* he could have sued the company for damages for the deceit of its directors, though in that case he would recover the amount of the loan as damages in tort and not under the contract. In addition, there is an action against the directors, as agents, for breach of warranty of authority, though this action is against the directors personally (see *Weeks v Propert*, 1873, p. 558). The company is not vicariously liable as it is when the directors commit the tort of deceit.

(ii) If a company's memorandum shows that its power to enter into a transaction is limited, an outsider who fails to enquire as to the validity of a transaction may find it is *ultra vires* and unenforceable unless it can be brought within s. 35.

An act beyond the objects clause cannot be validated by the subsequent agreement, even of all the shareholders. It may, however, be enforceable under s. 35.

41. Ashbury Railway Carriage and Iron Co *v* Riche (1875) LR 7 HL 653

The company bought a concession for the construction of a railway system in Belgium, and entered into an agreement whereby Messrs Riche were to construct a railway line. Messrs Riche commenced the work, and the company paid over certain sums of money in connection with the contract. The company later ran into difficulties, and the shareholders wished the directors to take over the contract in a personal capacity, and indemnify the shareholders. The directors thereupon repudiated the contract on behalf of the company, and Messrs Riche sued for breach of contract. The case turned on whether the company was engaged in an *ultra vires* activity in building a complete railway system, because if so, the contract it had made with Messrs Riche would be *ultra vires* and void, and the claim against the company would fail. The objects clause of the company's memorandum stated that it was established—

'to make or sell or lend on hire railway carriages, wagons and all kinds of railway plant, fittings, machinery and rolling stock; to carry on the business of mechanical engineers and general contractors, to purchase and sell as merchants timber, coal, metal and other materials, and to buy and sell such materials on commission or as agents.'

Held—by the House of Lords—that the purchase of the concession to build a complete railway system from Antwerp to Tournai was *ultra vires* and void because it was not within the objects of the company. The words empowering the company to carry on the business of general contracting must be construed *ejusdem generis* with the preceding words, and must therefore be restricted to contracting in the field of plant, fittings and machinery only. In other words, the company could make things for railways, but not make railways as such. The contract with Messrs Riche was therefore void, and the directors were entitled to repudiate it. It was also stated that even if all the shareholders had assented to the contract, it would still have been void because there can be no ratification of an *ultra vires* contract.

Comment. The ruling in *Rolled Steel* (1985), p. 454, would not have applied here. The company had no provision *at all* in its objects clause under which it could build railways.

At common law the other party to a transaction with a company cannot enforce it if he had constructive notice that it was *ultra vires*.

42. Re Jon Beauforte (London) Ltd [1953] Ch 131

The company decided to carry on the business of manufacturing veneered wall panels, though by its memorandum it was empowered only to make ladies' clothing. The company had a factory built for the purpose and purchased veneers from a supplier, and also coke for use in the process of making the veneered panels. The company was wound up, and its liquidator would not accept as valid the claims submitted by the builder, the supplier of the veneers, and the coke supplier, on the grounds that they were *ultra vires* and void. The builders and the suppliers of the veneers had signed judgment against the company in actions which were undefended and where the question of *vires* was not raised. This action was brought to decide the validity of the liquidator's acts. It was *held*—

(i) That as regards the builders and the suppliers of the veneers the contracts were *ex facie* (on the face of it) *ultra vires* and void, i.e. if the two parties had compared their respective contracts with the company's memorandum, they would have seen that the contracts were *ultra vires*. They had not so compared the contracts, but the common law presumes knowledge of the contents of the memorandum, since it is a public document filed at the Companies Registry. The liquidator was, therefore, right in refusing their claims. With regard to the judgments they had obtained, the court said that no judgment founded on an *ultra vires* contract is inviolable unless it embodies a decision of the court on the question of *vires*; and since these actions were undefended and the question was not raised, the judgments could be set aside.

(ii) In the case of the coke supplier, the basis of his claim was that his contract was *ex facie intra vires*, i.e. if he had compared the contract with the memorandum, it would not necessarily have appeared *ultra vires* because coke might well be used in the business of manufacturing ladies' clothing, e.g. for heating workrooms. However, it appeared that the company had ordered the coke on notepaper describing the company as 'veneered wall panel manufacturers', and giving further particulars of its work in that capacity, and not referring to the clothing business. On this claim the court held that the fuel suppliers had clear notice that the fuel was required for use in the manufacture of veneered wall panels, and as they had also constructive notice of the contents of the company's memorandum, they were on notice that the transaction was *ultra vires* and the liquidator was right in rejecting the proof.

Comment. The creditors had *actual* knowledge of the use to which their goods and services were to be put (contrast *Re David Payne*, 1904, p. 461) and constructive knowledge that the use was *ultra vires*. Section 35 will now allow a claim if the requirements of the section are complied with. There is no constructive knowledge under s. 35.

A company has not only the express powers given in the memorandum but also those powers which are incidental to or consequential upon the express powers.

43. Deuchar *v* The Gas Light and Coke Co [1925] AC 691

The plaintiff was a shareholder in the defendant company and was also the secretary of a company which supplied the defendants with caustic soda. The plaintiff sought a declaration from the court that the manufacture of caustic soda and chlorine by the defendants, and the erection of a factory for the purpose, was *ultra vires* the company. He also asked for an injunction to restrain the defendants from manufacturing caustic soda and chlorine. Astbury J at first instance, had found that the activities were fairly incidental to the powers given in the objects clause, and the Court of Appeal affirmed this decision. On appeal to the House of Lords it appeared that the defendants derived their powers from a special Act of Parliament, the Gas Light and Coke Companies Act 1868, which gave the power to make and supply gas and deal with and sell by-products. The Act authorized the conversion of the by-products into a marketable state. One of the residuals of gas-making was naphthalene which could be converted into beta-naphthol and profitably sold, conversion being by the use of caustic soda. The company had formerly purchased this from the company of which the plaintiff was secretary, but later erected a factory on their land and began to make it themselves, though they only made what they required for their own use and did not make caustic soda for resale. Chlorine was a by-product of the manufacture of caustic soda, and the chlorine, it was admitted, was converted into bleaching powder and sold. *Held*—by the House of Lords—that the manufacture of caustic soda was fairly incidental to the company's powers, and although the sale of the bleaching powder was not incidental, the matter was trivial and on the basis of the maxim *de minimis non curat lex* (the law does not concern itself with trifles) the court would not interfere.

A loan within the borrowing powers of a company will not be invalid if it is used for an *ultra vires* purpose provided the lender had no knowledge that it would be.

44. Re David Payne & Co Ltd [1904] 2 Ch 608

In February 1902, the Exploring Land & Minerals Company lent the sum of £6,000 to David Payne & Co, this sum being within the borrowing powers of the latter company. The E company was given a debenture. Later David Payne & Co was wound up, and the liquidator said that the debenture given to the E company was void because the money had been used for an *ultra vires* purpose. It appeared that a Mr Kolckmann, who was a director of the E company, intended to use the loan to finance his own Die Press and Engineering Co, and that the loan to David Payne & Co was a sham, the money having been handed over to Mr Kolckmann. The liquidator suggested that because Mr Kolckmann was a director of the E company, his knowledge that the loan was for an *ultra vires* purpose must be imputed to the E company. *Held*—by the Court of Appeal—that the debenture was valid and enforceable. Where money is borrowed by a company within the limits of its powers of borrowing, there is no obligation on the lender to enquire for what purpose the borrowing is made, or whether the money borrowed is to be applied for objects within the powers of the borrowing company. Further, where a director of the lending company has in his private capacity knowledge as to the purposes of the borrowing, there is no duty on him to disclose it to the company, and his knowledge is not imputed to the company so as to render the loan void.

Comment. (i) If it is known that the loan will be used for an improper purpose it can be avoided. (See *Introductions Ltd*, 1968.[39])

(ii) The rule could also be applied to goods as in *Re Jon Beauforte*, 1953[42] where the coke supplier would have had a good claim because the coke could have been used in the *intra vires* part of the business.

He failed because he knew in fact what the company was doing and constructively that this was outside its objects.

A director is personally liable to a third party where he has acted beyond his own powers or those of the company and the third party is unaware actually or constructively of that fact.

45. Firbanks' Executors v Humphreys (1886) 18 QBD 54

Joseph Firbanks sued to recover damages from the first defendants who were directors of the Charnwood Forest Railway Company. It appeared that Mr Firbanks had contracted to make a railway, and had done work for which he was entitled to be paid in cash. The company could not pay and Mr Firbanks agreed to accept debentures which were issued to him by the directors. In fact, at the time, unknown to the directors, the company had issued all its allowed debenture stock and the plaintiff's debentures were valueless. Mr Firbanks then sued the directors for breach of warranty of authority, but he died during the course of the action and his executors were substituted for him as plaintiffs. *Held*—The defendants were liable on their implied representation that the debentures were good, and the damages were the nominal amount of the debenture stock which Mr Firbanks should have received, in this case, £18,400.

Effect on guarantees and other securities of a transaction infringing Part V, Chapter VI of the Companies Act 1985.

46. Heald v O'Connor [1971] 2 All ER 1105

In order to enable the defendant, a purchaser of shares in a company, to complete the purchase the vendors, the plaintiffs, made a loan of £25,000 to the company which was used by the defendant to buy the shares. By way of security for the loan the company gave the vendors a floating charge over its assets. The purchaser endorsed this debenture with a guarantee promising to pay the money that had become due under the debenture if the company defaulted in payment. The company did default in payment and the vendors sued the purchaser on his guarantee. *Held*—by Fisher J—that by entering into the debenture the company had in effect given financial assistance within the meaning of what is now s. 151 in the matter of the purchase of its own shares. Accordingly, the debenture was illegal and void. Therefore, since no money could become due under the debenture no action lay on the guarantee which was also void and unenforceable. In the course of his judgment Fisher J said—'It seems to me that the only true distinction is one of construction. Did the guarantor undertake to pay only those sums which the principal debtor could lawfully be called upon to pay but had not duly paid, or did he promise to pay those sums which the principal debtor had promised to pay but had not paid whether the principal debtor could lawfully be called on to pay them or not? I have no doubt that the promise made by the guarantor in the present case was the former. The promise was to pay the principal moneys which had become due under the debenture if the company did not. If the debenture was void then no money could become due under it. The decision in *Garrard v James* [1925] Ch 616 seems to have been based on the view that the promise made by the guarantors in that case fell into the latter class.'

Comment. It should be noted that although a transaction infringing what is now s. 151 is void and unenforceable, the directors who were responsible for the infringement can be sued for breach of trust as a means of compensating the company for any loss it may have suffered. (See *Wallersteiner v Moir*, 1974.[112])

Ultra vires: application of s. 35, Companies Act 1985.

47. International Sales and Agencies Ltd *v* Marcus [1982] 3 All ER 551

In this case the High Court considered what is now s. 35 which is concerned with *ultra vires* transactions. M was a director of a money-lending company, B Ltd. F borrowed £30,000 from B Ltd. F had not repaid this loan at the time of his death insolvent. F's friend X, who was a director of I Ltd and another company, J Ltd, told M that the £30,000 was in jeopardy. X and M came to an arrangement under which I Ltd gave B Ltd four cheques for £5,000 each and J Ltd gave B Ltd a cheque for £10,000. The other directors and shareholders of I Ltd and J Ltd learned about these payments and caused I Ltd and J Ltd to claim repayment of the sums involved, i.e. £30,000 in total, from M and B Ltd.

The main objects of I Ltd and J Ltd set out in the objects clause of their memorandums of association were commodity and steel dealing and property owning respectively and their objects clauses contained the usual common form lists of ancillary objects including the giving of guarantees and indemnities, drawing negotiable instruments and doing all things as might be deemed incidental and conducive to the attainment of the objects.

However, the payments totalling £30,000 were clearly *ultra vires* I Ltd and J Ltd and it was not contended otherwise.

The claims of I Ltd and J Ltd were defended on the basis that although the cheque transactions were *ultra vires*, and therefore void at common law, they were protected by what is now s. 35 which provides: 'In favour of a person dealing with a company in good faith, any transaction decided on by the directors is deemed to be one which it is within the capacity of the company to enter into and the power of the directors to bind the company is deemed to be free of any limitation under the memorandum or articles; a party to a transaction so decided on shall not be bound to enquire as to the capacity of the company to enter into it or as to any such limitation on the powers of the directors and is presumed to have acted in good faith unless the contrary is proved.'

Mr Justice Lawson held that the claims of I Ltd and J Ltd succeeded. M and B Ltd received the £30,000 as constructive trustees. M had *actual* notice that the payments were a consequence of X's breach of trust as a director of I Ltd and J Ltd; B Ltd had *imputed* notice by reason of M's actual notice.

Section 35 had no bearing on the liability of persons to return money held by them on constructive trust to its rightful owner. This decided the matter but Mr Justice Lawson did say in passing, or *obiter*, that what is now s. 35 did not apply in any event because although the dealings of I Ltd and J Ltd were decided on by their respective directors since X was the sole effective director to whom all actual authority to act for the boards had been effectively delegated, the payment did not arise from dealings with I Ltd and J Ltd. In other words, there had been no 'dealing with a company'. The cheques paid out by I Ltd and J Ltd were merely used by X as part of his personal desire to be generous to M and M's company B Ltd. Thus the dealings were not within the Act.

Furthermore, the defendants could not claim the protection of the Act because the plaintiff companies could prove that neither M nor B Ltd had acted in good faith which was a requirement of the section.

Lawson J said on the matter of good faith: '...the test of lack of good faith in somebody entering into obligations with a company will be found either in proof of his actual knowledge that the transaction was *ultra vires* the company or where it can be shown that such a person could not, in view of all the circumstances, have been unaware that he was a party to a transaction *ultra vires*.'

Under s. 4 the objects clause may be altered but only for certain purposes laid down in that section.

48. Re Egyptian Delta Land and Investment Co Ltd [1907] WN 16

The company was formed to acquire land in Egypt and wished to acquire land in the Sudan. *Held*—The additional power would be granted on condition that the company inserted the words 'and Sudan' after the word 'Delta' in its name.

49. Re Parent Tyre Co [1923] 2 Ch 222

In this case the company was petitioning the court to confirm a special resolution altering the objects under the provisions of s. 8 of the Companies Act 1908. The company was incorporated to manufacture rubber tyres and parts of vehicles, and to invest in companies which manufactured such goods. It wished to change to the business of finance, banking and underwriting. The company had not traded since 1912, but had made a business of investing within the limits allowed by the memorandum. *Held*—by Lawrence J—that the alteration would be upheld under the provisions of the Companies Act 1908 (now Companies Act 1985, s. 4), because it would enable the company to carry on a business which could be conveniently or advantageously combined with its existing business. The company was the best judge of what was convenient or advantageous.

Comment. (i) The company had never manufactured tyres but had always operated as a holding company. It wished to extend its financial activities because virtually all of its funds were invested in the Dunlop Rubber Co Ltd and Parent Tyre wished to spread its investment risks over a broader range of securities.

(ii) The alteration also allowed the company to deal in any kind of property, either real or personal, but the Court struck this power out and approved only the remainder of the alteration relating to the finance, banking, and underwriting aspects.

50. Re Cyclists Touring Club [1907] 1 Ch 269

The company's memorandum contained the following objects—
  (i) the protection of cyclists on the roads;
  (ii) to give legal aid to the same to enable them to enforce their rights; and
  (iii) to furnish road maps and routes for cyclists.
The company now sought the confirmation of the court, as it was then required to do, under the Companies Act 1890, of a special resolution changing the objects in order to add the following clause: 'to assist and protect the pastime of touring by the use of all vehicles.'

Held—by Warrington J—that the alteration was not permitted by the Act because the interests of pedal cyclists and other vehicle users often conflicted, and the company could not serve both masters properly.

Comment. It is rare for dissentient shareholders to apply to the court under what is now s. 5. However, there was an application in *Re Hampstead Garden Suburb Trust* [1962] 2 All ER 879. The memorandum provided for surplus assets on winding up to go to an organization with similar objects or that failing *any* charity. The company sought to amend that provision in favour of one specified charity instead. Dissentients objected. The court refused to confirm the alteration. It was not a proper use of what is now s. 4(*e*) (power to restrict or abandon any of the objects).

If there is a conflict between the memorandum and the articles, the memorandum prevails. If there is an ambiguity in the memorandum, the articles may be referred to in order to resolve it.

51. Re Duncan Gilmour & Co Ltd [1952] 2 All ER 871

The company had ordinary and preference shares, and the memorandum provided that the holders of the preference shares should have a preferential right to repayment of their capital in a winding up. The usual construction put upon such a provision by the court is that, if the preference shareholders have a preferential right to repayment of capital in a winding up, they have no right to participate in surplus assets in a winding up, where these exist. However, in this case, the company's articles provided that in a winding up the surplus assets should be divided among all the members in proportion to the capital paid up on their shares, both preference and ordinary. The company was not being wound up, the point having been raised by a scheme of arrangement which was designed to alter the rights of the shareholders. *Held*—The rights conferred by the memorandum on the preference shareholders were exhaustive. They were limited to a preference in the distribution of assets, and had no right to participate in the distribution of surplus assets in a winding up or otherwise. Although the articles may be used to clarify ambiguities in the memorandum, they could not be referred to here, because the memorandum was clear and so no question of ambiguity arose.

The articles may be altered by the unanimous, albeit informal, agreement of all the shareholders, even in the absence of an enabling regulation in the articles.

52. Cane v Jones [1981] 1 All ER 533

The articles of a family company Kingsway Petrol Station Ltd, gave the chairman of the board a casting vote at both board and general meetings. In 1967 by means of an agreement which they signed (but not together at a meeting) all three of the company's shareholders agreed that the chairman should not have a casting vote. The plaintiff Gillian Cane was a beneficiary under a trust containing 15,000 shares in the company and later became fully entitled to them, and a shareholder in her own right. This resulted in the voting being evenly distributed between Gillian and the two other members of the company, who were the son and daughter of Percy Jones a life director, they having 7,500 shares each. In these circumstances the casting vote of the chairman was crucial.

A dispute arose between Gillian and the Joneses and so long as the shares were held 50/50 Gillian could at least preserve the *status quo*. She would, however, be outvoted if Percy had a casting vote and used it, as he would, to support any plans of the Joneses.

In this action Gillian asked for a declaration that where there was an equality of votes Percy should not have a casting vote because of the 1967 agreement. Counsel for Mr Jones said that since the articles could only be altered by special resolution under what is now s. 9 the agreement of 1967 was ineffective. It was *held* by Michael Wheeler QC, sitting as a Deputy Judge of the Chancery Division, that s. 9 merely provided a method by which *some* of the shareholders could alter the articles but it was a basic principle of company law that *all* the members acting together could do anything *intra vires* the company and the unanimous agreement of 1967 was effective to change the articles.

Comment. (i) It should be noted that where a company's articles are in the form of *Reg 53 Table A*, the company can proceed under that Regulation which provides that a resolution in writing signed by or on behalf of each member who would have been entitled to vote upon it if it had been proposed at a general meeting at which he was present, shall be effective. This applies to public and private companies and to extraordinary and special resolutions as well. In practice written resolutions are only possible in companies with a small number of shareholders.

(ii) In *Cane* the company was governed by *Table A* to the Companies Act 1929 which did not have a provision relating to written resolutions. This was introduced by the Companies Act 1980 and does not affect companies registered before 22 December 1980. Such companies would have to change their articles to include it. It follows from *Cane*, therefore, that an informal resolution is valid whether or not there is a provision in the articles allowing this. The resolution would have to be evidenced in writing as in *Cane* otherwise it would not be acceptable to the Registrar with whom it must be filed.

The power to alter the company's articles must be carried out '*bona fide* for the benefit of the company as a whole'. Variation of shareholders' rights.

53. Greenhalgh v Arderne Cinemas Ltd [1951] Ch 286

The articles of the company originally required any member who wished to sell his shares to offer them to his fellow members before selling them to a stranger. A majority group of the shareholders procured an alteration enabling a member to sell his shares without first offering them to his fellow members if the company so resolved by ordinary resolution. The purpose was so that the majority could sell their shares to an outsider, a Mr Sheckman, for 6s per share and so give Mr Sheckman a controlling interest. Mr Greenhalgh, a minority shareholder, objected to the alteration although Mr Sheckman was prepared to pay 6s per share to any shareholder of the company, including Mr Greenhalgh. *Held*—by the Court of Appeal—that the alteration was valid even though its *immediate* effect was to enable the majority group to sell their shares to outsiders without first offering them to the minority shareholders, though the minority shareholders, not being able to pass an ordinary resolution, were still bound to offer their shares to the majority group before selling elsewhere.

Comment. (i) The alteration of the articles in this case was clearly justifiable under the objective test adopted by the courts since the hypothetical member might benefit equally with any other member in the future by the extension of his power to sell his shares to strangers. Furthermore, the alteration represented a *relaxation* of the very stringent restrictions on transfer in the article which had existed before the change.

(ii) In earlier litigation between the same parties [1946] 1 All ER 512 what would now be 10p ordinary shares had one vote per share and so did each 50p ordinary share. Greenhalgh held 10p shares and controlled 40 per cent of the vote and could block special resolutions. The holders of the 50p shares procured an ordinary resolution (as company legislation requires, see p. 97) to subdivide each 50p share into five 10p shares with one vote each, thus reducing G's voting power. It was held that the voting rights of the original 10p shares had not been varied. They still had one vote per share.

54. Rights and Issues Investment Trust v Stylo Shoes [1964] 3 All ER 628

The defendant company proposed to increase its issued share capital by issuing unissued shares and by creating new shares. In order to ensure continuity of management it was proposed to double the voting rights of the management shares from 8 votes per share to 16 votes per share. This was sanctioned by a special resolution at a class meeting of ordinary shareholders and on the same day the company passed a special resolution to that effect. The management shareholders did not vote at either meeting. Certain ordinary shareholders who had voted against the resolutions sought in this action to restrain the defendant company from acting on them on the ground that they were oppressive to the minority. *Held*—by Pennycuick J—that the action failed. 'The effect of the resolutions is, of course, that the holders of the management shares, although they take up no new shares so that their proportion of the issued capital of the company is correspondingly reduced, retain approximately the same voting strength as they did previously the percentage being now approximately 45 per cent instead of 47 per cent. They are retaining that existing voting strength without taking up any new capital in the company. ... Of course, any resolution for the alteration of voting rights must be passed in good faith for the benefit of the company as a whole, but, where it is so, I know of no ground on which an alteration would be objectionable and no authority has been cited to that effect. So here this alteration in voting powers has been resolved upon by a great majority of those members of the company who have themselves nothing to gain by it so far as their personal interest is concerned and who, so far as one knows, are actuated only by consideration of what is for the benefit of the company as a whole. I cannot see any ground on which that can be said to be oppressive ... '. (*per* Pennycuick J.)

Comment. Absence of discrimination was also shown by the fact that the management shares were not voted and Pennycuick J quite rightly gave weight to this.

55. Dafen Tinplate Co Ltd v Llanelly Steel Co (1907) Ltd [1920] 2 Ch 124

The principal shareholders of the defendant company were other steel companies, and it was hoped that the member companies would buy their steel bars from the defendants, though there was no contract to this effect. In the main the member companies did buy their steel from the defendants, but the plaintiff company began in 1912 to get its steel from a concern called the Bynea company in which the plaintiffs had an interest. The defendant company then sought to alter its articles to expel the plaintiff company. The alteration provided that the defendant company could by ordinary resolution require any member to sell his shares to the other members at a fair price to be fixed by the directors. The plaintiffs sought a declaration that the alteration was void. *Held*—by Peterson J—that the plaintiff company was entitled to such a declaration. The power taken by the articles was a bare power of expulsion, and could be used to expel a member who was not acting to the detriment of the defendant company at all. Therefore, whatever its merits in the circumstances of the case, it could not be allowed.

Comment. This power of expulsion was to be written in the articles and would last indefinitely. In addition, it would permanently discriminate between shareholders of the same class and as such could not benefit the future hypothetical member and was therefore void.

56. Sidebottom *v* Kershaw, Leese & Co [1920] 1 Ch 154

The defendant company, which was a small private company, altered its articles to empower the directors to require any member who carried on a business competing with that of the company, to sell his shares at a fair price to persons nominated by the directors. The plaintiff was a member of the defendant company, and ran mills in competition with it, and this action was brought to test the validity of the alteration in articles. The Vice-Chancellor of the Court of the County Palatine found for the plaintiff, regarding the alteration as a bare power of expropriation, though there was no dispute that the price fixed for the purchase of the shares was fair. *Held*—by the Court of Appeal— that the evidence showed that the plaintiff might cause the defendant company loss by information which he received as a member, and as the power was restricted to expulsion for competing, the alteration was for the benefit of the company as a whole and was valid.

Comment. (i) It was obviously in the interest of the company as a whole and of the 'hypothetical member' that the company's trade secrets should not be available to its competitors.

(ii) As Lord Sterndale MR made clear in his judgment in this case, the power of compulsory purchase of shares is valid if contained in the *original* articles. Such a provision would not be set aside on the 'benefit' ground; the concept is applicable only to changes in the articles as *Phillips v Manufacturers' Securities Ltd* (1917) 116 LT 290 decides.

57. Shuttleworth v Cox Brothers & Co (Maidenhead) Ltd [1927] 2 KB 9

The company's articles provided that Shuttleworth and four other persons should be permanent directors of the company, to hold office for life, unless disqualified by any one of the events specified in Art 22 of the company's articles. These events were bankruptcy, insanity, conviction of an indictable offence, failure to hold the necessary qualification shares, and being absent from meetings of the board for more than six months without leave. The company conducted a building business, and Shuttleworth, on 22 occasions within 12 months, failed to account for the company's money which he had received on its behalf. The articles were altered by adding another disqualifying event, namely, a request in writing by all the other directors. Having made the alteration, the directors made the request to Shuttleworth, and he now questioned the validity of his expulsion from the Board. *Held*— by the Court of Appeal—that the alteration and the action taken under it was valid, because it was for the benefit of the company as whole. Shuttleworth also claimed that no alteration of the articles could affect his contract with the company, but the Court of Appeal held, on this point, that since part of his contract (the grounds for dismissal) was contained in the articles, he must be taken to know that this was in an alterable document and he must take the risk of change.

An alteration in the articles which is inconsistent with, and in breach of a contract outside of the articles, will probably not be restrained but the company will be liable in damages for the breach.

58. Southern Foundries (1926) Ltd v Shirlaw [1940] AC 701

The appellant company was incorporated in 1926 as a private company, and was engaged in the business of iron founders. The respondent, Shirlaw, became a director of the company in 1929 under a provision in the articles. In 1933 he became managing director under a separate contract, the appointment to be for 10 years, and containing restraints under which Shirlaw agreed that he would not, for a period of three years after leaving the employment of the appellants, engage in foundry work within 100 miles of Croydon. In 1935 there was a merger between the appellant company and 10 other concerns, and the group was called Federated Industries. The members of the group agreed that they should make certain alterations in their articles regarding directors; the articles of each member were altered, and in their new form gave Federated Industries power to remove any director of the company, and also stipulated that a managing director should cease to hold office if he ceased to be a director. In 1937 Shirlaw was removed from office as a director, under the provision in the articles, by an instrument in writing, signed by two directors and the secretary of Federated Industries. This meant that Shirlaw could no longer be managing director of Southern Foundries, and since his contract had still some time to run, he brought this action for wrongful dismissal. The trial judge found for Shirlaw and awarded him £12,000 damages, and the Court of Appeal affirmed that decision. The company now appealed to the House of Lords. *Held*—by a majority—that Shirlaw's contract as managing director contained an implied term that the article making him a director would not be altered. Since it had been altered, there was a breach of contract and the company was liable for it. Lord Wright took the view that since there was no privity of contract between Shirlaw and Federated Industries, it was difficult to see how they could dismiss him. Lord Romer, dissenting, did not think a term against alteration of the articles could be implied and thought that Shirlaw took the risk of alteration. Lord Porter lent support in this case to *Punt v Symons*, 1903, and said that a company could not be prevented by injunction from altering its articles but that the only remedy for an alteration which had caused a breach of contract was damages.

Comment. (i) From statements made in this case it appears that any member who votes for the alteration will also be liable to the plaintiff for inducing the company to break its contract if the inevitable consequence of the alteration is that the contract will be broken.

(ii) In *Shirlaw* the articles said that a managing director was to be subject to the same provisions for removal as any other director 'subject to the provisions of any contract between him and the company'. There was an implied term in the contract of service which overrode the power of removal without compensation in the articles.

(iii) In *Nelson v James Nelson & Sons Ltd* [1914] 2 KB 770 a service contract appointing the plaintiff to act as managing director 'so long as he shall remain a director of the company' was also held to override an article giving a power of removal without compensation. Damages were awarded to the plaintiff because his contract was terminated by his removal from office as a director. That was a breach by the company of his contract as managing director which he could then no longer perform.

Directors who have earned fees payable under the articles of the company cannot be deprived of them by a subsequent alteration of the articles reducing the fees.

59. Swabey v Port Darwin Gold Mining Co (1889) 1 Meg 385

Swabey had served the company as a director under a provision in the company's articles which provided for his salary. The articles were altered so as to reduce that salary and it was *held*—by the Court of Appeal—that, although the alteration was effective to reduce the salary for the future, Swabey could not be deprived of his salary at the original figure for the period he had served prior to the alteration of the articles.

The court has no power to rectify the memorandum or articles of a company.

60. Scott v Frank F. Scott (London) Ltd [1940] Ch 794

The defendant company was a private company with three members, Frank, Stuart and Reginald Scott, the business of the company being that of butchers. On the death of Frank Scott, his widow, Marie Scott, became entitled under his will to certain preference shares and ordinary shares in the company, as executrix. When she sought to be registered in respect of the shares, Stuart and Reginald Scott claimed that under a provision in the articles the shares must on the death of a member be offered to the other members at par, but the article was not so well drafted as to make this clear beyond doubt. This action was brought to interpret the article, and also to ask the court to rectify the article to carry a right to pre-emption if the article was not so drafted as to achieve this. *Held*—by the Court of Appeal—that the article did give the right of pre-emption claimed by Stuart and Reginald Scott. However, if it had not done so, the court could not have rectified it; the alteration could only be carried out by special resolution.

The articles bind the members to the company and the company to the members.

61. Hickman v Kent or Romney Marsh Sheepbreeders' Association [1915] 1 Ch 881

The defendant company was incorporated under the Companies Acts in 1895. The objects of the company were to encourage and retain as pure the sheep known as Kent or Romney Marsh, and the establishment of a flock book listing recognized sires and ewes to be bred from. The articles provided for disputes between the company and the members to be referred to arbitration. This action was brought in the Chancery Division by the plaintiff because the Association had refused to register certain of his sheep in the flock book, and he asked for damages for this. It also appeared that the Association was trying to expel him, and he asked for an injunction to prevent this. *Held*—by Astbury J—that the Association was entitled to have the action stayed. The articles amounted to a contract between the Association and the plaintiff to refer disputes to arbitration. Astbury J, after accepting that the articles were a contract between a company and its members, went on to say: '...No right merely purporting to be given by an article to a person, whether a member or not, in a capacity other than that of a member, as for instance, a solicitor, promoter, director, can be enforced against the company...'.

Comment. It was held, by the Court of Appeal applying *Hickman*, in *Beattie v E and F Beattie Ltd* [1938] Ch 708, that a provision in the articles that disputes between the company and its members must be referred to arbitration did not apply to a person whose dispute was between the company and himself as *director* even though he was also a *member*.

62. Pender *v* Lushington (1877) 6 Ch D 70

The Direct United States Cable Company was a company registered under the Companies Act 1862. The articles of the company provided that every member should be entitled to one vote at a general meeting for every ten shares, but should not be entitled to more than 100 votes in all. The Globe Telegraph and Trust Company was a rival of the Direct United States Cable Company and held a large number of shares in it, but the provision prevented the use of all its potential voting power and it was limited to 100 votes. Accordingly the telegraph company transferred certain of its shares to the plaintiff so as to increase their voting power, and at a meeting of the cable company the chairman rejected the plaintiff's votes and would not allow them to be exercised, and accordingly declared lost a resolution proposed by Pender which would otherwise have been carried. The plaintiff brought this representative action against the cable company's directors for an injunction to restrain them from acting on the footing that the plaintiff's votes were bad. The defence was that this was a matter for the company to complain about, and if the directors chose to act contrary to the articles, the company was the proper plaintiff. *Held*—by Jessel MR in the Chancery Division—that this case also revealed a personal wrong to the plaintiff in that his votes had been rejected. He was, therefore, entitled on the basis of the articles to an injunction for breach of the contract expressed in the articles, and the rule in *Foss v Harbottle* (see p. 197) was no bar to the action.

Comment. (i) The case is also an example of the rule that there can be no notice of trust on the register of a company or in connection with its shares. (See s. 360.) 'It comes, therefore, to this that the register of shareholders, on which there can be no notice of a trust, furnishes the only means of ascertaining whether you have a lawful meeting or a lawful demand for a poll, or of enabling the scrutineers to strike out votes.

'The result appears to me to be manifest, that the company has no right whatever to enter into the question of the beneficial ownership of the shares. ... it is clear that the chairman had no right to enquire who was the beneficial owner of the shares, and the votes in question ought to have been admitted...' (*per* Jessel MR).

(ii) If the wrong is to the company, as where, e.g. the directors have made a secret profit from office, the action is *derivative*, not *personal*, and the rule in *Foss v Harbottle* applies. (But see p. 198.)

The articles bind the members to each other.

63. Rayfield *v* Hands [1958] 2 All ER 194

The articles of a private company provided by Art 11 that 'Every member who intends to transfer his shares shall inform the directors who will take the said shares equally between them at a fair value.' The plaintiff held 725 fully-paid shares of £1 each, and he asked the defendants, the three directors of the company, to buy them but they refused. He brought this action to sue upon the contract created by the articles without joining the company as a party. *Held*—by Vaisey J—that the directors were bound to take the shares. Having regard to what is now s. 14, the provisions of Art 11 constituted a binding contract between the directors, as members, and the plaintiff, as a member, in respect of his rights as a member. The word 'will' in the article did not import an option in the directors. Vaisey J did say that the conclusion he had reached in this case may not apply to all companies, but it did apply to a private company, because such a company was an intimate concern closely analogous with a partnership.

Comment. Although the articles placed the obligation to take shares of members on the *directors*, Vaisey J construed this as an obligation falling upon the directors in their capacity as *members*. Otherwise the contractual aspect of the provision in the articles would not have applied. (See *Beattie v E and F Beattie Ltd* [1938] Ch 708 p. 474.)

The company is not bound by the articles to persons who are not members, nor to members except in their capacity as members.

64. Eley v Positive Government Security Life Assurance Co (1876) 1 Ex. D 88

The articles contained a clause appointing the plaintiff as solicitor of the company. The plaintiff was not appointed by a resolution of the directors or by any instrument under the seal of the company, but he did act as solicitor for some time. The company ceased to employ him, and he brought an action for breach of contract. *Held*—by the Court of Appeal—that the action failed because there was no contract between the company and Eley under the articles. He was an outsider in his capacity as a solicitor, and even though he was also a member, he could not enforce the articles since they gave him rights in his capacity as solicitor only.

Comment. It was held by the court of first instance that a service contract on the terms set out in the articles was created because Eley had actually served the company as its solicitor. However, the contract was unenforceable because the articles contemplated his employment for an indefinite period of time, possibly longer than a year, and there was no written memorandum of the contract signed on behalf of the company as was then required by s. 4 of the Statute of Frauds, 1677. This statute is now repealed so that the case may have been decided differently today. This view is re-inforced by the decision in *Re New British Iron Co ex parte Beckwith*[65] because surely when Eley took office he did so on the terms of the articles and had an implied contract based upon the terms of those articles. Thus if a term as to tenure could be implied in the way that a term as to salary was in *Beckwith*,[65] then Eley should have been able to sue for breach of the implied contract. *Read's case*[66] suggests also that tenure of office may be based on the articles.

Where the articles contain the terms of a contract with an outsider and the contract has been partly performed, the contract will be regarded as having been entered into on the terms of the articles.

65. Re New British Iron Co ex parte Beckwith [1898] 1 Ch 324

Beckwith was employed as a director of the company, relying for his remuneration on the company's articles which provided that the directors should be paid £1,000 per annum. In this action by Beckwith for his fees, it was *held*—by Wright J—that, although the articles did not constitute a contract between the company and Beckwith in his capacity as director, yet he had accepted office and worked on the footing of the articles, and the company was liable to pay him his fees on that basis. Actually, the company was liable on an implied contract, the articles being merely referred to for certain of its terms.

66. Read *v* Astoria Garage (Streatham) Ltd [1952] Ch 637

The defendant company was a private company which had adopted *Art* 68 of *Table A* of the Companies Act 1929. The articles provided for the appointment of a managing director, and said that he could be dismissed at any time and without any period of notice, if the company so resolved by a special resolution. The plaintiff's contract made in 1932 appointed him managing director at a salary of £7 per week, but said nothing about notice. The directors dismissed him on 11 May 1949, at one month's notice, and later called an extraordinary general meeting of the shareholders and got the necessary resolution. The special resolution was passed on 28 September 1949, and Read's salary was paid until that date but not afterwards. Read now sued for wrongful dismissal, suggesting that he ought to have had more notice because a person holding his position would customarily have more notice than he had been given. *Held*—by the Court of Appeal—that since the plaintiff's contract was silent on the point, *Art* 68 was incorporated into the express contract. Once this was done, the notice he had been given was most generous and his claim therefore failed, his tenure of office being based on the articles.

Because the articles are a contract between the company and the members, those members may have a right to have the company's affairs conducted in accordance with the articles, e.g. that a power of allotment be used by the board for the proper purpose, i.e. to raise money for the company and not for any collateral purpose.

67. Hogg *v* Cramphorn [1966] 3 All ER 420

In order to prevent a take-over bid, which they honestly thought would be bad for the company as a whole, the directors used certain money belonging to the company which was standing in an account headed '"employees" benevolent and pension fund' to set up a pension scheme by issuing preference shares bearing 10 votes each. This had the effect of giving the trustees of the fund and the directors together control of the company. The directors had power to issue shares but not to attach more than one vote to each. This action was brought by a minority shareholder on behalf of the others except the directors against the company and the directors. The following points arose out of the judgment of Buckley J—

(i) That if directors issue, without power, shares bearing more than one vote each a minority of other shareholders who may suffer thereby can sue in the name of all other shareholders notwithstanding the rule in *Foss v Harbottle*, 1843 (see p. 197). This would seem to remove a major difficulty formerly facing a shareholder under the rule in *Foss v Harbottle*, i.e. he is not prevented from complaining of an improper act merely because it could be authorized in general meeting. A member may sue because the memorandum and articles constitute a contract between him and the company which he has a right to enforce, *provided, as here, that the improper act has not in fact been authorized in general meeting*.

(ii) Although directors will normally be authorized to issue further capital they will be liable if they exercise that or any other power in order to keep control of the company notwithstanding that they honestly believe it is in the best interests of the company.

(iii) The allotment could not stand unless confirmed in general meeting and a meeting should be convened to consider whether to approve what had been done. The court ordered that the increased votes should not be exercised by the directors at the meeting though they could exercise their original votes.

(iv) If directors have acted honestly in what they believe to be the best interests of the company but have exercised a power for a purpose other than that for which it was given, as here where a power of allotment which is given to raise capital for the company was used with other motives, their actions can be ratified by the company in general meeting, since the power could have been given initially and therefore can be given retrospectively.

Comment. It will be noted that now directors must have the permission of the members by ordinary resolution or in the articles in order to allot unissued share capital, and even then must offer it to existing equity shareholders first unless their pre-emption rights have been disapplied. (Ss. 80 and 89, see further pp. 137 and 138.)

68. Bamford v Bamford [1969] 2 WLR 1107

Under a power given by the articles of association the directors of Bamfords Ltd, agricultural machinery manufacturers of Uttoxeter, Staffordshire, allotted 500,000 unissued shares of 4s each to Frederick H Burgess Ltd for cash at par. At an extraordinary general meeting of Bamfords Ltd, held approximately one month after the shares were issued, *an ordinary resolution was passed ratifying and approving the allotment*, the holders of the newly issued shares refraining from voting.

The allotment and ratification was attacked by the plaintiffs who were minority shareholders. The plaintiffs' case was that the allotment was not made for the company's benefit but to thwart a take-over bid in that representatives of Frederick H Burgess Ltd would vote with the directors of Bamfords Ltd not to accept the bid, and thus provide the necessary majority to prevent the bid succeeding. It was unanimously *held* by the Court of Appeal that the ratification was valid and the allotment good. Acts by directors which were initially defective whether because of lack of quorum or because of some defect in their appointment or because their motives were improper, could be validated, after full disclosure of the facts by the shareholders in general meeting. Even assuming that the directors had acted in breach of duty when allotting the shares any impropriety had been waived by the company and the allotment must stand.

Comment. (i) It will be noted that now directors must have the permission of the members by ordinary resolution or in the articles in order to allot unissued share capital and even then the shareholders have pre-emption rights. (Ss. 80 and 89, see further pp. 137 and 138.)

(ii) Here the majority ratified the allotment *after* the proceedings commenced. If they had done so before would the rule in *Foss v Harbottle* (p. 197) have prevented as a matter of procedure the action proceeding to trial?

At common law an outsider who enters into a transaction with a company which is consistent with its public documents may presume that all matters of internal management have been properly complied with.

69. Royal British Bank *v* Turquand (1856) 6 E & B 327

The plaintiff bank lent £2,000 to a joint stock company called Cameron's Coalbrook Steam Coal & Swansea and London Railway Company, which was at the time of the action in course of winding up. Turquand was the general manager of the company and was brought into the action to represent it. The company had issued a bond under its common seal, signed by two directors, agreeing to repay the loan. The registered deed of settlement of the company (which corresponded to the articles of a modern company) provided that the directors might borrow on bond such sums as they should be authorized by a general resolution of the members of the company to borrow. In the case of this loan it appeared that no such resolution had been passed. *Held*—by the Court of Exchequer—that the bond was nevertheless binding on the company, because the lenders were entitled to assume that a resolution authorizing the borrowing had been passed.

The *Turquand* presumption does not apply where the internal authorization is a resolution registerable with the Registrar. In such a case the outsider will have constructive notice of the fact that authorization has not been given.

70. Irvine *v* Union Bank of Australia (1877) 2 App Cas 366

This was an appeal to the Judicial Committee of the Privy Council from a judgment of the Recorder of Rangoon. The action was brought by the bank to recover £15,296 17s. 6d. advanced to the company on a mortgage of its assets. Irvine, who was also brought into the action, was a director of the company which was called the Oriental Rice Company Limited. The directors of the company had borrowed the above sum of money, and their borrowing powers were set out in Art 50 of the company's articles, where it was stated that the directors should have power to borrow on the security of the company's property 'any sum not exceeding in the aggregate one-half of the paid up capital'. The articles also provided that one-half of the votes of the members, at a meeting called for the purpose, should be necessary to enlarge, extend, rescind or alter all or any of the provisions contained in the articles. As the members had never altered the article to extend the borrowing powers of the directors, the Recorder held that, since the paid up capital of the company was £17,100, the bank could only recover one-half of that sum, i.e. £8,550. Sir Barnes Peacock in delivering the judgment of the Privy Council said: 'Their Lordships are of the opinion that the learned Recorder was correct in holding that this case is different from *Royal British Bank v Turquand*.[69] In the present case if the bank had looked at the articles, they would have found that the directors were expressly prohibited from borrowing beyond a certain amount'. It was also said that if the members had met and extended the borrowing powers of the directors for the future, some record of their resolution would have been found in the records of the Registrar of Companies because it would have involved some alteration of the articles.

Comment. Section 35 could well protect the outsider in the circumstances of this case because those who rely on s. 35 do not have constructive notice of the company's constitution and therefore are not constructively aware of absolute prohibitions of the kind seen in this case, where the directors were expressly prohibited from borrowing beyond a certain amount.

A director who has no authority to act on behalf of the company in a transaction may rely on the *Turquand* presumption: usual authority of the chairman and managing director.

71. Freeman & Lockyer v Buckhurst Park Properties Ltd
[1964] 1 All ER 630

A Mr Kapoor carried on a business as a property developer, and entered into a contract to buy an estate called Buckhurst Park at Sunninghill. He did not have enough money to pay for it, and obtained financial assistance from a Mr Hoon. They formed a limited company with a share capital of £70,000, subscribed equally by Kapoor and Hoon, to buy the estate with a view of selling it for development. Kapoor and Hoon, together with two other persons, comprised the board of directors. The quorum of the board was four, and Hoon was at all material times abroad. There was a power under the articles to appoint a managing director but this was never done. Kapoor, to the knowledge of the board, acted as if he were managing director in relation to finding a purchaser for the estate; and again, without express authority of the board but with their knowledge, he employed on behalf of the company a firm of architects and surveyors, the plaintiffs in this case, for the submission of an application for planning permission which involved preparing plans and defining the estate boundaries. The plaintiffs now claimed from the company the fees for the work done, and the company's defence was that Kapoor had no authority to act for the company. The Court of Appeal found that the company was liable, and Diplock LJ, in considering *Turquand's case*[69] and similar cases since that time, said that *four conditions* must be fulfilled before a third party was entitled to enforce against a company a contract entered into on its behalf by an agent without actual authority to make it—

(i) *A representation must be made to the third party that the agent had authority.* This condition was satisfied here because the board knew that Kapoor was making the contract as managing director but did not stop him.

(ii) *The representation must be made by the persons who have actual authority to manage the company.* This condition was satisfied because the articles conferred full powers of management on the board.

(iii) *The third party must have been induced to make the contract because of the representation.* This condition was satisfied because the plaintiffs relied on Kapoor's authority and thought they were dealing with the company.

(iv) *That under the memorandum and articles the company was not deprived of the capacity either to make a contract of the kind made or to delegate authority to an agent to make the contract.* This condition was satisfied because the articles allowed the board to delegate any of its functions of management to a managing director or a single director.

The court also decided that although the plaintiffs had not looked at the articles, this did not matter; for the rule does not depend upon estoppel arising out of a document, but on estoppel by representation.

Comment. (i) The decision in this case may be regarded as an extension of *Turquand*[69] into non-collective acts of individual directors or simply as an example of the application of the general principles of agency to companies. The principle of agency involved is that of usual authority under which an agent has the actual authority which his principal gives him, and the usual authority of an agent of his class. The judgment would appear to cover all directors and give them a wide apparent authority but it should be remembered that the case was applied on its facts to a managing director who has a great deal of usual authority anyway.

(ii) The decision of the Court in *International Sales and Agencies Ltd v Marcus*, 1982[47] suggests that a managing director or a person acting as a managing director and in effect running the company with the whole-hearted consent of the board, may bind the company by a contract which is not only beyond his powers as in this case but also beyond the company's powers since s. 35 may be applied in these circumstances.

(iii) The usual authority of a managing director or a director holding another executive office is further strengthened by *Reg* 72 of *Table A* which provides that the directors may delegate to any managing director or other director holding any other executive office such of their powers as they consider desirable to be exercised by him. Thus even though the managing director has not had powers delegated to him, the outsider may assume he has. The extension in the latest *Table A* to directors holding 'another executive office' would extend usual authority to other executive directors in companies which adopt the latest *Table A* or have an individual article like it.

72. Hely-Hutchinson *v* Brayhead Ltd [1968] 1 QB 549

A Mr Richards, the chairman and managing director of a company signed, on behalf of the company, a guarantee and indemnity in favour of the plaintiff who was also a director of the company. In this action the plaintiff was trying to enforce the contract but it was alleged that the chairman (who had never been formally appointed as managing director) had no power to bind the company in a transaction of that kind; he had in fact no express power to bind the company in such a transaction. Furthermore, since the plaintiff was himself a director of the company he could not claim to be an outsider and avail himself of the rule in *Turquand's Case.*[69] *Held*—by the Court of Appeal confirming the decision of Roskill J—that the plaintiff succeeded in enforcing the guarantee and indemnity against the company. A director acting in his private capacity who contracts with his company through another director is not automatically to be treated as having constructive knowledge of any defect in the latter's authority. Where the acts done by him are not so closely interwoven with his position as director as to make it impossible to say that he did not know of the limitations on the powers of those he dealt with, he may take advantage of the *Turquand*[69] rule. *Morris v Kanssen*, 1946[73] and *Howard v Patent Ivory Manufacturing Co*, 1888,[15] distinguished.

Comment. It is not true to say that all the judges in this case felt that a chairman had any greater authority than an ordinary director. Lord Wilberforce (in the Court of Appeal), for example, doubted whether he had. The case may therefore simply establish the greater authority of the managing director because Mr Richards was with the approval of the board acting as a managing director, though never formally appointed. It should also be noted that Lord Denning was of the opinion that Mr Richards had actual authority, such authority being implied from the circumstances that the board by their conduct over many months had acquiesced in his acting as their chief executive and committed Brayhead Ltd to contracts without the necessity of sanction from the board.

The *Turquand* presumption cannot be relied upon by 'insiders'. Thus a director who has acted on behalf of the company is under a duty to know the circumstances of the transaction and cannot rely on *Turquand*.

73. Morris *v* Kanssen [1946] 1 All ER 586

Kanssen brought this action to have determined who were the lawful directors and shareholders in a company. The original shareholders and directors were Cromie and Kanssen. Between 1940 and 1942 Cromie, in alliance with Strelitz held 'meetings' without Kanssen and concocted minutes purporting to record that Kanssen had been replaced by Strelitz as a director. Later C and S held a meeting at which they appointed Morris a director and C, S and Morris as directors then allotted all the unissued shares in the company to themselves in roughly equal parts. None of the parties realized that by virtue of a provision in the company's articles, all the directors had ceased to hold office on 31 December 1941, having not come before a general meeting before that time and there had since been no directors properly appointed. It was held at first instance that the allotment to Morris was valid by reason of what is now s. 285 but this decision was reversed by the Court of Appeal and the Court of Appeal was confirmed by the House of Lords on the ground that whereas s. 285 could operate to cure a defective appointment, it could not validate the acts of persons who had not been appointed at all. Morris also contended that he was entitled to rely on the rule in *Turquand's Case*[69] but it was held that as an 'insider' he could not.

CAPITAL AND ITS MAINTENANCE

A share which by its class rights is preferential as to dividend has no right to share in profits remaining after the preferential dividend has been paid. The express provisions relating to class rights are in general exhaustive.

74. Will *v* United Lankat Plantations Co Ltd [1914] AC 11

The plaintiff was a preference shareholder in the company and claimed that the preference shares which he held—
(i) were entitled to a preferential dividend of 10 per cent, and had preference as regards payment of capital; and
(ii) carried a right to participate in any further profits made by the company after the 10 per cent preference dividend had been paid. The resolution under which the shares were issued certainly provided for a preference dividend of 10 per cent and gave the shares preference as to repayment of capital. The articles provided that, subject to any priorities that might be given upon any new issue of shares, the profits of the company available for dividend should be distributed among the members in accordance with the amounts paid on the shares held by them. *Held*—by the House of Lords—the articles were expressly made subject to any other priorities, and as the terms of issue of the preference shares had given the preference shareholders a priority as to dividend of 10 per cent and as to repayment of capital in a winding up, these rights were exhaustive. The preference shares could not, therefore, participate further in the profits in the absence of an express provision in the articles to that effect, a provision which the articles did not contain.

Preference shares—arrears of dividend in a winding up.

75. Re Crichton's Oil Co [1902] 2 Ch 86

The capital of the company consisted of preference and ordinary shares all fully paid, the preference shares being entitled to a cumulative dividend. The preference dividend was paid for some time, but for three years the company was carried on at a loss and no dividends were declared. The next year a profit of £1,675 was made, but again the directors did not declare a dividend.

The company went into voluntary liquidation, and after payment of debts and 7s per share to the ordinary and preference shareholders as repayment of capital, the £1,675 remained in the hands of the liquidator as profit and not capital. The ordinary shareholders claimed that this should be distributed rateably among all the shareholders, whilst the preference shareholders said it should be employed in paying the arrears of preference dividend. The liquidator asked the court to settle the matter. *Held*—by the Court of Appeal—since the dividend on the preference shares had not been declared, they were not entitled to the arrears unless there was an express provision in the articles, which was not the case here. The court ordered that the sum of £1,675 be divided as if it were capital, i.e. rateably among all the shareholders, both ordinary and preference.

76. Re Roberts and Cooper Ltd [1929] 2 Ch 383

The capital of the company consisted of 4,000 'A' preference shares of £10 each, 4,000 'B' preference shares also of £10 each, and certain ordinary shares. The preference shares were entitled under the memorandum to receive a fixed cumulative dividend, which at the relevant time was 5 per cent, and it was provided that, on a winding up, preference shares were to receive in full from the assets of the company the amount of their paid-up capital, together with any arrears of dividend due on that date, in priority to the claims of all other shareholders. It was also provided that the 'A' preference shareholders should be entitled to receive in full all capital and arrears of dividend before the 'B' preference shareholders were to receive anything. In April 1925, the company resolved to wind up, and at that time no preference dividend had been declared or paid for four years. In the winding up all the creditors of the company were duly paid, and the 'A' preference shareholders were paid £10 per share, and the 'B' preference shareholders £7 17s. 6d., there being still £10,000 available for distribution. If it were held that four years' dividends were due, this would entail a further payment of £8,000 to the 'A' preference shareholders, the remaining £2,000 being payable to the 'B' preference shareholders. If the dividends were not due, then the 'B' preference shareholders would be entitled to a repayment of £2 2s. 6d. per share, i.e. £8,500, leaving £1,500 for the ordinary shareholders. The liquidator asked the High Court to determine the question. *Held*—since no dividends had been declared between 1921 and 1925, they were not due in the sense meant by the memorandum, and the preference shareholders were not entitled to any arrears of dividend. £1,500 was, therefore, available for the ordinary shareholders.

Comment. It is usually provided in the terms of issue of preference shares that the preference dividend shall be deemed to be due on a certain date or dates during the year in order to avoid argument based on the decisions in *Crichton* and *Roberts*, above.

COMPANY FLOTATIONS

A document which offers to acquire the shares of members in one company for shares to be issued by the company making the offer is not a prospectus within the Companies Act 1985 nor the Financial Services Act 1986 and thus need not comply with either of the two Acts.

77. Governments Stock and Other Securities Investment Co Ltd *v* Christopher [1956] 1 All ER 490

On 12 November 1955, the British & Commonwealth Shipping Co Ltd made an offer in writing to acquire the whole of the preference and ordinary shares and stock of the Union Castle Mail Steamship Co Ltd and the Clan Line Steamers Ltd in exchange for shares in British & Commonwealth. The offer was conditional on acceptance by not less than 90 per cent of all the share and stockholders in the two companies, and on permission being obtained to deal on the London Stock Exchange. The circular setting out the offer contained a form of acceptance and transfer. The plaintiffs, on behalf of themselves and all the other share and stockholders of Union Castle, except the directors of the company, asked for an injunction to stop the defendants from proceeding with the offer, contending that the circular was a prospectus and that the contents must comply with what is now Sched 3 of the 1985 Act. The defendants admitted that if it was, it did not comply with the provisions of the Act. *Held*—by Wynn-Parry J—that the prospectus provisions applied only where shares were offered for 'subscription or purchase'. Here there was no purchase, the shares being unissued and to be received direct from the issuing company; and there was no subscription because they were not to be taken for cash. The offer was to exchange shares and consequently the plaintiffs failed.

Comment. These offer documents are governed by Rule 23 of the City Code which requires that they be drafted with the same standard of care as a prospectus within the meaning of the relevant statutes and Rules.

A company is answerable for statements of fact in an expert's report included in a prospectus unless there is an express disclaimer.

78. Re Pacaya Rubber and Produce Co Ltd, Burns' Application [1914] 1 Ch 542

The company published a prospectus inviting the public to subscribe for certain shares, and included an expert's report by a Mr Hassell on the condition of certain rubber estates. This report contained errors in that it overstated the number of rubber trees which were mature enough to yield latex. Burns applied for shares on the faith of the prospectus, and was allotted 800 shares on 30 March 1910. On 11 October of the same year he discovered the misrepresentations and immediately wrote to the company rescinding the contract to take the shares. He then had a nervous breakdown and was unable to attend business until June 1911. On 28 July 1911, the company sued him for calls due, and he defended the action by pleading the misrepresentation, but on 7 February 1912, when the company commenced to wind up compulsorily, the liquidator put Burns on the list of contributors. In this case Burns asked the court to rescind his contract and remove his name from the list because of the misrepresentation in the prospectus under which he bought the shares. *Held*—by Astbury J, that—

(i) Burns was not guilty of *laches* or delay because he had repudiated his contract by writing to the company as soon as he discovered he had been misled.

(ii) Where a company issues a prospectus and invites applications based on statements of fact made by an expert, the accuracy of those statements is *prima facie* the basis of the contract, and unless the company expressly dissociates itself from those statements, any contract to take shares can be rescinded if the statements are material and false, as they were here.

In order to be actionable as a contractual misrepresentation a false statement in a prospectus must be one of fact and not intention or opinion.

79. Aaron's Reefs Ltd v Twiss [1896] AC 273

A prospectus which a gold-mining company issued was held by the House of Lords to be misleading because it described the mine to be acquired by the company as rich and merely in need of machinery to start production at once. In fact the mine had been worked unsuccessfully by three previous companies. The reports which were quoted to show that the mine was rich were all more than three years old and the purchase price which was to be paid for the mine, which the prospectus did not disclose, would in fact take up so much of the capital which the company hoped to raise by the issue that it would not have enough capital left to work the mine.

80. Edgington *v* Fitzmaurice (1885) 29 Ch D 459

The plaintiff was induced to lend money to a company by representations made by its directors that the money would be used to improve the company's buildings and generally expand the business. In fact the directors *intended* to use the money to pay off the company's existing debts as the creditors were pressing hard for payment. When the plaintiff discovered that he had been misled, he sued the directors for damages for fraud. The defence was that the statement they had made was not a statement of a past or present fact but a mere statement of intention which could not be the basis of an action for fraud. *Held*— by the Court of Appeal—The directors were liable in deceit. Bowen L J said: 'There must be a misstatement of an existing fact; but the state of a man's mind is as much a fact as the state of his digestion. It is true that it is very difficult to prove what the state of a man's mind at a particular time is, but if it can be ascertained, it is as much a fact as anything else. A misrepresentation as to the state of a man's mind is, therefore, a misstatement of fact.'

Comment. (i) Statements of opinion may be actionable in damages under the *tort* of negligence. (See *Hedley Byrne & Co Ltd v Heller & Partners Ltd*, 1963, p. 494.)

(ii) Although the action is for damages for fraud the case is relevant to the remedy of rescission which also requires a false statement of existing fact.

A statement is untrue if because of what it fails to say it is misleading even though what it does say is true.

81. R. *v* Kylsant [1932] 1 KB 442

A prospectus contained a statement to the effect that the company had paid dividends in every year between 1921 and 1927. This statement, which was true, gave the impression that the company had made trading profits during each of those years. However, it appeared that in fact the company had incurred considerable trading losses and had been able to pay the specified dividends only by drawing on secret reserves. The trading losses were not disclosed. It was *held* by the Court of Criminal Appeal that the prospectus was false in that it placed before intending investors figures which did not truly disclose the existing position of the company. Lord Kylsant, who was a director of the company and knew that the statements were misleading, was guilty of an offence under the Larceny Act 1861, s. 84 (see now the Theft Act 1968, s. 15). Although the statements made in the prospectus were in themselves true, the omission to state that dividends had been paid only by drawing on secret reserves had resulted in the prospectus giving a false impression of the company's position which was enough for the purposes of the offence.

Comment. This case was a criminal prosecution but the same principles of falsity apply in civil cases. Thus in *Coles v White City (Manchester) Greyhound Association Ltd* (1929) 45 TLR 230, a prospectus stated that certain land was 'eminently suitable' for greyhound racing. It failed to say that before buildings for kennels and stands could be built, local authority approval was necessary. In an action by the plaintiff to rescind the contract to take shares the Court of Appeal held that the land was misleadingly described and rescission was granted.

The purpose of the statements in a prospectus is to invite persons to apply for shares in the company, i.e. to induce a contract with the company. So far as remedies for contractual misrepresentation are concerned, it cannot be relied upon by those who purchase shares from some other source.

82. Peek *v* Gurney (1873) LR 6 HL 377

The respondents were the directors of a bill-broking company and had issued a prospectus containing material false statements of fact going to the company's solvency, and in particular had concealed the precise nature of the company's bad debts. The business had in fact been carried on at a loss for some years. Peek became a purchaser of 2,000 shares in the company, and now sued the directors for damages for fraud because the shares had lost value owing to the company's insolvency. It appeared that Peek was not an original allottee but had taken the shares by transfer, though he had relied on the prospectus. *Held*—by the House of Lords—The force of the prospectus was spent once it had induced the original allottees to subscribe for shares under it, and since Peek was not an original allottee, he had no claim against the directors in respect of their false statements.

Comment. (i) The decision has a somewhat unfortunate effect because, at those times, when public issues are oversubscribed, it is most likely that those persons who did not receive an allotment or an adequate allotment as subscribers will try to purchase further shares within a short time on the Stock Exchange. These people will clearly be relying on the prospectus, but in view of this decision would have no claim in respect of false statements in it.

(ii) A claim in tort for damages for a negligent misstatement should be available under *Hedley Byrne* (p. 494) in that those who publicly advertise a prospectus must surely in the modern context foresee that it will be relied upon by subscribers *and* by those who purchase from subscribers on the stock market for a reasonable time after the issue of the prospectus. (See s. 146, Financial Services Act 1986 at p. 130.)

In appropriate circumstances the court may hold that a prospectus was intended to induce persons to purchase shares as well as to induce subscribers. Where this is so the rule in *Peek v Gurney* will not be applied.

83. Andrews *v* Mockford [1896] 1 QB 372

The defendants were father and son, and they prepared a prospectus for a gold mining company called the Sutherland Reef Company which never existed, the whole thing being a sham. The prospectus was issued to the public, and early in 1889 the plaintiff received a copy of it but decided that he would not buy shares under it. The issue was not very successful and so the defendants caused to be published in the *Financial News* in September 1889, an article based on a telegram sent by another son to his father from Africa. This confirmed certain statements in the prospectus and said—'Mockford, London. Sutherland Reef main shaft down 50 feet discovered good body of pay ore assays 24 ozs. per ton'. This telegram was again a mere sham. Andrews read the article in the *Financial News* and decided to buy some shares in the company on the market. On later discovering the fraud, he sued the defendants for damages, and their defence was that the plaintiff had relied on the article in the *Financial News*, and that the plaintiff's loss was too remote if he had bought the shares on the strength of the article. *Held*—by the Court of Appeal—That as a *matter of fact* the force of the prospectus was not spent in this case, and the defendants were liable since it was one continuous fraud.

A misrepresentation in a prospectus must have been material to the plaintiff if he is to rely upon it successfully.

84. Smith v Chadwick (1884) 9 App Cas 187

This action was brought by the plaintiff, who was a steel manufacturer, against Messrs Chadwick, Adamson and Collier, who were accounts and promoters of a company called the Blochairn Iron Co Ltd. The plaintiff claimed £5,750 as damages sustained through taking shares in the company which were not worth the price he had paid for them because of certain misrepresentations in the prospectus issued by the defendants. The action was for fraud. Among the misrepresentations alleged by Smith was that the prospectus stated that a Mr J. J. Grieves, MP, was a director of the company, whereas he had withdrawn his consent the day before the prospectus was issued. It was *held* by the House of Lords that the statement regarding Mr Grieves was untrue but was not material to the plaintiff, because the evidence showed that he had never heard of Mr Grieves. His action for damages failed.

A person who has been misled by a false statement in a prospectus is not prevented from obtaining a remedy merely because he failed to check the accuracy of the statement.

85. Central Railway Company of Venezuela v Kisch (1867) LR 2 HL 99

The prospectus of a railway company stated that it had entered into a contract to build a railway in Venezuela 'at a price considerably within the available capital of the company'. This statement was false because it turned out that the company would have to pay £50,000 for the concession to build the railway, and it would then cost £420,000 to make it, and this was not really covered adequately by the available capital of the company. The prospectus also stated that the engineer's report, maps and plans could be inspected and further information obtained at the offices of the company. An examination of these documents would have revealed the true position, but the plaintiff relied on the statements in the prospectus, and did not inspect the documents or ask for additional information. He now asked for rescission of his contract to take shares in the company. *Held*— by the House of Lords—the fact that he had not inspected the documents or asked for further information was no bar to his action for rescission. He had chosen to rely on the prospectus which he was entitled to do.

A false statement is not fraudulent unless it was made knowing it to be false, without belief in its truth, or recklessly not caring whether it be true or false.

86. Derry v Peek (1889) 14 App Cas 337

The Plymouth, Devonport and District Tramways Co had power under a special Act of Parliament to run trams by animal power and, with the consent of the Board of Trade, by mechanical and steam power. Derry and the other directors of the company issued a prospectus inviting the public to apply for shares in the company and stating that the company had power to run trams by steam power and claiming that considerable economies would result. The directors assumed that the Board of Trade would grant its consent as a matter of course, but in the event the Board refused permission for certain parts of the tramway, and the company went into liquidation. Peek, who had subscribed for shares under the prospectus, brought this action against the directors for fraud. *Held*—by the House of Lords—that before a statement can be regarded as fraudulent at common law, it must be shown that it was made knowing it to be untrue, or not believing it to be true, or recklessly, not caring whether it be true or false. On the facts of the case it appeared that the directors honestly believed that permission to run the trams by steam power would be granted as a matter of course by the Board of Trade, and thus they were not liable for fraud.

Comment. (i) This case gave rise to the Directors' Liability Act, 1890, and s. 67 of the Companies Act 1985, which provides for compensation even where the directors' statements are not made fraudulently.

(ii) Fraud must be proved to the criminal standard, i.e. beyond a reasonable doubt; not to the civil standard, i.e. on a balance of probabilities. It is thus not easy to sustain an action based on fraud. Furthermore, it will be noticed from this case that the mere fact that no grounds exist for believing a false statement does not of itself constitute fraud. Dishonesty is required.

(iii) A person is not guilty of fraud if he made a false statement which, as a result of his personal misunderstanding, he thought was true. Thus in *Akerhielm v De Mare* [1959] 3 All ER 485, the defendant issued a circular inviting subscriptions for shares in cash and stating that about one-third of the company's capital had already been 'subscribed'. The word 'subscribed' is normally taken to mean 'paid for in cash'. In fact the company had not received any money for its shares since they had been allotted for promotion services and the sale of patent rights to the company. The defendant did not understand the meaning normally given to 'subscribed' and was not guilty of fraud.

Damages for fraud against the company will not be granted unless the contract to take the shares has been rescinded. Thus damages cannot be claimed if an action for rescission has not been taken or if rescission is no longer possible.

87. Houldsworth v City of Glasgow Bank (1880) 5 App Cas 317

The bank was an unlimited company registered under the Companies Act 1862. In February 1877, the plaintiff purchased stock in the bank and was entered on the Register of Members and received dividends. On 22 October 1878, the bank commenced to wind up and the plaintiff's name was put on the list of contributories. It appeared that the directors of the bank had made various fraudulent misstatements to and concealments from the plaintiff when he took the stock, and he now sued the bank as vicariously liable for the frauds of its officers, commencing his action on 21 December 1878, i.e. after the commencement of the winding up. *Held*—by the House of Lords—A person who is induced to take shares in a joint stock company by the fraud of the agents of that company cannot bring an action for damages against the company whilst he remains a member of it, but must first rescind the contract. If that becomes impossible, as it had here by the commencement of the winding up, then his action for damages becomes irrelevant and cannot be maintained.

Comment. (i) The decision is somewhat anomalous because the House of Lords failed to recognize fully the fact that a company is a *persona* at law and therefore a member is not suing himself, as a partner would be if he sued the firm. The decision seems to be based on capital maintenance, i.e. the fact that the courts have always regarded the share capital of a company as a creditors' fund, not to be attacked by shareholders in priority to creditors, particularly in a winding up. Rescission is not permitted once a winding up has commenced, and to allow an action for damages would allow a shareholder to attack the company's assets along with the creditors by the device of suing for fraud. Additionally, as Lord Cairns and Lord Selborne said, a plaintiff cannot sue the company for damages so long as he remains a shareholder because while he does he is bound by the contract between him and the company and his fellow shareholders which is implied from the fact of his membership. One of the terms of that contract is that the company's property shall be used only for the purpose of achieving its objects. This does not include the payment of compensation to shareholders who have been defrauded.

(ii) The rule in *Houldsworth* does not apply to an issue of debentures.

The measure of damages in an action for fraud is the tort measure, i.e. the price paid for the shares less the actual value at the date when the shareholder took issue of them.

88. McConnel *v* Wright [1903] 1 Ch 546

The plaintiff was a shareholder in the Standard Exploration Co Ltd, and sued the defendant for damages for misrepresentation contained in a prospectus issued by him as a director of the company. The prospectus stated that the directors had acquired on behalf of the company a controlling interest in an undertaking operating successfully in the Pandé Basin and mining copper. This interest had not been acquired when the prospectus was issued but was in an advanced state of negotiation and was acquired within a few days of the issue of the prospectus. The company failed and the plaintiff sued Mr Wright who was chairman of the board. The defence to this action was that there could be no damage to the plaintiff because the interest had now been got in. *Held*—by the Court of Appeal—The true measure of damages was the difference in value which the shares would have had on the date of allotment if the statement had been true, and the value which they would have had on that day if it had been known that there was only a mere possibility of acquiring the interest. An enquiry was directed for the purpose of ascertaining the damages on that basis.

Comment. This was a claim under the Directors' Liability Act 1890 (later s. 67, Companies Act 1985). The court decided also that the measure of damages would have been decided in the same way if the action had been in tort for deceit. If the contract measure, i.e. represented value less actual value, had been used there would have been no damages because the representation regarding the mining interest came true. It was later acquired.

When a person has been induced to subscribe for securities on the faith of a prospectus containing a material misrepresentation he may, depending on the circumstances of the case, have a claim for damages in negligence.

89. Hedley Byrne & Co Ltd *v* Heller & Partners Ltd [1963] 2 All ER 575

The appellants were advertising agents and the respondents were merchant bankers. The appellants had a client called Easipower Ltd, who were customers of the respondents. The appellants had contracted to place orders for advertising Easipower's products on television and in newspapers, and since this involved giving Easipower credit, they asked the respondents, who were Easipower's bankers, for a reference

494

as to the creditworthiness of Easipower. The respondents said that Easipower Ltd was respectably constituted and considered good, though they said that the statement was made without responsibility on their part. Relying on this reply, the appellants placed orders for time and space for Easipower Ltd, and the appellants assumed personal responsibility for payment to the television and newspaper companies concerned. Easipower Ltd went into liquidation, and the appellants lost over £17,000 on the advertising contracts. The appellants sued the respondents for the amount of the loss alleging that the respondents had not informed themselves sufficiently about Easipower Ltd before writing the statement, and alleging that they were therefore liable in negligence. *Held*—by the House of Lords—In the present case the respondents' disclaimer was adequate to exclude the assumption by them of the legal duty of care, but, in the absence of the disclaimer, the circumstances would have given rise to a duty of care in spite of the absence of a contract or fiduciary relationship. The dissenting judgment of Denning L J, in *Candler v Crane, Christmas*, 1951 (see p. 584) was approved, and the majority judgment in that case was disapproved.

Comment. This case decided that there could be a duty of care in the tort of negligence arising from a negligent misstatement which had resulted in monetary loss. It opened up the possibility of actions in negligence where such statements were made in a prospectus although it has never been tested in that context.

SHARES AND THEIR TRANSFER

Where, as is usual, the post is the means of communication which is contemplated by the parties, the allotment is complete when the letter of allotment is posted.

90. Household Fire Insurance Co *v* Grant (1879) 4 Ex D 216

The defendant handed a written application for shares in the company to the company's agent in Glamorgan. The application stated that the defendant had paid to the company's bankers the sum of £5, being a deposit of 1s. per share on an application for 100 shares, and that he also agreed to pay 19s. per share within 12 months of allotment. The agent sent the application to the company in London. The company secretary made out a letter of allotment in favour of the defendant, and posted it to him in Swansea. The letter never arrived. Nevertheless the company entered the defendant's name on the share register and credited him with dividends amounting to 5s. The company then went into liquidation and the liquidator sued for £94 15s., the balance due on the shares allotted. *Held*—by the Court of Appeal—that the defendant was liable. Acceptance was complete when the letter of allotment was posted.

An application for shares lapses after the passage of a reasonable time.

91. Ramsgate Victoria Hotel Co *v* Montefiore (1866) LR 1 Exch 109

The defendant offered by letter dated 8 June 1864 to take shares in the company. No reply was made by the company, but on 23 November 1864, they allotted shares to the defendant. The defendant refused to take them up, the company by then being financially unsound. *Held*—by the Court of Exchequer—his refusal was justified because his offer had lapsed by reason of the company's delay in notifying their acceptance.

Conditional acceptance for shares may be made.

92. Re Universal Banking Co, Rogers' Case, Harrison's Case (1868) 3 Ch App 633

Rogers wished to be appointed the local manager for a joint stock banking company. He was informed by an agent of the company that before he could be appointed he would have to purchase 100 shares. Rogers applied for the shares and the agent sent the application form to the directors with a letter saying that the application was made on condition that Rogers was appointed branch manager. Shares were allotted to Rogers but he could not pay the deposit on them, and the directors refused to give him the appointment, but did put his name on the register of members. The company was then wound up, and the question of Rogers' liability to pay for the shares arose. *Held*—Rogers' application was conditional upon being appointed as branch manager, and he was not a member of the company until that event took place. Since it had not taken place, Rogers was not liable to pay for the shares.

Harrison's circumstances were similar, but he did not make his application conditional upon being appointed manager. It was held that he was liable, having become a shareholder. There is thus a distinction between a *conditional* application and an application for shares coupled with a *collateral agreement*.

In appropriate circumstances a company is estopped from denying against a *bona fide* purchaser of its shares that the person named in the share certificate concerned is entitled to it.

93. Re Bahia & San Francisco Railway Co (1868) LR 3 QB 584

Miss Amelia Tritten was the registered holder of shares in the railway company and left the shares in the hands of her broker. A transfer of the shares was made by the broker to a Mr Stocken and a Mr Oldham by means of a transfer on which Miss Tritten's name was forged. The transfer and the certificates were left with the company's secretary for registration, and he wrote to Miss Tritten advising her of the transfer. Having received no reply after ten days, he registered the transfer, removing Miss Tritten's name from the register, and substituting the names of Stocken and Oldham. Stocken and Oldham eventually transferred the shares to the Revd Burton and a Mrs Goodburn, and they were registered and certificates issued to them. When the forgery was discovered, Miss Tritten's name was restored to the register, and in this action the Revd Burton and Mrs Goodburn sued the company for damages. *Held*—by the Court of Queen's Bench—the company was estopped from denying the validity of the certificates, and must pay damages equal to the value of the shares at the date when the company first refused to recognize the Revd Burton and Mrs Goodburn with interest at 10 per cent also from that time.

94. The Balkis Consolidated Co Ltd v Tomkinson [1893] AC 396

This action was brought by Tomkinson to recover damages in respect of the refusal of the appellant company to register the purchasers from Tomkinson of shares in the company. It appeared that Tomkinson, who was a stockbroker, loaned the sum of £250 in December 1888, to a person named Powter. This loan was made on the faith of, and in exchange for, the transfer of shares in the appellant company which Powter purported to use as a security. The loan was given for the deposit of a certificated transfer which indicated that shares to the value mentioned were registered in Powter's name and that the certificate was left with the company. The loan of £250 was paid off in January 1889, and further loans were afterwards made on the faith and security of the same certificated transfer. In May 1889, Tomkinson, with the consent of Powter, decided to convert his equitable mortgage into a legal mortgage, and inserted his name in the certificated transfer as transferee, and lodged it with the company for registration. In July

1889, the company issued a certificate to Tomkinson stating that he was the owner of the shares set out in the certificated transfer. In August 1889, Powter owed Tomkinson £193 14s. 6d. and Tomkinson still held the shares as security. Powter told him to sell the shares and realize the debt that way and so Tomkinson sold the shares to various purchasers on the strength of the certificated transfers, the company certifying yet again that Tomkinson was the owner of the shares. The company refused to register the purchasers from Tomkinson because it appeared that in March 1888, before Tomkinson's first loan to Powter, the company had certified a transfer from Powter to persons named Balfour and Maitland, who had actually been registered in January 1889. Tomkinson, being a stockbroker, had by virtue of custom to buy other shares in the appellant company to replace those in respect of which the purchasers from him could not obtain registration, and he now sued the company for the value of the shares which he had had to replace, regarding the company as estopped from denying his title to the shares. *Held*—by the House of Lords—the company was estopped from denying Tomkinson's title and must pay him the damages claimed.

Comment. Powter was able to sell the same shares twice, once to Balfour and Maitland, and once to Tomkinson, because some of the company's servants were in collusion with him.

95. Longman *v* Bath Electric Tramways Ltd [1905] 1 Ch 646

In April 1904, Peter Bennett became the registered owner of shares in the tramway company and certificates were made out in his name but were not sent to him. On the same day a transfer by Bennett to Messrs Houselander and Madders was presented to the secretary of the company, and the instrument of transfer was certified by him to the effect that certificates were lodged at the company's office showing a *prima facie* title in Bennett. The certificated transfers were returned to Houselander and Madders, and they executed them and returned them to the company, thus becoming the registered owners of the shares. On 22 April 1904, the company secretary, when sending Bennett some other certificates to which he was entitled, enclosed by mistake the certificates for the shares which Bennett had transferred to Houselander and Madders, and later the plaintiffs lent money to Bennett on the security of those certificates. The loan was not repaid and the plaintiffs sent the certificates to the company for registration. The company refused to register the plaintiffs who now sued for damages on the ground that the company was estopped from denying Bennett's title to the shares and, therefore, by inference, the title of the plaintiffs. *Held*—by the Court of Appeal—the plaintiffs were not persons who could rely on the estoppel arising out of the certificates made out in Bennett's name. There was a duty on the company to retain the certificates when a transfer had been certificated, but the duty did not extend to the whole world but only to the transferee under the certificate transfer. The certificates were *prima facie* evidence of the title only and were not in the nature of a warranty. The court did say that if there had been fraud here by the company or its secretary, as distinct from mere negligence, the company might have been liable.

Comment. The basis of this decision would seem to be that the *proximate cause* of the loss was the fraud of Bennett, not the negligence of the company.

96. Dixon *v* Kennaway & Co Ltd [1900] 1 Ch 833

In January 1897, the plaintiff employed Liddell, a broker, to buy some shares for her in the company. Liddell was also the secretary of the company. Liddell prepared a transfer of 30 shares, the transferor being his clerk, who had never owned any shares in the company and who was a man of no means. The certificates were issued to the plaintiff, the directors relying throughout on Liddell's assurance that the transfer was good. In June 1898, Liddell was dismissed by the company, and in August 1898, was adjudicated bankrupt. The plaintiff now sued the company for damages because she had not in fact obtained any shares under the forged transfer, and she claimed that the company was estopped from denying her title because they had issued certificates to her. *Held*—by the High Court—although in the normal way the company would not have been estopped by the issue of the certificates under a forged transfer, they were in this case, because the plaintiff had relied on the certificates to her detriment in that she had now lost all her remedies against Liddell who was bankrupt.

Comment. Although it is the general rule that a person cannot invoke the rule of estoppel when he presents for registration a forged transfer in his own favour, he can do so if (*a*) someone else presented it, and (*b*) he can show reliance to his detriment on the certificate as in the above case where Liddell had become bankrupt.

Estoppel in terms of a share certificate may operate, not only as to title, but also as to the sum paid up.

97. Bloomenthal *v* Ford [1897] AC 156

Bloomenthal lent £1,000 to a company, the inducement being that he would have as a security certain 7 per cent preference shares fully paid up. The company issued the certificates to the plaintiff, the said certificates stating that the shares were fully paid up. No money had in fact been paid on the shares which were issued direct from the company to Bloomenthal, but he believed that someone else had paid for the shares in full. The company went into liquidation, and Bloomenthal was placed on the list of contributories by the liquidator, Ford. Bloomenthal now asked the court to remove his name from the list, claiming that the company was estopped from denying that the shares were fully paid because the certificates said they were. *Held*—by the House of Lords—the company was so estopped, and Bloomenthal's name must be removed from the list of contributories.

A share certificate which is forged is a nullity and is not binding on the company.

98. Ruben *v* Great Fingall Consolidated [1906] AC 439

Rowe was the secretary of the company and he asked the appellants, who were stockbrokers, to get him a loan of £20,000. The appellants procured the money and advanced it in good faith on the security of the share certificate of the company issued by Rowe, the latter stating that the appellants were registered in the register of members, which was not the case. The Certificate was in accordance with the company's articles, bore the company's seal, and was signed by two directors and the secretary, Rowe, but Rowe had forged the signatures of the two directors. When the fraud was discovered, the appellants tried to get registration, and when this failed, they sued the company in estoppel. *Held*—by the House of Lords—a company secretary had no authority to do more than deliver the share certificates, and in the absence of evidence that the company had held Rowe out as having authority to actually issue certificates, the company was not estopped by a forged certificate. Neither was the company responsible for the fraud of its secretary, because it was not within the scope of his employment to issue certificates. This was a matter for the directors.

Calls on shares must be made equally on all shareholders of the same class unless an arrangement under s. 119(a) exists. The Proper Purpose Rule.

99. Galloway *v* Hallé Concerts Society [1915] 2 Ch 233

The defendant society was registered in 1899 as a company limited by guarantee without the addition of the word limited to its name, as being formed for the promotion of art and with the intention that its profits should be applied in promoting its objects without payment of dividends to its members. Its object was the promotion of concerts known as the 'Hallé Concerts' in Manchester. Under the provisions of the memorandum each member was to contribute on a winding up such amount as should be required to pay the company's liabilities, not exceeding £5 per member. Article 7 of the company's articles provided that each member should be liable to contribute, and should pay on demand to the society, any sum or sums not exceeding in the aggregate £100 (called the contribution) as and when called. The plaintiffs, Galloway and Holt, were members of the society but disagreed with certain of its policies. They objected to calls being made upon them in respect of the contribution and had not paid previous calls made, although one such call had been recovered by the society in a county court. On 31 March 1915, the committee of the society resolved to call up the whole of the contributions of Galloway and Holt, but no corresponding call was made on the other members. The plaintiffs claimed a declaration that the resolution was invalid and the call unenforceable. *Held*—by Sargant J—there is an implied condition of equality between shareholders in a company, and it is generally improper for directors to make a call on part of a class of members without making a similar call on all the members of the class. Further, even if the articles give power to discriminate, the fact that the members are dilatory in paying previous calls would not be sufficient reason for enforcing a discriminatory power in the articles.

Comment. It should be noted that the act of making the call was not in any sense beyond the powers of the directors and was even in a sense exercised for the benefit of the company because, having called up the whole of the share capital of Galloway and Holt, they could have been sued once for all for its recovery if they had not paid it. However, in spite of the fact that the directors had the power and were probably motivated in the company's benefit, the power was not exercised for the proper purpose and was struck down for this reason.

Even if the articles allow the making of calls in different amounts, at different times from different shareholders, the directors cannot except themselves under such an arrangement from liability to pay calls on their shares. The Rule in *Foss v Harbottle*.

100. Alexander *v* Automatic Telephone Co [1900] 2 Ch 56

This action was brought by Alexander and Gibbs, suing on behalf of themselves and all the other shareholders in the defendant company, against the company and three of the directors, Margowski, Cohen and Sworn, asking for a declaration that the above-mentioned directors were bound to pay on their shares the amount paid by other shareholders. It appeared that the other members had been required to pay 6d. on application and 2s. 6d. on allotment but that the three directors, who had taken their shares under the memorandum, had not paid anything. Their defence was that they were given power by the articles to discriminate in this way, and indeed such a power was given by Art 5 of the company's articles. *Held*—by the Court of Appeal—in spite of the provisions of Art 5, it was a breach of duty by the directors to act in this way, and they must pay 3s. per share on each of the shares held by them. They were depriving the company of the use of money to which it was entitled. Further the court held that it could entertain this representative action by two shareholders on behalf of the others, since the case was not one of mere internal management under the rule in *Foss v Harbottle*, 1843. (See p. 527.)

Minor irregularities will not invalidate a call.

101. Shackleford, Ford & Co Ltd *v* Dangerfield (1868) LR 3 CP 407

The company sued two of its members, Dangerfield and Owen, for calls made but unpaid by them. The defence was that the calls were unenforceable since they were made in the new name of the company, although at the time the calls were made the company's name had not been officially registered by the Registrar of Companies. The defendants were aware of the change because the company had resolved to alter the name, but at the time of the call the Registrar had not issued a new certificate. *Held*—by the Court of Common Pleas—when a company changes its name, the change is not complete until the new name is entered on the Register of Companies and a certificate of incorporation issued. Nevertheless the call was good because the shareholders were aware of the change of name, and a minor irregularity such as this did not invalidate the call.

The power to accept calls in advance must be exercised in good faith for the benefit of the company and not for the benefit of the directors. However, the directors are not trustees of the power for the creditors.

102. Re European Central Railway Co, Sykes' Case (1872) LR 13 Eq 255

The directors had a power under the articles of the company to receive payment of calls in advance. The directors paid into the company's bank the full amount remaining uncalled on their own shares, and on the same day paid their own directors' fees. There were no other assets available to pay the fees at the time. The company went into liquidation and the liquidator put the directors on the list of contributories, including Colonel Sykes who was the chairman of the board. The directors claimed that their shares must be treated as fully paid and they should not be regarded as contributories. *Held*—by the Court of Chancery—there was in this case *no bona fide payment of calls in advance*. The directors were bound to exercise the power of making calls in advance for the benefit of the company and not with a view to their private interest. They were, therefore, still liable to pay the money due on their shares, ignoring the payment of calls in advance.

103. Poole's Case (1878) 9 Ch D 322

The directors of an insolvent company paid in advance the amount of their calls and used the money to discharge the company's bank overdraft which they had guaranteed. By so doing the directors—(*a*) discharged their own liability under the guarantee and (*b*) preferred one of the company's creditors, i.e. the bank, before the others. Nevertheless it was *held* by the High Court that the shares were fully paid up. They were not trustees for the company's creditors.

Transfer of shares: for the purposes of s. 183 a proper instrument of transfer is a written document which attracts stamp duty under the relevant fiscal legislation whether or not it complies with the company's articles.

104. Re Paradise Motor Co Ltd [1968] 2 All ER 625

In 1948 W caused a transfer of 350 shares owned by him in the company to be made to his stepson. The transfer carried the purported signature of the stepson as transferee though he was not named in the transfer as such. The register of members also showed a transfer to the stepson. In 1964 an order was made for compulsory winding up of the company and in 1965 the liquidator informed the stepson of the above matters and asked whether he claimed to be a shareholder. The stepson replied in the negative. In the liquidation of the company it became necessary to determine who owned the shares. By Art 8 of the company's articles of association a transfer of shares had to be signed by both transferor and transferee, and by what is now s. 183 it was not lawful to register a transfer unless a proper instrument of transfer was delivered to the company. The court accepted the stepson's evidence that he did not execute the transfer. *Held*—by the Court of Appeal, affirming the decision of Pennycuick J—that the phrase 'proper instrument' in s. 183 meant an instrument such as would 'attract stamp duty under the relevant fiscal legislation'. It did not have to be an instrument which complied with the articles. In the circumstances the fact that the stepson had not signed the 1948 transfer amounted only to an irregularity and the gift of shares to him was effective under the transfer thus making him owner at that point of time. However, his subsequent disclaimer was effective so that he could not be regarded as owner for the purposes of the liquidation of the company. The company's register could be rectified without a further transfer signed by the stepson because the disclaimer of the shares by him had rendered the original gift void. In such circumstances the register is rectifiable as of right.

A company which refuses to register a transfer must notify the transferor within two months of lodgment under s. 183. If the company does not do this it will usually be safe to say that the transfer cannot be rejected.

105. Re Swaledale Cleaners [1968] 3 All ER 619

On 3 August 1967, the shareholding of the company was: H (deceased) 5,000; S 4,000; A (deceased) 500; L 500. S and L were directors of the company which was a private one. The company's articles provided that the quorum of directors should be two although a sole continuing director had power to appoint an additional director. At a combined board meeting and annual general meeting held on 3 August 1967, L retired by rotation and was not re-elected a director. The personal representatives of H and A had executed transfers of H and A shareholdings in favour of L, but S as director refused to register them purporting to exercise a power of refusal contained in the articles. There was no resolution either of the board or of the shareholders on the matter of refusal to register the transfers. On 11 December 1967, L began proceedings for rectification of the register and on 18 December 1967, S appointed an additional director and the two directors formally refused to register the transfers. Held—by the Court of Appeal—the register must be rectified to show L as the holder of the shares of H and A. The power to refuse a transfer must be construed strictly because a shareholder ordinarily has a right to transfer his shares. Furthermore, the delay in exercising the power of refusal, i.e. four months, had been unreasonable and the power was no longer capable of being exercised.

On a sale of shares the equitable interest passes to the purchaser on contract but not if subject to a condition precedent unless this is solely for the benefit of the purchaser who is prepared to waive it.

106. Wood Preservation Ltd v Prior [1969] 1 All ER 364

A company called Silexine owned three-quarters of the issued share capital of Wood Preservation Ltd. Part of the business of Silexine was wood preserving but this part of the business was disposed of to Wood Preservation Ltd who in consequence took over a contract with a German company, Desowag-Chemie, to which Silexine had formerly been a party. This contract could be terminated without notice for what were described as 'important reasons'.

On 25 March 1960, British Ratin Ltd offered to purchase the whole of the issued share capital of Wood Preservation Ltd on certain terms and conditions. One was that within a month of acceptance of the offer Wood Preservation Ltd would produce to British Ratin Ltd a letter from Desowag-Chemie confirming that the sale of the share capital would not be regarded as an 'important reason' entitling Desowag-Chemie to terminate their agreement. Another condition was that all the holders of the issued share capital of Wood Preservation Ltd accepted the offer within seven days. The second condition was fulfilled and on 18 May 1960, British Ratin waived the requirement of the production of the letter from Desowag-Chemie and the transfer took place. In their accounting periods up to 9 May 1960, Silexine had incurred losses on their wood preserving business and Wood Preservation Ltd now wished to set off these losses against its own future profits. The claim turned on who was the beneficial owner of Silexine's holding in Wood Preservation immediately prior to 9 May 1960. It was necessary to decide when the property in the shares passed from Silexine to British Ratin. The contract with British Ratin was subject to two conditions precedent and one was fulfilled when all holders of the issued share capital of Wood Preservation had agreed to sell, i.e. on or about 1 April 1960. However, the second conditions relating to the letter from Desowag-Chemie was not waived until 18 May 1960, and ordinarily the property in the shares would not have passed to British Ratin until 18 May 1960, but would have been vested in Silexine until then so that Silexine's losses could be set off. *Held*—by the Court of Appeal—that in a contract to purchase shares the property passes, at least in equity, when the contract is made but not if the contract is subject to a condition precedent. Where this is so the property does not pass until the condition has been performed or waived. But here the condition was solely for the benefit of British Ratin who could waive it. If they did so the property would pass and they could obtain specific performance. As a result Silexine were virtually trustees of the shares for British Ratin and the property had passed so as to prevent Wood Preservation Ltd from setting off the losses of Silexine.

Where a person requests the registration of a share transfer which a company is under a duty to effect there is implied in that request a warranty that the transfer is genuine.

107. Sheffield Corporation *v* Barclay [1905] AC 392

Two persons, Timbrell and Honnywill, were joint owners of corporation stock. Timbrell, in fraud of Honnywill, forged a transfer of the stock and borrowed money from the respondents on the security of the stock. The respondents sent the transfer to the corporation asking for registration, and they were duly registered. Later the respondents sold the shares and the corporation issued certificates to the purchasers who were also registered. Honnywill, after the death of Timbrell, discovered the forgery, and the corporation replaced the stock which was the best course open to them, because if they had taken the ultimate purchasers off the register of stockholders, they would have had to pay damages to them by virtue of the doctrine of estoppel. The corporation now sued the respondents for an indemnity on the grounds that they had presented the forged transfer. *Held*—by the House of Lords—The corporation succeeded. The person presenting a transfer warrants that it is good, and the fact that he is innocent of any fraud does not affect this warranty. The corporation, therefore, was entitled to recover from the respondents the value of the stock replaced, leaving them to such remedies as they might have against Timbrell's estate.

A person who takes shares as a security will not rank in front of a company's lien on those shares unless he gives the company notice of his charge before the company's lien arises.

108. The Bradford Banking Co Ltd *v* Henry Briggs, Son & Co Ltd (1886) 12 App Cas 29

The respondents were a trading company carrying on the business of a colliery. The articles of the company provided that it should have 'a first and permanent lien and charge available at law and in equity upon every share for all debts due from the holder thereof'. John Easby, a coal merchant, became a shareholder in the respondent company, and deposited his certificates with the bank as security for the overdraft on his current account. The bank gave notice to the company that the shares had been so deposited. Easby owed the respondent company money, having done trade with it, and he also owed money to the bank. The question for decision was whether the company was entitled to recoup its debts by exercising a lien and sale on the shares, or whether the bank was entitled to sell as mortgagees. *Held*—by the House of Lords—that the respondent company could not claim priority over the bank in respect of the shares for money which became due from Easby after the notice given by the bank. The notice served by the bank was not a notice of trust under s. 30 of the Companies Act 1862 (now s. 360), but must be regarded in the same light as notice between traders regarding their interests.

The power to forfeit shares must be exercised for the benefit of the company and not to give some personal advantage to a director or shareholder.

109. Re Esparto Trading Co (1879) 12 Ch D 191

Two persons, Finch and Goddard, agreed at the request of one Noble, who was forming the Esparto Trading Co, to become subscribers of the memorandum, and they took shares but regarded themselves as making up the necessary number of subscribers only. Finch was entered in the register for one share of nominal value £500, and Goddard was entered in the register for four such shares. Goddard was named as a director by the articles and was eventually appointed managing director. Another article provided that a director's share qualification was four shares and that his office would become vacant if he ceased to hold the stated number of shares. Goddard remained in the office of director and managing director for two months in 1866, i.e. in the first year of the company's life. Finch and Goddard were later called upon to pay the sums due on their shares, the directors at the time feeling that if Finch and Goddard were holding shares, they ought to pay for them whatever the original arrangement. Finch and Goddard asked the board to forfeit their shares, and this was done by a resolution of the board under a power in the articles. The company was later wound up, and the liquidator wished to place Finch and the executors of Goddard, who had died, on the list of contributories. *Held*—by the High Court—Finch must be put on the list for one share and the executors of Goddard for four shares. The forfeiture was invalid; it was not done for the benefit of the company because Finch and Goddard could not pay but was done primarily to relieve them of their liability on the shares, and at their own request. The power to forfeit shares lay only where a shareholder could not pay for his shares, and not where he simply did not want to pay for them.

507

A company cannot evade the rules relating to reduction of capital by taking a surrender of its partly-paid sharers.

110. Bellerby v Rowland & Marwood's SS Co Ltd [1902] 2 Ch 14

Three directors of the company, Bellerby, Moss and Marwood, agreed to surrender several of their shares to the company so that they might be re-issued. The object of the surrender was not that the directors could not pay the calls, the shares being of nominal value £11 with £10 paid, but to assist the company to make good the loss of one of its ships, the Golden Cross, valued at £4,000. The surrender was accepted but the shares were not in fact re-issued. The company survived the loss and became prosperous, and in this action the directors sought to be returned to the register as members, claiming that the earlier surrender was invalid. *Held*—by the Court of Appeal—It was invalid since the surrender was not accepted because of non-payment of calls or inability to pay them, and so the directors must be restored to the register of members.

MEMBERSHIP AND CONTROL

A contract by a minor to take shares in a company is voidable at any time before the minor reaches full age and for a reasonable time thereafter. Money paid for them cannot be recovered unless there has been total failure of consideration.

111. Steinberg v Scala (Leeds) Ltd [1923] 2 Ch 452

The plaintiff, Miss Steinberg, purchased shares in the defendant company and paid certain sums of money on application, on allotment and on one call. Being unable to meet future calls, she repudiated the contract whilst still a minor and claimed—

(*a*) rectification of the register of members to remove her name therefrom, thus relieving her from liability on future calls; and

(*b*) the recovery of the money already paid.

The company agreed to rectify the register and issue was joined on the claim to recover the money paid.

Held—The claim under (*b*) above failed because there had not been total failure of consideration. The shares had some value and gave some rights, even though the plaintiff had not received any dividends and the shares had always stood at a discount on the market.

Financial assistance by a company for the purchase of its own shares—
an infringement illustrated.

112. Wallersteiner v Moir [1974] 3 All ER 217

The relevant facts in this case were as follows—

(a) On 30 March 1962 Camp Bird Ltd, a public company, made an agreement with a Dr Wallersteiner to sell to the Rothschild Trust its shares (an 80 per cent holding) in Hartley Baird Ltd for £518,787.

(b) The Rothschild Trust was registered in Liechtenstein and was controlled by Dr Wallersteiner.

(c) The money for the Camp Bird shares was not found by the Rothschild Trust (in effect Dr Wallersteiner). It was found—

(i) by loans which Hartley Baird Ltd made to Dr Wallersteiner (in the name of his company Investment Finance Trust Ltd of Nassau);

(ii) by regarding as cancelled certain sales commissions which Camp Bird owed to Dr Wallersteiner's various Liechtenstein companies. It was alleged that these commissions were not really owed but fabricated.

All this was achieved because Dr Wallersteiner had a controlling interest in the various companies involved who could in consequence be made to do what he wanted.

These transactions came to the notice of Mr Moir, a minority shareholder in Hartley Baird Ltd and he made statements to the press and applied to the Department of Trade for an investigation into Hartley Baird's affairs. This resulted in an action by Dr Wallersteiner for libel. The libel action was struck out and on other matters relevant to company law the Court of Appeal decided—

(i) the loan by Hartley Baird Ltd to the Rothschild Trust assisted the acquisition of Hartley Baird shares by the Rothschild Trust and was a plain breach of what is now s. 151. Dr Wallersteiner was liable to repay the loan to Hartley Baird Ltd.

(ii) Since Dr Wallersteiner was a director of Hartley Baird Ltd there was also an infringement of the provisions relating to loans to directors. (See now ss. 330–334.)

(iii) The corporate veil. In the course of his judgment Lord Denning MR said: 'It is plain that Dr Wallersteiner used many companies, trusts or other legal entities as if they belonged to him. He was in control of them as much as any "one man company" is under the control of the one man who owns all the shares and is the chairman and managing director. He made contracts of enormous magnitude on their behalf on a sheet of notepaper without reference to anyone else. ... Counsel for Dr Wallersteiner repudiated this suggestion. It was quite wrong he said, to pierce the corporate veil. The principle enunciated in *Salomon v Salomon & Co Ltd* (1897)[1] was sacrosanct. If we were to treat each of these concerns as belonging to Dr Wallersteiner himself under another hat, we should not, he said, be lifting a corner of the corporate veil. We should be sending it up in flames.' After accepting that the various concerns were distinct legal entities Lord Denning went on to say: 'Even so, I am quite clear that they were just the puppets of Dr Wallersteiner. He controlled their every movement. Each danced to his bidding. He pulled the strings. No-one else got within reach of them. Transformed into legal language, they were his agents to do as he commanded. He was the principal behind them. I am of the opinion that the court should pull aside the corporate veil and treat these concerns as being his creatures—for whose doings he should be, and is, responsible. At any rate, it was up to him to show that anyone else had a say in their affairs and he never did so.'

Comment. (i) This case is an example of a common malpractice under previous legislation where a take-over bidder uses the victim company's funds to acquire shares in it. Such conduct would be forbidden under the provisions of the 1985 Act, ss. 151–158, because it would seem that the principal purpose of the assistance is the acquisition of the victim company's shares.

(ii) The case also shows that although a transaction in contravention of s. 151 is void and unenforceable (see *Heald v O'Connor*, 1971[46]) directors responsible can be sued for breach of trust to compensate the company for any loss it has suffered.

A company may provide assistance for the purchase of its own shares under s. 153(4)(a) where the lending of money is part of the ordinary business of the company, and the lending of money by the company is in the ordinary course of its business. In this connection a mere power to lend money is not enough. The lending must be part of the general business of the company as in the case of a bank.

113. Steen v Law [1963] 3 All ER 770

In June 1959, International Vending Machines Ltd, a company incorporated in New South Wales, lent £200,000 to another company, A M Holdings Ltd, in order that the latter company could buy shares of IVM Ltd so making it the subsidiary of A M Holdings Ltd. The shares were purchased from the two appellants, who were the only directors of IVM, and another relative of theirs. The object was to avoid paying tax on the undistributed profits of IVM. In May 1961, an order was made for the winding up of IVM, and the respondent, who was the liquidator, sought to make the appellants repay the loan on the grounds that it was unlawful under the Companies Act 1936,

s. 148(1) of New South Wales, which allowed (as does s. 153(4)(*a*))
a company to lend money for the purpose of buying its own shares
where *inter alia* the lending of money is part of the ordinary business
of the company. *Held*—by the Privy Council—that the applicants were
liable to repay the loan. A mere power in a company to lend money
is not enough; lending must be the ordinary business of the company
and this predicates moneylending, as by a bank or registered money-
lender.

Comment. This case is still authority on what is lending 'in the
ordinary course of business'.

**Shares in a company can legally be held by a trustee upon trust for
the company itself.**

114. Kirby *v* Wilkins [1929] 2 Ch 444

A partnership business was sold to a company, known as the Derby
Paper Staining Co Ltd, the purchase price being satisfied by an allotment to the partners of 16,000 fully-paid shares in the company of
£1 each. It was later discovered that the company had paid £3,000
more for the business than it was worth, and the partners voluntarily
transferred to the chairman of the board of directors of the company
3,000 shares upon trust to use or sell them for the benefit of the company. The plaintiff, a shareholder of the company, claimed that the
shares were held in trust for individual shareholders and could not
be held on trust for the company, and he sought an injunction to
restrain the chairman from voting at any meeting of the company
as holder of the shares. *Held*—by Romer J—the transaction did not
offend against any principle laid down by any of the decided cases.
The chairman did not hold the shares for the benefit of individual
shareholders but for the benefit of the company.

115. Re Castiglione's Will Trusts [1958] 1 All ER 480

A testator, Edwin James Castiglione, by his will directed his trustees
to hold 1,000 fully-paid shares in a private company called Castiglione,
Erskine & Co Ltd in trust for his son for life, and after his death
without leaving issue, to transfer them to the company. The son died
in 1956 without leaving issue, and the question of the validity of the
bequest of shares was raised. *Held*—by Danckwerts J—the shares could
not be transferred to the company itself, but could be transferred to
nominees to hold on trust for the company.

Comment. Since s. 143(3) allows companies limited by shares to acquire their own fully paid shares by way of gift, there is now no need to put such shares in the name of a trustee for the company.

Shares may be regarded as paid for in cash if the company pays *an existing debt* by an issue of shares to the creditor.

116. Re Harmony and Montague Tin and Copper Mining Co, Spargo's Case (1873) LR 8 Ch App 407

A company purchased a mine from Spargo and he made an agreement to buy shares in the company. The moneys owed by Spargo to the company for his shares and by the company to Spargo for the mine were payable immediately. Under a further agreement between Spargo and the company he was debited with the amount payable on the shares and credited with the purchase price of the property making up the difference in cash. It was *held* by the Court of Appeal in Chancery that Spargo must be deemed to have paid for his shares in cash.

Comment. The provisions of the Companies Act relating to an issue of shares for a non-cash consideration seem not apply to set-offs of this kind which are regarded as cash transactions. Section 739(2) provides in effect that the issue of shares to satisfy a liquidated sum, i.e. an existing quantified debt, as in this case, is not an issue for a consideration other than cash.

In private and public companies the consideration for shares must not be past but in private companies it need not be adequate, provided it is not wholly illusory.

117. Re Eddystone Marine Insurance Co [1893] 3 Ch 9

The company proposed to raise capital from the public, but passed a resolution before going to the public to allot £6,000 worth of fully-paid shares to the existing directors and shareholders for a consideration other than cash. A copy of the agreement was filed in which the consideration was said to be services rendered by the allottees to the company during its formation. There was in fact no such rendering of services. Eighteen months later the company was wound up, and the liquidator proposed to regard the shares as unpaid on the grounds that there was no consideration given for them. *Held*—by the Court of Appeal—

the allottees must contribute the nominal value of the shares. There was in fact no consideration because the services had not been rendered, but even if they had, they would not have supported the contract to take the shares because the consideration would have been past.

Comment. Section 99(2) provides that a public company shall not accept at any time in payment up of its shares or any premium on them, an undertaking given by any person that he or another should do work or perform services for the company or any other person. If shares are issued for services by a public company the holder is liable to pay the nominal value and any premium to the company plus interest, which under s. 107 is currently 5 per cent *per annum.*

118. Re Wragg Ltd [1897] 1 Ch 796

Messrs. Wragg and Martin were the proprietors of a livery stable business and they agreed to sell it to a company, Wragg Ltd, which they formed. The business was sold to the company for £46,300, among the assets being horses and carriages valued for the purposes of the sale at £27,000. The company paid for the business by issuing shares and debentures to Wragg and Martin, and later, when the company was being wound up, the liquidator asked the court to declare that the shares were not fully paid up because it appeared that the horses and carriages had been overvalued and were really worth only £15,000 at the date of sale. It was *held* by the Court of Appeal that—

(i) Where fully-paid shares are allotted to vendors under a contract registered in accordance with the Companies Acts, it is not illegal for the said vendors or promoters to make a profit, though disclosure is required. In this case disclosure did not arise, since Wragg and Martin and certain nominees of theirs became the only shareholders in Wragg Ltd, and they were aware of the details of the transaction.

(ii) The court will not go behind a contract of this sort and inquire into the adequacy of the consideration unless the consideration appears on the face of the contract to be insufficient or illusory. This was not the case here for if the company had received advice on the purchase of the business, some advisers might have thought that, looking at the business as a whole, it was a good bargain at £46,300.

(iii) Where persons, as vendors, make an agreement with themselves and their nominees in the character of a limited company it is, following *Salomon v Salomon & Co*, 1897,[1] an agreement between independent legal entities and is valid.

Comment. The Companies Act 1985 places restrictions on public companies in regard to the allotment of shares for a non-cash consideration by requiring, amongst other things, a valuation of that consideration. However, in private companies the company's valuation of the consideration will still be accepted as conclusive in the absence of, e.g. fraud.

119. Hong Kong & China Gas Co Ltd v Glen [1914] 1 Ch 527

The company agreed that in return for a concession to supply gas to the city of Victoria, Hong Kong, it would allot the vendor of the concession 400 shares of £10 each, fully paid; and it further agreed that if and when it increased its capital in the future, the vendor or his executors, administrators or assigns should have as fully paid, one-fifth of the increased capital. In this action the company asked the court to decide whether the part of the agreement relating to the one-fifth share of any increase in the capital of the company was binding. *Held*—by the High Court—it was not. The insufficiency of the consideration appeared on the face of the contract, for the company had agreed to give at any future time or times a wholly indefinite and possibly unlimited value for the purchase of the concesssion.

Debentures can be issued at a discount but not if they are capable of conversion immediately into shares of the equivalent par value.

120. Mosely v Koffyfontein Mines Ltd [1904] 2 Ch 108

The company proposed to issue to its shareholders certain debentures at a discount of 20 per cent, the debentures to be repayable by the company on 1 November 1909. The debenture holders were to have the right at any time prior to 1 May 1909, to exchange the debentures for fully-paid shares in the company on the basis of one fully-paid share of £1 nominal value for every £1 of nominal value of debentures held. The court was asked in this case to decide whether the proposed issue of debentures was void. *Held*—by the Court of Appeal—it was void, because the exchange of debenturers for fully-paid shares would lead to the issue of shares at a discount whenever the right was exercised.

Comment. Issue of shares at a discount was permitted prior to the Companies Act 1980, but only if, amongst other things, there had been an ordinary resolution of the members, together with the permission of the court. Issue at a discount is now forbidden by s. 100 of the Companies Act 1985.

Shares which are not issued for cash may still be issued at a premium under the terms of s. 130.

121. Henry Head & Co Ltd *v* Ropner Holdings Ltd [1952] Ch 124

Ropner Holdings was formed as a holding company, its main object being to acquire the whole of the issued share capital of the Pool Shipping Co Ltd and the Ropner Shipping Co Ltd for the purposes of amalgamation. Ropner Holdings issued the whole of its authorized capital of £1,759,606 (this being equal to the sum of the issued capitals of the two shipping companies) to the shareholders of Pool Shipping and Ropner Shipping on the basis of £1 share for each £1 share held in the two shipping companies. The value of the assets of the two shipping companies, when Ropner Holdings acquired the shares, was £6,830,972, and the difference between this figure and £1,759,606, less formation expenses, was shown on the balance sheet of Ropner Holdings as 'Capital Reserve—Share Premium Account' so as to comply with s. 56(1) of the Companies Act 1948. The plaintiffs, who were large shareholders in Ropner Holdings, asked that the company be required to treat the reserve as a general and not a capital reserve because otherwise no payment out of the reserve could be made unless the procedure for reduction of capital was followed. *Held*—by Harman J—Ropner Holdings had, in effect, issued its shares at a premium within the meaning of what is now s. 130, and was bound to retain the reserve as a capital reserve.

Comment. The case is still authority for the statement that a share premium account must be raised even where the consideration is not cash. However, in the circumstances of the case merger relief would presumably have been available.

An order rectifying the register of members can be made even when the company is being wound up.

122. Re Sussex Brick Co [1904] 1 Ch 598

On 16 January 1901, W. Belcher transferred shares in the company to G. B. Browne and D. G. H. Pollock. The transfers were deposited with the company for registration but, owing to unnecessary delay on the part of the company, they were not registered. In April 1903, the company passed a special resolution to wind up voluntarily for the purpose of reconstruction. No notice of the meeting was sent to Browne or Pollock, but they did give notice of dissent to the liquidator, requiring him to abstain from carrying the resolution into effect or to buy them out. The liquidator would not accept the notice as valid because Browne and Pollock were not on the register of members. This action was brought by Browne and Pollock to rectify the register, and to rectify it retrospectively so that the notice of dissent served by them would be good. *Held*—by the Court of Appeal—that there was a jurisdiction to rectify the register even when the company was in liquidation. It was, therefore, ordered that the register be rectified, the rectification to operate retrospectively so as to render valid the notice of dissent.

The power of the court to rectify the register of members is not confined to the circumstances set out in s. 359.

123. Burns *v* Siemens Bros Dynamo Works Ltd [1919] 1 Ch 225

The plaintiffs, Burns and Hambro, were the joint owners of shares in the defendant company. The shares were entered in the company's register in the joint names of Burns and Hambro. The company's articles provided that, where there were joint holders, the person whose name appeared first in the register of members, and no other, should be entitled to vote in respect of the shares. The result was, of course, that Hambro had no voting rights. This action was brought by Burns and Hambro asking that the register be rectified so as to show roughly half of the joint shareholding in the name of each joint holder. *Held*—by the High Court—the court had jurisdiction to make such an order, and the company was required to rectify the register, showing shares numbered 1 to 10,000 in the names of Burns and Hambro, and shares numbered 10,001 to 19,993 in the names of Hambro and Burns.

Notice of any trust, express, implied or constructive, must not be entered on the register of a company registered in England.

124. Simpson *v* Molson's Bank [1895] AC 270

This was an appeal to the Privy Council in England from the Court of Queen's Bench for Lower Canada. It appeared that the bank was incorporated by an Act of Parliament, and that by s. 36 of that Act the bank was not bound to take notice of any trust over its shares. (The provision was similar to the one contained in s. 360.) The executors of the Hon John Molson were given ten years by his will to wind up his estate. After the expiration of that time, and in breach of the terms of the will, they made a transfer of certain shares in the bank. The plaintiffs, who had an interest in the residuary estate of John

Molson, brought this action claiming damages from the bank because it had registered a transfer knowing that transfer to be in breach of trust, such knowledge being derived from the fact that a copy of the will was deposited at the bank, and that William Molson, the testator's brother, was one of the executors who signed the transfer and was also the President of the bank. *Held*—The bank was not liable for registering the transfer although they had notice that it was in breach of trust, because s. 36 of the Act of Parliament incorporating the bank provided specifically that it should not take notice of any trust over its shares.

It follows from the 'no-trusts' rule that where there are two or more lenders on the security of the same shares by way of equitable mortgage, the first in date has priority, not the first to give notice to the company.

125. Société Générale de Paris *v* Walker (1885) 11 App Cas 20

James Walker was the registered owner of 100 shares in Tramways Union Ltd, and he created two charges over the shares, one on 9 March 1881, in favour of James Scott Walker, who took the certificates and a blank transfer, and one on 1 December 1882, in favour of the appellants, the latter charge being created by means of a blank transfer, duly executed but without the deposit of the share certificate. The appellants tried to obtain registration first, but Tramways Union Ltd would not register the transfer without the certificates, and later the executors of James Scott Walker informed the Tramways Union that they had the certificates. This action was brought to decide who had the title to the shares. The articles of Tramways Union Ltd provided that the company should not be bound to recognize any equitable interest in its shares. The appellants claimed that because they notified first the fact of their equitable interest in the shares, they were entitled as against the executors of James Scott Walker. *Held*—by the House of Lords—they were not, because neither the company nor its officers could be treated as trustees for the purpose of notifying equitable interests over the shares. The title to the shares was in the person eventually registered by the company, and the company was right in refusing to register a person who could not produce the share certificates. The respondents were entitled to the shares.

Where the shares are purchased in the name of a nominee, the company cannot go behind the nominee in order to make the beneficial owner

liable to pay for the shares unless the nominee is a fictitious person or someone who never agreed to act as nominee.

126. Re National Bank of Wales Ltd [1907] 1 Ch 582

In 1893 the bank was in the course of a voluntary winding up. At the commencement of the winding up a Mr Sparke was the registered holder of 50 shares in the bank. On 26 April 1894, Sparke transferred the shares to a person named Littlejohn. The liquidator sanctioned the transfer and entered Littlejohn on the register of members. On 30 May 1894, Littlejohn transferred 20 of the shares to one Davis, and he was ultimately registered as the holder of the shares. Calls were made on the shares but never paid, and in March 1906, the liquidator asked the court to rectify the register, substituting the names of Giffin and Massey in place of Littlejohn and Davies. The liquidator's case was that Littlejohn was, on the date he purchased the shares, aged 16, and was employed as an office boy by a firm of stockbrokers named Giffin and Massey, and that he was a mere nominee for the two stockbrokers in acquiring the shares from Sparke. *Held*—There was no contractual relationship between the company and Giffin and Massey, and they could not be placed on the register.

127. Re Hercules Insurance Co, Pugh and Sharman's Case (1872) LR 13 Eq 566

A Mr Sharman held a large number of shares in the insurance company and wished to take more, but the directors refused to let him take any more shares in his own name. On the suggestion of the company secretary and with the concurrence of a local agent of the company at Leighton Buzzard, he sent in an application for shares signed by his daughter, Mrs Pugh, who happened to be visiting Sharman at the time. Her father's residence was stated in the application and the allotment moneys were paid by Sharman, and all dividends were sent to him, as were all notices relating to meetings and other matters. Mrs Pugh signed the application without being informed as to what it was, and she did not tell her husband that she had signed it. In the liquidation of the company Mrs Pugh was put on the list of contributories, and Mr and Mrs Pugh now applied for rectification of the register to put on the name of Sharman in substitution for Mrs Pugh. *Held*—The case was really one in which the shares were applied for in the name of a fictitious person. Mrs Pugh was not a nominee, her name having been used as a mere alias for Sharman, and the register must, therefore, be rectified, and Mr Sharman's name substituted for that of Mrs Pugh.

Minority rights: power of the court to wind up the company on a petition by a minority: s. 122(1)(g), Insolvency Act 1986.

128. Loch v John Blackwood Ltd [1924] AC 783

This was an appeal to the Privy Council from the West Indian Court of Appeal. Loch, who was a shareholder, petitioned on behalf of herself and the other shareholders of the company, apart from the directors, for the winding up of the company on the grounds that the directors, one of whom was the majority shareholder, had failed to hold general meetings, or submit accounts to the members, or recommend a dividend, and had generally kept the shareholders in ignorance of the company's affairs with the object of forcing them to sell their shares at an undervaluation. *Held*—The petitioners were entitled to a winding-up order on the grounds that it was, in the circumstances, just and equitable that the company be wound up.

Comment. This case might now more appropriately have been made the subject of proceedings under Part XVII (protection of company's members against unfair prejudice). The minority in this type of case would nearly always be satisfied to be bought out at a fair price by the majority. Winding the company up in order to achieve a distribution of its assets is a clumsy way of achieving this when s. 461(2)(d) states that the court order may provide for the purchase of the shares of an unfairly prejudiced member, either by other members or by the company itself, at what the court thinks is a fair value. The position where the prejudice alleged is denial of a say in management is more difficult, but *Re A Company*, 1983 and more recent cases (see p. 521) suggest that Part XVII is applicable also in that type of case.

129. Ebrahimi v Westbourne Galleries [1972] 2 All ER 492

Since 1945 Mr Ebrahimi and Mr Nazar had carried on a partnership which dealt in Persian and other carpets. They shared equally the management and profits. In 1958 they formed a private company carrying on the same business and were appointed its first directors. Soon after the company's formation Mr George Nazar, Mr Nazar's son, was made a third director. By reason of their shareholdings, Mr Nazar and George had the majority of votes at general meetings. The company made good profits all of which were distributed as directors' remuneration and no dividend was ever paid. In 1969 Mr Ebrahimi was removed from the position of director by a resolution at a general meeting in pursuance of what is now s. 303. Mr Ebrahimi presented a petition seeking an order under s. 210 of the Companies Act 1948 (see now Part XVII) that Mr Nazar and George should purchase his shares or, alternatively, an order under what is now s. 122(1)(g), Insolvency Act 1986 that the company be wound up. At first instance Plowman J refused the order under s. 210 because the oppression alleged was against Mr Ebrahimi in his capacity as director and not that of member. However, the petition for a compulsory winding up was granted because, in the opinion of Plowman J, it was just and equitable that the company should be wound up. The Court of Appeal affirmed the decision of Plowman J under s. 210 but dismissed the petition for a compulsory winding up regarding it as an unjustifiable innovation in the company situation. On further appeal the House of Lords reversed the Court of Appeal and restored the decision of Plowman J that an order for winding up should be made. The major points arising from the case are as follows—

(i) the majority shareholders, Mr Nazar and George, had made use of their undisputed right under what is now s. 303 to remove a director, namely Mr Ebrahimi. Could such use of a statutory right be a ground for making a compulsory winding up order under what is now s. 122(1)(g), Insolvency Act 1986? In other words, could the exercise of a legal right be regarded as contravening the rules of equity which are the basis of what is now s. 122(1)(g) (*ibid*)?

(ii) The House of Lords answered these questions in the affirmative, at least for companies founded on a personal relationship, i.e. for companies which in essence were partnerships, though in form they had assumed the character of a company. '... a limited company is more than a mere judicial entity, with a personality in law of its own: ... there is room in company law for recognition of the fact that behind it, or amongst it, there are individuals, with rights, expectations and obligations *inter se* which are not necessarily submerged in the company structure. That structure is defined by the Companies Act 1948 and by the articles of association by which shareholders agree to be bound. In most companies and in most contexts, this definition is sufficient and exhaustive, equally so whether the company is large or small. The "just and equitable" provision does not, as the respondents suggest, entitle one party to disregard the obligation he assumes by entering a company, nor the court to dispense him from it. It does, as equity always does, enable the court to subject the exercise of legal rights to equitable considerations; considerations, that is, of a personal character, arising between one individual and another, which may make it unjust, or inequitable, to insist on legal rights, or to exercise them in a particular way.' *per* Lord Wilberforce.

(iii) The case is thus an illustration of the rule that if the common law (including in this context statute law) and equity conflict, equity shall prevail, at least where the company is founded on personal relationships. However, not every private company will fall into that class.

(iv) The decision makes an important contribution to the movement for harmonization of European company law. The concept of the private company founded on a personal relationship has been approximated to the continental European concept. For example, it is accepted in Germany and France that the private company is a special association and not merely a variety of a general concept of companies and they are governed by different enactments.

(v) The partnership analogy is an example of the drawing aside of the corporate veil, i.e. treating a company as a partnership. Once this has been done then partnership law applies and under this each general partner is, in the absence of contrary agreement, entitled to a say in management (see s. 24(5), Partnership Act 1890). Furthermore, the definition of partnership requires that the partners be in business 'in common' which they obviously are not if one or more of them is deprived of a say in management. A partner who is deprived of a say in management is, in the absence of a contrary agreement, entitled to dissolve the firm.

Comment. (i) The reasons for the refusal of Plowman J at first instance to grant Mr Ebrahimi a remedy under what was then s. 210, Companies Act 1948 (now repealed), i.e. because the conduct of the majority shareholders in excluding him from participation in management following his removal as a director did not affect his rights as a member, is not necessarily applicable to claims under s. 459 of Part XVII of the Companies Act 1985. The wording of s. 459(1) differs significantly from that of old s. 210. It states that a member can petition the court if the business of the company is being conducted 'in a manner which is unfairly prejudicial to the interests of some part of the members (including at least himself) ...'. Section 210 required that the affairs of the company were being conducted 'in a manner oppressive to some part of the members (including himself)'; there was no reference in s. 210 to the 'interest' of members. It is possible to take the view that the 'interests' of a member could be his holding of a position as director.

In *Re A Company* [1983] 2 All ER 854 the petitioner (T) had made an application for winding up under what is now s. 122(1)(g), Insolvency Act 1986. He was one of three directors, each of whom held one-third of the total share capital of the company. Following the collapse in the relationship between the three, the other directors, C and R, excluded T from participation in management of the company. T proposed a sale of his shares to C and R at a price which included compensation for loss of office. A counter-offer for T's one-third shareholding was made by C and R, based upon a price formula of 'fair market value as fixed by an independent expert'. This proposal was rejected by the petitioner, who subsequently applied to the court for a just and equitable winding up. The grounds of the petition included unfair exclusion from participation in the company's management. The other directors applied for a striking out of T's petition, under what is now s. 125 (*ibid*), claiming that an alternative solution to a winding up was available to T under what is now Part XVII. Since it had been suggested that exclusion from management did not constitute grounds for the application of the unfair prejudice principle, counsel for the petitioner suggested that T was entitled to the 'last resort' remedy of a winding up order as no alternative solution was available. However, Vinelott J expressed the opinion that the intention of what is now Part XVII was to extend relief against oppression beyond the prejudice of strict shareholder rights. An order for 'such remedy as the court thinks fit' under Part XVII would thus always be an alternative to a winding up order where a petitioner complained of exclusion from management of the company and the purchase of his shares could, for example, be ordered. However, Vinelott J's actual grounds for refusal of the winding-up petition were based on the remedy being restricted to circumstances in which continuance of the company would be unjust, where the injustice could not be remedied by alternative means. Further, the just and equitable remedy is discretionary and should not be enforced if making a winding-up order would be unfair to the other shareholders. Vinelott J considered that the alternative solution for agreement of a fair price met all T's reasonable objections and his seeking to enforce a winding up was, therefore, unreasonable. The case suggests that Part XVII is to be applied to prejudice of shareholder 'interests' beyond strict shareholder 'rights' and diminishes the importance of the 'last gasp' winding-up remedy under what is now s. 122(1)(g), Insolvency Act 1986.

(ii) In *Re R A Noble & Sons (Clothing) Ltd* [1983] BCLC 273 Nourse J accepted that what is now Part XVII of the Companies Act 1985 could cover expulsion from management which could be regarded as unfairly prejudicial. He also agreed with Lord Grantchester QC in *Re A Company (No 004475 of 1982)*, 1983[133] where he said that unfair prejudice could occur when the value of a shareholding of a petitioner had been seriously diminished or jeopardized *but* that jurisdiction under what is now Part XVII was not limited to such a case. On the facts in *Noble* Nourse J did not accept that the exclusion of the particular director, Mr B, from management was unfairly prejudicial. The situation arose because Mr B became disinterested in the company's affairs and the other director, Mr N, merely wanted to get on with the management of the company. Mr B was not removed from office but decisions were taken without consulting him. However, Mr N did not act in any underhand way. Since, however, mutual confidence had been destroyed, Nourse J was prepared to wind up the company under what is now s. 122(1)(g).

Nourse J also decided in *Re Bird Precision Bellows* [1984] 2 WLR 869 that exclusion from management could be unfair prejudice under what is now Part XVII of the Companies Act 1985.

(iii) In *Re London School of Electronics, The Times* 9 April 1985, Nourse J again affirmed that exclusion from management could be unfair prejudice and also that where the claim was under Part XVII the petitioner need not necessarily come to the court with clean hands as is required for a winding up order on the just and equitable ground under s. 122(1)(g). The petitioner had been excluded from management in the London School of Electronics and had set up the London College for Electronic Engineering *and had taken a number of students who had previously enrolled with, or made enquiries of, the London School of Electronics.* Nevertheless, Nourse J allowed his petition under what is now Part XVII to proceed and made an order for the purchase of his shares in the London School by the only other shareholder in that company.

(iv) For an interesting application of that passage of Lord Wilberforce's judgment set out at (ii) in the summary of the case *outside of the context of winding up*, see *Clemens v Clemens Bros Ltd*, 1976, p. 533.

130. Re A & B C Chewing Gum Ltd [1975] 1 All ER 1017

The petitioners, Topps Chewing Gum, held one-third of the ordinary shares in A & B C on the basis of a shareholders' agreement that they should have equal control with the two Coakley brothers, Douglas and Anthony, who were directors of and held a two-thirds interest in the ordinary shares of A & B C. In order to achieve equality of control the company adopted a new set of articles which allowed Topps to appoint and remove a director representing them in A & B C, and for board decisions to be unanimous. On the same day Topps, the Coakleys and A & B C signed and sealed the shareholders' agreement setting out the terms referred to above. Topps appointed Douglas Coakley to represent them but later removed him and appointed John Sullivan, their marketing director. Douglas and Anthony Coakley refused to accept the change so that Topps were effectively prevented from participating in management. *Held*—by Plowman J—that it was just and equitable that the company be wound up under what is now s. 122(1)(g), Insolvency Act 1986. The Coakleys had repudiated the relationship in the agreement and the articles. The case was one of expulsion and *Westbourne Galleries*[129] applied. It is interesting to note that in applying *Westbourne Galleries*[129] Plowman J took the view that Lord Wilberforce's judgment spoke of entitlement to management participation as being an obligation so basic that if broken the association must be dissolved, even though it is not a company arising out of a partnership.

Comment. (i) A & B C Chewing Gum was presumably regarded as a 'personal relationship' company, analogous to a partnership, so that the partnership principle could be applied as in *Westbourne*.[129] A personal relationship company would appear to be one in which the directors are also the only shareholders (or proprietors). This situation brings in the partnership analogy because in a partnership the general partners are managers and also supply the capital.

(ii) Although Plowman J purported to be applying the equitable principles of *Westbourne*,[129] he was in fact merely enforcing the petitioner's contract rights set out in the shareholders' agreement. He could have granted an injunction to prevent the breach of that contract by the Coakley brothers; a less drastic remedy than winding the company up.

Statutory protection of members against unfair prejudice: ss. 459–461: court's power to regulate conduct of the company's affairs in the future.

131. Re H R Harmer Ltd [1958] 3 All ER 689

The company was formed in July 1947, to acquire a business founded by Mr H R Harmer who was born in 1869. The business of the company was stamp auctioneering, and dealing in and valuing stamps. Two of Mr Harmer's sons, Cyril and Bernard Harmer, went into the business on leaving school. The nominal capital of the company was £50,000, and Mr Harmer senior and his wife were between them able to control the general meetings of the company, and could even obtain special and extraordinary resolutions. Mrs Harmer always voted with her husband. The father and his two sons were life directors under the articles, the father being chairman of the board with a casting vote. The sons claimed that their father had repeatedly abused his controlling power in the conduct of the company's affairs so that they were bound to apply for relief under s. 210 of the Companies Act 1948 (see now Part XVII of the Companies Act 1985). Mr Harmer senior had, they said, always acted as though the right of appointing and dismissing senior staff was vested in him alone, and this right he also extended to the appointment of directors. He also considered that no director should express a contrary view to that expressed by himself, and had generally ignored the views of his sons and the other directors and shareholders. In particular he had opened a branch of the company in Australia in spite of the protests by the other directors, and the branch had not proved profitable. In addition, he dismissed an old servant and procured the appointment of his own 'yes-men' to the board. He drew unauthorized expenses for himself and his wife and engaged a detective to watch the staff. He also endeavoured to sell off the company's American business which severely damaged its goodwill. Roxburgh J, at first instance, granted relief under s. 210, and the Court of Appeal confirmed the order, saying that the relief was properly granted because the circumstances were such that the court would have been justified in ordering a winding up. Roxburgh J's order provided *inter alia* that the company should contract for the services of Mr Harmer senior as philatelic consultant at a salary of £2,500 per annum; that he should not interfere in the affairs of the company otherwise than in accordance with the valid decisions of the board; and that he be appointed president of the company for life, but that this office should not impose any duties or create any rights or powers in him.

Comment. The court's order had the effect of changing the provision in the articles under which Mr Harmer was a director for life with a casting vote.

Statutory protection of members: court's power to order purchase of petitioner's shares.

132. Scottish Co-operative Wholesale Society *v* Meyer [1958] 3 All ER 66

The appellants and the respondents went into the business of manufacturing rayon cloth, the appellants owning a weaving mill and the respondents providing the formulae, knowledge and experience, and the licences to purchase the necessary yarn which was then controlled. A private company was formed, as a subsidiary of the appellant company, for the purpose of conducting the business. The issued capital of this private company was 7,900 £1 shares of which 4,000 were held by the appellants and 3,900 were held by the respondents. The company had five directors, the respondents being two members of the board, and the other three directors being nominees of the appellants. The respondents supplied the yarn and the appellants made it up at their mill, and then sold it to the private company which re-sold it on the market. The arrangement was quite successful. However, after the parties had traded together for some time, the appellants wished to acquire further shares in the private company at par, the value of a £1 share in the company being at that time £6. The respondents proposed that the appellants pay £6 each for the shares but this was not accepted, and from that time on hostility developed between the appellants and the respondents. Control over yarn ceased in June 1952, and after that time the appellants could get yarn without a licence. They then adopted the policy of starving the private company of supplies of rayon cloth from their mill on which the company was dependent. In 1953 the respondents offered to sell their shares to the appellants at £4 16s. but the appellants refused and continued to let the company decline. The respondents petitioned under s. 210 of the Companies Act 1948 (see now Part XVII, Companies Act 1985), on the ground that the affairs of the company were being conducted in a manner oppressive to some part of its membership, i.e. the respondents. *Held*—by the House of Lords—the appellants were acting in an oppressive manner so much so that a winding up would have been justified on the grounds of oppression. The court ordered the appellants to buy out the respondents at a price of £3 15s. per share.

133. In Re A Company (No 004475 of 1982) [1983] 2 WLR 381

A testator who died in July 1980 left 1,844 shares in a private company. These were held by his executors for his two minor children. The shares were unquoted. There were no pre-emption provisions in the articles, though the directors had power to refuse transfers. The shares were the only assets available for the maintenance and the education of the children. The company sold two subsidiaries in June 1981 and had substantial liquid assets. The net value of the company at 31 December 1981 was £1,284,513, and the shares held by the executors were in consequence worth £172,893. The company proposed to use the liquid reserves to form a new company, with business activities which were unrelated to the company's existing business, but had not formally decided to go ahead with the proposal. The executors thought that it was in the best interests of the children that the shares be sold. They first proposed a reconstruction under what is now s. 110, Insolvency Act 1986, i.e. that the company be wound up and the shares be exchanged for shares in a new company. The executors, being dissentients, would have to be bought out under what is now s. 110 (*ibid*), the shares being valued not at an open market value, but as if the company was being wound up and its assets distributed, as distinct from being transferred to another company. This method of valuation for the purchase of dissentients' shares by a liquidator under s. 110 (*ibid*) results from the decision in *Re Mysore West Gold Mining Co* (1889) 42 Ch D 535. Section 110 (*ibid*) cannot be implemented unless the members agree by special resolution.

In the event a s. 110 scheme proved unacceptable to the members. The executors then suggested that a scheme should be put forward for the purchase by the company of the shares under what is now

s. 162. The company made an offer, valuing the shares on an open market basis, of £112,373. This was not acceptable to the executors, who then petitioned the court under what is now Part XVII. The petition did not allege any improper conduct by the directors, but did allege that the failure by the company to propound either a scheme of reconstruction under s. 110 or a purchase of the executors' shares pursuant to s. 162, was unfairly prejudicial to the executors pursuant to Part XVII, as was the making of proposals to diversify the business into unrelated activities. A motion by the company asked that the petition be struck out on the ground that it disclosed no reasonable cause of action or was otherwise an abuse of the court. Lord Grantchester QC, sitting in the Chancery Division as a Deputy High Court Judge, ordered that the petition be struck out. He decided that failure by the company to propound the scheme of reconstruction under s. 110 or to purchase the shares under s. 162, was not unfairly prejudicial. Certain statutory rights were available to shareholders once such schemes had been propounded to ensure that they were carried out fairly, but shareholders could have no interest in a non-existent hypothetical scheme.

Comment. (i) It should be noted that refusal or failure to make capital payments is not, according to this case, unfairly prejudicial. Whether failure or refusal to pay dividends would be actionable under Part XVII was not in issue here, and is a matter which remains to be decided.

(ii) Lord Grantchester also said that a petitioner under what is now Part XVII would have to show a diminution in the value of his shares to satisfy the requirement of unfair prejudice. (But see now Nourse J in *Re R A Noble (Clothing) Ltd*, 1983, p. 522.)

(iii) In *Re London School of Electronics*, 1985 (see p. 523) Nourse J ordered the purchase of the holding of an unfairly prejudiced minority shareholder/director who had been excluded from management and stated that the price should not be discounted because it was a minority holding not carrying the ability to control the company.

Where it is alleged that there has been a wrong to the company the proper plaintiff is the company itself: the principle of majority rule.

134. Foss *v* Harbottle (1843) 2 Hare 461

The plaintiffs, Foss and Turton, were shareholders in a company called 'The Victoria Park Company' which was formed to buy land for use as a pleasure park. The defendants were the other directors and shareholders of the company. The plaintiffs alleged that the defendants had defrauded the company in various ways, and in particular that certain of the defendants had sold land belonging to them to the company at an exorbitant price. The plaintiffs now asked the court to order that the defendants make good the losses to the company. *Held*—by Vice Chancellor Wigram—since the company's board of directors was still in existence, and since it was still possible to call a general meeting of the company, there was nothing to prevent the company from obtaining redress in its corporate character, and the action by the plaintiffs could not be sustained.

Foss: there is no exception allowing a petitioner to proceed to trial where the court's order could be rendered ineffective by an ordinary resolution: no injunction to prevent removal of director under s. 303.

135. Bentley-Stevens v Jones [1974] 2 All ER 653

The plaintiff complained that he had been removed as a director of the company by the resolution of a general meeting which had been irregularly convened. The irregularity was that the decision to call the meeting had been made by two of the four directors of the company but not at a properly convened board meeting. It appeared that the two directors concerned had sent the plaintiff a letter notifying him that a board meeting would be held next morning for the purposes of convening an extraordinary general meeting to remove the plaintiff from the board. The plaintiff did not receive the letter until after the other two directors had met and passed the resolution. In all other respects, e.g. as regards notice, the general meeting and the resolution for the plaintiff's removal were entirely correct within the terms of the Companies Act. On this point Plowman J decided that the court could not intervene. He took this view for the reason that the irregularities in terms of the board meeting could all be cured by the members in general meeting so that any order which the court might make would inevitably be rendered futile.

The plaintiff also claimed that his removal was a breach of the principles established in the *Westbourne Galleries*[129] case. On this point Plowman J *held* that even if this company, which was admittedly a small private company, had a 'personal relationship' basis (which had not been established) the *Westbourne Galleries*[129] case merely decided that a removed quasi-partner/director could be given equitable relief in the form of a winding-up order under what is now s. 122(1)(g), Insolvency Act 1986. It was not authority for the proposition that an injunction could be granted to prevent his removal.

Foss: Situations which cannot be remedied by ordinary resolution: *ultra vires* acts: breaches of company's memorandum and/or articles.

136. Simpson *v* Westminster Palace Hotel Co (1860) 8 HL Cas 712

The company was established 'for the erection, furnishing and maintenance of an hotel, and the carrying on of the usual business of an hotel and tavern, and the doing of all such things as are incidental or otherwise conducive to the attainment of these objects.' The directors, while the hotel was in the course of being built, agreed to let for a short period a large portion of it to the head of a Government Department for use as an office, and the plaintiff, a shareholder, brought this action saying that the letting was *ultra vires*. The evidence showed that the letting was advantageous to the company and its intended business because it brought in income and was for a short period only, and further it appeared that the majority of the shareholders had sanctioned the act by a resolution which, though it would not have been effective to cure an *ultra vires* act, indicated the mood of the majority. *Held*—by the House of Lords—(i) The plaintiff's action in this case was not defeated by the rule in *Foss v Harbottle*, 1843[134] because the plaintiff was pleading an *ultra vires* act by the company. (ii) However the letting was valid because it was within the words 'all such things as are incidental or otherwise conducive to the attainment of these objects.'

Comment. This was a personal action where the company was the real defendant because the remedy was required against it and not on its behalf.

137. Salmon *v* Quin & Axtens Ltd [1909] 1 Ch 311

The memorandum of the company included among its objects the purchasing of real or personal property. By the articles the business was to be managed by the directors, but no resolution of the board to purchase or lease any premises of the company was to be valid unless two conditions were satisfied, namely, notice in writing must be given to each of the two managing directors named in the articles, and neither of them must have dissented therefrom in writing before or at the meeting at which the resolution was to be passed. In August 1908 the board passed resolutions for the purchase of certain premises by the company, and for leasing part of the company's property. The plaintiff, who was one of the managing directors, dissented, but at an extraordinary general meeting of the company held in November 1908, resolutions similar to those passed by the board were passed by an ordinary resolution of the members. The plaintiff brought this action for an injunction to stop the company from acting on the resolutions as they were inconsistent with the articles. *Held*—eventually by the House of Lords (see *Quin & Axtens v Salmon* [1909] AC 442) that an injunction would be granted. The defence that the company ought to have been the plaintiff because the acts were not *ultra vires* but mere matters of internal management, as in *Foss v Harbottle*, 1843,[134] did not apply, because the ruling in that case did not apply where the company was in breach of some provision of its memorandum or articles. These documents can only be altered by a special resolution.

Comment. The plaintiff in fact sued on behalf of himself *and other shareholders*, in a representative action to prevent the majority and the company from acting contrary to the company's constitution.

Could the above decision be used to enable a solicitor who was also a shareholder indirectly to enforce a provision in the company's articles that he is to be the company's solicitor by saying to the company 'conduct business in accordance with the articles'? (See *Eley v Positive Government Security Life Assurance Co*, 1876[64].)

Foss: a minority action is permitted where the notice of a resolution does not give fair and full particulars of the business of the meeting.

138. Baillie *v* Oriental Telephone and Electric Co Ltd [1915] 1 Ch 503

The directors of the defendant company were also the directors of the Telephone Company of Egypt Ltd which was a subsidiary of the defendant company which held practically the whole of the shares in the subsidiary. In 1907 the directors of the defendant company, by using the company's voting powers in the subsidiary, obtained the passing of a resolution by which the articles of the subsidiary were altered giving the directors an increase in remuneration and also a percentage of the profits. In 1913 the auditors of the defendant company pointed out to the directors that the increase in remuneration ought to be sanctioned by the shareholders of the defendant company. An extraordinary general meeting was convened to pass a special resolution ratifying the acts of the directors in 1907, and authorizing them to retain the sums already received, and also altering the articles to allow them to retain remuneration as directors of subsidiaries without being accountable for it. The notice of the meeting was accompanied by a circular setting out the proposed resolutions, but neither the notice nor the circular gave particulars of the very large remuneration which had actually been received by the directors from the subsidiary, i.e. £44,876. The resolutions were passed by the required majority and confirmed. The plaintiff, who held 387 ordinary shares, brought this action on behalf of himself and other shareholders of the company against the majority for a declaration that the resolutions were not binding because of insufficient notice, and for an injunction to restrain the company and its directors from acting on them. Astbury J, at first instance dismissed the action on the ground that the plaintiff could not sue without joining the company, but it was *held*, by the Court of Appeal, that a representative action was permissible here and that the notice was insufficient and the resolutions were not binding on the company.

139. Kaye *v* Croydon Tramways Co [1898] 1 Ch 358

This action was brought by Major-General Kaye on behalf of himself and the other members of the defendant company, except the defendant directors, for a declaration that an agreement between the defendant company and the British Electric Traction Company Ltd for the sale of the undertaking of the defendant company to the traction company, and a resolution approving the same passed at a meeting of the shareholders of the defendant company held on 14 December 1897, were *ultra vires* and ought to be set aside; and for an injunction restraining the defendants from carrying out the agreement. The plaintiff, it appeared, was the holder of £25 ordinary stock in the defendant company, and the basis of his complaint was that the agreement between the two companies involved the payment of a substantial sum to the directors of the defendant company as compensation for loss of office. This was not mentioned in the notice convening the meeting which simply described the agreement as for the sale of the undertaking. *Held*—by the Court of Appeal—

(i) The provision for compensation for loss of office did not render the agreement *ultra vires*.

(ii) The notice, by reason of its omission to refer to the compensation provision, did not fairly disclose the purpose for which the meeting was convened. The notice of a meeting must be capable of being understood by ordinary minds.

(iii) The company would, therefore, be restrained from carrying out the agreement until it was duly sanctioned by the shareholders of the defendant company at a properly convened meeting.

(iv) The rule in *Foss v Harbottle*, 1843[134] was no bar to a representative action in this sort of case.

Foss. Fraud on the minority: misappropriation of corporate property.

140. Menier *v* Hooper's Telegraph Works Ltd (1874) 9 Ch App 350

Company A (European and South American Telegraph Co) was formed to lay a transatlantic cable to be made by Hooper's, the majority shareholder in company A, from Portugal to Brazil. Hooper's found that they could make a greater profit by selling the cable to another company B, but B did not have the government concession to lay the cable which company A had. After much intrigue with the Portuguese government trustee of the concession, he agreed to transfer the concession to company B, and company B then bought the cable from Hooper's. To prevent company A from suing for loss of the concession Hooper obtained the passing of a resolution to wind up company A voluntarily and arranged that a liquidator should be appointed whom Hooper could trust not to pursue the claim of company A in respect of the loss of its contract. Menier, a minority shareholder of company A, asked the court to compel Hooper to account to company A for the profits made on the sale of the cable to B. *Held*—by the Court of Appeal in Chancery—where the majority shareholders of a company propose to gain a benefit for themselves at the expense of the minority, the court may interfere to protect the minority. In such a case one shareholder has a right to bring a derivative claim to seek relief and the claim is not barred by the rule in *Foss v Harbottle*.[134] This was a blatant case of fraud and oppression and Hooper's were trustees of the profit and had to account to company A for it.

141. Cook v Deeks [1916] 1 AC 554

This action was brought in the High Court Division of the Supreme Court of Ontario by the plaintiff, suing on behalf of himself and other shareholders in the Toronto Construction Co Ltd, against the respondents, who were directors of the company. The plaintiff claimed a declaration that the respondents were trustees of the company of the benefit of a contract made between the respondents and the Canadian Pacific Railway Co for construction work. It appeared that the respondents, while acting on behalf of the company in negotiating the contract, actually made it for themselves and not for the company, and by their votes as holders of three-quarters of the issued share capital, subsequently passed a resolution at a general meeting declaring that the company had no interest in the contract. *Held*, by the Privy Council—

(i) That the contract belonged in equity to the company, and the directors could not validly use their voting powers to vest the contract in themselves, in fraud of the minority;

(ii) In cases of breach of duty of this sort, the rule in *Foss v Harbottle*[134] did not bar the plaintiff's claim.

Comment. In *Industrial Developments v Cooley*, 1972 (see p. 548) there was a not dissimilar misappropriation of a corporate opportunity. However, in the *Cooley* case there was no need to resort to a derivative claim because Mr Cooley had made the profit for himself. The whole board were not involved and were clearly anxious to bring the company into court in order to sue Mr Cooley for recovery of the profit.

Foss: Fraud on the minority: expulsion of the minority: benefit of the company.

142. Brown *v* British Abrasive Wheel Co [1919] 1 Ch 290

The company required further capital. The majority who represented 98 per cent of the shareholders were willing to provide this capital but only if they could buy up the 2 per cent minority. The minority would not agree to sell and so the majority shareholders proposed to alter the articles to provide for compulsory acquisition under which nine-tenths of the shareholders could buy out any other shareholders. *Held*—by Astbury J—that the alteration of the articles would be restrained because the alteration was not for the benefit of the company. In addition, the rule in *Foss v Harbottle*[134] did not bar the plaintiff's claim.

Foss: Fraud on the minority: inequitable use of majority power.

143. Clemens *v* Clemens Bros [1976] 2 All ER 268

In this case the issued share capital of £2,000 in a small but prosperous family company was held between the plaintiff (45 per cent) and her aunt (55 per cent), the aunt being one of the five directors of the company. The directors proposed to increase the company's share capital to £3,650 by the creation of a further 1650 voting ordinary shares. The four directors, other than the aunt, were to receive 200 shares each, and the balance of 850 shares was to be placed in trust for the company's long-service employees. The plaintiff objected to the proposed resolution to put this scheme into effect since the result would be to reduce her shareholding to under 25 per cent. At the extraordinary general meeting called to approve the scheme, the aunt voted in favour of the resolutions which were passed. The plaintiff sought a declaration against both the company and the aunt that the resolutions should be set aside on the ground that they were oppressive of the plaintiff. The defendant contended that if two shareholders honestly hold differing opinions, the view of the majority should prevail, and that shareholders in general meeting were entitled to consider their own interests and to vote in any way they honestly believed proper in the interest of the company. In giving judgment in favour of the plaintiff, Foster J made it clear that in the circumstances of this case Miss Clemens (the aunt) was not entitled to exercise her majority vote in whatever way she pleased. The judge found difficulty, however, in expressing this as a general principle of law, in terms, for example, of expressions such as '*bona fide* for the benefit of the company as a whole', 'fraud on a minority', and 'oppressive'. He came to the conclusion that it would be unwise to try to produce a principle because the circumstances of each case are infinitely varied. He did, however, say, following a phrase of Lord Wilberforce in *Westbourne Galleries*,[129] that the right of a shareholder to exercise voting rights in any way whatever is subject always to equitable considerations which may in particular circumstances make it unjust to exercise votes in a certain way. Dealing with the facts before him, Foster J then went on to say: 'I cannot escape the conclusion that the resolutions have been framed so as to put into the hands of Miss Clemens and her fellow directors complete control of the company and to deprive the plaintiff of her existing rights as a shareholder with more than 25 per cent of the votes, and greatly reduce her rights. They are specifically and carefully designed to ensure not only that the plaintiff can never get control of the company, but to deprive her of what has been called her negative control. (Here the judge is referring to her ability to block special and extraordinary resolutions.) Whether I say that these proposals are oppressive to the plaintiff or that no-one could honestly believe that they are for her benefit, matters not. A court of equity will in my judgment regard these considerations as sufficient to prevent the consequences arising from Miss Clemens using her legal right to vote in the way she has and it would be right for a court of equity to prevent such consequences taking effect.'

Comment. (i) The case is quoted to show the very wide power which equity reserves to itself to control the activities of majority shareholders. On the particular facts of this case, of course, the pre-emption rights given to shareholders by s. 89 should prevent the sort of prejudicial conduct towards a minority which was alleged in this case. The plaintiff could, of course, have prevented the other members from effecting the dissapplication of pre-emption rights under s. 95 because a special resolution is required for this.

(ii) Although Foster J was not prepared to put the case into any existing category of *Foss* exceptions, fraud on the minority seems a possible one.

144. Estmanco (Kilner House) Ltd *v* Greater London Council [1982] 1 All ER 437

Estmanco were the owners of a block of flats known as Kilner House. The company was formed by a Conservative controlled GLC with the object of selling the flats into the private ownership of the tenants.

The new owners of the flats would obtain voting rights in the company but not until all the flats were sold. The GLC was to exercise the voting rights attaching to the company's shares until that time.

At a later stage control of the GLC passed from Conservative to Labour. The GLC then told its nominees on the board of Estmanco not to proceed with the private ownership arrangement and they stopped the prosecution of a legal action by Estmanco which had been commenced by its original board. A member who had purchased a flat but whose share had as yet no voting rights, carried on the action as a derivative claim on the basis of fraud on the minority. Her action succeeded, Megarry J granting an injunction to restrain the GLC from preventing Estmanco from pursuing its objectives of privatization.

Foss: **fraud on the minority: is negligence covered by the expression 'fraud'?**

145. Pavlides *v* Jensen [1956] 2 All ER 518

The directors of the Tunnel Asbestos Cement Co Ltd sold an asbestos mine to the Cyprus Asbestos Mines Ltd in which the TAC Ltd held 25 per cent of the issued capital. The mine was sold for £182,000 but the sale was not submitted to a general meeting of TAC for approval. The plaintiff, who was a minority shareholder in TAC, claimed that the defendant directors were negligent because the mine was worth £1,000,000, and this price or something like it should have been obtained. He sued the directors with the company as a nominal defendant for a declaration that the directors were in breach of duty, and for an inquiry into the damage caused to TAC by their negligence and for payment of that sum by the directors to TAC. On the preliminary point as to the competence of the plaintiff as a minority shareholder to bring a derivative action in these circumstances, it was *held*—by Danckwerts J—that the action was not maintainable because the sale was *intra vires* and, since no acts of a fraudulent character were alleged by the plaintiff, the sale could be approved by the majority of shareholders and it was a matter for them.

Comment. (i) The plaintiff was alleging negligence which is a common law claim and derivative actions are creatures of equity, the judiciary being reluctant to extend them to common law claims such as negligence (but see *Prudential v Newman*, p. 554, and Part XVII of the Companies Act 1985, p. 193).

(ii) This line of reasoning was followed in *Multinational Gas v Multinational Gas Services* [1983] 2 All ER 563 where two judges in the Court of Appeal were of opinion that a claim for negligent mismanagement could not be brought even by a liquidator against directors whose actions had been approved by a majority of the members who were not a disinterested majority because they had appointed the directors as their nominees.

Foss: negligence resulting in benefits to the wrongdoers at the expense of the company is 'fraud' for the purposes of the 'fraud on the minority' exception.

146. Daniels *v* Daniels [1978] 2 All ER 89

Mr Douglas Daniels, Mr Gordon Daniels and Mrs Soule, three minority shareholders in Ideal Homes (Coventry) Ltd, wished to bring an action against the majority shareholders (who were also the directors), Mr Bernard Daniels, Mrs Beryl Daniels and the company. In their claim the minority alleged that in October 1970 Ideal Homes, acting on the instructions of the majority shareholders, sold and conveyed freehold property in Warwick to Mrs Beryl Daniels for £4,250 when they knew, or ought to have known, that the correct value of the land was higher. The majority, in reply to these allegations, said that they adopted a valuation made for probate purposes in June 1969 on the occasion of the death in that month of Mr Joseph Daniels, the father of the minority shareholders and Mr Bernard Daniels. Against this the minority shareholders alleged that probate valuations were conservative as to amount and usually less than the value obtainable on open market between a willing seller and buyer.

In 1974 the land was sold by Mrs Daniels for £120,000 and although the majority had every intention of denying the allegations, they asked at this stage that the claim of the minority be struck out as disclosing no reasonable cause of action or otherwise as an abuse of the process of the court. It was argued, on behalf of the majority, that since the minority was not alleging fraud against the majority no action on behalf of the alleged loss to the company could be brought because under the decision in *Foss v Harbottle*, 1843[134] the court could not interfere in the internal affairs of the company at the request of the minority. The minority said they were unable to allege fraud because they were not able to say precisely what had happened beyond the matters set out in their claim.

Templeman J who had not been asked to try the action but only to say whether there was an action at all, reviewed the decisions under the rule in *Foss v Harbottle*, 1843[134] and his judgment made clear that if the breach of duty alleged turned out to be a breach of fiduciary duty, then it should be allowed to proceed under the rule in *Cook v Deeks*, 1916[141] because the majority could control general meetings. Furthermore, if the breach of duty alleged was one of skill and care, i.e. negligence at common law, then it should also be allowed to proceed as an exception to *Foss v Harbottle*, 1843[134] because the alleged negligence had resulted in a profit to one of the directors which distinguished this case from *Pavlides v Jensen*, 1956.[145]

Foss: no derivative claim to challenge the form in which a company's accounts are prepared.

147. Devlin *v* Slough Estates Ltd (1982) 126 SJ 623

Mr Devlin, in a claim on behalf of the company against its directors, asked the High Court to declare that the accounts of Slough Estates for the year ended 31 December 1979 were not prepared in accordance with the Companies Acts in that they did not contain a note of the company's contingent liability in respect of proceedings for alleged breach of contracts in France. The company's defence was that the liability was not sufficiently material to be disclosed, being a sum of £529,000, whereas the assets of the company in 1979 were £371m, and that the plaintiff had no *locus standi* (right to be heard).

Mr Justice Dillon, without commenting on materiality, struck out Mr Devlin's claim on the basis that he had no *locus standi*. Shareholders could bring a derivative action on behalf of the company to redress a wrong to it but the purpose of such an action was normally to prevent misapplication of the company's money and assets; it was not an appropriate vehicle open to any shareholder seeking merely declaratory relief as to the form in which accounts for a prior year ought to have been drawn. There were many matters in accounts which had to be a matter of opinion for which there was no one correct answer. A shareholder had protection in that the accounts had to be audited and he could with sufficient support requisition a meeting. The formulation of accounts involved matters of business judgment with which the court could not interfere where there were no allegations of bad faith.

Foss: a procedural rule of law: the parties cannot waive the rule.

148. Heyting *v* Dupont [1964] 2 All ER 273

The plaintiff and the first defendant were the only directors of the Dupont Pipe Co Ltd. The company was incorporated for the purpose of exploiting an invention by the first defendant being a machine for laying plastic pipe for conveying liquids which could travel overground while laying the pipe. The issued capital of the company was 5,021 shares of £1 each, Dupont holding 3,003 and the plaintiff 2,003, the remaining 15 shares being held by five shareholders. Because of the way in which the articles were framed it was not possible to conduct the business of the company properly, and it became paralysed and the invention was not really exploited at all. Under the articles the election of the directors after the first required a three-quarters majority. The quorum of the board was three and the first board had consisted of four members. However, one resigned and one died and neither were replaced Thus either the plaintiff or the defendant could by staying away prevent a board decision. For all these misfortunes the plaintiff blamed the first defendant and the first defendant blamed the plaintiff. The plaintiff sued on behalf of himself and the other shareholders of the company, the relief claimed being the payment of damages by the first defendant to the company for the company's lost opportunities arising out of misfeasance. The statement of claim did not allege any *ultra vires* acts nor fraud on the part of the first defendant. There was no suggestion of any misappropriation of the company's assets by him in fraud of the minority, but the statement of claim did allege that it was impossible in the circumstances for the company to sue in its own name against the first defendant. There was a counterclaim by which the first defendant brought similar claims against the plaintiff. *Held*—by Plowman J—the plaintiff's action and the first defendant's counter-claim could not be entertained when all that was alleged was misfeasance. The case did not come within any of the exceptions to the rule in *Foss v Harbottle*.[134] Exceptions to the rule will not be granted merely because the justice of the case demands it (and see *Prudential v Newman*, p. 554). Although in this case it was impossible for the company to bring an action in its own name, the rule in *Foss v Harbottle*[134] was one of procedure and therefore the court had no jurisdiction to hear the case.

Comment. Misfeasance is a common law claim and the court was saying in effect that derivative actions cannot as a matter of procedure be brought for common law claims (but see *Prudential v Newman*). (See p. 554.)

MEETINGS AND RESOLUTIONS

In the absence of a contrary provision in the articles, see e.g. *Reg* 39 of *Table A*, notice must be given to all those entitled to notice of the meeting: failure to do so renders resolutions passed void.

149. Young *v* Ladies Imperial Club [1920] 2 KB 523

Mrs Young, who was a member of the club, was expelled by a resolution passed by the appropriate committee. The Duchess of

Abercorn, who was a member of the committee, was not sent a notice of the meeting, it being understood that she would not be able to attend. In fact she had previously informed the chairman that she would not be able to attend. Nevertheless, in this action which was concerned with the validity of the expulsion, it was *held*—by the Court of Appeal—that the failure to send a notice to the Duchess invalidated the proceedings of the committee and rendered the expulsion void.

'Every member of the committee ought, in my view, to be summoned to every meeting of the committee except in a case where summoning can have no possible result, as where the member is at such a distance that the summons cannot effectively reach the member in time to allow him or her to communicate with the committee. Extreme illness may be another ground, though I should myself require the illness to be extremely serious, because a member of the committee receiving a notice to attend may either write to ask for an adjournment of the meeting or express his views in writing to the committee, and I should require the illness to be such as to prevent that form of action being taken on receiving notice of such a meeting.' *Per* Scrutton L J.

Failure to give notice of a meeting: effect of *Reg* 39, *Table A*.

150. Re West Canadian Collieries Ltd [1962] Ch 370

The company failed to give notice of a meeting to certain of its members because their plates were inadvertently left out of an addressograph machine which was being used to prepare the envelopes in which the notices were sent. The proceedings of the meeting were not invalidated it being *held* in the High Court to be an accidental omission within an article of the company similar to *Table A, Reg* 39.

151. Musselwhite v C H Musselwhite & Son Ltd [1962] Ch 964

The company failed to give notice of a general meeting to certain persons who had sold their shares but had not been paid and remained on the register of members. The directors believed that the mere fact of entering into a contract of sale had made them cease to be members. *Held*—in the High Court—the proceedings of the general meeting were invalidated since the error was one of law and not an accidental omission within an article of the company similar to *Table A, Reg* 39.

539

As a general rule one shareholder cannot constitute a meeting: exceptionally the Department of Trade and Industry under s. 367 and the court under s. 371 can order the holding of meetings with a quorum of one.

152. Sharp *v* Dawes (1876) 2 QBD 26

The Great Caradon Mine was run by a mining company in Cornwall and was carried on on the cost-book system, being controlled by the Stannaries Act 1869. The company had offices in London, and on 22 December 1874, notice of a general meeting was properly given. The meeting was held, but only the secretary, Sharp, and one shareholder, a Mr Silversides who held 25 shares, attended. Nevertheless the business of the meeting was conducted with Silversides in the chair. Among other things a call on shares was made, and the defendant refused to pay it. He was sued by the secretary, Sharp, who brought the action on behalf of the company, and his defence was that calls had to be made at a meeting and there had been no meeting on this occasion. *Held*—by the Court of Appeal—the call was invalid. According to the ordinary use of the English language a meeting could not be constituted by one shareholder.

153. In Re London Flats Ltd [1969] 2 All ER 744

The company was in liquidation and a meeting was called under what is now s. 92(1), Insolvency Act 1986 to appoint a successor to the liquidator who had died. At the meeting X, one of the only two shareholders, proposed that he be appointed liquidator and put forward an amendment to the resolution before the meeting which substituted his own name in the resolution for the person named therein who was a chartered accountant. The other shareholder, Y, left the meeting saying 'I withdraw from the meeting, you now have no quorum'. The meeting continued and the amended resolution was put to the vote. There being one vote in favour and none against, X as chairman declared the amendment carried thus making himself liquidator. Y made application to the court under what is now s. 108(2), *ibid*, for the removal of X and the appointment of a liquidator by the court on the ground that the appointment of X was invalid, the meeting having consisted of only one shareholder. *Held*—by Plowman J—that the appointment of X was invalid. He said that as a general rule one shareholder could not constitute a meeting except where it could be shown that the word 'meeting' had a special meaning and could include a single shareholder. There were such instances under what are now s. 367 (power of DoTI to call an AGM) and s. 371

(power of court to order a meeting) where clearly one shareholder could constitute a valid meeting. However, this did not apply to a meeting under what is now s. 92(1), *ibid* and therefore the appointment of X was a nullity. The court exercised its power under what is now s. 108(2), *ibid* and ordered the removal of X. The matter was then referred to chambers for the appointment of an independent liquidator. A chartered accountant unconnected with the parties was appointed.

154. XL Laundries Ltd, *The Financial Times*, 18 June 1969

In this case it was necessary for the company to pass a special resolution under what is now s. 135(1) in order to reduce its share capital prior to making an application to the court for confirmation of the reduction.

A Mr Johnson, who was the sole ordinary shareholder and, as such, the only person entitled to vote, attended the meeting alone. Later the validity of the meeting was questioned and the court *held*—

(*a*) that *prima facie* a meeting meant the coming together of at least two persons, though company legislation seemed to accept that there might be occasions on which a 'meeting' of one person would be valid (see ss. 367 and 371, Companies Act 1985);

(*b*) accordingly it seemed pointless for one of Mr Johnson's shares to be transferred to a nominee merely to hold a meeting, at which two shareholders were present, and the 'meeting' attended by Mr Johnson as sole ordinary shareholder and the resolutions passed thereat were valid.

Comment. In this case the court was clearly satisfied that the reduction was fair and reasonable and the judgment represents a practical approach. However, it should not be assumed that the court would be so co-operative in every case under s. 135(1).

155. Re El Sombrero Ltd [1958] 3 All ER 1

The applicant in this case held 90 per cent of the shares of the company which was a private company. The company's two directors held 5 per cent of the shares each. The company's articles provided that the quorum for general meetings was two persons present in person or by proxy, and if within half an hour from the time appointed for holding a meeting a quorum was not present, the meeting, if convened on the requisition of the members, was deemed dissolved. On 11 March 1958, the applicant requisitioned an extraordinary general meeting under what is now s. 368, to pass a resolution removing the two directors and appointing others in their place. The directors did not comply with the requisition, so the applicant himself convened an extraordinary general meeting for 21 April 1958. The two directors deliberately failed to attend, and since no quorum was present, the meeting was dissolved. The applicant took out a summons asking for a meeting to be called by the court under what is now s. 371 to pass a resolution removing the two directors, and for a direction that one member of the company should be deemed to constitute a quorum at such meeting. The application was opposed by the directors. *Held*—by the High Court—Since in practice a meeting of the company could not be convened under the articles, the court had a jurisdiction under what is now s. 371, to order a meeting to be held, and for one member to constitute a quorum, and such an order was made. The applicant was entitled to enforce his statutory right under what is now s. 303 to remove the directors by ordinary resolution, and the directors had refused to perform their statutory duty to call a meeting for the sole reason that, if a meeting was held, they would cease to be directors.

Comment. This case was followed in *Re HR Paul & Son, The Times*, 17 November 1973 where Brightman J ordered a general meeting to take place with a quorum of one where a 90 per cent shareholder could not get alterations in the articles because the minority had refused to attend general meetings. In cases such as this it is often impossible for the major shareholder to transfer a few shares to a nominee in order to make a quorum, either because there are pre-emption provisions in the articles or the remaining members are also directors who have a majority on the board and refuse to register the necessary transfers.

Weighted and special voting rights: application to removal of directors under s. 303.

156. Bushell v Faith [1969] 1 All ER 1002

Mrs Bushell, Mr Faith and their sister, Dr Bayne, each owned 100 shares in a family company which had an issued share capital of 300 fully paid shares of £1 each. The company had adopted *Table A* for its articles of association but a special art 9 provided that, in the event of a resolution being proposed at a general meeting for the removal of a director any shares held by that director should carry three votes per share.

Mr Faith's conduct as a director displeased his sisters and they requisitioned a general meeting at which an ordinary resolution was passed on a show of hands to remove him. Mr Faith demanded a poll, contending that, in accordance with art 9, his 100 shares carried 300 votes and that therefore the resolution had been defeated by 300 votes to 200.

Mrs Bushell then claimed a declaration by the court that the resolution had been validly passed and an injunction restraining her brother from acting as a director. Ungoed-Thomas J at first instance, granted the injunction *holding* that art 9 was invalid because it infringed what is now s. 303 and that therefore the resolution removing Mr Faith had been duly passed. The Court of Appeal did not agree with the decision at first instance and allowed Mr Faith's appeal. In particular Russell L J, stated that a provision as to voting rights in the articles which has the effect of making a special resolution to alter the articles incapable of being passed if a particular shareholder or group of shareholders exercise his or their voting rights against it is not a provision depriving the company of the power to alter its articles or any of them by special resolution, and so does not contravene what is now s. 9 and is valid. However, an article providing that no alteration shall be made in the articles without the consent of a particular person would be contrary to s. 9 and so would be invalid.

Mrs Bushell's appeal to the House of Lords ([1970] 1 All ER 53) was also dismissed, their Lordships *holding* that the provisions of what is now s. 303 did not prevent companies from attaching special voting rights to certain shares for certain occasions, e.g. to directors' shares on a resolution at a general meeting for the removal of a director.

Comment. In the House of Lords, Lord Reid pointed to what is now *Reg* 2 of *Table A* as justifying the weighted voting provisions. *Table A*, *Reg* 2 provides 'any share may be issued with such rights or restrictions as the company may by ordinary resolution determine'. This to Lord Reid indicated that there was no reason why shares should not have weighted voting rights if the company wished that to be the position.

DIRECTORS AND SECRETARIES

The articles may require a director to hold qualification shares 'in his own right'. Even so, he need not be the absolute owner of the relevant shares.

157. Pulbrook *v* Richmond Consolidated Mining Co (1878) 9 Ch D 610

The company's articles provided that 'No person shall be eligible as director unless he holds as registered member in his own right capital of a nominal value of £500 at least'. Pulbrook was elected director on 23 August 1877, but in January 1877 he had mortgaged his shares to a William Cuthbert, although it was agreed that the transfer should not be registered. On 28 January 1878, Cuthbert in error had the transfer registered in his name as holder of the shares and, notice of this entry having been given to the directors, they refused to allow Pulbrook to sit on the board. Pulbrook applied to the court for rectification to the register, and Cuthbert's name was struck out and his own restored. He then took his seat on the board and produced the court order but was refused permission to act, so he brought this motion to restrain the directors by injunction from interfering with his rights. *Held*—by Jessel M R in the Chancery Division—he was validly elected in August 1877, his period of office had not expired, and at the time of his election he had the required qualification. The words 'in his own right' cannot mean he must be a beneficial owner since no notice of trust can be entered on the register. The company cannot look behind the register as to beneficial interest but must take the register as conclusive. The fact that Cuthbert was registered was irrelevant. The effect of rectification is that he is struck off and it is as though he had never been on at all. Thus Pulbrook was and always had been a director, and the injunction was granted.

Comment. In *Grundy v Briggs* [1910] 1 Ch 444 a director was held to be qualified where he held shares jointly with other persons as the personal representatives of a deceased member.

The members may by ordinary resolution ratify an act of the board which is *intra vires* the company but beyond the authority or competence of the board.

158. Grant *v* United Kingdom Switchback Railways Co (1888) 40 Ch D 135

The articles of association of Thompson's Patent Gravity Switchback Railways Co (the second defendant) disqualified any director from voting at a board meeting in regard to any contract in which he was interested. The directors of Thompson's agreed to sell the company's undertaking to the United Kingdom Co (the first defendant) despite the fact that they were also the promoters of the purchasing company. An action was brought by a shareholder in Thompson's for an injunction to restrain Thompson's from carrying into effect the contract of sale on the grounds that they had no authority to enter into it since the articles prohibited a director from voting upon a contract in which he was interested, and here all the directors but one were interested. However, it appeared that a general meeting of the shareholders of Thompson's had been properly held and that they had passed an ordinary resolution approving and adopting the agreement and authorizing the directors to carry it into effect. *Held*—by the Court of Appeal—that the contract was valid and an injunction was refused.

The members by ordinary resolution may override the exercise by the board of a concurrent power.

159. Scott v Scott [1943] 1 All ER 582

The plaintiffs were two members and the defendants the remaining members of a private limited company, Frank F. Scott (Liverpool) Ltd, which had adopted as its articles *Table A*. Resolutions were passed in general meeting to the following effect—
(1) that certain payments in respect of interim dividend be paid to preference shareholders;
(2) that Messrs. A Hallett & Co be instructed to investigate the financial affairs of the company for the last two financial years;
(3) that A. Hallett & Co should be auditors for the ensuing year.
The plaintiffs contended that the resolutions were invalid and had applied to the Board of Trade to appoint auditors on the footing that the company had failed to appoint them. *Held*—by the Court of Appeal—
  (i) The first two resolutions were invalid as being attempts by the company in general meeting to usurp the directors' powers of financial control derived from the articles.
  (ii) The appointment of A. Hallett & Co as auditors was valid.
  Comment. (i) A remedy of the shareholders in general meeting when they are dissatisfied with the directors is not to attempt to usurp their powers but to remove them.
  (ii) As regards the resolution instructing a financial investigation, the members might have asked for a Department of Trade investigation under what is now s. 431(1) which requires application by 200 members or those holding one-tenth of the shares issued.
  (iii) In fact the provisions of *Table A* give the directors powers of financial control in terms of dividends. What is now *Reg* 102 provides that the company in general meeting may declare dividends but no dividend shall exceed the amount recommended by the directors. What is now *Reg* 103 says that the directors may from time to time pay to the members such interim dividends as appear to the directors to be justified by the profits of the company.
  (iv) At the time when this case was brought the power to appoint auditors was concurrent. Now, under s. 384, the primary duty to appoint auditors falls on the members alone. Nevertheless, the *Scott* case is a valid illustration of the effect of the different exercise of concurrent powers by directors and members.

(v) In a company governed by the latest *Table A*, the members could presumably have directed, by special resolution, the appointment of the auditors to undertake a financial investigation. (See *Reg 70.*) However, the dividend position is unchanged.

Unauthorized payments to directors: directors may be excused of misfeasance if they acted honestly and reasonably: s. 727

160. In Re Duomatic [1969] 1 All ER 161

The share capital of the company was made up of 100 £1 ordinary shares and 50,000 £1 non-voting preference shares. At one time E, H and T held all the ordinary shares between them and in addition were directors of the company. E and T did not consider that H was a good director. Although they could have voted him off the board they decided instead to pay him £4,000 to leave the company perhaps largely because he was threatening to sue the company and generally to cause trouble if he was removed against his will. On payment of the £4,000 H left transferring his shares to E. No disclosure of the payment of the £4,000 was made in the company's accounts.

It was also the practice for each director to draw remuneration as required and for the members to approve these drawings at the end of the year when the accounts were drawn up. The amounts drawn were as follows:

In period A (E, T and H sole directors and ordinary shareholders) £10,151 paid to E
£5,510 paid to H

In period B (E and T sole directors and ordinary shareholders) £9,000 paid to E but no final accounts agreed,

In period C (when additional persons had become shareholders) E informally agreed to limit his drawings to £60 per week but in fact drew approximately £100 per week

The company then went into voluntary liquidation and the liquidator began proceedings against E and H—

(*a*) for repayment of the sums paid to E and H as salaries on the ground that these had never been approved in general meeting;

(*b*) repayment of the £4,000 paid to H for loss of office; and

(*c*) declarations that E and T had been guilty of misfeasance.

Held—by Buckley J—that—

(i) repayment of the sums of £10,151 and £5,510 could not be ordered since thay had been made with the approval of all the shareholders;

(ii) although E had not obtained the approval of all the shareholders to the payment of the £9,000, final accounts not having been agreed, in the circumstances and in view of the general practice E ought to be excused repayment of the £9,000 under what is now s. 727;

(iii) since there had been no disclosure to the preference shareholders of the payment of £4,000 compensation to H required by what is now s. 312, E and T had misapplied the company's funds and were jointly and severally liable to repay the sums. Furthermore, H held the money on trust for the company and if necessary could be required to repay it. E and T had not acted reasonably in this matter and could not be excused under what is now s. 727.

A director whose appointment is defective and void may be entitled to remuneration by way of *quantum meruit* for work carried out. *Quantum meruit* is not available if the director has a contract. If he has he must abide by its terms.

161. Craven-Ellis *v* Canons Ltd [1936] 2 KB 403

The plaintiff was employed as managing director by the company under a deed which provided for remuneration. The articles provided that directors must have qualification shares, and must obtain these within two months of appointment. The plaintiff and other directors never obtained the required number of shares so that the deed was invalid. However, the plaintiff had rendered services, and he now sued on a *quantum meruit* for a reasonable sum by way of remuneration. *Held*—by the Court of Appeal—he succeeded on a *quantum meruit*, there being no valid contract.

162. Re Richmond Gate Property Co Ltd [1964] 3 All ER 936

The company was incorporated on 19 January 1962, and a resolution for a voluntary winding up was passed on 20 September 1962, a declaration of solvency being filed. Walker, one of the two joint managing directors, lodged proof of a salary claim which the liquidator rejected. Walker was appointed on terms that he should receive 'such remuneration as the directors may determine', and in fact no remuneration was fixed. He claimed £400 either in contract or on *quantum meruit*. *Held*—by Plowman J—the liquidator was right in rejecting the proof. There was no claim under the contract which was only for 'such remuneration as the directors may determine' and none had been so determined. Moreover, the existence of an express contract in regard to remuneration automatically excluded a claim on a *quantum meruit*.

Comment. Although the decision seems harsh and represents the law, in this case there had been an understanding that until the company got on its feet, which it never did, no remuneration should be paid.

The relationship of a director with his company is fiduciary. He is therefore required to account to the company for any secret or unauthorized profit made from his position as a director: the relationship also means that there can be no unauthorized use of confidential information acquired from office.

163. Industrial Development Consultants v Cooley [1972] 2 All ER 162

The defendant was an architect of considerable distinction and attainment in his own sphere. He was employed as managing director by Industrial Development Consultants who provided construction consultancy services for gas boards. The Eastern Gas Board were offering a lucrative contract in regard to the building of four depots and IDC was very keen to obtain the business. The defendant was acting for IDC in the matter and the Eastern Gas Board made it clear to the defendant that IDC would not obtain the contract because the officers of the Eastern Gas Board would not engage a firm of consultants. The defendant realized that he had a good chance of obtaining the contract for himself. He therefore represented to IDC that he was ill and because IDC were of the opinion that the defendant was near to a nervous breakdown, he was allowed to terminate his employment with them on short notice. Shortly afterwards the defendant took steps which resulted in his obtaining the Eastern Gas Board contracts for the four depots for himself. In this case IDC sued the defendant for an account of the profits that he would make on the construction of the four depots. *Held*—by Roskill J—that the defendant had acted in breach of duty and must account. The fact that IDC might not have obtained the contract itself was immaterial. 'Therefore it cannot be said that it is anything like certain that the plaintiffs would ever have got this contract ... on the other hand, there was always the possibility of the plaintiffs persuading the Eastern Gas Board to change their minds; and ironically enough, it would have been the defendant's duty to try and persuade them to change their minds. It is a curious position under which he should now say that the plaintiffs suffered no loss because he would never have succeeded in persuading them to change their mind.' *per* Roskill J.

164. Baker v Gibbons [1972] 2 All ER 759

The plaintiff was a working director of Megafoam Ltd, the third defendants in these proceedings. The first defendant, Gibbons, and the second defendant, Cameron, were directors and shareholders of Megafoam Ltd, the objects of which were the marketing of specialized cavity wall insulation. Megafoam operated its business through 16 agents each of whom covered an area in the United Kingdom and all of whom worked on commission. The contract of service between the plaintiff and the company had no covenant against competition after its termination. In December 1971 the first and second defendants removed the plaintiff from the office of director of Megafoam under what is now s. 303. The plaintiff then set up in business under the name of J. C. Baker (Insulation) Ltd and began to market a produce called Supafoam. The plaintiff commenced proceedings against the first two defendants and the company as third defendants in regard to his dismissal and the latter contended that the plaintiff was seeking to entice the company's agents away from it. The company asked for an injunction pending the trial of the action restraining the plaintiff from soliciting any employees of the company to terminate their employment with Megafoam. Pennycuick V-C refused the injunction. He referred to the general principle that a person who had obtained information in confidence was not allowed to use it as a springboard for activities detrimental to the person who made the confidential information available. This principle did not depend on implied contract but it depended on the broad principle of equity that he who had received information in confidence should not take unfair advantage of it. Pennycuick V-C also observed that this principle applied with particular force between a director and his company, in view of the fiduciary character of the relationship between them. In the present case, however, he *held* that the company had not made out its case. It would be impossible to maintain as a principle of universal application that in every instance in which a director during the term of his office learned the name and address of a particular employee of his company, that information must necessarily be regarded as received in confidence and remain confidential. It was not alleged that the plaintiff had taken with him a written list of the names and addresses of the agents employed by Megafoam Ltd. In the circumstances of the present case the names and addresses of individual agents could not be treated as confidential information, and this conclusion was not affected by the fact that the plaintiff was a director of the defendant company and as such owned a fiduciary duty to it.

165. Regal (Hastings) Ltd v Gulliver [1942] 1 All ER 378

The Regal company owned one cinema and wished to buy two others with the object of selling all three together. The Regal company formed a subsidiary so that the subsidiary could buy the cinemas in question but the Regal company could not provide all the capital needed to purchase them and the directors bought some of the shares in the subsidiary themselves thus providing the necessary capital. The subsidiary company acquired the two cinemas and eventually the shares in the Regal company and in the subsidiary were sold at a profit. The new controllers of the Regal company then caused it to bring an action to recover the profit made. It was *held* by the House of Lords that the directors must account to the Regal company for the profit on the grounds that it was only through the knowledge and opportunity they gained as directors of that company that they were able to obtain the shares and consequently to make the profit. In particular the House of Lords stated that directors were liable to account to the company once it was established—

(*a*) that what the directors did was so related to the affairs of the company that it could properly be said to have been done in the course of their management and in utilization of their opportunities and special knowledge as directors; and

(*b*) that what they did resulted in a profit to themselves.

Comment. This same question was considered by the House of Lords in *Boardman v Phipps* [1967] 2 AC 46 where the *Regal* case was followed. It is generally felt that the fiduciary duty to account which was placed in the directors in these two cases is rather high. In the *Regal* case the directors did not have a majority of shares in the company. It would have been possible for them to obtain ratification of their acts by the company in general meeting. Furthermore it was always conceded that they had acted in good faith and in full belief in the legality of their action, so that it had not occurred to them to obtain the approval of a general meeting. It is also true to say that the directors had not deprived the company of any of its property. The shares in the subsidiary were bought with their own money and those shares had never been the company's property on the facts as the court found them. It would seem that the mere possession of information which results from the holding of office as a director is sufficient to raise the duty to account.

A director is entitled to take up a business opportunity for himself if his company has considered that opportunity and following full disclosure by the director has decided to reject it.

166. Peso Silver Mines Ltd (NPL) v Cropper (1966) 58 DLR (2d) 1

The board of directors of Peso was approached by a person named Dikson who wanted to sell to Peso 126 prospecting claims near to the company's own property. The board of Peso rejected this proposal after *bona fide* consideration. However, a syndicate was then formed by Peso's geologist to purchase Dikson's claim. A company called Cross Bow Mines Ltd was incorporated by the syndicate for the purpose. Cropper was a director of Peso and had taken part in the earlier decision of the Peso board and also became a shareholder in Cross Bow Mines. This action was brought claiming that Cropper was accountable to Peso for the Cross Bow shares which he had obtained. *Held*—by the Supreme Court of Canada—that he was not bound to account. On the facts Cropper and his co-directors had acted in good faith solely in the interest of Peso and with sound business reasons for rejecting the offer. There was no evidence that Cropper had any confidential or other information which he concealed from the board. The court also found that when Cropper was approached to join the syndicate it was not in his capacity as a director of Peso but as an individual member of the public whom the syndicate was seeking to interest as a co-adventurer.

Directors' duty of skill and care: negligent mismanagement and other common law claims for damages caused by breach of duty and misfeasance.

167. Overend & Gurney Co Ltd v Gibb (1872) LR 5 HL 480

This action was brought by a company which was in liquidation against the directors of the company, seeking to make them liable for loss sustained by reason of the directors having purchased a bill broking and money dealing business which turned out to be a losing concern. The directors were authorized by the company's memorandum and articles to purchase the business. The main claim of the plaintiff company was that the directors had acted negligently in making the purchase. *Held*—by the House of Lords—they had been imprudent in buying the business but even so they were not liable. The imprudence must be so great and manifest as to amount to gross negligence, and the evidence in this case did not show the great degree of negligence required to make the directors personally liable.

Comment. This case and other similar cases were decided in the days of non-technical directors. In modern times, directors often have expertise in a particular branch of the company's activities and it is doubtful whether the duty of care they owe to the company is as low as that found in the early cases involving non-technical directors. (For an example of the modern view, see case 169 below.)

168. Re City Equitable Fire Insurance Co [1925] Ch 407

In this case the chairman of the company committed frauds by purporting to buy Treasury Bonds just before the end of the accounting period and selling them just after the audit. By this method a debt due to the company from a firm in which the chairman had an interest was considerably reduced on the balance sheet by increasing the Gilt-edged securities shown as assets. With regard to the duty of auditors it was *held* that they might have been negligent in that they had not asked for the production of the Treasury Bonds but appeared to have trusted the chairman. However, they were held not liable mainly because this was one item in a very large audit. The case does, however, show a movement towards a situation in which the auditors cannot necessarily implicitly trust the company's officers. The case is also concerned with the duties of directors in that it appeared that the directors of this insurance company had left the management of its affairs almost entirely to the chairman and it was perhaps because of this that he had more easily been able to perpetrate his frauds. In the course of his judgment Romer J laid down the following duties of care and skill required of directors and the general view is that these are not unduly burdensome. '... (1) A director need not exhibit in the performance of his duties a greater degree of skill than may reasonably be expected from a person of his knowledge and experience. A director of a life insurance company, for instance, does not guarantee that he has the skill of an actuary or of a physician ... (2) A director is not bound to give continuous attention to the affairs of his company. His duties are of an intermittent nature to be performed at periodical board meetings ... He is not, however, bound to attend all such meetings though he ought to attend whenever, in the circumstances, he is reasonably able to do so. (3) In respect of all duties that, having regard to the exigencies of business, and the articles of association, may properly be left to some other official, a director is, in the absence of grounds for suspicion, justified in trusting that official to perform such duties honestly.'

Comment. A classic illustration of the above principles is to be found in the earlier *Marquis of Bute's case* [1892] 2 Ch 100 where the Marquis was made president of the Cardiff Savings Bank at six months old by inheriting the office from his father. He attended one board meeting in 38 years and was held by Stirling J not liable for certain irregularities in the lending operations of the bank.

169. Dorchester Finance Co Ltd v Stebbing [1977] (unreported) (Noted (1980) 1 Co. Law. p. 38)

On 22 July 1977 Foster J dealt, in the Chancery Division, with this case which concerned the duties of skill and care of company directors. The decision was not officially reported, which is unfortunate since it seems to be the first decision in this area of the law since *Re City Equitable Fire Insurance Co Ltd*.[168] The case concerned a moneylending company, Dorchester Finance, which at all material times had three directors. Only one, S, was involved in the affairs of the company on a full-time basis. No board meetings were held and P and H, the other directors, made only rare visits to the company's premises. S and P were qualified accountants and H had considerable accountancy experience, though he was in fact unqualified. It appeared that S caused the company to make loans to other persons and companies with whom he had some connection or dealing, and that he was able to achieve this, in part at least, because P and H signed cheques on the company's account in blank at his request. The loans did not comply with the Moneylenders Acts and adequate securities were not taken so that the loans could not be recovered by the company which then brought an action against the three directors for alleged negligence and misappropriation of the company's property. Foster J held that all three directors were liable in damages. S, who was an executive director, was held to have been grossly negligent and P and H were also held to have failed to exhibit the necessary skill and care in the performance of their duties as non-executive directors, even though the evidence showed that they had acted in good faith throughout. The decision is of particular importance in regard to P and H because the judge appears to have applied a higher standard for non-executive directors than that laid down in the *Re City Equitable* case.[168] In particular the judge rejected any defence based upon non-feasance, i.e. the omission of an act which a person is bound by law to do. Contrary to *Re City Equitable*, therefore, it would seem from this case to be unreasonable for a non-executive director not to attend board meetings or to show any interest in the company's affairs and merely rely on management, or, according to the judge, on the competence and diligence of the company's auditors.

Comment. It is not possible to say with certainty whether this decision affects the liability of non-executive directors who are not qualified or experienced in a discipline relevant to company administration. It was obviously of importance that P and H were experienced accountants and one would have expected a more objective and higher standard to be applied to such persons, even in their capacity as non-executive directors. The matter is really one which should be dealt with by legislation but there is nothing which is relevant to this problem in the Companies Act 1985.

170. Prudential Assurance Co Ltd v Newman Industries Ltd [1980] 2 All ER 841

The facts of this case date from the failure of the stock market in 1974 when a Mr B and a Mr L were respectively chairman and vice-chairman of Strongpoint Ltd, which was owned by them, Thomas Poole and Gladstone China Ltd (TPG), an investment group with holdings in a wide range of companies, and Newman Industries Ltd (Newman). Strongpoint owned 35 per cent of TPG's issued ordinary shares and TPG held 25·6 per cent of Newman shares. By December 1974 the value of TPG's holdings was much reduced in the stock market collapse and new sources of finance were not easy to obtain and existing loans difficult to extend so that TPG faced a severe financial crisis. By agreement of 3 June 1975 Newman agreed to purchase all TPG assets (except its holding in Newman and a debt of £100,000 owed by Strongpoint to TPG) in return for Newman assuming all TPG's liabilities and a payment of £325,000 in cash, this figure being arrived at after deducting £1,171,000 liabilities from £1,496,000 of assets. Because of the common directorship of Mr B and Mr L and their ownership of Strongpoint, the agreement was conditional on approval by the shareholders of Strongpoint and Newman. Without full consultation with the board of Newman that company was caused to issue a circular to shareholders recommending the acceptance of the scheme to buy TPG for £325,000. Newman's auditors had been brought in to make a valuation and a partner in the firm of auditors, on the basis, it was alleged, of false information supplied to him by Mr L, placed a valuation of £235,000 on TPG. Later, by means of a telephone conversation with Mr L, the partner was persuaded to increase the valuation to £325,000. There was opposition to the deal from one non-executive director, who was later removed from the board, and from some shareholders, including the institutions led by the Prudential which held 3·2 per cent of Newman's shares. However, the TPG proposal was eventually approved by the shareholders of Newman at a meeting in July 1975. Following this the Prudential, who established at the trial that Newman could have acquired TPG for £450,000 less than the price paid for it, i.e. a nil price with the assumption of a few liabilities, served a writ on Mr B, Mr L, Newman and TPG. The Prudential's allegations were as follows—

(a) *That* in order to meet TPG's pressing obligations, Mr B and Mr L conspired to use moneys belonging to Newman secretly and by instalments which could be met out of Newman's ordinary cash flow and were therefore unlikely to attract attention.

(*b*) *That* this was deliberately concealed from other members of the Newman board.

(*c*) *That* by means of a valuation prepared by a partner of the firm of auditors on false information supplied to him and from whom they concealed relevant information, they misled the board.

(*d*) *That* by a tricky and misleading circular, sent to the shareholders, they conspired to induce them to approve the agreement which was designed to benefit TPG at Newman's expense.

The form of the Prudential's action was unusual since they proceeded with three actions simultaneously as follows—

(i) a direct action in which they claimed damages for themselves from the defendants;

(ii) a representative action on behalf of all other shareholders;

(iii) a derivative action for damages on behalf of Newman.

The direct and the representative action succeeded. As regards the representative action, the judge did not actually award damages to all the shareholders but gave a declaratory judgment saying that they were entitled to them in law. Thus shareholders who wished to take advantage of the judgment need only prove actual loss since the declaratory judgment operated in favour of all of them and the action need not be tried out again in each case. This aspect of the judgment tends to explode the theory hitherto held that damage to the company is not damage to its shareholders. This argument, said the judge, pressed the distinction between a company and its shareholders too far. The success of the representative action also meant that shareholders could associate together and pool their resources to bring such an action in the name of one shareholder. They would then all share in the proceeds and their costs would be reduced accordingly.

As regards the derivative action, this has generally been allowed when the directors who are alleged to have caused the company loss also control the company and are therefore unlikely to bring the company into court to claim that loss. Control has usually been linked to voting control (see *Cook v Deeks*, 1916[141]) but that was not the case here and Vinelott J in holding that the derivative action succeeded regarded control as *de facto* control, regardless of voting power. Thus the judgment has made directors who do not have voting control responsible to shareholders for breaches of duty owed to the company through which they receive a benefit by allowing shareholders to sue in the name of the company. It is conceivable, therefore, that this principle could be applied to shadow directors under the Companies Act 1985, being those who may control a company without having a seat on the board. Furthermore, the judgment rather anticipated the enactment of what is now s. 459 which provides that 'any member of a company may apply to the court by petition for an order ... on the ground that the affairs of the company are being ... conducted in a manner which is unfairly prejudicial to the interests of some part of the members'. This section then goes on to provide that civil proceedings may be brought 'in the name of or on behalf of the company'.

Comment. (1) The actions were brought for the tort of conspiracy but might extend to actions in negligence where the directors had failed to exercise skill and judgment in the exercise of their duties, thus causing loss. Such actions are permitted in the United States and if permitted here would cause company directors urgently to consider the matter of insurance against this sort of liability. As regards the issue as to whether derivative and representative claims could be brought for common law claims (see p. 200), Vinelott J said they could as an exception to the rule in *Foss v Harbottle*, 1843[134] and that there could be an exception made to that rule: 'whenever the justice of the case requires it'.

(2) As regards the statement which misled the partner in the firm of auditors, what is now s. 393 provides that an officer of a company who knowingly or recklessly makes a statement to auditors which is misleading, false or deceptive, shall be guilty of an offence and liable to imprisonment. However, it appears that s. 393 applies to an audit but not to the case of a valuation carried out by auditors.

(3) Vinelott J also suggested in his judgment that the Stock Exchange might tighten up its regulations in regard to transactions in which directors have an interest and also that a company's auditor might not be sufficiently independent to carry out a valuation of a transaction in which the directors have a material interest.

(4) There was an appeal to the Court of Appeal in this case (see *Prudential v Newman industries* (No. 2) [1982] 1 All ER 354). The Court of Appeal reversed Vinelott J in part as follows:

(i) The findings against Mr B and Mr L of conspiracy and fraud were substantiated only in regard to points (a) and (b) of the main summary. They had concealed payments of £216,000 to TPG and they were then forced at a later date to conceal it from Newman's auditors and from Newman shareholders. Since the £216,000 was part of a plan to buy TPG's assets this concealment caused the auditors of Newman to over-value TPG's assets.

(ii) As regards actions (i) and (ii) in the main summary, the Court of Appeal decided that these should not have been allowed to succeed and they reversed Vinelott J. The loss of value of shares is 'not a personal loss' but merely a reflection of the company's loss. A shareholder's right is that of participating in the company as by attending meetings and so on. This right is not affected by a fall in the value of the shares.

(iii) The Court of Appeal did not consider the rule in *Foss v Harbottle* 1843[134] in any depth because Newman had decided to join in the action and to take advantage of any judgment in its favour. Thus, the claim was not a derivative one from that time on. However, the Court of Appeal did say that they thought Vinelott J's view that a derivative claim could be heard 'whenever the justice of the case requires it' was not an exception to *Foss*.

(iv) The *de facto* control concept of Vinelott J was not favoured by the Court of Appeal. It does require some form of evidence necessitating a trial approach and yet allegations that *Foss* does or does not apply to a cause of action should, according to the Court of Appeal in this case, be heard as a preliminary procedural matter. (See below.)

(v) Finally, the Court of Appeal ruled that where derivative claims are defended on the basis that the rule in *Foss* prevents them from proceeding the preliminary *Foss* point should be cleared first. Vinelott J had decided that the *Foss* issue could be more conveniently decided *after the action had been tried*. This was wrong said the Court of Appeal. The parties had been subjected to a trial of 30 days to prove the allegations whereas proof of a *prima facie* case would have been enough. Once the Court has ruled on *Foss* the parties should be left to decide whether to proceed to trial.

Company directors are not in a fiduciary relationship with the share-holders as such.

171. Percival *v* Wright [1902] 2 Ch 421

The plaintiff wished to sell shares in the company and wrote to the secretary asking if he knew of anyone willing to buy. After negotiations, the chairman of the board of directors arranged the purchase of 253 shares, 85 for himself and 84 for each of his fellow directors at a price based on the plaintiffs valuation of £12 10s. per share. The transfers were approved by the board and the transactions completed. The plaintiffs subsequently discovered that prior to and during the negotiations for the sale, a Mr Holden was also negotiating with the board for the purchase of the company for resale to a new company, and was offering various prices for shares, all of which exceeded £12 10s. per share. No firm offer was ever made, and the negotiations ultimately proved abortive, and the court was not satisfied that the board ever intended to sell. The plaintiff brought this action against the directors asking for the sale of his shares to be set aside for non-disclosure. *Held*—by Swinfen Eady J—The directors are not trustees for the individual shareholders and may purchase their shares without disclosing pending negotiations for the sale of the company. A contrary view would mean that they could not buy or sell shares without disclosing negotiations, a premature disclosure of which might well be against the best interests of the company. There was no unfair dealing since the shareholders in fact approached the directors and named their own price.

Comment. The Company Securities (Insider Dealing) Act 1985 would not seem to affect this decision since it does not apply its insider dealing provisions to private dealings in shares but only to dealings on a recognized stock exchange or through recognized dealers off-market. In any case, the Act gives no civil claim but merely contains criminal sanctions.

If the directors agree to act as agents for the shareholders they owe fiduciary duties towards them in the carrying out of that agency.

172. Allen *v* Hyatt (1914) 30 TLR 444

In this case the directors induced the shareholders to give them options for the purchase of their shares so that the directors might negotiate a sale of the shares to another company. The directors used the options to purchase the shares themselves and then resold them at a profit to the other company. It was *held* by the Privy Council that the directors had made themselves agents for the shareholders and must consequently account for the profit which they had obtained.

Comment. There are disadvantages in this agency arrangement. It was *held* by the House of Lords in *Briess v Woolley* [1954] 1 All ER 909 that where shareholders employ the directors to negotiate a sale of their shares, the shareholders will be vicariously liable in damages to the purchaser if the directors fraudulently misrepresent the state of the company's affairs to the purchaser of the shares.

A director impliedly warrants that he and the company have authority and power to make the contract he is negotiating. If this is not so he is liable in damages to the third party for breach of warranty of authority.

173. Weeks *v* Propert (1873) LR 8 CP 427

The defendants were the directors of a railway company and they issued a prospectus inviting persons to lend money to the company on the security of debentures. Weeks was a trustee of certain funds and he lent £500 of the trust money to the company, obtaining a debenture. The company had, unknown to Weeks, already exceeded its borrowing powers so that it was not possible to sue the company, the loan being *ultra vires*. Held—by the High Court—The plaintiff succeeded in this action against the directors. The latter were in breach of warranty that the company had power to borrow, which could be implied from the prospectus.

Comment. (i) The plaintiff in this case was Walter Weeks who was seeking redress against the directors, having failed to obtain his money from the company. (See *Fountaine v Carmarthen Railway Co*, 1868.[40])

(ii) The misrepresentation here was one of fact, i.e. that the company was not exceeding its borrowing powers. The statute which set up the company gave it borrowing power limited to £60,000 so if Mr Weeks had compared his contract of loan with the statute, his contract of loan would not have been patently *ultra vires* but a mere limitation on powers indicated and it was the extent to which the company had already borrowed which the directors misrepresented and that was a misrepresentation of fact.

Section 303 is additional to any other means of removal that may be provided by the articles.

174. Bersel Manufacturing Co Ltd *v* Berry [1968] 2 All ER 552

Berry and his wife were the first directors of a private company and were appointed permanent life directors by art 11 of the company's articles of association. In addition art 16(H) provided that—'The permanent life directors shall have power to terminate forthwith the directorship of any of the ordinary directors by notice in writing.' Mr Berry's wife died in 1962. The question before the court in this case was whether or not the power given in art 16(H) could only be exercised during the joint lives of Mr Berry and his wife and ceased to be exercisable when she died. *Held*—by the House of Lords—that the power was not vested in the permanent life directors as recipients of a joint confidence but for the securing of their joint interests, and the principle that a bare power could not be exercised by the survivor of joint holders did not apply. Furthermore, the principle that a power annexed to an office passed to successive holders of the office was not conclusive since the office in question died with the death of the survivor of the two occupants of the power. Therefore, on a true construction of the articles the power conferred by art 16(H) remained exercisable by Mr Berry after the death of his wife. In these circumstances it was possible for Mr Berry to terminate the directorship of any of the ordinary directors by a notice in writing.

Comment. The power to remove a director in the articles is effective even if the directors who exercise the power have acted with ulterior motives as in *Lee v Chou Wen Hsian* [1984] 1 WLR 1202 where a director who was asking for information about the company's dealings and not receiving all the information he wanted asked the secretary to convene a board meeting but was removed by the other directors two days before the meeting under a power in the articles. A removal under s. 303 would seem to be effective in a similar situation.

Effect of appointment of administrative receiver: directors' powers.

175. Newhart Developments Ltd v Co-operative Commercial Bank Ltd [1978] 2 All ER 896

A scheme for housing development in North Wales was to be carried out by a company formed specially for the purpose and jointly owned by Newhart Developments Ltd (Newhart) and the Co-operative Commercial Bank Ltd (the bank), finance being provided by the bank. The scheme got into difficulties and the bank appointed a receiver of Newhart under the provisions of a debenture in common form. In particular, clause 2(c) provided that the company should not deal with its books or other debts or securities for money otherwise than by getting in and realizing the same in the ordinary course of business. Clause 5 provided that the receiver should have power to take possession and collect and get in the property charged by the debenture and for that purpose to take any proceedings in the name of the company or otherwise. Newhart took the view that they might have a claim against the bank for breach of contract arising from the development scheme. They issued a writ and the bank applied to the court to have it set aside because it had been issued by the directors of Newhart without the receiver's consent. The bank's application was successful in the High Court but Newhart appealed to the Court of Appeal which allowed the appeal thus enabling Newhart's claim to proceed to trial.

Shaw L J said that the function of a receiver was to protect the interests of debenture holders; he was not like a liquidator whose function was to wind the company up. During a liquidation directors were divested of their powers but not so in a receivership. The fact that a receiver had been appointed did not prevent the directors of the company concerned from exercising their powers as the governing body of the company provided that their acts did not threaten the assets which were subject to the debenture holders' charge. In this case the receiver was put into a curious and unenviable position because the action by Newhart was against the bank which had appointed him. Nevertheless, where a receiver had in his discretion chosen to ignore an asset such as a right of action there was nothing in law to prevent the directors pursuing it in the company's name. A company might have creditors other than the debenture holders and those creditors were entitled to expect the directors to bring an action which, if successful, might provide a fund out of which to pay them. If the claim succeeded the receiver would have an interest in the disposition of any money received but if he decided not to pursue a claim of this kind the directors could do so provided that nothing in the course of proceedings would influence the security of the debenture holders.

A company secretary owes the same fiduciary duties to the company as its directors.

176. Re Morvah Consols Tin Mining Co, McKay's Case (1875) 2 Ch D 1

James Hammon, the owner of a mine, arranged with McKay to get up a company to buy the mine for £6,000, and McKay was to receive from Hammon £3,000 in 600 £5 paid-up shares. An agreement was made on behalf of the intended company for the purchase by McKay from Hammon of the mine for £6,000, half in cash and half in shares. The company was registered on 7 November 1871 with a capital of £15,000 in 3,000 shares of £5 each, and the agreement to purchase was adopted by the articles. McKay was appointed secretary of the company and remained so until 2 March 1872 when at a meeting of the directors 1,000 shares were allotted to Hammon who on 12 April transferred 600 shares to McKay. By then McKay had left England, but before going he had signed a transfer to himself, and had handed a blank transfer to one Fisher enabling him to deal with the shares. Fisher transferred 100 shares to a Colonel Holland, but 500 remained in McKay's name. In 1874 McKay returned to England and became a director, and in 1875 the company was ordered to be wound up in the Stannary Court, from the decision of the Vice-Warden of which McKay appealed. *Held*—confirming the Vice-Warden's decision—that McKay stood in a fiduciary relation to the company and had been guilty of misfeasance. He was, therefore, liable on the shares and the measure of damages was the highest value of the shares transferred to him. As some of the company's shares had been allotted to solvent shareholders, this value must be taken to be the value of the shares and he was liable for this amount.

A company secretary has usual authority to enter into contracts and do acts on behalf of the company for the purpose of carrying out its administration.

177. Panorama Developments (Guildford) Ltd v Fidelis Furnishing Fabrics Ltd [1971] 3 All ER 16

The plaintiff company trading as Belgravia Executive Car Rental sued the defendant company for £570 in respect of car hiring. Belgravia had a fleet of Rolls Royce, Jaguar and other cars. Fidelis was a company of good reputation which employed a new man, X, as their secretary. He got in touch with Belgravia and booked cars which he wanted to drive for the company to meet important customers when they arrived at Heathrow Airport. On the first occasion X wrote a cheque on his own account and it was met. In January 1970 he gave a list of dates for which he required cars on hire to Belgravia. They confirmed that the cars would be available and sent a written confirmation to Fidelis and not to X. Belgravia allowed the cars to go out on credit asking for references. X gave references of the company which proved to be satisfactory. The printed forms of hiring and insurance agreements showed that X, the company secretary, was the hirer. These forms were signed by X or the sales manager of Fidelis. X used the cars which were never paid for. Belgravia sent the statement of account to Fidelis but they did not pay. Later the managing director of Fidelis found many unpaid bills in the company's name and disputed X's authority to act on behalf of the company. *Held*—by the Court of Appeal—that the defendants were liable for the hire because, amongst other things, X as company secretary had ostensible authority to enter into the contracts for the hire of the cars on behalf of the defendants. 'The second point of counsel for Fidelis is this. ... He says that, on the authorities, a company secretary fulfils a very humble role; and that he has no authority to make any contracts or representations on behalf of the company. He refers to *Barnett Hoares & Co v South London Tramways Co* where Lord Esher M R said "a secretary is a mere servant; his position is that he is to do what he is told, and no person can assume that he has any authority to represent anything at all ...." Those words ... are referred to in some of the textbooks as authoritative. But times have changed. A company secretary is a much more important person nowadays .... He is an officer of the company with extensive duties and responsibilities .... He is certainly entitled to sign contracts connected with the administrative side of a company's affairs, such as employing staff, and ordering cars and so forth.' (*per* Lord Denning MR.)

DIVIDENDS AND PROFITS

Loans to pay dividends already declared: the trust concept.

177. Barclays Bank v Quistclose Investments [1968] 3 All ER 651

In the spring of 1964 Rolls Razor Ltd was in financial difficulties having an overdraft of £484,000 with the bank against a permitted limit of £250,000. The bank informed the company that it would cease to do business unless the position improved. Rolls Razor then obtained a loan of £209,719 from Quistclose on condition that it was used to pay an ordinary share dividend declared by Rolls Razor on 2 July 1964. The bank was aware of this condition and the money was paid into a separate account.

On 27 August 1964, Rolls Razor went into voluntary liquidation and the dividend had not been paid. Quistclose brought an action against Rolls Razor and the bank claiming—

(i) that the money which they had lent had been held on trust to pay the dividend;

(ii) that the trust having failed the money was held on a resulting trust for Quistclose;

(iii) that the bank having had notice of the trust could not retain the loan by way of set-off of Rolls Razor's indebtedness to the bank in respect of the overdraft.

Plowman J at first instance upheld the bank's claim to set-off but the Court of Appeal reversed his decision. On a further appeal to the House of Lords it was *held*—

(1) that not only was the Rolls Razor company under a contractual duty to repay Quistclose the money lent but since the particular and only purpose of the loan had failed the money was subject to a resulting trust for Quistclose; and

(2) that it was plain that the bank knew of the purpose of the loan and was therefore a constructive trustee of the money for Quistclose.

The bank was therefore ordered to pay back the sum of £209,719 to Quistclose.

Comment. Since the fund did not belong to the Rolls Razor Company, it was not available to the liquidator of that company for distribution to the creditors of Rolls generally. Instead, it had to be paid back to Quistclose who otherwise would have had to prove in the liquidation of Rolls in the hope of receiving such dividend as the company's assets could provide which would obviously have been far less than £209,719.

BORROWING POWERS

Trading companies have implied power to borrow as being a matter incidental to their objects.

178. General Auction Estate and Monetary Co v Smith [1891] 3 Ch 432

The company had among its objects the sale and purchase of estates and property, the granting of advances on property intended for sale, and loans on deposit of securities and the discounting of approved commercial bills. It had no express power to borrow money under either the memorandum or articles. The company did considerable business, discounting bills on a large scale, and accepting deposits payable at short notice or even on demand. The executors of a Mr Thunder, a depositor, and other creditors, were pressing for payment, and the defendant, Robert Thomas Smith, a director of the company and an unsecured creditor for £433 16s. 7d., offered to advance the company £666 3s. 5d., if this advance and his debt, £1,000 in all, were secured by an equitable mortgage on certain real estate belonging to the company. The proposal was accepted and the security authorized by the board, but the company was ordered to be wound up within six months. The liquidator sought to set aside the security as *ultra vires* the company. *Held*—by Stirling J—

(i) The company was a trading company and had an implied power to borrow money for the purposes of its business.

(ii) The borrowing in question was fairly incidental to the business of the company. The deposits were valid loans; the company could borrow money to repay them, and it could also give security' to the person making the advance.

Widely differing types of document are within the definition of 'debenture'.

179. Lemon v Austin Friars Investment Trust Ltd [1926] Ch 1

The defendant company issued £1,400,000 income stock payable out of profits, of which the plaintiffs subscribed £2,100. In a document called an income stock certificate, the company acknowledged its debt to the plaintiffs, the debt to be paid only out of profits. Three-fourths of the net profits of each year were to be used for paying off the income stock *pari passu* (on an equal footing). The company had an obligation to keep a register of these certificates which the plaintiffs wished to inspect. They requested permission to do this, and the company refused the request, so the plaintiffs applied for an injunction restraining the company from interfering with this statutory right. *Held*—by Lawrence J—and the Court of Appeal—

(i) The certificates fulfilled the *primary* qualification of a debenture, namely, they contained an acknowledgment of indebtedness even if only payable in the future and on a contingency of profits being earned.

(ii) They also contained a further common characteristic, namely, a charge on the assets although consisting only of a proportion of profits as and when ascertained.

The certificates were, therefore, debentures within the meaning of the Companies Act, and the plaintiffs were entitled to an injunction.

If several debentures are secured on the same property they rank for repayment in the order of their creation unless they are expressed to rank *pari passu*.

180. Gartside *v* Silkstone and Dodworth Coal and Iron Co Ltd (1882) 21 Ch D 762

The company issued 150 debentures of £100 each on the same day. They were issued in two lots, one lot being numbered 501–600 and the second lot from 601–650. Each of the debentures contained a provision that it was to rank *pari passu* with the others, but the first group referred to the amount of £10,000 and the second to £5,000, this being the only difference in the respective provisions. Nevertheless this suggested that they were independent issues. The company was in liquidation and the question of priority arose. When two deeds are executed on the same day, the court must inquire which of them was executed first, but if there is anything in the deeds to show such an intention, they may take effect *pari passu* or the later may even have priority. *Held*—by the High Court—the company could, therefore, choose to give security in the form of a second floating charge of the kind outlined, and this was valid and did rank equally with the first charge because they were expressed to be *pari passu*.

Debentures: exclusion of equities by express provision in the terms of issue of the debentures.

181. Re Goy & Co Ltd, Farmer *v* Goy & Co Ltd [1900] 2 Ch 149

In a voluntary winding up of the company a liquidator, W. H. Doggett, had been appointed, and judgment had been given in a debenture holder's action against the company. At this point, Chandler, a former director, transferred £600 of debentures to G. D. Robey by way of security for a loan. The conditions of the debentures provided that on complying with certain formalities, the principal and interest secured by the debentures would be paid without regard to any equities between the company and the original or intermediate holder. After Robey had taken the transfer, it was discovered that Chandler had been guilty of misfeasance and he was ordered to pay £300 to the liquidator. Robey, who had no notice of this cross-claim, sent his transfer to the liquidator, who was also receiver in the action, for registration. The liquidator declined to register it, and claimed the right to deduct the £300 owed by Chandler. *Held*—by the High Court—the right to transfer and have the transfer registered was not affected by the winding up or by the judgment in the action against Chandler, and Robey was entitled to receive the full dividend payable on the debentures without deduction.

Section 193 allows a company to create debentures which are irredeemable before the agreed term ends.

182. Knightsbridge Estates Trust Ltd *v* Byrne [1940] AC 613

The plaintiffs were the owners of a large freehold estate close to Knightsbridge. This estate was mortgaged to a friendly society for a sum of money which, together with interest, was to be repaid over a period of 40 years in 80 half-yearly instalments. The company wished to redeem the mortgage before the expiration of the term, because it was possible for them to borrow elsewhere at a lower rate of interest. *Held*—by the House of Lords—the company was not entitled to redeem the mortgage before the end of the 40 years because the effect of what is now s. 193 was to remove the application of the equitable doctrine of no postponement of the right of redemption from mortgages given by companies. Therefore Knightsbridge were not entitled to redeem the mortgage except by the half-yearly instalments as agreed.

Debentures: an administrative receiver is not in a stronger position than the company giving the charge. He is subject, e.g. to a debtor's right of set-off and an unpaid creditor's lien on the company's property arising before and possibly after crystallization.

183. Rother Iron Works Ltd *v* Canterbury Precision Engineers Ltd [1973] 1 All ER 394

A bank had a floating charge on all the assets of Rother under a mortgage debenture. On the 4 October 1971 Rother owed the defendants £124 under previous contracts. On 18 October 1971 Rother contracted to sell goods to the defendants for £159. On 21 October the bank appointed a receiver and the floating charge crystallized. The goods ordered by the defendants were delivered on 3 November 1971. In this action by the receiver in the name of Rother against the defendants for £159 the defendants claimed to set off the debt owing to them. *Held*—by the Court of Appeal—that the defendants were entitled to set off the debt so that the receiver was entitled only to a judgment for £35.

Comment. It was held in *George Barker (Transport) Ltd v Eynon* [1974] 1 All ER 900 that a contractual lien arising on goods collected by a carrier *after crystallization* of the floating charge had priority and the receiver had to pay the charges owing for carriage before he could obtain the goods. The decision weakens the security provided by a floating charge and seems incorrect. Obviously, a lien arising on property of the company acquired before crystallization is correctly subject to a creditor's lien.

The registration of a charge under s. 395 does not give constructive notice of the details of the charge, such as the fact that the company will not create further charges.

184. Wilson *v* Kelland [1910] 2 Ch 306

In 1901 the Bedford Brewery Company executed a trust deed and issued debentures for £100,000 secured by way of a floating charge on present and future property, and prohibiting the creation of any charge ranking in priority to or *pari passu* with this particular charge. Particulars of the trust deed and debentures were registered in accordance with the Companies Act. In June 1904, the company agreed to purchase a brewery and other property from A. W. and L. A. Kelland for £5,350, of which £3,000 should remain on mortgage on the property which was freehold. Conveyances were duly executed and a legal mortgage created over the property in favour of the Kellands, who had no notice of the debentures and made no inquiry or search into the company's title. In June 1906, the company mortgaged the premises with the plaintiff Wilson for £3,000, Wilson having notice of the debentures and the trust deed. In a foreclosure action it was *held* by Eve J that, in the case of the Kellands' mortgage, whether they had or had not notice of the trust deed or debentures, any equity attached to the purchased property in favour of debenture holders or trustees was subject to the paramount equity of the unpaid vendors. The Kellands' mortgage took priority over any charge to persons claiming through the company. If priority had turned on notice, the particulars registered would have amounted to constructive notice of a charge affecting the property, *but not of any special restrictions upon the company's dealings if the charge was a floating charge.* There was ambiguity between the trust deed and the debentures of 1901, but on their cumulative effect, the court held that the mortgage of 1906 must be postponed to their earlier one.

A company may have power to create a second floating charge over its undertaking to rank before an earlier one, but only if the earlier charge expressly permits this.

185. Re Automatic Bottle Makers Ltd [1926] Ch 412

A debenture trust deed created a floating charge of £50,000 over all the company's undertaking and assets both present and future, but the company reserved the right to create in priority to that charge such mortgages or charges as it should think proper 'by the deposit of dock warrants, bills of lading, or other similar commercial documents, or upon any raw materials, or finished or partly finished products and stock for the purpose of raising moneys in the ordinary course of business of the company'. The company exercised this power and raised £12,000 by creating a floating charge on all these documents, materials and stock, to rank in priority to the floating charge previously created. *Held*—by the Court of Appeal—the power reserved to the company was unlimited, provided it was exercised within the subject matter and for the purpose mentioned. The company could, therefore, choose to give security in the form of a second floating charge of the kind outlined, and this was valid and could have priority over the first floating charge. This was so even though a second charge might alternatively have been made over specific assets.

Debentures: goods on hire purchase as part of the security if attached to realty.

186. Re Morrison, Jones and Taylor Ltd [1914] 1 Ch 50

George Mills & Co supplied (and erected) a patent automatic sprinkler fire extinguisher to Morrison, Jones & Co on 11 November 1910, for £237 payable by annual instalments, and in default of payment of any instalment, the whole of the unpaid balance and interest was to become due. The agreement also provided that the sprinkler was to remain the property of George Mills & Co until the whole sum of £237 was paid, and in default, they might enter the premises and remove it. The defendant company was incorporated in December 1911, and took over the assets and liabilities of Morrison, Jones &

Co including the interest in the agreements. In December 1911, Morrison, Jones & Taylor issued a series of first mortgage debentures secured by a floating charge. On 18 October 1912, the debenture holders appointed a receiver and manager to enforce their security. On 21 October the last instalment under Mill's agreement fell due and was not paid. The debenture holders had no notice of the agreement. George Mills & Co applied to enter on the premises to remove the sprinkler. *Held*—by Eve J, and the Court of Appeal—the hire-purchase agreement gave George Mills & Co an equitable interest in the land on which the sprinkler was fixed, and authority to enter and remove it. The interest of the debenture holders was also equitable so that the ordinary principles of priorities applied. The applicants' interest was first in time, so George Mills & Co could remove the sprinkler.

Section 245, Insolvency Act 1986: money paid to the company includes cheques which are met by a bank on behalf of the company: effect of *Clayton's case* on a bank account.

187. Re Yeovil Glove Co Ltd [1965] Ch 148

The company was in liquidation and had an overdraft of £67,000 with the National Provincial Bank Ltd. The overdraft was secured by a floating charge given less than 12 months prior to winding up at a time when the company was insolvent. The charge was therefore void under what is now s. 245, Insolvency Act 1986. However, the company had paid in some £111,000 and the bank had paid cheques out to the amount of some £110,000. The Court of Appeal held that under *Clayton's case* (1816) 1 Mer 572 under which the earliest payments into an account are set off against the earliest payments out and *vice versa*, the overdraft, which was not validly secured, had been paid off and the floating charge attached to the money drawn out because the company had received consideration for this. It did not matter that the floating charge did not require the bank to make further advances. It did, however, expressly secure uncovenanted loans.

Comment. The Cork Committee said that this case defeated the object of what is now s. 245. They thought it should be repealed by statute so that for the purposes of s. 245 payments into the account should be treated as discharging debit items incurred after the creating of the floating charge before those incurred before it. (See Cmnd 8558, para 1562.)

A floating charge to secure a loan to repay an existing unsecured debt is invalid unless made in good faith to assist the company to carry on its business and not merely to secure an existing debt.

188. Re Matthew Ellis Ltd [1933] Ch 458

The company owed £1,954 to the firm of Arthur Tipper for goods supplied on credit, and Arthur D. Tipper, a partner in the firm, who was the chairman of the company, advanced £3,000 to the company on the security of a debenture, the agreement being that £1,954 should be used to liquidate the debt of the firm of Arthur Tipper, and the balance was to be paid to the company in cash. Arthur Tipper continued to supply goods to the company for the purposes of its trade, but the company went into liquidation within six months of the issue of the debenture. The liquidator claimed it was invalid as to £1,954, and valid only as to the balance paid to the company in cash. *Held*—by the Court of Appeal—looking at all the circumstances, the transaction was in substance a payment of £3,000 to the company. 'Cash paid' does not necessarily mean cash paid with no conditions as to the way it is to be applied. The following points were made—

(i) that the company's business was worth saving;

(ii) that in order to continue its business it must have goods supplied to it;

(iii) that Arthur Tipper were the only firm from which further goods could be obtained on credit; and

(iv) that if such extended credit were to be obtained to keep the business going, it was right that the debt owing should be paid.

Debentures: certificate of registration of charge: conclusive evidence.

189. In Re C L Nye Ltd [1969] 2 All ER 587

The company was granted a loan and overdraft facilities by a bank, the security being *inter alia* the company's business premises. On 28 February 1964, the company handed transfers of certain premises, relevant land certificates and a charge sealed by the company to the bank. The transfers and charge were undated. A solicitor acting for the bank was to effect the registration of the charge but by oversight this was not done. On 18 June 1964, the oversight was noticed and on 3 July the solicitor applied for registration of the charge under what is now s. 395, including 18 June 1964 as the date on which the charge was created. On 16 July 1964, the company went into a creditor's voluntary liquidation. Three years later on 16 November 1967, the Registrar's certificate required by what is now s. 401(2) was granted. (There is no explanation in the report of this delay.) This section provides that the Registrar's certificate shall be 'conclusive evidence that the requirements of ... this Act as to registration have been satisfied'. The liquidators of the company claimed that the charge was void against them on the ground that it was registered too late. The two main questions before the court were therefore—

(i) was the charge registered in time, i.e. within twenty-one days of its creation; and

(ii) if not did the registrar's certificate constitute 'conclusive evidence' of the date of registration which could not be contraverted.

Held—by Plowman J—that a declaration would be made that the charge was void as against the liquidators and creditors of the company because the charge had not been registered in due time, i.e. within 21 days of its creation, and the certificate of registration gave the bank no protection against its own misstatements on the principle that no man can take advantage of his own wrong. In consequence the bank's charge was registered out of time. This decision was reversed by the Court of Appeal [1970] 3 All ER 1061. The Registrar's certificate was conclusive evidence that the Act had been complied with. The charge must be regarded as created on 18 June 1964, and registered on 3 July 1964 (i.e. within 21 days), and was valid and enforceable by the bank.

Comment. (i) The morality of the practice of altering the date of creation of the charge is dubious but in any case the practice could be dangerous if the company went into liquidation, because each time the date of creation is artificially pushed forward, the greater risk of its invalidation should s. 245 of the Insolvency Act 1986 apply because the debenture holder will not be able to establish that the debt secured was in respect of cash paid (or goods supplied) to the company *at the time of the charge or subsequently.*

(ii) Where in the past the Registrar of Companies has received a charge for registration within 21 days but not containing all the necessary particulars, he has allowed those registering the charge to submit amended particulars and these have been registered in some cases after the period of 21 days from creation of the charge had elapsed. In *R v Registrar of Companies, ex parte Esal (Commodities) Ltd, The Times* 26 November 1984 where this had happened, Mervyn Davies J would not regard the certificate of registration as conclusive and decided, in effect, that the charge was registered out of time. In a statement issued in 1985 the Registrar said that he would no longer be permitted to accept any Form 395 (particulars of a mortgage or charge) outside the 21-day period, either in an original or amended form. He would only do this following an application to the court under s. 404 of the Companies Act 1985 for permission to register the charge out of time, unless the errors are minor.

Debentures: charge: effect of late registration under permission of the court.

190. Watson v Duff Morgan and Vermont (Holdings) Ltd
[1974] 1 All ER 794

On 21 January 1971 a company created a first debenture in favour of the plaintiff and a second debenture in favour of the defendants. Both were secured by floating charges and gave the right to appoint a receiver should principal moneys become payable. The second debenture was made expressly subject to and ranking immediately after the first one. The second debenture was properly registered within 21 days under what is now s. 395. The first was not, and initially therefore became void on 12 February 1971. In October the plaintiffs secured an order under what is now s. 404 extending the time for registration to 11 November 1971 'without prejudice to the rights of any parties acquired prior to the time when the said debenture is to be actually registered'. It was registered on 5 November and the plaintiff appointed a receiver on 8 November. In the meantime the defendant had appointed a receiver under the second debenture on 28 October. In a subsequent winding up of the company its assets were insufficient to satisfy either of the debenture holders. The defendants suggested that the terms of the order granted under s. 404 made the first debenture subject to the second, or, alternatively, that the first debenture was subject to rights they acquired when it became void for non-registration or when they appointed their own receiver on 28 October. *Held*—by Templeman J—that the plaintiff was entitled to a declaration that his first debenture took priority. The proviso to the order in October related only to rights acquired while the first debenture was void. The rights of the defendants had been acquired earlier, on execution of their debenture. Therefore no rights were conferred on the defendants by the mere expiration of the 21-day period for registration of the first debenture. Nor did they acquire rights by appointing a receiver, for this was merely the exercise of a power acquired earlier when their debenture was created.

Comment. This case produces the odd result that a second mortgage created 22 days after the first mortgage (unregistered) is protected, but one created within 21 days is not.

The appointment of an administrative receiver out of court operates to dismiss directors only if the continued exercise of their powers conflicts with the exercise of the administrative receiver's powers.

191. Griffiths v Secretary of State for Social Services [1973] 3 All ER 1184

Griffiths was employed by a company as managing director under a contract of service subject to the general supervision and control of the board. The debenture holders appointed a receiver and manager but Griffiths continued working until his resignation four weeks after the appointment, there having been no fresh agreement between Griffiths and the receiver. In determining questions under the National Insurance Acts, the Court of Appeal *held* that the appointment out of court by debenture holders of a receiver and manager to act as agent of the company does not terminate contracts of employment unless—

(i) the appointment accompanies the sale of the company's business; or

(ii) soon after his appointment the receiver enters into a different contract of employment with the employee; or

(iii) the continuation of any particular employee's employment is inconsistent with the role and functions of the receiver and manager.

Since, in this case, the receiver was not appointed full time the continued employment of Griffiths was not inconsistent with that of the receiver and his employment continued until the company accepted his resignation. It would appear that if the receiver had been appointed full time the court may have taken a different view with regard to Griffiths' employment which might well have been terminated by a full-time appointment.

The other party to a contract with a company in receivership cannot obtain an injunction to restrain the receiver from ignoring the contract.

192. Airlines Airspares Ltd v Handley Page Ltd [1970] 1 All ER 29

The plaintiffs had acquired by assignment a contract with Handley Page under which the latter company agreed to pay a special commission on sales of Jetstream aircraft. On 7 August 1969, a receiver and manager was appointed by the debenture holders of Handley Page Ltd. The receiver caused Handley Page Ltd to form a subsidiary company, Aircraft Ltd, and all the business relating to Jetstream aircraft was transferred to that company. The receiver then entered into negotiations for the sale of the shares of Aircraft Ltd to American interests and made it clear to the plaintiffs that he was not prepared to go on with the contract made by Handley Page. The plaintiffs were granted an interim injunction on 29 August 1969, restraining Handley Page and their receiver Mr Kenneth Cork, from selling the shares in Aircraft Ltd until such time as provision had been made for the payment to the plaintiff company of their special commission in respect of all future sales of Jetstream aircraft. The plaintiffs brought this action for the continuance of the injunction. Graham J in the vacation court *held* that a receiver and manager appointed by debenture holders was in a stronger legal position than the company itself in regard to contracts between unsecured creditors and the company. Although on the authority of *Southern Foundries Ltd v Shirlaw* 1940,[58] a company was not entitled to put it out of its own power to perform contracts it had entered into, a receiver was entitled to repudiate a contract provided the reputation would not—

(i) adversely affect the subsequent realization of the company's assets; and

(ii) weaken its trading position if it were able to trade again.

Accordingly, within the limitations stated above, the receiver was in a better position than the company regarding repudiation of contract and the receiver in doing what he proposed to do in connection with the transfer of the shares of Aircraft Ltd was not doing anything that the plaintiffs were entitled to prevent. The interim injunction was therefore discharged.

Comment. The case was concerned with *preventing* the breach of contract by the receiver. It will be appreciated that if the receiver does break a contract, as was the case here, the other party has a claim for damages against the company.

Petition to court for appointment of a receiver. When assets are in jeopardy.

193. Re Victoria Steamboats Ltd, Smith *v* Wilkinson [1897] 1 Ch 158

The debenture holders of the company wished to enforce their security because a petition for winding up was presented and was still pending, so they applied to the court for the appointment of a receiver and also for a manager on the ground that the security was in jeopardy. *Held*, by Kekewich J that, although the charge had not yet crystallized, the winding-up order put the security in jeopardy, because on a winding up the interests of the creditors are inimical to those of the debenture holders. A receiver could, therefore, be properly appointed since that is a mere protection. The question of a manager was more difficult since the company was still in being as a going concern, and the appointment of a manager postulates the necessity or probability of a sale and the charge had not yet crystallized. In view of the probability of a winding-up order, when the charge would crystallize, the receiver, Mr Ogle, was also appointed manager for a fortnight only, by which time the position would be clarified.

194. Re London Pressed Hinge Co Ltd [1905] 1 Ch 576

The plaintiffs, debenture holders, had a floating charge on the undertaking and its property, but nothing was due in respect of principal or interest. The plaintiffs applied for a receiver to be appointed because the assets were in jeopardy, a creditor having issued a writ and signed judgment so that he was in a position to issue execution. The appointment of a receiver would mean that the company could no longer pay the creditor to whom money was due in priority to debenture holders to whom nothing was due. *Held*—by Buckley J—the effect of this state of affairs means that many businesses are carried on for the benefit of debenture holders, and so long as the security floats, the creditor has a prospect of being paid. As soon as he attempts to enforce his legal remedies, the debenture holders can apply for a receiver and close the door against him. Nevertheless that is the law, and the plaintiffs were entitled to an order for a receiver.

195. McMahon *v* North Kent Ironworks Co [1891] 2 Ch 148

The plaintiff, on behalf of himself and the other holders of debentures which were due for repayment on 1 January 1892, and which were secured by a floating charge, asked in February 1891, for a receiver to be appointed. The company owned freehold land and works at Erith, but owing to its having become insolvent, the works had been closed and the workmen discharged. A petition for winding up had been presented by a creditor, who claimed a lien on part of the company's property, but the petition was adjourned since the company proposed to pass resolutions for voluntary winding up. The company was insolvent. Although there had been no default on the payment of interest, other creditors were pressing for payment and threatening actions, thus placing the assets in jeopardy. *Held*—by the High Court— The application for the appointment of a receiver should be granted.

196. Re Tilt Cove Copper Co Ltd [1913] 2 Ch 588

The Tilt Cove Copper Co was incorporated in 1888 to purchase and work copper mines in Newfoundland. In November 1888, the company issued debentures to the value of £80,000, secured by a floating charge and protected by the usual trust deed. By 1912 the mines were worked out, the land, plant and machinery were worthless, the company's share capital was gone, and all that remained was a reserve fund of some £10,000 and some £2,240 in cash. The debenture interest had been regularly paid. The company now proposed to distribute the reserve fund to shareholders but an action was brought to determine the parties' rights. *Held*—by Neville J—There was here a case of jeopardy, and since the mortgagees' rights ought to prevail over those of the mortgagors, a receiver ought to be appointed in the interests of the debenture holders.

PRIVATE COMPANIES: HOLDING COMPANIES

A member is not bound to sell his shares to other members under a pre-emption arrangement unless one or more of them are prepared to purchase all the shares he wishes to sell.

197. Ocean Coal Co Ltd *v* Powell Duffryn Steam Coal Co Ltd [1932] 1 Ch 654

The capital of the Taff Merthyr Steam Co, a private company, was £600,000 in £1 shares held in equal parts by the plaintiff and defendant companies. The articles of association of the Taff Merthyr Co provided that a member wishing to sell any of his shares to a third party must notify the board of the number, price proposed, and the name and address of the proposed transferee. The board must then offer the shares to other shareholders at that price, and if the offer is accepted, the shares must be transferred to the shareholders concerned. If the offer is not accepted, the holder may transfer them to third parties approved by the board. Powell Duffryn notified the board that they wished to sell 135,000 shares to third parties at £2 per share. The board offered the 135,000 shares to Ocean Coal Co, who wished to exercise their option to buy 5,000 only at the proposed price. *Held*—by the High Court—The price proposed was for the whole block of shares, not £2 per share. The offer was for the block of shares and not for individual shares up to that number. Ocean Coal Co were not entitled to purchase only 5,000; they must either accept or reject the offer for the full 135,000. Powell Duffryn were, therefore, entitled to sell the shares to a third party.

Pre-emption arrangements apply in a take-over bid. Shareholders wishing to sell to the bidder must comply with the articles if the company invokes them.

198. Lyle & Scott Ltd v Scott's Trustees [1959] 2 All ER 661

Lyle and Scott Ltd, a private company, prohibited a registered holder of more than 1 per cent of its shares from selling them if any other ordinary shareholder was willing to buy them, and required such a would-be seller to inform the secretary in writing of the number of shares he wished to transfer, so that notice could be sent to the holders of ordinary shares for offers. Scott's Trustees held more than 1 per cent of the shares, and, in common with the other shareholders, were approached on behalf of Hugh Fraser, who had no shares in the company, with an offer to buy shares. The respondents agreed that, if the offer became unconditional, which it did, Fraser's nominee would be authorized to use general proxies, and that they would deliver their share certificates and execute transfer deeds when called upon to do so. Fraser paid for the shares. The company sought a declaration that the respondents were bound to implement the articles. *Held*—by the House of Lords—They were. Having agreed to sell their shares to Fraser, they could not deny that they were 'desirous of transferring their shares' within the meaning of Art 9 merely because it suited the purchaser to delay the registration for the time being. There was an unequivocal desire to sell, and the secretary must be notified, and the machinery of the articles set in motion.

Comment. Here the company sought and obtained a declaratory judgment which would be complied with once the legal position was known. If there was no intention in the seller to comply with the articles, an injunction would be the more appropriate remedy.

Rejection of transfers: requirement of good faith by the board.

199. Re Accidental Death Insurance Co, Allin's Case (1873) LR 16 Eq 449

The company's deed of settlement provided that when a shareholder wished to transfer his shares, he should leave notice at the company's office, and the directors should consider the proposal and signify their acceptance or rejection of the proposed transferee. If they rejected the proposed transferee, the proposed transfer would still be considered approved unless the directors could find someone else to take the shares at market price. The company arranged to transfer its business to the Accident and Marine Insurance Corporation Ltd. The shareholders acquiesced in an arrangement to exchange their shares for shares in the corporation, but the company was not wound up. A year later, the former directors of the company reversed the procedure, and the company proposed to resume its former business. Notice of this was given to shareholders, and shortly afterwards the corporation was wound up. Under an arrangement to release certain shareholders of liability, Allin transferred 200 shares in the company to Robert Pocock for a nominal consideration. He gave notice to the directors at a meeting at which he was present, and the transfer was agreed. Later the company was wound up. *Held*—by the High Court—The transfer was invalid, and Allin must be a contributory. The clauses were not intended to be in operation for the purpose of enabling individuals to escape liability when the company had ceased to be a going concern.

Rejection of transfers: giving reasons for rejection: effect of provisions in articles.

200. Berry and Stewart v Tottenham Hotspur FC Ltd [1935] Ch 718

Berry held one ordinary share in Tottenham Hotspur and he transferred his share to Stewart, both of them subsequently trying to register the transfer. Registration was refused, and Art 16 of the company's articles specified four grounds on which this was allowable, and also stipulated that the directors were not bound to divulge the grounds upon which registration was declined. The plaintiffs brought an action for a declaration that the company was not entitled to decline to register the transfer, and sought interrogatories directed to find out which of the four grounds was the basis of the refusal. *Held*—by Crossman J—Art 16 excused the directors from the need to disclose this information, and this was binding not only on Berry, as a member, but also on Stewart who was applying to be a member. An action coupled with a demand for interrogatories could not be used to oust the agreement.

Rejection of transfers: effect of equality of votes in the board.

201. Re Hackney Pavilion Ltd [1924] 1 Ch 276

The company had three directors, Sunshine, Kramer and Rose, each of whom held 3,333 shares in the company. Sunshine died, having appointed his widow as his executrix. Her solicitors wrote to the company, enclosing a transfer of the 3,333 shares from herself as executrix to herself in an individual capacity. At a board meeting at which Kramer, Rose and the secretary were present, Rose proposed that the shares be registered, but Kramer objected in accordance with a provision in the articles. There was no casting vote. The secretary then wrote to the solicitors informing them that his directors had declined to register the transfer. *Held*—by the High Court—The board's right to decline required to be actively expressed. The mere failure to pass the proposed resolution for registration was not a formal active exercise of the right to decline. The right to registration remained, and the register must be rectified.

Rights of rejection of transfer and pre-emption; renounceable letters of allotment.

202. Re Pool Shipping Ltd [1920] 1 Ch 251

The applicants were shareholders of the company which had capitalized £125,000, part of a reserve fund, for distribution among the registered shareholders or their nominees, at the rate of one share for every four shares issued. All but one of the shareholders renounced their right to allotments, and requested the company to allot the shares to Coulson who had agreed to accept them. The managers refused to issue the shares or register them to him when he presented the letters of renunciation in his favour, so the applicants moved for rectification of the register by the insertion of Coulson's name. The company had no directors but was controlled by Sir R. Ropner & Co Ltd, who were described as managers and who relied on various clauses in the articles as grounds for refusal. *Held*—by the High Court—Letters of renunciation do not amount to transfers of shares so as to come within the provisions of the articles of association dealing with the transfer of shares already registered. The managers were wrong in thinking they could refuse to register Mr Coulson, and the register must be rectified.

AUDITS AND INVESTIGATIONS

An auditor must make a proper investigation. If he is not given sufficient time to do this he must refuse to make a report or qualify it.

203. Re Thomas Gerrard & Sons Ltd [1968] Ch 455

The managing director of the company had falsified the accounts by three methods one of which involved including non-existent stock and altering invoices. The auditors who were put on inquiry by alterations of invoices negligently failed to investigate the matter and gave a falsely favourable picture of the profits of the company as a result of which it declared dividends it would not otherwise have declared which in turn resulted in extra tax being payable. The company was wound up and in misfeasance proceedings under what is now s. 212,

Insolvency Act 1986 against the auditors they claimed that they had not been given enough time to do their work. *Held*—this was no defence and the auditors must repay the dividends, the cost of recovering the extra tax and any of the extra tax not recoverable. In the course of his judgment Pennycuick J made the following points—

(i) if directors do not allow the auditors adequate time to make proper investigations they must either refuse to make a report at all or qualify it;

(ii) while leaving open the question whether the auditors would have been in breach of duty had the only fraud been falsification of stock, the judge held that once they were on notice of the altered invoices they had a duty to make an exhaustive inquiry. Having failed to do so they were liable to the company under what is now s. 212, Insolvency Act 1986.

An auditor does not guarantee that the company's accounting records show the true state of the company's affairs.

204. Re London and General Bank [1895] 2 Ch 166

The greater part of the capital of the bank, which was being wound up, had for some years been advanced to four of the 'Balfour' companies and a few special customers on securities which were insufficient and difficult of realization. The auditors drew attention to the situation in a confidential report to the directors, stressing its gravity, and ending by saying—'We cannot conclude without expressing our opinion unhesitatingly that no dividend should be paid this year'. The chairman, Mr Balfour, persuaded the auditors to strike this sentence out before the report was officially laid before the board of directors. The certificate signed by the auditors and laid before the shareholders at the annual general meeting stated that 'the value of the assets as shown on the balance sheet is dependent on realization'. As originally drawn, it also said—'And on this point we have reported specifically to the board'. But again Mr Balfour persuaded them to withdraw this statement by promising to mention this in his speech to the shareholders which he did without drawing special attention to it. The directors declared a dividend of 7 per cent. *Held*—by the Court of Appeal, affirming the decision of Vaughan Williams J—that the auditors had been guilty of misfeasance, and were liable to make good the amount of dividend paid. It is the duty of an auditor to consider and report to the shareholders, whether the balance sheet exhibits a correct view of the state of the company's affairs, and the true financial position at the time of the audit. He must take reasonable care to see that his certification is true, and must place the necessary information before the shareholders and not merely indicate the means of acquiring it. In the course of his judgment Lindley L J said—'An auditor ... is not an insurer; he does not guarantee that the books correctly show the true position of the company's affairs; he does not even guarantee that his balance sheet is accurate according to the books of the company ... but, he must be honest, i.e. he must not certify what he does not believe to be true, and he must use reasonable care and skill before he believes that what he certifies is true. What is reasonable care in any particular case must depend upon the circumstances of the case.' Theobald, the auditor, stated the true position to the directors, and if he had done the same to the shareholders, his duty would have been discharged.

Auditors must know their duties under the articles of the company as well as under the Companies Act.

205. Re Republic of Bolivia Exploration Syndicate Ltd [1914] 1 Ch 139

A solicitor who became a director of the company three months after incorporation was later paid sums of money for the agreed costs of its incorporation and other sums for costs, rent of office, and clerical assistance, the payments being confirmed by the board of which the solicitor was a member. These payments were passed by the auditors without drawing attention to the fact that, since the company was governed by *Table A* (1906), there was no power in a director to contract with the company, and the solicitor could not charge profit costs, the payments being therefore unauthorized. *Held*—by Astbury J—company auditors are bound to know or make themselves acquainted with their duties under the company's articles and under the Companies Acts for the time being in force. They are *prima facie* responsible for *ultra vires* payments made on the faith of the balance sheet, but whether and to what extent they are liable for not discovering and calling attention to illegal payments made prior to the audit, depends on the special circumstances of the case. In the circumstances of the case the auditors escaped liability. They were also held not liable, in the circumstances, for passing certain other *ultra vires* payments not authorized by *Table A* which governed the company in the absence of special articles.

Auditors may be successfully sued in damages for loss caused by breach of their duty as auditors.

206. Leeds Estate, Building and Investment Co v Shepherd
(1887) 36 Ch D 787

The articles of association provided *inter alia* that when the company should pay a dividend of 5 per cent, the directors should receive a fixed sum for attendance, and further fixed sums for each additional 1 per cent of dividend; that the directors might declare dividends out of profit but not out of capital; that they should lay proper accounts before the company; and that these accounts should be properly audited. The company made no profits, except in one year when they were less than 5 per cent, but from 1870 onwards, the directors declared a dividend of 5 per cent and upwards and remunerated themselves correspondingly, and also paid bonuses to the manager. The payments were in fact made out of capital. The balance sheets were prepared by the manager and were false, being framed so as to show a profit available for dividends. The auditor did not look at the articles of association but accepted the statements of the manager, and certified the accounts submitted as true copies of those shown in the books of the company. The directors never knew the true state of affairs but relied entirely on the manager and the auditor. The company was being wound up, and the action was brought to render the directors, manager and auditor liable for payment dividends out of capital.
Held—by the High Court—

1. The directors had fallen short of the standard of care required of them, and since they could not show that the dividends were paid out of profits, they were jointly and severally liable for the dividends, remuneration and bonuses wrongly paid out.

2. The auditor should not have confined himself to verifying the arithmetical accuracy of the balance sheet, but should have inquired into its substantial accuracy, and endeavoured to see that it contained the particulars specified in the articles of association, and was properly drawn up so as to contain a true and correct representation of the state of the company's affairs.

3. The improper payments by the directors were the natural and immediate consequences of the breach of duty by the manager and auditor, and the manager and auditor were liable for the amounts so paid.

Comment. The auditor's liability was subject to the Statute of Limitations, which was specially pleaded.

An auditor is not under a duty to take stock. In the absence of suspicion an auditor may rely on the certificate of an apparently responsible manager or employee.

207. Re Kingston Cotton Mill Co [1896] 2 Ch 279

The directors of a company were enabled to pay dividends out of capital because the stock in trade of the company was overstated for several years. The auditors had not required the production of the stock records but had accepted the certificate of the company's manager regarding the value of the stock. *Held*—by the Court of Appeal—the auditors were not liable. It was stated that an auditor is 'a watch dog not a bloodhound'. He can assume that the company's servants are honest and can rely upon statements they make unless there are suspicious circumstances which would give reason for distrust. 'It is the duty of an auditor to bring to bear on the work he has to perform that skill, care and caution which a reasonably competent, careful and cautious auditor would use. What is reasonable skill, care and caution must depend on the particular circumstances of each case. An auditor is not bound to be a detective, or, as was said, to approach his work with suspicion, or with a foregone conclusion that there is something wrong. He is a watchdog, but not a bloodhound. He is justified in believing tried servants of the company in whom confidence is placed by the company. He is entitled to assume that they are honest and to rely upon their representations, provided he takes reasonable care. If there is anything calculated to excite suspicion, he should probe it to the bottom; but in the absence of anything of that kind he is only bound to be reasonably cautious and careful.... It is not the duty of an auditor to take stock; he is not a stock expert; there are many matters on which he must rely on the honesty and accuracy of others.' *per* Lopes L J.

Comment. The rule laid down in the above case has been modified by subsequent cases.

In *Westminster Road Construction and Engineering Company Ltd* (1932) unreported, a company paid dividend out of profits which were overstated by reason of the overvaluation of work in progress. This figure was supplied by the manager and secretary and it was held that the auditor was liable to repay the money paid out as dividend because he had accepted the certificate given by them without making proper enquiries which would have revealed that the valuation was inflated.

See also *Re City Equitable Fire Insurance Co Ltd*, 1925.[168]

Contrast American law which requires the auditor to check the stock or at least to qualify his report that he has not done so. (*Stanley L. Block Inc v Klein* (1965) 258 NYS 2d 501.)

Criminal liability of auditor under the Companies Act.

208. R *v* Shacter [1960] 1 All ER 61

In 1950 one Maurice Shalam, who had formed two companies, appointed Shacter as auditor at an annual general meeting in 1953, and his appointment was continued from year to year. One of the companies got into financial difficulties. Shacter, in order to help in obtaining an overdraft from the bank, put forward false figures concerning the stock position. Shacter and Shalam were charged with falsifying the books and with frauds and default by officers of a company, and with making a false entry in a book or paper. At the trial the judge directed the jury that the appellant was an officer of the company by virtue of holding the position of auditor. The appellant appealed against the conviction on the ground of misdirection. *Held*— by the Court of Criminal Appeal—an auditor appointed by a company to fill an office (as distinct from an auditor appointed for a particular purpose) was an officer of the company for the purpose of liability under s. 223, and what are now ss. 206 and 207, Insolvency Act 1986.

Auditor: duty of care in negligence.

209. Candler *v* Crane, Christmas & Co [1951] 2 KB 164

The defendants, a firm of accountants and auditors, prepared the accounts and balance sheet of a limited company at the request of the managing director, knowing that they were required to induce the plaintiff to invest money in the company. The plaintiff, relying on the accounts, invested £2,000 in the company. The accounts were, it was alleged, negligently prepared and did not give an accurate picture of the company's finances. The company was wound up and the plaintiff lost his money. He now sued the accountants in negligence. *Held*— by the Court of Appeal—that, in the absence of a contractual or fiduciary relationship between the parties, the defendants owed no duty of care to the plaintiff in preparing the accounts. Denning L J thought that the defendants might have a duty because they knew that the accounts were to be shown to the plaintiff, though he would not have found them liable to complete strangers.

Comment. The dissenting judgment of Lord Denning in this case marks the beginning of the modern law of liability for careless misstatements causing monetary loss. However, he did restrict liability to those whom it was *known* would rely on the careless misstatement and *Hedley Byrne*[89] perpetuated this 'knowledge' requirement. The *JEB Fasteners* case (see p. 367) takes the principle further to the objective test of foresight.

INVESTIGATIONS

Investigations: obstruction of inspectors treated as contempt of court:
mere refusal to answer incriminating questions.

210. McClelland, Pope & Langley v Howard, *The Times*, 31 March 1966

Inspectors had been appointed by the Board of Trade under s. 165(b)
of the 1948 Act (now s. 432), to conduct an inquiry into the affairs
of Fiesta Tours Ltd and Travel and Holiday Club Ltd. The inspectors
were of the opinion that the appellant company had acted as agent
of one of the companies under inspection and using their powers under
what are now ss. 434 and 436 extended their inquiry to the appellant
company. Two of the directors of the appellant company attended
and gave evidence on oath. During the cross-examination by the inspectors one of the directors complained that the answers might incriminate
him but was told that he was not entitled to refuse to answer on
that ground and in consequence he answered the questions under protest. One of the grounds on which this appeal to the House of Lords
was founded was that the taking of the evidence at the inquiry was
contrary to natural justice as the inspectors had insisted that the
director concerned was not entitled to refuse to answer questions on
the ground that the answers would incriminate him. The appellant
company asked for an order prohibiting the inspectors from using
the evidence given. The House of Lords dismissed the appeal from
the Court of Appeal and refused the order. In the course of his judgment
Lord Upjohn said that it was unfortunate that the inspectors had
insisted that the director was not entitled to refuse to answer questions
on the ground that the answers would incriminate him. What is now
s. 436 of the Companies Act made it clear that a witness might
refuse to answer questions. The consideration of whether refusal was
proper was not a matter for the inspectors but for the court if the
inspectors so referred the matter. The wrongful assumption of power
by the inspectors did not, however, entitle the appellants to an
order of prohibition. Although the questions were answered under
protest they were not obtained by trickery or under duress. In these
circumstances no prohibition could lie to stop the use of the answers
given.

Proceedings before inspectors: administrative, not judicial or quasi-
judicial: inspectors must nevertheless act fairly.

211. Maxwell v Department of Trade and Industry [1974] 2 All ER 122

Inspectors had been appointed in September 1968 under s. 432 to investigate and report on the affairs of Pergamon Press of which the plaintiff was at the material time chairman and chief executive. In their first interim report the inspectors were very critical of the plaintiff who sought a declaration that as these criticisms had not been put fully to him so as to give him the opportunity of answering them the inspectors had failed to observe the rules of natural justice. *Held*— by the Court of Appeal—that the inspectors had conducted their inquiry and made their report with proper regard to the principles of natural justice. They had undertaken their work with conspicuous fairness and on nearly every criticism they had given the plaintiff a proper indication of the matter to enable him to explain and answer it. The Court of Appeal also made it clear that a court cannot set aside a report in whole or in part or declare it or any part of it null and void. All it can do is to grant a declaration that, for example, the inspectors had not acted honestly or reasonably. It also appears from the judgment that such a declaration will only be made in a very rare case where, for example, the inspectors have behaved so unfairly that the public interest requires the court to say so in a declaratory judgment.

RECONSTRUCTIONS AND AMALGAMATIONS

Section 425: there must be a 'compromise or arrangement'.

212. NFU Development Trust Ltd [1973] 1 All ER 135

The company was limited by guarantee without a share capital and had 94,000 members. All members could vote at general meetings and in the event of a winding up had a right to the surplus assets of the company in such proportions as the directors should determine. The company proposed a scheme of arrangement whereby in order to reduce the expense of administration in sending out notices and other communications to the 94,000 members, the number of members of the company would be reduced to seven, all the other members being deprived of their membership. At a meeting to consider the scheme 85 per cent of the votes were cast in favour of it. Application was then made to the court to sanction the scheme. *Held*—by Brightman J—that the scheme could not be approved. It was not a compromise or arrangement within the terms of s. 425. The rights of members were being expropriated without any compensating advantage and in this sense it could not be said that they were entering into a compromise or arrangement with the company.

Comment. Section 425 had to be used here, albeit unsuccessfully, because the company did not have a share capital, which meant that the variation of rights procedure under s. 125 was not available. Brightman J suggested that the solution was that members who were not interested in receiving, e.g. reports and accounts should be asked to resign.

Section 110, Insolvency Act 1986: dissenting shareholders' rights.

213. Payne v The Cork Co Ltd [1900] 1 Ch 308

The company, by its articles, gave the liquidator in the case of a voluntary winding up, an additional power, irrespective of his powers derived from the Companies Acts, to sell the undertaking and assets of the company for shares fully or partly-paid up, and to make an agreement to allot to the shareholders the proceeds of the sale in proportion to their respective interests in the company. The articles also provided that no member could require the liquidator to abstain from carrying out such a scheme, but upon request in writing of a dissentient member, the liquidator might sell his shares, and pay over to him the proceeds of sale. *Held*—The articles were *ultra vires* and inoperative in so far as they purported to deprive dissentient shareholders of their rights under the Act. Stirling J said: 'The legislature has conferred on voluntary liquidators a power of selling in a particular way, and it has attached to that power provisions which constitute a safeguard for the protection of dissentient shareholders, and in my opinion it is not competent for the company by articles framed in this way to deprive shareholders of that protection.... This article appears to be one more attempt to remove a statutory safeguard of the inexperienced intending shareholder.'

Section 429: power to acquire shares of dissenting minority not to be used to expel a minority.

214. Re Bugle Press Ltd [1960] 3 All ER 791

Holders of 90 per cent of the shares in a company formed a new company which made an offer for the shares of the old company. As was to be expected, 90 per cent of the shareholders accepted the offer and the new company then served notice on the holder of the other 10 per cent of the shares stating that it wished to purchase his holding. *Held*—by the Court of Appeal—that in substance the new company was the same as the majority shareholders, and the scheme was in effect an expropriation of the minority interest. 'What the section is directed to is a case where there is a scheme or contract for the acquisition of a company, its amalgamation, reorganization or the like, and where the offeror is independent of the shareholders in the transferor company, or at least independent of that part or fraction of them from which the 90 per cent is to be derived.' *per* Evershed MR.

WINDING UP

Liquidation: distribution of company's property *pari passu*: agreement to the contrary not binding.

215. British Eagle Airlines *v* Air France [1975] 2 All ER 390

Air France received services from British Eagle which exceeded in value those rendered to British Eagle by Air France. Both companies were members of an international clearing system for the payment of debts. Air France suggested that this net balance after set-off between them should be applied to reduce the net amount owed by British Eagle in respect of services provided by other airlines to British Eagle. *Held*—that to operate a multi-party set-off was to contract out of what is now s. 107, Insolvency Act 1986 for the payment of unsecured debts *pari passu*. This was contrary to public policy. The liquidator should collect from each airline the net amount owing to British Eagle after set-off, leaving net creditors to prove in the liquidation.

Disclaimer by liquidator or trustee in bankruptcy: effect of.

216. Re Hooley, ex parte United Ordnance and Engineering Co Ltd [1899] 2 QB 579

Hooley's trustee in bankruptcy disclaimed certain unpaid shares which Hooley held in the company, the shares being of low value. Hooley owed £25,000 under the contract to take the shares. The court assessed the damages payable to the company on the basis of the company's indebtedness. It appeared that the gross amount owed by the company was £16,169. The court deducted from this the cash in hand of £4,000 and directors' fees owing of £1,669, leaving a balance of £10,500. *Held*—this was the measure of damages which the company could prove for in the bankruptcy.

Index